LOCAL AREA NETWORKS

Second Edition

David A. Stamper

 **ADDISON-WESLEY**

An imprint of Addison Wesley Longman, Inc.

Reading, Massachusetts • Menlo Park, California • New York • Harlow, England
Don Mills, Ontario • Sydney • Mexico City • Madrid • Amsterdam

Publishing Partner: Michael Roche
Editorial Assistant: Ruth Berry
Production Supervisor: Louis C. Bruno, Jr.
Project Coordination: Electronic Publishing Services Inc., NYC
Text Designer and Illustrations: Electronic Publishing Services Inc., NYC
Cover Designer and Illustration: Linda Wade
Compositor: Electronic Publishing Services Inc., NYC
Marketing Manager: Michelle Hudson
Marketing Coordinator: Deanna Storey

Library of Congress Cataloging-in-Publication Data

Stamper, David A.
    Local area networks / David A. Stamper. — 2nd ed.
      p.   cm.
    Includes index.
    ISBN 0-8053-7729-8 (paperback)
    1. Local area networks (Computer networks)   I. Title.
TK5105.7.S784   1997
  004.6'8—dc21   97-15945
                                      CIP

ISBN 0-8053-7729-8

123456789—MA—0100999897

Networks

Second Edition

To Kay, Tae, and Shawn

Brief Contents

Detailed Contents   ix

Preface   xv

PART 1   ***INTRODUCTION TO DATA COMMUNICATIONS AND LOCAL AREA NETWORKS   1***
    1   Introduction to Data Communications   3
    2   Introduction to Local Area Networks   27

PART 2   ***HARDWARE   51***
    3   Hardware Introduction and LAN Media   53
    4   Topologies and Media Access Control   81
    5   LAN Hardware   113

PART 3   ***SOFTWARE   137***
    6   Software Introduction   139
    7   LAN System Software   163
    8   LAN Operating System Implementation   187
    9   Application Software   201

PART 4   ***INSTALLATION AND MANAGEMENT   233***
    10   LAN Installation   235
    11   LAN Administration: Users, Groups, and Security   257
    12   LAN Administration: The Printing Environment   281
    13   LAN Administration: Backup and Recovery   301
    14   LAN Administration: Reactive and Proactive Management   325

PART 5   ***CONNECTING TO OTHER SYSTEMS AND NETWORKS   351***
    15   Wide Area Networks   353
    16   Making Network Connections   377
    17   Other LAN Technologies   413

Glossary   427

Key Terms   430

Index   455

Detailed Contents

Preface   xv

PART 1   ***INTRODUCTION TO DATA COMMUNICATIONS AND LOCAL AREA NETWORKS   1***

CHAPTER 1   **Introduction to Data Communications   3**
    CHAPTER PREVIEW   3
    ESSENTIAL ELEMENTS OF COMMUNICATION   3
    NETWORK DEFINITION   7
    THE OSI REFERENCE MODEL   10
    GENERAL NETWORK IMPLEMENTATIONS   21
    SUMMARY   24
    KEY TERMS   24
    REVIEW QUESTIONS   24
    PROBLEMS AND EXERCISES   24

CHAPTER 2   **Introduction to Local Area Networks   27**
    CHAPTER PREVIEW   27
    WHY USE LANS?   27
    APPLICATION SOFTWARE   34
    CHARACTERISTICS OF LANS   37
    ADDITIONAL LAN RESPONSIBILITIES   40
    LAN SELECTION CRITERIA   41
    SUMMARY   48
    KEY TERMS   49
    REVIEW QUESTIONS   49
    PROBLEMS AND EXERCISES   50

PART 2   ***HARDWARE   51***

CHAPTER 3   **Hardware Introduction and LAN Media   53**
    CHAPTER PREVIEW   53
    THE LAN SYSTEM   53
    LAN MEDIA   54
    CONDUCTED MEDIA   55
    WIRELESS MEDIA   63
    MEDIA SELECTION CRITERIA   66
    ERROR SOURCES   69
    PREVENTION   71
    ERROR DETECTION   71
    ERROR CORRECTION   76
    SUMMARY   77

KEY TERMS   78
REVIEW QUESTIONS   78
PROBLEMS AND EXERCISES   79

CHAPTER 4   **Topologies and Media Access Control   81**
CHAPTER PREVIEW   81
LAN TOPOLOGIES AND THE PHYSICAL LAYER   81
DATA LINK AND MEDIA ACCESS CONTROL PROTOCOLS   89
LAN STANDARDS   98
BROADBAND AND BASEBAND TECHNOLOGIES   104
MAKING THE DECISIONS   106
SUMMARY   109
KEY TERMS   110
REVIEW QUESTIONS   110
PROBLEMS AND EXERCISES   111

CHAPTER 5   **LAN Hardware   113**
CHAPTER PREVIEW   113
SERVER PLATFORMS   113
BACKUP DEVICES   122
WORKSTATIONS   124
LAN ADAPTERS   125
PRINTERS   126
HUBS AND SWITCHES   127
MAKING CONNECTIONS   128
UNINTERRUPTIBLE POWER SUPPLY   130
OTHER HARDWARE   133
SUMMARY   134
KEY TERMS   134
REVIEW QUESTIONS   134
PROBLEMS AND EXERCISES   135

PART 3   *SOFTWARE   137*

CHAPTER 6   **Software Introduction   139**
CHAPTER PREVIEW   139
CLASSES OF SOFTWARE   139
GENERIC FUNCTIONS OF LAN SYSTEM SOFTWARE   145
SOFTWARE REQUIREMENTS FOR SHARED USAGE   149
SOFTWARE STANDARDS   154
SOFTWARE PROTECTION   154
SUMMARY   160
KEY TERMS   161
REVIEW QUESTIONS   161
PROBLEMS AND EXERCISES   162

CHAPTER 7   **LAN System Software   163**
CHAPTER PREVIEW   163
SERVER/WORKSTATION COMMUNICATIONS   163
THE NETWORK DIRECTORY   168
CLIENT/SERVER DIALOGUE   174
SPECIFICS OF SERVER SOFTWARE   176

SUMMARY   183
KEY TERMS   184
REVIEW QUESTIONS   184
PROBLEMS AND EXERCISES   184

CHAPTER 8   **LAN Operating System Implementation   187**
CHAPTER PREVIEW   187
NOVELL NETWORK OPERATING SYSTEMS   187
MICROSOFT NETWORK OPERATING SYSTEMS   195
IBM NETWORK OPERATING SYSTEMS   197
BANYAN VINES   197
ARTISOFT LANTASTIC   198
SUMMARY   199
KEY TERMS   200
REVIEW QUESTIONS   200
PROBLEMS AND EXERCISES   200

CHAPTER 9   **Application Software   201**
CHAPTER PREVIEW   201
DISTRIBUTED SYSTEM DEFINITIONS   201
EVOLUTION OF DISTRIBUTED SYSTEMS   203
DISTRIBUTED FILE SYSTEMS   205
CLIENT/SERVER COMPUTING   207
DATABASE SOFTWARE   214
DATABASE MANAGEMENT IN DISTRIBUTED SYSTEMS   217
WORKGROUP SOFTWARE   221
PRIMARY BUSINESS SOFTWARE   228
SOFTWARE STANDARDS   228
SUMMARY   230
KEY TERMS   231
REVIEW QUESTIONS   231
PROBLEMS AND EXERCISES   232

PART 4   ***INSTALLATION AND MANAGEMENT   233***

CHAPTER 10   **LAN Installation   235**
CHAPTER PREVIEW   235
ADMINISTRATIVE DETAILS   235
INSTALLATION TASKS   240
TRAINING   251
SUMMARY   254
KEY TERMS   255
REVIEW QUESTIONS   255
PROBLEMS AND EXERCISES   255

CHAPTER 11   **LAN Administration: Users, Groups, and Security   257**
CHAPTER PREVIEW   257
USERS AND GROUPS   257
SECURITY   260
VIRUSES   273
SUMMARY   278
KEY TERMS   279

REVIEW QUESTIONS   279
PROBLEMS AND EXERCISES   279

CHAPTER 12   LAN Administration: The Printing Environment   281
CHAPTER PREVIEW   281
INTRODUCTION TO PRINTING   281
CREATING A PRINTING ENVIRONMENT   283
A GENERIC SPOOLER   284
NOVELL SPOOLER CONFIGURATION   292
SUMMARY   299
KEY TERMS   300
REVIEW QUESTIONS   300
PROBLEMS AND EXERCISES   300

CHAPTER 13   LAN Administration: Backup and Recovery   301
CHAPTER PREVIEW   301
DATA BACKUP   301
RECOVERY   317
DISASTER PLANNING   320
SUMMARY   322
KEY TERMS   322
REVIEW QUESTIONS   323
PROBLEMS AND EXERCISES   323

CHAPTER 14   LAN Administration: Reactive and Proactive Management   325
CHAPTER PREVIEW   325
REACTIVE NETWORK MANAGEMENT   325
PROBLEM IDENTIFICATION AND RESOLUTION   327
PROACTIVE NETWORK MANAGEMENT   334
SYSTEM TUNING AND CAPACITY PLANNING   335
CONFIGURATION OF HARDWARE AND SOFTWARE UPGRADES   340
NETWORK MANAGEMENT SYSTEMS   342
NETWORK MANAGEMENT PROTOCOLS   345
SUMMARY   346
KEY TERMS   349
REVIEW QUESTIONS   349
PROBLEMS AND EXERCISES   350

PART 5   CONNECTING TO OTHER SYSTEMS AND NETWORKS   351
CHAPTER 15   Wide Area Networks   353
CHAPTER PREVIEW   353
WAN TERMINOLOGY   354
WAN NETWORK TOPOLOGIES   355
WAN DATA LINK CONTROL PROTOCOLS   358
WAN NETWORK LAYER FUNCTIONS   360
IBM'S SYSTEMS NETWORK ARCHITECTURE   365
PACKET DISTRIBUTION NETWORKS   369
COMPARING WANS WITH LANS   371
LAN-WAN INTERCONNECTIONS   373
SUMMARY   373
KEY TERMS   374

REVIEW QUESTIONS   375
PROBLEMS AND EXERCISES   375

CHAPTER 16   Making Network Connections   377
CHAPTER PREVIEW   377
LAN-TO-LAN CONNECTIONS   377
THE OSI REFERENCE MODEL REVISITED   379
SWITCHES AND VIRTUAL LANS   395
LAN-TO-HOST CONNECTIONS   401
INTERCONNECTION UTILITIES   407
REMOTE ACCESS   408
SUMMARY   409
KEY TERMS   410
REVIEW QUESTIONS   411
PROBLEMS AND EXERCISES   411

CHAPTER 17   Other LAN Technologies   413
CHAPTER PREVIEW   413
NONDEDICATED SERVERS AND PEER-TO-PEER LANS   413
DISKLESS WORKSTATIONS   415
ISDN   415
DIGITAL SUBSCRIBER LINE   416
HIGH-SPEED LANS   417
MULTIMEDIA ON LANS   418
MOBILE COMPUTING   420
INTERNET ACCESS   422
SERVERS   424
TECHNOLOGY AND NETWORK MANAGEMENT   425
SUMMARY   425
KEY TERMS   426

Glossary   427

Key Terms   430

Index   455

Preface

Over the past two decades, local area networks (LANs) have had an increasingly significant impact on the way companies conduct business. With the assistance of LAN technology, both large and small companies can take advantage of the ability to share valuable hardware and software resources among multiple users. These decades saw the rise of network-oriented software (groupware), which allows people working together on a project to share ideas and information more quickly and systematically. Furthermore, network interconnections between a company's wide and local area networks in addition to Internet and client/server technologies have created a vast information resource. Because LANs are becoming such an integral part of today's businesses, students of management information systems and computer information systems need fundamental LAN knowledge and experience. This experience can strategically position today's students for the growing opportunities in LAN management.

This textbook provides a good foundation in the theory and practical application of LAN use and administration. Because most LANs do not exist in isolation, this text also discusses how LANs can be connected to other LANs, wide area networks (WANs), and larger mainframe computers. Finally, this text provides readers with insight into emerging LAN technologies and their potential impact on the future of LANs.

Key Themes and Features

Focus on LAN Management

This text is written primarily from the perspective of LAN management. The focus is on administrative responsibilities and strategies, which range from selecting and installing LAN hardware and software to designing backup and recovery options. However, LAN administrators must often consider the issues important to other segments of the LAN community, such as users, so we provide appropriate coverage of these perspectives as well.

Complete, Up-to-Date Coverage

This text discusses a variety of the most popular LAN hardware and software technologies to help prepare students for any LAN environment. For consistency, most of the examples are based on Novell NetWare, the leading LAN operating system, which the majority of students will encounter as LAN administrators. Despite the rapid rate at which new LAN technology is being introduced, *Local Area Networks*, Second Edition, provides up-to-date coverage and anticipates emerging technology. The following is a sample of the topics covered in this text:

- Novell NetWare, Windows NT Server, and Banyan Vines (throughout the text)
- Basic data communication principles, including the OSI reference model (Chapter 1)

- LAN selection criteria (Chapter 2)
- LAN media (Chapter 3)
- Data link and MAC protocols (Chapter 4)
- Token passing versus CSMA/CD (Chapter 4)
- LAN hardware (Chapter 5)
- LAN system software (Chapter 7)
- Groupware (Chapter 9)
- LAN installation concerns (Chapter 10)
- Security options and virus protection (Chapter 11)
- Creating and maintaining the printing environment (Chapter 12)
- Backup, recovery, and disaster planning (Chapter 13)
- SNMP and CMIP network management protocols (Chapter 14)
- Wide area network overview (Chapter 15)
- Bridges, routers, and TCP/IP routing protocol (Chapter 16)
- Diskless workstations, peer-to-peer LANs, and multimedia on LANs (Chapter 17)

In-Text Learning Aides

Pedagogical features, such as boldfaced key terms, end-of-chapter summaries, review questions, and problems and exercises, are included to fully support a learning environment. In addition, examples are used throughout the text to illustrate practical applications of LAN management.

Part Openers

Each part begins with a part opener that gives an overview of the topics covered in each of the part's chapters.

Chapter Preview

Each chapter begins with a brief overview that outlines the goals of the material to be covered in the chapter.

Key Terms

Key words are boldfaced for easy identification when they are introduced in the chapter.

End-of-Chapter Material

The end-of-chapter material begins with a summary of the key concepts. Key terms are listed for review, and review questions are provided to help students recall important ideas and concepts. These review questions, along with problems and exercises, encourage students to apply their understanding of the concepts in the chapter.

Glossary

The extensive glossary includes acronyms for a comprehensive, easy-to-use reference guide.

Organization

The text is divided into five parts:

Part 1: Introduction to Data Communications and Local Area Networks

Part 1 introduces LAN technology and explores how LANs are used to extend the power of the stand-alone microcomputer.

Part 2: Hardware

Part 2 outlines criteria for evaluating network layouts and choosing hardware components that can be integrated to form a system.

Part 3: Software

Part 3 explores the role of network software in the successful interaction of application software, workstation system software, and server system software.

Part 4: Installation and Management

Part 4 explores the LAN administrator's core responsibilities, including creating and managing the user environment, security, backup and recovery, and strategies for managing planned and unplanned network changes.

Part 5: Connecting to Other Systems and Networks

Part 5 covers wide area networks (WANs) and interconnection between LANs and WANs. This part concludes with an overview of several important but less commonly used technologies and a look forward to emerging LAN technologies.

Supplements

Instructor's Disk

The Instructor's Disk includes additional exercises, solutions to end-of-chapter problems and excercises, case studies, lab exercises, and advice for setting up a networked lab. Available for the IBM PC and compatible machines on one 3-1/2 inch disk.

Of Related Interest

Also in the Addison-Wesley series on Information Systems are *Business Data Communications*, Fourth Edition, and *Essentials of Data Communications*, both by David A. Stamper; *Information Systems: A Management Perspective*, by Steven Alter; *Modern Systems Analysis and Design*, by Jeffrey A. Hoffer, Joey F. George, and Joseph S. Valacich;

Database Management, Fourth Edition, by Fred R. McFadden and Jeffrey A. Hoffer, and *Business and Information Systems* by Robert C. Nickerson.

Acknowledgments

Many thanks to the following reviewers for their feedback and suggestions:

Theodore Chrobak, Youngstown State University

Peter G. Drexel, Plymouth State College

Stephen Elky, Catonsville Community College

Deborah Fels, Ryerson Polytechnic University

Next, I wish to express my sincere appreciation to all the instructors and students who used the first edition of this book. I want to thank my wife, Kay, and sons, Tae and Shawn, for all their support and encouragement. A special thanks to the key people at Addison-Wesley who contributed to the success of this project: Editor Michael Roche and Editorial Assistant Ruth Berry ensured superior consistency and quality, and Production Supervisor Lou Bruno directed the efforts of numerous people.

David A. Stamper

PART 1

Introduction to Data Communications and Local Area Networks

Since the beginning of the computer era, data communications has been a significant segment of computing technology. Over time, hardware and software developers have extended existing capabilities and invented new ones to meet ever-changing communications requirements. As data communications evolved, a variety of methods were developed for connecting terminals to computers, computers to computers, and networks to networks. Furthermore, a variety of network types were created to satisfy changing computing needs, such as the following:

Connecting remote card readers and printers to a central computing system, a technology called remote job entry (RJE) that transmits record images from one location to another

Connecting local and remote terminals to a central host computer

Connecting computing systems geographically distributed over a country or the world, a wide area network (WAN)

Connecting computing systems in a limited geographic area, a local area network (LAN)

Connecting networks together, as in the Internet

Providing a utility for receiving messages in one location and routing them to one or more other destinations

This text is primarily about a specific type of network, a LAN. A LAN is one of several general types of networks. Underlying each of these network types is a common set of generic networking and application functions. Before we begin discussing the specifics of LAN technologies, in the introductory part of this text, we introduce the basics of data communications. The objective of this introductory material is to build a foundation for the ensuing discussion of LAN technology. There is an additional reason for looking at data communications and networking basics. In many of today's communications networks, LANs are connected to other LANs and to WANs. Therefore, LAN users and administrators alike will benefit from a fundamental knowledge of all types of networks. After we cover the basics of data communications in Chapter 1, in Chapter 2 we provide a brief introduction to LANs. The LAN introduction includes reasons organizations use LANs, an overview of the LAN environment, and a discussion of several LAN selection criteria.

Chapter 1
Introduction to Data Communications

Chapter 2
Introduction to Local Area Networks

Chapter 1

Introduction to Data Communications

CHAPTER PREVIEW

In the part opening, you read that there are a variety of networks; however, at the base level, these diverse network implementations share a set of common tasks. The objectives of these tasks have been described and categorized in a variety of ways by different companies and organizations. Regardless of the way in which they were stratified, the basic functions remained fairly constant. A detailed knowledge of these data communications and networks fundamental functional requirements is not essential to understanding LANs and their connection to other networks. However, to better appreciate LAN technology, you should be exposed to these data communications principles. The objective of this chapter is to give you a basic overview of data communications, introduce some of its terminology, and profile the various types of networks being used today. Understanding these concepts will help you understand the technical material in later chapters.

In this chapter you will learn about

the requirements for communication

what constitutes a network

the various types of networks in common use today

the OSI Reference Model

some of the basic terminology of data communications and networks

By the end of this chapter you should have a general understanding of the essential elements of communication, network types, and how data flows from one network computer to another. We begin by describing the essential elements of communication.

ESSENTIAL ELEMENTS OF COMMUNICATION

Networks are communications mechanisms. For communication of any type to occur, there must be four basic elements present: a message, a sender, a receiver, and a medium. Figure 1.1 shows the sender, receiver, medium, and message in a telephone connection.

3

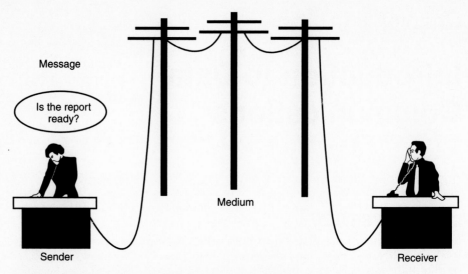

Figure 1.1   Essential Elements of Communication

In addition to these four basic elements, the message should be understandable and there should be an ability to detect errors that may occur during data transmission. Let us look at each of these elements.

The Message

Obviously, when communicating, a **message** is needed. A message can have several forms and be of varying length. You may have worked with a computer and computer networks. In doing so, you have originated and received a variety of messages. If you want to run a program, you type the program name or select an appropriate icon or menu message. When doing this, you are communicating with the computer's software by sending it a message to run the program. Occasionally, you may receive messages from the computer's software indicating that you have made a mistake or suggesting courses of action. On a network you may send and receive electronic mail (e-mail) messages. If you have used the Internet, a communications utility such as America Online, CompuServe, or Prodigy, or a bulletin board system, you may have transferred a file to or from your computer. In this instance the message being sent is the file itself. These are but a few of the types of messages exchanged in a computing system. Data communications message types include files, requests for services, responses to requests, device or network status messages, device or network control messages, and correspondence, such as e-mail.

The Sender

The **sender** is the transmitter of the message: a person, application, or machine with enough intelligence to originate a message or response without human intervention. The sender can also be a system user, sensor, badge reader, or other input device.

The Receiver

If a tree falls in a forest, does it make a sound? Your answer to this age-old logic question may affect your perception of this essential element of communication. Is the mere presence of a signal (sender, message, medium) sufficient for communications or must there be a receiver? For our part, we include a receiver as essential to communications. Bits being transmitted over a communications link are meaningless unless received. However, we sometimes use the term *communicating* to mean posting a letter or typing on a keyboard; what we really mean is that we are providing the initial steps to communications and the communication is realized only when it is read by the receiver.

Receivers include computers, terminals, remote printers, people, and devices such as drill presses, furnaces, and air conditioners. There can be a message and a sender without a receiver; however, without a receiver there is no communication. For instance, signals have been beamed into space in an attempt to contact intelligent life forms; until something receives these signals, no communication has taken place. In a LAN a message can be sent to all computers saying that a new system feature is available; if all computers happen to be turned off at that time, no communication occurs.

Three sender/receiver combinations can exist in a network: sender and receiver are in the same computer system, sender and receiver are in different computers that are directly connected, and sender and receiver are in different computer systems that are connected via intervening computer systems. In Figure 1.2, each of computers A, B, C, D, and X is a node. A **node** is a computer system connected to a network. The lines in the figure show that node A is directly connected to node B, and node B is directly connected to node C. Direct connections between two computers are called **links.** Nodes A and C are not directly connected; however, if node B forwards A's message, node A can communicate with node C. We call the connection between two nodes through an intervening node a **path.** In Figure 1.2 there are two paths between nodes A and X: path A $\longrightarrow$ B $\longrightarrow$ C $\longrightarrow$ X and path A $\longrightarrow$ D $\longrightarrow$ X. If a sender and receiver are directly connected to each other, like computers A and B in Figure 1.2, the message usually travels directly from computer A to computer B over that connection. Which of the two paths between nodes A and X is used depends on the networking software. The determination of a message path is called **routing,** and the method used to determine the route is called a **routing algorithm.** In large networks, there might be many possible paths; the routing algorithm should have sufficient intelligence to choose the best path available.

The Medium

Messages are carried from sender to receiver through some communication medium. For instance, in oral communication, sound waves are transmitted through air (the medium). LANs use several media to transmit data, including wires, **coaxial cable, fiber optic cable,** radio waves, and **infrared light.** Wires and cables are conductors that carry electrical or light signals. Radio waves and infrared light are wireless media. With wireless technologies such as broadcast radio and television, the signal is transmitted without using a wire or fiber optic cable. Each medium has several transmission characteristics that distinguish it from other media. For example, media vary with respect

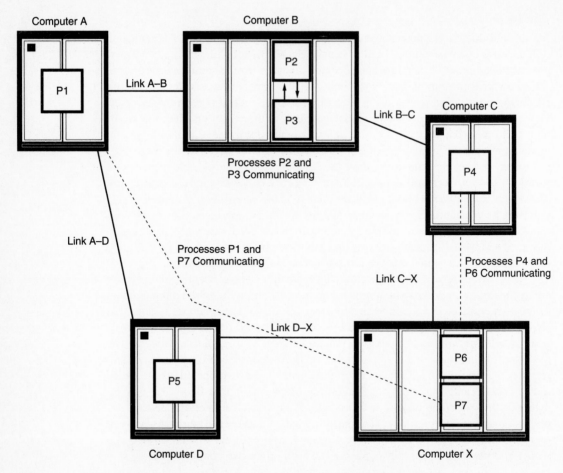

Figure 1.2   Sender/Receiver Combinations with Communicating Computers

to speed of transmission, security, cost, ease of maintenance, and susceptibility to errors. We examine the characteristics of LAN media in Chapter 3.

Understandability

Even if all four of the components just discussed are present, if the message is not understood correctly, then accurate communication has not taken place. In human communication the most obvious obstacles to understanding are language differences, for which translators or interpreters may be necessary. Computer systems have similar obstacles to overcome. Data appears in a variety of formats. Some data, such as the words in this book, are in text or character format. Video and audio data are stored and transmitted in a variety of different formats. Text data can be represented by any of several different codes, the two most common being the **American Standard Code for Information Interchange (ASCII)** and the **Extended Binary Coded Decimal**

Interchange Code (EBCDIC). It is becoming increasingly common for audio, video, and graphic data to be transferred through a network. If you have used the Internet or read articles about it, you are probably aware that telephone conversations, radio programs, video clips, and graphic images all may be transmitted or played over the network. These data types are represented in a variety of formats. The exact format used depends on the type of data and several formats exist for data of the same type. The key is that the recipient must be capable of understanding the format being used. Sometimes nodes must translate data from one format to another to ensure that data is interpreted correctly. You may have experienced other situations in which you received a message but did not understand it (for example, the message was in the context of other information you did not know, you only received part of the message, or the message was garbled). Similar situations may happen in computer communications, and it is important that these situations be recognized, a capability called error detection.

Error Detection

In human communication **error detection** is a common and basically simple task because humans can reason and interpret. Error detection is common because a variety of events—background noise, lack of concentration, ambiguous statements—can occur that prevent us from receiving the message as intended. A human receiver can usually correct grammatical errors, misspellings, and even some misstatements. Sometimes we must ask for the entire message to be retransmitted. But computer networks generally lack a reasoning ability, even when a human computer operator is involved. For example, if an operator realizes that a received message is erroneous, such as a student grade point average of 19.4, that operator may be unable to correct the error because he or she does not know the proper value, but only that the transmitted value is out of range. When the receiver is a piece of hardware, incapable of reasoning and unable to detect or correct errors, the user must employ special schemes for determining whether an original message has been distorted during transmission. All such schemes involve transmitting additional information along with the data to increase the chances of detecting errors; however, no error-detection scheme can detect every possible combination of errors. Error detection in networks occurs on several levels, such as node-to-node error checking across a link and end-to-end error checking over a path. We discuss some of these methods in Chapters 3 and 15.

NETWORK DEFINITION

This book is primarily about LANs. There are several types of networks, so the term *network* has a variety of connotations. As a prelude to discussing why people use networks and network applications, you should have an understanding of the term *network* as used in this text.

In electronic communications, there are two basic types of networks. The traditional network is a **terminal network.** Figure 1.3 shows that this network consists of a single host computer with attached terminals. In today's networks these terminals are probably microcomputers with software and hardware that allow them to emulate a standard terminal. In a terminal network the **host computer** does all or most of the processing, and the terminals simply act as an input/output (I/O) device through which a person gains access to the host's applications. When the terminal is a microcomputer, the microcomputer may download data from the host for local processing or upload new data to the host for incorporation into other application systems or for distribution to other terminal users. Except for the chapter on connecting a LAN to a host computer or WAN, this type of network is not addressed in this text.

The second type of network is a **network of computers,** as shown in Figure 1.4. This network consists of two or more nodes connected by a data communications medium. The individual nodes may have terminals attached to them. Thus a single node on this network can look just like the terminal network described in the previous paragraph. In a network of computers, communication can be from a terminal to its host (the computer to which the terminal is directly attached), a terminal to another node on the network, or among network nodes themselves. Henceforth, unless otherwise stated, the term *network* refers to this type of network.

Although later in this chapter we describe several network implementations, there are two general network subtypes: a **local area network (LAN)** and a **wide area network (WAN).** Network technology advances are tending to blur the distinctions between these two, but the fundamental differences between LANs and WANs are distance covered, transmission speed, media, and types of nodes. These differences are listed in Table 1.1.

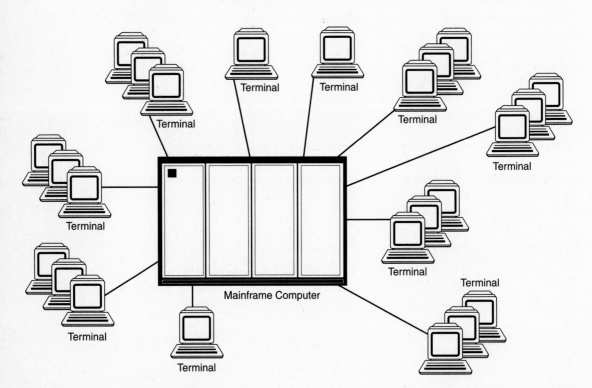

Figure 1.3   A Terminal Network

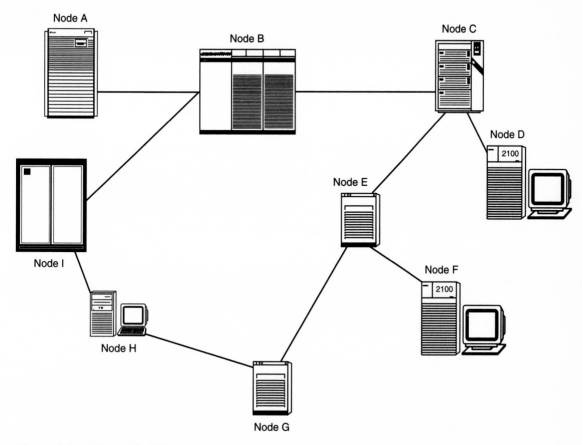

Figure 1.4   A Network of Computers

We could also define a third network subtype, a **metropolitan area network (MAN);** however, a MAN has the same characteristics as a LAN, with an extended distance ca-pability. A LAN's distance is generally restricted to a building complex, whereas a MAN can serve a metropolitan area spanning 60 miles or more.

A network may also consist of interconnected LANs and WANs, as illustrated in Figure 1.5.

As you can see, there are many ways a network can be implemented. Despite these varieties, each network performs a similar set of functions: message preparation, trans-mission, and receipt. In carrying out these functions, a number of tasks must be per-formed. These tasks have been codified by the **International Standards Organization (ISO),** an international agency for the development of a wide range of standards. The generic tasks are described in a model called the ISO **Open Systems Interconnection (OSI) Reference Model.**

Table 1.1   LAN/WAN Comparison

	LAN	*WAN*
Distance	Limited—typically less than 2500 m or 2 mi	Unlimited
Speed	High—typically above 10 Mbps	Slower—usually 1.5 Mbps or lower
Media	Locally owned—twisted-pair wires, coaxial cable, fiber optic cable, wireless (no satellite)	Locally owned and common carrier—twisted-pair wires, coaxial cable, fiber optic cable, wireless to include satellite
Nodes	Can be any, but most are desktop computers	Mostly mainframe and minicomputers

THE OSI REFERENCE MODEL

The basic objective of a network is for an application or device in one node to communicate with an application or device on another node. Although this may sound simple, some complexities are involved. Many different WAN and LAN implementations are possible and, consequently, so are many different types of interfaces. That is, you need one type of hardware and software to connect to one type of LAN, say a token-passing ring, a different set of hardware and software to connect to a contention bus LAN, and still another type of hardware and software to connect to a particular WAN. Because of the variety of network types available and the frequent need to interconnect them, a thriving business has been created for establishing connections among networks. Moreover the problem of network interconnection is so important that the ISO created the OSI Reference Model that describes the functions a generic network needs to provide. The OSI Reference Model has become the basis for many data communications standards. Because these standards are in the public domain, they are called **open standards** and lead to open systems. The advantage of open standards is that any company can build hardware or software for use on the network. If the standards are adhered to, multivendor components can interoperate correctly. Open systems allow for competition, which invariably leads to innovation and lower prices. In contrast, early network systems were proprietary. The implementation details were considered confidential by the designer and competition was suppressed. If you understand the OSI model, you will also understand the basic functions that must be carried out in moving a message from an application on one node to an application on another node. The OSI Reference Model has seven functional layers, as illustrated in Figure 1.6.

To help you understand the OSI Reference Model, let us ignore computer technology for the moment and look at how a worker might send a letter from his or her office to a colleague in another location. This simple act can closely resemble sending a message in an OSI network. A possible scenario for this transmission might be as follows:

1. The worker drafts the letter by recording it on a tape recorder and delivers it to her or his secretary (an OSI application layer function).

2. The secretary makes the letter presentable by typing it, correcting grammatical

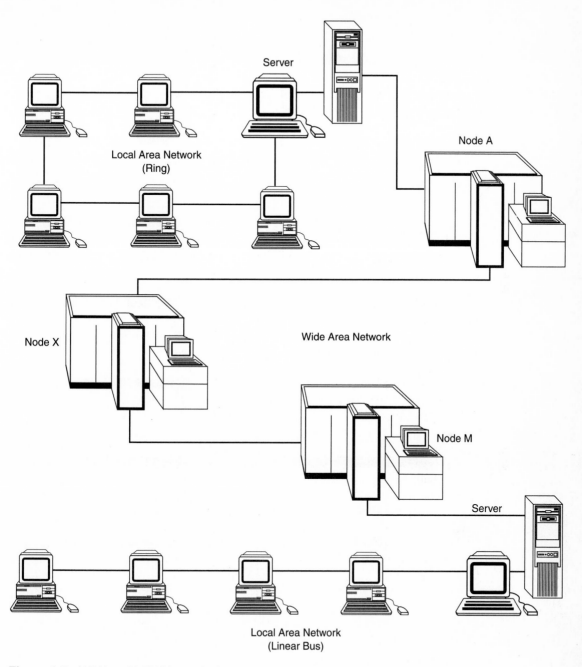

Server

Local Area Network
(Ring)

Node A

Node X

Wide Area Network

Node M

Server

Local Area Network
(Linear Bus)

Figure 1.5 WAN and LAN Networks Interconnected

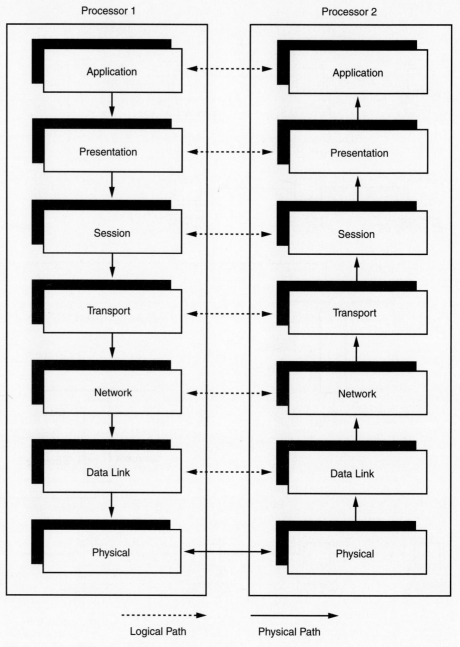

Figure 1.6   OSI Peer Layer Communication

mistakes, and so on. The secretary places the memo in an interoffice envelope and places it in the outgoing mailbox. This service is analogous to the OSI presentation layer function.

3. The mail room clerk picks up the mail, takes it to the mail room, sorts it, and determines the routing for the message. Possible routings are internal mail for local messages, postal mail, and private express mail carriers. Because this message must go to another distant office and no priority is assigned, the clerk places the interoffice envelope in an external mailing envelope, possibly with other correspondence for that office, addresses it, and deposits it in the external mailbox. These functions correspond to the OSI Reference Model transport and network layer functions (end-to-end delivery and routing).

4. The mail carrier picks up the mail, including the worker's message, and takes it to the post office, where it is sorted and placed on an outgoing mail truck. The letter is transported by a variety of conveyances, including trucks, airplanes, and the postal employee's mail pouch. Transportation of correspondence from one point to another corresponds to the OSI physical layer functions.

5. The post office physically delivers the mail to the mail room of the destination office. That mail room clerk opens the outer envelope and sorts its contents.

6. The mail room clerk delivers the memo in its interoffice envelope to the recipient's secretary, a routing and transport function.

7. The recipient's secretary takes the memo out of the envelope and prepares it for the recipient. For example, the secretary may time stamp it, summarize the memo, make comments, set a priority for the recipient's reading it, and so on. This is like a presentation layer function.

8. The recipient receives the memo, reads it, and reacts to the worker's message. Processing the message is an application layer function.

The preceding scenario describes a variety of different functions necessary to move a message from the sender's desk to the recipient's desk. The functions consisted of message composition, presentation services, address determination, enveloping, selecting transmission routes, physical transmission, and so on. In general these same functions must be performed when transmitting a message between computers in a network. The OSI Reference Model explicitly identifies seven functional layers for network communications: application, presentation, session, transport, network, data link, and physical. Each layer has several communications tasks to perform. Figure 1.6 represents the OSI layers in two network nodes.

In the letter-routing example above, each functional layer on the sending side performed a specific set of functions, and each function was performed for a peer layer on the receiving side. For example, placing the correspondence in the interoffice envelope was done by the sending secretary and undone by the receiving secretary. In the OSI model each layer in the sending network node performs a particular set of functions for its corresponding layer in the receiving network node. That is, the application layer in the sending node prepares the data for the application layer in the receiving node. The application layer then passes the message to the presentation layer. The presentation layer formats the message properly for the presentation layer on the receiving node and passes the data to the session layer, and so on. In Figure 1.6 the solid line shows the physical route of the message, and the dotted lines show the logical route, from peer layer to peer layer. Note also that each layer has a well-defined interface through which it communicates with adjacent layers.

The OSI Reference Model is simple in concept but the details can be complex. The model itself establishes a framework for data communication standards and implementations. In this chapter our objective is to give you an overview of the concepts.

Before we begin presenting an overview of the functions of the seven layers of the OSI Reference Model, let us first relate it to another everyday communication situation: a telephone conversation. When you decide to telephone someone, you have an application need. You might conduct business or just visit with an acquaintance. In order to communicate, you need to establish a session. This is accomplished by dialing the telephone and using the physical elements of the telephone company (telephone wires, wiring concentrators, and switching equipment) to establish a circuit. Once the conversation (application) begins, both parties engage in presentation activities. In our speech, we often use inflections to convey more information than the words alone. Our presentation of the words can convey additional meaning. While the telephone conversation (session) continues, each party unconsciously monitors the session for flow control and session breakdown. The conversation flow is usually one person talking and another listening, and the parties to the call alternate as senders and receivers. On occasion, both parties may speak at the same time, but this is generally a violation of the rules of dialogue. On rare occasions, the session may be broken (for example, the line may go dead). Either party may then attempt to recover the session by redialing. At the end of the call, the session is dissolved when the participants hang up. These functions (session establishment, recovery in the event of problems, flow control, and session dissolution) are OSI session layer functions. When the call is placed, some routing is done to establish a temporary circuit. In routing the call, the telephone company's switching equipment searches for an available path. When a path is found, the conversation is directed over that path for the call's duration. If the call is long distance, the telephone company gathers accounting data by measuring the length of the call. The accounting information is used to derive part of the charges for your next bill. These two functions (routing and accounting) are network layer functions. During the conversation, one of the parties may not understand the message. This can occur because of noise, such as a child crying in the background, interruption from a coworker, or interference on the telephone circuit itself. The receiving party realizes the lack of understanding and effects recovery by asking the sender to repeat the message. This is a form of error detection. Furthermore, during the conversation there are implicit rules as to when a party may talk (access the medium). For example, a pause in the sender's conversation may be a signal that it is the recipient's turn to talk. These two functions (error detection and media access control) are two functions of the data link layer. Thus, you can see that OSI Reference Model functions are inherent in all aspects of communication. The requirements of different kinds of communication vary; therefore, functions essential to one form of communication may be omitted from other forms. For example, a friend-to-friend conversation may not include accounting, whereas a client-to-attorney conversation probably will.

Functions of OSI Layers

The functions of each OSI layer are briefly described in this section. More extensive explanations of several of these layers are given later as needed.

Application Layer

The specific functions of the **application layer** depend on the application being executed. In general the application layer generates the data for the message to be transmitted, perhaps affixes a transaction identifier to it, and then passes the message to the presentation layer. An example of an application layer standard is the X.400 standard for electronic mail systems. This standard describes the application requirements for interconnecting different electronic mail systems.

Presentation Layer

The **presentation layer** accepts a message from the application layer, provides formatting functions, and then passes the message to the session layer. The types of presentation services that might be accomplished include data compression, encryption, and date conversion. Consider date conversion. The standard date format in the U.S. is mm/dd/yy, whereas in Australia it is dd/mm/yy. If a message containing date information is to be transmitted from Australia to the U.S the date must be converted to the recipient's standard. Because this is a function common to all messages containing dates, the conversion might be done by a presentation layer function.

Session Layer

Whenever one object communicates with another, a **session** is said to exist between the two. When you telephone someone you begin a session with that person. However, several events can occur when you call someone: The other party may not be there, they may already be using the telephone, or they may refuse to communicate with you. Each of these events may occur when network objects try to communicate. The general functions of the **session layer** are to set up the dialogue between two applications, set up the dialogue rules, and control the dialogue. Specific functions include controlling the data flow between the objects and providing recovery if a failure occurs.

Transport Layer

The **transport layer** ensures that all messages are delivered, that no messages are lost or duplicated, and that messages are free of errors. One mechanism the transport layer may use to account for messages is a message sequence number. If you send five packages to someone, you will probably label them 1/5, 2/5, 3/5, 4/5, and 5/5. This scheme allows the recipient to know whether all packages have been recovered and, if order is important, the proper sequence. The transport layer in the receiving node tells the transport layer in the sending node which messages have been successfully received. If a message is not acknowledged, it is sent again.

Network Layer

The **network layer** is responsible for collecting accounting data and routing the message. The accounting task is responsible for tracking the number of messages received and their source and destination. This data is used if an installation wants to charge users for network use (that is, the cost of packet forwarding). The routing task ranges between simple and quite complex. In LANs the task is simple: The message is broadcast to all network nodes. This is practical because the high speed of LAN transmissions and the limited geographical area ensures speedy delivery. In WANs and network interconnections, routing is considerably more complex. In WANs the communications links are usually slower than in LANs and distance is sometimes an obstacle. Different technologies are typically used in WANs to find the optimal transmission path. A variety of paths may exist along which the message can be sent. The network layer chooses the path most appropriate for the message. For example, a short, time-critical message may be transmitted via a leased communication line whereas a long file transfer may use a satellite link. We discuss how LANs route messages in Chapter 4 and WAN routing in Chapter 15.

Data Link Layer

The **data link layer** is responsible for preparing the message for physical transmission to the next node. Specific functions it performs are low-level error detection, delineation of data, and establishing the protocol by which a node can send and receive data. **Protocols,** which exist at all levels in the OSI Reference Model, are conventions for how one object interfaces to another. You may unknowingly observe protocols in your life for simple things such as talking. There is a classroom protocol for speaking (raise hand and wait until called on), a different protocol for polite conversation (do not interrupt, wait until no one is talking, and then talk), and yet another protocol for arguments (do not listen to the other party and talk loudly and continuously). In this text we investigate LAN and WAN data link and network layer protocols in some detail.

Physical Layer

The **physical layer** is responsible for physically transmitting data over the communications medium. It specifies how the data is represented on the medium, the physical connections that must exist between the medium and the computer, and the speed at which transmission occurs. Elements of the physical layer are discussed in Chapter 3.

The OSI Model at Work

Recall the office letter transmission example presented earlier in the chapter. The message as dictated by the sender underwent a variety of changes in its transmission. Additional data was added to the message and the message was encapsulated in several envelopes. Each envelope contained addressing information appropriate to a corresponding recipient at the receiving location. Similar actions occur when a message is transmitted over a network. An example of the changes a message might go through as it passes from layer to layer of the OSI model is illustrated in Figure 1.7. The example shows a message being transmitted from a client application in node A to a server application in node M in the network shown in Figure 1.5. A client application makes requests of server applications, and the application architecture based on this computing model is called the **client/server (C/S)** model. The C/S computing model is common to many LANs and is described in more detail in Chapter 9.

As in the letter example, in which the mail room at one location enveloped messages that were unwrapped at the receiving location, the data appended to a message by an OSI layer in the sending node is affixed for the benefit and interpretation of the corresponding receiving layer in the destination node. Thus, data link layers add data to be interpreted by the adjacent data link layer, network layer to network layer, and so on. Typically each OSI layer adds some control information to the message, a process sometimes called **enveloping** or **encapsulation.** The entity created when an OSI layer adds its data to the message received from the next higher layer is called a protocol data unit (PDU). The steps shown in Figure 1.7 are explained in the following sections. For specifics, we assume a banking transaction where node A in Figure 1.5 needs to communicate with node M.

Application Layer
The application on node A builds a record with a transaction identifier, the number of the account to be updated, the date and time of the transaction, and the amount

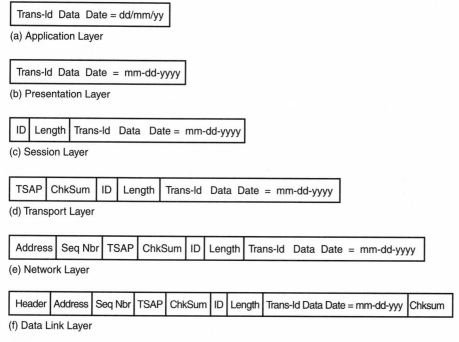

| Trans-Id Data Date = dd/mm/yy |
(a) Application Layer

| Trans-Id Data Date = mm-dd-yyyy |
(b) Presentation Layer

| ID | Length | Trans-Id Data Date = mm-dd-yyyy |
(c) Session Layer

| TSAP | ChkSum | ID | Length | Trans-Id Data Date = mm-dd-yyyy |
(d) Transport Layer

| Address | Seq Nbr | TSAP | ChkSum | ID | Length | Trans-Id Data Date = mm-dd-yyyy |
(e) Network Layer

| Header | Address | Seq Nbr | TSAP | ChkSum | ID | Length | Trans-Id Data Date = mm-dd-yyy | Chksum |
(f) Data Link Layer

Figure 1.7   OSI Reference Model Formatting

to be deducted. The transaction identifier tells the message recipient what to do with the record, inserts it, updates it, and so on. The message is illustrated in Figure 1.7(a). The client application then invokes a procedure call to send the message to the server process.

Presentation Layer

The application layer formatted each field in the record being transmitted according to its own format rules. The receiving application may have a different set of format conventions. For example, the sending application may view a date in one format, whereas the receiving application uses a different date format. The presentation layer is responsible for translating from one format to another. It can do this by changing to a standard transmission format that is converted by its peer layer or by converting it directly to the format expected by the receiving application. The message after such translation has taken place appears in the PDU shown in Figure 1.7(b). The presentation layer then sends the message to the session layer.

Session Layer

The session layer's major functions are to set up and perhaps monitor a set of dialogue rules by which the two applications can communicate and to bring a session to an orderly conclusion. A session dialogue can be one way (simplex) or bidirectional. Examples of one-way communication include radio and television; the station is always the sender only and the recipient receives but never sends a message back (at least not directly over the same medium). In bidirectional sessions messages flow in both directions. Ordinary conversations are bidirectional. In polite conversations people alternate between sending and receiving. Other situations benefit from having data flow in both directions simultaneously, a characteristic of regular mail and e-mail systems. One-way communication is called **simplex** communication. Bidirectional communication is called **half-duplex** when data transmission alternates between sender and receiver and **full-duplex** when data flows in both directions simultaneously. **Flow control** refers to setting up message transmission. Once the connection has been made and the dialogue rules established, data transfer can occur. The session layer appends an identifier and length indicator at the beginning of the data block creating its PDU, as illustrated in Figure 1.7(c). These two fields identify the function of the message (which contains user data as opposed to control functions such as session establishment or termination).

Transport Layer

The transport layer is the first of the OSI layers responsible for actually transmitting the data. The higher layers are oriented toward the data and application interfaces, not to data transmission. The transport layer uses an address called a **transport services access point (TSAP)** to uniquely identify session entities. TSAPs of the source and destination session entities, together with a checksum to detect errors and message sequence numbers, are appended to the message received from the session layer, creating the PDU shown in Figure 1.7(d). The message sequence numbers ensure that all parts of the message are received (recall your 1/5, 2/5, . . . package sequence) and place the parts in the proper order if they were received in a different order from the original sending order. Parts of a message may be received out of order because they have been sent over different paths.

Network Layer

The network layer provides accounting and routing functions. Upon receiving a message from the transport layer, the network layer logs the event to the accounting system and then prepares the message for transmission to the next node on the path to the destination, node M in our example. Some networks do this by looking up the destination address in the network routing table to find the next address along that path. A routing table for a node in a small network is shown in Figure 1.8. As already mentioned, routing in a LAN is done by broadcasting the message to all nodes. The address and a sequence number from the transport layer are appended to the message, as illustrated in Figure 1.7(e).

Data Link Layer

The data link layer is responsible for data delineation, error detection, and logical control of the link. In Figure 1.5 node X is between nodes A and M. The data link layer facilitates flow control between nodes A and X and again between nodes X and M. Note that data link flow control is for one computer to another, whereas transport layer flow control is end-to-end, that is, between source and destination applications. To fulfill its function, the data link layer appends a header and trailer to the message, creating the PDU illustrated in Figure 1.7(f). The header contains a flag to indicate the beginning of the message, the address of the recipient, message sequence numbers, and the message type (data or control). The trailer contains a checksum for the data link block and a frame-ending flag.

Physical Layer

The physical layer does not append anything to the message. It simply accepts the message from the data link layer and translates the bits into signals on the medium.

Receiving the Message

When node A physically transmits the message, the following sequence of events occurs:

1. The message is passed over the link connecting nodes A and X.
2. The message is passed to the data link layer in node X. The message is checked for transmission errors, the PDU information applied by node A's data link layer is removed, and the message is sent to node X's network layer.
3. Node X's network layer records the accounting information for the message and then strips off the network layer protocol data and examines the destination address. The destination is not node X, so the network layer consults its network routing table and determines the next link on the path to node M. Node X's network layer affixes the proper network layer protocol data and sends the message to node X's data link layer.

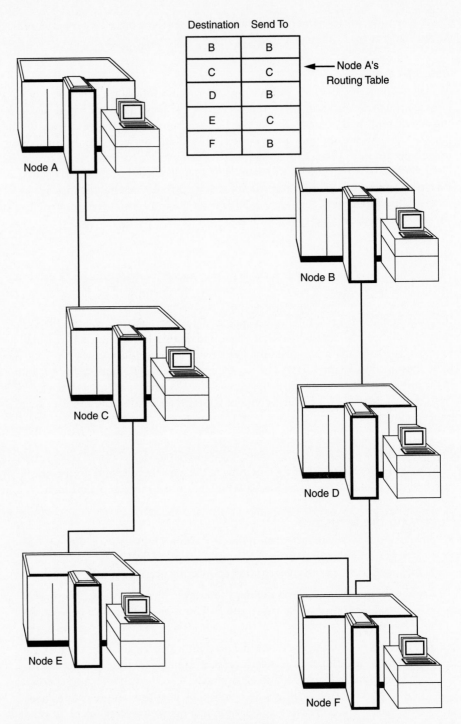

Destination	Send To
B	B
C	C
D	B
E	C
F	B

← Node A's Routing Table

Node A

Node B

Node C

Node D

Node E

Node F

Figure 1.8   Example of a Network Routing Table

4. Node X's data link layer creates its PDU and sends the message to node M.

5. Node M's data link layer receives the message, strips off node X's data link layer protocol data, checks for transmission errors, and passes the data up to node M's network layer.

6. Node M's network layer gathers accounting data, strips off the network layer protocol data, and finds that the message is destined for an application in this node.

7. The message is passed up to M's transport layer, where the sequence number is checked to ensure that no messages have been lost. The transport layer protocol data is removed.

8. The message arrives at the session layer, where relevant protocol data is examined and removed.

9. The message arrives at node M's presentation layer, where appropriate action is taken.

10. The message arrives at the application, where it is acted on.

Functional Layer Standards

You may realize by now that even though the OSI Reference Model cites seven functional layers, different strategies may be used at each layer. For example, there are many different data link layer protocols in use today, such as the asynchronous and synchronous protocols that are covered in Chapter 15. Likewise, at the network layer there are several widely used protocols for PDU formatting and routing, such as the internet protocol (IP) used on the Internet, LANs, and WANs. We have multiple standards at the various layers because of technology evolution and because different network types have their own special requirements.

GENERAL NETWORK IMPLEMENTATIONS

Earlier, we stated that there are two general network subtypes: LANs and WANs. Within these two subtypes, we have a variety of network implementations, each of which is optimized to fulfill one or more specific networking needs. Among the most common of these implementations are LANs, WANs, **value-added networks (VANs),** enterprise networks, internets, the Internet, and intranets. Because these network implementations often interface with LANs, we provide a brief overview of each. Additional details of some of these may be found in Chapter 15 (WANs) and Chapter 16 (WANs, VANs, internets, and the Internet).

LANs

A LAN serves a limited geographic area at high speeds—usually 10 million bits per second (Mbps) or higher. All components of the LAN are commonly owned by the organization that uses it. In contrast, a WAN often uses media and transmission facilities obtained from a **common carrier** such as a telephone company. The nodes in many of today's LANs are desktop systems such as personal computers. Henceforth, we also use the terms *workstations, clients,* and *servers* in referring to LAN nodes. The word **workstation** is used here to represent a LAN user's computer; other terms used in referring to a workstation are **client** and node. A **server** is a network node that is dedicated to providing services to client nodes. Services that may be provided include network printing, application sharing, and database sharing. We examine several classes of servers in Chapter 5.

MANs

A MAN (Metropolitan Area Network) is a high-speed network covering wider distances than a LAN. A MAN spans distances of approximately 100 miles; therefore, it is suitable for connecting devices in a metropolitan area. MAN speeds are typically 100 Mbps or higher. The most commonly implemented MAN is the Fiber Distributed Data Interface (FDDI). The FDDI is a standard developed by the American National Standards Institute (ANSI). It operates at 100 Mbps over fiber optic cable for distances up to 200 kilometers.

WANs

A WAN is the oldest type of network. WANs generally span a wide geographic area such as a state, province, country, or multiple countries. However, some WANs are confined to a limited geographic area. In these cases the WAN is distinguished from a LAN by the speed of transmission and the transmission protocols used. That is, a WAN in a limited geographic area could be easily extended over a wide area using the same technologies. The same is not true of a LAN. Furthermore, WANs typically use the transmission services of a common carrier. If a company were to set up a WAN with nodes in Australia, the U.S., and Europe, it is unlikely that the company would deploy its own communications media. Instead, the company would probably lease communications lines from a communications company. We discuss WANs in more detail in Chapters 15 and 16.

VANs

A VAN is a network owned by a communications utility that sells the services of the network to other companies. Suppose you wanted to deploy a network with nodes in 50 major cities. It would be quite costly to lease communications lines from a common carrier. An alternative might be to subscribe to the services of a VAN. The communications utility that owns the VAN would provide the connectivity to the 50 locations. Your company would connect to the VAN via a local telephone connection and pay the communications utility a flat monthly fee for the connection and a small fee for each packet of data you transmitted. The value added by the communications utility is the maintenance and management of the communications circuits. If you used the VAN extensively, the per-packet cost would eventually exceed the cost of leasing lines from a common carrier. VANs, also sometimes called **X.25 networks,** packet switching networks, and public data networks, are discussed in Chapter 16 as a method for interconnecting networks.

Enterprise Networks

An **enterprise network** is an organization's complete network. Before the widespread adoption of LANs, a company typically had one and only one network, their WAN.

With the advent of LANs, many companies installed departmental LANs to improve the productivity of work groups. These LANs were not originally connected to other LANs or the WAN. Soon, these companies realized that there was a benefit to having users on one LAN communicate with users or applications on other LANs or on the WAN, and the various networks were connected together to form one corporate-wide network, the enterprise network.

Internets

An **internet** (with a lowercase *i*) is the interconnection of two or more networks. The enterprise network just described is an example of an internet.

The Internet

The Internet (with an uppercase *I*) is a specific instance of an internet. The Internet is a global network of networks. The Internet is made up of hundreds of networks, thousands of nodes, and millions of users throughout most countries of the world. Represented on the Internet are companies, government organizations, educational institutions, independent service providers, and individuals. The Internet has evolved from a research-oriented network to a commercial, entertainment, social, political, and information utility.

Intranets

A popular feature of the Internet is the World Wide Web (WWW). The WWW is a mechanism for traversing the Internet and uses specific protocols to provide users with a variety of ways to view data. Organizations can set up web pages that contain information and hypertext links to other web pages. **Hypertext** is a method for working with documents. Hypertext allows a user to follow links embedded in a document. The links allow you to jump to another document (or to a different location in the current document) to gain additional information about the linked topic. Hypertext also allows you to return directly to a previously referenced location or to progressively return along the path of links you have followed. For example, you may be visiting the web page of a sports store in one city and see a reference to a new bicycle made by a company in a different city. The sports store might provide a link to the bicycle manufacturer's home page. By choosing to follow that link you can get additional details about the bicycle and the manufacturer. Following that, you might follow new links from the bicycle manufacturer to get more information about the company or the bicycle. At any time you can return directly to your original position in the sports store's page and perhaps place an order for the bicycle.

Hypertext Markup Language (HTML) is the language commonly used to prepare hypertext documents. HTML allows the document designer to format text (bold, underline, fonts, and character size), embed graphic images in the document, define paragraphs and headers, and establish links to other documents. With these capabilities, an organization can make a wide variety of information available to its employees and customers through an easy-to-use interface. The interfaces most widely used today are called **browsers,** and several browsers are widely used. Examples of browsers include Netscape Communications Corporation's Netscape, Microsoft's Internet Explorer, and the

National Center for Supercomputer Applications' Mosaic, all of which provide a graphical user interface and are available on most of the hardware and software platforms used to access the Internet.

An **intranet** is an organization's private web. Companies have found that WWW capabilities can improve the information flow and availability in a company. Rather than depending on printed matter, the companies can publish information and make graphics available on their private web. These companies use an intranet rather than publishing on the Internet because the information being provided is intended for corporate use only rather than the public at large.

SUMMARY

Data communications is a subset of communications in general. All forms of communication—oral, written, electronic, and so on—have common requirements. The four basic components of communication are a sender, a receiver, a medium, and a message. In addition the message must be understood and errors must be detected and corrected. Data communications networks must meet these basic requirements.

There are two major classes of networks: local area networks and wide area networks. A variety of different implementations exists for each of these types. Generally a WAN operates at lower speeds, uses different types of media, and spans a greater distance than a LAN. The main reasons for using networks are communicating, sharing resources, control, security, and cost-effectiveness.

Standards organizations have recognized that there are different types of networks and different ways to implement a particular type of network. For example, there are several different types of LANs. One of the major standards efforts is based on the International Standards Organization's Open System Interconnection (OSI) Reference Model. The OSI Reference Model defines seven functional layers: application, presentation, session, transport, network, data link, and physical. Each layer carries out well-defined functions. The OSI layer in the sending computer performs its functions for its peer layer in the receiving computer. Messages are passed between adjacent layers through well-defined layer interfaces.

Several network implementations have evolved. Among these are LANs, WANs, VANs, enterprise networks, internets, the Internet, and intranets. Each network type provide a set of capabilities that makes it desirable in certain situations.

Key Terms

American Standard Code for Information
    Interchange (ASCII)
application layer
browser
client/server (C/S)
client
coaxial cable
common carrier
data link layer

encapsulation
enterprise network
enveloping
error detection
Extended Binary Coded Decimal
    Interchange Code (EBCDIC)
fiber optic cable
flow control
full-duplex mode

half-duplex mode

host computer

hypertext

Hypertext Markup Language (HTML)

infrared light

International Standards Organization
 (ISO)

internet

intranet

link

local area network (LAN)

medium

message

network of computers

network layer

node

open standard

Open Systems Interconnection (OSI)
 Reference Model

path

physical layer

presentation layer

protocol

receiver

routing

routing algorithm

sender

server

session

session layer

simplex transmission

terminal network

transport layer

transport services access point (TSAP)

value-added network (VAN)

wide area network (WAN)

workstation

X.25 network

Review Questions

1. What are the four basic requirements for communication?
2. What does an error-detection scheme for data transmission do?
3. Compare a terminal network and a network of computers.
4. What are the seven layers of the OSI Reference Model?
5. List two functions performed by each layer of the OSI Reference Model.
6. Compare the transmission of a letter in paper form from one corporate location to another with transmitting messages under the OSI Reference Model.
7. What is meant by the following statement? "A layer in the OSI Reference Model's sending node operates on behalf of its peer or equivalent layer in the receiving node."
8. What are the general characteristics of a LAN?
9. Describe some differences between LAN and WAN characteristics.
10. Describe the characteristics of
    a. a LAN
    b. a WAN
    c. a VAN
    d. an enterprise network
    e. an internet
    f. the Internet
    g. an intranet

Problems and Exercises

1. The objective of the OSI Reference Model is to define and organize the functions required to move a message from an application on one node to a destination on another node. There are some parallels between the way the Reference Model sends messages and the way in which we send objects from one place to another. Compare the ways in which we prepare and transmit letters, large heavy packages, and new automobiles.

2. Identify the sender, receiver, medium, and error-detection methods for the following forms of communication:
    a. people speaking in a room
    b. people speaking on a telephone
    c. television and radio
    d. CB radio
    e. telegraphy
3. Security was not listed as an essential element of communication. Do you think that security is an essential element of communication? Justify your decision.

Chapter 2

Introduction to Local Area Networks

CHAPTER PREVIEW

Technologies such as telecommunications, typewriters, copy machines, and computers have significantly changed the ways companies conduct business, and this evolution of the modern office is continuing. Two computer technologies that flourished in the 1980s are microcomputers and data communications. It is only natural that these two technologies would combine to provide a computing environment with a greater impact than either technology alone could provide. In this chapter you will see how LANs are used to extend the power of the stand-alone microcomputer.

Specific topics you will read about in this chapter include

reasons organizations use networks

popular network applications

distinguishing features of LANs

situations in which a LAN can be useful

added management responsibilities when using a LAN

LAN selection criteria

By the end of this chapter, you should have an understanding of why we use LANs, the LAN application environment, and the items to consider when selecting LAN hardware and software.

WHY USE LANS?

We use networks for a variety of reasons. Most early microcomputer LANs were implemented for resource sharing. Since then additional advantages—communication, management control, cost-effectiveness, downsizing, and new application software—have materialized. Let us now look briefly at each of these purposes.

Resource Sharing

The need to share resources is still one of the primary reasons for using a network. A network consists of a variety of resources, such as disk drives, tape drives, printers, data, application programs, modems, scanners, and facsimile (FAX) machines. Dedicating re-sources of this type to each user is expensive. In a network some or all of these resources may be shared. For example, the stand-alone microcomputer **workstations** in Figure 2.1 illustrate three basic ways that a user can print a document: Each workstation can have its own dedicated printer, as illustrated in Figure 2.1(a). Alternatively, several worksta-tions can share one printer, either by using a data switch, as illustrated in Figure 2.1(b), or by the user of one workstation placing the data to be printed on a floppy diskette and carrying it to another workstation with an attached printer (a technique sometimes called sneakernet), as illustrated in Figure 2.1(c). A **data switch** is a hardware device to which two or more computers and one printer may be attached. The data switch allows

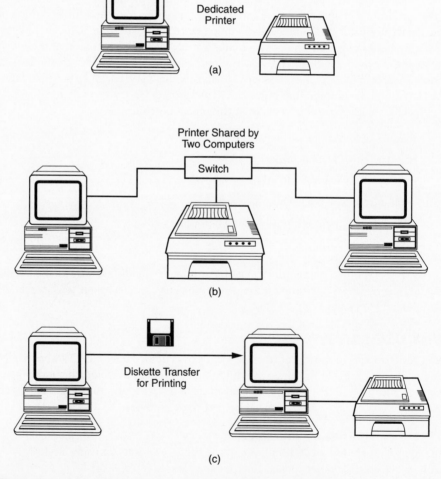

Figure 2.1   Stand-Alone Microcomputers and Printer Sharing

one computer to connect to the printer and use it exclusively. When that computer finishes printing, another computer can connect to the printer and print its output.

With a data switch a user needing access to the printer must activate the switch to connect his or her workstation to the printer. The switch may be a manual switch, as illustrated in Figure 2.2, a software switch activated through a software utility, or a switch that senses when an attached microcomputer wants to send printer data. In the latter case the switch continually rotates through connections with each microcomputer. If a microcomputer wants to print, the switch recognizes it and locks onto that channel until the entire job is printed. The switch then resumes sampling each available connection for other print jobs. With simple switches only one user can use the printer at a time. More sophisticated switches have memory that allows several users to write logically to an attached printer at the same time. This is accomplished by holding one job in the memory buffer while another job is being printed, as illustrated in Figure 2.3.

A third alternative is to connect the workstations and printers on a network, as illustrated in Figure 2.4. Each workstation has access to the network printers as though they were locally attached. Naturally, several users may request to use the same printer at the same time. A software application called a **spooler,** located within the network server, handles **contention** for the printer. The spooler accepts print jobs and saves them in a disk file. When the printer is available, the spooler selects a completed print job in the disk file and prints that job. When that job is done printing, the spooler selects another job for printing.

Resources other than printers, such as disks, files, FAX machines, and so on, can be shared among LAN users. A variety of techniques are used to accomplish sharing;

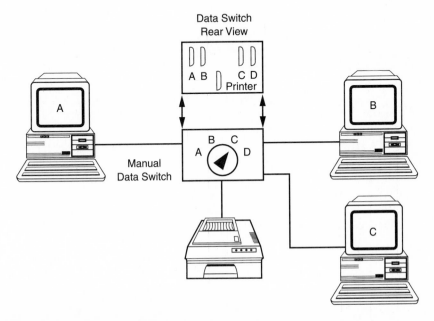

Figure 2.2   Manual Data Switch

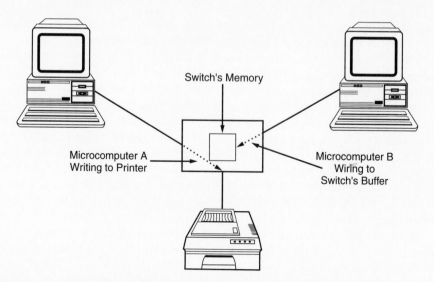

Figure 2.3   Switch Using Memory to Hold One Job While Printing Another

individual techniques, such as a spooler for printers, are tailored for each type of resource being shared. Some techniques used to share LAN resources are described in Chapter 5.

Communication

If you were asked why people use telephone networks, your likely response would be "to allow people to communicate." We use data communications networks for the same reason, but the objects that are communicating are not always people. Figure 2.5 shows a variety of users and applications communicating: Person-to-person communication is shown by a dotted line, person-to-application communication shown by a solid line, and application-to-application dialogue shown by a dashed/dotted line.

The messages being exchanged can also differ. The person-to-person communication may be an electronic conversation with the two parties exchanging messages in real time: When User A types a message on his or her terminal and hits the enter key, the message is immediately displayed on User B's workstation. The person-to-application communication may be a user making an inquiry into a corporate database to check on a shipment for a customer, for example. The application-to-application dialogue may be the transfer of a file from one node to another. Examples of other network applications are cited in a later section of this chapter.

Management Control

A third reason for using a network is management control. A LAN can help standardize the microcomputer environment. At the outset of the microcomputer age, some companies left the choice of software and hardware to individuals or departments. As a result they found a variety of software being used on hardware platforms that were not

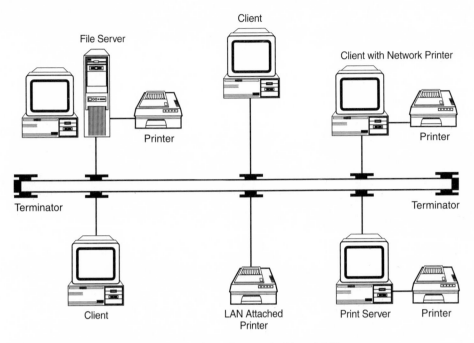

Figure 2.4   Printers and Workstations Connected to a LAN

homogeneous. That is, there were two or three different word processors, two or three spreadsheets, two or more database managers, and so on running on IBM-compatible, Apple-compatible, and other types of microcomputers. Having such a variety of software and hardware creates two immediate problems: portability and education. **Portability** is the ability to transfer an application or application data from one system to another. Files maintained on one word processor must be converted before being used by another user with different hardware or different word processing software, or users must learn to use several different software packages to perform the same function—a time-consuming and expensive proposition.

Furthermore, imagine a work environment in which each user maintains his or her own copy of the same data. Changes in the data are not reflected in all copies of the data at the same time. Thus if User A makes a change to an employee's address and telephone number in her database, that change is not immediately reflected in User B's database. Coordinating changes of data in several databases is usually not a simple task. The result is inconsistent data—the data equivalent of anarchy. With a network, users can share data and avoid data inconsistencies. Data consistency and integrity can be further enhanced through management control of data and file backups. In the stand-alone computing environment, each user is responsible for maintaining backups, and the frequency and completeness of backups is usually poor. With a LAN, management can carry out a comprehensive backup policy for shared data. This provides for better data and file protection against intentional or accidental data destruction.

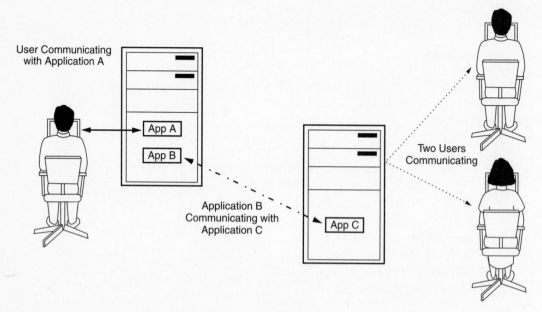

User Communicating
with Application A

App A

App B

Application B
Communicating with
Application C

App C

Two Users
Communicating

Figure 2.5   Objects Using a Network to Communicate

Application standards can be set up more easily in a network, because most application programs, such as word processors and spreadsheet programs, can be installed on one or more network nodes called **servers.** Users can then access these applications over the network. Thus, in a small network all users may run the same word processing program located on a specific network node. When all users use the same version of the same word processor, document interchange is a simple matter. Contrast this with two or more users having different versions of the same word processor, or worse yet, completely different word processing software. In this case documents created under one system must be converted and possibly reformatted before being used by the other word processing system.

LANs can also help control one of the most unsettling problems facing computer users today: **computer viruses.** With diskless workstations and **virus detection software,** management can reduce the risk of viral infections. A **diskless workstation,** as the name implies, has no local disk drives. This reduces the ways in which a virus can be introduced. An added security benefit of diskless workstations is the inability of a company's workers to copy software or corporate data for personal gain. The disadvantage of diskless workstations is their complete dependence on the network. They cannot be used in a standalone mode, nor can they be used in a location that does not have access to the network.

Cost-Effectiveness

Communicating, sharing, and management control are three of the benefits of using networks. In the final analysis, however, there is only one reason for using a network: cost-effectiveness. The ability to share resources has a direct impact on an organization's expenses. If users can share hardware, less hardware is needed. If a network were used only for resource sharing, it would be cost-effective when the cost of installing and operating the network is less than or equal to the cost of hardware, software, data preparation, and other costs in a nonnetworked environment. The less obvious cost-effectiveness comes from the ability of users to communicate and thus improve their productivity. A direct benefit of this ability is the reduction of paperwork.

Downsizing

In some companies LANs have been used to downsize the data processing hardware, software, and personnel requirements. **Downsizing** refers to using smaller computer platforms in place of large computers. Some companies have replaced their mainframe computers with one or more microcomputer LANs. These companies found that they could provide better data processing services at much lower hardware, software, and personnel costs. One company's experience with downsizing resulted in cutting the company's annual systems budget from $10 million to $2 million and reducing its information services staff from 70 programmers to 20. This represented an 80 percent cost savings. Diagrams of that company's computer configuration before and after downsizing are shown in Figures 2.6 and 2.7, respectively. Other companies that have tried downsizing have not realized the same gains as the company just cited. These companies found that downsizing did not meet their expectations of cost-effectiveness and the ability to effectively process applications. Each company must carefully evaluate its computing environment to determine whether downsizing will be effective. Downsizing is not a good alternative for every company.

New Application Software

Personal productivity applications are designed to help individual users to do their jobs better. One new application technology associated with networks is called **groupware:**

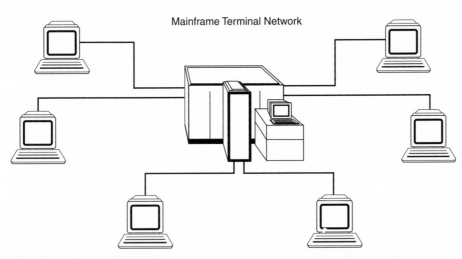

Figure 2.6   *Computer System Before Downsizing*

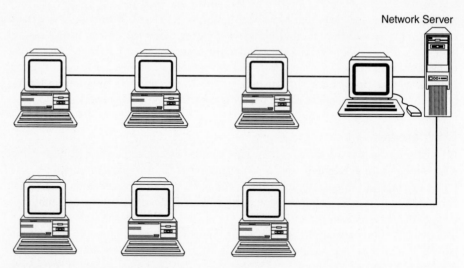

Network Server

Figure 2.7   Computer System After Downsizing

applications oriented toward improving the productivity of a group of people working together. Groupware automates work functions that require the communication and collaboration of two or more individuals. These tools raise office productivity and make LANs even more cost-effective.

The main reason we use computers is to solve problems, and it is the application software that actually goes about solving problems. We now look at both personal and **workgroup productivity software** and their relationship to LANs.

APPLICATION SOFTWARE

The scope of network application software is so varied that it would be a monumental task to describe each application. Let us look just at applications that allow users to make more effective use of their microcomputers on a LAN.

Personal Productivity Applications

Personal productivity software is single-user oriented. It helps improve the productivity of individual users. Personal productivity software is often found on LANs to provide hardware and software sharing. In contrast, groupware provides idea sharing.

Word Processing and Desktop Publishing

Microcomputer word processing and desktop publishing applications continue to expand in scope. Many of them are still single-user oriented, but document-processing competition is intense, and software vendors must improve their products to keep competitive. It is therefore reasonable to assume that future versions will allow several users to pull out sections of a single document at the same time, allow one user to update a document and let others concurrently view but not change it, and allow users to work concurrently on the same document and view or edit the document in concert. Each of these capabilities helps improve workgroup productivity.

Spreadsheets

Spreadsheet applications are used extensively on LANs, primarily for applications that require the manipulation of numbers. Examples of specific uses include budgeting, cost analysis, preparation of financial statements, and performing what-if analyses. **What-if analysis** is a form of modeling that allows a user to see the effects of changing parameters in a specific situation. For example, a marketing analyst can see the effects of price and interest rate changes on profits. Using spreadsheets on a LAN, users can easily share templates and multiple users can access, modify, and print completed spreadsheets. However, most spreadsheets in use today do not allow several users to work simultaneously on the same spreadsheet.

Today's spreadsheet software is expanding to encompass multiple files. For example, one spreadsheet file might be linked to another, so changes in one are automatically reflected in the other. A LAN can provide the setting for widespread sharing. At the same time, the LAN can provide protection against unauthorized changes to spreadsheets and against update contention.

Database Management

A **database management system (DBMS)** gives you the ability to define, use, and manage data. Not only can you create, retrieve, modify, and delete data, but also most modern DBMSs have high-level data languages, report generators, and application generators. With these facilities nontechnical people can direct the DBMS to produce tailored reports and respond to ad hoc enquiries. With LAN-oriented databases users share the database. This reduces the amount of redundant data storage that occurs when individuals maintain their own databases on stand-alone systems. Reduction in data redundancy also helps eliminate data inconsistencies. When a DBMS allows data sharing, it must also reconcile problems arising from data contention.

Presentation Services

Presentation services refers to the generation and use of graphics. Graphics hardware and software can be expensive. A LAN allows these expensive resources to be shared, providing a cost-effective way of distributing graphics capabilities.

Workgroup Applications

One motive for having a LAN is communication. For years workers have been communicating in person, via telephones, and with printed material. The first two methods require the correspondents to be at the proper place at the proper time and also to be available for the dialogue. Written material does not require this coordination but often lacks the timeliness and spontaneity of oral communication. An ideal communication system provides the timeliness, spontaneity, and interaction of oral communication with the scheduling independence and recording of written communication. One part of workgroup applications, or groupware, addresses this issue. Although we have not yet attained the ideal, we are constantly getting closer.

One of the most explicit communication applications is electronic messaging. The most publicized electronic messaging application is electronic mail, but other types, such as voice mail, time-staged message delivery systems, and **electronic conferencing,** are also in use. These applications are written explicitly for networks and may eventually surpass resource sharing as the primary motive for a LAN.

Electronic Mail

One of the earliest workgroup applications was **electronic mail (e-mail).** An e-mail system has many of the capabilities of a conventional postal system, such as collecting and distributing correspondence of various sizes and types and routing the correspondence to recipients in a timely manner. However, we have come to expect many more capabilities from an e-mail system than from a conventional postal system. Today's e-mail systems allow correspondents to exchange communications containing text, graphics, and voice images in batch or real-time mode. For many companies, e-mail has become a primary mode of communications.

Electronic Appointment Calendars

Electronic appointment calendars are stored on the network. One user can consult other users' appointment calendars to find a time at which each user is available for a meeting. The electronic calendar system can then schedule the meeting for each participant.

Electronic Filing Cabinets

E-mail and other machine-readable documents can be stored in disk folders that are equivalent to file folders in conventional filing cabinets. Messages and documents in the folder can later be retrieved, modified, or deleted. Most filing systems maintain an index of the folders and their contents.

File Exchange Utilities

File exchange utilities allow files to be easily copied from one network node to another.

Project Management Systems

Project management systems assist in planning projects and allocating resources. The introduction of LAN implementations has allowed these systems to be integrated more completely into the workgroup. A manager and team member can agree on the parameters of a task, the team member can update his or her progress, and the manager can monitor the progress. Projects can therefore be managed more effectively.

Group Decision Support Systems

Group decision support systems (GDSSs) assist individuals and groups in the decision-making process and help them set objectives. There are two levels of GDSSs. A lower-level GDSS does not have an underlying decision support system, but simply serves as a bulletin board for the exchange and development of ideas. A higher-level GDSS includes a decision support system that provides more tools for group users than a lower-level GDSS.

Electronic Meeting Systems

Electronic meeting systems (EMSs) go beyond simple teleconferencing. The inclusion of networks allows participants to exchange machine-readable information in the form of graphics, text, audio, and full-motion video. If electronic meeting systems are combined with decision support system software, meeting participants can work in parallel to reach solutions.

Document Management Systems

Document management systems help an organization manage and control its documents. Capabilities include indexing documents, finding documents based on keywords contained in the document, controlling document changes, and allowing several users to collaborate on document editing.

These groupware applications are only a few of those being used today. The future holds even greater promise. In a future work scenario, two car designers in different locations might work together on the design of a new car model. Each designer can see immediately the work done by the other. Moreover, the designers can change the contours of the automobile body by molding it with an electronic glove, much like a sculptor molds a clay figure. The difference is that the car model designers form a graphic image, and that image can be changed by two or more designers working together but in different rooms or locations.

CHARACTERISTICS OF LANS

Let us look now at the general characteristics of LANs, which are listed in Table 2.1. In later chapters we go into detail about LAN hardware and software. In this section we compare LAN technology with **wide area network (WAN)** technology when appropriate. These comparisons will help you understand the place of each technology.

Transparent Use

One of the objectives of most LANs is to achieve transparent use; that is, users connected to a LAN should detect few differences between using a stand-alone microcomputer and using one connected to a LAN. Access to the file server's disk should be carried out as though it were a locally attached disk drive. Printing to a network printer ought to be done in the same manner as directing output to a local printer. The only

Table 2.1   LAN Characteristics

Transparent use

Mixed hardware and software

Limited geographical area

High speed

Resource sharing

Communication protocols

Local ownership

major difference between stand-alone and LAN microcomputers should be security. The network user usually must log onto a LAN by providing a user ID and a password.

Mixed Hardware and Software

Most LANs in operation today are microcomputer based; that is, most nodes on LANs are microcomputers. However, LANs also connect large computing systems, and it is not uncommon for large systems to be nodes on a LAN with microcomputers of various types, in which case the large computer often functions as a server. A server is a computer (usually) dedicated to providing one or more services to the other nodes. For example, a file server provides file and disk access services, and a printer server provides printing services. Thus a node may access data on a file server and route its printed output to a printer server. In contrast, most of today's WANs have only minicomputers, mainframes, or supercomputers for nodes. Moreover, LANs may include a variety of microcomputers. With these mixed hardware LANs, it is also common to find a variety of operating systems and applications being used. Having mixed hardware and software allows users to use the right equipment for the right job and to make good use of existing equipment. Mixed hardware and software also complicates the job of LAN administration.

Limited Geographical Area

A LAN is designed to operate in a limited geographical area. The limits depend on the type of network. Appletalk, a network for Apple Macintosh computers, spans 300 m. In an Ethernet network, the maximum network distance is 2500 m. A third network, the fiber distributed data interface (FDDI), spans distances up to 200 km. As you can see there are considerable variances in the limited area LANs can serve. In contrast, a WAN can be either geographically distributed or confined to a local area; that is, there are no restrictions on the media distances for WANs.

High Speed

The speed of a LAN, like the distance spanned, depends on the specific implementation. In general the speeds exceed 10 Mbps, with speeds of 4, 10, 16, and 100 Mbps common for microcomputer LANs. The transmission speeds have been constantly increasing, and speeds of 1 billion (G) bps will soon be a reality. The FDDI LAN cited in the previous paragraph and Ethernet LANs operate at 100 Mbps. Fiber optic LANs in the laboratory have reached speeds of 2 Gbps. To put this speed into perspective, an average textbook contains about 1 million characters, or 8 million bits of text. Thus, a speed of 2 Gbps is roughly equivalent to transmitting all the characters from 250 texts each second! In contrast, a common WAN speed is 56,000 bps. This is approximately 1800 times slower than a 100-Mbps LAN, and it would take 142 seconds to transfer just one book. Higher WAN speeds of just over 1 Mbps are available, but are less common. WAN speeds are also increasing, and WANs may soon operate at LAN speeds. When this occurs, you can expect to see many of the differences between LANs and WANs disappear.

Resource Sharing

As discussed earlier, one of the basic goals of networks is resource sharing. Data, programs, and hardware (such as printers and disks) are all resources that can be shared.

LAN Media

Attaining high LAN transmission speeds requires a high-capacity communications medium. Most early LANs used **coaxial cable** as the transmission medium. Today the popularity of coaxial cable is giving way to **twisted-pair wires** for low-speed LANs (150 Mbps or lower) and **fiber optic cables** for both low- and high-speed LANs. Wireless LAN media, such as **infrared light,** broadcast radio, and microwave radio, operate at speeds up to 15 Mbps, and one vendor has said it will provide wireless speeds up to 100 Mbps. A LAN configuration using a conducting medium such as twisted-pair wires, coaxial cable, or fiber optics is shown in Figure 2.8. Use of a radiated medium such as infrared light and a LAN using radio waves is illustrated in Figure 2.9. WANs use each of the media used by LANs. In addition a WAN might use satellite transmission. Often a WAN's transmission medium is obtained from a common communications carrier, such as a telephone company, whereas a LAN medium is usually owned by the LAN proprietor.

Media Access Control Protocols

Each network has specific ways in which it gains access to the communications medium, transmits data over the medium, and routes messages. LANs generally differ from other networks in their methods for doing this. The technical details of **media access control (MAC)** protocols are covered in Chapter 3.

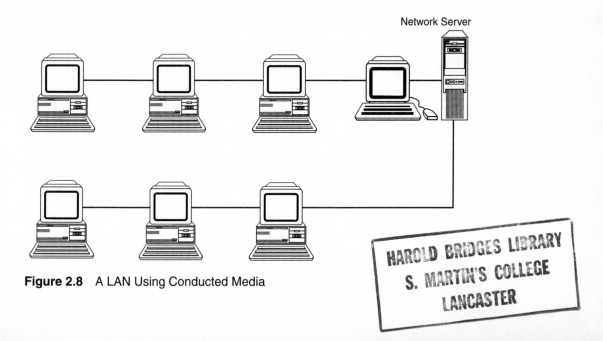

Network Server

Figure 2.8 A LAN Using Conducted Media

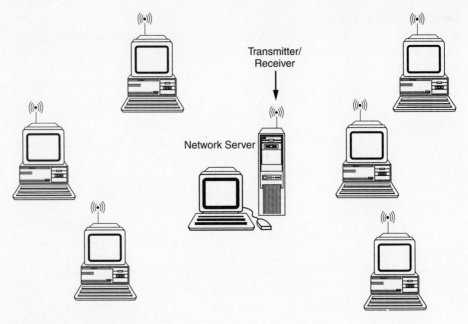

Figure 2.9   A Wireless LAN

Local Ownership

Usually, a LAN is completely owned and managed by the using organization. That is, the organization is responsible for all of the equipment and software, including installing and controlling the communications medium. In contrast, most WANs use media supplied by a common carrier such as a telephone company.

ADDITIONAL LAN RESPONSIBILITIES

Thus far we have mentioned several problems that a LAN can help solve and benefits that can result from implementing a LAN. A LAN also comes with added responsibilities. Earlier we mentioned that in stand-alone computer systems, each user is also the computer operator. As such, users are principally responsible for making backups, keeping the system running, reporting problems, replacing paper in the printer, and so on. With a LAN many resources can be shared, but one thing that should not be shared is the responsibility for managing the LAN. When management is everyone's responsibility it is also no one's responsibility. Thus a LAN must be managed, and there must be someone given that responsibility and authority. We devote several chapters to this important topic. For now suffice it to say that a well-managed LAN requires additional skills beyond those usually required by individual microcomputer users.

LAN SELECTION CRITERIA

You have not learned much about the details of LANs and LAN management; however, it is appropriate to introduce LAN selection criteria here. These criteria also establish the environment of LANs and hence will establish a basis for learning about LANs and evaluating competing technologies that are discussed in subsequent chapters. Table 2.2 lists the major factors to consider when selecting a LAN. You need to provide prospective vendors with sufficient information to size the system. This is best done by analyzing the problems you are trying to solve and any factors that may constrain your selection. Some of these constraints must be communicated to the potential vendors, whereas others (for example, your budget) should not be given to vendors. (If you tell vendors how much money you intend to spend or are able to spend, you will be surprised at how many configurations will cost this amount of money.) The effects of the criteria given in Table 2.2 on the selection process are described in this section.

Cost

If cost were not a consideration, LAN selection would be easier. You could buy the fastest, biggest workstations and servers available and use the most comprehensive LAN software available. Deciding which hardware and software modules fit this description would not be simple, but lack of price constraints would make selection much easier. For most of us, however, cost is an overriding constraint, and you must choose the best solution within your budget. Usually cost is the most inflexible constraint under which you must operate, and in the final analysis the LAN must be a cost-effective solution to your problem.

In general, as the speed of a LAN increases, so does the cost. For instance, the **LAN adapters** that provide computer-to-LAN medium connection for a high-speed LAN are more expensive than those for a low-speed one. Also, as the number of users and workstations increases, so does the cost of the LAN. Each workstation needs a LAN adapter, each of which may cost $200 or more (LAN adapter prices start under $50), and wiring hubs (a hardware device used in some networks to connect wires from workstations) may be needed to connect the workstations to each other. Each workstation must have LAN software, often paid for on a per-station basis. As the number of concurrent users increases, so does the amount of work required of the server. Increased demands on the server require you either to obtain a more powerful computer as a server (sometimes

Table 2.2 LAN Selection Criteria

Cost	Distance and Medium	LAN Software and Hardware
Number of workstations	Speed	Adherence to established standards
Type of workstations	Applications	Vendor
Number of concurrent users	Expandability	Vendor support
Type of use	Device Connectivity	Manageability
Number and type of printers	Connectivity with other networks	Security

called a platform) or to buy several servers. Moreover, installing cabling can be an expensive proposition, particularly in an existing building. An existing building has barriers such as ceilings and walls that restrict your ability to install new cabling. You must pull cables through ceilings and walls rather than simply stringing it in the exposed areas of a new building.

Hardware and software are not the only costs you will incur. Other costs you must plan to incur include the immediate and recurring costs shown in Table 2.3.

Immediate Costs

You may already have some equipment—workstations, printers, and so on—that can be integrated into the LAN. This equipment may need upgrading to function on the LAN. Workstations may need extra memory because the LAN software uses some of each workstation's memory. Workstations will need to have a LAN adapter card. All personnel involved in working with the LAN must be educated. Even if your company assumes the responsibility for doing this, it will incur an expense in people, time, and materials. You must provide users, operators, and administrators with the proper documentation to allow them to do their jobs effectively. Some of this documentation may come with the system. Additional copies of vendor-supplied documentation may need to be purchased. An organization might also need to write and distribute user procedures for using the LAN.

Installing a LAN usually requires some site preparation. You may need to dedicate work space for the server nodes, which ideally are located in a room with restricted access to protect it from unauthorized use. If you use a conducted medium, you must arrange for a safe way to string the cables between the workstations. Cables should be placed in floor channels, dropped from the ceiling, or otherwise distributed to prevent people tripping over or accidentally pulling on cables and breaking the connections. You must install LAN hardware; at a minimum this means cabling and LAN adapters.

Another installation task is to load or install the application and system software on the server and the network software on the workstations and test the system. To make the LAN easier to use, each user ought to have a **LAN environment.** A user's LAN environment consists of a wide variety of specifications that control the user's access to LAN resources as well as his or her workstation settings. The environment assists in the

Table 2.3   Immediate and Recurring Costs of a LAN

Immediate Costs	Equipment upgrades	Training users, operators, administrators
	Documentation	Site preparation
	Installation of cabling	Hardware installation
	System software installation	Installing applications
	Creating user environments	Testing
	Space required for new equipment	Supplies and spares
Recurring Costs	LAN management; personnel costs	Hardware and software maintenance
	Consumable supplies (toner, paper, etc.)	Training new users, administrators

logon process, maps the user to a home directory, and sets search paths for application software. For example, if a user needs to use word processor, spreadsheet, and database applications, the environment is set up to make running those applications easy. Some of the items that might be specified in a user's environment are listed in Table 2.4.

The LAN must be tested after being installed, and each user environment must be tested to ensure that it meets the user's specific needs. Work space must be allocated to store the new equipment, supplies, and spare parts.

Recurring Costs

Some of the costs you incur in setting up a LAN are ongoing. A LAN must be managed. For small LANs this may be a part-time duty for an existing employee. For large LANs it is a full-time responsibility. In either case LAN management is a recurring expense. The hardware and software you use must be kept up to date, and you need to use preventive maintenance on the hardware to keep it running correctly. This can be accomplished by paying for the services when needed or by subscribing to hardware and software maintenance services.

To keep your network operational and to reduce downtime, you may want to stock spares of parts that have a short life or are consumable. For instance, you need to stock toner cartridges for laser printers, printer paper, and so on. These supplies are required for stand-alone systems, so this expense may not differ significantly from your stand-alone needs. Typically an organization will also stock extra LAN adapters and cables. Finally, you will probably need a continuing education program. Again, training is required for stand-alone systems; however, users must learn some additional material to use a LAN effectively.

Number of Workstations

The effect the number of workstations has on the immediate costs of attaching a LAN has already been discussed. The number of workstations is also a key factor in network configuration. Each LAN is physically capable of supporting some maximum number of workstations. If you exceed that number, you must make some provision for extending the maximum number. A variety of techniques exist for doing this, and each increases the cost of the LAN. Several of these techniques are explained in Chapters 5 and 16.

Type of Workstations

The type of workstations you use will have a significant influence on your LAN alternatives. If your LAN will consist of Apple Macintoshes, a number of Windows- or DOS-oriented LAN systems will be eliminated. Similarly, if your workstations are IBM-compatible systems, Apple LANs will be eliminated. The same logic applies if your LAN consists of any of the other possible workstation platforms, such as those of Sun Microsystems. The LAN hardware and software must be compatible with the

Table 2.4   Some Items Specified in a User's Environment

Default disk drive	Default disk directory	Disk drive mappings
Disk drive/directory search paths	Printer mappings	Initial program/menu

workstations used. If you need to mix the types of workstations on the LAN, for example, allowing both Apple and IBM-compatible workstations, you will again eliminate a number of LAN options and perhaps increase the cost somewhat.

Number of Concurrent Users

The number of concurrent users may differ from the number of workstations. Some networks have restrictions regarding the number of active users. For example, one network operating system allows four concurrent users, but more than four workstations can be attached. As the number of concurrent users goes up, so does the LAN workload. As the LAN workload increases, you have two basic choices: You can allow system responsiveness to decrease, or you can increase the work potential of the system to maintain or improve the responsiveness. Naturally the second option involves higher costs. Some ways to improve LAN responsiveness are to select a faster LAN (one with higher transmission speeds), use additional or more powerful servers (which means more expensive computers), or use more efficient (and typically more costly) LAN software. The number of concurrent users of an application also affects the cost of the application. Software vendors vary in their user license provisions; in general, however, application costs are directly proportional to the number of concurrent users. That is, as the number of concurrent users goes up, so do software costs.

Type of Use

The impression you may have gained from the preceding paragraph is that having more concurrent users increases the LAN workload. However, you need to understand more about the effect of concurrent users on LAN performance. To do so, let us look at two very different LAN usage profiles.

Suppose the primary LAN application is word processing, and the operating mode is as follows: LAN users access the word processing software on the file server at the beginning of their work shift, they save their documents on a local disk drive, and they periodically print a document. What demands are there on the LAN? The demand is heavy when a user starts the word processing program. It must be **downloaded,** or transferred from the server to the workstation. The user does not need LAN services again until he or she prints a document or, in some cases, requires an overlay module for the word processor. An example of an overlay is a spelling checker module. Today's microcomputer software is so rich in capabilities that all the functions cannot always be included in one memory-resident module. An overlay module overcomes this constraint by sharing memory with other overlay modules. LAN requests are therefore infrequent, but the amount of data transferred is large. Adding users may not significantly increase the LAN workload if there is a considerable amount of idle time. If you have used a LAN in a classroom situation, you probably have experienced this type of usage. At the beginning of the class, LAN response is slow because many students are starting an application at nearly the same time, and the demand for LAN resources is high. After that, however, LAN responsiveness improves because the LAN usage becomes intermittent.

Suppose instead that the primary LAN activity is database access. That is, users are continually accessing and updating a database. In this case the LAN is constantly busy transferring large and small amounts of data. Adding new users in this instance can have a noticeable impact on LAN performance.

Number and Type of Printers

The number and distribution of printers can affect your LAN decision as well. Some LAN operating systems require that network printers be attached to file servers, and each file server can support only so many printers. With such systems, if you need a large number of printers, you may need to add server hardware and software simply to provide printing services. Also, you must be sure that the LAN you select is capable of supporting the types of printers you will be using. Each printer requires printer driver software to direct its operation. The driver software knows how to activate the special printer features needed to print special typefaces, underlining, graphics, and so on. Recall that spooler software is responsible for writing printed output to shared printers. If follows that there must be an interface between the spooler and the printer drivers. Often the drivers are included as part of the server software. When selecting a LAN you must ensure that the printers you plan to use are supported. Also, you must ensure that they are supported in the manner in which you plan to use them. For example, a certain printer may be supported for printing text but not for printing graphics.

Distance and Medium

LANs serve a limited geographical area at high speeds. Distance and speed are related. Attaining high speed over long distances can be very expensive. Thus each LAN has a maximum distance it can cover. Moreover, different types of LANs have different distance limitations. The distance is measured in wiring length. If you snake a cable back and forth through an office complex, you may not cover a wide geographical area, but the cable distance can be quite long. In general, as the distance your LAN needs to cover increases, your LAN options decrease. Distances for popular microcomputer LANs range from a few hundred meters to several thousand meters.

The type of medium also influences the selection process. If your facility already has wiring installed, you may select a LAN that can use that type of wiring. Each medium has speed and error characteristics. Twisted-pair wires support lower speeds than fiber optic cable and are more susceptible to errors than either coaxial cable or fiber optic cable. If your LAN wiring must pass through areas that can induce transmission errors (for example, areas that produce electrical or magnetic interference) you may need to select a LAN that can use a more noise-resistant medium, such as coaxial cable or fiber optic cable. One company came to this realization the hard way. In wiring the building with unshielded twisted-pair wires, the company ran the wiring through the shaft of a freight elevator. The freight elevator was seldom used; however, every time it was operated, the motor interfered with the data being transmitted on the LAN, causing numerous failures. Replacing the cabling in the elevator shaft with more error-resistant wiring eliminated the periodic failures.

Speed

LAN speeds can be somewhat deceptive. A LAN speed quoted by the vendor is the speed at which data are transmitted over the medium. You cannot expect the LAN to sustain this speed at all times. Time is required to place data onto the medium and to clear data from the medium. This is done in a variety of ways, and you will learn more about them in Chapter 3. It is important, however, to select a LAN capable of meeting your performance goals. For example, suppose that you expect access to data on your LAN's file server to have a transfer rate comparable to that of a hard disk, say 5 Mbps. This requirement eliminates a number of low-speed LANs. Common LAN speeds available for microcomputers are 4, 10, 16, and 100 Mbps, and the trend is for increasing speeds.

Applications

Most major application software packages are now available in LAN-compatible versions. However, this does not mean that all applications can run on all LANs. Applications communicate with the network through interfaces called **application program interfaces (APIs),** and a variety of APIs are in use. If the application uses an interface not supported by a particular LAN, then the application probably will not work on that network. Moreover, some software is not LAN compatible. Either it cannot run on a LAN at all or it does not support sharing on a LAN but can be used by one user at a time. If you have custom-written applications, they may not be LAN compatible. It is important to determine whether software you need to use will work on the LAN you are considering.

Expandability

After installing a LAN you probably will need to add workstations to it or move workstations from one location to another. The ease of doing this varies among implementations. In some instances the ease depends on the medium used and on the way in which the medium was installed. For example, adding new nodes to some systems using twisted-pair wires or coaxial cable is fairly easy. Adding a new node to a fiber optic cable may require cable splicing, which means that you must cut the cable, add the connectors, and rejoin the cable so the light pulses can continue along the cable. Fiber optic cable splicing technology has improved and is not difficult; however, the ease of adding a new node is still more difficult than for twisted-pair wires or coaxial cable.

Device Connectivity

Some organizations need to attach special devices to the LAN, such as an optical disk. LAN interfaces for such devices may not be available on some LANs or on some LAN file servers. This reduces your options to the LANs and servers that support the interface.

Connectivity to Other Networks

A LAN is often only one part of an organization's computing resources. Other facets may be a WAN, a large stand-alone computer, other LANs, or the Internet. If there are other LANs, they may be of different types. When a variety of computing resources are available, it is often desirable to connect them. Thus a node on the LAN can communicate with a node on a WAN or can access data on a central mainframe system. A variety of connection capabilities exist, but a given LAN may not support all of them. If you have immediate connectivity needs or anticipate them in the future, you need to select a LAN that will support the connection protocols you expect to use.

LAN Software and Hardware

If you already have microcomputers and associated software and hardware, you probably want to preserve your investment in them. That means that you need to select LAN software and hardware that will be compatible with your existing equipment. Furthermore, there are notable differences in the capabilities of LAN software and hardware. These differences may be important in making your LAN selection.

Adherence to Established Standards

There are several standards for LAN implementation. Some LANs conform to these standards, but others do not. Several nonstandard LANs have been adopted by many users and have thus become de facto standards. Other LANs are neither covered by standards nor so widely adopted that they have become de facto standards. A LAN's adherence to a standard does not necessarily mean that it superior to nonstandard LANs. However, there are benefits to choosing a LAN that conforms to a standard. Because standards are published, any company is able to design components that work on the LAN. This creates competition, gives users alternative sources of equipment, and usually drives down the cost of components. Because adopting a standardized LAN is often regarded as a safe decision, the community of users is often large. This in turn generates a body of expertise that new users can tap for either information or personnel. On the other hand, a nonstandard LAN may provide innovative features that are not yet covered by standards. Adopting such a LAN can place an organization ahead of competition that is using a more conventional system. You can read about LAN standards in Chapter 4.

Vendor and Support

When you select a LAN, you are selecting much more than hardware and software. You are selecting a vendor or vendors with whom you expect to have a long-term relationship. Your vendors ought to be available to help you in times of problems, provide you with maintenance and support, and supply you with spare parts, hardware and software upgrades, and new equipment. You can be more successful with a good vendor and a less capable LAN than with a poor vendor and a superior LAN, especially if your vendor can quickly resolve problems, obtain needed equipment, and so on. Thus you should evaluate prospective vendors and their support policies as carefully as you evaluate the equipment itself.

Manageability

Do not underestimate the time and effort required to operate and manage a LAN. Even a small, static LAN requires some management once installed and set up. Occasionally a new user might be added or deleted, new applications added or existing ones updated, and so on. The major ongoing activity will be making backups of files, taking care of printer problems, and solving occasional user problems. In a large LAN, however, management can be a full-time job, perhaps for more than one person. In Part 4 you will learn the details of LAN management. During the selection process you must ensure that your LAN will have the necessary management tools or that third-party tools are available. Third-party tools are those written by someone other than the LAN vendor. The tools you need depend on the size of the LAN and complexity of the users and applications involved. At a minimum you should be able to easily accomplish the tasks listed in Table 2.5.

Table 2.5   Basic LAN Management Tasks

User/Group Oriented	Add, delete users and groups	Set user/group security
	Set user environment	Solve user problems
Printer Oriented	Install/remove printers	Set up user/printer environment
	Maintain printers	
Hardware/Software Oriented	Add/change/delete software	Establish connections with other networks
	Add/change/delete hardware	Diagnose problems
	Plan and implement changes	
General	Make backups	Maintain operating procedures
	Carry out recovery as necessary	Educate users
	Plan capacity needs	Monitor the network for problems and to gather statistics for capacity planning
	Serve as liaison with other network administrators	

Security

With stand-alone microcomputers **security** generally is not an issue because they are usually single-user systems, so no security provisions were built into the operating systems or application software. As a result, access to the system is tantamount to access to all data stored on that system. By contrast, data in a LAN is shared. However, sharing should not imply that all users have unlimited access to all data. The LAN software must have the ability to control access to data. For each user you should at least be able to establish read, write create, and delete rights for each file. Chapter 11 gives a more comprehensive coverage of LAN security.

Now you know why we use LANs, the general characteristics of LANs, and the OSI Reference Model's description of how messages travel from one node in a network to another, and some of the factors we must consider when choosing LAN hardware and software. With this information, we can begin to look at the details of LAN systems.

SUMMARY

Microcomputers and data communications combined in the 1980s to add a new dimension to corporate computing. The expanded power of microcomputer hardware provided the ability for microcomputers to do more than could be done with early microcomputer systems. Taking advantage of expanded hardware and software capabilities on stand-alone microcomputers not only is expensive but also can lead to data inconsistencies and less-efficient use of resources. LANs help overcome these problems by providing a way to share hardware, data, and programs and to provide additional management controls over microcomputing. In some companies LANs have even replaced large computer systems and reduced the data processing budget. Replacing large computers with small computers is called downsizing.

The use of LANs has required changes in the way microcomputer software works. Specifically, provisions had to be made to provide security, control contention for resources, and allow applications to be tailored to individual workstations and user preferences.

Many network applications are available today. For microcomputer networks, applications can be separated into personal productivity applications and workgroup applications. Personal productivity software is available on stand-alone microcomputers. Workgroup productivity applications require the use of a network. The principal personal productivity applications are word processing, desktop publishing, spreadsheets, database management, and presentation services. Workgroup applications, also called groupware, include e-mail, data interchange, conferencing, meeting systems, and scheduling. The main reason for using LANs today is resource sharing. The ability to increase workgroup productivity may eventually be a more important reason for using a LAN than resource sharing.

There are two general classes of networks: local area networks and wide area networks. Each has characteristics that make them suitable for certain networking situations. Implementing a LAN creates a new layer of responsibility: LAN management. Stand-alone computing relies on distributed management: Each user of a stand-alone system is responsible for managing the resources of that computer. LANs require that an individual or group be responsible for operating and maintaining the shared LAN resources as well as providing assistance at the individual workstation level.

When selecting a LAN you must understand your application and how LAN technology can be applied to meet your application needs. Many general and technical considerations will influence your decision.

Key Terms

application program interface (API)	LAN adapter
coaxial cable	LAN environment
computer virus	manageability
contention	media access control (MAC) protocol
database management system (DBMS)	personal productivity software
data switch	portability
diskless workstation	presentation services
downloaded	security
downsizing	server
electronic appointment calendar	spooler
electronic conferencing	twisted-pair wire
electronic mail (e-mail)	virus detection software
electronic meeting systems (EMS)	what-if analysis
fiber optic cable	wide area network (WAN)
groupware	workgroup productivity software
infrared light	workstation

Review Questions

1. Explain how a local area network can help people communicate.
2. Explain how a network is used to share resources. What resources are commonly shared?
3. What are personal productivity applications? List four examples of personal productivity applications.

4. What is groupware, or a workgroup productivity application? Identify four workgroup applications.
5. Why is the security need for microcomputers on a LAN different from the security required for stand-alone microcomputers?
6. What are the differences between managing a stand-alone microcomputer and a LAN?
7. What are the general characteristics of a LAN?
8. Describe some differences between LAN and WAN characteristics.
9. Distinguish between immediate and recurring costs. Give two examples of each.
10. Explain how each of the following influences the selection of a LAN:
    a. cost
    b. number of workstations
    c. type of workstations
    d. number of concurrent users
    e. type of use
11. Explain how each of the following influences the selection of a LAN:
    a. number and type of printers
    b. distance and medium
    c. speed
    d. applications
    e. expandability
12. Explain how each of the following influences the selection of a LAN:
    a. device connectivity
    b. connectivity to other networks and nodes
    c. LAN software and hardware
    d. adherence to established standards
    e. vendor and support
    f. manageability
    g. security

Problems and Exercises

1. If you have access to a LAN, describe what users must do differently when using the LAN (compared to using a stand-alone microcomputer).
2. Identify three responsibilities of a LAN manager.
3. Diskless workstations provide an extra dimension of management control. At a college, diskless systems can help prevent the introduction of computer viruses and the piracy of software. What are the disadvantages of having diskless workstations in an academic LAN environment? Do these disadvantages also apply to corporations? Why or why not?
4. Describe a networking situation in which a WAN might be used in preference to a LAN.

PART 2

Hardware

A LAN administrator is often confronted with the task of evaluating different LAN systems and choosing from a variety of vendors. In Chapter 3 we explore the media used for LANs, and you will read how to evaluate the capabilities, strengths, and weaknesses of each medium. Chapter 4 presents the primary LAN topologies and media access control protocols. The topology is the way in which the LAN is laid out. Media access control protocols provide data link layer functions. In Chapter 5 you will learn the roles of various hardware components in a LAN and some of the considerations to be made in selecting this equipment. The key to successful LAN implementations is choosing components that can be integrated to form a system. In this section you will read about the ways in which hardware can be combined and some of the advantages and disadvantages of key technologies.

Chapter 3
Hardware Introduction and LAN Media

Chapter 4
Topologies and Media Access Control

Chapter 5
LAN Hardware

Chapter 3

Hardware Introduction and LAN Media

CHAPTER PREVIEW

A LAN is basically made up of hardware, software, and a medium. In building a LAN, you have a wide variety of options. You can choose from over three types of media, three basic network layouts, a variety of network operating systems, two or three fundamental network methodologies (such as server-based or peer-to-peer), and a multitude of computer platforms and client operating systems. There are literally thousands of possibilities. The challenge is to select from the available options and configure the components into a network that both meets your objectives and is cost-effective. We are ready to begin helping you to meet this challenge.

In this chapter you will read about

what makes up a LAN system

several of the leading LAN media

characteristics of LAN media

error sources, detection, and correction

We first discuss what we mean when we talk about a LAN system and follow with a discussion of LAN media and their characteristics.

THE LAN SYSTEM

If you evaluate vendor responses for a LAN procurement, the vendors may introduce their proposals with statements intended to give you a general idea of the type of solution proposed. Here are some examples:

"We are happy to propose a Novell NetWare IEEE 802.3 network for your consideration."

"We believe an IBM OS/2 Warp Server token ring network will best suit your purposes."

"Our solution uses Microsoft's Windows NT Server software and Ethernet."

53

These statements basically encapsulate three major LAN components: the LAN software, the topology, and the media access control (MAC) protocol. A network **topology** is the model used to lay out the LAN medium and connecting computers to the medium. A **MAC protocol** is part of the OSI data link layer and describes the way in which a network node gains access to the medium for transmitting data. The combination of these three components together with the medium provides much of the uniqueness of a LAN. When building a LAN a network designer must consider

a variety of media (twisted-pair wires, coaxial cable, fiber optic cable, and several less common wireless media)

three basic topologies (ring, bus, and star)

two basic media access control protocols (contention and token passing)

hardware from many vendors

network operating systems from several vendors

network utilities

application software

A LAN takes a medium, MAC protocol, and a topology and combines them with hardware and a network operating system (NOS) to create the LAN system. The major distinctions between one token ring, contention bus, or token bus and another are in the NOS, the hardware, and the medium. A number of vendors, such as Artisoft, Banyan, IBM, Microsoft, and Novell, provide networking software.

In selecting a LAN's components, one idea is paramount: You are selecting a *system*. The system has many components, and the overall success of the LAN is how well these components are integrated to form a system. Interoperability is the key, not the efficiency of a single component. For example, you must be able to attach workstations to the LAN and support each workstation's operating system. The LAN might have IBM or IBM-compatible workstations together with Apple Macintosh or compatible systems, with a variety of operating systems and printers. In this case the system you choose must support all of these components. Some network operating systems do not.

We now examine the media commonly used for a LAN.

LAN MEDIA

In Chapter 1 we examined the essential features of communication, one of which was a medium. We also briefly discussed the OSI Reference Model, including the physical layer. Media is a component of the OSI physical layer. Here we look at the various media available for transporting information over a LAN and the strengths and weaknesses of each medium. In this chapter we address only the primary LAN media, that is, media to which network nodes are directly attached. We can access a LAN in two basic ways: via nodes directly attached to the LAN medium and via remote connections. With remote connections, a user may access LAN resources from home, a distant office, or a mobile, portable workstation. In accessing the LAN remotely,

Table 3.1   Primary LAN Media Options

Conducted	Unshielded twisted-pair	Shielded twisted-pair
	Coaxial cable	Fiber optic cable
Wireless	Microwave radio	Spread-spectrum radio
	Broadcast radio	Infrared light

media other than the primary LAN medium are used, and coverage of remote connections is deferred until Chapter 16.

The transmission media commonly used in today's data communications networks can be broken down into two major classes: conducted and wireless. **Conducted media** systems use a conductor to move the signal from sender to receiver. Conducted media in a LAN include twisted-pair wires, coaxial cables, and fiber optic cables. **Wireless media** systems use radio waves of different frequencies or infrared light broadcast through space. Wireless media do not need a wire or cable conductor to transmit signals. Radiated media include broadcast radio, microwave radio, spread-spectrum radio, and infrared light. The primary media options are listed in Table 3.1. The discussion in this chapter focuses on the characteristics that make each medium desirable or undesirable in different situations, including speed, security, distance, susceptibility to error, and cost. These attributes form the basis of the medium selection criteria covered later in the chapter.

CONDUCTED MEDIA

Early LANs primarily used two types of medium. Coaxial cable was the most common medium and was used for higher-speed LANs (those faster than 1 Mbps). Wires were used for LANs operating at 1 Mbps or lower. With the technology of the early 1980s, speeds over 1 Mbps using twisted-pair wires were not possible. Since that time, transmission technologies have improved considerably, and speeds of 150 Mbps over high-quality twisted-pair wires are now attainable. In the forthcoming gigabit LAN standard, wires will probably be used as the medium over short distances.

Wires are the earliest and currently the most commonly used LAN transmission medium. In wide area networks wires are used to connect terminals to host computers, and until recently most telephone company facilities were wire based. You may be familiar with cables of this general type because telephone cables are twisted-pair wires, and the cable you use to connect your computer to a modem consists of several strands of individual wires; however, there is generally a difference between modem cables and telephone wires or wires used as LAN media.

Modem cables are usually straight wires. With straight wires, the individual wires are enclosed in an outer covering that provides protection and holds the wire bundle together. The wires themselves are passed straight through the covering. This wire configuration is suitable for the short distances and lower speeds common to modem connections; however, the error characteristics of straight wires make them unsuitable for high-speed LANs. For LANs we use twisted-pair wires.

Twisted-Pair Wires

Twisted-pair wiring consists of a bundle of color-coded wires (usually four or eight). Two of these wires with matching color codes form a pair that are twisted about each other as illustrated in Figure 3.1(a). One such color code scheme uses a solid color and a solid color with a white stripe as a pair; for example, a solid blue covered wire and a blue-and-white striped covered wire form one pair, and an orange and orange-and-white striped wire form another pair. One pair may be used to transmit data whereas the other is used to receive data. Twisted-pair wires are classified in several ways:

by **American wire gauge (AWG)** rating

by shielding, either **unshielded twisted-pair (UTP)** or **shielded twisted-pair (STP)**

by categories that define the wire's rated acceptable speed and error characteristics

AWG Rating

The AWG is a measure of the thickness of the copper conductor in the cable. The higher the AWG rating, the smaller the diameter of the wire; that is, a wire with an AWG rating of 12 is thicker than one with an AWG rating of 24. Twisted-pair wires for LANs have an AWG rating of 22–26. Standard telephone wires may be smaller, with an AWG rating of 28. When selecting LAN wiring, you ordinarily do not need to consider the AWG rating of the wires because it is included in the specifications used to define wire categories.

UTP and STP

You might have been wondering about the significance of twisted wires as opposed to straight wires. When electrical signals are transmitted over wires, an electromagnetic field is created along the axis of the wire. This electromagnetic field may affect the sig-

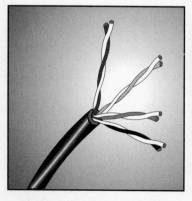      

(a) Unshielded Twisted-Pair Wires   (b) Shielded Wires   (c) Coaxial Cable

Figure 3.1   Copper Wire Configurations

nals being transmitted along adjacent wires. When the wires are twisted about each other with at least two twists per foot, the effect of the electromagnetic field is minimized. This type of error, called **crosstalk,** is measured in decibels and is discussed later in the section on error sources. Straight wires are more susceptible to crosstalk than are twisted-pair wires.

Twisted-pair wires have two basic configurations: unshielded and shielded. Even though twisting pairs of wires together minimizes crosstalk, it does not eliminate it and there are other sources of transmission errors. Some of these errors can be reduced by shielding the wires. STP wires have a metal foil or wire mesh wrapped around individual wire pairs, with a metal braided shield around the twisted-pair wire bundle itself; the entire bundle is enclosed in a polyvinyl chloride (PVC) jacket. The STP wire bundle is illustrated in Figure 3.1(b). Twisting pairs of wires helps eliminate interference from neighboring wires; the metal shielding helps prevent ambient distortion from heavy-duty motors, electrical or magnetic fields, and fluorescent lights. UTP wires, as the name implies, have no protective metal covering. Consequently, UTP wires are more susceptible to environmental noise that can disrupt the signal. When the signal is disrupted, transmission errors are likely to occur. When errors are detected, the data must be retransmitted, and the efficiency of the network is reduced. Companies use UTP because it is cheaper than STP. UTP may safely be used in environments where external disruptions are rare, such as the typical office environment.

In addition to being classified as UTP or STP, twisted-pair wires are also classified by categories. Several different rating classifications exist. One of the principal classifications was developed by the **Electronics Industries Association (EIA)** and the **Telecommunications Industries Association (TIA).** This classification, the **EIA/TIA-568 standard,** defines five categories of cables. In general, the distinctions between categories are the thickness of the wire, as defined by the AWG standard, and the error characteristics. Also included in the specification are connector types to be used in making the connection of the wires to wiring hubs and wiring closet punchdown blocks. A **punchdown block** is used as a terminal point for multiple wire cables. Figure 3.2 shows a variety of wire connection panels.

Category 1 Wire
Category 1 wire is the traditional telephone wire. It uses thin copper conductors and is not rated for LAN speeds.

Category 2 Wire
Category 2 wire is certified for speeds up to 4 Mbps. This type of wiring is used in older networks that operate at or below this speed. Because most of today's LAN implementations operate at 10 Mbps or higher, category 2 wires should be avoided in new LANs.

Category 3 Wire
The specifications for category 3 wires are more stringent than those for categories 1 and 2. **Category 3 wire** must have at least three twists for every foot of wire and no two pairs should have the same number of twists per foot. This configuration provides better protection from crosstalk and provides more error-free transmissions than categories 1 and 2.

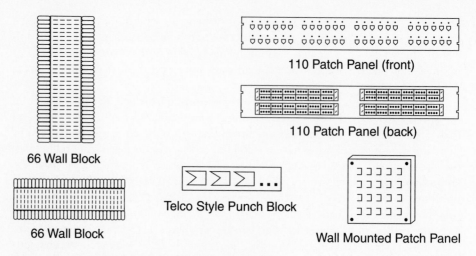

Figure 3.2   Assorted Wiring Panels and Blocks

Category 3 wire is common in LANs operating at 10 Mbps, and some 100-Mbps implementations allow category 3 wires over short distances.

Category 4 Wire

Category 4 wire is common in 16-Mbps LANs. It must meet tighter constraints for attenuation, crosstalk, and capacitance than lower categories. Capacitance is a measure of the energy stored by the cable. If the stored energy is high, transmission errors are more likely than if the energy level is low.

Category 5 Wire

Category 5 wire is the best of the five categories. It is certified for speeds of 100 Mbps, and as the speed threshold for twisted-pair wires increases, category 5 wires will probably be the only one of these five categories supported. Category 5 wire is scheduled for inclusion in 150-Mbps and 1-Gbps LAN specifications. The attenuation and crosstalk characteristics for category 5 wires are better than those for category 4.

Connectors

Two connectors for twisted-pair wires are defined by the EIA/TIA-568 standard. An 8-pin modular connector, typically a telephone-like **RJ-45 jack** as illustrated in Figure 3.3, is used to connect to a wiring hub or wall outlet.

Table 3.2 summarizes the characteristics of the five wire categories, and Figure 3.4 illustrates a generic twisted-pair wiring layout. Wire classifications other than those just described exist. For example, the IBM Corporation established a wiring classification and cable layout plan using four wire classification types: type 1, type 2, type 6, and type 9. Like the EIA/TIA classification, these classifications specify different AWG specifications and error characteristics. The relative cost column in Table 3.2 indicates cost

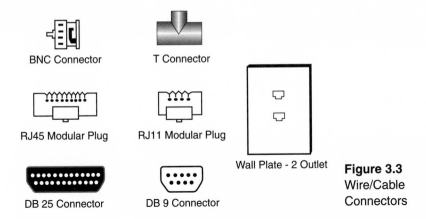

BNC Connector

T Connector

RJ45 Modular Plug

RJ11 Modular Plug

DB 25 Connector

DB 9 Connector

Wall Plate - 2 Outlet

Figure 3.3
Wire/Cable
Connectors

differentials. For example, if category 1 cable costs 5 cents per foot, category 2 cable will be approximately 7.5 cents per foot and category 5 cable will be 20 cents per foot. Thus, category 5 cable will cost approximately 33 percent more than category 4 cable. Cable costs per category can vary by as much as 15 or 20 cents per foot for category 5 cable. As of this writing, category 1 cable costs begin at about 5 cents per foot.

An additional configuration for twisted-pair wires is **plenum cables.** Normal cables are insulated with polyvinyl chloride (PVC). In the case of fire, PVC cables may emit a hazardous gas and building codes may prohibit the use of such cable in certain areas.

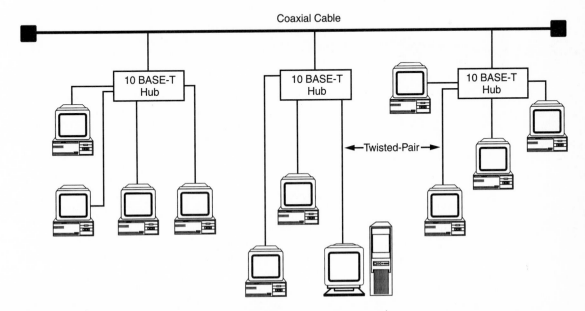

Figure 3.4   A Generic Twisted-Pair Wiring Layout

Table 3.2   Twisted-Pair Wire Category Summary

Category	Maximum Data Rate	Typical Use	Cost (relative to Category 1)
1	1 Mbps	Telephones	1
2	4 Mbps	Token-ring LANs	1.5
3	10 Mbps	Ethernet LANs	2
4	16 Mbps	Token-ring LANs	3
5	100 and 155 Mbps (1 Gbps likely in the future)	Ethernet and fast Ethernet LANs, copper distributed data interface LANs, and asynchronous transfer mode (ATM)	4

Plenum space is defined as the air space between the ceiling and the next floor, and ordinances may require that cables in plenum areas be enclosed by metal conduits or be plenum rated. Plenum cables are coated with a coatings such as Teflon that will not emit noxious gasses during fires. Plenum cables are somewhat more expensive than non-plenum cables.

In Chapter 4, we will see how these wires are deployed in connecting the LAN nodes. The advantages of twisted-pair wires are their ability to support high speeds at a low cost. Their disadvantages include susceptibility to signal distortion or error and lower transmission speeds when they are deployed over longer distances (relative to other types of media). For example, in one LAN standard, the maximum wire distance between a workstation and the wiring hub is 100 meters. Longer cable distances for this same technology are possible for coaxial cable and fiber optic cable.

Coaxial Cable

Most early microcomputer-based LAN implementations used coaxial cable as the medium. It was the medium of choice because twisted-pair wires were not generally capable of supporting the higher LAN speeds (more than 4 Mbps) and coaxial cable technology was well developed through its use in preexisting LANs of mainframe and minicomputer systems.

Coaxial cable is packaged in a variety of ways, but essentially it consists of one or two central data transmission wires surrounded by an insulating layer, a shielding layer, and an outer jacket, as depicted in Figure 3.5. The shielding layer protects the transmission wires from electromagnetic interference. Coaxial cable has several advantages as a LAN medium. The television industry has helped develop coaxial cable technology, including the capabilities to add stations or tap into a line with minimal interruption to existing users. In an environment where workstations are regularly added, moved, or deleted, the ability to alter the equipment configuration without disrupting existing users is significant. On the other hand, the ability to tap into the cable without disrupting service is a disadvantage if a high degree of security is required. Coaxial cable shielding provides a high degree of immunity to externally caused signal distortion. In LANs of less than a half-mile range (the distance

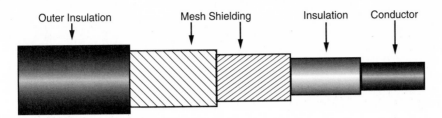

Figure 3.5 A Single Conductor Coaxial Cable

varies with specific implementations), signal loss or attenuation is not a concern; for longer distances, however, **repeaters** that enhance the signals are necessary. Data transmission rates over coaxial cable of up to 100 Mbps are not uncommon, and the theoretical bit rate is more than 400 Mbps.

Coaxial cable is most commonly used in two types of LANs: Ethernet and ARC-NET. **Ethernet** is widely used and supports speeds of 10 to 100 Mbps. **ARCNET** is an older, slower technology that is seeing declining usage because of low speeds (2.5 Mbps) and limitations on the number of allowed workstations per LAN (255). Ethernet supports two types of cable: thick and thin. LANs using the thick cable are called **thicknets** and those using the thin cables are called **thinnets.** As you might deduce, the primary difference between the two Ethernet cables is the cable thickness. The primary, less obvious difference is the distance that can be spanned by the cables. Thicknet LANs can span distances roughly 2.5 times longer than thinnet cables. More details regarding Ethernet specifications can be found in Chapter 4. ARCNET cables have different characteristics from Ethernet cables. ARCNET is also discussed in more detail in Chapter 4.

Security may be considered both an advantage and a disadvantage of coaxial cable. If a very secure medium is required, with taps being difficult to make and easy to detect, coaxial cable presents a serious problem. Whenever distances are great, attenuation becomes a problem, as does the cost of the greater amount of cable and the repeaters that must be installed to enhance the signal over longer distances. The allowed distances vary by LAN type. For thinnet LANs a single cable segment cannot exceed 185 meters, and for thicknet LANs the distance is 500 meters. In each instance, four repeaters can be used, making the total cable distances 925 and 2500 meters for thinnet and thicknet LANs, respectively.

Despite the advantages just cited, coaxial cable use is decreasing significantly. With UTP and STP wires capable of supporting speeds above 100 Mbps at lower costs than coaxial cable, coaxial cable's market share has been eroded for lower-speed LANs. Furthermore, twisted-pair wires are lighter and easier to work with than coaxial cable. Today, coaxial cable's primary use is in connecting LAN segments where distance is a factor. UTP and STP wire lengths vary somewhat with different wiring standards; in one implementation the maximum wire length is 100 meters from a station to a wiring hub (see Chapter 5). Longer distances are possible with coaxial cable, so two wiring hubs may be connected via coaxial cable, as illustrated in Figure 3.6. For extremely fast

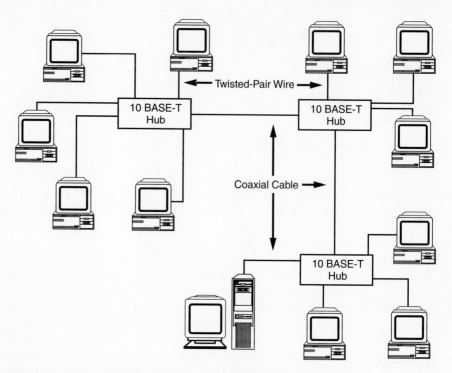

Figure 3.6   Coaxial Cable Connecting Wiring Hubs

LANs, fiber optic cable is preferable to coaxial cable, so coaxial cable has lost market share at the high end as well.

Fiber Optic Cable

Fiber optic cable is a newer technology than either twisted-pair wires or coaxial cable. It is now extensively used by telephone companies in place of long-distance wires. It is also used by private companies in implementing high-speed LANs.

Fiber optic cables come in two varieties, multimode and singlemode, each with a different way of guiding the light pulses from source to destination. Multimode fiber optic cable has a larger-diameter core than singlemode cables. The typical light source for multimode is a light-emitting diode (LED). Multimode light pulses are reflected from the walls of the core; consequently, some distortion of the light pulses can occur and this restricts the speed and distances supported by multimode fiber optic cables. The smaller core of singlemode fiber optic cables ensures that the light pulses travel in a straighter line. A laser is used as the light source and a single light beam is transmitted though the core. Singlemode is capable of higher data rates and longer distances than multimode fiber. Although the light source and the way the light is guided through the medium differ, fiber optic cables all have the same basic composition and characteristics. One or more glass or plastic fibers are woven together to form the core of the cable. This core is surrounded by a glass or plastic layer called the cladding. The

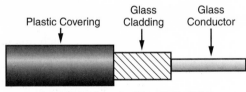

(a) A Side View of a Fiber Optic Cable

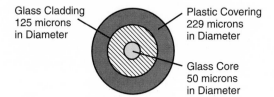

Figure 3.7   Views of a Fiber Optic Cable

cladding in turn is covered with PVC or some other material for protection. Figure 3.7 shows a cross-section of a fiber optic cable. All three cable varieties require a light source, with laser and light-emitting diodes (LED) being the light sources most commonly used.

One of the shortcomings of fiber optics is the inability to add new nodes. Although it is now easy to splice the fiber optic cable and add new stations, the network or a portion of the network must be down while the splice is being prepared. Fiber optic links for very short distances cost more than wires, but as distance or the required transmission rate increases, fiber optic cables become cost-effective. Fiber can carry signals for long distances without repeaters. The cost breakeven point generally occurs when the distance is so great that coaxial cable or wires would require expensive signal-enhancing equipment or when the required data transfer rate would require multiple twisted-pair wires or coaxial cables. A significant advantage of fiber optics over copper wires is its reduced size and weight; it is about 20 times lighter and five times smaller than equivalent copper wire (either coaxial or twisted-pair). Very low error rates and immunity to environmental interference such as electromagnetic fields are additional benefits. Furthermore, fiber cables do not conduct electricity, so the danger of high voltages (due to lightning strikes) being carried to and ruining computing equipment is eliminated. Fiber optic cables do not corrode, so they can be used in environments unsuited for copper media.

WIRELESS MEDIA

Mobile computing and obstacles to premises wiring have given rise to the development of wireless LANs. Mobile computing requires portable workstations. When these portable workstations are brought into in an office, they are often used in a variety of locations. Wireless media makes it easier to accommodate equipment mobility because the workstations do not need to be tethered to a conducted medium. Sometimes the expense of delivering wires to a location makes wireless media attractive. For example, if delivering a wire-based medium requires drilling through 6 inches of concrete, a wireless connection may be more practical. Wireless technology is newer and less common than conducted media but its market share is growing. In general, wireless technologies provide lower speeds, more limited distances, worse error characteristics, and less security than conducted media. The most common wireless technologies are broadcast radio, microwaves, spread-spectrum radio, and infrared light.

Broadcast Radio

Broadcast radio uses not only the radio frequencies typical of AM and FM radio stations, but also short-wave or short-distance radio frequencies, with an available frequency range from 500,000 to 108 million cycles per second. Broadcast radio's primary applications are in paging terminals (the devices carried by people who are on call), cellular radio telephones, and wireless local area networks. A good example of radio broadcast for data communications is in the AlohaNet at the University of Hawaii. Broadcast radio was chosen to overcome the difficulty of setting up wire links in the islands, and it proved quite effective when the number of stations was small. As more stations were added, however, contention between broadcasting stations increased, collisions or interference became more frequent, and effective use dropped. Furthermore, the medium proved to be susceptible to interference from other radio broadcast sources. The AlohaNet transmission rate was 9600 bps. When broadcast radio is used with LANs, cables connecting each microcomputer are eliminated. The elimination of cables makes installation and changing of workstations easier and reduces the problems of loose connections that can occur as a result of people walking or pulling on cables.

Mobile computing and communications have expanded the role of broadcast radio in data communications. The importance of mobile computing and communications is such that major evaluation and reallocation of the available radio frequencies may result. Of course, mobile computing requires a wireless medium and broadcast radio is being increasingly used in this manner. This new application of radio transmission is placing ever higher demands on a limited range of broadcast frequencies. The demand is reaching the point where some experts suggest that countries need to reevaluate the entire use of the frequency spectrum and use radio-frequency transmission only for mobile communications. Nonmobile communications such as television would be delivered exclusively by conducted media, thus freeing radio frequencies for mobile communication devices such as portable computers and personal communicators.

The most common media for mobile computing communications are cellular radio, radio nets, and low-orbit satellites. Cellular radio as currently implemented tends to be costly and operates at low speeds, typically 19,200 bps or lower. Therefore, cellular radio is suitable primarily for transfers of small amounts of data such as electronic mail messages. Cellular radio transmission for data is also subject to high error rates.

Radio nets using dedicated frequencies over large areas are also used for mobile computing. These networks require the use of a radio modem to send and receive data. Currently radio nets operate at speeds up to 19,200 bps, but higher speeds are likely as this technology expands. Low-orbiting satellites offer another communication alternative.

Unlike geosynchronous satellites, low-orbit satellites do not remain in a fixed position relative to the earth. However, using several low-orbit satellites ensures that at least one is always in position to accept and relay signals. Use of this technology for commercial mobile computing is still in its infancy. Each of these three technologies has the disadvantages of low speed, possibility of signal interference, and lack of security.

Microwave Radio

The original use for **microwave radio** data transmissions was long-distance communications. The first commercially implemented digital microwave radio system was installed in Japan by Nippon Electric Company in 1968. Long-distance microwave transmission rates range up to 45 Mbps. Microwaves are now also being used as a medium for wireless LANs. For networks where installation of conducted media is difficult or too expensive, microwaves provide a high-speed media alternative. The microwaves are generated at a lower power than long-distance microwave transmission to minimize the effects on humans. Despite the lower power, the waves are able to penetrate thin office walls. Microwaves as a LAN medium provide transmission speeds of 10 Mbps, and higher speeds are inevitable.

Microwave transmission offers speed, cost-effectiveness, and ease of implementation; however, it is susceptible to interference from other radio waves. LAN microwave transmissions are insecure because they can be intercepted by anyone with a receiver located within the service area. Microwaves can also be affected by environmental conditions. Transmissions at the same or nearly the same frequencies can interfere with each other, and some atmospheric conditions, such as high humidity, can affect the signal.

Spread-Spectrum Radio

Spread-spectrum radio (SSR) has long been used by the military to provide reliable radio communications in battlefield environments, where signal jamming can be expected. This characteristic of reliability in environments where signal interference is likely makes SSR well suited for LAN transmissions.

Two methods, frequency hopping and direct sequencing, are used to provide SSR signals. With frequency hopping, data is transmitted at one frequency and then the frequency is changed and data is transmitted at the new frequency, and so on. Each piece of data is transmitted over several frequencies to increase the probability that it will be successfully received. Direct sequencing sends data over several different frequencies simultaneously. When used in wireless LANs, SSR distances are limited to approximately 1000 feet, making it useful for small LANs or as the medium for small segments of larger LANs. SSR signals can penetrate normal office walls but signal strength is reduced considerably by concrete and metal walls. As is typical with radiated media, SSR has the disadvantage of being susceptible to signal interference and signal interception. Moreover, the speed of data transmission of 2 Mbps is lower than that of most of today's LANs using conducted media.

Infrared Transmission

Infrared transmission uses electromagnetic radiation of wavelengths between visible light and radio waves. Infrared transmission is a line-of-sight technology. It can be used

Table 3.3   Wireless Media Frequencies

Frequency (Hz)	
10^{16}	X rays, gamma rays
10^{15}	Ultraviolet light
	Visible light
10^{14}	Infrared light
10^{13}	
	Millimeter waves
10^{12}	
10^{11}	Microwaves
10^{10}	UHF television
	VHF television
10^{9}	VHF TV (high band)
10^{8}	FM radio
	VHF TV (low band)
10^{7}	Shortwave radio
10^{6}	AM radio
10^{5}	
10^{4}	
10^{3}	Very low frequency
10^{2}	
10^{1}	

to provide LAN connections between buildings and also is the medium used in some wireless LANs. Data transmission rates are typically on the order of 100 Kbps or less.

Radiated Media Frequencies

The frequencies of various wireless media are given in Table 3.3.

MEDIA SELECTION CRITERIA

Several factors influence the choice of a medium for a LAN. These factors are given in Table 3.4. Because every configuration has its own set of constraints, not all factors apply in every situation; in some situations, there may even be only a single viable alternative. However, system designers must consider each criterion, either implicitly or explicitly. In most situations, the factors may influence one another. For example, a strong correlation often exists between a medium's application and its required speed, so much so that the application usually dictates a minimum acceptable transmission speed (although other factors such as cost and expandability can also pertain).

Table 3.4   LAN Media Selection Criteria

Cost	Security
Speed or capacity	Distance
Availability	Environment
Expandability	Application
Error rates	Maintenance

Cost

The costs associated with a given transmission medium include not only the costs of the medium but also ancillary fees, such as the costs for additional hardware (repeaters, for example) that might be required. A deferred ancillary cost that is important to consider when making an initial selection is the cost of expansion. Suppose a company begins the implementation of LAN technology with a department-oriented LAN with 15 users whose primary activity is word processing. It is likely a 4- or 10-Mbps LAN with one server will satisfy this application's requirements and the LAN can be implemented with category 4 UTP. However, suppose that the same company expands its plans and adds more users and applications such as multimedia that require much higher data capacities than 10 Mbps. Moreover, suppose that some of the LAN medium must pass through an area that has a high potential for electromagnetic interference. A better LAN medium is category 5 STP or fiber optic cable. This expansion would probably require the removal of the category 3 UTP and its replacement by a higher-capacity medium.

Speed

A tremendous range of transmission speeds is available. Low-speed LANs transmit at rates under 1 Mbps, and high-speed LANs at over 100 Mbps. You have already read that different media types are rated for different speeds. Within a given medium, higher speeds typically mean higher costs, which are not entirely attributable to the medium itself. Higher data transmission rates require more sophisticated (expensive) communications equipment. For example, in a LAN the interface between the computer and the medium is made by a piece of hardware called a LAN adapter or network interface card (NIC). Lower-speed NICs are less costly than higher-speed NICs. Two factors dictate the required speed of a medium: response time and aggregate data rate.

Response Time

Response time is the time between when a LAN request is made and when the results of that request are received. For example, if a user makes a request to run a word processing program, the response time is the interval between making the request and having the program downloaded and ready to run; for a database request, it is the time between making the request and receiving the result. Response time has two components, transmission time and processing time, and each of these can be broken down into subcomponents. Suppose the design objective is a response time of 3 seconds for downloading the word processor software. If processing takes 1 second, then transmission must take 2 seconds or less. If the transaction involves the exchange of 400,000 characters of information, then the speed of the medium must be at least 200,000 characters per second (400,000 characters divided by 2 seconds), which represents approximately 2 Mbps using the rough estimate of 10 bits per character. We use a 10-bit-per-character estimate because as you read in the first chapter about the OSI Reference Model, we envelope the actual data to be sent with additional error-checking and control information. The calculated speed of 2 Mbps assumes there is no sharing of the communications link. If other users are making requests at the same time, a higher speed is required to service the other requests and maintain a speed of 2 Mbps.

Aggregate Data Rate

The **aggregate data rate** is the amount of data that must be transferred per unit of time. In discussing deferred costs, we suggested that higher speeds would probably be required for multimedia applications. These applications typically provide both video and audio data and both data streams must be synchronized so that the audio corresponds to the movement of lips in the associated video. Full-motion video and audio to one workstation alone can require transmission speeds of 10 Mbps or higher. If a company plans to use multimedia applications, a high-speed medium is essential.

Expandability

Often it becomes necessary to expand the scope of a data communication configuration, either by adding more devices at a given location or by adding new locations. Some LAN media, such as coaxial cable, are easier to expand than others, such as fiber optic cables. LANs must be designed for the future as well as for immediate needs. Expandability is a problem not just of media availability but also of hardware. When a system has reached its maximum capacity with respect to the available number of devices, additional hardware and software may be required. Recall, for example, that an ARCNET LAN allows a maximum of 255 nodes. If a company using this technology needs to expand beyond that limit, it must have two separate LANs and the hardware and software necessary to connect the two. Expansion also includes running at higher data speeds over the existing infrastructure because the cable plant infrastructure should last at least 15 years.

Error Rates

All transmission media are subject to signal distortion, which can produce errors in the data. The propensity for error influences not only the quality of transmission but also its speed. As the number of errors increases on a medium, the effective data rate drops because we need to retransmit the data that is found to be in error. Later in this chapter we discuss the types of errors that might occur and how to detect and overcome them.

Security

The lack of security in data communications networks has been made clear by several widely publicized incidents of hackers or espionage agents penetrating several major networks. Although most of the hacker incidents reported relate to WANs, similar concerns apply to LANs. As already noted, wireless media are generally less secure than conducted media and there are security differences between conducted media. A

Table 3.5 Characteristics of Common LAN Media

Medium Type	Common Speeds (Mbps)	Error Characteristics
Unshielded twisted-pair	1, 4, 10, 16, 100, 1000	Less capable than other conducted media
Shielded twisted-pair	1, 4, 10, 16, 100, 1000	Better than unshielded; less capable than fiber optic or coaxial cables
Coaxial cable	10, 16, 50	Good; less capable than fiber optic cable
Fiber optic cable	10, 16, 50, 100, 1000, 2000	Excellent
Broadcast radio	2	Subject to interference
Spread-spectrum radio	2, 10, 16	Good
Microwave radio	5.7	Subject to interference
Infrared light	4, 10, 16	Objects can block transmission

company installing a LAN needs to weigh the security needs of the network when selecting the proper medium.

Distance

Every LAN has a maximum distance it can cover. The distance is typically the longest length of conducted medium or maximum radius for radiated media. In some instances, distances can be extended with repeaters. Before deploying a medium, LAN designers need to determine the distances that must be covered and ensure that the wiring configuration or wireless configuration does not exceed the distance limitations of the technology being used.

Environment

The constraints of environment can eliminate certain types of media. For instance, if the LAN medium must be strung through areas with considerable electrical or magnetic interference or other impediments, such as chemicals or severe weather conditions, the chosen medium should be resistant to such interference.

Application

Certain applications (such as environmental monitoring) use devices designed to connect to a system in a very specific way and at specific speeds. In such applications, the characteristics of the required equipment may dictate the type of medium and interfaces to be used. Furthermore, the particulars of an application help determine other required characteristics of the medium, such as speed and security.

Media Comparison

Table 3.5 summarizes the characteristics of common LAN media.

ERROR SOURCES

You have already read that UTP wires are more susceptible to errors than fiber optic cables. However, *all* data transmissions are subject to error regardless of the medium. There are a number of error sources. We now look at the primary error sources and then discuss how errors are detected and corrected. For completeness and to allow you to compare error detection schemes, we also discuss error-detection algorithms that are used in data communications networks but not commonly used in LAN transmissions. Figure 3.8 illustrates the impact of **noise** on a data communications signal.

White Noise

White noise, also called thermal noise or Gaussian noise, results from the normal movements of electrons and is present in all transmission media at temperatures above absolute zero. The amount of white noise is directly proportional to the temperature of the medium (hence the term *thermal noise*). White noise also is distributed randomly throughout a medium (hence the term *Gaussian noise*). White noise in telephone circuits is sometimes heard as static or hissing on the line. Usually, the magnitude of white noise is not sufficient to create data loss in wire circuits, but it can become significant in radio-frequency links such as microwave and SSR.

Impulse Noise

Impulse noise is characterized by signal spikes. In LANs it can be caused by lightning striking the medium, by jarring loose connections, or by transient electrical impulses such as those occurring on a shop floor. The various pieces of equipment on a shop floor require large amounts of electricity. Moreover, this equipment often cycles up and down, drawing more and less power. Setting an electrical charge in motion generates a magnetic field, and magnetic fields can, in turn, affect electrical transmissions. Thus UTP wires passing through a shop floor in close proximity to current-carrying wires can have their signals affected. Impulse noise usually is short (several milliseconds), with varying levels of magnitude.

Crosstalk

Crosstalk occurs when signals from one channel distort or interfere with the signals of a different channel. In telephone connections, crosstalk sometimes appears in the form of another party's conversation heard in the background. Crosstalk in wire-pair transmission occurs when wire pairs interfere with each other as a result of strong signals, improper

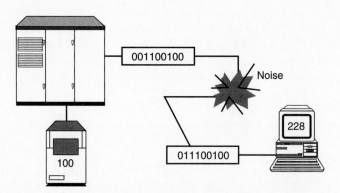

Figure 3.8   The Impact of Noise on a Data Communications Signal

twisting of the wire pairs, or improper shielding. Crosstalk is directly proportional to distance, bandwidth, signal strength, and proximity to other transmission channels; it is inversely proportional to shielding or channel separation.

Echo

Echo is essentially the reflection or reversal of the signal being transmitted. This is most likely to occur at junctions where wires are interconnected or at the end of a line in a LAN. In LANs where echo might be a problem, terminators are attached to open cable ends to suppress the echo.

Attenuation

Attenuation is the weakening of a signal as a result of distance and characteristics of the medium. Attenuation can produce a significant number of data errors. For a given gauge of wire and bit rate, a signal can be carried for a certain distance without enhancement. Beyond that distance, however, a repeater would have to be included to ensure that the receiving station can properly recognize the data.

Impact of Data Errors

Figure 3.9 shows the possible effects of impulse noise of various duration, for different line speeds. It is significant that fewer bits are subject to error when transmission is at lower rather than higher speeds. Although the table applies to any type of noise for the same duration, impulse noise was chosen because it is one of the most common types of noise affecting LANs. The most significant thing shown by Figure 3.9 is that the potential number of bit errors increases with both duration of the noise and line speed. The ideal is to eliminate all errors in data, but a goal of fewer than one error per 1 million bits is considered satisfactory.

PREVENTION

The best way to guard against data errors is to eliminate their source. Eliminating all noise is impossible, but error-prevention techniques can reduce the probability of error corruption in the data. Such techniques include reducing transmission speed, adding shielding and line drivers, and using better-quality equipment.

ERROR DETECTION

Unfortunately, the remedies just cited to minimize the number of errors may be impractical from either a cost or a feasibility standpoint. Also, because error elimination is impossible, it is necessary to determine whether a transmission error has occurred and, if errors have occurred, to return the data to proper form. Error-detection algorithms in data communications networks are based on the transmission of redundant information. In telegraphy, one way to ensure correctness of data is to transmit each character twice. Because even this is not entirely error-proof, it could be taken one or more steps further by sending each character three or more times. However, although this might increase the reliability of the transmission, line capacity drops dramatically. As the error rate approaches zero, so does the effective use of the medium. Obviously, some middle-ground

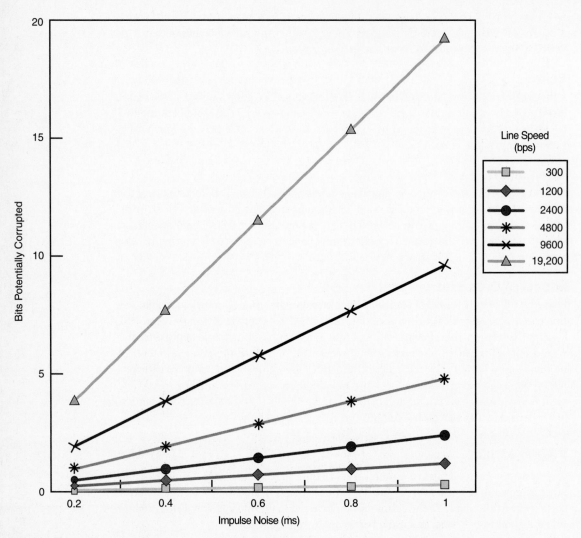

Figure 3.9   Potential Number of Corrupted Data Bits

approach is required that can detect almost all errors without significantly reducing the data-carrying capacity of the medium. In the following discussion we cover the error-detection techniques common to data communications on all types of networks.

Parity Check

One of the simplest and most widely used forms of error detection is known as a parity check or **vertical redundancy check (VRC).** A parity check involves adding a bit—known as the parity bit—to each character during transmission. The parity bit is selected so that the total number of 1 bits in the code representation of each character adds up to either an even number (even parity) or an odd number (odd parity). Each character is checked upon receipt to see whether the number of 1 bits is even or odd. Consider the string of characters *DATA COMM,* as coded in 7-bit ASCII with odd parity. The representations of these characters plus the parity bit for odd parity are given in Table 3.6. It can be seen that the number of 1 bits in each 8-bit sequence (octet) is always odd (either one, three, five, or seven); it is the parity bit that ensures this. If even parity were chosen, the parity bit would be selected so that the number of 1 bits would always be an even number.

Besides even and odd parity, you can have no parity, a parity bit with no parity checking, mark parity, or space parity. If there is no parity bit or if the parity bit is not checked (called no parity check), the ability to detect errors using this method is lost (although other methods, to be described later, could be used). Mark parity means that the parity bit is always transmitted as a 1 bit, and space parity means that the parity bit is always transmitted as a 0 bit. Clearly, mark and space parity are ineffective as error-detection schemes. If two stations attempting to communicate disagree on the parity scheme, all messages will be seen as being in error and will be rejected.

In the odd parity example in Table 3.6 each character transmitted consists of 8 bits: 7 for data and 1 for parity. Parity enables the user to detect whether 1, 3, 5, or 7 bits have been altered in transmission, but it will not catch whether an even number (2, 4, 6, or 8 bits) has been altered. One common error situation involves burst errors, or a grouping of errors (recall the possible effect of impulse noise during high transmission rates). The likelihood of detecting errors of this nature with a parity check is approximately 50%. At higher transmission speeds this limitation becomes significant. (A burst error for the duration of 2 bits does not necessarily result in 2 bit errors; 0, 1, or 2 bits could be affected.)

Longitudinal Redundancy Check

We can increase the probability of error detection beyond that provided by parity by making, in addition, a **longitudinal redundancy check (LRC).** With LRC, which is similar to VRC, an additional, redundant character called the block check character (BCC) is appended to a block of transmitted characters, typically at the end of the

Table 3.6   Parity Bit Generation

Letter	ASCII	Parity Bit	Transmitted Bits
D	1000100	1	10001001
A	1000001	1	10000011
T	1010100	0	10101000
A	1000001	1	10000011
Space	0100000	0	01000000
C	1000011	0	10000110
O	1001111	0	10011110
M	1001101	1	10011011
M	1001101	1	10011011

block. The first bit of the BCC serves as a parity check for all of the first bits of the characters in the block, the second bit of the BCC serves as parity for all of the second bits in the block, and so on. An example of LRC is provided in Table 3.7. Because an odd parity scheme has been chosen to perform the redundancy check, each column has an odd number of 1 bits.

LRC combined with VRC is still not sufficient to detect all errors (indeed, no scheme is completely dependable). Table 3.8 presents the same *DATA COMM* message transmission, with errors introduced in rows and columns marked by an asterisk. Although both LRC and VRC appear correct, the data received is not the same as that transmitted. Adding LRC to VRC brings a greater probability of detecting errors in transmission.

Cyclic Redundancy Check

A cyclic redundancy check (CRC) can detect bit errors better than either VRC or LRC or both. A CRC is computed for a block of transmitted data. The transmitting station generates the CRC and transmits it with the data. The receiving station computes the CRC for the data received and compares it to the CRC transmitted by the sender. If the two are equal, then the block is assumed to be error-free. The mathematics behind CRC requires the use of a generating polynomial and is beyond the scope of this book.

If the CRC generator polynomial is chosen with care and is of sufficient degree, over 99 percent of multiple-bit errors can be detected. Several standards exist—CRC-12, CRC-16, CRC-32, and CRC-CCITT—that define both the degree of the generating polynomial and the generating polynomial itself. Because CRC-12 specifies a polynomial of degree 12, CRC-16 and CRC-CCITT specify a polynomial of degree 16, and CRC-32 specifies a polynomial of degree 32, the BCC will have 12, 16, or 32 bits. CRC-16 and CRC-CCITT can

detect all single-bit and double-bit errors

detect all errors in cases in which an odd number of bits are erroneous

Table 3.7   LRC Generation

Letter	ASCII	Parity Bit	Transmitted Bits
D	1000100	1	10001001
A	1000001	1	10000011
T	1010100	0	10101000
A	1000001	1	10000011
Space	0100000	0	01000000
C	1000011	0	10000110
O	1001111	0	10011110
M	1001101	1	10011011
M	1001101	1	10011011
BCC	1000011	0	10000110

Table 3.8 LRC Transmission Errors

Letter	ASCII	Parity Bit	Transmitted Bits
D	* * 1000100	1	10001001
A	1000001	1	10000011
T	*1100100	0	10101000
A	*1110001	1	10000011
Space	0100000	0	01000000
C	1000011	0	10000110
O	1001111	0	10011110
M	1001101	1	10011011
M	1001101	1	10011011
BCC	1000011	0	10000110

detect all burst errors of 16 bits or fewer (32 bits or fewer for CRC-32)

detect over 99.998 percent of all burst errors greater than 16 bits (32 bits for CRC-32)

Because of its extra reliability, CRC-32 is the error-detection scheme used by most LANs.

Sequence Checks

When a data communications network is simple enough that sending and receiving nodes are connected directly, the receiving station receives all transmissions without the intercession of other nodes. However, large communications networks may have one or more intermediate nodes responsible for forwarding a message to its final destination, and one complete message may be divided into a number of transmission blocks. Furthermore, these blocks may not all be routed along the same path and hence could be received out of order. In such a case, it is important to assign sequence numbers to each block so that the ultimate receiver can determine that all blocks have arrived and can put the blocks back into proper sequence.

Suppose you send someone one letter per day for five days through the postal system. There is no guarantee that the letters will be received in the order sent. Several might arrive on the same day (and out of order), one might be lost, or all five might arrive at the same time. If the letters are intended to be read in order, you can number them sequentially, such as 1/5, 2/5, 3/5, and so on. This alerts the recipient to the order and allows him or her to detect missing messages. A similar scheme can be used for data communications messages.

One sequencing technique appends a message sequence number to each data block transmitted between two stations. If a processor is communicating with two different stations, each link would have its own sequence number. Every time a message is transmitted, the sequence number is sent along with the message. The receiving station compares the received sequence number with a number maintained in its memory. If the message numbers agree, no messages have been lost; if the received message number disagrees with the expected message number, an error condition is created and the receiver requests that the sender retransmit the missing messages. In a data communications network, the transport layer of the OSI Reference Model is responsible for end-to-end reliability and affixes sequence numbers to message packets when reliable communication is needed.

Packet Sequence Numbers

In some networks, messages are segmented into smaller transmission groups, or packets. If there are multiple communication paths between sender and receiver, the packet routing strategy may use several of the paths simultaneously to speed delivery of the entire message, in which case the packets could arrive out of order. To ensure that such a message can be reassembled in proper sequence, packet sequence numbers are appended to each packet. These sequence numbers also allow for error control.

In any of the situations just discussed, if a data block arrives and an error is detected, or if some of the blocks in a sequence have not been received, the recovery method is to ask the sending station to retransmit the erroneous or lost data. Usually, an acknowledgment is sent for all blocks received correctly; if a block is not positively acknowledged, the transmitter must resend it. This obligates the transmitting node to retain all transmitted blocks until they have been acknowledged. Being able to request that a message be retransmitted implies that the flow control is either half duplex or full duplex. If an error is detected on a simplex line, the recipient cannot send a request for retransmission. The only recourse in this case is to ignore the message or to use the message as received.

Error-Correction Codes

Some error-detecting schemes allow the receiving station not only to detect errors but also to correct some of them. Such codes are called forward error correcting codes, the most common of which are called Hamming codes. As with straight error-detection codes, additional, redundant information is transmitted with the data. Error-correcting codes are convenient for situations in which single-bit errors occur, but for multiple-bit errors, the amount of redundant information that must be sent is cumbersome. Because the effectiveness of forward error-correcting codes is reduced by transmission noise that often creates bursts of errors, these codes are not used as commonly as are error-detection schemes. Error-correcting codes have good applications in other areas, however, such as memory error detection and correction, where the probability of single-bit errors is higher. Some semiconductor memories use a 6-bit Hamming code for each 16 bits of data to allow for single-bit error correction and double-bit error detection.

ERROR CORRECTION

Whenever an error is detected, it must be corrected. If an error-correcting code is used, the transmitted data can be corrected by the receiver. However, this is seldom the case in data communications. The most common error-correction mechanism is to retransmit the data. In asynchronous transmission, individual characters are retransmitted, whereas in synchronous transmissions, one or more blocks may need to be retransmitted. This type of correction is known as ARQ, which stands for automatic request for retransmission or automatic request for repetition.

Message Acknowledgment

The mechanism used to effect retransmission is positive or negative acknowledgment, often called ACK and NAK, respectively. When a station receives a message, it computes the number of error detection bits or characters and compares the result with the check number received. If the two are equal, the message is assumed to be error-free and the receiver returns a positive acknowledgment to the sender; if the two are unequal, a negative acknowledgment is returned and the sending station retransmits the message. Of course, the sending station must retain all messages until they have been positively acknowledged.

Retry Limit

In some instances the second message is also received in error, perhaps due to an error-prone communications link or to faulty hardware or software. To cut down on continual retransmission of messages, a **retry limit**—typically between 3 and 100—can be set. Thus, a retry limit of five means that a message received in error will be retransmitted five times; if it is not successfully received by the fifth try, the receiving station either disables the link or disables the sending station itself. The objective of a retry limit is to avoid the unproductive work of continually processing corrupted messages. Once the cause of the problem has been corrected, the communications path is reinstated.

SUMMARY

Media used to set up a LAN can be divided into two broad categories: conducted and wireless. Conducted media are twisted-pair wires, coaxial cable, and fiber optic cable. Wireless technologies include broadcast radio, microwave radio, spread-spectrum radio, and infrared light. Conducted media are more commonly used than wireless media. In general, conducted media support higher speeds, have better error and security characteristics, and are less expensive than wireless alternatives.

Twisted-pair wires are used for LANs with speeds up to 155 Mbps and will probably be used for 1-Gbps LANs in the near future. Fiber optic cable is used for high-speed LANs with speeds ranging from 100 Mbps to several Gbps. Coaxial cable, once the primary LAN medium, is being used less often because of the increased capabilities of twisted-pair wires and the lower costs and increased ease of use of fiber optic cables.

Wireless media are used primarily when workstations are often moved and when it is impractical to install conducted media. Wireless LAN technologies are newer than conducted media and we can expect their speed and market share to increase. A variety of factors influence the choice of a LAN medium. The primary decision factors are cost, speed, response time, aggregated data rate, availability, expandability, and error characteristics.

Transmission errors are always a matter of concern in data communications. There are several sources of errors including white noise, impulse noise, crosstalk, echo, and attenuation. In selecting a medium, LAN designers must consider the environment and equipment being used and select media whose error characteristics are compatible with that environment.

Key Terms

aggregate data rate	microwave radio
American wire gauge (AWG)	noise
ARCNET	plenum cable
broadcast radio	punchdown block
category 1 wire	repeaters
category 2 wire	response time
category 3 wire	retry limit
category 4 wire	RJ-45 jack
category 5 wire	sequence checks
coaxial cable	shielded twisted-pair wires (STP)
conducted media	spread-spectrum radio (SSR)
crosstalk	Telecommunications Industries
cyclic redundancy check (CRC)	Association (TIA)
echo	thicknet
EIA/TIA-568 standard	thinnet
Electronics Industries Association (EIA)	topology
Ethernet	twisted-pair wiring
fiber optic cable	unshielded twisted-pair wires (UTP)
impulse noise	vertical redundancy check (VRC)
infrared transmission	white noise
longitudinal redundancy check (LRC)	wireless media
media access control (MAC) protocol	

Review Questions

1. What is a LAN topology?
2. What are the basics a designer should consider when building a LAN?
3. What are the primary LAN conducted media?
4. What are the primary LAN wireless media?
5. Compare shielded and unshielded twisted-pair wires.
6. Describe the five EIA/TIA twisted-pair wire categories.
7. Describe the composition of coaxial cable.
8. What are the advantages and disadvantages of coaxial cable?
9. What are the differences between thicknet and thinnet coaxial cables?
10. What are the advantages and disadvantages of fiber optic cable?
11. Compare the primary LAN conducted media.
12. Compare the primary wireless LAN media.
13. When would it be expedient to use wireless media instead of conducted media?
14. Describe five media selection criteria.
15. Describe six sources of transmission errors.
16. How can transmission errors be prevented?
17. How are transmission errors detected?

Problems and Exercises

1. Suppose a LAN transmits data at 10 Mbps. If an impulse error of 1 ms occurs, how many bits may be corrupted by this error?
2. Give three instances or environments in which it would be beneficial or necessary to use shielded twisted-pair wires rather than unshielded twisted pairs.
3. What are the current costs for the following media?
   a. Category 5 UTP
   b. Category 5 UTP plenum cable
   c. Category 5 STP
   d. 10-Mbps Ethernet coaxial cable
   e. 100-Mbps fiber optic cable
4. Describe a situation in which a wireless LAN would be preferable to a wire-based LAN.
5. Suppose you needed to install a wire/cable-based LAN in an environment in which there was the possibility of considerable electromagnetic noise. What type of medium would you recommend? Justify your recommendation.
6. Suppose you have a large file and a small file to transfer between two computers. The size of the large file is 2 million bytes and the small file is 1000 bytes. Compare the time required to transfer each file if the mode of transfer is
   a. sneakernet
   b. 28,800 bps
   c. 1 Mbps
   d. 10 Mbps
   e. 16 Mbps
   f. 100 Mbps
   g. 1000 Mbps

Chapter 4

Topologies and Media Access Control

CHAPTER PREVIEW

When you select LAN hardware and software, you will probably investigate the capabilities provided by a variety of vendors. You will discover a variety of ways in which you can build a LAN, and you might also hear conflicting statements about the relative merits of these ways. In this chapter you will learn about the network layouts that vendors most commonly propose. The objective of learning about this technology is not only to understand the different available capabilities but also to understand their strengths and weaknesses.

In this chapter you will read about

LAN topologies

media access control protocols

common ways in which topologies and media access control protocols are combined

LAN standards

strengths and weaknesses of different LAN configurations

The LAN components covered in this chapter exist at the OSI physical and data link layers.

LAN TOPOLOGIES AND THE PHYSICAL LAYER

What do we mean when we talk about a LAN topology? First, the term *topology* derives from a mathematics field that deals with points and surfaces in space—that is, with the layout of objects in space. The LAN **topology** is the physical layout of the network. Another way you can look at a topology is as a model for the way in which you configure the medium and attach the nodes to that medium. In general, LAN topologies correspond to the OSI physical layer described in Chapter 1.

LANs have three basic topologies: ring, bus, and star. Each of these configurations is illustrated in Figure 4.1. Let's take a closer look at each topology.

Ring Topology

In a **ring topology,** illustrated in Figure 4.2, the medium forms a closed loop, and all stations are connected to the loop or ring. Let us first look at the basics of a ring and then at some specifics of two implementations.

On a ring data is transmitted from node to node in one direction. Thus if node A in Figure 4.2 wants to send a message to node E, the message is sent from A to B, from B to C, and so on, until it reaches node E. Usually node E then sends an acknowledgment that the message was successfully received back to node A, the originator of the message. The acknowledgment is sent from node E to F, and then from F back to A, completing one journey around the loop.

Nodes attached to the ring may be active or inactive. An active node is capable of sending or receiving network messages. An inactive node is incapable of sending or receiving network messages; for example, an inactive node may be powered down. Naturally, nodes may go from the inactive state to the active state and from active to inactive. For example, when a worker leaves at night, she might turn her workstation off, placing the workstation in an inactive state. In the morning she powers up her system and brings it into the active state. A failed or inactive network node must not cause the network to fail; an overview of how this happens is covered later in this chapter.

One type of network that uses a ring topology is a high-speed metropolitan area LAN, sometimes called a metropolitan area network (MAN), which is designed to cover a wider geographical area than a typical LAN. The ANSI standard for this type of network is called the **Fiber Distributed Data Interface (FDDI)** standard. It uses fiber optics for the medium and spans distances of up to 200 km at a speed of 100 Mbps. An alternative to FDDI is the **Copper Distributed Data Interface (CDDI),** which uses shielded or unshielded twisted-pair wires as the medium. As LAN workstations become more powerful and the volume of data transmission increases (perhaps because of the transmission of graphic and video images), high-speed LANs may be used to connect microcomputers in one department within a company. Currently one use for an FDDI LAN is as a backbone network connecting microcomputer LANs within a company complex or within a metropolitan area. A **backbone network,** illustrated in Figure 4.3, is used to interconnect other networks or to connect a cluster of network nodes.

A **token-passing ring** is the most common microcomputer ring network. **Token passing** is one way in which a node gains access to the medium and passes messages. A token is a unique type of message that is passed from node to node and gives a node that receives the token the right to transmit data. A node that receives the token can send a message to another node, or if the node does not have a message to send, it must pass the token to the next node. Once a node has used the token to send a message, it must relinquish the token by sending it to the next node. Thus one node cannot monopolize the medium by keeping the token indefinitely. Token passing is a type of media access control (MAC) protocol and is discussed later in this chapter.

IBM chose the token ring as its principal LAN topology and MAC protocol. IBM's LAN approach has been widely adopted and conforms to the **IEEE 802.5 standard,** so

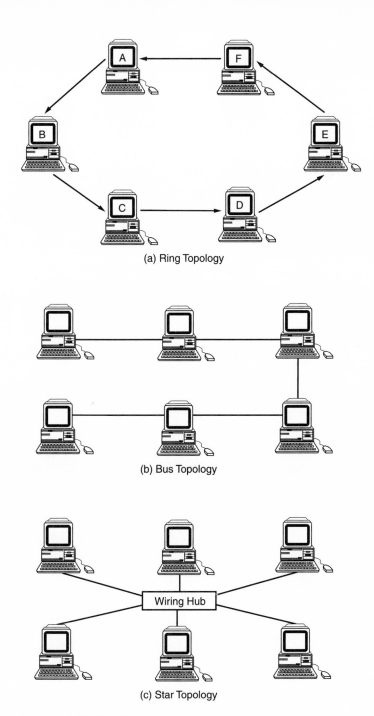

(a) Ring Topology

(b) Bus Topology

(c) Star Topology

Figure 4.1 Basic LAN Topologies

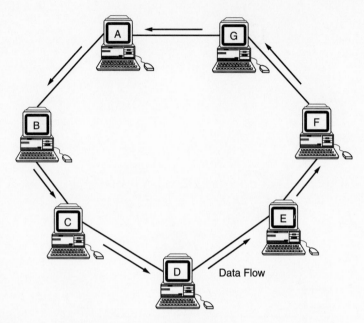

Figure 4.2   A Token-Passing Ring Configuration

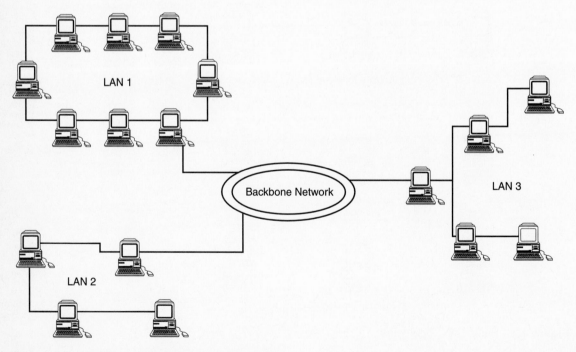

Figure 4.3   Backbone Network Connecting LANs

we describe it here. However, we are discussing only the topology and MAC. The token-passing ring we are describing can be implemented using a variety of different network operating systems, including Novell NetWare, Banyan Vines, Microsoft's Windows NT Server, and IBM's OS/2 Warp Server.

In IBM's Token Ring network, stations (nodes) are connected to a **multistation access unit (MAU or MSAU),** as shown in Figure 4.4. You can see that this configuration looks somewhat like the star configuration of Figure 4.1(c): The MAU forms the ring internally. Figure 4.5 shows the connection of two MAUs. IBM Token Ring speeds are 4, 16, and 100 Mbps using twisted-pair wires or fiber optic cable as the medium. Both of the lower speeds are supported within the same LAN; that is, transmission between two stations can be at 4 Mbps while two other stations communicate at 16 Mbps.

Bus Topology

In a **bus topology,** illustrated in Figure 4.6 (a), the medium consists of a single wire or cable to which nodes are attached. Unlike in a ring, the ends of the bus are not connected. Instead the ends are terminated by a hardware device aptly called a **terminator.**

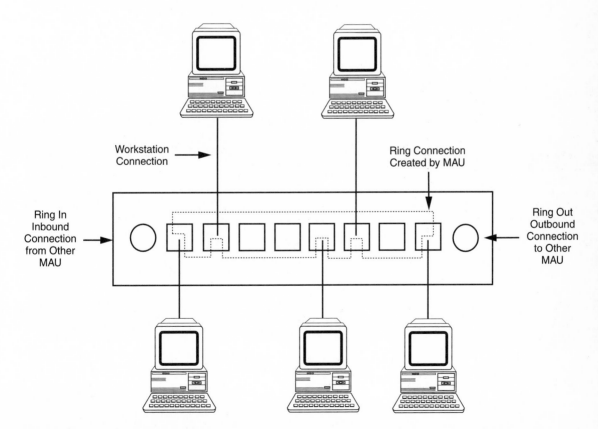

Figure 4.4   A Multistation Access Unit

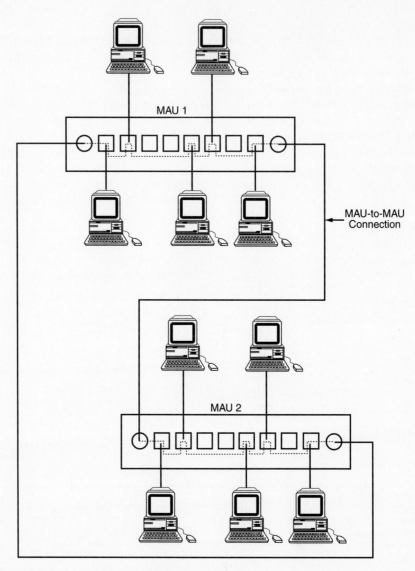

Figure 4.5   Token-Passing Ring Using a MAU

The purpose of the terminator is to eliminate signal feedback or signal loss at the endpoints. A variation of a bus topology, illustrated in Figure 4.6(b) has spurs to the primary bus formed by interconnected minibuses. This variation of the bus topology is quite common.

As with ring topologies, there are several standards that describe a bus implementation. The most common of these is an implementation originally known as **Ethernet.** Ethernet LAN specifications were originally proposed by Xerox Corporation in 1972.

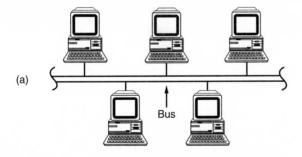

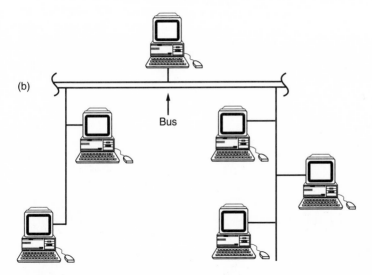

Figure 4.6   Bus LAN with Spurs

Soon thereafter Xerox was joined in establishing the Ethernet standard by Digital Equipment Corporation (DEC) and Intel Corporation. The IEEE 802 committee then developed the **IEEE 802.3 standard,** which encompasses most of the premises of the original Ethernet specification. Thus the IEEE 802.3 standard is sometimes called an Ethernet implementation. Another bus topology, **100VG-AnyLAN,** is one of two 100-Mbps Ethernet implementations and is covered by the **IEEE 802.12 standard.** The **IEEE 802.4 standard** also proposes a bus technology. The primary difference between the two is the MAC protocol. The IEEE 802.3 standard specifies a contention protocol, whereas the 802.4 standard uses a token-passing protocol. Again, these protocols are covered later in this chapter.

The common speeds of bus LANs are 1, 2.5, 5, 10, and 100 Mbps, with 10 and 100 Mbps the most commonly used. Versions of the IEEE 802.3, 802.4, and 802.12

standards specify one or more of these speeds. Speeds of 50 and 80 Mbps exist but are less common. Furthermore, a 1-Gbps standard is being developed. IEEE 802.3, 802.4, and 802.12 media are either twisted-pair wires, coaxial cables, fiber optic cables, or microwaves.

Star Topology

Figure 4.7 shows a **star topology,** which consists of a wiring hub to which nodes are directly connected. This type of topology is common in microcomputer networks. In a star-wired LAN, wiring hubs are used to form the connection between network nodes. The most common star-wired LAN is specified in the IEEE 802.3 10BaseT standard, covered later in this chapter.

ARCnet technology was developed in the 1970s by Datapoint Corporation to form networks of their minicomputers. ARCnet is another example of a star-wired LAN. The technology was well developed when microcomputer LANs were evolving, and the technology was readily adopted for microcomputer LANs. Because it has been so widely used, ARCnet has become a de facto microcomputer LAN standard and also has been submitted to ANSI for formal standardization. An ARCnet configuration, illustrated in

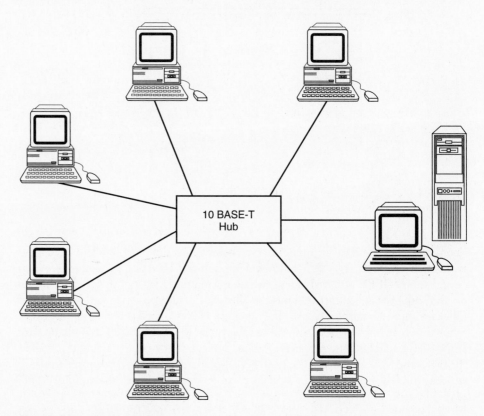

Figure 4.7   Star Topology

Figure 4.8, uses both active and passive hubs to connect network nodes. An **active hub** allows cable runs of up to 2000 feet between the hub and a workstation. A **passive hub** allows cable runs between a workstation and a passive hub of 100 feet. The reason for this difference is that the active hub regenerates the signal before transmitting to a node, but a passive hub splits the signal. ARCnet speeds are 2.5 Mbps and 20 Mbps, and both speeds can be used in the same network. ARCnet media are usually either twisted-pair wires or coaxial cables. Fiber optic cables are also used for ARCnet LANs, primarily in high-speed implementations.

At one time, ARCnet was widely used. Its speed was competitive with other LANs and the cost of implementing an ARCnet LAN was quite low. However, a number of factors have reduced the popularity of ARCnet LANs, and the number of new ARCnet implementations is constantly dropping. The factors adversely affecting ARCnet are lack of a formal standard, low transmission speeds, limited number of nodes per LAN, and price competitiveness.

StarLAN technology was developed by the American Telephone and Telegraph (AT&T) Corporation. The topology was also adopted and marketed by several other companies and has been included as a low-cost, low-speed option in the IEEE 802.3 standard. Originally the StarLAN speed was 1 Mbps, but today 10-Mbps implementations are also available. A star-wired topology is shown in Figure 4.7. Note that the configuration is also similar to that of the ARCnet configuration shown in Figure 4.8. The primary medium used for StarLAN implementations is twisted-pair wires.

LAN topology forms half of the LAN's circulatory system—its veins and arteries. The second half of the LAN circulatory system is the functions of the heart, pumping data through the system's medium. These functions are known as MAC protocols. Referring back to the OSI reference model discussed in Chapter 2, MAC functions are found in the data link layer. Let us now look at these important functions.

DATA LINK AND MEDIA ACCESS CONTROL PROTOCOLS

The physical layer of the OSI reference model describes the medium, the connectors required to attach workstations and servers to the medium, and the representation of signals using the medium, such as voltage levels or frequencies.

Once connected to the medium, a network node must have the ability to send and receive network messages. This function is described by the data link layer of the OSI reference mode. A convention, or protocol, must exist to define how this function is accomplished. The method by which a LAN workstation is able to gain control of the medium and transmit a message is called a MAC protocol. The MAC protocol is implemented in LANs as one of two sublayers of the OSI reference model's data link layer. The other sublayer is the **logical link control (LLC)** layer. The LLC provides a consistent interface between the network layer and the data link layer. Regardless of which MAC protocols and network layer protocols are being used, the LLC provides an interface that allows interoperability of different protocols.

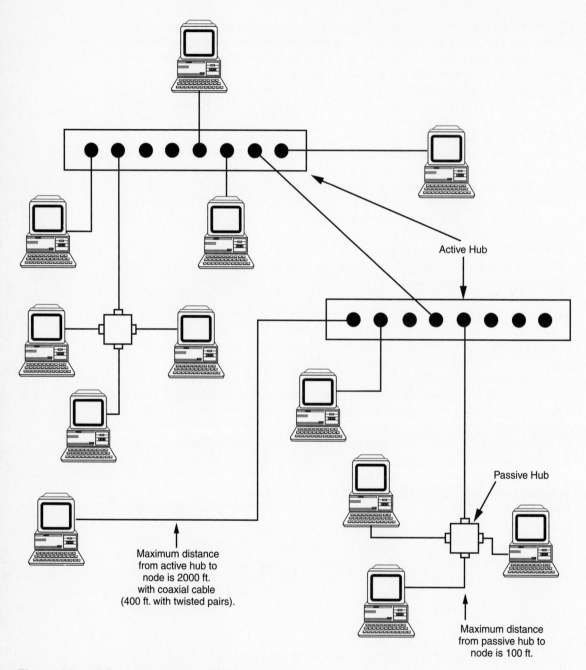

Active Hub

Passive Hub

Maximum distance
from active hub to
node is 2000 ft.
with coaxial cable
(400 ft. with twisted pairs).

Maximum distance
from passive hub to
node is 100 ft.

Figure 4.8   ARCnet with Active and Passive Hubs

Data Link Protocols

In general, a **data link protocol** establishes the rules for gaining access to the medium and exchanging messages. To do this, the protocol describes several aspects of the message-exchange process. Six of the most important are

> media access
>
> delineation of data
>
> error control
>
> addressing
>
> transparency
>
> code independence

Media Access

You practice media access in everyday life. Recall from Chapter 1 the different types of conversation: polite, classroom, and arguments. In each of these, there was a well-defined method for speaking (gaining access to the medium). Media access defines how a node gains the right to transmit data on the medium.

Delineation of Data

A data link protocol must define or delineate where the data portion of the transmitted message begins and ends. For the moment, consider a primitive communications situation: a terminal communicating with a host computer. In this situation we do not need the facilities of the OSI layers above the data link layer. The terminal probably uses one of two data link protocols, asynchronous or synchronous. The object is for the terminal to send the data an operator typed on the terminal to a host application to which it is attached. You may recall from the discussion of the OSI reference model in Chapter 1 that each layer may add data to the message it receives from the layers above it. The data link layer is no exception to this. Some of the characters or bits it adds to the message may include line control information, error-detection data, and so on. When these fields are added, a data link protocol must provide a way to distinguish between the various pieces of data. This can be accomplished in two basic ways: by framing the data with certain control characters or by using a standard message format wherein data is identified by its position within the message.

The framing technique is used in two types of data link protocols: asynchronous transmission and binary synchronous transmission. Asynchronous transmission sends one character at a time. Each character is framed by a start bit and a stop bit, as illustrated in Figure 4.9(a). In binary synchronous transmission multiple characters are transmitted in a single block. Special characters from the selected character set are reserved for data link control purposes (for example, to indicate where fields begin and end within the message and the presence of a header). For example, in Figure 4.9(b)

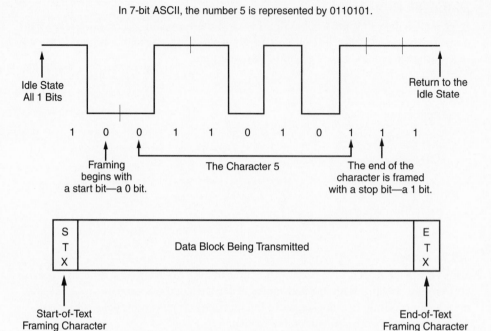

(b) Binary synchronous data link control characters: STX and ETX.

Figure 4.9   Character Framing

the STX characters indicate the beginning of the data, and the ETX characters indicate the end of the data.

Each LAN has a standard data link format for sending data, and Ethernet LANs may recognize several different frame formats. As the Ethernet technology matured, new frame formats were developed to enable new capabilities. Several of these formats are shown in Figure 4.10. From the figure you can see that each Ethernet message has several distinct parts. The message frame begins with a 64-bit synchronization pattern. The synchronization bits give the receiving node an opportunity to sense the incoming message and establish time or synchronization with the sending node. The message is a stream of continuous bits, so the receiving node must be able to clock the bits in as they arrive. The IEEE 802.3 standard uses a 64-bit synchronization pattern; however, the standard divides this into a 56-bit group and an 8-bit group. The first 56 bits are for synchronization, and the 8 bits that follow signal the start of the frame and thus indicate where the first bit of the remaining frame can be found. The next two fields are the addresses of the destination node and the sending node. Each address is 48 bits long.

The 16-bit field type is a control field. In the IEEE 802.3 standard, this represents the length of the data field that follows. The length is expressed as the number of octets of data. An **octet** is a group of 8 bits. If the message is short, extra bits may be added to make the entire message long enough to allow it to clear the length of the

Preamble	Destination Address	Source Address	Type Field	Data Field	32-Bit CRC

(a) Original Ethernet_II Frame

Preamble	Start Frame Delimeter	Destination Address	Source Address	Length Field	Data Field	32-Bit CRC

(b) IEEE 802.3 Frame

Preamble	Start Frame Delimeter	Destination Address	Source Address	Length Field	IEEE 802.2 Control	Data Field	32-Bit CRC

(c) IEEE 802.2 Frame

Preamble	Destination Address	Source Address	Length Field	DSAP	SSAP	CTRL	Data Field	32-Bit CRC

(d) Ethernet_SNAP (an 802.2 variant)

Figure 4.10 Ethernet Message Formats

network before the sending node stops transmitting. This is essential to ensure correct transmission. The frame check sequence is a 32-bit **cycle redundancy check (CRC)** field. This is used for error detection.

Error Control

Error control is used to determine whether data is corrupted during the transmission. This might happen if lightning strikes a wire carrying the data or if there is a loose connection at the wiring interface. To detect errors, additional data is attached to the message, such as the 32-bit CRC field in the Ethernet messages of Figure 4.10. The additional data allows the recipient to make a check to see whether errors have occurred. In Chapter 3 we discussed VRC and LRC, which are other error-detection methods. Compared to CRC these are rather primitive techniques. Today most state-of-the-art data link protocols and almost all LANs use the more efficient CRC error-detection scheme.

Addressing

Communication between two network nodes is accomplished through an addressing scheme. Network addressing is similar to addressing we use for postal mail. A postal address is a hierarchical addressing scheme, with the hierarchy being individual recipient, street address, city, state, country, and zip code. Networks also use a hierarchical addressing scheme, with the hierarchy being application, network node, and network. Consider an internet. Like postal addresses, network addresses must be unique; otherwise ambiguity arises as to which node is the recipient. A process in one internet node may need to send an e-mail message to a process in a node on another network. A process in a node has an address, sometimes called a port or socket number, that is unique among all processes running in that node. Each node on a specific network has an address that is unique among all nodes on that network. Each network in an internet has an identifier that uniquely distinguishes it from all other networks on that internet. Thus, the combination of process, node, and network addresses describe a unique entity on the internet. At the data link layer we are concerned only with network node addressing, not network or application addressing.

Each network has a specific way in which it forms station addresses. In Ethernet and the IBM token-passing ring, each address is 48 bits long. Each Ethernet or IBM token-ring LAN adapter card has its address set by the manufacturer. This ensures that all nodes, regardless of location, have a unique address. In ARCnet a node address is an 8-bit entity, and the LAN administrator typically sets the node address through switches on the LAN adapter. On a LAN, node source and destination addresses typically are included in the data link and network layer headers of messages being transmitted.

Transparency

Transparency is the ability of the data link to transmit any bit combination. In the binary synchronous data link protocol (shown in Figure 4.9(b)), the start-of-text and end-of-text framing characters have special meaning. These characters can be sent as part of the data only when special considerations are made. Without these special considerations, the protocol is not transparent. For example, in the binary synchronous protocol, if an ETX character were embedded in the data portion of the transmission frame, the receiving node would interpret it as the end of the message, not part of the data. The messages would be prematurely terminated and the error-detection field would not check correctly. We like protocols to be transparent because they can be used to transfer binary data such as object programs as well as text data. LAN data link protocols ordinarily provide transparency: No bit patterns in the data field can cause confusion in the message.

Code Independence

Code independence means that any data code, such as ASCII or EBCDIC, can be transmitted. These codes use different bit patterns to represent many of the characters. Code independence is important because often you must communicate with or through a computer having a different data code than your computer. In LAN protocols this is accomplished by sending data in groups of 8 bits, called octets. The 8 bits are not tied to any particular code, so any code can be used. If your computer uses a 7-bit code, like one of the two ASCII codes, the only requirement is that the total number of bits transmitted in each subfield of the frame be divisible by 8. Thus, if you are sending 100 7-bit characters, the total number of bits in the data portion must be 704. The last 4 bits are added to pad out to an integral number of octets. ($700/8 = 87.5$, and an integral number of octets must be transmitted; 704 bits are necessary because 704 is a multiple of 8.)

MAC Protocols

LAN technology adheres to two primary MAC protocols: token passing and contention.

Contention

In a pure contention MAC protocol, each network node has equal access to the medium. Variations of this protocol exist, some of which allow for node priorities. Contention is similar to the polite conversation protocol we discussed in Chapter 1.

Contention works like this: Each node monitors the medium to see whether a message is being transmitted. If no message is detected, any node can begin a transmission. The act of listening to the medium for a message is called carrier sensing, because when a message is being transmitted, a carrier signal is present. Several nodes can have messages to send. Each of them may detect a quiet medium, and each may begin to transmit at one time. The ability for several nodes to access a medium that is not carrying a message is called multiple access. If two or more nodes begin to transmit at the same time, a **collision** is said to occur. Multiple simultaneous transmissions cause the messages to interfere with each other and become garbled. It is imperative that collisions be detected and that recovery be effected. When a collision occurs, the messages will not be transmitted successfully. On detecting a collision, the sending nodes must resend their messages. If both nodes immediately attempt to retransmit their messages, another collision might occur. Therefore, each node waits a small, randomly selected interval before attempting retransmit. This reduces the probability of another collision.

There is only a small time interval during which a collision can occur. For example, suppose that two nodes at the extremities of a 1000-m bus network have a message to send and that the medium is not being used. The collision interval is the time it takes for a signal to travel the length of the cable. Because the signal travels near the speed of light, the collision window is the time it takes for the signal to travel 1000 m, the signal's propagation delay. The propagation delay is approximately 5 nanoseconds per meter, so for a 1000-m segment, the maximum propagation delay is approximately 5 microseconds (5 millionths of a second). Although this interval is small, collisions can still occur.

The MAC technique just described is known as **carrier sense with multiple access and collision detection (CSMA/CD)** and is used for Ethernet LANs. It is the most common of the access strategies for bus architectures. The CSMA/CD MAC protocol, sometimes called listen-before-talk, is summarized in Table 4.1. You should note that the CSMA/CD protocol is a broadcast protocol. All workstations on the network listen to the medium and accept the message. Each message has a destination address. Only a workstation having an address equal to the destination address can use the message. Using a broadcast technique makes it easy for new workstations to be added and taken off the network.

CSMA/CD is known as a fair protocol, meaning that each node has equal access to the medium. In a pure CSMA/CD scheme, no one node has priority over another. Variations of this protocol exist that give one workstation priority over another and minimize the likelihood of collisions. One of these protocol variations divides time into transmission slots. The length of a slot is the time it takes a message to travel the length

Table 4.1   CSMA/CD Media Access Protocol

1. Listen to the medium to see whether a message is being transmitted.
2. If the medium is quiet, transmit message. If the medium is busy, wait for the signal to clear and then transmit.
3. If a collision occurs, wait for the signal to clear, wait a random interval, and then retransmit.

of the medium. Nodes on the network are synchronized and can begin a transmission only at the beginning of its allocated time slot. This protocol has been proven to be more efficient for networks with lots of nodes and message traffic.

A variation of CSMA/CD is **carrier sense with multiple access and collision avoidance (CSMA/CA).** This protocol attempts to avoid collisions that are possible with the CSMA/CD protocol. Collisions are avoided because each node is given a wait time before it can begin transmitting. For example, suppose that there are 100 nodes on the network and the propagation delay time for the network is 1 millisecond (ms). Node 1 can transmit after the medium has been idle for 1 ms. Node 2 must wait 2 ms before attempting to transmit, node 3 must wait 3 ms, and so on. Each node, therefore, has a specific time slot during which it can transmit and no collisions will occur. However, the node with the lowest time slot may experience long delays in getting access to the medium.

Token Passing

The second major MAC protocol is token passing. It is used on both bus and ring topologies. Token passing is a round-robin protocol in which each node gets an equal opportunity to transmit. With token passing, the right to transmit is granted by a token that is passed from one node to another. Remember that a token is a predefined bit pattern that is recognized by each node. In a ring topology, the token is passed from one node to its adjacent node, as illustrated in Figure 4.2. On a token-passing bus, the order of token passing is determined by the address of each node. The token is passed in either ascending or descending address order. If it is passed in descending order, the station with the lowest address passes the token to the node with the highest address. The routing of a token from high to low addresses in a token-passing bus is illustrated in Figure 4.11.

When a node receives the token, it has two options: It can transmit a message or, if it has no message to send, it can pass the token to the next node. If the node has a message to transmit, it keeps the token by changing the format of the message header from *token* to *transmit* and sends the message. The message recipient keeps the message, changes the format of the frame to acknowledge receipt, and then transmits it back onto the network. The message eventually arrives back at the sending node. When a node receives the message it sent (the node's address matches the sender's address in the frame), it accepts the message as an acknowledgment that the message was received successfully. The transmitting node then activates the token by sending it to the next node. The token-passing protocol does not allow a node to monopolize the

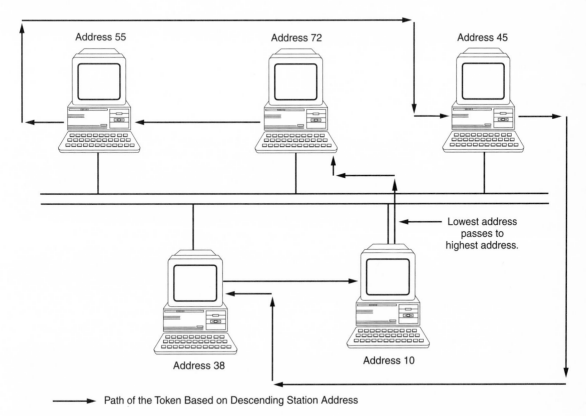

Figure 4.11   Token-Passing Bus

token and hog the network. Note that, unlike the CSMA/CD protocol, the token-passing protocol does not allow collisions.

Token-Passing Ring

In token passing, the token can become lost if a node holding the token fails or if transmission errors occur. To allow recovery from this loss, one node is designated as the active monitor. Other nodes are designated as standby monitors. The active monitor periodically issues a message indicating that it is active. The standby monitors accept this status and remain in standby mode. If the active monitor message fails to appear on time, a standby monitor assumes the active monitor role. A major function of the active monitor is to ensure that the token is circulating. If the token does not arrive within a certain amount of time, the active monitor generates a new token. This technique is guaranteed to work, as the token transmit time is very predictable.

Token-Passing Bus

Token passing is a bit different on a **token-passing bus.** On a bus the token is passed from one workstation to another based on station addresses. As mentioned earlier, the token

Table 4.2 Token-Passing Media Access Control Protocol

1. Wait for transmit token.
2. If transmit token is received and there is no message to send, send the token to the next node.
3. If transmit token is received and there is a message to send, then
   a) Transmit message
   b) Wait for acknowledgment
   c) When acknowledgment is received, pass token to next node

can be passed in ascending or descending address order. Let us assume that the token is passed in descending address order, so the station with the lowest address forwards the token to the station with the highest address. This token-passing scheme is outlined in Table 4.2. Such a protocol must allow for new workstations to be inserted and for active ones to be deactivated.

Suppose node 72 in Figure 4.11 attempts to send the token to the next node, node 55, and that station has been shut down. Recovery must be possible when a station goes from active to inactive status. For example, when a sending station does not receive the token back in a prescribed interval, the sending station transmits the token to its neighbor again. If a second failure occurs, the sending station assumes that the neighboring station is inactive and issues a "who is next" message, asking for the address of the next station. The "who is next" message contains the address of the unresponsive station. The successor of the failed station, node 45 in this example, recognizes the address in the "who is next" message as its predecessor station and responds to node 72. If node 45 has also failed, node 72 sends another "who is next" message with the entire address range of the LAN. If any other stations are active, they respond.

Allowance also is made in the token-passing bus protocol for new stations to enter the LAN. Periodically stations issue a "solicit successor" message. This message contains the sending station's address and the address of that station's current successor node. Stations receiving this message inspect the addresses of the sender and the successor in the message. If a station has an address that falls in between these two addresses, it responds to the message. Two stations can respond at the same time. In this case a collision occurs, as in CSMA/CD, and collision resolution is effected. This allows an orderly process for insertion of new stations.

LAN STANDARDS

If you have the opportunity to build a LAN from the beginning, you will be faced with a multitude of decisions. In Chapter 3 we discussed LAN media, and with media alone there are two major categories: conducted and wireless. Within each of these categories there are three or four major options, and most options have suboptions. Therefore, if we just consider media, we have about 20 viable options. When you combine these 20 options with the multitude of options covering hardware, software, and LAN layout, the number of combinations is staggering. The issue becomes how to make the proper choices. For many people, the answer lies in standards.

Standards exist covering most aspects of LAN technology. Furthermore, as technology advances, new standards come into being. For many LAN designers, standards provide the framework for building a LAN. A set of standards stipulates things such as the LAN medium, number of allowed nodes, LAN layout, speeds, and types of adapters and wiring hubs. Implementing according to established standards generally results in the availability of components from multiple vendors, competition among vendors, and lower prices. In contrast, if a designer chooses to implement only established standards, new technology that has not yet been sanctioned by a standard may be eliminated from consideration. Furthermore, one of the LAN implementations that has been popular in the past, ARCnet, was not sanctioned by any official standards organization. In this section, we briefly introduce you to some of the most important LAN standards and standard-making bodies.

The organizations that have been most active in developing LAN standards are

the **American National Standards Institute (ANSI)**

Electronics Industries Association (EIA)

Institute of Electrical and Electronic Engineers (IEEE)

International Standards Organization (ISO)

International Telecommunications Union (ITU)

Object Management Group (OMG)

Open Software Foundation (OSF)

SQL Access Group (SAG)

Telecommunications Industries Association (TIA)

As you read in Chapter 3, the EIA and TIA have established standards for LAN media. The organizations most active in setting standards for LAN topologies and MAC protocols are the IEEE and ANSI, and their primary contributions are discussed here. Standards from the other organizations are covered in later chapters. The most prolific standards group for specifying the basics of LAN implementations is the IEEE.

IEEE Standards

The IEEE established a standards group called the 802 committee. This group is divided into subcommittees, each of which addresses specific LAN issues and architectures. The subcommittees and their objectives are described below.

802.1: High-Level Interface

The high-level interface subcommittee addresses matters relating to network architecture, network management, network interconnection, and all other issues related to the

OSI layers above the data link layer, which are the network, transport, session, presentation, and application layers.

802.2: Logical Link Control

IEEE has divided the OSI data link layer into two sublayers: Logical Link Control (LLC) and MAC. The MAC sublayer implements protocols such as token passing and CSMA/CD. Figure 4.12 illustrates the relationship between the LLC and the MAC sublayers. The objective of the LLC is to provide a consistent, transparent interface to the MAC layer, so the network layers above the data link layer are able to function correctly regardless of the MAC protocol.

802.3: CSMA/CD

The IEEE 802.3 standard covers a variety of CSMA/CD architectures that are generally based on Ethernet. Several alternatives are available under this standard. Some of these are as follows:

- 1Base5 is a 1-Mbps baseband medium with a maximum segment length of 500 m (a baseband medium is one that carries only one signal at a time, as opposed

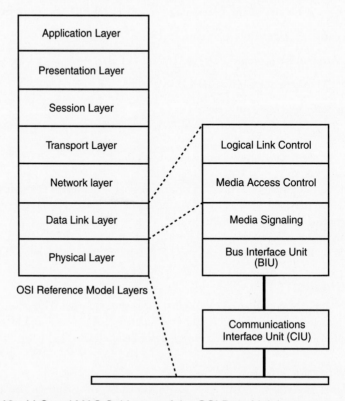

Figure 4.12 LLC and MAC Sublayers of the OSI Data Link Layer

to a broadband medium that can carry multiple signals simultaneously). The segment length is the length of cable that can be used without repeaters to amplify the signal. This standard encompasses implementations commonly known as StarLAN.

- 10Base5 is a 10-Mbps baseband medium with a maximum segment length of 500 m.

- 10Base2 is a 10-Mbps baseband medium with a maximum segment length of 185 m. The cable used in this implementation is commonly called thinnet or cheapernet.

- 10Base-T is a 10-Mbps baseband medium with twisted-pair wires as the medium using a star-wired topology.

- 10Broad36 is a 10-Mbps broadband medium with a 3600-m segment length.

- 100Base-T is a 100-Mbps baseband medium with twisted-pair wires as the medium using a star-wired topology.

- 100Base-FX is a 100-Mbps baseband medium using fiber optic cable.

- 100VG-AnyLAN is a specification of the IEEE 802.12 subcommittee. This specification competes with 100Base-T for the 100-Mbps Ethernet market. The specification calls for twisted-pair wires and can support either CSMA/CD or token-passing technologies.

You may infer from this nomenclature that, in general, the initial number represents the speed of the medium in millions of bits per second. The *base* or *broad* designators represent *baseband* and *broadband*, respectively. With four exceptions, 10Base-T, 100Base-T, 100Base-FX, and 100VG-AnyLAN, the last number represents the segment length of the medium in hundreds of meters in a bus topology LAN.

802.4: Token Bus

The IEEE 802.4 standard subcommittee sets standards for token bus networks. The standard describes how the network is initialized, how new stations can insert themselves into the set of nodes receiving the token, how to recover if the token is lost, and how node priority can be established. The standard also describes the format of the message frames.

802.5: Token Ring

The IEEE 802.5 standard subcommittee sets standards for token-ring networks. The standard describes essentially the same functions as those described by the token bus network.

802.6: Metropolitan Area Networks (MANs)

The FDDI family of technologies is not the only MAN proposal. The IEEE 802 LAN standards committee has also developed specifications, IEEE 802.6, for a MAN. The

IEEE 802.6 standard has also been adopted by ANSI. The standard is also called the distributed queue dual bus (DQDB) standard.

As the name indicates, the DQDB architecture uses two buses. Each bus is unidirectional, meaning that data is transmitted in one direction on one bus and in the other direction on the second bus, as illustrated in Figure 4.13. Each node must therefore be attached to both buses. The specification also allows for a variation called a looped bus. The looped bus still uses two one-direction buses; however, each bus forms a closed loop, as illustrated in Figure 4.14. Several speeds are defined in the standard. Speeds depend on the medium used. With coaxial cable the speed is 45 Mbps; the speed is 156 Mbps over fiber optic cable. Distances up to 200 miles are supported. This subcommittee sets standards for networks that can cover a wide area and operate at high speed. Distances of up to 200 miles and speeds on the order of 100 Mbps are being considered for MANs. A MAN could transmit voice and video in addition to data.

802.7: Broadband Technical Advisory Group

This group provides guidance and technical expertise to other groups that are establishing broadband LAN standards, such as the 802.3 subcommittee for 10Broad36.

802.8: Fiber Optic Technical Advisory Group

This group provides guidance and technical expertise to other groups that are establishing standards for LANs using fiber optic cable.

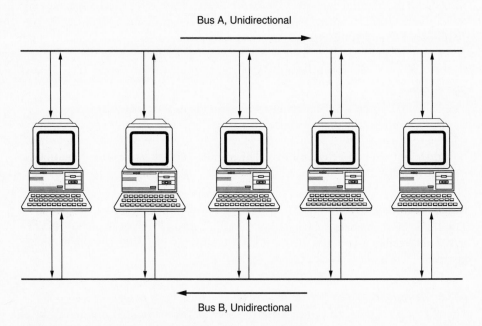

Figure 4.13   ANSI Distributed Queue Dual Bus LAN

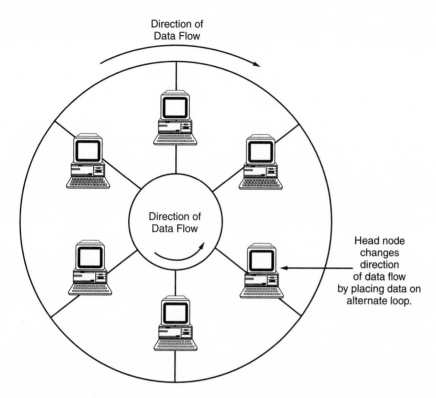

Direction of
Data Flow

Direction of
Data Flow

Head node
changes
direction
of data flow
by placing data on
alternate loop.

Figure 4.14   ANSI Looped Bus LAN

802.9: Integrated Data and Voice Networks
This committee sets standards for networks that carry both voice and data. Specifically, it is setting standards for interfaces to the Integrated Services Digital Networks (ISDNs).

802.10: LAN Security
This committee addresses the implementation of security capabilities such as encryption, network management, and the transfer of data.

802.11: Wireless LANs
This committee sets standards covering multiple transmission methods to include infrared light, as well as a variety of broadcast frequencies to include spread-spectrum radio waves and microwaves.

802.12: Demand Priority Access Method
This subgroup is developing the specifications for the 100VG-AnyLAN protocol. The protocol specifies 100-Mbps speeds over twisted-pair wires.

In the standards for IEEE 802.3 two transmission methods, baseband and broadband, were mentioned. These terms refer to how the medium is used in transmitting signals. Let us look at each of these.

BROADBAND AND BASEBAND TECHNOLOGIES

Broadband transmission and **baseband transmission** are different ways in which you can use a medium. Broadband transmission divides the medium into several channels, thus allowing the medium to be used for distinct transmission needs. Baseband transmission dedicates the entire data-carrying capacity of the medium to the LAN. Most of today's microcomputer LANs use baseband transmission. In the future, broadband LANs may become more common, so you should understand both technologies and the advantages and disadvantages of each.

Broadband Transmission

In a broadband system one communications cable can carry multiple signals simultaneously. For broadband transmission to be practical for a LAN, the medium must have sufficient carrying capacity to allow at least one channel to be fast enough for LAN communication. For small LANs this might be 250 Kbps or faster; for bigger LANs, speeds of 1 Mbps or more are needed to provide proper performance levels. Recall from Chapter 3 that the speed you need depends on how the LAN is being used.

The technique that allows one medium to carry multiple signal channels is similar to a technique used by telephone companies to carry several different telephone conversations over one telephone line. With this technique, called frequency division multiplexing, the total bandwidth of the medium is divided into separate subchannels, or frequency bands. The **bandwidth** of a medium is the range of frequencies that the medium can carry without incurring signal disruption. Also described as the carrying capacity of a medium, the bandwidth is measured in hertz, a measure of electrical frequency that represents one cycle per second, or megahertz (MHz), which represents one million cycles per second. The bigger the bandwidth, the greater the data-carrying capacity of the cable. Coaxial cable is the primary medium used for broadband transmission. Because twisted-pair wires do not have the bandwidth to support a wide range of broadband channels, they are seldom used as a medium for broadband systems.

A proposal for broadband channel allocations is shown in Figure 4.15. Notice that the channels include voice, video, low-speed data, and high-speed data bands.

The voice channel shown in Figure 4.15 can be used for telephones, and the video channel can carry a closed-circuit television channel used for training. The low-speed data channel can have several low-speed subchannels, which can be used to connect terminals to a host system. The high-speed data channel may operate at speeds of 10 Mbps or higher and can be used as the LAN channel. Thus one cable system can meet many of the communications needs of an organization.

Devices are connected to a broadband system through a radio-frequency modem. Suppose that a terminal is set up to use the low-speed data band to communicate with

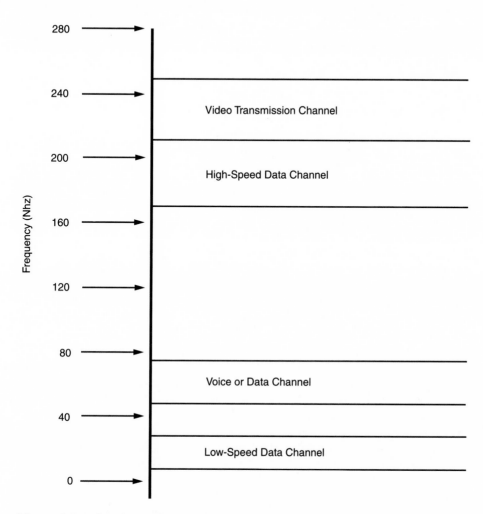

Figure 4.15 Suggested Broadband Frequency Allocations

a host computer. The terminal's modem places data on the cable at the frequencies designated for that terminal's subchannel. A workstation using the high-speed LAN band places its data signal on the cable at the frequencies designated for the high-speed data band, and so on.

Broadband Standards and Use

The IEEE has adopted several standards for implementing broadband LANs. Broadband standards are a part of the 802.3 and 802.4 specifications. Another broadband implementation is covered by the manufacturing automation protocol (MAP) LAN specifications proposed by General Motors Corporation. MAP conforms in some respects to the IEEE 802.4 standard.

Because a broadband system can provide a wide range of communications capabilities, it would seem preferable to a baseband system, which can carry only one data signal. However, broadband transmission has disadvantages. The equipment required for a broadband system is more expensive than that required for most baseband systems. Moreover, broadband systems, being more complex than baseband systems, are more difficult to install and manage. For example, frequency allocations must be designated for each subchannel, and cable disruptions can impair an organization's entire communications system.

Let's take a closer look at baseband transmission.

Baseband Transmission

Baseband transmission allows only one signal to be transmitted on the medium at one time. Most microcomputer LANs use this technology because it is easier and cheaper to implement than a broadband system. Baseband systems are implemented on all three primary media types—twisted-pair wires, coaxial cable, and fiber optic cable—as well as on wireless media. A wide variety of speeds are supported, ranging between several hundred thousand bits per second at the low end to over 100 Mbps on the high end. Speeds of over 2 Gbps have been attained in the laboratory using a fiber optic medium.

Broadband and baseband technologies address how we use the medium. Another issue that must be decided is how we arrange the nodes on the medium: the LAN topology. We introduced topologies in Chapter 3. We explore the workings of LAN topologies in more detail in the following sections.

The ANSI Fiber Distributed Data Interface (FDDI) Standard

The IEEE 802.6 committee's charter is to set standards for MANs. The ANSI also has set standards for MANs. The ANSI standard was established before the IEEE standard and is more widely adopted than the IEEE standard. ANSI has set two standards, the Fiber Distributed Data Interface (FDDI) and the Copper Distributed Data Interface (CDDI). As the names imply, the primary difference between the two is the medium; FDDI uses fiber optic cables and CDDI uses UTP or STP wires. CDDI and FDDI speeds are 100 Mbps and use token passing as the MAC protocol. CDDI distances are limited to 100 m from the wiring closet to the network node. FDDI covers distances up to 200 km.

MAKING THE DECISIONS

Even without considering the software alternatives, the number of alternatives available in choosing a LAN is large. You have three basic conducted media choices (with suboptions in each class) or four wireless medium choices, three major topology choices, two primary MAC choices, and a wide variety of vendor choices. The issue then becomes which is the best configuration. If there were one clear option that was superior for all applications and for all users, the choice would be easy. However, applications vary significantly with respect to the number of nodes, number of concurrent users, data access needs, distance spanned, and cost. To help you make the right decision, we can offer only tradeoffs for you to consider.

Token Passing and CSMA/CD Compared

The pros and cons of each MAC protocol are summarized in Table 4.3. Note that each protocol has its advantages and disadvantages. In practice both have been noted to have good performance.

Topology and Protocol Tradeoffs

We consider the three primary combinations of topology and protocol: CSMA/CD bus, token bus, and token ring. The StarLAN model LAN is covered under the IEEE 802.3 standard, and its characteristics are similar to those of the CSMA/CD bus. Because wireless media occupy such a small segment of the market, we do not include them in the discussion. When specifics are required, we use popular implementations as examples: Ethernet or an IEEE 802.3 implementation for CSMA/CD buses, ARCnet for token buses, and IEEE 802.5 for token rings. Table 4.4 is a summary of the topologies and protocols, which are described in the following sections.

CSMA/CD Buses

Most CSMA/CD bus implementations use either twisted-pair wires or coaxial cable. Less commonly, fiber optic cable and microwave radio are used. Common speeds for these LANs are 10 and 100 Mbps. At present, 10 Mbps is the more common but a large number of new LANs being installed operate at speeds of 100 Mbps and 10-Mbps LANs are being converted to 100 Mbps. The distances spanned by these networks vary, but the IEEE 802.3 standard, which covers several implementations, specifies maximum medium lengths of 925, 2500, and 3600 m. The number of supported nodes also varies. In the IEEE standard one implementation allows 150 nodes, and another allows 500. The number of nodes allowed is a hardware-based limit and addresses the issue of connectivity. The network operating system and performance needs may also limit the number

Table 4.3   Comparison of Token-Passing and CSMA/CD Media Access Control Protocols

Token Passing	CSMA/CD
Equal access for all nodes.	Equal access for all nodes.
Predictable access window.	Access window can be unpredictable.
Maximum wait time to transmit is token circulation time.	Maximum wait time to transmit is unpredictable and depends on collisions.
Average wait time to transmit is predictable (half the maximum circulation time).	Average wait time to transmit is unpredictable.
Network congestion does not adversely affect network efficiency.	Network congestion may result in collisions and reduce network efficiency.
A node needs to wait for the token before being able to transmit.	A node may be able to transmit immediately.
One node cannot monopolize the network.	One node may be able to monopolize the network.
Large rings can result in long delays before a node obtains a token.	A node can transmit when the network is quiet.
Consistent performance for large, busy networks.	Unpredictable performance for large, busy networks due to possibility of collisions.

Table 4.4   LAN Topology and Protocol Summary

	IEEE 802.3: Ethernet	IEEE 802.5: Token Ring	FDDI/CDDI
Speed (Mbps)	10, 100, 1000	4, 16, 100	100/100
Medium	Twisted-pair wires, coaxial cable	Twisted-pair wires or fiber optic cable	Fiber optic cable/ twisted-pair wires
Distance	500 meters for thick cable, 185 meters for thinnet cable segments; five segments can be connected with repeaters to give maximum lengths of 2500 and 925 meters	366 meters for the main ring; can be extended to 750 meters with repeaters and to 4000 meters with fiber optic cable	200 kilometers/ 100 meters node to patch panel
Number of Stations	802.3: 100 per thick cable segment, 30 per thinnet segment Ethernet-1024	255	1000
Standards	IEEE 802.3: 10Base5, 10Base2, 10Base-T, 100Base-T, 100Base-FX, 10Broad36, and IEEE 802.12 100VG–Any LAN	IEEE 802.5	ANSI X3T9.5 ISO 9314
Cost for NIC	Under $40 for 10Base-T Under $140 for 100Base-T	Under $200 for 4/16 Mbps	$1200

of network nodes. Some network operating systems restrict the number of network nodes. We discuss network operating systems in Chapter 8.

One of the things you will want to know about a network is its performance. Performance depends on both the hardware and the software. The number of combinations of hardware and software is large, so let us look at the general outlook for CSMA/CD bus systems. The major concern people have voiced regarding CSMA/CD bus performance is its capacity under load. As the number of users and the number of messages being sent increase, so does the probability of collisions. If the collision rate is high, the effectiveness of the LAN decreases. That is, when the LAN is busy, the efficiency may drop, and you might lose effectiveness just when you need it most. LAN vendors and researchers have run numerous tests to gauge the effect of high collision rates. Under these tests the performance characteristics did not drop appreciably. The true test of performance comes from actual use. Under light load conditions, access to the medium and the ability to transmit are good; there is little waiting time to transmit. Performance under heavy loads can be unpredictable but in practice there are many large CSMA/CD LANs in operation that provide excellent performance.

Token Buses and Token Rings

We discuss these two implementations together because their MAC characteristics are similar. ARCnet can be implemented in a bus or a star-wired topology. ARCnet operates at speeds of 2.5 or 20 Mbps on twisted-pair wires, coaxial cable, or fiber optic cable.

Both speeds can be used in the same LAN because the 20-Mbps cards can work at either speed. The maximum distance that can be spanned by ARCnet is 20,000 feet (6110 m). An example of an ARCnet configuration is shown in Figure 4.8.

IBM's Token Ring operates at 4 or 16 Mbps using twisted-pair wires or fiber optic cable as the medium. Transmission at 16 Mbps requires the use of Category 4 twisted-pair wires or fiber optic cable. Shielded twisted-pair wires are less error-prone than unshielded twisted-pair wires and were originally specified to support the higher speed. Stations on the LAN connect to a MAU, as illustrated in Figure 4.5. A typical MAU contains ports for eight workstations plus an input and output connector, called the ring-in and ring-out, respectively, to allow one MAU to be connected to another MAU, as illustrated in Figure 4.5. The ring is established by interconnections within the MAU, as illustrated in Figure 4.5. The distance spanned by a ring is 750 m. The maximum number of nodes allowed per ring is 255. Multiple rings can be connected with bridges.

Predictability is the key to describing token-ring LAN performance. Because access to the medium is through the possession of a token, and because each station is assured of receiving the token, you can accurately predict the maximum, minimum, and average times a station needs to be able to transmit a message. The problem of collision, inherent in contention LANs, does not exist. Thus, when network traffic is light, a station may need to wait longer than a station on a contention bus; however, when network traffic is heavy, the token-passing station may wait less time. Regardless of the wait time, a station is assured that it can transmit in a predictable time. The maximum time a station must wait is the number of stations, minus 1, times the message transit time. That is, a station that has just passed the token to its neighbor may become ready to send a message. That station must wait until the token comes around. The worst case is that every other station has a message to transmit. Thus, the station must wait on every other station to transmit and pass the token. On average, the station must wait for half the other stations.

Of the common microcomputer LAN implementations, token-passing solutions are the lowest- and highest-cost solutions. In general, ARCnet LANs have a lower per-station cost than Ethernet LANs, and Ethernet LANs have a lower per-station cost than token rings. This statement is based on the cost of the hardware (LAN adapters, MAUs, wiring hubs, cables, connectors, wiring, and so on). Because prices fluctuate over time and from one vendor to another, you should verify these costs.

For high-speed token rings, you may select from FDDI and CDDI. FDDI has the added benefit of spanning longer distances than any of the other LANs described here. Moreover, to enhance performance, FDDI supports the ability to have multiple tokens circulating at once and for a message to be piggybacked in the same frame with other messages.

SUMMARY

There are two basic ways in which LANs use a transmission medium. In broadband transmission the carrying capacity of the medium is divided into separate transmission bands. Each transmission band is able to support a data transmission type. One band may be used for video transmission, one for voice, one for high-speed data (a LAN band), and some bands may be available for low-speed data transmission. Thus one transmission medium, usually coaxial cable, can become the delivery mechanism for a corporation's various communications capabilities. In baseband transmission only one signal is allowed on the medium at one time. A baseband system is simpler to implement and manage and costs less than a broadband system.

A LAN topology is the pattern used to lay out the LAN. The main LAN topologies are bus, ring, and star. Coupled with the topology is the way in which a station interfaces with the medium, known as its MAC protocol. The main MAC protocols for LANs are CSMA/CD and token passing. CSMA/CD is used on bus topologies and star topologies. Token passing is used on bus and ring topologies.

The primary media used for implementing LANs are unshielded twisted-pair wires, shielded twisted-pair wires, coaxial cable, and fiber optic cable. Newer LAN technology features wireless LANs. Wireless LANs use broadcast radio, infrared light, and microwave radio waves to communicate between workstations and servers.

Key Terms

100VG-AnyLAN
active hub
American National Standards Institute
   (ANSI)
backbone network
bandwidth
baseband transmission
broadband transmission
bus topology
carrier sense with multiple access and
   collision avoidance (CSMA/CA)
carrier sense with multiple access and
   collision detection (CSMA/CD)
code independence
collision
Copper Distributed Data Interface
   (CDDI)
cycle redundancy check (CRC)
data link protocol
Ethernet
Fiber Distributed Data Interface (FDDI)
IEEE 802.3 standard
IEEE 802.4 standard

IEEE 802.5 standard
IEEE 802.12 standard
Institute of Electrical and Electronics
   Engineers (IEEE)
International Telecommunications Union
   (ITU)
logical link control (LLC)
multistation access unit (MAU or
   MSAU)
octet
passive hub
ring topology
StarLAN
star topology
star-wired LAN
terminator
token passing
token-passing bus
token-passing ring
topology
transparency
wireless LANs

Review Questions

1. Compare baseband and broadband transmission.
2. What are the advantages and disadvantages of broadband transmission? of baseband transmission?
3. What is a topology?
4. What are the primary LAN topologies?

5. What is a media access control protocol?
6. What are the primary LAN media access control protocols?
7. What are the IEEE 802.3, 802.4, 802.5, and 802.12 standards? What does each specify?
8. What is the ANSI fiber distributed data interface (FDDI)?
9. Distinguish between FDDI and CDDI LANs.

Problems and Exercises

1. The Hyperchannel is a high-speed (50-Mbps) LAN used to connect large computing systems. From a data communications text, determine what topology and MAC protocol the Hyperchannel uses. Which of the three technologies—token ring, token bus, or contention bus—is closest to the Hyperchannel architecture?
2. The AlohaNet, an early example of a local area network, was developed by the University of Hawaii. Research the literature to find the details of this network's architecture.
3. What are some of the uses of a MAN such as the Fiber Distributed Data Interface?
4. What are the advantages and disadvantages of LAN standards?
5. Suppose you had a LAN application in which guaranteed access to the medium within a specified time was essential. Which MAC protocol would you choose? Justify your choice.
6. Suppose you wanted to install a LAN in a small office. The LAN will have ten workstations. Which medium would you choose? Justify your choice.

Chapter 5

LAN Hardware

CHAPTER PREVIEW

Physical and data link layer conventions, topology, and network architecture are important aspects of your LAN decisions. Choosing the right hardware and software is also critical. In this chapter we look at the principal hardware components of a LAN. A wide variety of components are available—servers, workstations, adapters, and so on— but the key to success is choosing components that can be integrated to form an effective system.

In this chapter you will read about

servers

backup devices

workstation hardware

LAN adapters

printers

miscellaneous hardware

Some hardware components are tightly coupled with software and should be discussed at the same time. Some hardware components that are closely coupled to enabling software are mentioned in this chapter but the discussion is deferred until Chapter 7, where the two are covered as a single entity. By the end of this chapter you should understand the role each component plays in a LAN and some of the considerations to be made in selecting this equipment.

SERVER PLATFORMS

In an ideal world your decisions regarding medium, topology, and media access would ensure the success of a network. But you can negate even the best decisions in each of those areas by making a poor choice of server hardware. To make an informed decision regarding server hardware, you must understand what the server does. Services provided by a server include file, print, terminal, modem, and facsimile services. File services are the most common and are the focus of our attention here.

File Services

File services are one of the primary jobs of a server. The objective of file services is to allow users access to data, programs, and other files stored on the server's disk drives. From the user's perspective it ought to be transparent that the data or files he or she is using are located on the server's disk drives. Over time several technologies have been used to provide file services, including disk, file, and database servers. File and database services are the most commonly used today, and disk servers are of historical interest only.

Disk Servers

A **disk server** has one or more hard disks that can be used by someone at a workstation. Each user is given a dedicated portion of the disk server's disks. Essentially the disk drive is divided among the user base, as illustrated in Figure 5.1. Suppose you are a user of a disk server, and you need to use word processing, spreadsheet, and database applications. A portion of the disk server's disk is dedicated to your needs, and each application you need is placed in your dedicated area. Thus the *disk* is shared, not the files. If ten users need to use word processing applications, then ten copies of the word processing software must reside on the disk server's disk, one copy per user. Disk servers do not make efficient use of disk space.

File Servers

Disk servers soon gave way to **file servers.** A file server allows users to share files. In the scenario of the preceding paragraph, only one copy of the word processing, spreadsheet, and database software must reside on a file server. Individual users share these applications. When a user enters a command to start an application, that application is downloaded into the user's workstation, as it is with the disk server, but the file server gives each user a copy of the same file (provided software license agreements are adhered to). File server technology is illustrated in Figure 5.2.

   When a user needs data from the file server, that data is transferred to the user's workstation. This is suitable for small files, but consider the impact of such technology when accessing a large database. If a user enters a request that requires looking at thousands of records, each record must be transferred over the LAN to the user's workstation. For example, suppose you want to determine the average grade point average (GPA) for all students in your school. Suppose further that there are 40,000 records in the student file. With file server technology the database application runs on your workstation. It is downloaded to your workstation when you start the application. When you make your request to find the average GPA, each student record is transferred over the network to your workstation, where the GPA data is extracted and computations are made. Transferring all 40,000 database records over the network can place a heavy load on the medium and reduce its performance. In a case like this it is more efficient to have the server do the calculations and pass only the response over the network. A database server operates in this way.

Database Servers

The **database server** was developed to solve the problem of passing an entire file over the medium. The most common example of a database server is the **SQL server.**

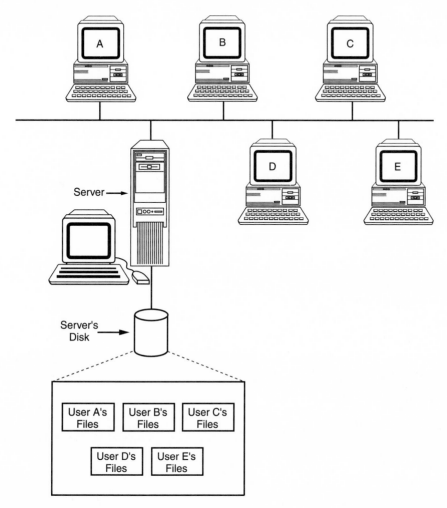

Figure 5.1 Disk Server Technology

Structured query language (SQL) is a standard database definition, access, and update language for relational databases. An SQL server accepts a database request, accesses all necessary records locally, and then sends only the results back to the requester. In the GPA example all 40,000 student records still must be read, but the computation is done by the SQL server. Only one record containing the average GPA is sent back over the network to the requester. This reduces the load on the network medium, but it does place an extra load on the server. In addition to accessing the records, the server also must perform some database processing. This can affect other users who are also requesting SQL services. The SQL server must be powerful enough to provide effective services and avoid becoming a performance bottleneck.

Also, an interface must exist between the application software making the database request and the SQL server. The interface must be capable of translating an application's

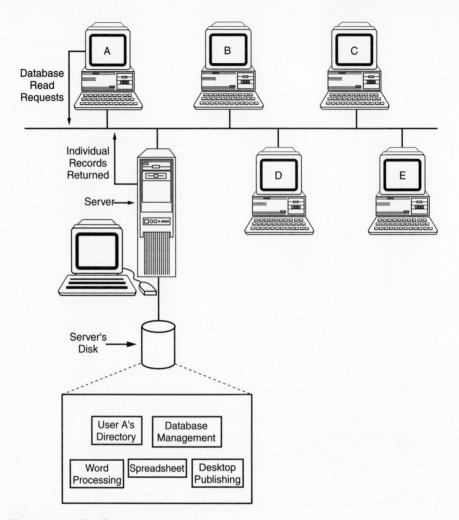

Figure 5.2 File Server Technology

data needs into an SQL statement. Thus an SQL server cannot work unless the application or an application interface exists that can generate the SQL syntax. SQL server technology is illustrated in Figure 5.3.

Server Disk Drives

Disk, file, and database servers all share a common need: to efficiently access data. Thus, when choosing a server, you should carefully select the server's disk subsystem. Two factors are critical when choosing a disk drive: storage capacity and average access time.

Disk drives on servers typically are high-capacity units; that is, they can store large amounts of data and have fast access times. The capacity to store large amounts of data is important because the server must store many data and program files. A file server, for

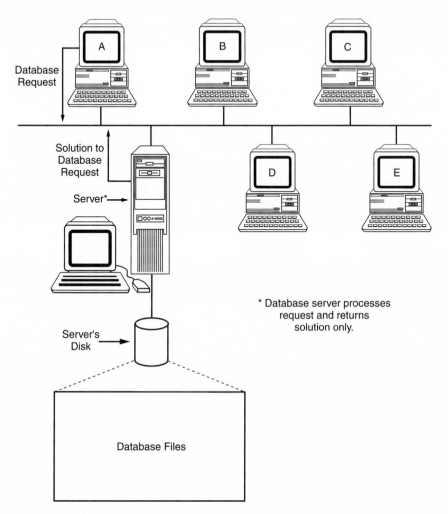

Database
Request

Solution to
Database
Request

Server*

Server's
Disk

* Database server processes
request and returns
solution only.

Database Files

Figure 5.3   SQL Server Technology

example, is essentially each user's hard disk. Individual data storage, together with shared storage needed for application software, databases, several versions of operating system software, utility programs, and electronic mail messages, can easily require hundreds or thousands of megabytes of storage. For example, the space required for one office software suite (word processor, spreadsheet, database management, and presentation) is approximately 65 million bytes (MB). This does not include the disk space required for data and document files. Furthermore, the network operating system (NOS) that resides on the server may require on the order of 75 MB. Thus, a very minimal workable system requires at least 140 MB of disk space.

The need for large amounts of data storage might be satisfied with one high-capacity drive or with several low-capacity ones; both alternatives offer benefits. Having few disk drives provides a configuration that is easier to manage. However, having several smaller drives is beneficial because several disks can be working simultaneously to satisfy user requests. For example, suppose you need 2 gigabytes (GB) of storage. You could select one 2-GB drive or two 1-GB drives. With one drive it is simple to determine file allocation because all files are placed on the drive. With two drives you must place the data carefully to equalize access to each drive; that is, your objective should to be to spread the files over the two drives so that each is equally busy.

Suppose your application calls for 45 disk accesses per second. A single fast disk drive may have difficulty keeping up with this load. However, with two drives and a good distribution of files, you end up with only 22.5 requests per disk per second, usually an easy objective to attain. This configuration is a bit more expensive but provides better performance. Remember, for file or SQL server disk drives, you should select those with sufficient storage capacity and speed to meet your performance objectives. A powerful processor with a slow disk subsystem can cripple your network. We cannot overemphasize this point.

A second factor to consider when choosing a disk drive is the **access time** of the disk itself. The three components of disk access are seek time, latency, and transfer time. The **seek time** is the time required to move the read/write heads to the proper cylinder. Once the heads are positioned, you must wait until the data revolves under the read/write heads; this is called **latency.** The average latency is one-half the time required for the disk to make a complete revolution. **Transfer time** is the time required to move the data from the disk to the computer's memory. Fast disks have average access times of approximately 10 ms. In contrast, many floppy disk drives have access times on the order of 200 ms. As you can see, there is considerable difference between average access times. In general, your file server should have disks with fast average access times.

Finally you also need to consider the **disk drive interface,** or the **controller.** The disk drive interface sets the standards for connecting the disk drive to the system and the software commands used to access the drive. There are a variety of disk drive interfaces. Some are well suited for server operations and some are too slow for most LANs. Moreover, you must choose an interface that is supported by the LAN operating system you choose. The two interfaces most commonly used for microcomputer-based servers are the small computer system interface (SCSI, pronounced "scuzzy") and the integrated drive electronics (IDE). Both interfaces provide high-speed data transfers and large-capacity disk drives. The SCSI interface provides more drives per controller (7–15 depending on the SCSI version used) and more efficiency and is currently the interface of choice. There are several SCSI specifications: the original SCSI, SCSI-2, SCSI-3, fast SCSI, wide SCSI, and fast–wide SCSI. The specification has been enhanced to allow wider data paths (32-bit data paths in wide SCSI, as opposed to 8 or 16 bits in the original SCSI) and higher data transfer rates (up to 40 Mbps with fast–wide SCSI, as opposed to 5 Mbps with 8-bit SCSI). Another efficiency afforded by the SCSI bus is the ability to have several devices on the bus working simultaneously. You can initiate a sequence of disk accesses that cause several disks to operate simultaneously. This parallelism increases the throughput of the system. In contrast, only one disk on an IDE interface can work at one time.

Server Memory

A server is a combination of hardware and software. The software should be designed to take full advantage of the hardware, and in Chapter 6 you will read about some techniques for ensuring this compatibility. Memory is often a good hardware investment, because many software systems can take advantage of available memory to provide better performance. Some LAN software systems do this by using memory as an extension of the disk drives, a technique called **disk caching.** Disk caching is similar in function to cache memory that is used on high-performance processors. **Cache memory** is a high-speed buffer for slower main memory. Main memory can, in turn, serve as a high-speed buffer for slower disk drives. Assuming that you choose a LAN operating system that does this, you need to configure the server with sufficient memory to make caching effective.

The fundamental premise of disk caching is that memory accesses are faster than disk accesses. A disk cache therefore attempts to keep highly accessed data in memory. Caching works as follows: If a user's request is received for data, cache memory is searched before the data is physically read from the disk. If the data is found in cache memory—a process known as a logical read—then the data is made available almost instantly. If the data is not found in cache memory, then it is read from disk, which is called a physical access. As data is read from disk, it is also placed into cache memory so any subsequent read for that data might be a logical read.

Disk caching, taken to the fullest extent, results in all data residing in memory and all reads being logical reads. Of course, this is rarely the case. However, it should be clear that effective use of cache memory can improve performance. Because disk caching requires memory, sufficient memory must be available to provide a large percentage of cache hits. A cache hit occurs when the data being read is found in cache memory. Consider the following example, which illustrates the effects of having too little memory.

Suppose that LAN data requests cycle through four records, A, B, C, and D. Furthermore, you only have enough cache memory for three records. When additional space is needed, the cache-management scheme typically replaces the record that has been dormant the longest with a new record. Suppose that records A, B, and C have been read in that order and are in cache memory, as illustrated in Figure 5.4(a). A request is issued for record D, but it is not in cache memory, so a physical read is required. Record D is read and must be inserted into cache memory. Because record A is the least recently used, record D replaces record A, as illustrated in Figure 5.4(b). Next a request is received for record A. Because it is not in cache memory, a physical read is issued, and record A replaces the least recently used record, record B. Cache memory now looks like Figure 5.4(c). A request is made for record B, which is also not in cache memory. Record B is read and replaces record C. Unfortunately, record C is the next record to be read and again requires a physical read. It is read into cache memory, replacing record D. Then the cycle repeats again. In this simple, contrived example, the cache is one record too small and is totally ineffective. In fact, it is counterproductive, as it incurs extra overhead for searching cache memory for records that are not cache resident.

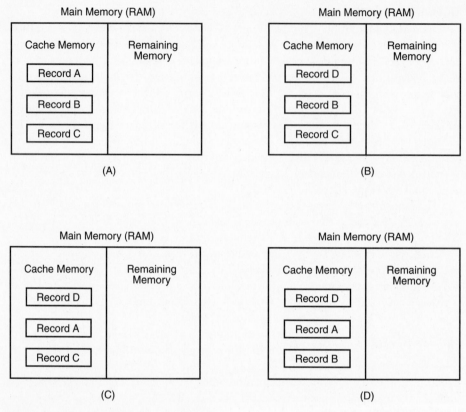

Figure 5.4 Example of Disk Caching

The problem of insufficient cache memory can be corrected by expanding it. In the example shown in Figure 5.4, just one more record slot results in 100 percent cache hits after the four initial reads. Again, this example is contrived, and 100 percent cache-hit rates are rarely attainable. However, you should learn from the example that there is a critical threshold for cache memory. If the available memory is under this threshold, cache can be ineffective. When the available cache memory is over this threshold, cache can be very effective. Some users have experienced cache hits on the order of 80 to 90 percent. The hit rate depends on the access patterns, so do not expect this figure to hold true for all systems.

An ample amount of memory is important for reasons other than disk caching. You should also have sufficient memory available to avoid **disk swapping.** Most of today's memory management schemes are based on **virtual memory** management, which uses the disk as an extension of memory so each program has virtually all the memory it needs. Virtual memory management allows the real memory of a system to be less than the aggregate memory required by all the applications. To do this, application code and data are swapped back and forth between the disk and memory.

If the available memory is too small, the swap rate goes up. When the swap rate increases, the operating system is spending extra time managing memory, and less time is available for doing application work. Thus the amount of application work done per unit of time decreases as the swap rate increases.

Processors and Processor Speed

The processing power of the server is also a critical factor. It seldom makes sense to select a server that has fast disks and plenty of memory but a slow CPU. In general, the server ought to be one of the fastest, if not the fastest computer on the network. There are a few exceptions to this generalization, such as a server providing small amounts of data to graphics workstations. Most graphics applications require high-speed processors to create and print graphic images. In these networks the workstation computing power may equal or exceed that of the server. For additional processing power in one server, multiple-CPU systems area available. Multiple-CPU systems can be **symmetrical multiprocessing (SMP)** or asymmetrical multiprocessing systems. A SMP system generally has CPUs that are alike and that share memory, processing responsibility, and I/O paths. In asymmetrical systems the processors may be of different types and one processor may be dedicated to I/O operations while another is dedicated to application processing. SMP systems allow for load balancing, whereas asymmetric systems do not. Thus, in an asymmetrical multiprocessing system, one processor can be extremely busy while another has little to do. Most multiprocessor servers are SMP servers. The presence of multiple processors is not sufficient for multiprocessing. The server's operating system (OS) must support the SMP configuration because it is the OS that schedules the use of the processors.

Processor Bus

A variety of buses are available. The bus is the path over which data is transferred between the CPU, memory, and peripherals. The original IBM Industry Standard Architecture (ISA) was an 8-bit bus, meaning that 8 bits of data were transferred in parallel over the bus. Today we have 32- and 64-bit buses and these are preferred for servers. Being able to transfer more bits over the bus at one time makes the system more efficient. For servers based on the IBM architecture, the best bus options are the Enhanced Industry Standard Architecture (EISA) bus or the Peripheral Component Interconnect (PCI) bus. Of the two, the PCI bus is preferable because it allows for multiple processors and processor independence. The principal IBM-compatible system buses are shown in Table 5.1.

Table 5.1   IBM-Compatible System Buses

Industry Standard Architecture (ISA)	Video Electronics Standards Association (VESA)
Enhanced Industry Standard Architecture (EISA)	Peripheral Component Interconnect (PCI)
Micro Channel Architecture (MCA)	PC-Card (formerly PCMCIA)
VESA Local (VL-Bus)	

Expansion and Power

A server should have sufficient expansion capability and the power to effectively use the expansion slots. Network server capacity can be expanded by adding hardware to the existing server or by adding additional servers. Expanding the capabilities of an existing server is less expensive than adding a new server, so the server you choose should be able to support expansion. For example, you may eventually want to add more memory, disks, printers, or other hardware devices that users can share, such as modems, facsimile machines, tape drives, and compact disc drives.

Compatibility

The server platform you choose must be compatible with the topology, MAC protocol, applications, and system software on the network. These components form an integrated package. Each component you choose may be optimal, and yet you may still have a poor LAN system if the individual components do not fit together well.

BACKUP DEVICES

No LAN is complete without a backup device. One of the LAN administrator's most important duties is to make periodic file backups. A **backup** is a copy of files at a specific time that is used to restore the system to a workable state following a system failure or an event that damages the data, or to restore data that is needed only on a periodic basis. For example, research data that is needed only once or twice a month and year-end payroll data that is needed temporarily to file worker's tax notices can be backed up and then replaced on disk on an as-needed basis.

The principal backup device is a magnetic tape drive, a variety of which are available. Removable disk drives and optical disk drives are alternatives. The primary backup technologies are listed in Table 5.2.

Table 5.2   Primary Backup Technologies

Diskette backup	1.44 MB	2.88 MB	20 MB
Hard drive, fixed	Multiple capacities		
Hard drive, removable cartridge	40 MB to over 1 GB		
Tape backup, 4 mm or 1/4 inch	To 15 GB	60 MB	150 MB
	160 MB	500 MB	1.2 GB
	2.2 GB	15 GB	30 GB (compressed)
Tape backup, 8 mm or VCR	To 2.2 GB		
Tape backup, 9-track	To 100 MB		
Optical drives, WORM	To 4 GB		
Optical drives, rewritable	To 4 GB		
Digital Versatile Disks (when available)	10–14 GB		

Floppy Diskette Drives

You may use floppy diskettes as the backup medium. The diskette drives may be server or workstation drives. The major disadvantage of this backup method is the low capacity and speed of the backup media. Typical diskette capacities of IBM-compatible systems are 1.44 MB and 2.88 MB. Diskettes with capacities of up to 20 MB are also available. Often the capacity of server drives is 1 GB or more. A large LAN may have tens of billions of bytes of disk storage. Backing up this amount of data to 1-MB (or even 20-MB) diskettes is cumbersome. The advantages of diskette backup are high availability on workstations and servers and low cost. Diskette backup for LANs with small disk requirements or for backing up a few small files can be practical, but for large-disk systems, the number of diskettes needed to store all the data is high. This process is slow and subject to errors, and requires handling many diskettes.

Hard Disk Drives

A hard disk drive on either a server or a workstation may also be used for backup. The arguments for and against this alternative are much the same as those for diskettes. The major difference is that the capacity of hard disk drives is greater than that of diskettes. If the hard disk is not removable, it is difficult to keep multiple generations of backups, a procedure that is important for a comprehensive backup plan. For example, you should have at least three generations of backups, which means that if you take a backup weekly, three weeks' worth of backups are always available. Some hard drives have removable disk cartridges, which are an excellent backup alternative because they provide high capacity (up to 1 GB per cartridge) and rapid access.

Optical Disk Drives

Optical disk drives are gaining popularity as backup devices. The reasons for this are their decreasing costs and large storage capacity, and the recently introduced ability to erase and write to optical disks. There are two classes of optical disk drives: WORM (write once, read many) and erasable drives. As the name implies, WORM technology allows you to write to the medium only once. You cannot erase a WORM disk. This can make the cost of backups expensive because the cost of cartridges for many such drives on microcomputers is over $100. An advantage of WORM technology is that the data cannot be changed, so the backup cannot be accidentally destroyed. Erasable optical drives have generally replaced WORM drives as the preferred optical technology. The cost of erasable drives and CD media now start at under $1000 and $10, respectively, with 650 MB of storage per CD. An emerging CD standard, the digital versatile disk (DVD), promises to provide up to 14 GB of storage per CD.

Magnetic Tape Drives

As mentioned earlier, a magnetic tape drive is the usual choice for a backup device. Magnetic tapes are less expensive than the other options. They hold large volumes of data, are easy to use and store, and generally provide good performance. A variety of tape backup devices are available. The drives themselves are less expensive than disk or optical drives with comparable storage characteristics, and you can choose from a wide

Table 5.3   Magnetic Tape Backup Functions

Back up all files	Create new index on tape and disk
Back up all files modified since a particular date	Maintain cross-reference of tape serial numbers and backup
Back up by directory	Back up manually
Back up by list of files	Back up automatically by time or calendar
Back up all but a list of files to be excluded	Start backup from workstation or server
Back up by index	Compress data
Back up by interface to a database	Back up multiple volumes
Back up using wildcard characters in file names	Generate reports

range of data capacities. Tape drives vary in the size of the tape and recording method. If more than one tape drive is to be used in one organization, it is best to establish a standard tape configuration so the tapes can be exchanged among the different drives. The main magnetic tape backup options are summarized in Table 5.3.

Like other hardware discussed in this chapter, the tape drive must be compatible with the server or workstation on which it is installed. A drive usually has a controller that must be installed in the computer, so you must select a drive that has a controller compatible with your equipment. A SCSI interface is currently preferred. You also need backup software and procedures to make your backups. Backup software is covered in Chapter 7 and backup procedures are discussed in Chapter 13.

WORKSTATIONS

Some LANs are homogeneous; that is, all the workstations are of the same basic type, all are running the same level of the same operating system, and all use essentially the same applications. It is easier to configure this type of network than a heterogenous one, but homogeneous networks are less common. Often a network is assembled from workstations acquired over time. These workstations usually represent different levels of technology and perhaps use different versions of operating systems. For example, consider a network with the following workstations:

IBM or compatible with an industry standard architecture (ISA) bus

IBM or compatible with an extended industry standard architecture (EISA) bus

IBM or compatible with a microchannel architecture (MCA) bus

Apple Macintosh or compatible

Sun workstation

When you are selecting components for a heterogenous network, your hardware and software options are more limited than those for a homogeneous network. For example, you may be more limited in your choice of network operating systems (see Chapter 7) or LAN adapters. The limitations arise from the inability of some LAN software to support different workstations or from the unavailability of required hardware, such as a

LAN adapter. You will find many options for LANs with only IBM-compatible workstations and several for LANs with only Apple workstations, but few options can support both types of microcomputers.

Diskless Workstations

When configuring your LAN, you may want to consider **diskless workstations.** As the name implies, a diskless workstation does not have any local disk drives. Instead, a diskless workstation has its boot logic in a read-only memory (ROM) chip located on the LAN adapter. This chip contains the logic to connect to the network and download the operating system from the server. Thus a diskless workstation cannot be used in a stand-alone mode; it is fully dependent on the server for all of its software, and it cannot function if the network or server is not operating. This is the disadvantage of a diskless system. Its advantages are cost, security, and control.

Because diskless workstations have no disk drives, they are inherently less expensive than those with disks. Moreover, the maintenance costs for diskless systems are less than for systems with disk drives. Diskless systems provide extra security because users are unable to copy the organization's data onto local hard or floppy disk drives. This is important because an organization's primary security risk is its employees. Diskless systems also provide a greater measure of control because employees cannot introduce their own software into the system. This not only ensures that standard software and data are used but also reduces the chances of computer viruses being introduced into the network.

Workstation Memory and Speed

Like servers, workstation memory configurations are important. If you have stand-alone microcomputer systems, each with the minimum application memory configuration, you may need to add more memory to those systems to run the same applications on a network, because LAN software must also run in the workstations. Moreover, LAN software stays memory resident. Suppose you have a microcomputer with 1 MB of memory and that this is just enough to load the operating system and your database management system. Placing that same microcomputer on a network requires that some of the memory be allocated to the LAN interface; thus, you may be unable to run your database management system because of insufficient memory. The solution, of course, is to expand the computer's memory. The amount of memory required for LAN software varies from one LAN to another. Some require less than 20 KB, and some require over 70 KB of resident memory.

The speed of the workstation's processor must be compatible with the type of work for which it is being used. If you use the workstation for word processing, a low-speed processor probably is satisfactory. However, a workstation used for graphics work requires a high-speed processor. Basically it is the application, not the LAN, that determines the power of the workstations.

LAN ADAPTERS

If you have chosen an architecture, medium, and media access control protocol, you have narrowed the options for **LAN adapters,** also known as a **network interface card (NIC).** LAN adapters provide the connection between the medium and the bus of the workstation or server. LAN adapters are designed to support a specific protocol using a specific medium, although a few can support two or three different medium types. For example, there is one type of Ethernet card for twisted-pair wires, another Ethernet card for coaxial cable, and a combination adapter that supports both types of connectors. After the medium and protocol are matched, there are additional alternatives regarding vendor and architecture.

The choice of a LAN adapter vendor determines the support, quality, and price of the LAN adapter. Just as you should be careful when selecting a LAN vendor, you should also be careful regarding the vendor of individual components, such as a LAN adapter. The LAN adapter that is initially the least expensive may prove to be more costly in the long term if it is of inferior quality, it does not have a good vendor-support policy, or replacement LAN adapters are difficult to obtain if the vendor goes out of business.

LAN adapters are installed in each workstation and server. Naturally the LAN adapter must be compatible with the hardware architecture of the computer into which it is installed. Moreover, you need to ensure that a LAN adapter is available for each type of network node you anticipate having. Certain combinations of equipment may not be supported. For example, you may have difficulty finding ARCnet cards for each node in a network consisting of a Digital Equipment Corporation VAX server and Apple Macintosh, Sun, and IBM workstations. You also need to ensure that LAN adapters are compatible with the bus of the host computer. Thus, for IBM microcomputer-based LANs, you may need ISA-, EISA-, MCA- or PCI-compatible cards.

LAN adapters also have an architecture. For example, LAN adapters for IBM or compatible systems often come in 16-bit, 32-bit, and 64-bit architectures and are designed for one or more bus architectures. In general, as number of bits in the architecture increases, so does the speed at which the adapter operates and so does the cost of the adapter. By saying that the speed of an adapter increases, we mean that a 32-bit card can transfer data between the computer and the medium faster than a 16-bit card, and so on; it does not affect the speed at which data is transferred over the network medium. A 32-bit card is faster than a 16-bit card because it transfers data 32 bits at a time, whereas the 16-bit card transfers data in 16-bit groups.

PRINTERS

One major factor that affects the success of a LAN is printer support. Some LANs have restrictions regarding the distribution of printers and the number of printers that can be supported by one server. For example, suppose that network printers must be attached to a server, and each server can support a maximum of five printers. An organization that needs 20 printers, therefore, must have at least four servers. This early LAN restriction is uncommon today, but each LAN operating system has restrictions regarding the number of printers that each server can support and the distribution of those printers within the network.

You must be concerned not only with the number of printers but also with the type of printers supported and the way in which they are supported. A **printer driver** is a software module that determines how to format data for proper printing on a specific type of printer. The printers you intend to use must be supported by the software drivers provided by the LAN operating system or printer vendor. For example, you may find that a laser printer you attach to the LAN can operate in text mode but is restricted in its graphic mode operation or in its ability to download soft fonts. Again, you need to consider interoperability of hardware and software components to ensure that your needs are met. Some LAN systems provide a utility program that allows you to tailor a generic printer driver to meet the needs of a specific printer you want to use. This utility allows you to define printer functions and the command sequences essential to invoking those functions. Because new printer technologies are constantly appearing, this utility is quite useful. Printing is discussed further in Chapter 12.

HUBS AND SWITCHES

Some LAN architectures use **wiring hubs** to provide device interconnection. A token-ring LAN may use a multistation access unit to provide the connection between a node and the ring. Ethernet LANs using twisted-pair wires use wiring hubs for the same purpose. ARCnet LANs use both active and passive hubs for connectivity. Naturally, hubs designed for one architecture, such as Ethernet, will not work in another architecture. Therefore, the first choice you need to make in selecting a wiring hub is to ensure that it is of the proper architecture. Beyond that, you have a variety of options.

Hubs vary in the number of ports available. A very common configuration is 8 ports, with 12- and 16-port hubs as common alternatives. Hubs may be stand-alone or stackable. When used in a stand-alone manner, the hub is usually enclosed in a chassis and has two or more ports that allow wire-based connections to other hubs. Stackable hubs are modular hubs that can be stacked on top of each other or mounted in a wiring rack. Stackable hubs share a backplane, so multiple hubs can be attached and treated as a single hub. Furthermore, the common backplane provides a high-speed interconnection between the hubs. By concentrating the hub connections into a stackable unit, the network administrator creates one central location for resolving wiring problems. Some hubs have reliability and maintenance features that help minimize the possibility of failure and streamline the repair process. A reliability feature is dual power supplies with shared power. During normal operation the hub draws power from both power supplies; if one of the power supplies fails, the remaining one is capable of providing power for the entire hub. A maintenance feature is hot-swappable components; *hot-swappable* means that the hub can be repaired while it is functioning, thus minimizing or eliminating downtime. For example, the power supply that failed in the reliability scenario could be replaced while the hub is operating and reliability could be restored without interrupting network operations.

As a key component of the LAN, it is important to have the ability to manage wiring hubs. Some hubs collect data about network traffic and make this data available through one of several available network management standards. The principal network management standards are the Simple Network Management Protocol (SNMP) and the Common Management Information Protocol (CMIP). SNMP is part of the Transmission Control Protocol/Internet Protocol (TCP/IP) protocol suite and CMIP is an ISO standard. More information on these two network management protocols is provided in Chapter 14.

LAN **switches** physically resemble wiring hubs but their function is quite different. For specifics, let us consider an Ethernet hub. When a node transmits a packet, the hub sends the packet out on all other ports so each node receives the packet. In contrast, a switch examines the packet and finds the address of the recipient. A connection between the sender and recipient is established and the packet sent directly between the two nodes. While that connection is being used, two other nodes can also be communicating over a different connection. Switches therefore have the ability to increase the aggregate data rate on the network. Switches also have additional LAN interconnection capabilities, and we look at those capabilities and specific types of switches in Chapter 16.

MAKING CONNECTIONS

Thus far we have discussed the medium, the network nodes, and the LAN adapter. All that remains is to connect the nodes to the medium. Connections can be made in a variety of ways. You have already learned that you must pick a LAN adapter that is compatible with the medium you choose. Therefore, it is the medium that primarily influences the way in which physical connections are made. Let us look at the problem from a generic perspective.

The objective of network connection—that is, connecting a computer to the LAN medium—is to provide a data path between the medium and the computer's memory. To accomplish this there must be a connection to the medium and a connection to the computer's bus or channel. The interface or connection to the medium is called the **communications interface unit (CIU),** and the interface or connection to the computer's bus is called the **bus interface unit (BIU).** These functions are illustrated in Figure 5.5 and for most microcomputer LANs are provided by the LAN adapter.

A key component of the network connection is a **transceiver,** which establishes the connection to the medium and implements the transmit and receive portions of the protocol. In a few Ethernet LANs, the transceiver is connected directly to the medium. In most of today's Ethernet implementations, the transceiver is located on the LAN adapter, as illustrated in Figure 5.6.

The physical connection between the computer and the medium is established through **connectors.** There are many different types of connectors that are used, but the principal ones are

BNC, TNC, or N-Type connectors for coaxial cable

RJ-11, RJ-45, or DB-nn (DB-25 or DB-15) connectors for wires

SMA connectors for fiber optic cable

The type of connector you need is determined by your LAN adapter and cable type. A wide variety of connector adapters allow you to change connector types. For example, one adapter can change a BNC connector to a TNC connector. **Baluns** are adapters that change coaxial cable connectors to twisted-pair wire connectors. These

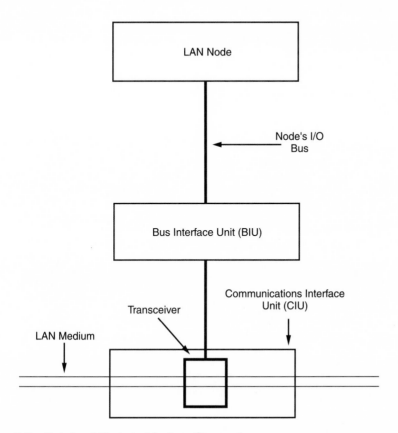

Figure 5.5 Details of Node-to-Medium Connection

adapters allow you to transfer from one medium to another or from a connector for one medium to a different medium.

In some networks, connecting a computer to the medium is sufficient for making that computer active on the network. Some LAN implementations use wiring hubs to provide node-to-node connection. Several kinds of connection hubs are commonly used. For example, in an IBM token ring, individual stations are connected to a wiring hub called a multistation access unit (MAU). Externally this wiring scheme looks like a star-wired architecture. The ring is established via internal connections within the MAU, as illustrated in Figure 5.7.

An ARCnet LAN may use active and passive hubs for node connections, as illustrated in Figure 5.8. An active hub provides signal regeneration and allows nodes to be located at distances of up to 2000 feet from the hub. A passive hub does not provide signal regeneration, so nodes can be located no more than 100 feet from the hub. Ethernets that use twisted-pair wires also use a wiring hub or concentrator similar to a MAU.

A variety of other hardware components are sometimes needed to make the network function. For example, on bus networks or networks using wiring hubs, terminators are often needed to prevent signal loss. A terminator is used at the ends of a bus

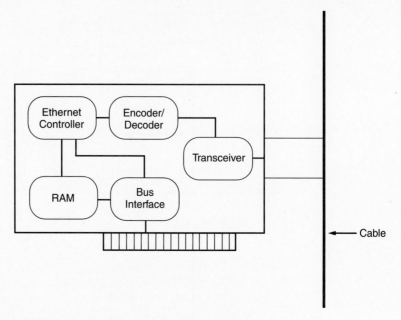

Figure 5.6   Transceiver Located on a LAN Adapter

to prevent echo, and terminators are required on unused passive hub ports in an ARCnet network for the same reason. The locations of terminators in a LAN configuration are shown in Figure 5.9.

Sometimes LAN connections go further than simply connecting a node to the medium. You may also need to connect one LAN to another or connect a LAN to a WAN. We discuss this subject in detail in Chapter 16.

UNINTERRUPTIBLE POWER SUPPLY

One of the features we mentioned for wiring hubs was power supply reliability. This is a reliability function only if power is available. There are many ways to improve the reliability of a network, particularly network servers. However, if there is a power outage, those reliability capabilities may not work. Fortunately, there is a reliability option that covers this problem. An **uninterruptible power supply (UPS)** is a hardware device that provides power to devices in the event of a power outage. Every server and related components should be protected by a UPS because the cost of a UPS is small relative to the cost of servers crashing because of power loss. An unexpected server crash can result in a time-consuming recovery. Recall the discussion of disk cache. A server keeps a considerable amount of data (such as end-of-file locations for open files, changes to user accounts, and the last updates to files) memory resident. A server crash can cause this data to be lost. Furthermore, the crash may occur in the midst of a related set of file operations and result in inconsistent file data. For example, a related set of updates for index

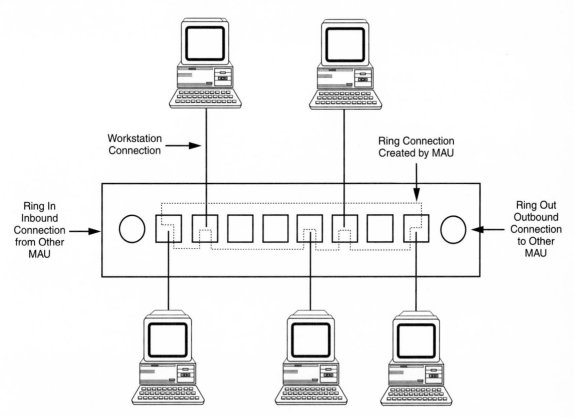

Figure 5.7 Implementation of a Ring Using a MAU

tables for a database access method may be in progress at the time of failure. If an entry is made in one index table and the corresponding update in another index is nullified by a server failure, data pointed at by the index tables may be unable to be located.

A UPS uses batteries as a source of power when a power outage occurs. During normal operation, power is available from the main power supply. This power is passed through the UPS and maintains the charge on the batteries. If the main power source fails, the UPS battery power takes over and continues to supply power to the connected devices. The duration of UPS power varies depending on the power load drawn by the equipment and the capacity of the UPS itself. The power load drawn relies on the total ratings of the equipment being sustained by the UPS, so different configurations consume different amounts of power. UPSs come in different sizes, and the size is usually measured in volt-amps (VA), but wattage is sometimes used to describe the power rating. The higher the VA rating is, the more power available. Generally, LAN administrators configure the power of the UPS to sustain the equipment it powers for approximately one hour. UPS sizes run the gamut from the ability to provide power for a small microcomputer for a few minutes to supplying power for large mainframe systems for several hours. Other capabilities of a UPS include

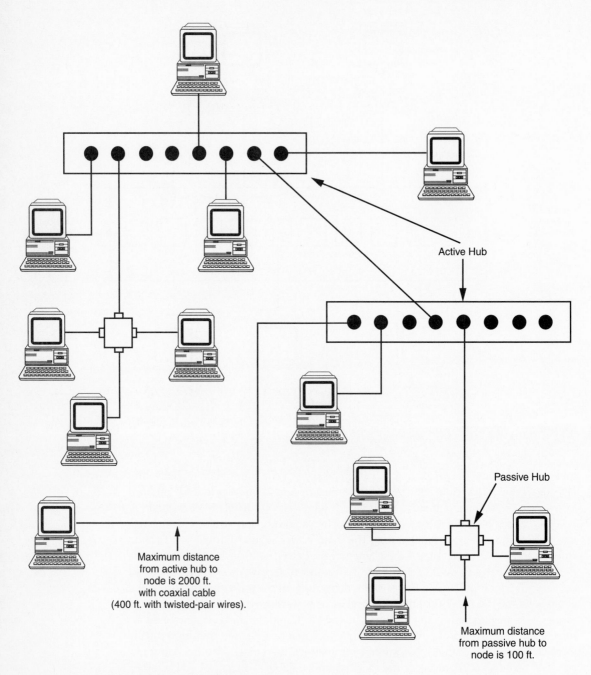

Active Hub

Passive Hub

Maximum distance
from active hub to
node is 2000 ft.
with coaxial cable
(400 ft. with twisted-pair wires).

Maximum distance
from passive hub to
node is 100 ft.

Figure 5.8   ARCnet with Active and Passive Hubs

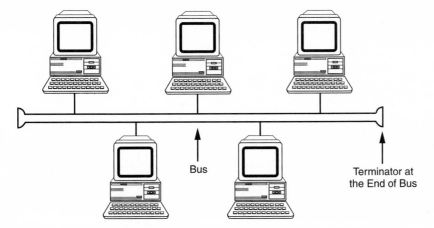

Figure 5.9   Terminators on a Bus Network

- surge protection
- power smoothing
- battery level indicators
- brown-out protection

Some UPS systems are combined with software to provide management capabilities. The UPS typically communicates with the computer via a serial connection. Software in the computer can interrogate statistics maintained by the UPS and report on those statistics. Information that might be reported includes high and low power levels supplied by the main power source, battery condition, power consumption over time, and temperature. Software features also include some management capabilities such as automatically shutting the system down and starting the system at a certain times and initiating alarms for out-of-tolerance situations such as low battery or overload situations.

OTHER HARDWARE

Some of the other hardware components you may find in a LAN are

Terminal servers, which allow terminals to access the network; however, a terminal attached to a LAN will not have the same functionality as a microcomputer attached to a LAN.

Modem servers, which allow users to share one or more modems. A modem is used to transmit digital data over analog communications lines (such as telephone lines).

Facsimile (FAX) machines, which may be attached to a server and shared by network users.

These services are important but are less common than either file or print services, so we shall not devote more coverage to them at this time. You may read more about these servers in Chapter 14.

SUMMARY

LAN hardware consists mainly of server platforms, workstations, LAN adapters, a medium, printers, backup devices, a UPS, and connectors. The hardware combines with software to provide the LAN services. LAN adapters are protocol and medium oriented. Thus one LAN adapter supports CSMA/CD on twisted-pair wires, another supports CSMA/CD on coaxial cable, and a different LAN adapter is necessary for token passing using fiber optic cable. Servers must be properly configured to provide the performance and backup services required by an efficient LAN. The key to meeting this requirement is having sufficient memory, a powerful processor, high-performance disk drives, and a file backup unit. Naturally, the software must also be available to exploit the hardware configuration.

A UPS is an important adjunct to server software. The UPS can preserve the state of a server in the event of power loss or brown-outs. Because the server's state is preserved, time-consuming recovery processes can be avoided. You can choose from many combinations of hardware and software when you are building a LAN. The key to success is combining the alternatives so that the hardware and the software form an effective team.

Key Terms

access time	hot-swappable
backup	LAN adapter
baluns	latency
bus interface unit (BIU)	network interface card (NIC)
cache memory	printer driver
communications interface unit (CIU)	seek time
connectors	SQL server
controller	structured query language (SQL)
database server	switches
disk caching	symmetrical multiprocessing (SMP)
disk drive interface	transceiver
diskless workstation	transfer time
disk server	uninterruptible power supply (UPS)
disk swapping	virtual memory
file server	wiring hub

Review Questions

1. What are the generic functions of a server?
2. Distinguish between file and SQL server technology.
3. What must you take into consideration when you select a server disk drive?
4. How do servers use memory to improve performance?
5. Explain how disk caching works. What is its benefit?

6. Why should servers have high processor speeds?
7. How do diskless systems work? What advantages do they have over disk systems? What are the disadvantages of a diskless system?
8. What is data backup? What devices are used to perform backup?
9. Why is a diskette usually ineffective as a backup device?
10. What options must be considered in selecting a LAN adapter?
11. What does an uninterruptible power supply (UPS) do?

Problems and Exercises

1. Suppose you need to establish a small network having one server and 15 workstations. Draw up a configuration for the server and the workstations. Make all workstation configurations the same. Choose a network topology and medium access control protocol. Consult one or more recent magazines to help you determine the hardware costs for your LAN. Include the server, workstations, LAN adapters, a backup tape device, three laser printers, and three dot-matrix printers in your cost estimates. Configure the server with at least 2 GB of disk storage and 32 MB of memory.
2. Suppose you have a file server with 600 MB of data. If you use 1.4-MB diskettes to back up this data, how many diskettes are necessary? Suppose your backup utility provides data compression and you get 2:1 compression for your files. A 2:1 compression ratio means that on the average, 2 bytes can be compressed into 1 byte. How many diskettes are required?
3. Examine the literature and give an example of how each of the following are used:
   a. a terminal server
   b. a modem server
   c. a FAX server
   d. an uninterruptible power supply
4. Suppose a company has an IBM or IBM-compatible microcomputer with an 486/33 processor, 4 MB of memory, and an 80-MB disk drive. The company wants to know if this computer will work as a file server for a 25-node network. The primary applications are word processing, spreadsheets, and desktop publishing. What would your response be to this inquiry? Justify your response.
5. Assuming that you decided the microcomputer in Problem 4 could handle the job if it is upgraded, what upgrades would you recommend?
6. Suppose a disk drive rotates at 7200 rpm. What is the average latency of this drive? Now, suppose that the average seek time is 1/50 ms per cylinder. If the read/write heads are positioned at cylinder 40 and a read request for data in cylinder 740 is received, what is the access time (seek plus latency) for this request?
7. Given the disk specifications in Problem 6, what will be the average access time for the disk if the average number of cylinders per seek is 400?

PART 3

Software

The success of a LAN in establishing communications capability depends on the interoperation of hardware with application software, workstation system software, and server system software. In Chapter 6 we begin our discussion of software with an overview of the software environment and software protection. Chapter 7 covers the generic functions of LAN operating system software and an overview of specific implementations of network operating systems is given in Chapter 8. In Chapter 9 you will read about LAN-oriented application software.

Chapter 6
Software Introduction

Chapter 7
LAN System Software

Chapter 8
LAN Operating System Implementation

Chapter 9
Application Software

Chapter 6

Software Introduction

CHAPTER PREVIEW

In Part 2 you read primarily about LAN hardware. In this section we begin the discussion of software. It is the conjunction of hardware, software, people, procedures, and data that makes up the LAN system. The software enables access to the hardware and manipulates data to produce information. We start the discussion of LAN software by looking at generic software functions and requirements.

By the end of this chapter you should understand

the distinction between the different classes of software

the generic requirements of workstation software

the generic requirements of server software

software requirements for shared access

how software can be protected on a LAN

some of the standards covering LAN software

the need for and general provisions of software license agreements

Let us begin by looking at the different classes of software that make up a system.

CLASSES OF SOFTWARE

The reason for having a computing system is to solve problems and accomplish work. The software that does this is called application software. Ordinarily application software operates in an environment that makes writing and using the application software easier. This environment-creating software can be separated into the following functional classes: **operating system (OS),** database management, utilities, network management, development, and network access. We start the discussion with application software.

Application Software

As we mentioned at the beginning of this section, the main reason we use computing systems is to solve business or scientific problems. Thus, the computer and its extension, the network, are simply problem-solving tools. Throughout history, humankind has constantly built new tools and improved on those already invented. At the beginning of the computing era, computers were quite primitive tools (at least by today's standards). Programmers at the dawn of the computing age needed to know not only the nuances of the problem they were solving but also many of the intricacies of the hardware their solution would be running on. In today's application environment, we have a supporting cast of software that helps to create an application environment that is mostly hardware independent.

Operating System Software

Today we are so used to using OSs to create the system environment that we take them for granted. However, we were into the second generation of computers before OSs appeared and into the third generation of computers before OSs became common. You may correctly infer from this that OSs are not absolutely necessary, and in the early years of personal computing, a variety of applications ran without using the services of an OS. The IBM Personal Computer (PC) came equipped with a BASIC interpreter in read-only memory. Thus, if you did not have the disk operating system (DOS) you could still use your computer by writing and running BASIC programs. Without DOS, BASIC was the operating environment. Furthermore, a few early programs functioned in a stand-alone mode. These programs were on a diskette and were loaded when the computer was booted. In this mode, if you wanted to run another program, you swapped disks and rebooted.

Without an OS, the application program is responsible for accomplishing many hardware-oriented functions such as input/output (I/O) and memory management. Because these tasks are common to all applications, software engineers developed OS software. The OS manages the resources of the computer and creates an application environment in which it is easier to develop and use application software because the OS takes care of a variety of functions formerly done by applications. Some of these functions are

memory management

file management

user interface

I/O interfaces

resource allocation

accounting

protection

Today, systems running on a LAN are more sophisticated than the early systems that ran without an OS; a LAN node without an OS is unthinkable.

Memory Management

When the computer is started, the OS is loaded into memory. A certain portion of the available memory is constantly occupied by the resident portion of the OS. The OS manages the remaining memory and allocates it among itself and the requesting processes according to a memory management scheme adopted by the OS designers. Most current OSs use a memory management algorithm called virtual memory. With **virtual memory,** the disk is used as an extension of real memory. A process may be thought of as consisting of pages of data and code. When there are fewer demands for real memory than there is available memory space, each request for memory can be satisfied. When the demand for real memory exceeds the supply, the virtual memory algorithm makes real memory available by **swapping** a portion of a program in real memory onto the disk. The portion of memory that was swapped to disk is now available to be used by the process making the memory request. Later, if the swapped portion of the program is needed, it can be read into memory from the disk image. The advantage of virtual memory management is that demands for real memory space can almost always be realized (there must be sufficient room on disk for swapping). The disadvantage is that if the demand for memory constantly exceeds the supply, excessive swapping may occur and the performance of the system degrades severely.

There are other memory management algorithms, but the point is that the management of this resource is the responsibility of the OS.

File Management

A disk is a raw storage device. It has the ability to store bits of data but inherently does not have the ability to organize those bits into files, files into directories, and so on. The OS provides this level of disk organization. It establishes the disk structure that allows users to create partitions, directories, volumes, and other disk subdivisions. Some file management systems allow multiple disks to be combined into one logical disk. The file management system allows users to create, delete, and access files. The file management system maintains the directory structure and stores directory and file information such as the date and time last modified, end-of-file pointer, and the file or directories' location on disk. Obviously, these are fundamental aspects of using a system.

User Interface

When a programmer begins to write a program, an environment is created for that user. When another user uses a workstation to access a database or create a document, an environment exists to enable her to carry out the desired activity. Creating these environments or user interfaces is an OS function. If you have ever used a computer you have worked with such an interface. If you are a DOS user, you use a command line interface, in which you enter commands that are interpreted and acted on by the OS. If you are using a graphical user interface (GUI) such as Microsoft Windows, your OS interface consists of selecting icons and options with a mouse or other pointing device. If you are a programmer you may need to use a text editor, compiler, link editor, and **application program interface (API),** which allows you to use OS procedures to carry out activities such as creating a new file, opening a file, or starting a new process. Sometimes a compiler or interpreter includes the API interfaces.

I/O Interfaces

When you access a disk file, you create a flurry of activity. Your request includes an address, which is probably the identifier of a specific record in a file or a certain portion of a document. But the disk drive has no sense of record identifiers or document pages. The disk knows about addresses in terms of cylinders, read/write heads, and sectors. Between your request of "give me record 15,829 in the Product File" and the physical work to accomplish this, the OS gets involved. The OS and file management system and perhaps the database management system translate the request into an address the disk can act on. Your request may be put into a queue of other requests for access to that disk drive. When it comes time for your request to be acted on by the disk, low-level OS commands cause the read/write heads to move to the proper cylinder (a **seek**), the proper head is selected for reading, the read must wait until the proper sector rotates under the read/write head selected (**latency**), the data is physically read from the disk, and the data is transferred into memory. Once the requested data is in memory, the OS must deliver it to the requesting program. It does this by alerting the program that the I/O is complete (usually via a signal called an interrupt) and then places the program in a state that allows it to continue processing. The OS provides similar, appropriate interfaces to other I/O devices such as tape drives, printers, and the LAN medium.

Resource Allocation

A computing system has resources other than memory and disks that must be managed. A prime example of a managed resource is the CPU itself. Most OSs allow multiple tasks to run concurrently; however, if there is only one CPU, only one of the tasks can actively execute instructions at a given instant. The process that is using the CPU and executing instructions is in a state called running. A process that is not actively executing instructions may be in one of several states: ready, waiting, or suspended. A ready process is waiting for the CPU to become available; the ready process has all the resources it needs to run except for the CPU. Process in the wait state are not ready to run because a resource it needs (other than the CPU) is not available; for example, a process in the wait state may be waiting for an I/O to complete. A process in the suspended state has been stopped by the OS because a fault has been detected or it may be stopped temporarily by a computer operator.

The OS has an algorithm that determines which ready process gets access to the CPU and the conditions under which a running process maintains control of the CPU. A variety of algorithms exist, including first-come-first-served, time-sharing, and job priority. In managing access to the CPU, the OS may be preemptive or nonpreemptive. With preemption, the OS transitions a running job to the ready state and gives another ready job the opportunity to run. A prime example of this is time sharing, where each process is allowed to run for a short time and then is preempted to allow the next process in the ready queue a time slot. With nonpreemption, the OS will not remove a running job. The job must remove itself by voluntarily giving up the CPU or by entering a wait state. A job might enter a wait state while awaiting the completion of an I/O operation.

Generally, for a LAN OS some sort of preemption is important because it prevents situations where one or two processes consume most of the CPU time and another process with important work to do is unable to get its work done. Important characteristics for a network OS are multiprocessing and OS preemption. Consequently, DOS is not a good candidate for a network OS because it has neither of these qualities.

Accounting

Some installations, particularly those with large computing systems shared among users and departments, must account for system usage. Note that a LAN is a large, shared computing system. For example, each department may be budgeted for a certain amount of computer resource use. In this case, computer usage must be tallied so management can determine how well departments are adhering to their budgets. Accounting data can also be used to spot trends in system usage. For example, the accounting data may show that CPU use is increasing and that if the increases continue, the capacity of the machine will soon be exceeded. Information of this type can be used for capacity planning. Capacity planning will recognize the impending need for additional resources or a reallocation of existing resources. Good capacity planning allows system administrators to upgrade the system before performance problems occur. Accounting information may be compiled by jobs, departments, or other entities identified by the system administrators. Items that may be collected by the accounting system include

CPU usage (CPU seconds)

lines printed

disk space used (KB or MB)

transactions submitted (by type)

data communications medium usage (characters transmitted)

bytes read from and written to disk

Protection

Today, nearly everyone is aware that security is an important aspect of computer usage. The OS provides the base on which security is established. We expect the OS to prevent user programs from crashing the system and to protect the intrusion of one program into the memory occupied by another program's data. In shared systems, we also expect the OS and the file management system to provide certain levels of file security. Commonly, an OS will at least provide capabilities that allow administrators to define which users can read, write, or erase a file. Furthermore, most OSs allow file attributes that define a file as read-only, hidden (so it will not appear in a standard directory listing), and execute-only (so the file cannot be illegally copied).

Database Management

A **database management system (DBMS)** extends the OS file management capabilities. A DBMS provides software that allows the user or database administrator to

> define records, files, and file relationships (the data definition language)
>
> access, update, and delete data in the database (the data manipulation language)
>
> set up security
>
> establish, maintain, and use a data dictionary (a compendium of database structures, user information, and access rules)
>
> use **host language interfaces** that allow the database to be manipulated by standard programming languages such as COBOL, C++, Visual Basic, and Java

The DBMS is a tool that allows a company to organize its data and share that data among multiple concurrent users. Because data is the raw material of information, a system that helps a company organize its data and use it effectively is fundamental to the operation of the business.

Utility Software

Often an OS is accompanied by a set of utility programs. Furthermore, many installations purchase additional utility programs from third-party vendors. Utilities augment the function of the OS or other subsystem, such as the database management system or the data communications subsystem. For example, a set of file utility programs may be available that allow users to copy files, sort a file, and concatenate files. A low-level disk editor may allow a system administrator to fix files that have become corrupted. Peripheral utility programs may allow a system administrator to bring devices such as a printer on-line, take a printer off-line, start and stop devices, and reconfigure peripheral components.

Development Software

Development software provides the means by which to create new software and modify existing software. Development software includes text editors, text formatters, compilers, interpreters, link editors, cross-reference programs, testing utilities, and related programs and utilities.

Network Management Software

Because this book is about LANs, it is appropriate to single out this special-purpose software. Once a network has been established and is running, it must be managed. Effective management requires the use of both software and hardware tools. Network management includes a variety of activities such as backups, problem resolution, capacity planning, and establishing user environments. These activities are the focus of Part 4.

Network Access Software

Again, because this text deals with LANs, it is appropriate to single out this software component. We can configure the hardware necessary for a network, but without a corresponding software system, the hardware is useless. Network access software for a LAN includes the components that allow us to access LAN resources from directly attached workstations and remote workstations. Other access capabilities include software that allows one network to connect to another network and utilities that allow some computers to emulate the functions of other devices such as terminals or cluster controllers. We address these capabilities in later chapters.

GENERIC FUNCTIONS OF LAN SYSTEM SOFTWARE

Application software is designed to solve business problems. It is assisted in this goal by supporting system software such as the OS, DBMS, and data communication systems. Like all system software, LAN system software is essentially an extension of the OS. It carries out hardware-oriented LAN tasks such as interfacing to the medium, and I/O oriented tasks such as directing print jobs and disk read/write requests to a server. A few OSs are specifically designed for LAN work and have these functions integrated. Other LAN system software implementations operate in partnership with a general-purpose OS such as UNIX or OS/2. We sometimes call the LAN OS a **network operating system (NOS).**

The purpose of system software is to insulate applications from hardware details such as I/O and memory management. System software provides an interface through which the applications can request hardware services without needing to know the details of how the services are carried out. That is, the applications make requests for services, and system software contains the logic to interpret and carry out those requests for a specific type of hardware. For example, there are several types of disk drives. An application makes disk access requests independent of the type of disk drive being used. A disk driver is a component of the OS that tailors the request and carries it out for a specific type of disk drive.

LAN system software resides in both the application's workstation and in the server, as illustrated in Figure 6.1. The workstation's LAN system software includes the redirector and the medium interface software. Let us look at a specific example of a workstation's environment and use that example to examine the interaction between workstation and server software components.

A Workstation Environment

Consider an application in an IBM-compatible LAN workstation and a server that provides file and printer services. The workstation has local disk drives A, B, and C.

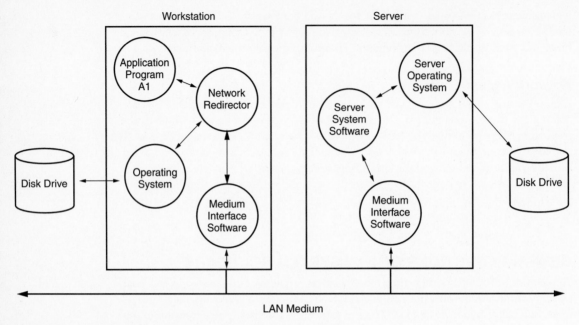

Figure 6.1   LAN System Software in Server and Workstation

The file server's disk drives are known to the workstation as drives F and G. The workstation's local printer ports are LPT1 and LPT2. There is a local ink-jet printer attached to LPT1. Output to LPT2 is directed to a high-speed, color network laser printer. The key to making this environment work is transparent access to all devices. From the user's perspective, printing to a network printer and accessing a network disk drive are transparent. That is, the workstation's user accesses remote drives F and G in exactly the same way as he or she accesses the local drives A, B, and C, and the user prints to the laser printer as though it were locally attached. This transparency is carried out by the LAN system software. Let us see how it is accomplished by considering an application that issues a read for a record that is located on the file server.

System Software Functions

You read in Chapters 3, 4, and 5 that the hardware provides the physical connection between a workstation and a server. The software forms the logical connection; that is, the software uses the hardware to carry on sessions between applications on a workstation and the server. The first function of the LAN software is to set up these logical connections. A variety of protocols are used to do this, and you will learn some details of these later. For now assume that this is done by the user issuing a server logon request. If the logon is successful, the user can use the server in accordance with his or her security controls.

The OS running in the workstation is aware only of the devices physically attached to that workstation. In our example it is capable of handling requests to drives A, B, and C and to LPT1 on its own. However, it cannot handle I/O requests to drives F and G or direct output to the network printer, LPT2. Ordinarily, when the application issues any file or print request, the request is accepted by the OS, and the OS carries out the request. If a request is made to access a device not attached to the workstation, the OS returns a "device not found" error message. In the LAN situation, to prevent the error message being returned, the requests for drives F and G must be intercepted before they get to the OS or the OS must be able to pass them on to a network software module. The software that does this is generically called a **redirector.**

The redirector is a software module that intercepts all application I/O requests before they get to the workstation's OS. The redirector passes requests for access to locally attached devices to the OS. Local device access requests are carried out as usual. If the redirector gets a request for a LAN server, it sends the request over the network to the server. This process is illustrated in Figure 6.2.

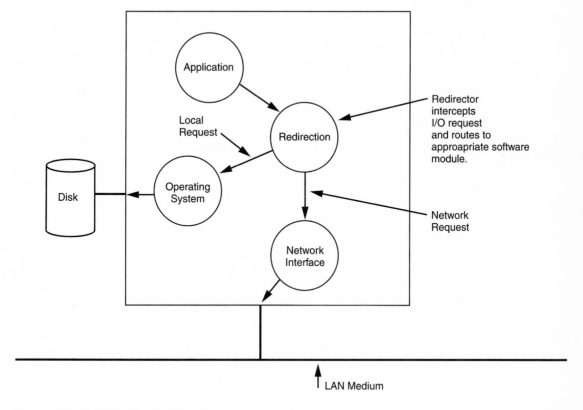

Figure 6.2 LAN Redirector Functions

The server receives the request from the workstation. Assume for now that the request is for a database record; we will look at printer services later. Many workstations are attached to the network, and any of them can make server requests at any time. Thus the server may receive several requests at nearly the same time. Efficiency requires that the server be able to work on multiple requests at once. This capability is know as **multithreading,** because the server can have multiple transactions in progress at the same time. The server software must keep track of the progress of each transaction.

Suppose, for example, that the server simultaneously receives two requests for a database record, three requests to write to a network printer, and one request to download an application program. These requests arrive in single file, as illustrated in Figure 6.3. The server accepts the first request, a database record read, and searches disk cache memory. If the record is not in cache memory, the server issues a disk read to satisfy it. It also remembers the address of the workstation that requested the read. While the disk is working to find the requested record, the server takes the next request, a printer write request, and issues a write to the print file. The server then accepts the next request, one for downloading the application program, and issues a read request for the first segment of the program.

At this point the server is notified that its read for the first database record has been completed. The server recalls the address of the workstation making the request and sends the record back to that workstation. Following that, the server takes the next request, a database read, and issues the read that satisfies the request. Thus the server software spends most of its time changing between accepting requests, issuing reads or writes to satisfy them, reacting to completions of those reads and writes, and sending the results back to the requester.

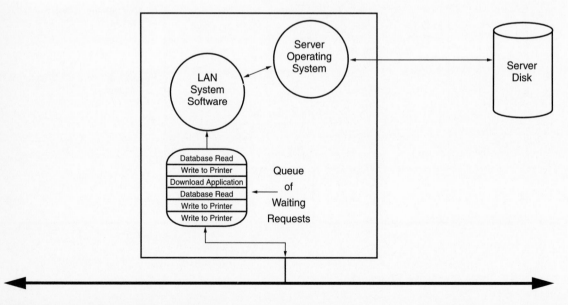

Figure 6.3   LAN Server Request Queue

The application/server protocol just described is called a **client/server** or **requester/server protocol.** You should realize the importance of the multithreading capability of the server. A real-world example of **single-threading** versus multithreading will show why. Suppose you went to a restaurant and your waiter could wait on you only when all tables ahead of you were done. You would end up waiting a long time before getting service, but the service would be great when you finally got it. However, the waiter would have large amounts of idle time waiting for the food to be cooked and so on. In a small restaurant, such as a quick-order restaurant, you may be willing to wait for the person ahead of you in line to be served before placing your order. Likewise, in a small LAN such a service protocol might work. However, the larger the LAN, the more likely there will be multiple, concurrent requests and the more important multithreading becomes.

SOFTWARE REQUIREMENTS FOR SHARED USAGE

Most early microcomputer applications were written for single-user systems, which means that the software developers could make certain simplifying design decisions. To use these applications in a shared LAN system, accommodations must be made by the LAN administrators, by the LAN system software, or by the application itself. Let us now look at the required changes.

Hardware Configuration

Software written for a single user need not be concerned with problems of computer configuration. You are probably aware that microcomputers may be configured with a variety of options. The primary variations are in memory, disk configurations, printer configuration, and monitor support. In a stand-alone system the application software is set up to match the configuration of that system. However, a LAN might have many different workstation configurations, and application software ought to support each configuration as much as possible. This can be done in several ways.

Some applications support only one configuration. The hardware settings of such applications are stored in a single file. One way to use this type of application is to configure the application for the lowest common denominator of hardware and have each user get essentially the same configuration. Users with high-resolution color graphics monitors might have images displayed in monochrome at low resolution, or a user with a hard disk drive might have to use a flexible disk drive rather than the hard disk for some files. Usually LAN administrators can avoid this type of configuration by storing multiple versions of the application in different disk directories. Users can then use the configuration that most closely matches their computer's profile.

Some applications allow several configuration files and decide which to use by a runtime parameter or by making a default choice if the startup parameter is not specified. LAN administrators can provide each user with a tailored environment by virtue of a batch startup file.

Applications that are designed for LAN use usually have a user-oriented configuration file. Each LAN user has his or her personal configuration that is custom-tailored for a specific user and his or her specific hardware. This provides users with the most flexibility and requires little or no customization by the LAN administrator. These options are summarized in Table 6.1.

Application Settings

The software equivalent to hardware configurations are application settings. Ideally users tailor application settings to meet personal preferences. For example, one word processor user might prefer green characters on a black background with tab stops every five character positions. Another user might prefer white characters on a blue background with tab stops every four character positions. Each user ought to receive these settings as the default. Application settings can be defined in a way similar to setting hardware options.

Contention

You already learned a little about contention in Chapter 2. Remember that whenever two users can access the same resource at the same time, **contention** for that resource can occur. In Chapter 2 you read how the spooler resolved contention for a printer: First the print outputs are captured on disk, and then the spooler schedules each job to be printed when the printer is available to accept new print jobs. You experience similar problems when accessing files.

One of the classic examples of a contention problem is illustrated by two users working on one document, file, or record at the same time. Suppose two users, Juan and Karen, are working on a group report for their Systems Analysis class. Juan is responsible for the second section of the paper and Karen for the third section. If the document is divided into two separate files (each of which represents a section) or if Juan and Karen do not work on the document at the same time, there are no contention problems. However, if they are able to update the document at the same time, a contention problem can exist. Figure 6.4 illustrates the consequences of this problem. The same type of problem can occur when two users access and update the same database record.

A primitive way to handle contention is simply to avoid it by scheduling user activities so they do not interfere with each other—for example, by allowing only one user at a time to update the database. On LANs with only a couple of users this may be possible, but as the number of concurrent users increases, this method becomes clumsy. Rather than avoiding contention, an application or LAN software should prevent contention problems. Contention is prevented by exerting controls over files or records.

One contention prevention mechanism is activated when an application opens a file. There are three basic file **open modes:** exclusive, protected, and shared. In **exclusive open mode,** an open request is granted only if no other user has the file already open.

Table 6.1   User Configuration Options

Default disk drive	Disk drive/directory search paths
Default disk directory	Printer mappings
Disk drive mappings	Initial program/menu

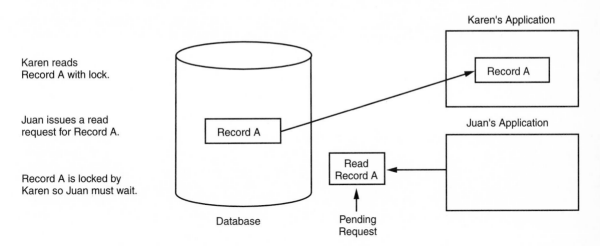

Karen reads
Record A with lock.

Juan issues a read
request for Record A.

Record A is locked by
Karen so Juan must wait.

Figure 6.4   A Contention Problem

Moreover, file open requests from other users are denied until the application having an exclusive open closes the file.

Exclusive opens may be too restrictive for some applications. Suppose, for example, that Karen and Juan are both working on the same word processing document. Karen needs to update the document, and Juan only needs to read it. In this case Juan will not interfere with the work being accomplished by Karen. A **protected open mode** can satisfy both users' needs. Protected open mode is granted only if no other user already has been granted exclusive or protected mode. Once the document is open in protected mode, only the application with protected open can update the document. **Shared open mode** allows several users to have the file open concurrently. In **shared update mode,** all users can update the file. In **shared read-only mode,** all users can read the file but cannot write to it. For example, if Karen opens the document in protected mode and Juan opens the document in shared read-only mode, Karen can read and update the document and Juan can read it. However, Juan cannot open the document in exclusive, protected, or shared update mode while a protected open exists.

Sometimes, a read-only application must be protected against file updates. For example, an application that is doing a trial balance of an accounting file must prohibit updates during the reading and calculations. If another application makes changes while the file is being read, the figures may not balance. The trial balance application can protect against this by opening the accounting file in protected read-only mode. This disallows other processes from opening the file in update mode while allowing processes to open the file in shared read-only mode. Table 6.2 shows the combinations of exclusive, protected, and shared open modes.

Exclusive and protected open modes are sufficient for meeting some contention problems, such as the word processing one described earlier. However, they are overly restrictive for other applications, such as database processing. One objective of database applications is for several users to share data. Exclusive opens allow only one user

Table 6.2   Exclusive, Protected, and Shared Open Combinations

	Currently Opened As			
Open Mode Requested	*Exclusive*	*Protected*	*Shared Update*	*Shared Read-Only*
Exclusive	Denied	Denied	Denied	Denied
Protected	Denied	Denied	Denied	Granted
Shared, update	Denied	Denied	Granted	Granted
Shared, read-only	Denied	Granted	Granted	Granted

at a time to use the data. The problem with file open contention resolution is overcome by exerting controls at a lower level, the record level. Record-level controls are called **locks.**

Suppose that our two users, Karen and Juan, want to update a database. As long as they are using different records, they will not interfere with each other. However, suppose that at some time both Karen and Juan need to update and access the same record. Contention problems such as those experienced in updating the word processing document might occur. However, if Karen locked the record when accessing it, Juan's read request would be denied until Karen unlocked the record. This is illustrated in Figure 6.5. Note that Juan waits until the record has been unlocked before being allowed to proceed.

However, record locking can cause another problem: **deadlock,** or **deadly embrace.** To illustrate this, suppose that Karen and Juan are accessing the database. Karen's application reads and locks record A, and at nearly the same time, Juan's application reads and locks record B. After reading record A, Karen attempts to read record B and, of course, waits because the record is locked. If Juan then attempts to read record A,

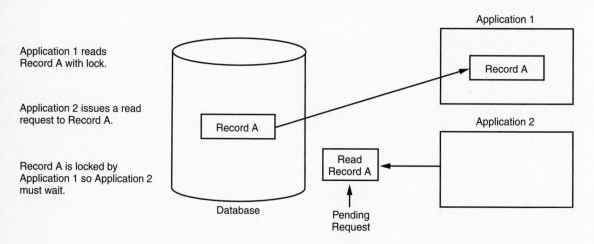

Application 1 reads Record A with lock.

Application 2 issues a read request to Record A.

Record A is locked by Application 1 so Application 2 must wait.

Figure 6.5   Waiting for Lock Release

deadlock occurs: Karen and Juan are waiting for each other, and neither can continue until the record they are waiting for is unlocked, which can never happen because there is a circular chain of users waiting on each other. Note that three or more users can also be involved in this circular chain of events. The deadlock problem is illustrated in Figure 6.6. Deadlock avoidance or resolution methods exist but are beyond the scope of this next. You can read about these methods in many database texts.

Some database systems take care of contention for users. They recognize when contention is occurring and prevent the problems associated with it. One convention used to do this is outlined as follows:

1. User A reads record X.

2. User B reads record X (and the read is allowed).

3. User A updates record X (and the update is allowed).

4. User B attempts to update record X.

5. The database management system recognizes that the record has been changed since User B read it.

6. The database management system sends the revised copy of record X to User B and notifies the user that the update was rejected because the record was changed by another user.

7. User B reissues the update or takes another course of action.

In selecting LAN software, it is critical that you understand the problems of configuration and contention. Without a resolution to these issues, the effectiveness of the

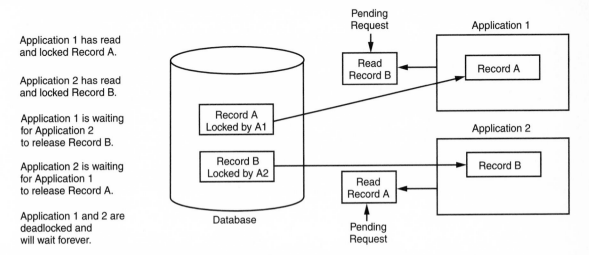

Figure 6.6   Deadlock Situation

system is reduced or, worse yet, the data becomes corrupted. Sharing data has another side effect that must be addressed: security.

Access Security

Early OSs, and many current ones for stand-alone microcomputers, do not provide file security. Even though only one user can use a microcomputer at one time, several users might use one system. Without security these users not only have access to another user's sensitive data, but also might accidentally (or intentionally) remove another user's files. Access to the computer essentially provides access to all data stored on that computer. A user might store sensitive data on a stand-alone microcomputer's disks, but those users are limited with respect to their ability to protect that data from unauthorized reading, changes, or destruction. The user could store the data on a removable disk and store it in a secure place when it is not being used, but many removable drives have low capacities. Another alternative is buying an application that provides password security or allows hiding or encrypting data to protect it from misuse.

When you install a LAN, data that must be shared and was once stored as private data on one or more stand-alone systems will probably end up being placed in a database on a server. Without security all data on the servers can be accessed, updated, and deleted by any LAN user. For most applications this is not acceptable. Therefore, the LAN system software must provide protection through security. Other security concerns include protecting against software piracy and preventing the introduction of computer viruses. We discuss security in more detail in Chapter 11.

SOFTWARE STANDARDS

Most of the LANs in operation today are called **open networks,** meaning that they adhere to a set of standards formulated by organizations such as ISO, ANSI, IEEE, and EIA. These standards are placed in the public domain and are called **open standards.** Open standards allow any company to build network hardware and software, secure in the knowledge that if they adhere to open standards their products will interoperate with other vendors' software written in conformance with the same or related open standards. Open systems stimulate competition among software and hardware vendors. This competition often leads to innovative products and lower prices, both of which benefit the consumer. As a side effect, a user often has several sources to rely on for replacement or additional network components. We have already discussed several standards in earlier chapters. We discuss other standards, as appropriate, in later chapters.

SOFTWARE PROTECTION

One of the most important things to know about your software is its licensing agreement. Virtually all software you buy is covered by a **license agreement.** This is true for both system and application software. The license agreement covers the rules under which you are allowed to use the product. It is a way of protecting both the manufacturer and the user of the product. To better understand the need for license agreements, let us first look at an analogy.

Consider a book you purchased for school. It was probably rather expensive. Of course, the publisher does not pay nearly that much to print the book. Part of the cost of your book goes to profit, of course, but the publisher incurs other expenses: One or more authors wrote the material, editors worked with the authors to develop the format and content, designers laid out the style (graphics and pages formats), marketing analysts determined a marketing strategy and created advertising brochures, and salespeople were told about the book, its target markets, and key selling points. All of this activity required a considerable investment. Some books never become popular, and the publishing company loses money on them. Others become very popular and the publishing company makes a profit. Some of that profit is used to offset losses on other projects. Now suppose someone decides to illegally reprint and sell a successful book. With today's technology it does not cost much to print such copies. This person could sell the copies for much less than the publisher, because he or she has not had to make the investment of developing the work, paying the salaries of editors and production workers and royalties to the developers, and so on.

Patent and copyright laws protect the investment of designers, artists, filmmakers, authors, publishing companies, and so on. You may be asking, "How do these examples relate to software?" Software companies also make a sizable investment in creating each application or system software. System analysts designed the product, programmers wrote and debugged the code, marketing analysts created a marketing plan, advertising campaigns were developed and implemented, manuals were created, a support organization was staffed and trained, and the product was brought to market. Several years probably elapsed from the time the product was conceived to the point at which it was ready to sell and make a profit. Thousands of dollars were probably spent before there was any opportunity to sell the software. Moreover, once a software product is released, expenses continue. Support staff must be paid and new enhancements designed. Like the book publisher, the software company can see its profits from all this effort eroded by illegal copying. To give you an idea of the magnitude of this problem, at the end of the 1980s, several software piracy shops in Hong Kong were raided. Some estimate the annual loss of revenues to software companies resulting from software piracy being conducted in one building alone to be hundreds of millions of dollars.

Software vendors must therefore take steps to protect their investment. Software is protected in six basic ways:

- The code is kept secret so other software houses cannot use special algorithms developed by the company to write a competing system.
- The code is copyrighted to prevent another company from copying the code and writing a competing system.
- Legislation penalizing those who do not adhere to the copyright and license restrictions is enforced.

- The software is copy-protected to deter someone from making an illegal copy.
- License agreements are used to establish the terms of ownership and use.
- The software requires WAN/Internet verification before it is activated.
- The software requires a special hardware device to run.

The first two measures protect the source code from being used by someone else. During software development companies commonly keep the source code of the software secret. However, after the product has been released, it is always possible to derive the source code, even if the software is released only in object code format. Deriving the source code from object code is done through reverse engineering. To protect itself from reverse engineering, software manufacturers usually copyright their software. **Copyright laws,** originally intended to cover books, films, and works of art, have been extended to include software. Moreover, new legislation has been enacted to further define the restrictions and penalties for unauthorized software copying.

Software piracy has always been a problem, even before the introduction of microcomputers. Minicomputers and mainframe systems make software piracy easier to detect, so its incidence is negligible relative to its occurrence on microcomputers. Large-system software piracy is easier to detect for two reasons. First, large computers are used by large organizations with professional data processing departments. Software piracy is difficult to hide in such organizations, and anyone found using pirated software is subject to dismissal and the company subject to lawsuits. Second, large-computer sites typically work closely with the software vendor's personnel. The vendor's employees are aware of the software its customers are authorized to use, and it is easy to detect the presence of unauthorized software. Piracy detection is not nearly so easy with microcomputer software.

A few software companies protect their software by requiring the use of a special hardware device that attaches to a serial or parallel port. The device and an application work together to provide application security. When started, the application attempts to read data encoded in the device. If the device is not attached, the application terminates. One disadvantage to this approach is that if you have several applications, you need a different device for each one. Because the number of serial or parallel ports is limited, changing from one application to another may require changing the device. Other companies have accomplished somewhat the same effect by requiring a **key disk.** The key disk usually is a flexible disk that must be in a disk drive when the application is run. The application uses the key disk only to verify its presence. This technique is seldom used today and, of course, cannot be used with diskless systems.

Originally many microcomputer software vendors used copy protection to deter software piracy. That is, the software diskette was encoded to prevent someone copying it using a standard OS copy facility such as DOS's COPY or DISKCOPY command. In general, copy protection only gave rise to a new software industry: software that allows copying of copy-protected software. Of course, vendors of such software were careful to point out that the sole purpose of their software was to make a backup copy, not to make illegal duplicate copies. Today, many companies that once copy-protected their software have abandoned that practice because it proved ineffective. Instead of, or in addition to, copy protection, software vendors now rely on copyright protection together with software license agreements.

Software License Agreements

When you buy software, the medium that holds the software often is sealed in an envelope. Written on or attached to the envelope is text regarding the license agreement and a message that when you open and use the software, you make a commitment to adhere to the stipulations of that license agreement. The license agreement states the conditions under which you are allowed to use the product.

In essence, when you buy software you do not get ownership of that product; you are simply given the right to use it. An attorney might quibble with this statement, but the basic premise is correct. Some license agreements explicitly state that you own the medium (diskette or CD-ROM) but not the contents of the medium. Thus you may not make copies of the software to give to your friends, you cannot run it on several workstations at the same time, you cannot reverse-engineer it to produce source code for modification or resale, and so on. Your rights to the software are limited to using the software in the intended manner. If you like, you can destroy it, cease to use it, sell it, or give it as a gift. In the latter two cases, you also transfer the license agreement to the recipient and cease using it yourself. Some software vendors go so far as to state that transferring ownership of the software must be approved by the software vendor. Moreover, in some cases the software license covers the use of the accompanying documentation as well.

When selecting your application and system software, you must take care to understand fully all the conditions of the license agreements. You want each user to have the necessary software services available. Differences in license and pricing policies between competing products can result in substantial differences in availability to your users or cost to your company.

One of the problems with license agreements is that no standards have been established. If you buy two different applications, you are likely to find two different license agreements. To protect yourself and your organization from civil and criminal suits, you must understand the provisions of each agreement. Several companies, including several major state universities, have been investigated for illegally copying software, found guilty of the offense, and forced to pay heavy fines. Therefore, it is important that a company and individuals respect the license agreements. In general, license agreements take one of the following forms:

single-user, single-workstation licenses

single-user, multiple-workstation licenses

restricted number of concurrent users licenses

server licenses

site licenses

corporate licenses

Single-User, Single-Workstation License

A **single-user, single-workstation license** agreement is the most restrictive. It specifies that the software is to be used on one workstation only and by only one person at a time. For example, if you have a multiuser microcomputer, only one user can run the software at any time. In most instances, restricting the software to only one machine also implies a single user.

This license agreement also means that if an office has two or more computers, a separate copy of the software must be purchased for each machine on which it is to be used. Thus, if you have two employees, one on the day shift and one on the night shift using the same software but on different workstations, each needs an individual copy of the software. In this situation the software is never used concurrently, yet two copies are required. One of the ways in which software vendors enforce this policy is through the software installation procedure, which counts the number of installations. When you install the product the counter is decremented to zero and you are not able to install the program on another system. To move the software to another system you must deinstall the software, a process that removes the application from the computer's disks and increments the installation count.

Single-User, Multiple-Workstation Licenses

The constraints of the single-user, single-workstation agreement are relaxed by the **single-user, multiple-workstation license** agreement. It usually relies on the honor system for enforcement. The software vendors that use this agreement recognize that different people may want to use the software and at different workstations, such as in the office and on a portable computer. The purchase of a single copy of the software allows the owner to install it on several systems. However, the license restricts the use of the software to one user at a time per software copy. For example, suppose an office with ten workstations must do word processing. At some time each employee can use the word processor, but at any time, only five employees can be using the product concurrently. With this license agreement, the company can buy five copies of the software and install them on ten different systems. As long as five or fewer employees use the word processing application at any one time, the company has lived up to the license agreement. Note also that it is possible for six users to inadvertently use the application at the same time, in violation of the license agreement.

Restricted Number of Concurrent Users Licenses

On a LAN, commonly several users run an application concurrently. Three employees may be doing word processing, ten may be using the spreadsheet software, and twenty-five may be using the database software. With file or database server technology, only one copy of each application is on the server's disks. Most LAN-compatible software is designed for multiple users; however, some software vendors limit the number of concurrent users with a **restricted number of concurrent users license** agreement. The main idea behind this strategy is to charge by the number of users.

Consider the database needs of the company just mentioned, where the maximum number of concurrent database users is 25. Suppose the database vendor has a license agreement that allows 10 concurrent users for a certain fee. The company also has an expansion policy that allows additional concurrent users to be added in groups of 10, with an additional fee for each such group. The company must purchase three modules to satisfy its need of 25 concurrent users. This type of license typically is enforced by a meter program that controls the concurrent use of the application. When a user starts the application, the meter program increments a counter by 1. When a user exits from the application, the counter is decremented by 1. If the license agreement is for 30 users, a user can run the application as long as the counter is 29 or below. If the counter is 30, a user requesting the application receives an error message indicating that the file is not available.

Server Licenses

A **server license** allows an application to be installed on one server. All users attached to that server may use the application. If a company has several servers, say three, and wants to use the application on each of them, the company must purchase three licenses or three copies of the software.

Site Licenses

A **site license** gives the user unlimited rights to use the software at a given site. The site may be a single LAN or multiple LANs at one location.

Corporate Licenses

A **corporate license** gives the corporation unlimited use of the software at all locations. Some companies restrict a corporate license to all locations within one country. Sometimes, the right to reproduce documentation is also granted.

License Control

Some license provisions are easy to control, whereas others require special considerations. Controlling server, site, and corporate licenses is straightforward. Controlling restricted number of concurrent user licenses requires more effort. Typically, this is accomplished by a metering program. Metering programs have become sophisticated, allowing license loaning. Consider a company that has an enterprise network with LANs in different time zones. For example, suppose there are offices in Australia and Europe, where the time zones differ by 12 hours. Consequently, people in Europe are generally working while those in Australia are not and vice versa. A meter program that supports loaned licenses will "borrow" the licenses not used in Australia for use in Europe. Although this arrangement conforms to the letter of the license agreement, it probably does not adhere to the spirit of the agreement. Consequently, changes are likely in number of concurrent user license agreements. Furthermore, efforts are under way to formulate industry standards for licensing. These standards will probably have several options covering several of the above options.

Owners' Rights

The license agreement is intended primarily to protect the rights of the manufacturer. However, the owner of a license agreement also has certain rights:

The owner can transfer or assign the license to another user.

The owner can get a refund if the product is defective or does not work as stated.

The owner has legal rights granted by certain states or countries regarding the exclusion of liability for losses or damage resulting from the use of the software.

The owner can terminate the license by destroying the software and documentation.

SUMMARY

A LAN system consists of hardware, software, people, procedures, and data. The software enables the capabilities of the hardware. Software may be divided into several functional classes, including application, OS, database management, utilities, network management, development, and network access. The interaction of these classes provides us with the capabilities we need to establish and maintain the working network environment.

In a LAN, a workstation periodically needs to access network resources such as a file server or print server. To access resources that are not local to the workstation, networking software must be present to augment the capabilities of the workstation's OS. The network request must be diverted from the control of the local OS to the control of the network software. Generically the software that routes this request is called the redirector. The redirector sends the network request to another workstation network component, the network interface software, which is responsible for transmitting and receiving network messages. A LAN server also has software that enables its capabilities. Servers contain the network interface software that communicates with the workstations' network interface software. Additionally, a server has software components that allow it to carry out its designated services.

When we use networks, we share resources. Sharing resources can lead to problems such as contention and deadlock. To resolve these problems, the software must have the ability to systematically control access to devices and data. OSs control files by limiting the manner in which they can be opened and by providing the ability to lock records. The OS uses similar mechanisms to control access to other shared resources such as printers and certain system memory locations. To provide efficiency, software controlling shared resources should allow multithreading. This allows a higher level of concurrency than does single-threaded software.

Standards address functions at all layers of the OSI Reference Model. When these standards are placed in the public domain, the systems adhering to the standards are called open systems. Open systems create an environment in which multiple vendors can develop hardware and software components that will interoperate with standard components produced by other vendors. Open systems promote competition, which in turn leads to innovation, lower prices, and multiple sources of hardware and software.

Vendor and user companies need to protect their investment in software. A variety of mechanisms have been developed to do this. One important mechanism is the software license agreement. The software license agreement details how the software may be used, where the software may be used, and how many users can access it concurrently. It is important that users understand the license agreements and adhere to their stipulations. Each software vendor is free to develop its own license strategy, so a variety of license agreement provisions exist.

Key Terms

application program interface (API)
client/server protocol
contention
copyright laws
corporate license
database management system (DBMS)
deadlock
deadly embrace
exclusive open mode
host language interface
key disk
latency
license agreement
locks
multithreading
network operating system (NOS)
open mode
open network

open standard
operating system (OS)
protected open mode
redirector
requester/server protocol
restricted number of concurrent users
   license
seek
server license
shared open mode
shared read-only mode
shared update mode
single-threading
single-user, multiple-workstation license
single-user, single-workstation license
site license
swapping
virtual memory

Review Questions

1. Explain the functions of the workstation redirector software.
2. Explain how an application's network request is processed by both the workstation and the server.
3. Why may a stand-alone workstation need a memory upgrade when added to a LAN?
4. Explain why multithreaded server operation is important.
5. What is a client/server or requester/server protocol? Give an example.
6. What is an application program interface (API)?
7. What is the purpose of I/O optimization? Give two examples.
8. Describe two ways in which data contention can be avoided.
9. What is deadlock? Give an example.
10. Briefly describe each of the following general classes of license agreements:
    a. single-user, single-workstation license
    b. single-user, multiple-workstation license
    c. restricted number of concurrent users license
    d. server license
    e. site license
    f. corporate license
11. In a restricted number of concurrent users license agreement, how does an organization control the number of concurrent users?

Problems and Exercises

1. Evaluate a LAN-compatible database management system to determine how it resolves contention. Is contention resolution the responsibility of the user or the database management system? Systems you may want to examine include Paradox and dBASE 5 from Borland, FoxBase and Access from Microsoft, Oracle, and Sybase.
2. Compare the software license agreements from three different software vendors.
3. Your company is considering purchasing a software product that provides a layered pricing scheme for licensing. A five-user system costs $1000 and includes two copies of documentation. Additional user licenses may be added in increments of five users for $500. The incremental licenses do not include documentation. Additional documentation sets can be purchased for $35. Your company has 75 workstations, but it has been determined that the maximum number of concurrent users for this software package is 53. What is the total cost of the software and documentation if 40 additional sets of documentation are required?

Chapter 7

LAN System Software

CHAPTER PREVIEW

In Chapter 6 we described the functions of an **operating system (OS).** In this chapter we look at LAN network operating systems (NOS) and supporting software, which we call system software. System software resides in servers and workstations. The success of the LAN depends on how the system software and application software interact in setting up the communications capability. In this chapter we look at functions we expect in system software, and in Chapter 8 you will read about specific examples of NOSs.

Specific topics you will read about in this chapter include

generic LAN system software functions

workstation system software functions

server system software functions

Let us now look at LAN system software in more detail. We will do so by looking at how a workstation and server establish a session and carry on a dialogue. In our discussion we provide a generic view of how communications is established and maintained. Because this is a generic view, it may differ somewhat from some of the available network OSs.

SERVER/WORKSTATION COMMUNICATIONS

When a server is powered up, like most of today's computers, it loads the OS. On completion of the loading process, the server is available to begin handling requests. In the following discussion, we assume that all servers and workstations have been powered up, their OSs have been loaded, and they are operational. Ordinarily, as part of the startup procedures for the workstation, the network software is also loaded. Finally, suppose that there is one available server on this LAN, which we will call SERVER1. Furthermore, suppose this LAN, which we will call LAN A, is connected to another LAN, LAN B, by a device called a router, as depicted in Figure 7.1. LAN B has a server, which we will call SERVER2. We describe the functions of a router in Chapter 16. For now, just realize that the router can determine whether a message originating on LAN A is destined for LAN B and route it to LAN B accordingly. Likewise, messages originating on LAN

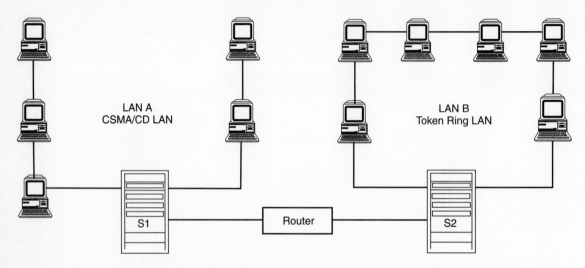

Figure 7.1   LANs Connected by a Router

B destined for LAN A are routed to LAN A. Intra-LAN messages, such as those between one LAN A node and another LAN A node, are not routed to the other network.

The network software within the workstation includes the **redirector,** which interfaces with the workstation's OS, and the network interface module, which we shall call LANCom. The redirector's functions were discussed in Chapter 6. LANCom performs several functions. On the communications medium side it provides the data link support—CSMA/CD or token passing—as discussed in Chapter 4. On the workstation side it interfaces to the redirector software. In between these interfaces, LANCom performs some of the functions found at the network and transport layers of the OSI reference model. Physically, the redirector and LANCom could be one process or several processes; it is the function we are addressing here, not the implementation. This software configuration is illustrated in Figure 7.2.

The first problem the workstation must address is connecting to one of the two servers. A workstation could connect to any of the two. Several mechanisms may be used to choose which server a client will connect to. First, the user may designate which server to attach to. To access the network, a user must issue a logon command. Some networks allow the name of the server to be included as part of the logon command. Thus the user may select the server by typing in a command such as

```
LOGON SERVER2 username
```

where username is the user's logon ID. A second method for determining which server to attach to is to specify the preferred server's name as part of the workstation network software loading process. The only difference between this option and the first is that the user does not need to specify the server name in the LOGON command. A user may want to connect to a specific server, say SERVER1, because the LAN administrator has designated primary servers for each user to balance the servers' workloads or because that

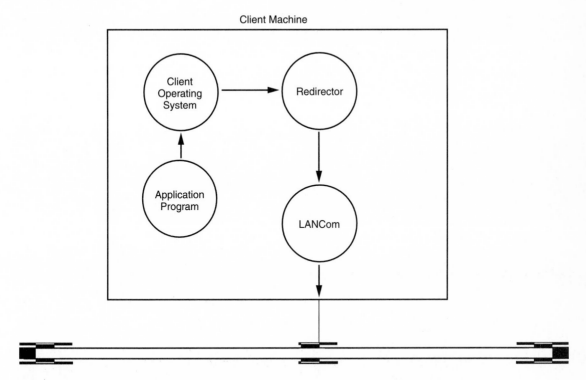

Client Machine

Figure 7.2 Network Interface Software

server contains the files and applications the user needs. Finally, the selected server could simply be the first one noticed by the workstation. In all scenarios, the workstation must discover the server's address; in the last scenario, the workstation must also somehow discover the existence of a server, and to determine how this is done, we need to look at several implementation alternatives.

The address of the server with which the workstation must communicate is essential because the address is part of the data link message header. Furthermore, at the network layer we build a network layer header that also includes the source and destination addresses. These addresses are used by the router to determine whether the message must be routed to the attached network. The format of CSMA/CD and token ring frame formats can be found in Chapter 4. Two network layer protocol formats, one for Novell's IPX protocol and one for TCP/IP's IP protocol, are shown in Figure 7.3. Note that each frame has the addresses of both the sending and receiving stations and that although the frames are similar, the exact format differs. Thus, the IPX and IP protocols are not interchangeable; nodes communicating at the network layer must have a common network layer protocol.

A workstation knows its own address, so to send a message it must discover the address of the recipient, in this case the desired or defaulted server. To accomplish this, we need a protocol that allows stations to exchange addresses. This protocol can be implemented

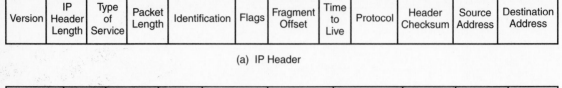

(a) IP Header

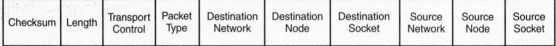

(b) IPX Header

Figure 7.3   IP and IPX Header Formats

in a variety of ways and could be initiated by the server or workstation or both, depending on the algorithms chosen by the NOS designers. We will look at three options: Novell's Services Advertising Protocol, TCP/IP's Address Resolution Protocol, and network directory resolution.

Services Advertising Protocol

In Novell NetWare LAN implementations, the Services Advertising Protocol (SAP) is implemented at the OSI application layer. Inherent in this protocol is the presence of a server table in each server and router. A generic server table is shown in Table 7.1. The server tables contain the name, address, and server type—file, print, application, and so on—of all servers known to the device. Servers find out about each other by advertising themselves. When the server is initiated, one of its startup functions is to broadcast a SAP message. A broadcast message has a distinct destination address that allows it to be accepted by all nodes. The SAP message identifies the server's name, address, and the types of services it can provide. Other active servers and routers accept this message and store the data in their server table. The router also enters the data into its server table and forwards the message onto the other LAN so that the servers (and possibly other routers) there can get the information. In this way, all servers and routers in the internet eventually learn of the existence of the new server.

Whenever a server goes down, the entries for that server in the remaining server and router server tables are eventually deleted. This can happen in two ways. First, if the server is shut down correctly, it will broadcast a server down message alerting the network that it is being shut down. Devices receiving this message remove that server's entry from their server tables. If the server is not shut down gracefully (for example, if the server crashes), other servers will also determine that the server is no longer available. Periodically, usually every 60 seconds, each server broadcasts a SAP message announcing itself. If this message does not arrive by the proper time, servers and routers will delete the entry for that server from their server tables. Note that in a large network with many servers, these SAP messages can generate considerable data traffic. In these instances, network administrators may filter the messages at a router to keep them from

Table 7.1   A Generic Server Table

Server Name	Address	Server Type	Hops
MktgSvr	A12B634A	File	1
AcctSvr	DDC3958B	File	2
SWDevSvr	DD84A124	File	0
HRSvr	A12C583D	SQL	1
MfgSvr	29837CAB	File	1
RanDSvr	834AB3E7	File	0
ExOffL	5602C0A1	Printer	1
unused			

being propagated throughout the entire internet. This minimizes the network traffic but has the consequence of making servers on some LANs invisible to users on another LAN. We are now ready to see how a client connects to a server using this algorithm.

When a client machine wants to connect to a server, the client's network software sends a message to find the nearest server or, if a specific server has been designated, to find a server by name. If the request is for the nearest server, the first server that replies with its address is the one to which the user is attached. If the request is for a named server, then the address is provided from information from a server's server table. In either case, the client receives the destination address.

Address Resolution Protocol

LANs using the TCP/IP protocol have a different method, the Address Resolution Protocol (ARP), for resolving addresses. In a TCP/IP network, nodes have an IP address that is used at the network layer and a physical address that is used at the data link layer. The physical address is the MAC address set in the LAN adapter, whereas the IP address is assigned by network administrators. Within a network both physical and IP addresses are unique; however, once assigned, the IP address for a node remains constant whereas the physical address may change. Recall that for Ethernet and token ring cards the physical address is placed on the card by the manufacturer. Therefore, if a LAN adapter goes bad and needs to be replaced or if it is upgraded to a faster model, the physical address will change. For this reason, the IP address is a better descriptor for a node than the physical address.

If one node on a network needs to communicate with another node on the same network, it needs the physical address for the MAC protocol. If the sending node has recently communicated with this node, the address will probably be in the sending node's ARP cache; if not, the sending node needs to find the recipient's physical address. To do so, the sending node issues a broadcast ARP packet containing the IP address of the recipient and the IP and physical address of the sender together with a few additional descriptor fields. If a node's IP address matches the one sent in the ARP packet, it responds with its physical address. A direct response is possible because the sending node included its physical address in the message. Both nodes save the physical address of the correspondent in their ARP cache for use in subsequent communications.

A number of problems can arise when using an address in the ARP cache. The recipient can be down. The recipient may be brought back up with a new physical address because the LAN adapter failed and a new one was installed. Transmitted packets may be lost. All these problems are addressed by the ARP protocol but are beyond the scope of this discussion.

In TCP/IP networks, nodes can also be found by name. The best TCP/IP address is the 32-bit IP address. However, 32-bit numbers are not as easy to work with as names. If you have ever used the Internet, you probably worked with node names, not their IP addresses. Occasionally, you may see an IP address that has been translated from a name or used an IP address in sending a message. IP addresses are usually written as four numbers separated by periods, a convention called a dotted quad. Each of the four numbers represents one 8-bit portion of the 32-bit address. Thus a dotted quad number may look like 207.17.188.2. Name servers are used to support name lookups that return an IP address.

In a large network, if all servers periodically broadcast their presence, many network messages may result and network efficiency declines. An alternative approach is a technique used in large networks, where broadcast messages are time-consuming. In this protocol, a node receives information from its neighbor nodes and builds its view of the network from that information. This protocol is similar to the way in which rumors are propagated. The rumor starts with one person. That person tells a neighbor, the neighbor then propagates the rumor to the next neighbor, and soon everyone knows the rumor.

In the case of networks, this method can be implemented by each server containing a network routing table similar to the server table. The primary difference between these two algorithms is that periodic messages advertising the services are not necessary. If a new server comes up, it is detected and its presence is noted. Each server or router sends this message to neighboring networks, so the information is propagated to all network servers and routers and is recorded in the network routing table. Unless there is a change in the status of the server, no additional messages are required. In very large networks, the network routing tables become excessively large. A solution to this problem is to have name servers, whose primary function is to resolve resource name to address problems.

There is another method: network directories by which clients can identify network resources. This method is suitable for large and small networks alike and is becoming the principal method for storing information about network resources and for disseminating this information to network users. However, the network directory is far more than a tool for address resolution, and we discuss its composition and other uses.

THE NETWORK DIRECTORY

In a LAN with 5 to 10 users, one server, and 2 or 3 printers, keeping track of users, user e-mail addresses, and LAN resources is not too difficult. Originally, most LANs stored information of this nature in a server-oriented database. A user connected to a server could find information about resources controlled by that server, but information about network resources managed by another server was unavailable. To use or find out about resources on another server, the user needed to attach to that server. Moreover, users needed user IDs and passwords for each server. This type of resource management is called server-centric.

Suppose you are a user on a LAN with hundreds of users and their associated e-mail addresses, approximately 60 printers, and 7 servers and want to send an e-mail message to a user, Kim Burton, with whom you do not regularly communicate. Because Kim is not one of your regular correspondents, you do not know her e-mail address. Or, suppose you want to print a document on a printer in the marketing department. How would you determine whether there were such a printer and its network designation?

In a large LAN with hundreds of users, hundreds of e-mail addresses, dozens of printers, and 5 to 10 servers, keeping track of the names and locations of people and equipment is a significant effort. If we take the next step and connect several LANs of this magnitude together with a wide area network (WAN), we have an even greater logistics problem. Consider the enterprise network in Figure 7.4. This network has LANs in numerous cities connected by a WAN. Moreover, in each location there may be several interconnected LANs, as shown in Figure 7.4. The enterprise network consists of thousands of users and dozens of servers.

In all cases it would be beneficial to have a support system to assist in recording the existence and location of network users, hardware, and software. A server-centric solution is not well-suited to this environment because a user will need to find the server that contains the desired resources and attach to that server. What is needed is a network-oriented or network-centric solution. The tool that provides this capability is the network directory.

One NOS vendor, Banyan Systems, Inc., has had a network directory, **StreetTalk,** as an integral part of its **Vines** NOS for many years, and a CCITT network directory standard, X.500, was available in 1988 and has been revised several times since then. Banyan Vines with StreetTalk has been a popular NOS for large LANs and LAN internets because Vines was the only LAN NOS supporting network directory services. Other NOS vendors who were oriented primarily to smaller LAN configurations lacked a comprehensive network directory until the mid-1990s. In the 1990s the LAN industry saw a significant rise in individual LAN sizes and in LAN interconnections. As result of this expansion, NOS vendors who did not have a network directory saw the need for them and network directories have become an essential LAN feature for companies installing large LANs. All of the leading LAN NOS vendors now have a network directory or have announced plans to have one available soon.

A network directory is fundamentally a database of LAN objects, properties of those objects, and values for properties. One such object is a server and a property of a server might be its physical and network layer (IP or IPX) addresses. The server's addresses could be determined by looking up the server's name in the network directory.

For another example, consider an object called a User. This user has properties such as name, e-mail address, telephone number, and password. The telephone property may have several values such as work, home, beeper, and cellular telephone numbers. The password property may have only one value, the user's current password, or it could be a list of passwords, one of which is the current password, with the others being past passwords. The past passwords may be used to ensure that the user does not use the same

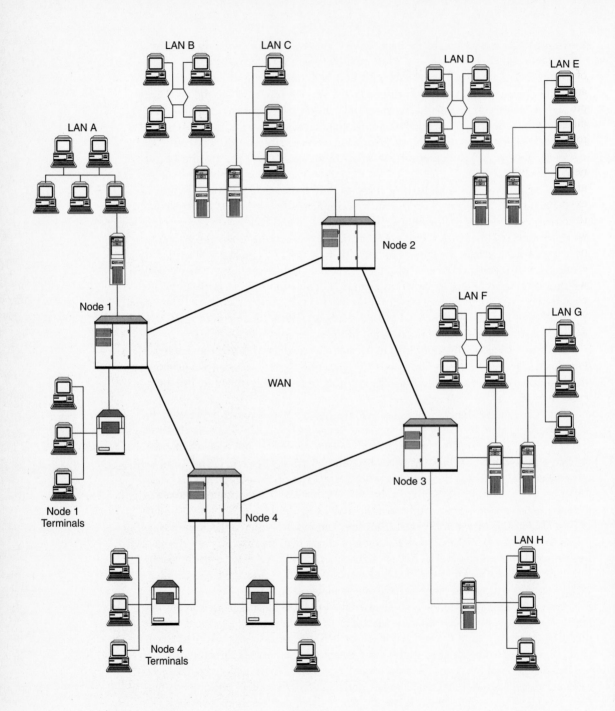

Figure 7.4   An Enterprise Network

passwords over and over. A LAN network directory will probably contain the objects and properties given in Table 7.2. The items in the table are intended to give you an idea of the makeup of the directory; actual implementations generally contain more objects and more properties per object. A network directory provided by a NOS vendor will probably have available a number of predefined objects such as those in Table 7.2. In addition, the directory system should be flexible enough to allow network administrators to define company-specific objects, properties, and values.

If we place the description of network objects in a network directory, we obviously need to be able to update and access the directory. If the network resources are distributed and the entire directory must reside on one node only, several potential problems exist. First, there is a reliability concern. If the directory resides on one node only and that node is not available to some users, those users will be unable to find needed network resources. The other potential problem is performance. Consider again the enterprise network shown in Figure 7.4. Distributed LAN users in some locations may experience long wait times when interrogating the directory. If the network directory were located on a server in Paris, Hong Kong, and Sydney users would probably experience delays of several seconds. If you have used the Internet to look at remote locations, you may have experienced such delays. The solution to both of these problems is the ability to distribute and replicate all or portions of the directory.

Replicating portions of the directory means that portions are copied and stored on multiple servers. Replication is sometimes called partitioning; however, *partitioning* has several other meanings so we use the term *replication* unless the context requires the use of the term *partitioning*. When replicating information, the directory software must contain the logic to maintain consistency among the replicated portions. Thus, if the London LAN administrator updates information in the directory in London, the directory software should also automatically make the same update to replicated versions of that part of the directory structure in New York and New Delhi.

Another concern raised by replication is time synchronization. Because the data is replicated, updates might occur at nearly the same time but in different locations. It takes a bit of time for the updates in one location to be propagated to the other. When this occurs, the updates might not occur in the same sequence. For example, suppose that an administrator deleted a user and then readded the same user. These activities must also take place at a replicated location. However, the user add transaction may arrive at the replicated location

Table 7.2   Possible Contents of a Network Directory

Object	Properties		
Server	Name	Network address	Location
User	Login name	Full name	Telephone
	Address		E-mail address
Printer	Name	Location	Operator name
	Print queues	Print server	
Disk volume	Name	Server name	Capacity
	Interface	Manufacturer	

before the deletion. If there were no time stamps involved, the add would fail because the user object would already be in place. The delete would then occur, resulting in the user object being deleted in the replicated portion of the directory. For reasons such as this, directory systems use time stamps to indicate when an activity occurs. When this activity can occur at two locations simultaneously, it is important that the time stamps be consistent. Thus, a mechanism should exist to ensure that the times used by all servers are consistent.

Distribution means that all or part of the directory can be placed on any suitable server in the enterprise network. Consider the directory structure shown in Figure 7.5. It represents all of the resources of the enterprise network. Logically it appears as a single entity. However, it is probably reasonable to distribute portions of the directory to place information about resources close to the users who are most apt to need them. A possible distribution configuration of the directory tree given in Figure 7.5 is shown in Figure 7.6. It is possible to both distribute and replicate portions of the directory.

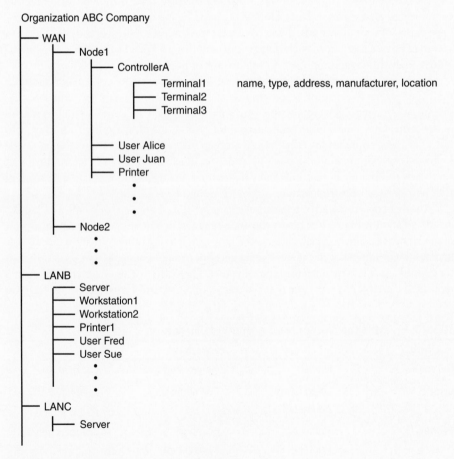

Figure 7.5   A Network Directory Structure

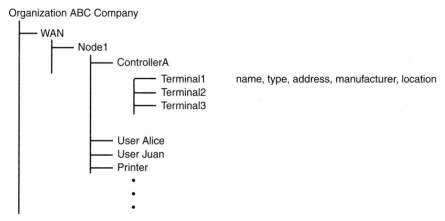

Organization ABC Company

name, type, address, manufacturer, location

This portion of the tree is stored on Node 1.

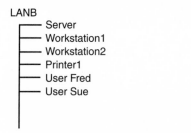

This portion of the tree is stored at Server on LANB and replicated on LANC.

This portion of the tree is stored at Server on LANC and replicated on LANB.

Figure 7.6   Distributing and Replicating a Network Directory Structure

From the users' perspectives, the network directory simplifies access to network resources. With one logon, all the resources of the enterprise network to which a user has
access are available; contrast this with the user needing to have multiple user IDs, passwords, and knowledge of needed server locations to accomplish his work. From a network administration perspective, setting up an enterprise network directory takes more
planning than multiple server-centric systems (which tend to be rather self-defining) but
the net results are far superior and are well worth the effort.

Currently, one of the problems network administrators and implementers face is **interoperability** of directories. Several NOS vendors have network directory capabilities. Although several NOS vendors are porting their directory structures to other LAN OSs, these efforts are just beginning and much work still must be done. If a company uses servers running under different NOSs, it may be difficult to establish a network directory that encompasses all network components. We can expect this situation to improve over the next several years. To further complicate issues, there are several competing standards for directory implementations. We have already mentioned the X.500 standard. The Open Systems Foundation's (OSF) Distributed Computing Environment (DCE) contains a standard for Directory and Security Services (DSS). The directory is based on the X.500 standard. It is being implemented by IBM in its **OS/2 Warp Server.** Novell has implemented a directory called Novell Directory Services (NDS), which is based on the X.500 standard. Although both are based on the same standard, they currently do not interoperate. At this writing, Microsoft is preparing a directory service for its Windows NT Server product. This technology is currently in flux as vendors attempt to establish their products and provide interoperability with existing NOSs and with the Internet.

CLIENT/SERVER DIALOGUE

Once the client and server have connected, a **client/server dialogue** can begin. Work performed at a client node may use local or server-based resources. Local requests are handled by the local OS. Server requests require the intervention of the LAN system software. When an application makes a request that must be handled by a server, the redirector process gets involved. This can occur in two ways: The local OS gets the request and passes it to the redirector or the redirector gets the request and passes local operations to the client's OS. These alternatives are illustrated in Figure 7.7.

When an application requests a service from the OS, it does so by issuing a signal called an **interrupt.** A computer's OS recognizes many interrupts, some generated by application software and some generated by the hardware (for example, to signal an I/O completion). Each interrupt reflects a different class of service. For example, one type of interrupt is used to request monitor output and another interrupt is used to read data from the keyboard. Naturally, neither of these interrupts would be of interest to a client's LAN software. If the redirector catches the interrupt before it gets to the client's OS, it must change the interrupt handler. Generally, a computer has an interrupt vector in memory; the vector contains addresses of interrupt handler routines. To trap an interrupt, the redirector changes the addresses in the interrupt vector for the interrupts it wants to look at. In this way, the redirector reacts to the interrupt and decides whether it is a LAN request or a local request. Note that the redirector must know which interrupts to intercept. In the bottom half of Figure 7.7 the client's OS receives all the interrupts and passes those that are for a LAN server to the redirector. In this instance, the client's OS must be able to differentiate between local and server requests and react accordingly. For example, DOS versions 3.3 and beyond have this ability. Even though the client OS has this capability, the redirector intercept method can also be used.

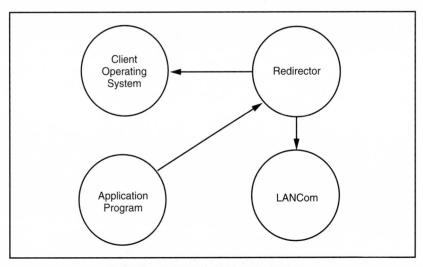

Redirector receives application requests and
routes local requests to the client OS and network
request to LAN communication process.

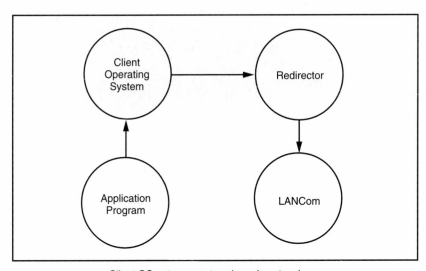

Client OS gets request and sends network
requests to the redirector.

Figure 7.7 Redirector Implementations

Once the redirector has the request, it must formulate a server message to indicate which service is to be provided. It formats a message with the proper request codes and sends the message to the LANCom process. The LANCom process creates a network layer protocol data unit (PDU) and passes it on to the MAC protocol layer. Examples of network layer protocol formats are given in Figure 7.3. The network layer PDU is encapsulated by the MAC protocol data and the frame is transmitted over the medium. The server recognizes its address in the MAC destination address portion of the frame and captures the message. The MAC layer checks for errors, strips off the MAC protocol data, and sends the network layer PDU up to the network layer process. The network layer removes the protocol data affixed by the client's network layer and sends the request to the server's OS for action. The request is fulfilled and the response is formatted by the server and sent back to the client in much the same manner as the client used in sending the message to the server.

SPECIFICS OF SERVER SOFTWARE

As previously stated, server software is more complex than workstation software because server software usually is multithreaded and because the software must work well with the hardware to provide efficient service. We have already discussed the benefits and general strategy of multithreading. Let us now look at several other functions that might be found in LAN server system software.

Server Operating Systems

Two basic approaches are taken in creating server software. One approach is to integrate the server and OS functions into one complete software package. The other approach is to write LAN functions that run under an existing OS, such as UNIX or OS/2. There are advantages and disadvantages to each approach. Table 7.3 lists several of the leading LAN network OSs.

Novell's **NetWare** is the leading example of the integrated software approach. The primary advantage of this approach is that the designers can optimize the software for LAN operation. That is, the system is designed specifically to provide server functions and can be custom-tailored for that one purpose. The disadvantage of this approach is it requires writing complex software that may already be provided by an existing OS. This makes the development effort longer and the maintenance more complex.

Creating LAN software that runs under an existing OS overcomes the disadvantages cited for the integrated approach. Examples of LAN software that run under an existing OS are Banyan Vines, which runs under UNIX, and IBM's OS/2 Warp Server, which runs under OS/2. The disadvantages are that a general-purpose OS may be less efficient than one designed to carry out only the special functions required for LAN services.

Some OSs, such as MS-DOS, are not well suited for hosting a LAN, primarily because of their inherent memory limitations, single-user orientation, and lack of security provisions. Despite these limitations, some LAN software runs under DOS and is successful in

Table 7.3   Several Leading LAN Operating Systems

LAN Name	Vendor Name	Topology	Protocols—Layers 2, 3, and 4
Apple Talk	Apple Computers, Inc.	Bus	CSMA/CA, CSMA/CD, token passing, Datagram Delivery Protocol (DDP), AppleTalk Transaction Protocol (ATP)
NetWare	Novell, Inc.	Ring or bus (supporting Ethernet, token ring, ARCnet)	CSMA/CD or token passing, TCP/IP, SPX/IPX
OS/2 Warp Server Advanced	IBM Corporation	Ring or bus	CSMA/CD, token passing, NetBEUI, TCP/IP
Windows NT Server	Microsoft, Inc.	Bus or ring	CSMA/CD, token passing, TCP/IP, SPX/IPX, NetBEUI
Vines	Banyan Systems, Inc.	Ethernet, token ring, and ARCnet	CSMA/CD, token passing, TCP/IP, SPX/IPX, NetBEUI
LANtastic	Artisoft, Inc.	Bus	CSMA/CD, token passing, NetBIOS, TCP/IP
PowerLAN	Performance Technology	Bus, ring	CSMA/CD, token passing, SPX/IPX, TCP/IP, NetBEUI

supporting LANs with few workstations or with limited server requirements. The OSs that most commonly host LAN software are UNIX and OS/2.

Let us look at some of the functions you might find in a LAN OS.

LAN Operating System Functions

A LAN OS provides a variety of special capabilities. Among these are I/O optimization and fault tolerance.

Optimized I/O

One of the main services provided by a server is file access. Optimizing this task, or **I/O optimization,** improves the performance of the server. This can be done in a variety of ways. Some methods are hardware oriented, and some are software oriented. One technique that is often used is disk caching, discussed in Chapter 5.

Another I/O optimization technique is **disk seek enhancement.** A disk read requires that the read/write heads be positioned to the proper disk location. The act of moving the read/write heads is called a seek. The place to which the heads are moved is called a cylinder or track. Disk requests typically arrive in random order. Disk seek enhancement arranges the requests in order so the read/write heads move methodically over the disk, reading data from the nearest location. This is illustrated in Table 7.4. In Table 7.4(a) you can see the order in which several disk requests are received. Table 7.4(b) shows the optimum way to access those records and the savings in

Table 7.4   Disk Seek Enhancement Example

(a) Disk read requests (cylinder or track) in order of arrival 50, 250, 25, 300, 250, 50, 300	Number of cylinders moved (assume a starting position of cylinder 0) 50 + 200 + 225+ 275 + 50 + 200 + 250 = 1250 cylinders
(b) Disk read requests (cylinder or track) in optimal order 25, 50, 50, 250, 250, 300, 300	25 + 25 + 0 + 200 + 0 + 50 + 0 = 300 cylinders Savings = 950 cylinders

number of cylinders when processing the requests in the optimum order. Reducing the seeks improves performance.

Fault Tolerance

Some network OSs provide increased reliability through a feature called **fault tolerance.** If you have only one server and it fails, the network is down. A LAN with fault tolerance allows the server to survive some failures that would ordinarily be disabling. Fault tolerance usually is provided by a combination of backup hardware components and software that is capable of using the backup hardware.

The lowest level of fault tolerance is the ability to recover quickly from a failure. That is, a failure that shuts the server down may occur, but the system can quickly be recovered to an operational state. One technique that makes this possible involves writing backup copies of critical disk information, such as disk directories and file allocation tables, to an alternative disk drive. Another helpful technique is called **read-after-write.** After writing data to a disk, the system reads the data again to ensure that no disk write errors occurred. If the data cannot be read again, the area of the disk containing that data is removed from future use and the data is written to a good area.

Fault tolerance also can be provided by **mirrored disks,** which are two disks that contain the same data. Whenever a disk write occurs, the data is written to both disk drives. If one of the disks fails, the other is available and processing continues. Mirrored disks have an additional benefit: Two disk drives are available for reads, so both disks can work simultaneously on behalf of two different requests. For added support some LAN servers also allow duplexed disk controllers. In such a configuration a controller can fail and another is available to continue working. Thus you can survive a controller failure and a disk failure.

Mirrored disk reliability can be extended using **redundant arrays of independent disks (RAID)** (sometimes the letter *I* in *RAID* stands for *inexpensive,* not *independent*). RAID technology spreads data over three or more disk drives. The stored data consists of the actual data plus **parity data:** additional data that provides the ability to reconstruct data that has been corrupted. Thus, if one drive fails, the data stored on that drive can be reconstructed from data stored on the remaining drives. Parity data can reconstructed because the remaining parts of the file are still available. If a section of the file is lost, it can be reconstructed from the parity data and the remaining parts of the file. The advantage of RAID over mirroring is that fewer disk drives are required for redundancy. For example, with mirroring, two drives of data require four disk drives; with RAID, the same information can be stored on three drives with the same level of reliability. Disk mirroring and RAID technology, illustrated in Figure 7.8, can provide more efficient data access because they make available multiple disk drives for reading and writing.

The best fault tolerance is provided by **duplexed servers.** With this configuration one server can fail and another is available to continue working. Even though it appears that this fault tolerance capability is primarily hardware oriented, software must exist that takes advantage of the duplexed hardware. A fault-tolerant duplexed server is illustrated in Figure 7.9. The key feature of duplexed servers is that any hardware or software component of the server may fail and the server remains available. Fault tolerance has been provided commercially by large systems since Tandem Computers introduced them in 1977. Today fault tolerance features are available in most of the leading NOSs.

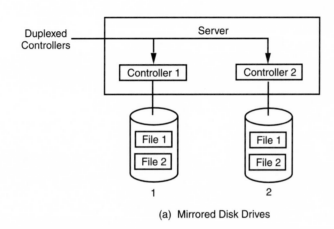

(a) Mirrored Disk Drives

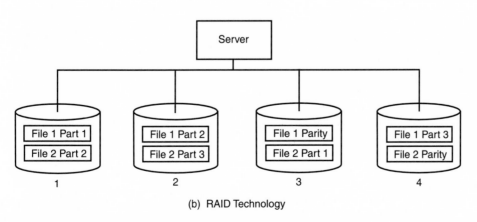

(b) RAID Technology

Figure 7.8 Mirrored Disk Drives and RAID Technology

As usual, one vendor's solution may differ from another's. Here we provide an overview of one system, Novell's **System Fault Tolerance (SFT) Level III,** that corresponds to Figure 7.9.

Two computers make up the duplexed server configuration. Each should have exactly the same configuration. Although configuration variations are allowed, the servers run at the lowest common configuration. Thus, if one server had 128 MB of memory and the other had only 64 MB, both would use 64 MB only. Both servers are attached to the LAN medium. An additional high-speed connection between the servers is used to allow the computers to exchange information without placing an extra load on the LAN medium.

One of the server machines is designated as the primary and the other as the backup. The primary's job is to satisfy client requests and send information to the backup server. Based on these messages, the backup server updates its memory and disks to keep them

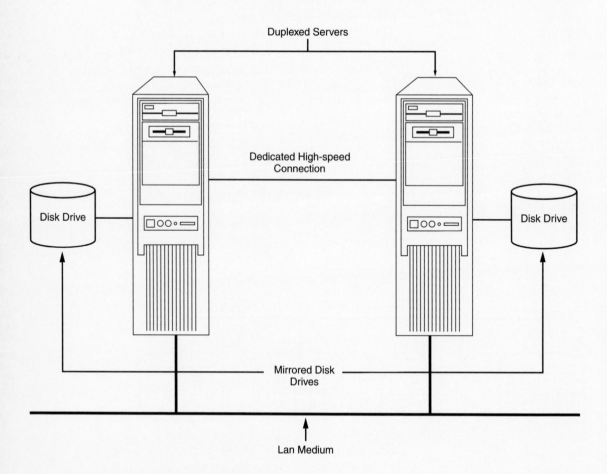

Figure 7.9   A Fault-Tolerant Duplexed Server

in step with the primary server's memory and disk images. If the primary fails, the backup server takes over and begins processing client requests.

UPS Software

In Chapter 5 we talked about uninterruptible power supplies (UPS) and the associated software. You may want to review that information at this time. A UPS system is an essential component of fault tolerance.

Print Spooler

LAN users share LAN printers. It ought to be obvious that only one user can be physically printing to a printer at one time and yet several users need to logically write to one printer at the same time. Logically writing to a printer means that the user has opened a printer and has written to that printer; however, the printed output may not be physically written to the printer at that time. The output is first written to a disk file and is printed after the complete output has been collected. The software subsystem that allows several users to logically write to one printer at the same time is called a spooler. The operation of a spooler is graphically shown in Figure 7.10. Let us trace the activity of a print job through the spooler.

The user at one workstation is using a word processing program to create a report, and the user at another workstation is using a spreadsheet program to prepare a budget. At nearly the same time, each user prints the document he or she is working on. The output is directed to LPT2 on each system. On each system LPT2 is mapped by the network software to the laser printer attached to the server. Before writing to the printer, each application first opens the printer. The redirector at each system directs the open request to the server. When the server receives the printer open request, it is passed to the spooler software. The spooler software prepares to receive each workstation's printed output into a disk file. When each application receives an acknowledgment that the spooler is ready, it begins to send output to the printer.

The spooler receives the output from each workstation and stores it in that workstation's print file on disk. This process continues until each workstation is done. When the application closes the printer file, the print job is ready to be physically written to the printer.

Be aware that some applications do not close the print file until the user explicitly chooses a close printer option or until the application terminates. For example, this was true of some early spreadsheet software. If this occurs, a user may not get a printout when expected. For example, suppose that Maria is working on a spreadsheet and prints a portion of it. If the printing had been sent to a locally attached printer, it would print immediately. With a spooler, however, the spreadsheet program does not close the printer, and the job is left open. This allows for another portion of the spreadsheet to be printed directly after the first print range. The spreadsheet program continues to hold the file open until Maria exits from the spreadsheet. Her job then is scheduled for printing. In this case printing on a LAN differs from printing to a local printer and may not be what Maria wants. She may want the range to be printed immediately so she can use that information for her further work. For such instances some spoolers also allow the print job to be closed if a certain time elapses before the spooler receives additional print data. This feature allows the user to obtain the printed results without exiting from the application.

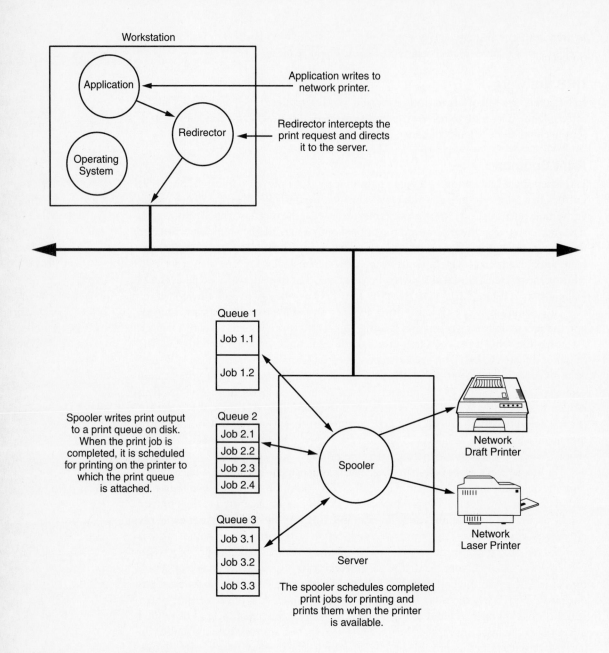

Figure 7.10   Spooler Operating Environment

When a print job is closed, the spooler schedules it for printing. Spoolers have a priority scheme by which they decide which job prints next. Some spoolers print the jobs in the order in which they became ready to print (first in, first out); some print the smallest available job; others print jobs according to user-assigned priorities. When the job has been

Table 7.5   Some Spooler Options

Collect printed output	Set/change job priorities
Direct print jobs to designated printers	Add/delete printers
Hold jobs in disk queue after printing	Start/stop printers
Hold jobs in disk queue before printing	Start/stop spooler process
View jobs on hold in print queue	Print banners
Set number of print copies	Close print jobs based on timeout interval
Delete jobs from print queue	Print statistical reports
Attach/detach printers from print queue	

printed, it may be removed from the disk to make room for other print jobs. Alternatively, the job may be held on disk for printing at a later time, for printing to a different device, or for perusal from a workstation. Spooler systems provide a variety of options regarding the association of logical print devices with physical printers and the treatment of jobs captured in the spooler files. Some of these options are listed in Table 7.5. We also discuss the set up and management of the printing environment in Chapter 12.

Backup Software

Chapter 5 discussed backup hardware. The software used to perform the backups is as important as the hardware. **Backup software** is responsible for reading the files being backed up and writing them to the backup device. During recovery a restoration module reads the backup medium and writes the data back to disk. Several backup software options are available. They all provide the basic functions of backing up and restoring data. They differ with respect to how they do this, the options they provide, the devices they support, and their ease of use. Backup devices often come with a backup/restore program (both capabilities are contained on one program) and most LAN system software includes a backup/restore module. For example, Novell's backup/restore program for one version of their network software is NBACKUP. However, some LAN administrators choose to purchase a separate, more functional backup system than the LAN or backup device versions. In Chapter 5, Table 5.3 lists some of the features supported by backup software. Backup procedures, disaster planning, and additional coverage of backup and recovery are found in Chapter 13.

Utility and Administrative Software

A LAN administrator must have utility and administrative software to assist in performing the administrative and management tasks of configuration changes, system monitoring, security, problem diagnosis, tuning, and capacity planning. These software modules are discussed in later chapters where appropriate.

SUMMARY

LAN software can be separated into two classes: system software and application software. LAN system software in the servers and workstations is responsible for carrying out the LAN functions. Application software solves business problems. LAN system software is found on servers and workstations.

Workstation system software is responsible for intercepting application I/O requests and deciding whether the request is local or network. If the request is a local one, the workstation's LAN software passes it along to the workstation's OS. If the request is for a network resource, the workstation's LAN software formats a network message and sends it over the network for processing. The workstation's LAN software is also responsible for accepting LAN messages and passing them along to the proper application. Because LAN workstation software must remain resident in the workstation's memory, a stand-alone workstation may need a memory upgrade to run some LAN applications.

LAN server software is more complex than workstation software. Some functions it may provide are I/O optimization, printer services, utility and administrative support, access security, fault tolerance, file backup and restoration, and contention resolution. These functions help to make performance better, improve reliability, or protect data from accidental or intentional damage.

When choosing LAN software, it is important to consider how that software will interoperate with other software, other networks, and your hardware. Poor interoperability increases the complexity of using a LAN and decreases its usability.

Key Terms

backup software
client/server dialogue
disk seek enhancement
duplexed servers
fault tolerance
interoperability
interrupt
I/O optimization
mirrored disks
NetWare

operating system (OS)
OS/2 Warp Server
parity data
read-after-write
redirector
redundant arrays of independent disks
  (RAID)
StreetTalk
System Fault Tolerance (SFT) Level III
Vines

Review Questions

1. Explain the workings of the services advertising protocol (SAP).
2. Explain the address resolution protocol (ARP).
3. What services are provided by the network directory?
4. Explain how an application's network request is processed by both the workstation and the server.
5. What is the purpose of I/O optimization? Give two examples.
6. What is the benefit of fault-tolerant servers?
7. Describe three fault tolerance capabilities.
8. Explain how a print spooler works.
9. Compare RAID and disk mirroring.
10. Describe Novell's SFT III capability.

Problems and Exercises

1. Use the literature to identify and briefly describe five capabilities of fault tolerance systems, such as Novell's SFT system or Tandem's NonStop systems. The following magazine sources

may prove helpful: *Network Management, LAN Times, LAN,* and *Network Computing.* You may use CD-ROM sources, such as *Computer Select.*

2. Research the literature for references to a LAN server that runs under the DOS operating system. How many users does the system support? Attempt to determine the expected level of performance.

3. Investigate one of the backup/restore software packages available. What functions does it provide?

4. You have been asked to configure the hardware for a LAN to provide automation capabilities for a small office. The office manager wants you to provide a LAN that will use four IBM 586 systems with 8 MB of memory, two 386 systems with 2 MB of memory, two 486 systems with 4 MB of memory, one laser printer, and two dot-matrix printers that the office currently owns. Draw a network diagram of your proposed LAN using a bus topology. Label all hardware components in your diagram. Prepare a report to accompany your diagram that gives the following details:

   a. the equipment, software, and cabling that will be needed to connect each device to the LAN

   b. necessary upgrades to any of the existing hardware to make it LAN-usable

6. Consider the office LAN described in Problem 5. Suppose that some employees want to access the LAN from their home to transfer files and do remote printing. Configure the hardware, software, and communications capabilities required at the LAN and user end of the connection.

7. Suppose the office described in Problem 5 wants to add FAX capabilities to the network. The capabilities needed include the ability to send and receive FAX transmissions and to store FAX images on disk. Images sent and received may be in either hard copy or disk image format. Describe the hardware, software, and communications equipment necessary to create this capability.

Chapter 8

LAN Operating System Implementation

CHAPTER PREVIEW

In Chapter 7 we described the generic functions of a network operating system (NOS). In this chapter we look at representative implementations of NOSs. We cannot cover all implementations; instead, we have chosen NOSs that are widely adopted or that provide unique capabilities. We have also chosen to discuss peer-to-peer NOSs as well as server-oriented NOSs. Peer-to-peer implementations are used primarily for LANs with few users. NOSs covered in this chapter include products by the following vendors:

Artisoft

Banyan

IBM

Microsoft

Novell

We start our discussion with the most widely implemented NOS.

NOVELL NETWORK OPERATING SYSTEMS

Over time Novell has offered several versions of network operating systems. Today, Novell offers three basic systems with a variety of configuration options for two of the versions. For small networks using peer-to-peer workstations, Novell offers Personal NetWare. A **peer-to-peer network** is one that has no dedicated servers, and the network administrator can make the resources of each network node accessible to other network nodes. For high-end networks Novell offers **NetWare 3.x** and **NetWare 4.x.**

Personal NetWare

Personal NetWare (PNW) debuted as NetWare Lite. Its primary attributes are simplicity, flexibility, and the ability to share files, printers, modems, and CD-ROMs. Novell provides PNW as an entry-level system. Small offices with up to 25 desktop systems may find PNW adequate for resource sharing, and up to 50 concurrent users

187

can be supported. As the network grows, customers will probably migrate to a more robust NOS such as NetWare 3.x or 4.x.

As a peer-to-peer network, PNW allows more configuration flexibility than its server-based relatives NetWare 3.x and 4.x. In configuring the network, almost any computer's peripheral devices can be shared; alternatively, one or more computers can be identified as servers and only components of those servers will be shared. In between these configurations lies a continuum of sharing. That is, the network designer can choose which resources are shared and which resources are private to a computer.

PNW runs under DOS version 3.3 and above and Microsoft Windows 3.1 or above. Note that Microsoft Windows for Workgroups and Windows 95 also provide peer-to-peer networking capabilities. Users of these operating environments may elect to use the networking capabilities of those products rather than investing in additional software for PNW. It is the author's opinion, however, that PNW is easier to install and work with than the networking in either of these Windows products.

The hardware requirements for PNW are the LAN adapter, cabling, 640 KB of RAM for DOS or 2 MB of RAM for Windows, and 8 MB of available disk space. That is, a minimal system is capable of running PNW and expensive upgrades are not necessary for most of today's desktop systems. The software supports Ethernet, token ring, and ARCnet LAN adapters. The software cost per node is under $75.

For small workgroups who simply want to share applications and printers, PNW is a good low-cost option. On the other hand, PNW lacks security capabilities, fault tolerance, management tools, and some of the capabilities we have come to expect of NOSs.

NetWare 3.x

NetWare 3.x (formerly known as NetWare 386) and NetWare 4.x are Novell's server-based NOS offerings. NetWare 4.x is newer than 3.x, but NetWare 4.x at the outset was not marketed as a direct replacement for NetWare 3.x. Both products are actively marketed and supported. The primary difference between the two NOSs is the way in which network information is stored. NetWare 3.x uses a server-oriented bindery whereas 4.x uses a network-oriented directory like that discussed in Chapter 7. Eventually, NetWare 3.x will probably be phased out.

The NetWare 3.x network information database is called the **bindery.** The bindery consists of three files that contain the names of objects (such as users, print queues, and groups) properties of objects, and values associated with those properties. For example, for a group object we might have a property called members and multiple values for members of that group. The bindery is server-centric. This means that it primarily contains data specific to that server. Thus, if a user needs access to two servers, that user would have a user entry in the bindery of each server; furthermore, on each server would be values for the properties of that user, such as passwords. The information stored on the different servers is not synchronized. This can result in unnecessary duplication and inconsistency in the user's stored data. Also, if a user were allowed to use ten servers, ten separate entries would need to be made, one for each server. In contrast, in a network directory, only one entry would be required. NetWare 3.x is well suited to LANs with one or two servers. As the number of servers increases, the effectiveness of NetWare 3.x decreases relative to NetWare 4.x and other NOSs.

Lack of a network directory makes NetWare 3.x less suitable for large networks; however, for smaller networks, it provides a robust set of capabilities enhanced by a vast collection of third-party hardware and software. Let us now look at some of the specifics of NetWare 3.x.

A single server can support up to 16 printers in a variety of configurations. The print server process that runs in NetWare 3.x server can support at most 16 printer definitions, and only one print server can run on a server at a time. Printers may be directly attached to the server, attached to dedicated printer server systems, or attached to a nondedicated print server. A dedicated print server system does nothing but control printers and interface to the server's print server software module. For example, some installations have used outmoded computers such as 286 CPU systems as dedicated print servers. Nondedicated print servers allow printers attached to client machines to be shared among network users. The disadvantage of nondedicated printers is the ability of a user to disable network printing by turning their computer off or by running a program that causes their system to hang. The printer alternatives are illustrated in Figure 8.1. We discuss NetWare printing specifics in Chapter 12. NetWare printing is used as the specific example in that discussion.

NetWare security in NetWare 3.x is greatly enhanced over the capabilities provided in the previous version, NetWare 2.x. Installations that upgraded from 2.x to 3.x found a significant increase in security capabilities. Security provisions address file access, printer access, user requirements, and intruder detection.

When we think of security, we usually think first of controlling unauthorized users and unauthorized access to files. Every user on the system has a user ID. Network administrators have the option of making passwords mandatory. Security-conscious installations use this option rather than the alternative, which is having passwords a user option. Passwords can be set up so that they must be changed periodically and must have a minimum number of characters. A password history can be used to ensure that new passwords are created when the password expiration time arrives or whenever users change their passwords. File access security is based on a user, groups to which a user belongs, inherited rights, and rights given explicitly to a user. The scheme is both comprehensive and complicated. Details of setting up security and determining a user's access rights are given in Chapter 11. NetWare security is used as the specific example for security implementations.

Like many network systems, network management tools are severely lacking in NetWare 3.x but improvements in this situation are constantly being made. A variety of Novell and third-party network management utilities are available, but there is no comprehensive, coordinated management capability. Network administrators must therefore assemble a set of tools from a variety of sources to provide an adequate level of diagnostic and monitoring capabilities. Backup and restore software are included with the system, but many installations prefer to purchase more comprehensive backup software.

NetWare 3.x allows for disk mirroring, disk duplexing, and RAID drives. It also provides read-after-write capabilities and the ability to move bad areas of the disk to another part of the disk. In addition, NetWare 3.x supports a Transaction Tracking System (TTS) that is able to restore the integrity of data files by reversing work done on transactions that do not complete successfully. Using TTS will help prevent data inconsistencies following a failure. System Fault Tolerance (SFT) III, which allows server duplexing (as discussed in Chapter 7), is also available.

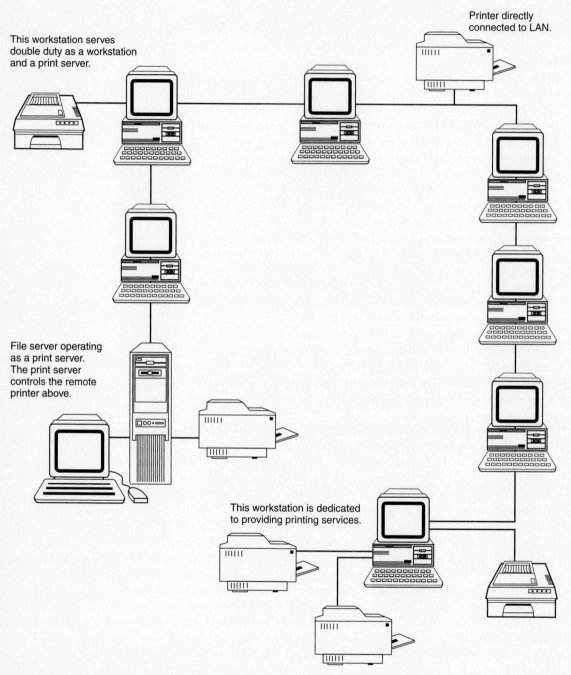

This workstation serves double duty as a workstation and a print server.

Printer directly connected to LAN.

File server operating as a print server. The print server controls the remote printer above.

This workstation is dedicated to providing printing services.

Figure 8.1   LAN Printer Configurations

I/O optimization features include disk caching and elevator seeking. With **elevator seeking,** disk access requests are ordered according to their location on the disk. Elevator seeking allows the read/write heads to move systematically over the disk from the inner tracks to the outer tracks and back again. This prevents excessive disk seeking. Faster access to files on disk is provided via directory hashing. Hashing allows a file's location to be determined more quickly than is possible with a sequential search.

A rudimentary accounting facility is available but is generally not widely used. Accounting allows an installation to track such events as connect time, disk space used, disk reads, disk writes, and service requests. The information reported by the accounting system allows an installation to apportion costs among users or to perform basic capacity planning.

Starting with NetWare Version 3.11, Novell included Message Handling Services (MHS), which provides for delivery of messages among servers. Also included as part of MHS is a basic electronic mail system.

NetWare 4.x

NetWare 4.x is currently the flagship of the Novell NOS line. Naturally, the next version is already on the drawing board and 4.x will eventually give way to 5.x. NetWare 4.x provides nearly all the capabilities of 3.x versions, although the user interfaces have changed considerably in some areas. Version 4.x also includes several important new features. As mentioned in the discussion of NetWare 3.x, the major distinguishing feature of NetWare 4.x is the network directory called **Novell Directory Services (NDS).** In NetWare releases 4.0 and 4.1, NDS was called NetWare Directory Services (also NDS). Novell has made NDS available for NOSs other than NetWare, so the name change was appropriate. By making NDS available to other OSs, Novell can position its product at the heart of the network, the repository of information on the enterprise network.

NDS is a global, hierarchical directory that allows replication and distribution. A sample directory tree is shown in Figure 8.2. In the sample directory tree, some objects are subordinate to other objects. Objects that can have subordinate items are called container objects. Some of the container objects defined in NetWare include Country, Organization, and Organizational Unit. Objects that cannot have subordinate objects are called leaf objects. Some of the leaf objects available in the directory are Computer, Group, Server, Print Queue, Print Server, Printer, User, and Volume. Each directory tree has a unique top-level object called the Root object or the Top.

Distributed portions of the directory are called partitions. NDS uses a hierarchical naming convention, with the naming hierarchy up to 15 levels deep. Thus, a generic 4-level object name in the directory might be

```
company-name.region-name.department-name.user-name
```

NDS is a global directory because it can span the entire enterprise network. As you will see later, some directory services are restricted to network segments. We discussed the issues of replication and distribution in Chapter 7. The CCITT X.500 standard served as a model for the implementation of NDS, but NDS is not X.500 compliant.

Defining the directory tree is accomplished via two utilities: NWADMIN, which is a Windows application, and NETADMIN, which is a DOS-based menu application. The

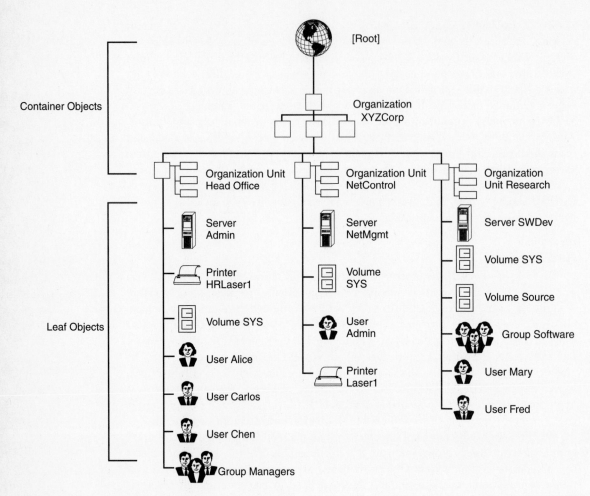

Figure 8.2   Novell Directory Tree

template for the directory definition is called the schema. The schema contains the definitions of the objects that can be included in the directory and the properties of those objects. Developers are able to extend the schema by adding new objects or new properties to existing objects. This is accomplished via application program interface (API) procedures available in a developers' toolkit. Some of the available objects and a partial list of the properties for each are given in Table 8.1.

   There are other differences between 3.x and 4.x. One of the shortcomings of NetWare 3.x is that it is not well suited to LANs with hundreds of users. NetWare 3.x generally can support up to 250 users. A design objective of 4.x was to support LANs of up to 1000 users. The user interface in 4.x has been upgraded. Although there are still some menuing and command line utilities, a graphical user interface (GUI) is available. GUIs make working with the network easier. Another key difference is that 4.x provides

Table 8.1 Sample NDS Objects and Properties

Object	Some Properties	
Computer	Network address	Server
	Serial number	Status
	Operator	Owner
Country (container)	Name	Description
Group	Common name	Full name
	Description	Members
	E-mail address	
NetWare server	Network address	Status
	Operator	Version
Organization	Name	Postal code
	Description	State/province
	Postal address	Telephone number
Print Server	Network address	Status
	Operator	
Printer	Default queue	Operator
	Host device	Status
	Network address	
Queue	Device	Server
	Network address	Volume
	Operator	
User	Account balance	Language
	Address	Last logon time
	E-mail address	Logon script
	FAX number	Password expiration time,
	Groups	change allowed, unique required,
	Home directory	required, minimum length
	Telephone number	User ID
Volume	Host server	Status

disk compression utilities that are not available with 3.x. Finally, with 4.x, Novell has provided support for symmetric multiprocessing (SMP) architectures. SMP systems have two or more CPUs that allow parallel processing and greater throughput.

The distribution CD-ROM includes a complete set of on-line documents and a document viewer. This allows the entire set of documents to be installed on-line. Unlike 3.x, NetWare 4.x comes with only a few manuals oriented to installation, upgrading from previous versions of NetWare, and explanation of NDS. Hard-copy documentation is available for an added cost. Navigating the on-line documents is easy and users can print portions of the document as needed.

NetWare 3.x's support for only 16 network printers on a network with 250 users can be a problem. In 4.x, each server can support up to 256 printers. Installing the print system in 4.x is easier than in 3.x. Chapter 12 presents additional details on 4.x printing.

NetWare 4.x generally provides all the security capabilities mentioned for NetWare 3.x, and 4.x extends those capabilities. Two significant enhancements have been provided. Perhaps the most significant is the ability to **audit** network activities. Users with administration privileges and hackers can disrupt the system and make unauthorized changes to files. NetWare 4.x provides an audit facility that allows a user independent of LAN administrators to monitor selected activities. A wide range of events can be selected to audit. Some of these are listed in Table 8.2. The key to the audit capability is the independence of auditing and administration. A LAN administrator is unable to see what events the auditor is monitoring and the audit data itself. Furthermore, the LAN administrator cannot delete the audit files unless the administrator is able to obtain the auditor's password. A second important security capability is the extension of security to NDS attributes. That is, a user may be given the ability to change the telephone number of a user object but be unable to view or change other attributes.

As with NetWare 3.12, the management software an installation needs will probably come from several sources. Included with NetWare 4.x are utilities for remote management that let administrators control a server from any network node. The Remote Management Facility (RMF) allows an administrator to execute console commands, load and unload **NetWare Loadable Modules (NLMs),** and reboot a file server. An NLM is an application-oriented software module that runs in the server. Both Novell and third-party software vendors provide NLMs that are dynamically bound to or unbound from the NetWare OS while the server is operational. For example, the print server application runs as an NLM. NDS maintenance can be effected via both a Microsoft Windows GUI and DOS menu interfaces. Beyond that, you need to purchase additional software, some of which is available from Novell. Novell and Intel have combined resources to provide ManageWise. ManageWise allows administrators to monitor server operations by recording information such as memory, CPU, and disk usage. It also provides information on the printing environment. Novell also sells NetWare LANalyzer, an NLM that monitors packets sent to and transmitted by a server. With LANalyzer, a network administrator can identify the type and source of protocol problems. Because the NDS is fundamental to the operation of 4.x, it is essential that tools be available for managing, maintaining, and recovering the NDS system. NDS tools are available that allow administrators to manipulate the NDS tree. Branches of the tree can be replicated and distributed and distributed branches can be merged.

For customers who have used or are also using NetWare 3.x servers, Version 4.x provides interoperability features. Version 3.x servers use the bindery files and many soft-

Table 8.2   Sample Audit Events

Create/delete directory	File open/close/create/delete	File read/write
File rename/move	User logon/logoff	User creation/deletion
Print queue create/delete	Server down/restart	Volume mount/demount

ware modules interface only to this form of directory. NetWare 4.x provides bindery emulation to support bindery-oriented interfaces.

NetWare 4.x provides interfaces to a variety of other networks and protocols, including

IBM System Network Architecture (SNA) gateway

X.25 gateway

LAN-to-LAN interconnection via X.25 or T-1 lines

Structured Query Language (SQL) server

Transmission Control Protocol/Internet Protocol (TCP/IP)

remote access services

World Wide Web server

Some of these features are also available in NetWare 3.x.

MICROSOFT NETWORK OPERATING SYSTEMS

Microsoft has had several NOS products. OS/2 LAN Manager was an NOS based on the OS/2 operating system. It was similar to an IBM product called OS/2 LAN Server, which has evolved into OS/2 Warp Server. Microsoft also provided peer-to-peer networking with its Windows for Workgroups product, an enhanced version of Windows 3.1. Both products have been replaced by **Windows 95** and **Windows NT Server** for peer-to-peer and server-based networks, respectively.

Windows 95

Windows 95's LAN capabilities are bundled with the software, so there is no additional software cost to set up a network. A Network Neighborhood icon is established on the desktop to help users identify the available servers and printers. Windows 95 allows users to connect to server-based networks such as NetWare and Windows NT Server as well as with other computers in a peer-to-peer mode. A user can provide security capabilities by password-protecting resources. For other users to gain access to those resources, they need to provide the correct password. Under this mechanism, if you have 10 shared directories (called **folders** in Windows 95), there will be 10 passwords involved, one for each folder. Of course, this could be a problem if one user needed access to all 10 folders. That user would need to remember 10 passwords and the folders to which they pertained. Security can be resolved on a name basis if a NetWare or Windows NT server is available. With user-level control, the above user could provide a user ID and a single password to the server. This user would then be allowed to access all resources for which she has been granted access without supplying an individual password for each. Sharing can be on a read-only basis or full-access basis. Peer-to-peer sharing can be done between Windows 95, Windows for Workgroups, and Windows NT client machines.

Windows NT Server

Windows NT Server (NTS) is enjoying considerably more success than its predecessor, OS/2 LAN Manager. NTS has gained market share and acceptance since its initial release. A portion of NTSs acceptance comes from its capabilities as an application server. At the beginning of this text we mentioned that a variety of services can be provided by a server. In the past, the principal services were file and print. A server role that has been expanding is application services. An application server does more than deliver files or records and handle printing. Application servers participate in the processing of the data. Thus, an application server allows the processing work to be divided between the client and the server. The popularity of NTS as an application server is attributable to the NT operating system. Because it is a 32-bit operating system, it can directly access up to 4 GB of main memory. NT supports preemptive multitasking and multithreading, which means that it can run several tasks concurrently and switch between them efficiently. Preemption means that a running process can be suspended by the OS to allow another process access to the CPU. Finally, NTS has good support for servers with multiple processors, allowing for parallel processing.

As of this writing, NTS does not have a global, distributed network directory; however, one has been announced and will probably be available by the time you read this. Instead, NTS provides a limited directory service called a domain. In a single-server network, a user logs on to the server and the user's capabilities are limited to that server. In a network with multiple servers, a user can do the same thing (log on to a given server and use that server's resources). As an alternative, a user could log on to a domain server and via that single logon gain access to the resources of multiple servers within that domain. Each domain has one primary domain controller and may have multiple backup domain controllers. Both primary and backup domain controllers contain a complete copy of the domain database. Backup domain controllers provide user authentication and authorization and may be promoted to a primary domain controller if the primary domain controller fails. All updates such as adding new users and password changes are made on the primary domain controller and then the changes are synchronized on the backup domain controllers. A domain may be geographically distributed. If a domain contains geographically distributed nodes, at least one server on each geographically distributed LAN segment should be a backup or primary domain controller. This avoids accessing the domain database over slower WAN links. For controlling access in department or campus environments, **domain services** is as effective as a global directory. Interdomain sharing is possible via a mechanism known as trusting. A trust relationship may be established between two domains and as long as this relationship is maintained, users in one domain can access resources in the other trusting domain. Companies that are geographically distributed or have completely separate networks will likely have several distinct domains, each of which will be administered individually; therefore, in the trusted domain situation, each domain database is maintained separately. Contrast this with the single-database concept of a global directory.

In the fault-tolerance area, NTS supports disk mirroring and RAID disk arrays. NTS can be installed in DOS-formatted disk drives (FAT format), high-performance file system formats (HPFS), or Windows NT file systems (NTFS). With FAT formats, installations lose some of the file security capabilities because the DOS file format does not support many file attributes. The benefit of this format is that NTS can be installed in disks that are currently in use and that disk can be used for DOS applications, Windows applications, and the NT server. This may be of benefit in small installations, where the server may also be needed as a desktop system. The HPFS format allows OS/2 disk access. The NTFS is preferred because it provides all the benefits of NTS security and performance. The management utilities are Windows-based, making the management tasks easier.

IBM NETWORK OPERATING SYSTEMS

Like Novell and Microsoft, IBM has both peer-to-peer and server-based NOSs. On the peer-to-peer side IBM provides OS/2 Warp Connect and on the server side it has OS/2 Warp Server. Both are obviously based on the OS/2 operating system. Both offerings are 32-bit OSs that provide multitasking and multithreading.

OS/2 Warp Connect

The LAN capabilities of **OS/2 Warp Connect** allow file and print sharing within a workgroup. Warp Connect allows connection not only to other Warp Connect systems but also to Windows for Workgroups, Windows NT, and Windows 95 systems. Also included are Internet browsers, protocols, and utilities. Installation of Warp Connect is made easier because the software is able to detect the installed network components and to automatically do some of the configuration that must be done manually with other peer networks.

Warp Server Advanced

Warp Server Advanced (WS) is the successor to IBM's first generation of NOSs, LAN Server. Both operating systems are based on the OS/2 operating system. Like Windows NT Server, the WS platform is well suited to application services as well as file and print servers. At this writing, support for multiprocessor systems is scheduled for release soon. WS supports up to 1000 users; a sister version, Warp Server, is available for smaller LANs of up to 120 users. WS does not currently support a global network directory; however, a global directory has been announced and, like multiprocessor support, it will be available soon. In the meantime, users can take advantage of domain directory services similar to those described for Windows NT.

BANYAN VINES

Banyan Vines is recognized for its support for large networks and network interconnections. Banyan Vines runs on UNIX-based servers. Being UNIX based gives Banyan a distinct advantage, because many WANs contain nodes running the UNIX operating system. This makes it easier for Vines systems to connect to those nodes. Moreover, a server based on UNIX can be effectively used as an application system in addition to providing LAN services; that is, the server platform can function not only as a server but also as a platform for running application programs. OS/2-based operating systems allow multitasking but not multiuser capabilities and thus cannot match UNIX-based machines, which allow several users to run applications.

One of the major strengths of Vines is its network directory, **StreetTalk.** For several years StreetTalk was the sole LAN network directory service. As you have already read, other NOSs now support this capability. StreetTalk can be replicated on any server in the

Table 8.3   Common NOS Capabilities

Password restrictions (minimum length, force changes, history)	Intruder detection	User account expiration dates
File level access control	Protocol support (TCP/IP, IPX/SPX, NetBIOS)	Printer support on server, client, directly connected to medium
Remote console	SNMP support	Client support (DOS, Macintosh, OS/2, Windows 3.1, Windows 95)

network, thus providing a measure of fault tolerance as well as making resource lookup more efficient. Like NDS, StreetTalk uses a hierarchical naming structure to define network objects. This format makes network object names easy to formulate and remember. A unique feature of StreetTalk that is particularly useful for international networks is the ability to store certain information such as status and error messages in several languages.

Common Capabilities

All of the server-based NOSs discussed so far have a wealth of common capabilities. Some of these are covered in Table 8.3.

ARTISOFT LANTASTIC

We have already mentioned several possibilities for peer networking, and several other alternatives exist. Here we cover one example, **Artisoft's LANtastic.** LANtastic has consistently been recognized for its continuing leadership in peer networking. Do not infer this to mean that LANtastic's competitors have inferior products; on the contrary, there are several outstanding peer NOSs from which you can choose.

LANtastic provides more than just the basic file- and print-sharing capabilities. Included in the system are e-mail, fax and modem sharing, file security, and Internet access. Software is available that runs on DOS, Windows, Macintosh, and OS/2 operating systems. LANtastic does not have a global directory, but this is not a disadvantage because you would not expect such a feature in a peer network. Each computer in the network has a name and any drive or printer on a LANtastic computer can be shared. A node that allows sharing becomes a network server as well as a client. Access to shared drives may be by drive mapping, where a drive letter is assigned to a nonlocal drive. Referring to files on that drive is exactly like referring to local drive files. As an alternative, you can browse the network neighborhood by selecting servers and drives.

LANtastic security is effected in two ways. Individual server nodes can have an access control list that allows or restricts access to the resources on that node. Alternatively, one server can be designated as a remote account server that controls access lists to networkwide resources. Access control can be based on individuals or groups and an access control list can be established for each shared object.

Interoperability of Server Software

If you have a large LAN, you may need more than one file server. (The point at which a second server is needed varies according to the number of active, concurrent users and their server access profiles.) If two or more servers are required, you must ensure that they

**Table 8.4   Possible Complications of Having Two
Network Operating Systems in One Network**

Compatibility of user identifiers and passwords

Synchronization of user identifiers and passwords across servers

Ability to simultaneously access data on two servers

Ability to access data on one server and print to spooler on another

Applications that can run from both servers

Support for common application program interfaces (APIs)

Support for common protocols at the OSI network and transport layers

Ability to use/have two redirector processes

operate correctly. Often, if all servers are using the same hardware and software platforms, they can operate correctly in concert. It is not always true, however, that two different server software packages can interoperate correctly. Although this problem is gradually being resolved as NOS vendors realize that heterogeneous networks are becoming more common, some incompatibilities still exist. Moreover, when new NOS versions are released, sometimes client software from other vendors is not immediately available.

What do we mean by interoperability? Basically **interoperability** is the ability of all network components to connect to the network and to communicate with shared network resources. With a global view this means the ability to interconnect different networks and to have nodes on one network able to communicate with nodes on the same network or another network (provided they have the appropriate security). On a single network it means that any node can access resources to which it has appropriate security. Interoperability is usually easy in a homogeneous network (one in which only one network operating system version is used and where the workstations are all of the same type and use the same operating system). Networks using a mixture of network operating systems and workstation platforms make interoperability more complex.

One of the current areas of concern for interoperability is in the area of network directory support. We now have two NOS vendors with directory service available and at least two more such releases are imminent. If two or more networks using directory services from two different NOS vendors are merged, it is necessary for the directories to be merged as well. Whose directory becomes dominant and how objects can be referenced requires some work. Some of the complications of interoperability are given in Table 8.4. How well the server operating systems can handle these issues affects the interoperability of the network.

SUMMARY

In this chapter we looked at specific implementations of NOSs. Some of these were peer-to-peer LANs that are appropriate for small LANs and some were dedicated server-based NOSs more suitable for larger LANs and internets. The major emphases in LAN development at this time are global, distributed, replicated network directories, Internet access, management tools, and interoperability.

Two of the four server NOSs, Novell NetWare 4.x and Banyan Vines, have network directories available. Microsoft Windows NT Server and IBM's Warp Server Advanced have domain services. Both Microsoft and IBM have plans for global network directories. All of the server-based NOSs and Artisoft's LANtastic provide Internet access and future releases of all products will probably include improvements and extensions of the current services. In general, all of the NOSs are weak with respect to management capabilities. Third-party tools can be used to supplement NOS vendor offerings. Interoperability with respect to client operating systems is generally good; most NOS vendors support DOS, Windows, OS/2, and Macintosh client OSs. Generally, clients are able to attach to servers running different NOSs. Interoperability of management tools and network directories needs improvement.

With the variety of NOSs available, most users' LAN operating system needs can be met.

Key Terms

Artisoft	NetWare 4.x
audit	NetWare Loadable Module (NLM)
Banyan	Novell
bindery	Novell Directory Services (NDS)
domain services	OS/2 Warp Connect
elevator seeking	peer-to-peer network
folders	Personal NetWare (PNW)
IBM	StreetTalk
interoperability	Vines
LANtastic	Warp Server Advanced (WS)
Microsoft	Windows 95
NetWare 3.x	Windows NT Server

Review Questions

1. Compare the network directory services of NetWare 4.x and Microsoft Windows NT Server.
2. Compare NetWare 3.x and 4.x.
3. Why is Windows NT Server well suited for application services?
4. Compare Personal NetWare and Artisoft's LANtastic.
5. What does the bindery do in NetWare 3.x.? What is its counterpart in NetWare 4.x?
6. What is elevator seeking? How does it improve performance?
7. Describe the Windows NT Server domain service.
8. How is security implemented in LANtastic?

Problems and Exercises

1. Choose one of the server-based NOSs discussed in this chapter. What is the current release level? What new features were added in the last release?
2. Research the literature and find the global network directory that is most widely implemented. What makes it the leading directory service?
3. Research another peer-to-peer NOS. Compare its features with those of LANtastic.
4. Use the literature to identify and briefly describe five capabilities of fault tolerance systems, such as Novell's SFT III system or Tandem's NonStop systems.
5. Research the literature for references to a LAN server that runs under the DOS operating system. How many users does the system support? Attempt to determine the expected level of performance.

Chapter 9

Application Software

CHAPTER PREVIEW

In the preceding chapters you read about LAN system software. Realize, however, that a LAN is simply a tool that allows its users to do their work more effectively. We use LANs because they provide cost-effective solutions to business problems. It is the application software that allows us to solve these problems. We can easily lose sight of this when we get involved in LAN technology. In this chapter you will read about the general considerations for choosing application software. Several key application software systems are covered in some detail.

Specific topics you will read about include

distributed computing

client/server computing

database software

workgroup software

primary business software

setting software standards

With stand-alone computers, all the processing is done on one computer. Networks give us another way to process data: sharing the processing among two or more computers. This kind of processing is called distributed processing or sometimes client/server (C/S) computing. We begin this chapter with an overview of distributed computing.

DISTRIBUTED SYSTEM DEFINITIONS

Systems can be distributed in a variety of ways. When you were reading about LANs in the preceding chapters, although it was not explicitly stated, many of the LAN's resources were distributed. For example, a LAN's processing load is split among servers and workstations, both acting in concert to help workers attain their objectives. In this use of the LAN, processing is distributed. Data also can be distributed over two or more nodes, such as on file servers, SQL servers, and workstations. However, although data is distributed, there is not always a distributed database management capability. In these instances, the distributed data is treated as islands of data without the benefit of the comprehensive, coordinated management of a distributed database management system.

The ultimate goal of distributed processing and databases is to essentially make the network the computer. In early computing systems, all data and processing were confined to one computer. In early networks, we were able to distribute the computing load among several computers by replicating what was done on individual computers. If a network had three nodes, processing was taking place simultaneously on all three computers, but most of the processing entailed a single program on one system accessing and processing data on the same system. The network was used primarily to transport completed reports, for data input on terminals attached to a remote computer, and so on. Ideally, we would like to have the aggregate resources of a network applied as appropriate to cooperatively work on problems. In this context, a single transaction might use processing resources of several computers, access and update data in a database distributed over multiple disk drives on multiple computer nodes, and perhaps output data in several geographically distributed places. Naturally, such distributed collaboration of hardware and software should be transparent to users of the system. Before we introduce the technology of distributed processing and distributed databases, we first define more precisely the various aspects of distributed systems.

First, there is a distinction between distributed processing and distributed databases. From the preceding paragraph, you may have an intuitive idea about these distinctions. Distributed processing is the geographic distribution of hardware, software, processing, data, and control. The data communications system is the glue that holds the distributed system together and makes it workable. Geographic distribution does not mean great distances. As stated earlier, a LAN is a distributed processing system and, by definition, serves a limited area. A company also can have a distributed LAN or WAN system contained in a single computer room. The key factor in having a distributed processing system is networking two or more independent computing systems where there is an interdependence among the nodes thus connected. The dependence can be for processing power, data, application software, or use of peripherals.

Often distributed systems also are characterized by distribution of control. If the nodes are placed in different locations, there is local responsibility for each node. A manufacturing organization may have processing nodes in the headquarters offices, regional offices, and warehouses. In each of these locations, there is an operations staff responsible for running the systems. There may also be a local support and development organization responsible for developing, installing, and maintaining applications and databases.

Data is often one of the objects distributed in a network. People often refer to data distribution as a distributed database. Simple data distribution, however, is not sufficient for having a distributed database. To have a true distributed database, there must be a comprehensive, coordinated system that manages the data, regardless of location. Later in this chapter you will learn about the requirements of a distributed database management system and how it differs from distributed file systems. Because distributed data and databases are an important aspect of distributed systems, a large portion of this chapter addresses the issues surrounding this topic.

One objective of distributed processing is to move data and processing functions closer to the users who need those services and thereby to improve the system's responsiveness and reliability. A second objective is to make remote access transparent to the system user, so the user has little or nothing special to do when accessing the other nodes of the system. How these objectives are met is explained later. First, we review how distributed systems evolved.

EVOLUTION OF DISTRIBUTED SYSTEMS

At the dawn of the computer age, computers were big and expensive, and operating systems were either nonexistent or incapable of supporting multiple job streams. As a result, for the organizations that could afford it, computer systems were acquired for every department needing computational power. In a manufacturing organization, one computer would be dedicated to inventory, one to accounting, and one to manufacturing control. These were decentralized processing systems, but they were considerably different from the current concept of distributed systems in one important respect: the sharing of resources.

Duplicated Databases and Inconsistent Data

Processors in early systems usually were not connected via communications links. As a result each maintained its own database, often with duplicated data. Both the warehouse database and the accounting database contained the same customer information, the former for shipping and the latter for invoicing. When a customer moved, the address change was not likely to be reflected in both databases at once, and in some instances not before a considerable amount of time had elapsed. Such redundant storage of data, with the attendant update problems, created data inconsistencies. Data inconsistencies often are manifested by conflicts in reports. Managers are generally intolerant of such conflicting reports. Perhaps more important, shipments or invoices could be sent to the incorrect address and perhaps be lost. Because each department was essentially the proprietor of its own system, there was little sharing of computer resources. This meant that one system might be completely inundated with work while another was idle. An early decentralized processing system is depicted in Figure 9.1.

Centralization

The early decentralized systems were far from ideal. In addition to data inconsistencies, there were extra costs for hardware, operations, maintenance, and programming. As systems grew larger and operating systems more comprehensive, there was a movement to large, centralized systems, as illustrated in Figure 9.2. Large, centralized systems had the benefits of a single operations center, control, and—according to some—economies of scale, as a single large system was likely to cost less than several smaller decentralized systems. In many organizations having centralized systems, a single programming department was established for all application development and maintenance. To reduce data redundancy and promote data sharing among users, centralized databases also were established.

Disadvantages of Centralization

It was later found that large centralized systems also have inherent problems. First, if the large central system fails, the entire system fails, and if a component fails, all or part of the application system also may be unavailable. In the decentralized approach, failure of one node results in part of the overall system being lost, but many processing functions can be continued. In this respect, decentralized systems are more reliable than the single centralized system.

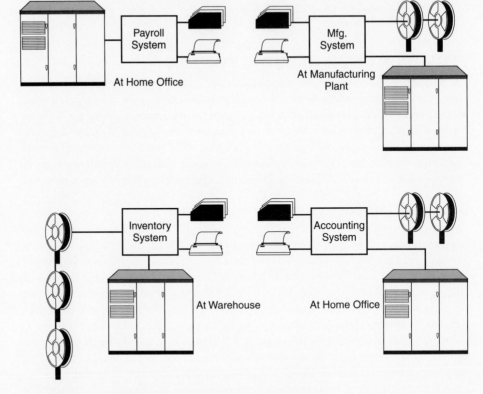

Figure 9.1 An Early Decentralized Processing System

Many end users of centralized systems—the accounting department, warehouse, and so forth—found their needs inadequately met by a centralized system. Because the system was shared, users often found it unresponsive, particularly regarding when jobs would be run and getting resources for new development. With a departmental system in a distributed or decentralized environment, a user contends only with other users in the department, so it was easy to establish priorities. However, setting interdepartmental priorities sometimes was not easy. The same held true for programming. In the centralized environment, a programming team may have been assigned to develop an application or a new report for a department. Because developers were not under the direct control of the department, it was sometimes difficult for the department to change priorities and directions.

Expansion and growth of the large centralized system posed another problem for some companies: controlling system growth. Too often growth was not in small, manageable increments but in giant steps, such as conversion to a larger processor with a different operating system. This conversion meant downtime while the new system was being installed. Sometimes programs had to be revised and new program bugs were encountered. The change was usually disruptive to all users. In contrast, when upgrading a distributed system, growth

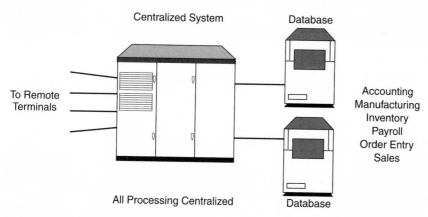

Figure 9.2   A Centralized System

was generally in smaller, more manageable increments. In addition, if a new processor became necessary, only those using that node were affected, not the entire user community.

Networked Systems

Networking provides some of the benefits of both centralized and distributed environments: more localized processing and control with shared data, processing power, and equipment. We use a LAN as an example; these comments generally apply to WANs as well. In a LAN, end users have a workstation capable of performing a variety of application functions such as word processing, working with spreadsheets, and so on. Each workstation is also able to call on the processing power and database capabilities of a server to accomplish more complex and time-consuming processing tasks. Some of the data required frequently by a user at a workstation may be resident on the workstation's local disk drives. This may include documents in process and budget data for spreadsheets. Data that either is infrequently used or is too big for the workstation's local disks can be maintained on a server. Despite this data being maintained by another node, the workstation can access that data as though it were stored locally. Workstations are also able to share other network resources such as printers and modems. The key to a distributed system is making resource distribution transparent to the users of the system. When the resources being distributed are data, sophisticated network software is necessary. The software responsible for doing this is called a Distributed File System (DFS).

DISTRIBUTED FILE SYSTEMS

In distributed systems, users must have the ability to locate and use remote files as though those files were locally resident. The objectives of a DFS are given in Table 9.1. Again, do not confuse a DFS with a distributed database management system. Although there are similarities between the two, distributed database systems significantly extend the capabilities of a DFS.

Table 9.1   Distributed File System Objectives

Provide transparent access to distributed files	Provide contention resolution
Provide operating system independence	Provide security
Provide file system independence	Provide file directory information
Provide architecture independence	Provide location independence

Transparent Access

Transparent access means that a user at one node must be able to access distributed files as though they were located on the user's local node. This means a user should be able to use the file system commands of the local system to access remote files, even if the remote file is located on a node with a different operating and file system.

Operating System Independence

In building a distributed system, a user should be able to configure heterogeneous systems. This may mean that different operating systems and file systems are involved. Not only should designers be able to build a system composed of different hardware and software, but also they must make these differences transparent to users.

File System Independence

With file system independence, different file systems, such as DOS, UNIX, and OS/2, may be used in one network. Just as important, the differences among the file systems should be transparent to users. For example, the local file system commands should be functional when a user accesses a file on a remote node having a different file system.

Topology Independence

The DFS should allow any network configuration (star, bus, ring, interconnected, and so on). Neither the topology nor the network software should limit the ability to distribute files.

Contention Resolution

The DFS ought to provide a mechanism that prevents data corruption due to contention. Such corruption can result when two or more users try to access and update the same file or record.

Security

A DFS must provide the requisite level of security. The DFS must be able to grant or deny requests based on the requester's ID and, perhaps, location. Inherent in this requirement is the ability to provide user identities for users on a node that does not support user IDs, such as a single-user microcomputer, and to control access among user IDs.

File Directory Information

The DFS is responsible for transparently satisfying user requests. This means that it must maintain a directory of remote files and their locations. When a user requests access to a file, the directory is consulted to find the node that houses the file.

Location Independence

Location independence means that a file can be located at any node in the network. A file also must be able to be moved from one node to another without disrupting applications or end-user access to that file.

Several DFS implementations exist. The one most often used for networks with equipment from a variety of vendors is the Network File System (NFS), developed by Sun Microsystems. It is implemented not only on Sun systems but also on a variety of UNIX-, VMS-, and Windows-based systems. Sun Microsystems has placed the NFS protocol specifications in the public domain to allow other vendors to implement it. The objective of publishing the protocol was to spread its use and establish NFS as a standard.

A UNIX operating system DFS, Remote File Sharing (RFS), currently runs only on UNIX-based systems. This protocol is supported by the American Telephone and Telegraph Company (AT&T), the originator of the UNIX operating system. One current limitation of RFS is its restriction to UNIX-based systems. With RFS, files that physically exist on one node can appear as though they are resident on other nodes. Thus, a user can access the remote file as though it were a local file.

CLIENT/SERVER COMPUTING

Networks changed the traditional way of computing and how we design application systems. Data processing has evolved from batch-oriented systems on stand-alone computers, to on-line transaction processing with terminals and a host computer, to distributed application processing using several computers in a network. One distributed software architecture on networks is called client/server computing. Recall from our discussion in Chapter 1 that client/server (C/S) computing divides the work an application performs among several computers. In C/S computing, one application (the client) requests processing services from another application (the server). In LAN systems, the client and the server processes typically run in different computers. Some of the more common server functions are database services in which a server processes database requests and mail services that route and store mail messages. A client process may use the services of several different server applications in carrying out its work.

C/S computing was developed neither for LANs nor for networking; however, networks in general and LANs specifically have created an environment amenable to C/S technology. Perhaps looking at the precursors of today's C/S environment will make it easier to understand the LAN implementations. Figure 9.3 shows a large computer to which many terminals are connected. Terminal users each have a set of applications and transactions they are allowed to run, and different users may have different sets of capabilities. A person's job needs determine which applications and transactions may be used. Figure 9.3 shows three classes of software components in the host processor: a transaction control process (TCP), applications, and database management system (DBMS).

Let us consider the needs of Kim, a specific terminal user. Kim works in the personnel department. Some of the functions she can do are adding employees, updating employee records, and deleting the records of employees who left the company more than three years ago. The add-employee transaction requires the services of three different applications, one each for employee, insurance, and payroll updates. When Kim

A Processor

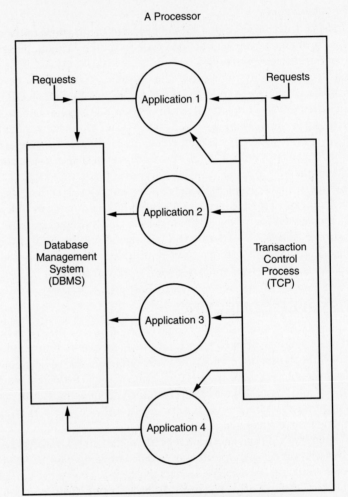

TCP has a role as a client with applications as servers.
Applications have roles as clients with DBMS as a server.

Figure 9.3   Client/Server Computing in a Mainframe Computer

requests that a certain transaction, such as adding an employee, be run, her request is received by the TCP. The TCP is responsible for routing the transaction to the appropriate applications. In this case, three applications must work on the transaction, a capability we can call cooperative computing. In this scenario, the TCP requests each application to perform a service. In some systems, the TCP is called a requester and the applications are called servers. In today's terminology the TCP could be called a client. The client makes requests that are carried out in whole or in part by other processes called servers. In this example, the applications in turn make requests of the database management system and the operating system for services they perform. Thus, a server can also become a client.

In WANs, some companies have extended the notion of this type of C/S technology by allowing the server processes to be on nodes different from the one on which the client is running. This provides a distributed processing environment in which the hardware, software, and data resources of several computers combine to solve a problem. In essence, with C/S computing the network becomes the computer. We can also talk about server classes. A server class is represented by one or more applications, all of which can carry out certain tasks. With server classes, a client does not need the services of a particular server process because any process in the class can perform the requested service.

A C/S LAN configuration is illustrated in Figure 9.4. This figure shows two instances of C/S computing; an e-mail server and a database or SQL server (SQL stands for structured query language, a standard database language). Earlier we described how a database server works. An **e-mail** server operates like a post office for its clients, performing functions such as supplying mail addresses given a user's name, distributing mail, interfacing to other mail servers, coordinating mail from different mail programs, and providing **mail agent** functions. There are several types of mail agents, one of which is a vacation agent. An e-mail vacation agent can provide services such as collecting incoming mail in an electronic folder or rerouting mail to another designated user while the original recipient is away.

In LAN C/S technology, clients typically run in workstations and request services from microcomputer, minicomputer, or mainframe nodes that operate exclusively as servers. Alternatively, C/S computing can be implemented in a peer-to-peer LAN. In a peer-to-peer C/S environment, server and client processes can be running in the same node. In Figure 9.5, both client A and server 1 are running in node 1.

Advantages of C/S Computing

System Expansion

Growth is one objective of many companies, and it is often accompanied by the need for additional computing power. With C/S computing the computing power is distributed over multiple processors. Because the computer is the network, in C/S computing we can expand the computer by adding hardware and software components to the network. Adding to the network can be done in small, manageable increments. This means the computer can be scaled up (or down) without incurring large expenses and major hardware upgrades. Applications also can be easily expanded. Once the C/S environment is set up, new applications can be quickly installed and can immediately take advantage of the services available. This growth is made easier because the application functions provided by the server processes are already in place, and the work of the application programmers is reduced.

Modular Applications

C/S applications are generally improved because applications are modular. Modularity can reduce the memory required for client applications and provide optimization for server processes. Part of the application logic is contained in the servers and hence does not need to be replicated in the client portion of the code. An analogy may be helpful here. If you are building a house, you would probably not do all of the jobs yourself

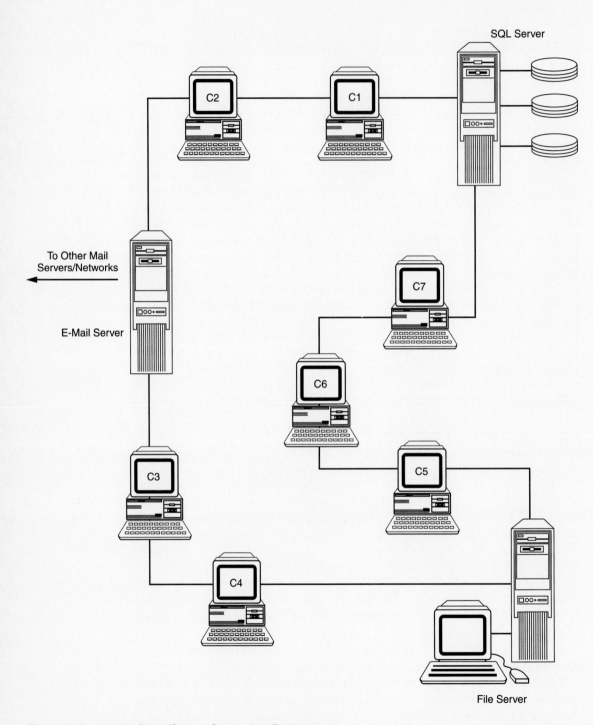

Figure 9.4   A LAN Client/Server Computing Environment

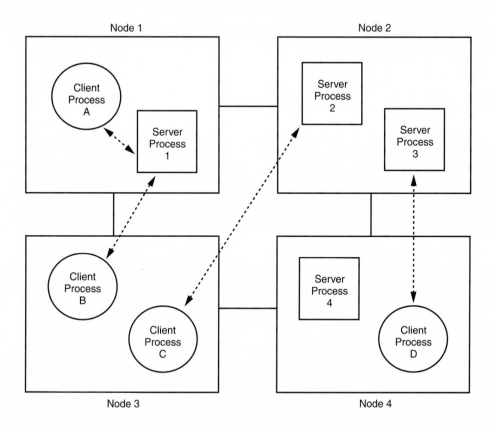

Figure 9.5 A Peer-to-Peer Client/Server Environment

because it would be difficult for you to learn all of the necessary carpentry, plumbing, electrical, and landscaping skills. However, if you become a client and use the services of those who already know how to do these things, you will probably get the job done faster and better. This analogy applies directly to the concept of C/S computing. Server modules are optimized to perform their function on behalf of their clients, and the clients do not need to be burdened with the logic essential to performing those tasks.

Portability

Some computer systems are better able to perform certain jobs than others. For example, some platforms are noted for their ability to do high-resolution graphics applications, such as computer-aided design and drafting (CAD), whereas other hardware and software combinations are well suited for office automation applications. The combination of hardware and software of an SQL server also enables the server to manage data more effectively than a general-purpose computer and operating system. As new technologies emerge, the C/S environment provides an easy way to integrate such technologies into the network. A company can switch among hardware and software vendors to find its ideal computing system. Ordinarily, these changes do not affect the remaining components. Using an SQL server as an example, if a new, more powerful server engine becomes available, it should be easy to install the new engine in place of existing SQL servers or to simply add the new server to augment existing servers.

Standards

As C/S develops we will probably see new standards for the way in which clients and servers communicate. Some of these are already in place. With interface standards available, software and hardware from many vendors can be integrated to create a modular, flexible, extendible computing environment.

Disadvantages of C/S Computing

One disadvantage of C/S technology on WANs is reduced performance because of the slowness of the communications links. With high-speed LANs, the communication link does not become an obstacle to performance. Another disadvantage of C/S computing on networks is the complexity of creating the optimum C/S environment. This disadvantage is common to WAN and LAN implementations.

C/S Technology

C/S technology on LANs is still new, but its direction has already taken shape. In this section we look at some of the technology that underlies C/S computing, the interfaces that exist between clients and servers, and standards that are being developed.

Clients and servers must have a way to communicate with each other. There are two basic ways in which this is done: remote procedure calls and messages. You may be familiar with programming languages that support local procedure calls. With local procedure calls, one segment of a program invokes logic in another program segment called a procedure. The procedure does its work, and then the results and processing control are passed back to the point in the program from which the procedure was called. You can think of the procedure as performing a service for the program. Remote procedure calls extend this concept to allow an application on one computer to call on the services of another process. The process being called could be running in the same computer or, as is typically the case in C/S computing, the process being called could be running in another computer. Moreover, the process being called may not be running at the time of the call. The remote procedure call in this instance must initiate the server process on the other computer.

Message exchange is a more flexible method of communication. The client and the server enter into a session (recall the OSI session layer) and exchange information. The client sends a request and the server responds with the answer to the request.

One issue to be resolved with C/S computing is how to find the server or servers that perform the needed functions. Today, we are looking primarily at clients and servers that are attached to the same LAN. It is logical to extend this to having servers and clients on different LANs. To maintain the modularity and flexibility of C/S computing, we would like to be able to add servers, delete existing ones, and perhaps move an existing server from one LAN to another. Changes of this nature also should be transparent to the clients, which means that the clients should not have to be reprogrammed. This problem can be solved by having servers "advertise" themselves. For example, they might place an entry into a network directory or send messages to all nodes registering their presence.

Clients communicate with servers through an application program interface (API), as illustrated in Figure 9.6. Standards are being developed that will make forming C/S interfaces easier. Having many different C/S interfaces should be avoided to maintain flexibility. It is better to have one or a few standard interfaces so a company can develop client applications that will be able to access servers created by other companies. These interfaces have come to be called middleware. The objective of middleware is to serve as an intermediary between clients and servers, which means that the middleware is responsible for making the connection between clients and servers. This is similar to the function performed by the logical link control layer, which, you may recall, is the interface between the network layer and media access control.

One example of middleware and its standardization efforts is the Distributed Computing Environment (DCE) specifications established by the Open Software Foundation. DCE addresses the use of remote procedure calls, security, name services, and messages for C/S computing. Another example is the Object Request Broker (ORB) established by the Object Management Group. A client communicates with a server through the services of the ORB. The ORB receives a client's request, finds a server capable of satisfying that request, sends the message to that server, and returns the response to the client. The ORB thus provides client and server independence. Any client that can communicate with the ORB is then able to communicate with any server that can communicate with the ORB. This provides both hardware and software independence.

We can use three models to represent the distribution of functions in a C/S environment. First, the majority of the application logic can reside in the client system, with only the specialized server logic residing in the server system, as illustrated in Figure 9.7(a). In this model, the server is less burdened and can be more responsive to volumes of client requests. This is usually the model used for database servers. In a database server, the server responds to a client's request for data and data meeting the constraints of the request are returned to the client for processing. This model is sometimes called the data management model.

A second model uses the client primarily to display or print data, and the data management and application logic reside on the server, as illustrated in Figure 9.7(b). This approach could be used for graphics applications wherein a high-speed server processor

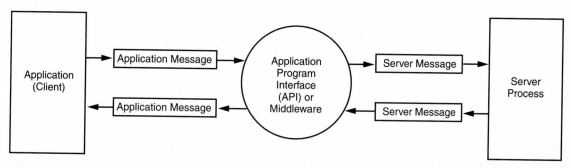

Figure 9.6   Client/Server Application Program Interface

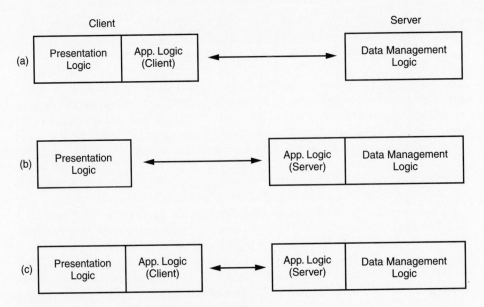

Figure 9.7 Client/Server Application Models

is used to generate the drawing details and the workstation is responsible for displaying the details on the monitor. This model can be called the presentation model.

The third possibility embeds application logic in both the client and the server, as illustrated in Figure 9.7(c). This model might be used in a transaction processing system where the application contains logic about customers and the server contains the application logic for banking accounts.

DATABASE SOFTWARE

Database management systems (DBMSs) have been mentioned earlier, so we concentrate here on additional LAN-oriented functions you must look for when selecting a DBMS. For several reasons, DBMS software selection may be one of your most difficult tasks. A DBMS is not only a personal productivity tool but also a key subsystem for workgroup productivity and corporate computing applications.

Often you will need to import and export database data, a task requiring interoperability between other application programs and other DBMSs. Also, databases files tend to be highly shared and thus more prone to contention problems than word processing documents, spreadsheets, and similar files. In a word processing or spreadsheet application, users typically do not use one file at the same time; in a database management system, users often need to use the same file simultaneously. If errors occur when a user is updating the database, the data could be left in an inconsistent state. Your DBMS choice should contain provisions to protect data from such risks.

Some of the issues of multiple concurrent users, the ability to have individual user profiles, and so on, have already been covered. We do not intend to lessen the importance of these issues in other software packages; however, the likelihood of contention and inconsistency problems is less for these applications when used in the normal way. For example, the normal way to use a word processing application for personal productivity is for each user to be working on a different document, not on different parts of the same document. Word processor users often open a file exclusively to avoid other users from inadvertently editing a file it is used by someone else, or they open the file in protected mode so only one user can update the document while others can access it for read-only purposes.

In Chapter 2 we introduced the concept of contention, and in Chapter 6 we showed how contention resolution can result in deadlock. You may wish to refer back to these chapters to refresh your understanding of contention and deadlock. In choosing a DBMS you should understand how the system resolves contention and how it deals with deadlock.

Another major concern when selecting a DBMS is how it supports **transaction processing.** Two fundamental methods are used to process data: batch and on-line transaction processing. In **batch processing,** you collect pieces of data over time and process them as a group. Often only one group of updates is processed at a time; that is, you have no concurrent updates to a file. In **on-line transaction processing,** you process events as they occur. In both cases you must be concerned with the integrity of data in the database. In batch processing you often make backups of files before beginning a batch update. If a fault occurs during the batch processing, the backup file allows you to return to a consistent state. Alternatively, you can use periodic synchronization points in the processing. At synchronization points you are assured that the database is consistent. If a failure occurs during processing, you can return the database back to its state at the last synchronization point by writing **before** and **after images** of the records you are updating. The techniques for doing database recovery are beyond the scope of this book.

With on-line transaction processing, two or more users may be involved in making updates at the same time. Ideally each user's work does not conflict with the work of other database users. However, unless you carefully schedule the work, you cannot count on this. Thus the ability of a DBMS to support transaction definition and recovery is important for databases that may be updated concurrently.

A **transaction** is a database activity that moves the database from one consistent state to another consistent state. A **consistent state** is one in which the data is accurate and complete. A transaction is an atomic unit of work, which means that the transaction either is completed in its entirety or leaves the database in the state it was in before the transaction started. Some database transactions only read data in the database. For example, you may run a database query to find the average employee salary. This transaction does not update the database and thus does not affect its consistency. From a database consistency perspective, we are interested only in transactions that perform updates.

Now, let us consider an update transaction and its problem potential. A bank account transfer transaction provides a simple illustration of the problem. Other transactions that update two or more records are similar to this example. This account transfer transaction moves funds from a savings account to a checking account. This transaction has two phases: In phase 1 the savings account record is read, the account balance reduced, and the record rewritten. In phase 2 the checking account record is read, the account balance increased by the amount of the savings account reduction, and the record rewritten. Clearly it is not appropriate to take the money out of the savings account while failing to put the money into the checking account. To do so leaves the database in an inconsistent state and the bank customer in an irate state. The database states for this transaction are illustrated in Figure 9.8. Your DBMS should prevent leaving the transaction in a state of partial update and leaving the database inconsistent.

To provide transaction integrity, the DBMS should support the ability to define a transaction and ensure either that the transaction ends successfully or, if it is unsuccessful, that any uncompleted transaction updates are reversed, thus leaving the database in the state it was in before the start of the transaction. Alternatively, the DBMS could ensure that the partially completed transaction is carried through to its successful conclusion, although this alternative is not often used.

The most common way to reverse an incomplete transaction is to have the application first declare the start of the transaction. Before a record is updated, its contents are saved in a before image record. If the transaction cannot complete, the before images replace the changes made by the transaction, thus returning the database to its state at the start of the transaction. When the transaction has completed, the application declares the end of the transaction and discards the before images. The account transfer transaction with its before images is illustrated in Figure 9.9. When a DBMS cancels a transaction and applies before images to return the database to a consistent state, it performs what is called a **transaction rollback.**

Another requirement of on-line transaction processing is that the records updated during one transaction remain unavailable for update by other transactions until that transaction ends. Preventing records from being updated by other transactions is necessary in the event that the transaction fails and must be rolled back. If another user has already made an update to a record being rolled back, the rollback reverses both

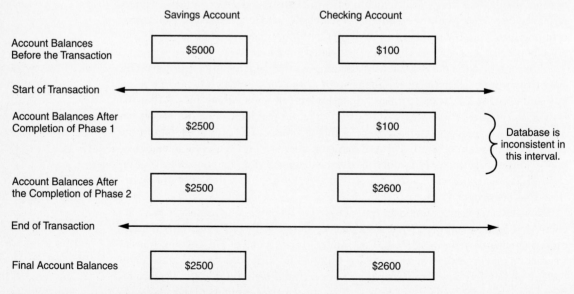

Figure 9.8   Account Transfer Transaction States

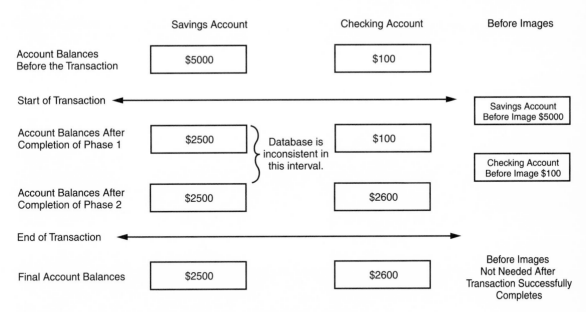

Figure 9.9   Account Transfer Transaction Using Before Images

updates. Again, the database you choose should ensure transaction integrity by preventing other transactions from updating a record being changed by another transaction. Exerting controls over records or files, generally called contention resolution, is discussed in Chapter 6.

A multiuser DBMS should also provide **recovery facilities** to assist with data restoration following a failure. A variety of failures can occur that damage database data. Among these are program logic errors, disk head crashes, server failures, and disasters such as fires and floods. You are already aware of backup and restore operations. File restoration is one component of database recovery. A restore utility returns the database to a consistent state. However, many transactions might have been processed since the backup was taken. Hundreds or thousands of update transactions per day are not uncommon. Most large-system DBMSs and a growing number of microcomputer DBMSs provide facilities for reconstructing the work done by transactions processed after the last backup. Moreover, these DBMSs usually provide automatic transaction rollback to a consistent database state following events such as a server failure. These recovery capabilities can help you avoid a considerable amount of manual work recovering from errors.

DATABASE MANAGEMENT IN DISTRIBUTED SYSTEMS

Having discussed how data can be manipulated with remote file systems, we now look at the more complex problem of distributed databases. Most current database management systems were designed to operate on only one node. There was no need to keep track of files or databases on another node or to manage transactions that span multiple nodes. In some instances the problem of distributed transactions is compounded by having two different database systems involved. One example is when one node uses one vendor's hardware and software and another node uses a different vendor's hardware and database management system. In such cases, it is not likely that the database management systems will cooperate with each other except through user-written programs or routines.

Rules for a Distributed Database

You have already read about the objectives of distributed file systems. A similar set of objectives or rules has been established for distributed databases. These rules are given in Table 9.2. Note that in some instances the rules are comparable to those for distributed file systems and that the rules extend the capabilities of remote file systems.

Rule 1

Local autonomy means that users at a given node are responsible for data management and system operation at that node. A local node has a certain amount of independence regarding these local operations. This independence is not unrestrained, however. As with individuals in a free society who have individual independence, the independence extends only where it does not adversely affect another member of the society. Thus, a local node does not typically have the independence to arbitrarily remove its node from the network if that action is detrimental to operating the distributed system. Another implication of local autonomy is that users at a node accessing only data local to that node should neither experience performance degradation nor need to interact with the system differently as a result of being part of a distributed system.

Rule 2

No reliance on a central site means that all nodes in the distributed system shall be considered as peer nodes, with no node identified as a supervisor. Furthermore, there shall not be one node on which other nodes must rely, such as a single node that contains a centralized data dictionary or directory.

Rule 3

Continuous operation means that adding nodes to the network, removing network nodes, or having one node fail will not discontinue availability of other nodes. Naturally,

Table 9.2   Twelve Rules for Distributed Databases

1. Local autonomy	7. Distributed query processing
2. No reliance on a central site	8. Distributed transaction management
3. Continuous operation	9. Hardware independence
4. Location independence	10. Operating system independence
5. Fragmentation independence	11. Network independence
6. Replication independence	12. DBMS independence

a single node failure will probably disrupt access for the users local to that node; however, users at other nodes can continue to use the distributed database, and their disruption is limited to an inability to access data stored only at the failed node.

Rule 4
Location independence means that data can be placed anywhere in the network and that its location is transparent to those needing access to it. Data can be moved from one node to another, and users or programs needing access to that data will not be disrupted.

Rule 5
In the personnel and payroll example cited earlier in this chapter, each regional node had personnel and payroll files for the employees in that region. Physically these were separate files, but logically their combination formed the corporate personnel file and payroll file. Fragmentation independence means that data that appears to users as one logical file can be transparently partitioned over multiple nodes. Thus, the personnel file is fragmented over several regional nodes. The corporate personnel director must be able to make inquiries regarding all employees, such as finding the average salary of all employees, and receive the answer consolidated from all fragments. The manager also must be able to initiate the query in the same way he or she would have if the table had not been fragmented. The distributed database management system is responsible for making the various fragments appear as a single file.

Rule 6
Storing the same file in multiple locations is called replication. Replication independence means that any file can be replicated on two or more nodes and that such replication is transparent to both users and applications. Replication is desirable for files that must be accessed by several nodes, such as a network directory. Replication can enhance performance and availability. The distributed database management system is responsible for managing updates to replicated data and keeping the replicated data consistent.

Rule 7
When we discussed access strategies for distributed files, three alternatives were given: remote access and local processing, partial remote processing, and total remote processing. The alternative used depended on the application program's logic. Distributed query processing means that a user at one node can start a query involving data on other nodes. Access and processing strategies such as those discussed earlier must be supported. The location of the data must be transparent to the user and the application. The query also must be completed in an optimum way. This might mean that database servers on several nodes cooperatively work on a portion of the query. In this way, the minimum amount of data is transmitted over the network to the requesting node. The database management system is responsible for determining the access strategy and carrying it out.

Rule 8
Distributed transaction management means that node-spanning transactions must be allowed. Moreover, transactions that update data on several nodes must be recoverable.

This requires that a transaction started on one node can update records on other nodes and that the database management systems on those other nodes coordinate their activities regarding locking, effecting transaction backout, and recovery.

Rule 9
Hardware independence means that the distributed network can consist of hardware from a variety of vendors. Nodes in the distributed system can come from a variety of vendors, such as Microsoft, Oracle, IBM, and Sybase.

Rule 10
When different hardware vendors supply network nodes, it is likely that different operating systems will be used. This capability is known as operating system independence.

Rule 11
Another consequence of Rule 9, hardware independence, might be that different network architectures, software, and protocols are used. If the vendors designed their network systems according to the OSI reference model and related standards, such interconnection will be easier. Network independence means that multiple kinds of network software may be used in connecting the nodes together. Some network nodes may be part of an Ethernet network, others may be members of a token ring network, and still others may be nodes on a WAN. Using disparate network systems must not adversely affect distributed database capabilities.

Rule 12
Database management system independence means that a variety of database management systems may be used in the distributed database. One node might use an IMS database, another might use DB2, and a third might use Oracle. Each database management system has a different data access and manipulation language, has different recovery mechanisms, and stores data in different formats. The distributed database management system must make these differences transparent to both users and applications. A user also should be able to access data managed by such a variety of database management systems without learning a variety of data access languages. Specifically, the user should be able to access distributed data using the same interface he or she uses to access data stored locally. This rule implies that database recovery systems should be coordinated and database language differences accommodated. Implementation of this rule is very complex.

Currently, there is no system that adheres to all of these rules. Creating a distributed environment that encompasses all 12 rules will require a considerable investment. Until then, those who want to implement distributed databases must settle for less than the capabilities implied by these rules. The best way to implement distributed databases today is to use hardware and software from one vendor only and to choose a vendor having a database system that supports distributed capabilities.

Distributed systems have become viable processing systems. They are currently at the frontier of database management systems and data communications systems. Many of the problems that impede their widespread use are in the area of database technology rather than data communications. Distributed data and distributed transactions may have a significant impact on the use of network resources. Specifically, data transfers, message transfers, and recovery messages can cause increased media traffic. Development in the problem areas should be spurred by potential advantages of distributing data to where it is most often used, sharing processing and data resources, and providing more control to end users.

WORKGROUP SOFTWARE

Most LAN implementations have the potential for effectively using **workgroup software,** often called **groupware.** In this section, you will learn what a workgroup is and some of the application tools used to increase the group's productivity. Before you can fully appreciate the functions of workgroup software, you must understand what we mean by a workgroup and the functions needed by the group. First, a group consists of two or more workers. In doing their jobs, these workers must share information, communicate with each other, and coordinate their activities. Specific work tasks that are group activities include meetings, office correspondence, and group decision making. Groupware is designed to make arranging and carrying out these tasks easier and less time-consuming.

The functions performed by groupware are not new. For years they have been done manually or with limited degrees of computer support. Networked systems in general and LANs in particular provide the communication link that was previously missing in computerizing many of these tasks. The groupware applications that have been created thus far fall into the following broad categories:

- electronic mail
- conferencing
- work-flow automation
- document coauthoring and document management
- decision support
- time-staged delivery systems

E-Mail Systems

One of the earliest workgroup applications was e-mail. An e-mail system has many of the capabilities of a conventional postal system such as collecting and distributing correspondence. An e-mail system also should be able to accept correspondence of various sizes and types—text, graphics, and audio—and route the correspondence to its recipients in a timely manner. However, we come to expect many more capabilities from an e-mail system. Before we discuss these, we first consider how an e-mail system might operate on a LAN by tracing a piece of correspondence through a hypothetical system. For specifics, suppose a LAN user, Maria, must send a mail message announcing a meeting to five other department heads: Alice, Mike, Tom, Shelly, and Chen.

Creating the Message

Before a message can be sent, it must be created. In general, there are two ways to create a message: through the facilities of the mail system or through an external word processing, desktop publishing, or other text/graphics system. If an external message creation facility is used, Maria can start that application, create the message, and save it on disk. Following that, she starts the mail application and imports the message into the mail system. Alternatively, most of today's e-mail systems allow users to designate their message creation software. Thus, the message can be composed from within the mail system itself (that is the word processor is invoked from the mail system and essentially becomes a mail job).

Sending the Message

Once the message has been created, it can be scheduled for delivery. The **mail administrator,** the person responsible for installation and management of the e-mail application, will have identified all eligible e-mail users and their associated mail addresses. In sending her message, Maria gives either the name of each user or the name of a predefined **distribution list** containing those names or perhaps a combination of these two alternatives. A distribution list contains the names of individual users or the names of other distribution lists, and thus provides a simple mechanism to send messages to workgroups. Maria may have defined a distribution list called DEPT-HEADS that includes the names of the other five department heads. The e-mail system takes care of breaking the distribution list into its individual components so each name on the list receives the message.

When the delivery system gets the message and a list of the recipients, it can route the message to the proper destinations. For each recipient, the mail message is delivered into a disk file called the user's **mailbox.** The message is available to each recipient almost immediately.

Reading the Message

A message is available for reading once it has been delivered. Suppose Chen has just logged onto the LAN. If mail is waiting, he receives a message that he has mail. If a mail message arrives while he is working at his workstation, he receives a mail-waiting message. To read his mail, Chen starts the mail application and receives a list of his mail headlines. After viewing the available messages, usually identified with the sender's identification and a subject line, Chen has several available options including (but not limited to) the following:

- He can ignore Maria's message altogether.
- He can leave the message in his mailbox for later viewing.
- He can delete the message without reading it.
- He can read the message and delete it.
- He can read the message and file it in an electronic folder.
- He can read the message and forward it to other mail users.
- He can read the message and send his response to the originator, Maria.

Responding to the Message

If Chen decides to read and respond to Maria's message, he can enter his comments on the message and choose the message response option. He also may send his comments to other recipients and to a third party. After responding, Chen may delete the message, print it, or file it in an electronic folder.

Other E-Mail Features

Other capabilities you may find in an e-mail system are described in this section.

Expiration Dates and Certified Mail   If the message is not read within a designated time limit, it can be automatically deleted from the user's mailbox. A sender can also send **certified mail.** When a recipient reads the message, the sender receives a notice that the message has been read. A notice is also sent if the message expires without being read.

Mail Classes and Mail Agents   There may be several classes of mail, such as first, second, and third classes. First class can be used for individual correspondence and second class for business news such as company stock quotes and product announcements. Third class can be used for junk mail such as garage sales, want ads, and social-group announcements. A mail agent is a software module that can automatically act on behalf of a user. For example, if a user goes on vacation, a vacation agent can forward the user's mail to another user or file the mail in an electronic folder. The vacation agent might also send each correspondent a message stating that the user is on vacation and name an alternative recipient.

Broadcast Messages and Message Attachment   A broadcast message is one sent to all users (or all but a few users) on the network. Broadcast capability is convenient for sending messages of general interest to all network users. Sometimes this correspondence is an assemblage of several discrete components. For example, a mail message may consist of text created by a word processor, graphic images created by a graphics or spreadsheet application, fax images, and digitized voice. The mail service may maintain an electronic bulletin board. Users can be notified that there are general-interest messages posted to the bulletin board. This keeps user mailboxes from being filled with messages while giving users an opportunity to read and post general-interest messages.

Miscellaneous Capabilities   Mail systems seem to be constantly expanding in capabilities as software vendors strive to surpass their competition or just remain competitive. Capabilities offered include

- spelling checker
- notification of mail arrival
- search messages for keywords
- message priorities
- voice overlay
- carbon copies
- security and message encryption

- notification of failure to deliver a message
- ability to create user profiles
- interactive mail

Electronic Conferencing Applications

Electronic conferencing applications range from simply arranging meetings to conducting the meetings themselves. Arranging a meeting or conference requires that the participants be notified and that a mutually agreeable meeting date and time be set. Conferencing applications provide assistance with one or more of these tasks. If each attendee has an **electronic calendar,** groupware can book the meeting at the best time. Given an interval during which the meeting must take place, the groupware application consults the calendars of the attendees. It notes the date and time that all attendees are available and schedules the meeting on their electronic calendars. If scheduling conflicts arise, the application can help resolve them. Some schedulers even double-book participants and allow them to choose which appointment to keep. Others report the conflicts and suggest alternative meeting times with no or reduced conflicts, allowing the person calling the meeting to find the best possible time. Once a meeting is scheduled, the electronic calendar software can issue an RSVP notice to the participants. Like personal calendars, groupware calendars can issue reminders of upcoming events. The reminder might be a mail message or an audio tone. Some groupware allows users to declare meetings to be recurring, such as weekly, monthly, or biweekly. The scheduler then automatically books these meetings for the attendees.

If the meeting is held with participants in different locations, teleconferencing groupware can also assist with communications among the attendees. Some teleconferencing applications allow images displayed on one computer monitor to be displayed on remote monitors. Individuals at all locations can modify the screen image and have the changes immediately reflected on the screens of the other participants. Thus, conference attendees can both view and modify computer-generated data and graphs. Viewing and modifying data coupled with audio transmission and freeze-frame or full-motion video allows geographically distributed conferences to be held, saving both travel costs and personnel time. Another conference or meeting communications aid is the creation and distribution of electronic minutes.

Work-Flow Automation

Attendees at a meeting may accept action items they must complete, or a workgroup manager may assign tasks to workgroup members. One responsibility of a workgroup manager is monitoring the progress of such tasks. Progress monitoring is not a new concept. For many years, managers have used **Program Evaluation and Review Technique (PERT)** charts or similar methods to track a project's progress and determine its critical path. The **critical path** of a project is the sequence of events that takes the longest to complete. Often, a project can be divided into several tasks. Some tasks can be done in parallel, whereas other tasks cannot start until one or more tasks have been completed. For example, when building a house, the roof cannot be put on until the building is framed. Plumbing and electrical wiring can be done concurrently. The project cannot be completed until the path with the longest duration is completed. Thus, project managers pay close attention to the project's critical paths to avoid delays. Although some project management work has been computerized for many years, much of the monitoring work was done by people. Groupware has extended the abilities of earlier systems by automating the tracking function.

Figure 9.10 is a PERT chart for selecting a LAN vendor. The critical path for the selection process is indicated by the heavier line. It is the critical path because it has the longest elapsed time between the start and the end points. Groupware helps in monitoring the critical path and keeps the group working together. Through the groupware application, group members can also keep aware of the status of other tasks that may affect their work.

With work-flow automation groupware, a manager can assign tasks to individuals or groups (through the group leader). The individual can either accept the task, negotiate a change, or refuse the task. Once a task is accepted, a completion date is set. The worker uses the groupware application to record his or her progress and to signal the completion of the task. The manager can then either agree that the task is complete and close it out or decide that the task has not been satisfactorily completed and refuse to accept the work. In the latter case, the worker is notified and must rework the task until the result is acceptable. The groupware work-flow application tracks all tasks and evaluates progress. The group manager can query the system and obtain reports of each task's status. If several tasks are in progress at once and other tasks are awaiting the outcome of those tasks, the groupware monitors the progress of the critical paths and helps the manager keep the project on schedule. Other functions that may be simplified with work-flow automation software include

- establishing and monitoring to-do lists
- task delegation

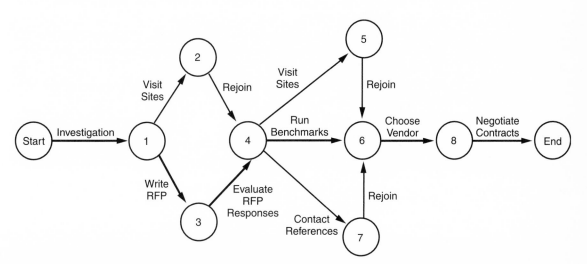

Figure 9.10   PERT Chart for Selecting a LAN Vendor

- holding completed tasks until released by a manager
- task deletion
- preventing a worker from modifying an accepted task
- setting or resetting task start and stop times
- adding, deleting, or changing the people responsible for tasks
- providing task and group reports

Document Coauthoring and Document Management

Word processing, text editors, and document exchange software were among the early computer applications. However, most of these systems were designed to allow only one person to manipulate a document at one time. If you have ever worked on a team to write a program, a report, or a manual, you are probably aware of the limitations inherent in these systems. If you and one of your team members wanted to work on the document at the same time, you found either that it could not be done or that concurrent document updates created contention problems. In a workgroup, it is often desirable and sometimes necessary to have several workers actively working on one document simultaneously. **Document coauthoring** and **management** applications provide this capability.

A full-function document coauthoring system allows two or more workers to work on one document concurrently. Concurrent processing presents some complex problems regarding posting changes to the same pages. Some current coauthoring systems do not provide this ability; however, they do provide the management and control abilities that allow a document to be shared without risk of contention problems. Some document managers help to control the flow of documents through the production cycle. Group users are identified as the principal document author, coauthors, or editors. The document manager assists in the production of the document by controlling the flow of the document from one designated user to another.

Document management software can control access to the document by a checkout mechanism. Workers can check out all or portions of the document. Once a portion is checked out, update access to that portion of the document by other users is typically restricted because the worker checking it out may change it. If a worker changes the document, the document management software monitors the changes and records the identity of the person making the change. When the document is ready for review, the application can route the document to the proper reviewers and editors. The reviewers and editors then can make notations and suggestions, with or without changing the document itself, and the application keeps track of the person making those remarks.

Other document management features include document organization, archiving, location, and full file searches. Imagine the number of documents generated per year by a large law office. Some law offices generate more than 50,000 documents per year including wills, contracts, legal briefs, and trial notes. Keeping track of this volume almost necessitates the use of a system that allows documents to be stored, archived to backup media, and retrieved when needed. For such large systems, standard directory and file naming conventions are often severely limited. A document management system allows users to store a single document under a variety of different subjects. As in a library card catalog, the document can then be found by attorney, client, subject, date created, last date accessed, project, department, author, and a variety of other descriptive categories. Some systems allow users to specify combinations of these attributes as well. Full file searches systematically search files stored on disk or archival directories looking for user-defined text strings.

Group Decision Support

Group decision support software on LANs facilitates the communication of ideas among the members of a group. Each participant has a workstation from which to make comments and suggestions, which are exchanged among the users in an anonymous way. This allows the lowest member in the organizational hierarchy to feel free to criticize suggestions made by the highest member. The key to making this work is protecting the source of ideas and comments. Included in the software are tools to gather and manipulate data from a variety of sources, such as a database, a spreadsheet, and graphic images. Companies that have used decision support technology have found that better decisions are reached in a shorter period of time.

It is important to emphasize that groupware is not intended to replace person-to-person interaction. Our future should not be one in which we get assignments via computers, are computer graded, and are fired or promoted via the computer. Instead, groupware complements person-to-person interactions. Groupware provides a tool for assigning and monitoring the group's tasks with the objective of making the group more productive.

Time-Staged Delivery Systems

Time-staged delivery systems have some characteristics of a mail system. Time-staged delivery software allows users to identify a transmission package, designate one or more recipients of the package, initiate the delivery of the package, and specify a delivery priority. If we compare time-staged delivery and e-mail to regular mail service, e-mail is like express mail service whereas time-staged delivery is equivalent to parcel post or surface mail. E-mail is usually oriented toward short messages of several pages or less. Time-staged delivery systems may be used for short messages, for transaction routing, or to transmit entire files.

With time-staged delivery, the user specifies a required delivery time. The system then schedules the message transmission to meet the requested goal. Suppose a user needs to send a lengthy report from New York City to each of five manufacturing plants, and that the message must be available at each plant by 9:00 A.M. local time. The report to London must arrive several hours before the one destined for California, so it has a higher priority in transmission than the California-bound package. The delivery system also can use the delivery time to defer transmission until a more convenient time. Rather than sending data in real time, when the system may be quite busy, it can delay transmission until a less busy time, such as early morning hours. In distributed processing environments, the ability to designate transmission packages and delivery times can be an important capability.

PRIMARY BUSINESS SOFTWARE

In some companies the LAN provides all computing resources. Some companies reached this level of LAN use through growth: They implemented a LAN when they were a small company, and the LAN grew with the company. Many companies reach this position from the opposite direction: Formerly users of minicomputers and mainframes, they **downsized** their data processing operations by substituting a microcomputer LAN for larger computers as the processing power of individual workstations and servers increased and the software available on LANs became more sophisticated. The reasons for downsizing vary, but three primary reasons are ease of use, lower cost, and the availability of primary business software.

Primary business software handles a variety of tasks, including personnel management, payroll, accounts receivable and payable, general ledger, inventory management, financial management, and manufacturing. LAN-compatible software packages for these applications are available, but some companies have developed their own primary business software using microcomputer software tools such as DBMSs, graphical user interfaces, and menuing systems. As the processing power of desktop systems continues to grow, LAN speeds increase, and new applications become available, the trend toward downsizing will likely continue.

SOFTWARE STANDARDS

Usually when we mention software standards we think of language standards, interface standards, and so on. However, many companies set up their computer systems with their own internal software standards. When you begin to acquire microcomputer systems, you should begin to think about setting up your internal software standards because they can reduce the costs of software, hardware, and training. One lesson some companies learned during the early days of microcomputer technology was that supporting several brands of the same software application soon became a management and control problem. To encourage the use of personal productivity tools and microcomputers in the early days of microcomputing, one company, let's call it Company X, originally took the approach that individuals could choose their own hardware platform and application software. Allowing individual hardware and software decisions resulted in a variety of hardware and software being used. Most of the hardware was based on either Apple or IBM technology, and variety of application packages were chosen. At one time six different word processing programs were in use! We will use word processing as the example in looking at the problems Company X experienced. On a smaller scale, the same problems existed with other software applications.

The mixture of hardware and software at Company X soon gave rise to several problems, the most critical of which was portability. The file formats of each word processing program were different, so transferring files among users was simple only if those users had chosen the same word processing application. For example, if Carlos used WordPerfect and Anita used Microsoft Word, they could not work on each other's documents without first going through a conversion. The company soon found it necessary to purchase file-conversion programs for the word processing applications. Having conversion programs helped reduce the problem of portability, but it did not completely eliminate it. Some word processors supported features not found in others. The use of those features was limited when porting documents from one word processor's format to another's.

The amount of user training required in Company X's mixed software environment was much greater than for similar companies that had established one standardized word processing package. Company X found that as new employees were added, they needed to be trained to use one of the products. Because the training was distributed over more products, classes were smaller and the number of classes was greater than was necessary for comparable companies. Moreover, users involved in document exchange had to learn the use of the conversion program, and extra time was required to do the conversion. Every time a new version of one of the word processing systems came out with new features, the conversion program also had to be upgraded. Sometimes the availability of new conversion software lagged behind the introduction of upgraded word processing software. After conversion, it was often necessary to do some manual formatting of the converted data.

The problems just described resulted in higher overall costs. The costs were seen in real dollars needed for conversion software and training and in intangible dollars for lost productivity resulting from workers doing conversions and manual formatting and from the reluctance of many users to get involved in document exchange. To avoid some of the problems Company X experienced because they did not set software standards, look for the following when choosing a software application:

Does the software run on a variety of hardware platforms and OSs?

What are the license agreement provisions?

What is the average cost per user? Factor in costs such as the need to buy 30 user licenses when there are only 25 concurrent users.

What functions are provided relative to other applications? For example, does the desktop publishing software accept the formats of the word processing software?

Is the application mature? That is, does it provide robust capabilities and is it free of bugs?

Does the software vendor provide good service? What kind of service is available (for example, do they offer on-site, telephone, or toll-free telephone service) and what is the cost?

Does the software come with complete and useful documentation?

Does the software vendor have a good record for enhancing the product?

Does the software depend on other software, such as a windows environment or specific operating system? If so, which ones?

Is the software LAN compatible? If so, on which LANs?

Is training readily available? Where? At what cost?

Is it likely that new employees will already be trained on this product?

Does the application interface readily with other software applications? For example, can the word processing application import graphs from spreadsheet programs, or can the spreadsheet program import data easily from the database management system?

What are the hardware requirements of the application? Memory? Disk? Mouse?

What hardware capabilities are supported? Graphics? Color? Other?

Are user profiles allowed? If so, how and to what degree?

Does the application allow for shared use?

Is an enabling hardware device required?

SUMMARY

There are two application environments for LANs. In one environment a workstation does all the processing, similar to processing on a stand-alone workstation. All that is accomplished by the network is file storage and printing services. The other environment distributes the work among network nodes. Essential to the distributed environment is software that allows the work to be divided and processed correctly. Distributed processing allows work to be accomplished on several different computers. One of the models for distributed computing is the client/server model. C/S computing is a LAN adaptation of a mainframe computing paradigm. On LANs, C/S computing has created a new class of software called middleware. Middleware establishes the interface between client and server software modules.

LAN application software can be separated into three major classes: personal productivity software, groupware, and primary business systems. Personal productivity software includes word processing, spreadsheets, graphics, and database management systems. These are the systems that are used as effectively on stand-alone systems as on LANs. Groupware needs workstation communications to operate. Of the personal productivity software, database management systems (DBMSs) need the most additional LAN support because databases are highly shared and concurrent usage problems must be avoided. In addition to the needs cited in earlier chapters, database management software for LANs should also support transaction processing and recovery to ensure the integrity of the database. Providing complete distributed processing capabilities requires a distributed database management system. Implementation of all distributed database capabilities is not likely in the next few years; however, we can expect to see improvements in distributed database capabilities.

A variety of groupware products are available, and new or improved applications are constantly being released. Some of the main groupware applications are e-mail, electronic calendaring and conferencing, work-flow automation, document coauthoring and management, and decision support. The features provided by individual application packages differ considerably, so care must be taken to choose the applications that are most consistent with your needs.

The use of a LAN as a vehicle for primary business system software may result from downsizing from a large computing platform or from upsizing a smaller company. The applications that fall into this category include personnel management systems, payroll, accounts receivable/payable, general ledger, and inventory control. This segment of LAN applications is increasing as LAN software and hardware expand.

Selecting software can be a difficult job because there is such a wide variety of choices. Some companies delegated software choice to their employees; thus, each employee was free to choose the software he or she wanted. Individual selection resulted in a variety of word processing, spreadsheet, and database systems being used and the associated problems of training users and exchanging data. To avoid this problem, organizations should establish organizational standards for widely used software. These standards define the brands and versions of application software that can be purchased and used. With a good set of standards in place, management can ensure that training and software costs can be better controlled and that the need for importing and exporting of data between products is minimized. Procedures for changing the application standard to add new applications or change existing ones should include testing to ensure that the application is LAN compatible.

Key Terms

after image
batch processing
before image
certified mail
consistent state
critical path
distribution list
document coauthoring
document management
downsize
electronic calendaring
electronic conferencing
e-mail
group decision support software

groupware
mail administrator
mail agents
mailbox
on-line transaction processing
primary business software
program evaluation and review technique
  (PERT)
recovery facilities
transaction
transaction processing
transaction rollback
work-flow automation software
workgroup software

Review Questions

1. Discuss the issues of remote file systems.
2. What is middleware? Why is it used?
3. Describe client/server processing.
4. What is a transaction?
5. Describe a problem that can occur if transaction integrity is not provided.
6. Describe the 12 rules for a distributed database management system.

7. What is a workgroup?
8. List five classes of workgroup software.
9. Describe five features that are likely to be found in e-mail systems.
10. What is work-flow automation? How does it help promote workgroup productivity?
11. How does a document coauthoring and management system differ from a word processing application?
12. How does time-staged message delivery differ from e-mail?
13. What are the advantages of group decision support systems?
14. What is downsizing? Why does a company downsize?
15. What are the advantages of having standard software products?
16. List ten items you should consider when selecting application software.

Problems and Exercises

1. Find a company that uses e-mail (LAN or WAN based). Interview several mail users to determine how often they use the mail, their likes or dislikes of e-mail, and the overall impact of the mail system on how they do business. How would their work be different if e-mail were not available?
2. Some people feel that work-flow automation, electronic calendaring, and e-mail are intrusive systems because they automatically schedule people for a meeting, monitor their work progress, report back to the originator of a message that the message has been read, and so on. Discuss the merits of this position. What are your personal viewpoints on these groupware applications?

PART 4

Installation and Management

After the LAN hardware and software have been selected, they must be installed, made operational, and administered. In Chapter 10 you will read about installation, perhaps the most difficult phase in a LAN's life cycle. Chapter 11 examines the LAN administrator's responsibility for creating and managing the user environment, including key issues such as security and virus protection. In Chapter 12 we present the LAN administrator's role in creating a printing environment that allows users to effectively share output resources. Chapter 13 explores the backup and recovery of a LAN. In Chapter 14 you will read about the roles of proactive and reactive management in the administrator's responsibilities.

Chapter 10
LAN Installation

Chapter 11
LAN Administration: Users, Groups, and Security

Chapter 12
LAN Administration: The Printing Environment

Chapter 13
LAN Administration: Backup and Recovery

Chapter 14
LAN Administration: Reactive and Proactive Management

Chapter 10

LAN Installation

CHAPTER PREVIEW

After you have selected the LAN hardware and software for your configuration, you must begin the process of installing it, bringing it to an operational status, and administering it. Installation is thought by some people to be the most difficult phase of a LAN's life cycle. Planning the installation begins as soon as you select the hardware and software. It continues until the entire LAN is operational. What determines when a LAN is operational varies. For our purposes it is when all hardware, system software, and application software have been installed, all user profiles have been created, security has been set up, and users are able to use the LAN in carrying out their tasks. In this chapter you will read about

administrative details such as contracts, support, and maintenance

hardware installation details such as site planning and cabling

testing and acceptance procedures

training for users, managers, and administrators

By the end of this chapter you should know some procedures to follow in setting up a new LAN. You should also realize that LAN installation can be quite complex, and installation details vary with the hardware, software, and LAN architecture you choose. This chapter contains general guidelines that are independent of particular implementations.

ADMINISTRATIVE DETAILS

LAN installation and testing can be complex tasks that require considerable planning and documentation. Plans provide the direction for equipment acquisition, installation, data conversion and loading, testing, and training. The LAN administrator should be aware of two key points during the installation process: First, plans may be incomplete or incorrect, so you must have a mechanism for changing the plans to meet the realities of the installation process. Second, people sometimes deviate from plans that you have set up, and these deviations can have unexpected and undesirable consequences. The rules for installation should be, if the plan is defective, change it; if the plan is correct, avoid deviations.

You have two choices when installing a LAN: You can be the primary contractor, acquiring yourself the essential hardware, software, documentation, and training you need from a variety of vendors, or you can select one or more vendors to handle the installation process for you. If you are the primary contractor, you may not need sophisticated contracts, and portions of this section may not apply to your situation. The reason the contracts may be less sophisticated is that you have assumed the responsibility for configuring the network and ensuring that it meets your needs. If a vendor has these responsibilities, the contract must include provisions for network acceptance and overcoming any deficiencies. The benefits of a company taking the role of primary contractor typically are lower costs and more control over the project. Several tasks must be carried out in LAN selection and installation, and if a company does not have personnel with experience in these areas, the equipment selected and the installation process may ultimately be more costly, error prone, and time-consuming than relying on outside network professionals.

After selecting your hardware and software, the first thing you usually do is contract with the vendors who will supply your LAN components. If you elect to have one company provide all your LAN needs, you will have one contract; if you choose several vendors, such as separate hardware and software vendors, you probably will have a contract with each; if you decide to be the primary contractor, you may need even more contracts. You must know when a contract is necessary and how to enter into a contract. The best source of information on this is an attorney, preferably one specializing in contract law. In large companies the people working in the purchasing department also have specialized knowledge of purchase contracts. We can offer you a few guidelines in establishing a relationship with your vendors, but these guidelines are not a substitute for an attorney.

Purchase Contract

When you purchase a system from a single vendor, you must have an understanding with that vendor about what is being supplied, when it will be ready, and what constitutes being ready. Too often the goodwill and good intentions that both the vendor and the user express at selection time turn to bitterness during system installation. Usually this happens because the vendor and the user have different ideas about what the results should be. A well-defined **purchase contract** clearly states the responsibilities of both parties and eliminates the ambiguities of what is to be done.

LAN installation has both tangible and intangible elements. Disagreements between the vendor and the user can arise from either element, but the intangible elements are more apt to cause disagreements and thus require more explicit contract terms. The most tangible elements of LAN installation are hardware components. There is little room for disagreement regarding the delivery and installation of 50 LAN adapters. Either the adapters work or they do not; either they are the correct type or they are not. Thus it is usually easy to write explicit contract provisions for hardware. Software is less tangible than hardware. You may receive software from your vendor that differs from your expectations in any of the following ways:

It does not provide the functions you expected.

It provides the functions you expected but is difficult to use.

It may be an older or newer version than you expected.

It may be produced by a software company other than what you expected.

It may not be functional because it does not match your hardware or software configurations.

It may not be functional because it has too many bugs.

It may not have the license provisions you expected.

Still less tangible than software are the conditions under which the vendor has satisfied his or her obligation to your company. That is, when are the terms of the contract met? A good contract can help make the intangibles more concrete. The more specific the contract is, the better. What specifics should you include in a purchase contract?

First, understand that when a vendor offers you a contract to sign, it probably has been drawn up by the vendor's attorneys and is designed to protect the interests of the vendor. This is not necessarily bad; however, the contract should also protect your interests. If you use a vendor's contract, you should definitely have it reviewed and approved by an attorney representing your interests. You can sign the vendor's standard contract, negotiate changes, or propose a contract drawn up by your attorney. Most contracts result from negotiation. Both parties agree that the terms are acceptable and they can abide by the terms.

Your contract should detail what, where, when, and how items are to be delivered. For hardware, the contract should specify the vendor, quantity, part numbers, and cost for each component or the aggregate cost for all components. For example, suppose the vendor is contracted to supply 50 LAN adapters. Simply specifying 50 of "Vendor X's Ethernet cards" is not sufficient. Vendors often have several models of Ethernet cards. You must include the vendor's part number or a more complete description. Making the correct choice of LAN adapter interface is another example of the importance of specification. One PCI bus card does not work in an EISA or ISA bus computer, and vice versa. ISA cards work in an EISA bus computer, but an EISA card does not work in an ISA bus computer. For example, the following LAN adapter options are available from one LAN adapter manufacturer:

8- or 16-bit ISA bus

16- or 32-bit EISA bus

16- or 32-bit MCA bus

32-bit PCI bus

8- or 16-bit PCMCIA bus

The vendor may want to use alternative sources for LAN adapter cards. In this case, again, be specific about the alternatives. For example, specifying "Vendor X's Ethernet LAN adapter Model 123-456 or equivalent" is not specific enough; you must qualify what constitutes equivalency or specify who determines what is equivalent.

Your contract should also set up a **payment schedule.** LAN installation often occurs in stages: First site preparation is done, wires or cables are installed, hardware is delivered and installed, software is delivered and installed, data is loaded, testing is conducted, and finally the system is accepted. Several months may elapse between starting and completing the installation. Vendors invest their money and time on the installation project, and they reasonably expect to be compensated for work completed satisfactorily. A payment schedule is usually established that allows the vendor to receive reimbursement at the completion of well-defined stages. For example, when the wiring installation is complete, a payment covering that portion of the network can be made. The payment schedule therefore represents **progress payments.** However, a substantial portion of the installation payment, say 15 to 25 percent, should be held until all conditions of the contract are fulfilled. The amount of the final payment should depend on the size of the contract and the number of progress payments in the payment schedule. The reason for holding the final payment is to ensure that the vendor completes final details. Sometimes a vendor that has been paid in full for an almost-finished project moves on to a new project, and the remaining installation tasks for your system become a low priority for that vendor.

A good contract identifies the conditions under which the network is complete. These conditions are often difficult to define. From both the user's and the vendor's perspectives, a specific set of events should be well defined. For example, simply defining completion as the installation of all hardware and software is usually not adequate. The user should also ensure that the system meets some minimum performance standards, that training is completed or at least scheduled, that the documentation is complete, and so on. The details of what must occur vary according to the size of the LAN and an organization's specific needs. Again, your attorney must ensure that the conditions are legally acceptable.

A company can take all the proper steps in setting up the final acceptance criteria but then jeopardize its legal status by placing the system into production before actually accepting it. Once a company begins to use the system in production, that company becomes dependent on the system. In some sense, until the system is accepted, it is still the responsibility of the vendor. Placing a LAN into production before it is formally accepted reduces the vendor's ability to make changes and gives the vendor a good argument for showing that the system has really been accepted.

As a final consideration regarding a purchase contract, you must attempt to protect yourself from losses in the event that the vendor is unable to live up to the conditions of the contract. Here are some things that can happen:

The vendor fails to meet completion schedules.

The system fails to meet performance objectives.

The vendor fails to complete delivery of all components.

The installation fails to meet building codes, such as wiring codes.

The vendor fails to deliver software custom-tailored to your environment.

The software fails to meet functional requirements (that is, it has too many bugs).

You can protect yourself from such problems by inserting **protection** or **penalty clauses** in your contract. A penalty clause holds the vendor liable for damages if the terms of the contract are not met. For example, the vendor might agree to a penalty clause that requires it to pay $1000 for each week beyond the scheduled completion date that the LAN is not acceptable. Thus, a vendor that is four weeks late in completing its obligations will have a $4000 penalty. For obvious reasons many vendors are uneasy about entering into contracts with penalty clauses; in fact, most vendors will not sign such contracts. Still, you should attempt to protect your company from losses resulting from the failure of the vendor to live up to the terms of the contract. Another possible penalty clause is to require the vendor to provide sufficient hardware to realize the performance or capacity goals. For example, suppose the contract specified a maximum time to download an application. If the hardware supplied is incapable of meeting that goal, the contract might require the vendor to add or substitute hardware to attain the stated performance level. In this situation the vendor may have to substitute a faster disk drive, add more memory, or install a faster server CPU. The expenses of such upgrades are absorbed by the vendor.

Support and Maintenance Agreements

When you purchase an expensive item such as a car or a house, you protect your investment through proper **preventive** and **restorative maintenance.** Just as you change the oil in your car periodically, paint your house every few years, and keep your lawn mowed, so must you protect your investment in LAN hardware and software, which is substantial. You will want to get software upgrades and bug fixes as they become available, repair or replace hardware components that fail, and carry out periodic preventive maintenance on the components. Your company may assume the responsibility for some of this maintenance. Some companies with large data processing organizations repair their own microcomputers. Some companies repair their equipment on an as-needed basis; if a device fails, the company takes it to a repair facility and pays for the repairs. Other companies subscribe to hardware maintenance contracts that cover preventive and restorative maintenance.

Microcomputer hardware and software are rapidly becoming more sophisticated. The hardware is still at a level that allows someone with modest technical skills to replace a defective printed circuit board, add new options, and so on. Moreover, much of the software is updated by purchases of an entirely new product or new version of the existing product. Some microcomputer software companies now offer maintenance services. With these services you can receive periodic interim releases that contain bug fixes and minor enhancements. As the sophistication of system components increases, so will the problems associated with them. Corporate users, particularly those who have large systems, are used to receiving periodic bug fixes to their software and hardware. These fixes usually come automatically under hardware and software maintenance agreements. You must decide which components, if any, are so critical that they should be covered by maintenance agreements. Multiple maintenance agreements may be necessary to cover all system components. For example, you may have a hardware and LAN software maintenance agreement with your LAN vendor and individual software maintenance agreements for each application.

If you are installing a LAN for the first time, you may need quite a bit of support during the first months or year of operation. Over time you build a level of expertise that makes you less dependent on technical help from others. If you are a new LAN user, it is usually wise to arrange for technical support from your vendor or from another source, such as a consultant. Many companies just entering the world of LANs hire consultants to make the transition easier. You should also consider subscribing to a support service for critical software, especially for software products with which you are unfamiliar. For example, if LAN system software, network mail, and groupware are critical to your users, and your organization is unfamiliar with those products, a support agreement can help you solve problems quickly and allow you to use the software more efficiently.

You also must evaluate the costs of hardware and software maintenance agreements carefully. Any agreement must be cost-effective. Occasionally a vendor has levels of maintenance and support; for example, at the highest level you may have permanent on-site vendor support personnel. At the next level you may find on-site support within a specified time, such as a 4-hour response time during normal working hours and an 8-hour response time during nonbusiness hours. A lower support level may offer unlimited telephone support; below that you may get measured telephone support, such as two free calls per week with added fees for additional calls; below that you would pay a fee for each call made to the support line. In general, a support and maintenance agreement compatible with your organization's technical expertise is a good investment, particularly during the first year of your LAN's operation.

Having negotiated your purchase, support, and maintenance contracts, you must prepare for the arrival and installation of the equipment. After an agreement is reached, planning and installation tasks begin in earnest.

INSTALLATION TASKS

Installing a LAN can be difficult because there are a multitude of details to attend to and a number of rules that must be followed. As the size of the LAN increases, so do the potential for problems and the chance to break rules about medium distances, number of nodes, distances between nodes, and so on. To illustrate what we mean by rules, Table 10.1 shows some of the restrictions outlined in the IEEE 802.3 standard for CSMA/CD bus LANs. In addition to these, you must know about technology, such as local codes for wiring, how to make connections between media and between a medium and nodes, and how to change from one medium to another, such as from coaxial cable to twisted-pair wires or from one type of coaxial cable to another.

LAN installation has several well-defined stages. Some of these stages can be worked on in parallel, and some phases require the completion of one or more other phases before they can begin. The major installation phases are

1. Documentation
2. Site planning
3. Medium installation
4. Hardware installation
5. Software installation

Table 10.1   IEEE 802.3 Distance Standards

Feature	Thick Coaxial	Thin Coaxial
Maximum segment length (meters)	500	185
Maximum number of segments	5	5
Maximum end-to-end cable length (meters)	2500	925
Minimum distance between nodes (meters)	2.5	0.5
Maximum nodes per segment	100	30

6. Conversion and data preparation

7. Creation of the operating environment

8. Testing and acceptance

9. Cutover

10. Training

Figure 10.1 is a PERT chart showing the relationships among these events and the critical path. The numbers in parentheses represent the expected completion time in days. The numbers in circles are nodes representing the completion of an activity. Neither set of numbers corresponds to the numbers of the installation phases. Let us now look at what is accomplished at each step.

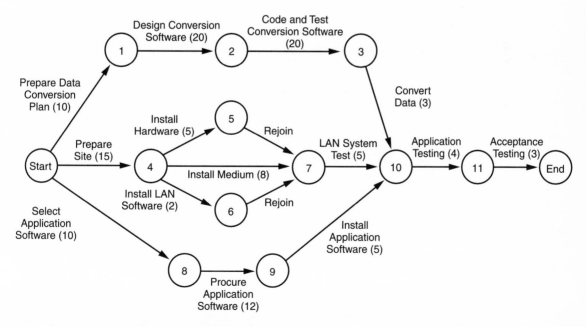

Figure 10.1   PERT Chart of Installation Activities

Documentation

Documentation is a part of each phase of LAN selection and implementation. When selecting the LAN, you must document your problem and your objectives, the options considered, the reasons for selecting and rejecting certain approaches, and so on. Because documentation is so pervasive, we will cite key documents you must create during certain phases of the installation.

Site Planning

Site planning defines the layout of the LAN and identifies the building and environment modifications necessary to house the components. During this phase you identify and plan the following:

workstation placement	printer locations
power requirements	building code conformance
power point locations	safety code conformance
medium locations	hardware relocation
ambient conditions	telephone line placement
server locations	network and computer interconnections

Site planning essentially produces the blueprints for laying out the network. During this phase you draw floor plans showing the location of cable runs (or transmitters and receivers for a wireless LAN), workstations, servers, printers, and wiring hubs. You also must ensure that your configuration conforms to your local building codes. These codes vary from one location to another. Some require that wires be strung through conduits or that cables on the floor be placed into recessed areas called **channels** or that plenum cables be used. Also, some building codes govern power distribution.

When planning your LAN layout, you must consider where to install the servers. Workstations and printers are located where users can easily access them. On the other hand, servers are often located in secure areas to avoid accidental or intentional disruption of LAN operations. For example, you do not want some well-meaning employee powering down the server because no one appears to be using it. Moreover, an employee intent on disrupting the organization's computing can cause problems by shutting down the server or destroying files located on the server. Therefore, it is usually a good idea to locate the server in a room that can be secured from casual access.

Sometimes LANs are connected to other LANs, to a WAN, or to a stand-alone host system. In such instances it is important to design the layout so that such connections are simple to make. For example, locating modem servers in close proximity to telephone lines is important for telephone-line connections. Locating servers in computer rooms provides for easy connection to a WAN or stand-alone host computer.

The primary maxim you should observe when doing the site planning is "Proper prior planning prevents poor performance." Try to anticipate everything. Be mindful of wiring lengths and interconnection points. Allow for extra cable lengths needed to keep wiring out of the way. Make sure all devices can be located where they are needed;

that is, be sure that maximum wire lengths between connecting points are not exceeded. It is important to identify all current and future equipment locations. Usually it is easier to install extra wiring during the initial wiring stages than to come back and add it later. Other site planning considerations include providing proper power supplies, cooling, and other ambient conditions such as proper humidity levels, distances from electrical and magnetic interference, and protection from direct sunlight. If you are working with a vendor, you should work closely with the vendor's staff to ensure that your plans are valid.

Medium Installation

After site planning you ought to be ready to install the medium. If you are working with a wireless LAN, installation is considerably easier than installing a wire-based LAN. With a wire-based LAN, you must find a way to string wires or cable through the areas housing servers, workstations, and printers. Often wires are strung through ceilings, walls, over the floor, along walls, through floors, through wiring closets, and so on. As mentioned earlier, when installing wiring you must be sure to comply with building codes.

Sometimes it is impossible or impractical for a company to install LAN wiring. This might be the case when wires must pass through concrete walls or between buildings. One company was prevented from installing wires between two buildings because the wires would have had to cross a public street. The company could not legally install wires over or under the street. The company had two options: contract with a common carrier for a line, or use a wireless medium such as microwave or infrared light. The company chose a wireless medium to connect LAN segments in the two buildings, as illustrated in Figure 10.2.

After the wire or cable has been installed, it should be tested to ensure that it was not damaged during the installation process. For example, a wire may have been crimped when it was bent around a corner. A wire crimp can cause transmission problems, so you should test the wires for continuity. You test cables with test equipment designed specifically for that purpose. Some cable test equipment manufacturers claim that over 50

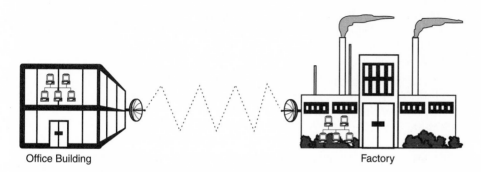

Office Building   Factory

Figure 10.2   Wireless Medium Connecting LANs in Two Buildings

percent of all LAN problems are cable related. For example, a cable tester can tell you the following information:

whether cable breaks exist

the distance from the test unit to the cable break

where faulty connections exist

whether twisted-pair wires can support the high speeds needed by Ethernet or token rings

components that are borderline

Do your testing while you still can make corrections easily. For example, if you are pulling wires through conduit, check the cables immediately. If errors are found, it is usually easier to correct them when the wires are exposed and the pulling wire is still in place than after the wires are connected or the pulling wire has been removed.

Hardware Installation

As illustrated in the PERT chart in Figure 10.1, hardware installation can begin before premises are wired. However, completion of hardware installation requires that both computer and medium hardware be installed. You must carry out several tasks during hardware installation. The primary task is installing the LAN adapters in the workstations and servers. Each workstation and server must have an available expansion slot to house the LAN adapter. Older LAN adapters have switch or jumper settings you must set before installing the adapter card in the computer; newer ones can be set up by software. Ethernet and token-ring cards usually have a unique address set by the factory. ARCnet cards have an 8-bit switch register in which the address must be set. Each LAN adapter must use an **interrupt request (IRQ)** to gain attention from the CPU. You must set the IRQ for each computer to a value not already being used by another device connected to that computer. Therefore, you must know about the devices already installed on the computer and the interrupts they are using. You must also indicate which I/O port the LAN adapter is going to use for reading and writing data and the memory address in RAM that is used to transfer data to and from the LAN. Again, these addresses should not conflict with those used by other devices. To keep these details straight, you should document each workstation's and server's configuration. A sample form you might use for doing this is shown in Figure 10.3. Some of your workstations may need additional memory. Recall that the overall memory requirement of each workstation increases as a result of the LAN system software.

You may decide that some servers also need additional memory. Typically LAN software vendors give you the necessary minimum hardware configurations for servers and workstations, but this configuration is usually just adequate. For best performance you should add memory beyond the minimum requirements. Recall that memory is often used to improve performance by caching disk records and increasing buffer sizes. The amount of memory required on servers is almost always greater than that required for workstations. Most large LAN systems require 16 MB or more of server memory.

Manufacturer _____

Vendor _____

Location _____

CPU: Type _____   Speed _____   Math-Coprocessor _____

Memory _____

Memory Management Software/Hardware _____

Monitor: Manufacturer _____   Graphics Adapter _____

           Screen Size _____   Color? _____

Disks: Drive   Type   Capacity   Comments

         _____   _____   _____   _____

         _____   _____   _____   _____

         _____   _____   _____   _____

         _____   _____   _____   _____

Network Interface Card _____   Manufacturer _____

Node Address _____   IRQ _____   I/Q Base Address _____

Operating System _____   Type _____   Version _____

LAN Interface Software _____

Printer: Type   Manufacturer   Network Address

           _____   _____   _____

           _____   _____   _____

           _____   _____   _____

           _____   _____   _____

Figure 10.3   Hardware Configuration Form

You should check the amount of available disk space when loading the LAN software on workstations and servers. A few LANs need considerable disk space on the workstation for storing network files. The disk space required on the file servers for LAN software alone can be great. For example, one LAN system requires 4 MB of disk storage space for its workstation network files and a minimum of 100 MB of server disk storage. The 100 MB is for the network operating system only; additional space is needed for spooler files, applications, database files, and so on. On your disk you must store not only the LAN software but also memory swap space for executing software, spooler files, and mail message files, and space for new applications such as groupware. The disk space required can easily exceed several hundred MB, and this does not include the storage required for application programs and databases. Moreover, if your workstations have a variety of operating systems, you may need to load operating system utilities from each version on the server disks. This allows workstations to access utilities from the network rather than from local disk drives. Each diskless workstation requires these operating system utilities.

Other hardware installation tasks include installing printers, backup units, modems, facsimile devices, and so on. Your site-planning documentation should indicate where these devices are located. Each can create special planning and installation problems. After the premises are wired and you have installed the LAN adapters and other hardware, you can begin connecting the hardware to the wiring. When this is done, you have the physical network in place.

Software Installation

The software installation process consists of three phases: LAN operating system software installation, application software installation, and utility software installation. Another task involved in software installation is setting up application and user environments. In this section we are concerned only with software that is stored on the server. Applications used by only one or two users can be installed on those users' workstations.

Installing LAN operating system software has two subphases: installing the workstation software and installing the server software. On workstations you must install the client system software discussed in Chapters 6 and 7. This is usually a rather simple process. The workstation software modules are generated for individual workstations or for groups of workstations. Earlier in this chapter you read about LAN adapter settings. These settings must also be defined for the software. The variations you must typically accommodate between workstations are

> operating system version
>
> interrupt requests
>
> memory addresses
>
> I/O port address

After the workstation's LAN system software is generated, it must be loaded onto the workstation. For DOS systems the **AUTOEXEC.BAT** and **CONFIG.SYS** files also are updated to set the environment and the startup parameters. An AUTOEXEC.BAT file contains commands that are automatically executed by DOS when the system is booted. Table 10.2 shows a simple batch file for a DOS workstation interface to a Novell NetWare server. The function of each of the lines is as follows:

> LSL: LSL stands for link support layer. The LSL interfaces between the network layer protocols, such as IPX and IP, and the LAN driver that provides the MAC layer protocol. LSL is an implementation of the Open Data-Link Interface (ODI) standard.
>
> EPROODI: EPROODI is the LAN driver for the adapter in this computer. It also conforms to the ODI specifications.

Table 10.2   Simple STARTNET.BAT File

LSL

EPROODI.COM

IPXODI

VLM

IPXODI: This provides the ODI network layer IPX protocol used by NetWare.

VLM: VLM stands for virtual loadable module. The VLM provides higher OSI layer functions and includes the redirector capability. Individual VLM modules can be loaded on a workstation to tailor the workstation to the network activity.

In a NetWare network an additional startup file, the NET.CFG file, may be used to provide parameters to the workstation environment. The general category of parameters that can be placed in NET.CFG include

MAC driver

link support

network layer support

redirector parameters

The CONFIG.SYS file contains system environment data. For instance, you can specify how many files can be open concurrently, the number of disk buffers allocated in memory, which device drivers are to be installed, and so on. Again, the steps you follow depend on the network you are using. A simple CONFIG.SYS file is shown in Table 10.3. In an OS/2 operating system, the STARTUP.CMD file is similar to DOS's AUTOEXEC.BAT file. With an OS/2 workstation the STARTUP.CMD file may need to be updated to make the network connection automatically.

Novell's 3.*nn* and 4.*nn* NetWare network operating systems (NOS) also have two **startup files** that are used automatically when the NOS is loaded. These files, named AUTOEXEC.NCF and STARTUP.NCF, contain commands the NOS automatically follows upon starting. Examples of an AUTOEXEC.NCF and STARTUP.NCF files are shown in Tables 10.4 and 10.5, respectively. The AUTOEXEC.NCF file shown provides the NOS with the name of the file server and the internal network number. The STARTUP.NCF file loads the disk drivers for the server disks. Further details of the startup files are beyond the scope of this chapter.

In addition to the LAN workstation software that interfaces to the operating system and the network, you must install workstation software to interface to network printers. We cover this topic in Chapter 12.

Usually, installing the LAN server software is more complex than installing the LAN workstation software. As mentioned earlier, some LAN server software is self-contained; that is, operating system and LAN software are integrated. Other

Table 10.3   Simple Workstation CONFIG.SYS File

DEVICE=C:\APPS\WINDOWS\SETVER.EXE
DEVICE=C:\SCSI\ASPI2DOS.SYS /D /Z
DEVICE=C:\APPS\WINDOWS\HIMEM.SYS
DEVICE=C:\APPS\WINDOWS\COMMAND\ANSI.SYS
REM BUFFERS=30
FILES=128
DOS=UMB
DOS=HIGH
DEVICEHIGH=C:\DSP16\DSP16.SYS /FC:\DSP16\dsp001.ld /I5 /D1 /J1
DEVICEHIGH=C:\CDROM\MTMCDAE.SYS /D:MSCD001 /P:310 /A:0 /M:32 /T:7 /I:10 /X
shell=C:\COMMAND.COM C:\ /p /e:2048
DEVICE=C:\SCSI\ASPIDISK.SYS /D

---

implementations load the LAN software as a set of tasks run under a general-purpose operating system such as UNIX or OS/2.

When installing the LAN software, you must understand the impact of the installation. If the LAN software is integrated with an operating system, it probably changes the format of the server's disk drives. An integrated LAN operating system may have a file and directory format different from those of a general-purpose operating system. For example, it may change the disk directory structure because the operating system uses different naming conventions and provides more security attributes for files. It may change the file allocation table because it allocates disk space by a method different from that used by a general-purpose operating system. If this is the case, before starting the installation, you should back up all files on the server's disks. This is a good idea even when installing LAN software that runs under the server's current operating system. Moreover, be sure that the backup is compatible with the eventual state of the system. For example, if you back up the data under the DOS operating system, and a new operating system is installed that does not allow you to run a DOS RESTORE program, be sure that a mechanism exists for getting those files back on the server.

LAN software is tailored to an individual server. You may need to generate an operating system version that is compatible with the hardware settings you indicated when installing the LAN adapter. The details of installing the LAN software vary from one LAN to another. In some cases it is a very simple process and requires little time. This does not imply that the LAN software is simple. For example, installing Novell NetWare 4.*nn* is quite easy, requiring only that you answer a few questions; it takes less than 30 minutes. However, NetWare 4.*nn* is one of the most sophisticated LANs for microcomputers.

Table 10.4   Sample AUTOEXEC.NCF File

FILE SERVER NAME NW41
IPX INTERNAL NET 30A38EAF

Table 10.5 Sample STARTUP.NCF File

SET RESERVED BUFFERS BELOW 16 MEG=200
LOAD AHA1520.DSK PORT=340
LOAD ASPICD.DSK int=0 int1=0 dma=0 dma1=0

In contrast, earlier, less capable versions of Novell LAN software, such as NetWare 2.*nn*, are noted for lengthy and complex installations.

A typical LAN also has utility software that provides a variety of functions. Some LAN software comes with utility software bundled in. Users often supplement this utility software with other utilities, such as

backup/restore utilities

LAN management/administration utilities

file transfer utilities

statistics and reporting utilities

diagnostics utilities

The type of utilities you need for your LAN varies according to the type and scope of the utilities bundled with your LAN software. Most LANs come with a backup/restore program, but some LAN administrators purchase another backup/restore system that is more comprehensive than the bundled version. The final installation phase is to customize the applications to the needs of individual users. Applications vary in their ability to accommodate individual users. How you do this customization is therefore application dependent.

Conversion and Data Preparation

Once all application and system software is installed, you must load the data. Sometimes data is converted from an existing computer system, and sometimes you must manually enter new data. When setting up a LAN, an organization must decide what is public data and what is private data. **Public data** is usually stored on a server. **Private data** may be stored at one or more workstations or in secured files on the server. Public data is shared by two or more users. In this section we are concerned only with public data. Some data starts as private data and when sufficiently prepared becomes public, such as budget data and marketing information for new products.

Creation of the Operating Environment

Installing software and user profiles is one aspect of creating the operating environment. Setting up security, user IDs, workgroups, and so on is another important aspect. This topic is discussed in Chapter 11.

Testing and Acceptance

After installing the hardware and software and setting up the operating environment, you are ready to conduct system testing. The objective of testing is to determine whether the system works according to contractual stipulations. Your purchase contract should detail the terms under which the LAN is acceptable. The testing conducted can be separated into two main parts: functional testing and performance testing.

During **functional testing** you test the system components to ensure that they all work correctly, both individually and collectively. Thus you check each application to verify that it works correctly. Recall that an application that works correctly on one network may not work at all on a different network, so you should not assume that your applications will all work correctly. For example, if you are using a client/server architecture, client and server software must be compatible. Because there are different middleware specifications, server and client software must be compatible in this regard. Moreover, you must check that the applications were installed correctly. One problem often encountered is improper security settings. When you check the applications, be sure you log on under the IDs of users who will be working with the applications. An application that works correctly for the LAN's supervisor may not work for a user with lesser privileges. You should also check that user profiles are correctly set up, the license provisions operate correctly, the printer system functions as it should, and the application modules can interoperate correctly. Functional testing can usually be conducted with a few users. These users should exercise each component of the systems they intend to use.

Performance testing, sometimes called stress testing, tests to see whether the network can sustain the anticipated workload. Again, the acceptance criteria in the purchase contract should indicate levels of required performance. This can be the time required to download an application, the response time to database requests, and the throughput of the system (the work that can be accomplished by the workgroup). Your testing must provide an environment that completely tests your system. You must define the functions that need testing and the environment necessary for conducting stress testing. Stress testing is ordinarily conducted in two ways: For the first approach a large group of users who are representative of all system users simulate the actual working environment by using the system. The second approach uses software that simulates the actual working environment by setting up a given number of users and a work rate. The first approach takes more personnel coordination and can be expensive if numerous employees must be paid overtime to conduct the tests. The second approach is not labor intensive but requires some software preparation. However, the stress testing software can be used again to tune the system and check the impact of adding new users and applications.

To perform effective acceptance testing, you cannot wait until the system is completely installed to prepare the suite of test programs. Proper testing is a well-planned event. The PERT chart for installation and acceptance in Figure 10.1 shows that you can begin planning for testing immediately after you select the system. Once you have accepted the system (or placed it into production without formally accepting it) you assume responsibility for making it work and keeping users satisfied with performance and capabilities. Acceptance testing helps you to ensure that the vendor has provided a system that works to your organization's satisfaction.

Cutover

After the system has been accepted, you must move users from the old system or way of doing things to the new system, a procedure known as **cutover.** Commonly when a new system is installed, it is run parallel to the old system for some time to confirm that the new system works the way it should. This may be difficult for a LAN because the old system of stand-alone workstations is likely to be integrated into the network. However, it may be a simple matter to revert to using the individual workstations as stand-alone systems. Thus, cutover usually can be accomplished after user training and system acceptance.

Even though cutover may be fairly straightforward, it still must be planned. The cutover plans should include when cutover is to occur and whether cutover is to be done all at once or in phases. The phased approach, often the most practical, adds users to the network in groups. Thus the network grows incrementally over time until all users are added to the network. Phased implementation allows you to build the network slowly, from both the users' and administrators' perspectives. If problems are encountered along the way, they can be overcome with a minimum disruption to the user community.

TRAINING

Three general classes of LAN users must receive training: administrators, group managers, and users. Before training is conducted, the roles of the participants must be decided. Some employees are users only, some are group managers, some are LAN operators, and at least one has the responsibilities of LAN administrator. The category or categories into which an employee falls depend on the employee's technical expertise, job functions, and interest. In an organization a group has a manager; however, this manager is not necessarily the person who should be assigned the task of group manager for LAN administration. A LAN group manager may need to carry out technical tasks, such as attaching users to printers, clearing jobs from the print queue, and so on. Someone in the workgroup with a technical aptitude may fulfill this responsibility better than the group's manager.

User Training

By far the least amount of training is needed for users, but user training often is the hardest to conduct, for two reasons. Users tend to have less computer expertise than the other two groups, so some users have a hard time learning technical details. Also, user training typically is done in-house by in-house staff, which means the trainees sometimes have their learning interrupted by work emergencies. Moreover, in-house training facilities sometimes lack the necessary equipment, and in-house trainers sometimes are less proficient than professional trainers.

Recall from earlier chapters that using a LAN ought to be transparent. In most cases this is true at the application level. That is, once a user environment has been established, the user works as though all the files needed are on a local disk drive. In a well-planned LAN, the LAN administrator sets up an environment that promotes transparency. One way to provide transparency is through startup files such as CONFIG.SYS and AUTOEXEC.BAT files and through **logon scripts.** A logon script is a set of system commands that creates a user's environment on the network. A logon script can set a user's default drive and directory, set a search path for executable files (such as those in the AUTOEXEC.BAT), map logical disk drives on the file server, set up a printing environment, display a message of the day, and so on. Taken to the ultimate level, the combination of startup files and logon scripts can log the user onto the LAN and automatically start a program for the user or display a familiar menu. A note of caution: Automatically logging a user onto the LAN in a startup file is a potential security hazard and typically should be avoided.

Even with startup files and logon scripts, users may notice that some operations are a bit different on a LAN than on a stand-alone system, including

directing printed output to different printers

changing a password

finding resources on the network or other networks

logging off

setting paths

using groupware

finding the disk drive mappings

running electronic mail

finding differences in application environment settings

setting file security

Naturally the type of training users need depends on the LAN software they will be using. Usually LAN users must know how to log on, use electronic mail, set up their own configuration for specific applications, and network differences in the applications they are using. For example, users might want to use a "send message to user" LAN utility, change passwords, change file security attributes for files they own, and look at their jobs in the spooler's disk queues.

Initial training may be conducted by your vendor, a software consultant, or your own staff. In the long term it is often best if several members of your organization provide the user training. Most organizations experience personnel turnover, so some people will always need training. Hiring outside consultants for this continual process can be expensive. Moreover, much of the training required can be done through self-paced user manuals, on-line tutorials, or videotapes.

Group Manager Training

Group managers are users with minor LAN administration responsibilities. A group manager must know everything that users know as well as group management tasks. The primary group management tasks are adding and deleting users from groups. A group manager may also be responsible for setting security for files and directories owned by the group. Other possible group management tasks include managing print queues, changing print job priorities, deleting jobs from the print queue, attaching and detaching a queue from a printer, printing specific portions of a job in a queue, and similar print tasks. The most likely source of this training is the LAN administrator.

Operator Training

An operator's responsibilities include starting the network, keeping it running, making data backups, and shutting the network down. Often these duties are carried out by the LAN administrator. Regardless of who is responsible for these tasks, training is necessary. Starting the system involves powering up shared components such as the file and print servers and loading essential software modules such as the spooler. When problems occur, the operator must know how to resolve them so the network continues to operate efficiently. Making data backups is another important responsibility of the operator (see Chapter 13). Finally, the operator must know how to bring the network to an orderly halt, ensuring that all users are able to complete their work and that no data is lost or corrupted in the process. These skills are often taught in LAN administration classes, and some sources for this training are given in the next section of this chapter.

LAN Administrator Training

Administration of a small, established LAN may require only a small amount of work, say several hours per week. However, a small LAN needs at least two qualified LAN administrators, one serving as an alternative or backup administrator. Suppose your organization has only one person who knows how to start, stop, and fix the LAN. If that person goes on vacation or a business trip, retires, quits, becomes ill, or for some other reason cannot be there to solve problems, your organization's work capability can be severely reduced when problems with the network arise.

LAN administration for large LANs can be a full-time job for one or more people. The amount of training required for a LAN administrator depends on the sophistication or complexity of the system. A large LAN may have hundreds of users; tens of servers; connections to other LANs, WANs, and stand-alone hosts; a wide variety of applications installed; and a high rate of personnel turnover. This system requires a LAN administrator with considerably more technical expertise than does a three-user LAN used primarily to share printers and disks.

The LAN administrator must know everything that users and group managers know, and a lot more. The administrator's education is usually more formal than that of users and managers. When a LAN is first implemented, the organization ordinarily hires an experienced LAN administrator or sends one of its employees to a LAN administration course oriented specifically toward the LAN chosen. For example, the LAN administrator

Table 10.6   LAN Administrator Responsiblities

Hardware options	Software options	Hardware installation
System software installation	Diagnostics and trouble shooting	User administration
Group administration	Printer administration	Security
Application installation	Backup and recovery	Problem reporting
Capacity planning	System tuning	Systems programming

will take several 1-week LAN administration courses, such as elementary LAN administration, LAN troubleshooting, advanced LAN administration, system programming, and performance and tuning. Training classes are often conducted by the LAN vendor. Other sources of training include in-house experts, consultants, professional education companies, the LAN manufacturer, and colleges and universities. LAN administrators also must have conceptual training oriented toward understanding the technology in general—topics such as data communication and LAN principles. It is definitely a good investment to train LAN administrators before they assume administrative duties. Learning as you go with self-taught on-the-job training has too much potential for costly and time-consuming errors. LAN administrators also must keep their administrative knowledge current. This is done through formal training classes, on-the-job training, and periodic additional formal training.

LAN administrators must learn all facets of administration. A partial list of topics they must know is given in Table 10.6.

SUMMARY

LAN selection leads naturally to LAN installation. During installation, problems often arise. Many times these problems result from misunderstandings between the organization and its LAN vendors. To guard against such misunderstandings, a company should have a detailed written contract with all vendors. The contract should protect the rights of the vendor and the organization alike. It should stipulate what is to be delivered, when and where delivery is to occur, and what constitutes acceptance of the system. An organization should have an attorney review the purchase and installation contracts.

Installation consists of several well-defined stages. Some stages can be done in parallel, and some must be done sequentially. A plan must be created that identifies the tasks, their order, and when they must be completed. A PERT chart is one way of organizing this plan. The main stages of installation are documentation, site preparation, medium installation, hardware installation, software installation, conversion, creation of an operating environment, testing, cutover, and training. Hardware installation may require upgrades to existing workstations. An organization should test for both functional completeness and adherence to stated performance goals.

Basic LAN training programs are needed for users, group managers, and LAN administrators. Users must know how the LAN environment differs from a stand-alone workstation and how to use the LAN resources effectively. Group managers need more training than users. Group managers are responsible for adding users, deleting users, setting security attributes for files and directories, and manipulating printer settings. LAN administrators need the most extensive training. Essentially LAN administrators must know about all aspects of the LAN: startup procedures; shutdown procedures; hardware and software installation; user, group, and printer management; troubleshooting; and so on. To ensure that an organization always has a LAN administrator available, at least two people should receive LAN administration training.

Key Terms

AUTOEXEC.BAT file
channels
CONFIG.SYS file
cutover
functional testing
interrupt request (IRQ)
logon script
payment schedule
penalty clause
performance testing

preventive maintenance
progress payments
private data
protection clause
public data
purchase contract
restorative maintenance
site planning
startup file

Review Questions

1. Why is a purchase contract important?
2. What is acceptance testing, and why is it necessary?
3. Why would you make progress payments? How do the vendor and customer benefit from progress payments?
4. What are penalty clauses? Give an example of a penalty clause.
5. Why are software and hardware maintenance agreements important?
6. What is accomplished during site planning?
7. What medium installation options are usually available?
8. What hardware changes might be required when converting a stand-alone workstation to a LAN workstation?
9. Describe the software installation process. In which computers must you install software? What types of files are created or modified to enable network access?
10. Describe eight differences a user may notice when going from a stand-alone environment to a LAN environment.
11. Compare functional and performance testing.
12. What are the four basic user groups that require training? Describe the training required for the four basic user groups.

Problems and Exercises

1. Write a list of tasks that should be completed as part of the site preparation for a LAN in your school or workplace. Examples of things you should consider are new power sources, construction to house a server in a controlled access room, and wiring.
2. Draw a PERT chart for the installation of a LAN for your school or workplace.

3. Suppose you wanted to install a new LAN in your school or workplace. What type of medium would be appropriate? Detail how the wires for a wire-based LAN (twisted-pair wires, coaxial cable, or fiber optic cable) would be installed. How would a wireless LAN be installed?

4. Suppose that you are installing a new application on the LAN. The new application replaces a manual system in which all data are kept on 3 × 5 file cards. Describe how you would convert the data to machine-readable form on the LAN.

5. Examine the literature to find the types of classes being presented by LAN vendors or consulting firms for data communication, LAN installation, LAN management, and LAN problem resolution. What are the costs of the course? Where are they held? What would be the cost of the such training for a LAN administrator in your area? Include the costs of travel, lodging, and meals.

Chapter 11

LAN Administration: Users, Groups, and Security

CHAPTER PREVIEW

LAN installation can be difficult, but it is a one-time task. LAN administration—keeping the system running properly—is an ongoing activity. How much time you spend on LAN administration depends on the number of users on your system, the variety of hardware, network software, and applications you have, and to a lesser extent on your LAN software itself. Many tasks of the LAN administrator relate to LAN users. Part of the responsibility of a LAN administrator is to help create a user-friendly environment by providing easy access to necessary applications and data and by making it easy for users to print or distribute their results. This chapter gives you some guidelines for creating and securing the user environment.

Specific topics you will read about in this chapter include

users and groups

system programming

security

virus protection

USERS AND GROUPS

When you implement a LAN, you are creating a community of users who share LAN resources. As in most communities, the members of a LAN community are not all alike. An individual LAN user does not always have the same rights and privileges as all other LAN users. One objective of LAN administration is to make available all the resources a person needs for his or her job while withholding or protecting the resources that are unnecessary. For example, a software engineer needs access to some program source files but not to payroll files. A payroll supervisor needs to access and update payroll files but not program source files. Studies have shown that the major security risk facing companies today is its employees, not outside intruders. Some security breaches are accidental, such as accidentally erasing a file; other breaches are intentional, such as disgruntled employees intentionally erasing files or providing sensitive corporate data to a competitor. The LAN administrator must create the environment that promotes both productivity and protection.

A network builds its user community primarily through two entities: users and groups. A group can be a workgroup or a collection of employees drawn along other organizational boundaries. However, before we go into the details of groups, let us first look at users.

Users

A LAN community of users may consist of all the organization's employees. In the typical organization, however, some employees must use the LAN to do their work, some simply use output created on the LAN, and others do not use the system at all. From the LAN administrator's perspective, the term *users* applies only to employees who use the LAN in doing their jobs. Because LAN users usually do not all have the same access privileges, it is important to be able to distinguish one user from another. Without such distinctions, the LAN software cannot enforce security.

The two most basic LAN administration tasks involving users are adding users and deleting them. Once a user has been added to the system, additional administrative tasks exist to customize that user's environment and to provide that user with access privileges and restrictions. The user's environment is often a matrix of rights covering printers, files, workstations, and time. That is, a user may have rights to use certain printers, have access privileges to certain files, and be restricted to using certain workstations at certain times. Let us look at these privileges and restrictions in more detail.

The **user ID** is a user's form of **identification** to the system. If security is in force, the user also must provide **authentication** of himself or herself by entering into the system information known only to that user, such as a **password.** More security-conscious systems use **biological identification and authentication** measures, such as retina scans, palm prints, or voice analysis. Once identified and authenticated, a user is granted access to the system. Exactly what access is allowed depends on the user's access rights, which are detailed later in the chapter.

Some systems allow functional user capabilities that correspond to a functional role rather than to a specific individual. For example, suppose several users need access to spooler control utilities. Furthermore, suppose these users have nothing else in common (they do not belong to the same workgroup or department, for example). LANs may provide several ways in which these users can be combined. Some of the options are through individual rights, group membership, use of a common user ID, and user profiles. NetWare 4.*nn* has an organizational role object that also provides these capabilities. It is well suited for the spooler situation just described. The print operators can be given their necessary privileges through affiliation with the organizational role object.

Many LAN systems automatically establish two types of users at installation time. One type of user has a common user ID, such as GUEST, with few or no network privileges. The other type of user is all-powerful, with all rights and privileges on the system.

In a Novell networks, this user is called SUPERVISOR or ADMIN depending on the NOS version. In UNIX the omnipotent user is called ROOT and under another OS, he or she is the SUPER user. We shall henceforth use the term *SUPERVISOR* when referring to this user. The major function of the SUPERVISOR is to set up LAN user, file, and printer environments, keep the system running correctly, install software and hardware, and solve network problems.

In most systems, adding users is simple. Some systems have a command language interface that requires you to use syntax such as ADD USER *<user-name>*. Some LANs have a menu or GUI interface that prompts you through the process of adding a user. Still other systems have a user ID file that you must edit with a text editor, inserting a new line to create a new user. The technique for adding new users is not as important as well-planned user administration. The LAN administrator should devise a plan for creating consistent user names, matching those user names with the users or functions that use them, and setting up user access rights.

Groups

A group is a collection of users. In some systems each user must belong to exactly one group. In other systems a user can belong to none, one, or several groups. The functions of a groups are to combine many users into a single entity and to use the group to implement security needs or grant capabilities common to groups of users.

You can think of a LAN as consisting of individual users, formally defined groups of users, and the entire community of users. Some LAN activities can be done by only one or two people, some things can be done by several people (a group), and some things can be done by everyone. Users and groups can do certain things on a LAN because they have been given **access rights,** or privileges. Examples of access rights for individuals, groups, and everyone are shown in Table 11.1. The LAN administrator must find an easy way to give proper access rights to all users. Shortly, we will look at security as it pertains to users and groups.

Table 11.1   User Access Rights

Rights Extended to Everyone	Logon and logoff	Run word processing and spreadsheet programs
	Send and receive electronic mail	
Rights Extended to All Members of a Personnel Group	Change employee addresses, telephone numbers, and names	Add new employees
	Retrieve employee data	Use department printers
Rights Extended to Only a Few Members of a Personnel Group	Change employee ratings	Delete employees
	Promote employees	Delete files
	Create files	
Rights Extended to Specific Members of a Software Development Group	Update source program	Delete source files

System Programming

The meaning of *system programming* depends on the whether the system is a mainframe or a LAN. In a mainframe environment, system programmers are responsible for maintaining system software, such as the operating system, database management system, and data communication system software. They install, patch, program, and test these system software components. On a LAN, system programming consists primarily of running the network, solving network problems, installing new software, writing network utilities, and personalizing users' environments.

One system programming task is creating logon scripts. A **logon script** is a file that contains commands to set the user's environment automatically when he or she logs onto the network. Through a logon script the a LAN administrator can usually carry out the following:

map server drives to the client's OS drive designators, such as F: in DOS

print messages to the user

run one or more programs

set the user's default drive and directory

synchronize the client's time to the server's time

Another system programming task is creating menus for users. Menus and graphical user interfaces (GUIs) make the system easier to use. If you are using a GUI, such as Windows, menus usually are created through the GUI's utilities. Some LAN applications also have utilities for building menus.

SECURITY

Setting up effective network **security** is critical task of the LAN administrator. The term *security* may conjure up images of protecting against hackers, industrial spies, or external disruption. Although security does guard against these types of outside intrusions, most commonly security protects an organization from accidental or intentional disruption from its own employees. Accidental disruption includes incidents such as accidentally erasing files and deleting or modifying data incorrectly. Intentional disruption includes intentionally deleting files or data, changing sensitive data (such as salary and invoice amounts), adding bogus records, and copying data to sell to competitors. Therefore, a comprehensive security program protects an organization from misuse or abuse from both employees and outsiders.

The administrator must realize several key facts about security. First, too much security makes a system hard to use. Total security means that no one can access the system. Too little security can result in the loss of data, money, or opportunity because everyone has access to everything. A good security system provides the necessary safeguards without unduly inhibiting the use of the system. Second, security does not deny access to a system. Anyone who wants to spend the necessary time, energy, and money can probably break any security system eventually. Security is merely a delaying factor. Its objectives are to make breaching security more costly than the expected gain or to deter intruders long enough to identify and apprehend them. Vigilance and flexibility in making changes in a security system are essential to keeping a system secure. Technology changes rapidly, for bad as well as for good. That is, some new technologies can render existing security ineffective. Therefore, the LAN administrator may need to constantly improve the security provisions of the system to overcome security loopholes that may arise.

Security is not absolute, and it is not free. The costs of security cover the labor that goes into setting up user IDs, passwords, access rights, and other security provisions, and for security hardware and software. Security hardware includes physical devices such as door locks, security guards, motion detectors, and encryption devices. Security software includes programs that analyze the security settings of a system and, perhaps, software that can be used to catch someone intentionally attempting to break security. It takes time, effort, and money to implement a good security system. If you can visualize a large LAN with hundreds of users, thousands of files, and many variations in access rights, you might begin to understand how much work can go into ensuring that each user gets access to everything he or she needs without giving access to critical data outside the user's job scope.

A comprehensive security program provides both physical security and data access security. **Physical security** is the traditional method of securing objects. It denies physical access to the objects being protected. Physical security includes measures such as door locks, security guards, closed-circuit television monitoring, and motion detectors. Although physical security still has a place in most networks, it is usually not a sufficient security measure. By nature, networks are distributed, making adequate physical security coverage difficult. For example, if a LAN has workstations distributed throughout an office complex, it is difficult to physically monitor each workstation to prevent unauthorized use. Furthermore, because an organization's own employees are its greatest source of security risks, monitoring a workstation to ensure that it is used only by an authorized employee is inadequate. Therefore, physical security must be augmented by data access security.

System access security controls a user's access to the system. This is usually accomplished via an identification and authentication procedure. Once a user gains access to the system, another set of security provisions—data and device access security—take effect.

Data and device access security uses software and hardware techniques to help protect data and define which devices a user is authorized to use. Data access security gives the proper access to data within the scope of an authorized user's job, denies access to data outside the scope of an authorized user's job, and denies access to unauthorized users altogether. Earlier you read about user identification and authentication. The use of passwords is one means of implementing data access security. Failure to supply a valid user ID and corresponding password results in system access being denied. Because this type of security is the cornerstone of many data security systems, let us look at passwords in more detail.

Password Administration

A properly secured LAN requires all users to identify themselves and then verify their identifications using passwords. In most LAN systems the LAN administrator has the option of making passwords mandatory or optional for individual users. We encourage the requirement of passwords for all users on all LANs.

Providing a user with an ID and a password grants that person access to the system. Access to the system does not necessarily imply access to all data and devices on the system, but it does usually provide the right to run certain programs and access certain data. The security of your LAN system depends to a great extent on your policy for creating and changing passwords. Table 11.2 lists some possible provisions of such a policy.

A good password cannot be discovered easily by an unauthorized person. The hardest passwords to discover are long (a minimum of six characters is suggested) and consist of random characters. If a password has up to eight characters (letters and digits only), the total number of passwords possible exceeds $36^8 = 2.8 \times 10^{12}$. This means that the average number of guesses to discover the password is also large: 1.4×10^{12}, or half the total number of passwords. To prevent systematic password guessing, a secure system disallows a user or program from attempting an arbitrary number of password guesses.

One way to handle unsuccessful logons is to use a **timeout value,** which causes the system to refuse to accept another logon attempt from a user ID, station, or both until after a designated interval, say 5 minutes. With a 5-minute timeout value, it would take approximately 13 million years for an unauthorized user to guess an 8-character password. A second approach for dealing with unauthorized logon attempts is to deactivate the user's account after some threshold number of unsuccessful passwords has been attempted. Once the user's account has been deactivated, no one, not even the proper user, can log in until the LAN administrator reactivates the account. For example, after three unsuccessful logon attempts, the security system will automatically deactivate that account, making it unavailable to the real user and intruder alike. Many automatic teller terminal machine (ATM) systems use a similar approach. If the customer fails to enter the correct personal identification number within three attempts, the machine keeps the ATM card and terminates the session.

Table 11.2   Suggested Password Policy

Change passwords regularly—at least once per month.

Passwords should be at least six characters long.

Do not write password down.

Do not use initials, month abbreviations, birth dates, and so on when making up a password.

Change a password if you suspect someone else knows it.

Make successive passwords unique; that is, do not use sequence numbers or letters (such as PW1, then PW2, then PW3, and so on).

Report any instances of suspected unauthorized logons.

Do not leave your workstation unattended while you are logged on.

A third method used to detect an intruder is for the system to fake a successful logon after the intruder has made several unsuccessful attempts. The **fake logon** establishes a controlled environment for the intruder and issues a security warning on the LAN administrator's control console. The objective of the fake session is to make the intruder think he or she has successfully gained access to the system. The session controls the type of access the intruder is given. While the intruder uses the system, thinking a successful security breach has been made, the LAN administrator can determine the workstation from which the intrusion is being made and take steps to apprehend the perpetrator.

The preceding steps are taken to thwart someone who is attempting to gain access through the trial-and-error method of password guessing. Commonly an intruder gains unauthorized access more directly, using more sophisticated measures than trial-and-error to find an authorized user's password. Often users select passwords that are easy for them to remember (their names, initials, birthdates, logon names, names of relatives, and so on). Such passwords are easy for an intruder to discover by trying likely combinations of user-relevant data strings. To be most effective, passwords should be lengthy— at least six characters long—and randomly created. However, such passwords are hard to remember, so users are more likely to write down their passwords, usually near their workstations. These passwords can then be discovered by an intruder with physical access to the area.

Users should be required to change their passwords within designated intervals, say at least once a month, as another way to thwart intruders. As part of a good security policy, administrators must specify a maximum time between password changes. If a user fails to change the password in that interval, the user ultimately is denied access to the system. Two main methods are used to force password changes. First, the user can be requested to change his or her password after it has expired and cannot logon until the password is changed. For example, in a UNIX-based system, a user attempting to logon with an aged password is prompted to change it. In a Novell network the administrator can grant a user several **grace logons.** For example, if an administrator allows a user two grace logons, the user can log on twice under an expired password. At each of the grace logons, the user is notified that the password has expired and is prompted to change the password. If the user does not change the password after two grace logons, the user's account is locked and he or she cannot make subsequent logons. The LAN administrator must then reactivate the password expiration date or number of remaining grace logons before the user can regain access to the system.

A security feature offered by some UNIX systems is a *minimum* period between changing passwords. On the surface this may appear to allow security problems to arise. The intent of this provision is to disallow a user from changing a password as required when the password expires and then immediately changing the password back to its previous value. An administrator also can instruct some security systems, such as UNIX and NetWare, to maintain a history of user passwords, say the 10 previous ones. A user is unable to use any of these 10 previous passwords, thus ensuring that the passwords are not recycled. Moreover, a few systems help guard against common passwords by checking that a user does not embed his or her user ID within the password.

Some installations like to maintain centralized control of the security system. One way of doing this is to prevent users from changing their own passwords. The LAN administrator is responsible for assigning all passwords. This policy ensures that the passwords assigned are changed with the proper frequency and that the passwords are suitably random. However, it also means that the passwords must be written down and sent to users, and the randomness of the passwords increases the probability that users will keep written copies of their passwords until they memorize them.

Logon Restrictions

Security can be further enhanced by controlling an authenticated user's access to the system. This requires the LAN administrator to restrict how and where users log on. One of the simplest of these controls is to limit the number of **concurrent logons** a user has. For example, suppose the LAN administrator limits each user ID to one concurrent logon. If you are logged onto the LAN, no other person can use your user ID to log on. Furthermore, if you attempt to log on and are denied because the logon limit will be exceeded, you know that either you or someone else is already using your ID. This is a good way to control user access, but it also has a disadvantage. Sometimes it is convenient to have a single user logged onto the network more than once. For example, you may have two workstations available and be conducting a simultaneous session on each, or you might be running a program on one workstation and documenting how the program works on the other or the administrator may log on as a specific user when attempting to resolve a problem that user is experiencing.

Another security feature is restricting the times at which a user can be logged on. For example, an organization may decide that employee salaries can be changed only during normal working hours. The LAN administrator can therefore restrict the logons for users having those access rights to the days and hours of normal operation. Typically this is done by setting up a work calendar. Anyone, including an authorized holder of a user ID, who attempts to use an ID that is restricted outside those specified hours will be denied access to the system. Thus, if payroll files can be updated only during normal working hours, payroll employees cannot be allowed to log onto the system on weekends, holidays, or on workdays outside of defined working hours.

An organization may restrict users to specific workstations. For example, suppose a LAN is used by several departments (personnel, payroll, software development, and marketing, for example). A good security policy for this organization might be to limit logons for payroll user IDs to workstations in the payroll department area and for personnel user IDs to be limited to logging on from workstations in the personnel department. Thus a programmer cannot log on as a personnel department clerk or a payroll clerk from his or her workstation in the software development department. This restriction has some disadvantages, however. For example, if a payroll clerk who cannot use a workstation outside his or her area is in a meeting in another area of the building and wants to log on and gather data needed during the meeting, the logon attempt would be unsuccessful. A personnel clerk may report a software problem to a programmer, who tries to access the system as a personnel clerk to investigate the problem but is denied access because of the logon restrictions. For user IDs with access to sensitive data, usually the benefits of logon restrictions outweigh such disadvantages.

A major breach of security occurs when a user leaves his or her workstation without logging off. For example, an employee may go to lunch and forget to log off. Without any security safeguards, an intruder could use that workstation and disrupt the system or make changes that enable him or her to circumvent security at a later time. Two countermeasures exist for this occurrence. First, a workstation can be automatically logged off in the absence of input. For example, with an automatic logoff interval of 5 minutes, whenever 5 minutes elapse without input from the workstation, the workstation is automatically logged off. If the timeout interval is too small, user progress is impeded; if it is too long, security is compromised. The UNIX system offers another technique to overcome the absentee user. Before leaving the workstation, a user can lock the terminal using the TLOCK utility. When run, TLOCK asks the user to enter a password. After the user enters the correct password twice (the second time for verification), the workstation is locked. It remains locked until the user correctly enters another password to reactivate the workstation.

Encryption

If you cannot always prevent users from gaining unauthorized access to data, you can take another measure, **encryption,** to prevent those users from using that data. Encryption is the process of taking data in its raw form, called **plain text,** and transforming it into a scrambled form, called **cipher text.** You have probably heard about "secure" telephone hookups that scramble conversations at the sending end and unscramble them at the receiving end, or perhaps you know about code machines that encode data for transmission and decode them upon receipt. The scrambling or encoding is encryption, and the decoding or unscrambling is called **decryption,** or **deciphering.** Anyone who gains access to encrypted data cannot understand that data simply through physical data access; the data must be decrypted to be useful. They key to good encryption is making the deciphering process time-consuming or expensive for unauthorized users. Data can be encrypted using hardware devices, software, or a combination of both. The most common encryption techniques are the **data encryption standard (DES),** originally established by the U.S. Bureau of Standards, and public key encryption.

You almost always find encryption being used on LAN files that contain user passwords. When a password is created by a user, it must be stored somewhere by the system. When the user provides a user ID and password during a logon, a record corresponding to the user ID is retrieved and the password in the record is compared to the password provided during logon. If the two agree, it is assumed the person has a legitimate right to use that ID; otherwise, logon security provisions take effect. Because passwords are stored in a file, access to the passwords in that file seriously jeopardizes system security if the passwords are stored in clear text. To overcome this problem, almost all systems encrypt the passwords before storing them on disk.

Generic Data Access Control

Data access control consists of a set of data access rights such as read, write, delete, and create together with a way in which these rights can be given to or taken from users, groups, or other objects. There are several ways in which rights can be granted. Within a given system, the implementers will probably choose one of the following methods.

Access Matrix

An access matrix is a grid in which users are listed over columns and files are listed at the beginning of a row (or vice versa), similar to a spreadsheet format. At the intersection of a row and column is a cell defining that user's rights to that file. Table 11.3 illustrates such a matrix. The rights represented are read (r), write (w), execute (e), and delete (d); a dash means no capability. Thus, User-1 can delete File-1 but User-3 cannot. User-3 has no access to File-2. When the numbers of users and files are large, the corresponding matrix can be unwieldy.

Access Control List

With an access control list, each file or device has a corresponding list of users, groups, or other objects that have rights for that file or device. A sample access control list corresponds to a row in the access matrix. For File-1 in the matrix in Table 11.3, the access control list is

```
File-1 ( User-1 (rwed), User-2 (rw), User-3 (r))
```

Access control lists are the most common method for recording access rights.

Capability Lists or User Profiles

A capability list is like an access control list except that it is user oriented. User-1's capability list would look like a column from the access matrix. For User-1 the capability list is

```
User-1 (File-1 (rwed) File-2 (r))
```

Let us now look at a specific example of file system security. Because Novell NetWare is the most commonly implemented NOS, we use it as an example. We have already discussed elements of NetWare 3.*nn* and 4.*nn*. Although there are some file access security differences between the two, for the most part they are the same. The following discussion is based on NetWare 4.*nn*. Also, be aware that the network directory in NetWare 4.*nn* also has a separate access security mechanism. If you are familiar with a predecessor of these versions, NetWare 2.*nn* (sometimes called NetWare 286), realize that the

Table 11.3   Access Matrix

	User-1	User-2	User-3
File-1	rwed	rw--	r- - -
File-2	r- - -	- - - -	- - - -

description that follows does not apply to that NOS; Novell made significant changes in access security in moving from NetWare 2.*nn* to 3.*nn*.

Novell NetWare Data Access Security

Before we can get into the details of how NetWare data access security is implemented, we must first define some of the terms Novell uses in setting up security. The basic goal of data access security is to give each user access to data essential to performing his or her job. Thus individual users may have different data access capabilities. For example, one user may be able to read and write data in a file and another user might be limited to reading data. The rights supported by NetWare's file management system are listed and briefly described in Table 11.4. These rights apply to files and directories. For the most part, the **file rights** have the same meaning for files and directories and the differences are not important for this discussion.

The access privileges a user enjoys are called the user's **effective rights.** Sometimes we enclose these rights in brackets ([ ]) and refer to them by their first letters. Within the brackets, missing rights are denoted by a space or a hyphen (-) to hold that right's position. Therefore, when we write [-RW—F—] we mean that the read, write, and file scan rights are given. Via several utilities, users and groups can be explicitly assigned rights to files and directories. Novell calls these assigned rights **trustee rights** because the user or group has been entrusted to exercise these rights. A user's effective rights accrue from the granting of individual rights, granting rights to a group to which the user belongs, and assigning rights to the directory or file being accessed.

To simplify administrative matters, many of a user's rights are assumed through groups to which the member belongs. This makes it easier to assign rights that are enjoyed jointly by several users. Rights that are limited to only a few users are granted on an individual basis. In a NetWare system a user may belong to no group, one group, or several groups. Generally every user belongs to a Novell-defined group called Everyone in 3.*nn* and [Public] in 4.*nn*. Although there is a difference between these two groups, the differences are not relevant to this discussion. These groups are created by the NetWare system at installation, and every new user defined is automatically inserted into the group. These groups are used to assign trustee rights held universally by all users.

To complete the picture, we need to introduce file attributes. In NetWare files can have a number of attributes, some of which affect access security. For example, a file can

Table 11.4   Novell NetWare File and Directory Rights

Supervisory	[S]	Supervisory rights to the directory and all subdirectories
Read	[R]	Read an open file
Write	[W]	Write to an open file
Create	[C]	Create a new file
Erase	[E]	Delete an existing file
File scan	[F]	List names of files or subdirectories in directory
Modify	[M]	Change file attributes, rename files, and rename directories
Access control	[A]	Pass rights to directory or file to another user

be assigned an attribute of read-only. Even though a user may be given the access write privilege for a file, the file cannot be written to if it has the read-only attribute set. Other attributes that can affect access security include delete inhibit, execute only, copy inhibit, and rename inhibit.

Determining File Access Rights

A user can gain access rights in three general ways: explicitly, implicitly, or via inheritance. A user gets rights explicitly by an administrator granting those rights. The administrator can be the SUPERVISOR or a user who has been granted the privilege of assigning rights. For example, a workgroup manager can be given the capability of assigning rights for a set of files used by the workgroup. In a large LAN, distributing the security capability helps reduce the workload of the LAN administrator and places the security decision in the hands of those closest to the data being secured. Therefore, Admin_Tom might be authorized to grant his employees the ability to read, write, modify, and file scan the CUSTOMER file in the DATABASE directory. At a minimum, Admin_Tom will have those rights.

A user gains rights implicitly in two ways: via group membership or security equivalencies. A user may be a member of one or more groups. Inherently all users are a member of the [Public] group. If a group has been given access rights, then all members of that group enjoy those rights. If a user, say Admin_Mary, is a member of several groups, she simultaneously gains all the rights enjoyed by all the groups to which she belongs. Another implicit security mechanism is user equivalence. A user can be made equivalent to another user. For example, an administrator might make Admin_Mary equivalent to Admin_Tom. Once the equivalence has been set up, Admin_Mary not only has her own rights but also all rights that Admin_Tom has. Equivalence is an expedient way to give two users equivalent rights. This could be done via a group, but if only two people need those rights, equivalence is easier. LAN administrators use equivalence with caution because equivalencing can have broader effects than originally anticipated. This is particularly true with equivalencing one user with the SUPERVISOR user.

Finally, a user can obtain rights through inheritance. In a LAN with many directories, files, and users, it would be a monumental task to assign all rights implicitly or explicitly. Recall the access matrix presented earlier. Every file, directory, user, and group would need to be represented. Inheritance is based on the directory tree. The basic premise of inheritance is that if a user has rights in a directory, those rights extend to all files and subdirectories in that directory. Furthermore, those rights flow downward through the directory tree to all subsequent subdirectories and files. For example, most users have a home directory. A user typically owns all files and subdirectories of his or her home directory. It makes sense to give a user all rights to his or her home directory, and as a consequence of inheritance, the user would gain all rights to all files and directories below the home directory. This basic premise holds true most of the time, but there are exceptions. For example, a directory may contain files that all members of the workgroup can read except for one, such as the manager's personnel notes. NetWare has a mechanism, an **inherited rights filter (IRF),** to handle these exceptions. Each directory and file has an IRF. In NetWare 3.*nn* the IRF is called an inherited rights mask.

The same rights a user or group can be granted can also be placed in the IRF for files and directories. IRFs are established in several ways. Whenever a directory is created, all rights are automatically inserted in the IRF. The SUPERVISOR or someone with **access control rights** in the directory must delete rights that should not be in the IRF. This is done via a utility called FILER. The LAN administrator can change an IRF to restrict a user's effective rights. The following examples show how inheritance, implicit, and **explicit rights** are used to determine a user's effective rights.

Table 11.5 shows the trustee rights assigned to four users and one group (Admin) and IRFs for a directory, its subdirectory, and two files. The IRFs for the subdirectory and files differ from the directory's IRF because they have been set explicitly by the LAN administrator to restrict the inheritance of rights. The tree structure of the directories and the files is given in Figure 11.1. We use these examples to show how a user's effective rights are determined. We assume that no user has gained rights through the [Public] group. All users with the user ID prefixed by *Admin* belong to the Admin group; thus, Mktg_Chen is the only user who does not belong to the Admin group. Chen and the other users may belong to other groups, but we assume that those groups do not have any rights to the directories and files listed.

Let us first consider user Admin_Sally. Sally has been given supervisory rights in the DATABASE directory. By virtue of this single right, Sally has all rights to all files and subdirectories in DATABASE. The supervisory right is powerful and absolute. It is not excluded by IRFs or any mechanism other than revoking that right. Naturally, LAN administrators use the utmost discretion in granting this right.

Next, consider Admin_Mary. Mary has not been given any personal trustee rights to DATABASE. However, Mary is a member of Admin and Admin has been assigned the rights of read, write, and file scan. Therefore, Mary has those rights to DATABASE. What are Mary's effective rights for SUB1? She has [-RWC—F-]. We know how she received RWC: They were granted as trustee rights. The F right was obtained via inheritance. Admin has that right in DATABASE and the IRF for SUB1 allows that right

Table 11.5 File and Directory Rights Matrix

Directory or File	Inherited Rights Filter	Admin (group)	Admin_Sally	Admin_Tom	Admin_Mary	Mktg_Chen
			Users, Groups, and Trustee Rights			
DATABASE (directory)	[SRWCEMFA]	[-RW---F-]	[SRWCEMFA]	[--------]	[--------]	[--------]
SUB1 (subdirectory of DATABASE)	[SRW---F-]	[--------]	[--------]	[---------]	[-RWC----]	[-RWCE-F-]
CUSTOMER (file in DATABASE)	[S--------]	[--------]	[--------]	[-RW--MF-]	[--------]	[--------]
NOTES (file in SUB1)	[SR----F-]	[--------]	[--------]	[-RW---F-]	[-RW---F-]	[--------]

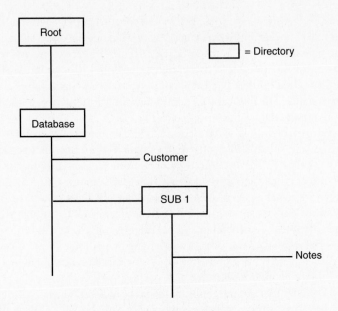

Figure 11.1   File/Directory Tree Structure

to be inherited. Therefore, Admin has the file scan right for SUB1 and Mary is a member of that group, so Mary also gets that right. Note that group and individual rights are additive. For the CUSTOMER file, Mary has not been given any trustee rights. Note that the CUSTOMER's IRF will not allow any rights to be inherited except supervisory, which could not be filtered even if the S were missing from the IRF. Mary has no rights for CUSTOMER and will not even see its existence in a directory listing because she does not have file scan capability. For NOTES, Mary has RWF, the trustee rights she was granted.

What are Admin_Tom's effective rights? He has no individual trustee rights for DATABASE but receives RWF implicitly from membership in the Admin group. Tom also has RWF for SUB1. He gets these rights via inheritance. Because Tom has RWF in DATABASE and because the IRF of SUB1 allows those rights to be inherited, Tom can read, write, and file scan in SUB1. Tom gets RWMF for CUSTOMER via individual trustee rights. For NOTES, Tom has RWF as a consequence of his individual trustee rights.

Finally, let us look at the rights Mktg_Chen has. Chen has no trustee rights except to the SUB1 directory, where he has been give read, write, create, erase, and file scan capabilities. Furthermore, Chen does not belong to any groups that have been given rights to the directories and files in question. Chen has no rights in DATABASE and CUSTOMER. For NOTES he has RF. Although he has RWCEF in SUB1, the IRF of NOTES allows only RF to be inherited and the WCE rights are filtered out by the IRF.

As you can see from these examples, a file or directory's IRF is used to limit the rights a user inherits in a directory or to a file. We did not look at the issue of equivalency in the above examples. If someone in authority decided that Mktg_Chen should have the same rights as Admin_Mary, an administrator could provide those rights individually or could make Chen security equivalent to Mary. Note that equivalence also means that Chen would have rights in Mary's home directory, a consequence that might make the equivalence option undesirable. To determine a user's effective rights to a file, you must know the following:

the user's effective rights to the directory (group rights plus individual rights)

the user's trustee rights to the file (group rights plus individual rights)

the file's IRF

the user's security equivalencies

The following summarizes the rules for determining a user's effective rights for a file.

Supervisory rights are paramount.

Explicit trustee rights supersede inherited rights.

Inherited rights masks act as a **maximum rights mask** to filter **directory rights** inherited from a parent directory or to filter file rights inherited from the directory containing the file.

Establishing Trustee Rights

Trustee rights are granted and rescinded in a variety of ways. First, consider NetWare 3.*nn*. There are two utilities, GRANT and REVOKE, that allow a LAN administrator to give and take away trustee rights. The administrator can also assign trustee rights with the FILER and SYSCON utilities and take them away with FILER, REMOVE, and SYSCON. A user can determine his or her rights in a directory with the RIGHTS command. FILER and SYSCON are menu utilities, and REMOVE, REVOKE, and GRANT are command-line utilities. In a menu utility you select the actions you want to take through menu selections. In a command-line utility you must use a command to carry out the desired task. A shortcut to granting security is to grant a user rights equivalent to those of another user. In NetWare 4.*nn* these tasks are accomplished by the NETADMIN, NWADMIN, FILER, and RIGHTS facilities.

File and Directory Attributes

In addition to file and directory security, Novell files and directories have **attributes** that control how files and directories are used. Tables 11.6(a) and 11.6(b) show file and directory attributes.

File attributes govern how the file may be used. A file can be flagged as shareable or non-shareable to prevent concurrent access. For example, a word processing document

Table 11.6 (a)   NetWare File Attributes

Read-Only	Can only be read.
Read-Write	Can be read from, written to, renamed, or deleted (default if Read-Only is not specified).
Normal	Non-shareable, Read-Write.
Shareable	Can be concurrently accessed by more than one user.
Non-Shareable	Can be accessed by only one user at a time.
Indexed	An index is built to speed access to large files.
Execute-Only	File can be executed but not read, erased, modified, renamed, or copied; prevents illegal copying.
Archive	File has been modified and archiving is needed on next backup.
Copy Inhibit	This attribute is for Macintosh users and prevents a file from being copied.
Delete Inhibit	Prevents a file from being deleted, even by users with erase access to that file.
Hidden	File does not appear in DIR or NDIR listings and prevents a user from copying or erasing the file.
Purge	File is purged when deleted and cannot be reclaimed by the SALVAGE utility.
Read Audit	Provides an audit trail of users who have read the file.
Write Audit	Provides an audit trail of users who have written to the file.
Rename Inhibit	Prevents a user from renaming the file, even if the user has the Modify trustee right to the file.
System	Used for DOS files needed for booting (these files are hidden from the user).
Transactional	Used with Novell's Transaction Tracking System (TTS) to ensure that all updates made to the file within a transaction can be backed out if the transaction cannot complete successfully.
Immediate Compress	Causes NetWare to compress the file as soon as possible.
Compressed	Indicates that file is compressed.
Can't Compress	Indicates that file should not be compressed because of insignificant savings.
Don't Compress	Indicates that file should not be compressed.
Migrated	Indicates that file has been migrated to near-line storage.
Don't Migrate	Indicates that file should not be migrated.
Don't Suballocate	Prevents file from being suballocated.

usually should not be edited concurrently by two users. Such files should be declared non-shareable to prevent the problems of simultaneous updates discussed in Chapter 2 and 9. Some files, such as program files, should be protected from accidental or intentional updates. Flagging such files as read-only or execute-only provides protection from updates.

One of the problems facing the microcomputer software industry is software piracy. When applications are placed on a file server and secured with read access, a user could

Table 11.6 (b)   NetWare Directory Attributes

Normal	Cancels other directory attributes.
Hidden	Directory does not appear in a directory listing.
System	Directory is used for proper functioning of system, directory does not appear in directory search.
Delete Inhibit	See Delete Inhibit for files above.
Rename Inhibit	See Rename Inhibit for files above.
Purge	See Purge for files above.

illegally make a copy of the application. Novell has a file attribute that prevents such copying. If a file is flagged with the execute-only attribute, the file can only be run and deleted, not opened and read, written to, or renamed, even by a user with SUPERVISOR capabilities. File attributes offer companies one means of protecting their software investment.

Security Utilities

In NetWare 3.*nn* a security-checking feature is implemented in a utility named SECURITY. It provides the SUPERVISOR with a list of possible security weaknesses. The listing gives a breakdown by user and group and checks for security weaknesses, such as those shown in Table 11.7. A sample list of the data reported by the SECURITY utility is shown in Table 11.8. In NetWare 4.*nn* an audit capability was added. Audit capabilities were discussed in Chapter 8.

VIRUSES

Many computer professionals recall worldwide concern among their colleagues as March 6, 1992 approached. The first exposure to the Michelangelo virus was scheduled to occur on that date. Computer professionals throughout the world hurried to protect their computers. Although the advanced publicity reduced the havoc of this virus, it still proved to be a major disruption to the computing industry. Since then, viruses have

Table 11.7   Possible Security Weaknesses

No password assigned

Passwords that are the same as the user name

Short passwords

Passwords that are not required to be changed periodically

User having security equivalent to the SUPERVISOR

User having unlimited grace logins

User having no login script

Users having SUPERVISOR privileges in the root directory of any volume

Users or groups having excessive rights to the four system directories

Table 11.8   Novell Security Utility Output

Novell Security Utility Output

File Server SECURITY Evaluation Utility

Checking for network security holes, please wait.

User DUMMY

    Has no logon script

    Has unlimited grace logons

    Is not required to change passwords periodically

    Can have passwords that are too short (less than 5 characters)

    Does not require a password

    Does not have a secure password

User DAVE

    Is security equivalent to user SUPERVISOR

    Has no password assigned

Group EVERYONE

    Has [WC M] rights in SYS:MAIL (maximum should be [WC])

continued to appear at a rapid rate. Some of today's virus scanners claim to detect over 9500 different strains.

In the past our primary security concern centered around people intentionally or accidentally jeopardizing the system's integrity. Today, we face another threat: computer viruses. A computer virus is so named because it imitates the activity of biological viruses. A biological virus uses a nonvirus or healthy cell to reproduce itself. Sometimes the virus destroys the healthy host cell. The primary objectives of a computer virus are to reproduce itself and avoid elimination. A computer virus uses a healthy file, program, memory area, or disk area to reproduce itself. Once the virus has been replicated, it starts on its second priority: disrupting the system.

A LAN administrator must protect the system from viruses. This is no easy task. In 1991 over 500 different viruses were been detected, and experts believe that new viruses are being introduced at the rate of over 50 per month (some predict that six new viruses will appear daily). By 1996, one antivirus software company had over 9625 viruses registered. Fortunately, antivirus technology is also growing at a rapid rate. A list of some of the common viruses is given in Table 11.9.

Viruses disrupt systems in a variety of ways, and some are more destructive than others. The most destructive viruses destroy files by overwriting or erasing them, corrupt disk directories, reformat disks, cause system failures, and so on. The more benign viruses are also destructive because they destroy productivity. These viruses do not destroy files, they just disrupt the working environment by displaying annoying messages, erasing the contents of the monitor, or similar activities. Both types hinder normal system operations.

Table 11.9   Some Common Viruses

ATOM	Azusa	Cascade	Dark Avenger
DMV	Empire.Monkey	Flame	Frankenstein
Hare.7610	Jerusalem	Junkie	Michelangelo
NYB	Quandrum	Satan Bug	Stealth_Boot
Stoned	Tequila	V_Sign	Werewolf
X.M. Laroux	Yankee Doodle		

Protecting Against Viruses

LAN administrators must have precautions and policies in place to prevent the introduction of viruses and to detect and eradicate them if they show up. All LANs should be equipped with current virus detection software. In this section we discuss some of the precautions, policies, and software used to keep a LAN virus-free. We look first at how a virus enters a system. We then discuss how to keep a LAN free of viruses through virus detection and virus eradication.

Introducing a System Virus

Viruses enter a clean system from a variety of sources. They may be introduced intentionally or unintentionally. A company programmer can deliberately create a virus within a program he or she is writing, or a LAN user can enter virus code directly from the keyboard. LAN users may also unintentionally spread a virus by using an infected disk, accessing data from another infected LAN, or downloading software from an external computer or network. A well-intentioned user may use a private, infected disk in his or her workstation. Immediately the virus attempts to spread itself to other parts of the system. A user may copy a file from a computer or a bulletin board outside the network and receive an infected file. Viruses have even been found in shrink-wrapped software produced by software vendors or by companies that distribute software or data files.

The best way to prevent users from *intentionally* introducing viruses is to hire trustworthy employees and to immediately deny network access to employees who are leaving the company, particularly those who are not leaving voluntarily.

One way to prevent unintentional infection is through employee education. Users must know how to scan a diskette for viruses before inserting it into the computer. When users find viruses, they must know how to eradicate them. Employees must also know about the importance of making system backups. Before backing up a file, a user must scan the file to ensure that it is not infected. If infected files are placed on a backup tape and then restored at a later time, the virus will be reintroduced to the LAN. A good procedure to follow is to ensure that all files and data entering and leaving the network are virus free. This can be accomplished by checking them as they are being moved or before they are moved.

Virus Detection

Viruses are detected in two ways. The most obvious but least desirable way is to experience the consequences of having a virus. The best way to detect a virus is to find it before it activates itself. A variety of **antivirus programs** are available for this purpose. Some of these are oriented to single computers and some are designed for both single computers and LANs. Naturally, a LAN administrator should select an antivirus program that protects servers and workstations.

Antivirus programs operate in different ways. Some programs are run on demand, whereas others are constantly running. A program that is run on demand does not continuously scan for viruses. On-demand programs must be explicitly run by a user or the LAN administrator. These programs scan for the viruses they know about and either remove or report viruses as they are found. If the detection program simply reports the existence of a virus, another program must be run to remove it. Programs that continuously scan for viruses remain memory resident while the computer is running. These programs check new data and programs for viruses as they enter and leave the system. An example of how a continuously running antivirus program works is shown in Figure 11.2. Continuously running virus detection programs are constantly using memory and CPU cycles and thus contribute to system overhead. This is one way in which viruses can be disruptive and costly. However, continuously running scanners generally provide better protection than on-demand antivirus programs.

LAN antivirus programs vary in capability. Some scan the server only, some primarily scan workstations, and some do both. Choosing a program that scans both the workstations and the servers is the best choice. Alternatively, a LAN administrator may

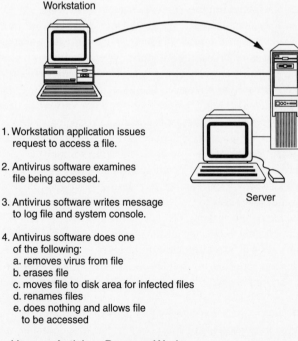

Figure 11.2   How an Antivirus Program Works

choose to use several virus scanners: one that is excellent at detecting workstation viruses and another that is excellent at protecting servers. A program that checks both servers and workstations must be more sophisticated because it has to be aware of at least two different operating systems and disk organizations. That is, an antivirus program that can detect viruses on a DOS computer cannot necessarily understand the memory and disk organization of a file server using a Novell, UNIX, or OS/2 operating system. An antivirus program that resides on a server and has the capability of checking workstation nodes typically downloads the antivirus software when the workstation logs onto the server. As an added precaution, an antivirus program could be loaded on the disk of each workstation and automatically started when the workstation is booted. On a DOS computer this can be done by placing the commands to run the antivirus program in the AUTOEXEC.BAT file.

Another way to reduce the risk of virus infection is to use diskless workstations. If individual workstations do not have disk drives, users cannot intentionally or accidentally introduce a new virus; however, a user intent on disrupting the system could still enter a virus via a diskless workstation's keyboard. Furthermore, a diskless system cannot be used when the network is down and must have a boot ROM or PROM that enables it to load the operating system over the network rather than reading if from a boot disk. Sometimes the ROM may need to be changed to enable the use of operating system upgrades. This does not happen often but is still a consideration in choosing diskless workstations.

It is best to have a stand-alone computer conveniently available for virus detection. A stand-alone computer is helpful for virus detection because it limits the potential for the virus spreading on the network before it can be found and removed by a LAN antivirus program. Likewise, when transferring data to or from networks or computers external to the LAN, a stand-alone computer can be used. After the data has been received, it and the stand-alone computer can be checked for viruses. After checking for viruses and removing any that are found, the administrator can move the data to the LAN. Naturally, following these steps takes longer and may be somewhat inconvenient, but they prevent catastrophic virus attacks.

Regardless of how viruses are detected, a company should have a procedure in place that requires users to report any suspected or confirmed incidence of a virus. A user at a workstation may detect and eradicate a virus found on that workstation. The user may believe that the infection from this virus has been completely eliminated from the LAN, but the virus may have already spread into other nodes. Cooperation of users in virus control is essential to a comprehensive antivirus plan.

Virus Eradication

We destroy biological viruses by being inoculated against them and building an immunity. The immunity is created when our bodies produce virus-killing antibodies that deactivate the virus when it appears. However, we can be inoculated only against known viruses, and new strains appear regularly. The same thing happens with computer viruses. Several companies provide software that searches for known viruses and eradicates them. The antivirus programs scan memory and disk drives, looking for traces of the virus. Once found, the virus can be removed, often without destroying the host.

However, the virus can be introduced again if an infected floppy disk is used on the system or if infected files are copied from another network or computer. Complete eradication from a network requires the examination of each disk drive and diskette used in the network.

Viruses are eradicated from a system either by the program that detected the virus or by a separate program designed for that purpose. The more convenient of the two methods is having the virus automatically removed on detection. Moreover, some antivirus programs automatically repair affected memory or disk areas. For example, if a virus is found in the boot sector of a disk, some antivirus programs remove the virus and restore the boot sector to its proper state.

We noted earlier that new viruses are appearing almost daily. As new viruses are introduced, new programs or program updates must be available to detect and remove them. A good LAN antivirus policy is to subscribe to the update service for the virus programs being used. This allows a company to keep pace with changing developments in the war against viruses. Keeping up with changes in viruses is important because new viruses have unique **signatures,** or bit patterns, that must be recognized. Moreover, the authors of viruses have begun to create viruses that are harder to detect. These are called **polymorphic viruses** because they can change their signatures. To further compound the problem, a **mutation engine** has been created that is a virus programmer's toolkit. The mutation engine enables programmers to make existing and future viruses polymorphic.

SUMMARY

One of the most important functions performed by the LAN administrator is to establish a proper user environment. This environment helps provide users transparency, gives them access to the data and applications they need, and protects other resources from inadvertent or intentional disruption. The administrator does this by setting up users, groups, and security provisions. In a large network this combination of needs can be complex.

User access is usually controlled through a process of identification and authentication, normally through entering a user ID and an associated password. To maintain a proper level of security, the LAN administrator must implement a comprehensive security policy. This may include setting up LAN parameters that require minimum password lengths, maximum and minimum intervals between password changes, requirements for unique passwords, and so on. The LAN software can assist the administrator by detecting intruder attempts, limiting the number of logons per user ID, automatically logging users off, and performing similar security tasks.

User security is just one dimension of a complete security policy. User and group security is usually coupled with directory and file security. Users are granted certain rights for directories and files. How this is implemented differs from one system to another; however, most of today's LANs give the administrator a way to set up a security matrix that gives users the rights they need while withholding the access rights that are outside their job scopes.

Viruses are an ever-present problem in today's LANs. The LAN administrator must implement a comprehensive plan for detecting and removing viruses and for educating users on proper virus prevention techniques. All viruses are disruptive, and keeping the LAN virus-free is essential to error-free LAN operations.

Key Terms

access control right

access rights

antivirus program

attributes

authentication

biological identification and
   authentication

cipher text

concurrent logon

data and device access security

data encryption standard (DES)

deciphering

decryption

directory rights

effective rights

encryption

explicit rights

fake logon

file rights

grace logon

identification

inherited rights filter (IRF)

logon script

maximum rights mask

mutation engine

password

physical security

plain text

polymorphic virus

security

signature

system access security

system programming

timeout value

trustee rights

user ID

Review Questions

1. Describe the relationships between users and groups.
2. Why do we define users and groups?
3. What are user access rights?
4. What is system programming on a LAN? Describe three system programming tasks.
5. Describe how security protects an organization's data from accidental or intentional misuse by the organization's employees.
6. What are identification and authentication? Describe two methods of identification and authentication.
7. List three biological identification and authentication methods.
8. Describe two ways of responding to unauthorized access attempts.
9. How do fake logons and timeout values help prevent unauthorized logons?
10. Why is it beneficial to limit concurrent logons?
11. What do encryption and decryption do? Where is encryption likely to be found in a LAN?
12. Describe file security in a Novell NetWare system.
13. What are viruses? What problems do they present to a LAN?
14. Describe how viruses are detected and eliminated.
15. What are polymorphic viruses? Why are they more difficult to detect?

Problems and Exercises

1. Select three different LAN operating systems.
   a. Describe how users and groups are set up in each system. What differences exist between user and group implementations?
   b. Describe the file and directory security attributes supported by each. List the differences between the systems.
   c. Describe the password security features of each. List the differences between the systems.
2. Draw up a comprehensive password security procedure for a business LAN. How does your system prevent password abuses?

Table 11.10 (a)   File and Directory Rights Matrix

Directory or File	Inherited Rights Filter	Users, Groups, and Trustee Rights				
		Admin (group)	Admin_Sally	Admin_Tom	Admin_Mary	Mktg_Chen
DATABASE (directory)	[SRWCEMFA]	[-R----F-]	[-RWCEMFA]	[-W-----]	[-RWCE---]	[--------]
SUB1 (subdirectory of DATABASE)	[SRWCE-F-]	[-RWCE---]	[--------]	[--------]	[-RWC----]	[-RW-EMF-]
CUSTOMER (file in DATABASE)	[S-------]	[-RW----]	[--------]	[-RW-EMF-]	[---------]	[--------]
NOTES (file in SUB1)	[SR----F-]	[--------]	[--------]	[-RW---F-]	[-RW---F-]	[--------]

Table 11.10 (b)   NetWare Rights Matrix

Effective Rights for	DATABASE		SUB1		CUSTOMER		NOTES	
ADMIN_SALLY	[	]	[	]	[	]	[	]
ADMIN_TOM	[	]	[	]	[	]	[	]
ADMIN_MARY	[	]	[	]	[	]	[	]
MKTG_CHEN	[	]	[	]	[	]	[	]

3. Table 11.10(a) shows the inherited rights for several directories and files and the trustee rights for several users and groups. Using the rules for effective rights in NetWare, complete Table 11.10(b) showing the effective rights for each user for each file and directory.

4. You are a LAN administrator and have just been notified that a LAN user has discovered the Stoned virus on her system. Plan a course of action to eradicate this virus from the system. You should realize that the virus may have affected other network nodes, may be on any of the diskettes that have been used on the LAN, and may be on some of your backup tapes.

5. The Michelangelo virus was considered to be widespread in 1992. The virus spread itself until March 6, at which time it overwrote the boot disk drive. As a LAN administrator, what steps (besides using an antivirus program) could you take to avoid activation of the virus?

6. Katie Hafner and John Markoff provide profiles of several hackers from three different hacking groups in their book *Cyberpunk*. Describe the methods used by these hackers to penetrate security.

7. Suppose you are a LAN administrator and have implemented what you consider to be effective security measures for your installations. One of the LAN users approaches you and brags about getting around the security. The user proves this claim by showing you a file outside his access scope in which he has placed some extra data to show that the file has been accessed. How should you and your company address this issue?

8. Suppose that a small office of 15 people has asked you to help them set up a LAN. Following discussions with the office manager, you outline your plans for setting up security. The office manager responds by saying that she trusts all of the employees and that security is not necessary. Furthermore, she tells you that if security were implemented, the workers would feel that they were not trusted, because security was never an issue before. How would you respond to these statements?

Chapter 12

LAN Administration: The Printing Environment

CHAPTER PREVIEW

In Chapter 11 we discussed how the LAN administrator helps create the proper user environment by setting up user IDs and user groups, and combining user and group access needs with directory and file security. These tasks are important to the overall success of the network. Less glamorous but perhaps equally important to user acceptance and network effectiveness is setting up a comprehensive printing environment. LAN administrators must not lose sight of their objective: to provide an environment in which users can be productive both individually and as a group. Creating an environment in which users can produce printed outputs on the right devices and at the right time is one part of this objective. In Chapter 7 we presented a generic overview of a print spooler. In this chapter we provide more details of the ways in which a printing environment can be established.

Specific topics covered in this chapter include

printing needs

the spooler system

connecting applications and users to printers

print management and administration

printing in a Novell LAN

INTRODUCTION TO PRINTING

A LAN user can get printed output on a LAN in three ways. The first way, using a dedicated local printer, is the same as the method used for stand-alone microcomputer systems: The printer is attached to a port on the microcomputer and the microcomputer's user has exclusive control of the printer. One disadvantage of this technique is that printers are dedicated to a specific computer so they remain idle for much of the time. Also, the cost of having one printer for each microcomputer can be excessive.

The second printing option is for several users to share a printer using a data switch, as illustrated in Figure 12.1. Before LANs this was the primary way of sharing printers. A variety of data switch capabilities are available. The disadvantage of this alternative is that only one microcomputer can print at once; if two microcomputers have jobs to print, one must wait until the other is done.

The third method of printing uses the services of the LAN. This is the method we are concerned with in this chapter. LAN printing does not have the disadvantages of the two other methods. Printers can be shared and multiple print streams can be active at once. With LAN printing, all users can be logically printing at the same time. A LAN user does not control a printer, as is the case in the first two printing alternatives. Instead, a print server controls the printer and serves as an interface between users and printers. Because all LAN users can print at the same time, the print server and its software, collectively known as a spooler, control all LAN print jobs. Shortly we describe how this is done. The important thing to realize at this time is that with LAN-based printing, you have less control over exactly when the printing occurs. Getting your printout immediately can be difficult because other print jobs are ahead of yours in the queue of jobs ready for the printer. On some occasions the wait for a printout might be quite long. For example, the spooler may be printing a 400-page manual, and several other jobs may be queued when your job arrives. Your printout may not be physically printed for several minutes, or even hours. However, from the application's perspective, the printing has been done, and you are free to move on to other computing tasks.

LAN Printing Configurations

The printer is physically connected to the microcomputer through an **I/O port,** usually a parallel or a serial port. This establishes the physical link between the computer and the printer. The printer driver directs its output to the port to which the printer is connected, thereby completing the connection between the application and the printer.

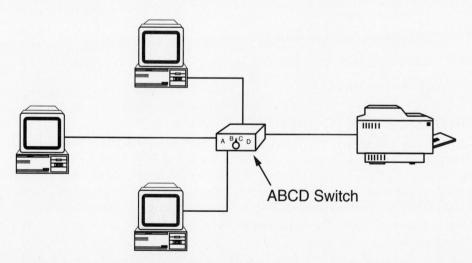

Figure 12.1   Printer Sharing Using a Switch

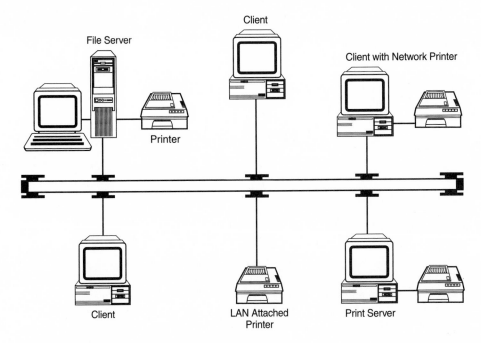

Figure 12.2 Network Printing Options

Printers may also be LAN ready, meaning that they have a built-in LAN adapter and can be connected directly to the LAN medium. Alternatively, special-purpose LAN print servers can serve as an interface between the medium and the LAN OS.

When a printer is connected to a computer, the computer can be a file server or another node. If the computer to which the printer is attached is not a file server, the computer can be either a dedicated or a nondedicated print server. A dedicated print server is one that has no other function on the network. The processing power of a print server is not great, so some companies use older computers as dedicated print servers. Nondedicated print servers have a dual role; they function as both a print server and client node. There are a few hazards when using nondedicated print servers. The computer operator may power the computer off and thus remove the printer from service. Printing activities will degrade application performance and vice versa. Finally, some applications are not well behaved and may disrupt network printing. For example, if the nondedicated print server is used by a software developer who encounters an infinite loop in testing, the computer may need to be reset to clear the problem. Naturally, such a circumstance will interrupt printing. Figure 12.2 illustrates the main printer configuration options.

CREATING A PRINTING ENVIRONMENT

Creating a printing environment is not always a simple task. Even in the stand-alone printing environment, illustrated in Figure 12.3, the basic configuration of an application that wants to print data on one side and a printer on the other side is complicated by one or more components between the printer and the application.

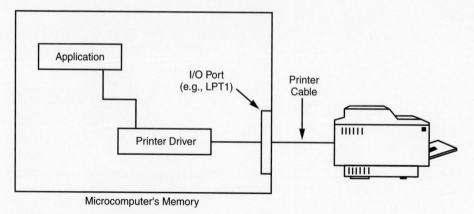

Figure 12.3   A Stand-Alone Printer Configuration

You have many different types of printers from which to choose, and each printer has a certain set of capabilities, including bolding, underlining, italics, graphics, fonts, color, and so on. These capabilities are enabled in different ways. Some can be set through the printer's control panel, and most can be set through commands transmitted to the printer from a program. Different printers may use different control commands to enable the same capability.

An application usually does not include the logic needed to invoke these capabilities for all types of printers. Instead, the application communicates with the printer through another program called the printer driver. Keeping printer-specific knowledge out of applications provides program–printer independence. If a new printer comes on the market, the application does not need to be changed; a new printer driver must be created that interfaces to the application and the printer. An application often comes with a set of printer drivers for the most common printers. The application knows how to interface to the printer driver, and the printer driver knows how to communicate with a specific brand of printer. The application sends a general code such as "turn bold on" to the printer driver, and the printer driver translates that code into the proper sequence of control characters for its printer.

A GENERIC SPOOLER

Chapter 7 includes a brief overview of how a spooler operates. Here we look at spoolers in more detail. From the preceding paragraphs you probably gained the idea that a spooler essentially acts as a switch between applications and printers, and this is correct. However, a spooler does much more than switch print jobs. We can separate the spooler's functions into four basic categories: hardware-oriented, application-oriented, administration-oriented, and user-oriented. Table 12.1 lists the various functions under each of these categories.

Table 12.1   Spooler Functions

Hardware-Oriented Functions	Serve as buffer between high-speed and low-speed devices (CPU and printer)
	Provide printer interface
	Provide for the introduction of new printers
Application-Oriented Functions	Provide application-level interface
	Provide operating system interface
	Close print jobs based on timeout interval
	Collect printed output
	Direct print jobs to designated printers
Administration-Oriented Functions	Provide statistical reports
	Add/delete printers
	Start/stop printers
	Start/stop spooler process
	View jobs on hold in print queue
	Delete jobs from print queue
	Attach/detach printers from print queue
	Set/change job priorities
	Provide user management interface
	Provide security
	Cancel print jobs
User-Oriented Functions (for user's jobs only)	Print multiple copies
	Print banners
	Hold jobs in disk queue after printing
	Hold jobs in disk queue before printing
	View jobs on hold in print queue
	Set print job priorities
	Delete jobs from print queue
	Set/change job priorities
	Print selected pages

Hardware-Oriented Functions

High-Speed Buffer

The primary function of a spooler is to serve as a buffer between the high-speed CPU and low-speed output devices such as printers. It does this by accepting output destined for the printers and storing it temporarily on disk or, less often, on tape. Because disk drives are much faster than most printers, the data can be stored on disk much faster than it can be physically written to the printer. A side effect of temporarily storing print jobs on disk is the ability to logically share a printer. Multiple users can concurrently direct their output to the same print device. The print jobs are collected on disk until they are finished and ready to print. Usually the spooler schedules the completed jobs for printing and prints them according to some priority scheme.

Printer Interface

Whenever you use a peripheral device such as a printer, you must have a software and hardware interface to the device. The typical **hardware interfaces** for printers are **serial** and **parallel interfaces** and **small computer system interfaces (SCSIs).** On a LAN the hardware interface may also be a LAN adapter connected directly to the LAN medium. The software interface is the printer driver. As we mentioned previously, printing devices provide a variety of different options, such as different colors or shades of gray, different fonts and font sizes, and graphic capabilities. Enabling these different printing capabilities is accomplished through the cooperation of an application, the spooler, and the printer driver. Let us look at how this occurs from the perspective of a word processing program.

To enable a printer's formatting capabilities, you must write a **control sequence** to it. For example, if you want to select the 8-point Roman font on a Hewlett-Packard laser printer, you must send the control sequence ESC(8U to the printer. Each change in characteristic, such as changing margins and bolding, has its unique enabling control sequence. Not all printers support functions such as an 8-point Roman font, and different printers may use different control sequences to enable the same capabilities. It is the printer driver that accommodates the individual capabilities of a specific printer.

A word processor user formats his or her document using the commands available within the word processing software. In most of today's word processors, you can specify underline, bold, fonts, font sizes, line drawing, and so on. These characteristics are stored in the text file in the word processor's format, a format independent of any printer. If the document is stored in a general format, it can be printed on a variety of printers. When the document is to be printed, the proper printer driver must be selected. It translates the word processor's formatting codes into those that the printer can interpret.

When you are using a spooler, two printer drivers may come into play: one that converts the word processor codes into printer codes and writes to the spooler, and one that reads the files from a spooler file and physically writes it to the printer. The first typically is provided by the word processing software, and the second usually is provided by the spooler itself.

Support for New Printers

The spooler's printer driver "talks" directly to the printer, so device support is an important consideration in spooler software selection. Widely used LAN spoolers support most commonly used printers. If one of your print devices is not supported by a standard printer driver, or if you get a new printer with a different command set, your spooler may provide a way to generate a new printer driver through a printer definition utility. Using this utility, you define the printer functions and the command sequences needed to carry out those functions. The printer definition utility then builds a command translate table that can be used by a printer driver program to enable print functions.

Application-Oriented Functions

Application-Level Interface

The best way for an application to interface with a spooler is to access it directly. You may recall that LANs provide an **application program interface (API)** for communicating with LAN software. The spooler has a **collector program** that accepts print data streams and writes them to disk. Through an API the application establishes a communication link with the collector program and writes the data to it directly. Some programs that are designed to run on LANs have the ability to do this. Usually these interfaces exist for specific LANs or specific LAN APIs.

Operating System Interface

If you have applications that do not write directly to a spooler collector, you probably can still use the applications on a LAN using a LAN spooler component known as a **redirector.** The redirector establishes itself between the application and the operating system. The job of the redirector is to intercept output destined for a specific operating system printer port (say LPT1 on a DOS system) and reroute the print stream to the spooler. The application assumes that it is writing to a local printer. The redirector filters the operating system calls for printing services and routes the appropriate job streams over the network to the spooler, much like the client redirector for nonlocal file access.

Timeout Interval

Some applications are designed to run on stand-alone platforms. When these applications are run on a network, their printing characteristics may not behave as expected. For example, a few spreadsheet programs open a printer and write to it continuously. Once open, the printer is not closed until the application terminates. When run on a stand-alone system, the output is directed to the printer immediately. Thus a user can issue print requests and have them printed without exiting the program. On a LAN, however, the spooler by default continues to accept input from an application and prints nothing until it receives a close message for the printer. This difference between printing on a LAN and on a stand-alone system may be a problem for some users.

Some spoolers provide a **timeout interval** that helps minimize the differences a user sees between printing on a stand-alone system and on a LAN. If a timeout interval is used, a print job is completed when the printer is closed by the application or no additional data is received for the period specified by the timeout interval. For example, suppose you are using the spreadsheet program just described. Without a timeout interval, your print output is scheduled for printing only after you exit from the spreadsheet program. Suppose instead that a 30-second timeout interval has been specified for your application. When the spooler begins to receive print data, it stores it on the disk as usual. When data stops arriving, the spooler starts a countdown timer at 30 seconds. If the timer counts down to 0 without receiving more input, the print job is closed and scheduled for printing. If more data is received after the interval has expired, it is treated as a separate print job.

A timeout interval is a compromise solution and is not without its problems. Sometimes in a spreadsheet program you want to specify several print ranges and have them printed at one time. If you are not able to specify the parameters for the second part of the print job before the timer expires, the first part is closed and printed. Furthermore, other print jobs may be directed to the printer between your first and second job fragments. Thus, it is important to use timeout intervals appropriately and to choose the timeout duration carefully. An interval that is too short makes manual concatenation of several print streams difficult. An interval that is too long delays printing. A graphics program can require considerable compute time to generate output, so a timeout interval of 60 seconds or more may be necessary. The timeout interval for a word processing program can be 15 seconds or lower. Ordinarily the timeout intervals are set for a printer, not a job, so the timeout specified should be the longest necessary for any of the applications being used.

Collect Printed Output and Direct Print Jobs to Designated Printers

The spooler collects print jobs and stores them on disk. It may do this by storing each job in a separate file, by storing jobs for one printer in the same subdirectory, or by storing all print jobs in one file. Logically all that is necessary is to be able to determine where each print job is located, where it begins, and where it ends. Once an entire print job has been collected, it can be scheduled for printing. Each print job must be directed to the proper printer. This can be accomplished in a variety of ways, as shown in Table 12.2.

Administration-Oriented Functions

Spooler administration may be divided among LAN administrators, printer operators, and users. These roles have a hierarchy of capabilities, with printer operators having a subset of the capabilities of a LAN administrator and users having a small subset of the capabilities of a printer operator. A LAN administrator has capabilities to start and stop the spooler system, remove any print jobs, place jobs on **hold,** and change printing priorities. A LAN administrator can also add or delete printers and change the printing configuration.

A printer operator is given control over a segment of the printing environment. For example, a print operator may be given discretion regarding a workgroup's printing environment. The operator can manipulate jobs submitted by the members of the workgroup. The workgroup print operator cannot affect print jobs in other workgroups. Printer operator capabilities may include starting print jobs, placing print jobs on hold, changing the priorities of print jobs, and maintaining the printer. The printer operator can also add and delete users who are allowed to use the printer.

Users have very limited rights. They can look at their jobs, place them on hold, release them from hold, and delete their own job. Typically, users are unable to take any action that affects other users. For example, they are unable to raise their job priority above another user's.

Table 12.2 Spooler Printing Alternatives

Queuing Mechanism	First in, first out (FIFO).
	Last in, first out (LIFO).
	Smallest job goes to head of queue.
	Smallest job goes to head of queue; each job passed over gets page count incremented by one, thus ensuring it eventually reaches the head of the queue and prints.
	Printing priority is the same as the job's priority in the CPU (for multiuser CPU print jobs).
	Priority depends on job queue.
	Priority set (or changed) by operator or user.
Mapping Jobs to Printers	Job is directed to printer by printer name.
	Job is directed to queue and queue is attached to printer.
	Job is directed to a queue and queue is attached to multiple printers.
	Job is directed to a queue and queue is not attached to printer; queue is later attached to one or more printers by a user or operator.
	Job is broadcast to multiple printers.
	Job is directed to local printer port; local printer port is redirected to a queue that is attached to none, one, or several printers.

All three classes of printer administration need support from the spooler system. Let us now look at several supporting capabilities.

Provide Statistical Reports

Information supports most management and administrative actions. To manage the printing environment effectively and keep it responsive to user needs, the LAN administrator must have information regarding the status of the printing environment. The spooler provides a wide assortment of statistical reports, as shown in Table 12.3. Let us take a closer look at a few of the user-oriented statistical reports produced by the spooler. A user should be responsible for his or her jobs in the spooler. The spooler can be used as more than just a staging area for jobs ready to print. For example, a software programmer can direct the output of compiler listings to the spooler with no intent of ever having the job printed. A programmer debugging a program may be intent only on eliminating syntax errors. Instead of directing the listing to the printer, the programmer can place it in the spooler in a location not attached to a printer. The job is automatically placed on hold. The programmer can then peruse the listing to find the syntax errors and then simply delete it from the spooler. Usually perusing a file on disk takes less time than waiting for printed output, and no paper is wasted. As another example, consider a technical manual writer who prints a document to the spooler and also places it on hold. Whenever another user needs a copy of the document, it can be printed and the document image kept in the spooler until the next print request is received. In the first example the programmer is responsible for removing the document when it is no longer

Table 12.3   Spooler Statistics

User-Oriented Statistics	Number of jobs collected
	Number of lines printed
	Number of jobs on hold
	Number of pages on hold
	Length of time jobs have been held
	Available printers
Administrator-Oriented Statistics	Number and size of jobs on hold
	How long jobs have been on hold
	Available space for new jobs
	Printer status
	Mapping of jobs or print queues to printers
	User-to-printer mappings
	Queue lengths for jobs ready to print
	Job print priorities
	Number of pages in print jobs
	Users responsible for each job
	Average time for a ready job to begin to print
	Maximum time for a ready job to begin to print

needed, and document stays in the spooler files for a short time. In the second example the document remains in the spooler's file for a long time. Both users are responsible for managing their spooler file. Using the user-oriented data maintained by the spooler, the user can manage his or her jobs by deleting jobs no longer needed or printing and removing jobs that have been placed on hold.

The administrator uses the spooler statistics to tune the spooler and make it adaptable to user needs. The administrator may have to remind users to delete unnecessary jobs when the spooler files near capacity. By keeping track of the queues of jobs waiting to print and printer status, the administrator can detect printing bottlenecks and take steps to eliminate or minimize them.

Printer Control

The LAN administrator occasionally has to add new printers, change printers from one location to another, or delete printers. The spooler must allow for such changes. Occasionally the administrator must take a printer out of service temporarily (for example, to change ribbons or toner cartridges and other maintenance tasks) and subsequently bring it back into service. At times the administrator must stop the spooler system altogether (for example, to install new spooler software or to shut down system over a weekend). The administrator must do each of these tasks with as little disruption to users as possible.

Job Control

Properly controlling jobs in a spooler can be critical in establishing user satisfaction. For example, it is disconcerting to many users to have a one-page job ready to print and have to wait several hours while long jobs are printed. Such problems can be avoided with proper job control. Spoolers have a **priority system** for determining which jobs to print next. The default priority usually is **first in, first out.** The LAN administrator can change the default priority to accommodate different situations. For example, the priority can be based on the number of pages to be printed, placing short jobs ahead of long jobs in the queue. Priorities also can be based on the queue to which the printer is attached. The Novell spooler allows several queues to service one printer, and each queue can be given different priorities. Jobs in **a high-priority queue** have precedence over jobs in a **low-priority queue.** Another alternative is to give print jobs priority numbers based on user or application priorities: High-priority applications have their jobs printed before lower-priority applications. A LAN administrator can manually change the order of jobs waiting to be printed. Naturally, once a job begins printing, it continues until done, and even higher-priority jobs queued after it must wait.

To expedite printing, the LAN administrator sometimes must move jobs from one queue to another, stop jobs that are currently printing, change job priorities, or even delete jobs from the spooler system altogether. Ordinarily this type of action is taken on an exception basis, not as a regular way to manage the spooler. If such manual activity is required on a regular basis, the spooler is probably not set up correctly and should be restructured to provide efficient service.

Security and Management Interface

The administrator must be able to monitor and alter the spooler system. This is done through a **spooler interface.** Portions of this interface may be used by printer operators or system users as well. However, users should not have the same privileges as the LAN administrator. Thus the spooler interface must provide for security. For example, users should be able to peruse jobs they have placed in the spooler system themselves but should not be able to peruse other users' jobs. Users should be able to delete their own jobs from the system but not the jobs of other users. A LAN administrator can also decide to allow users to print on certain printers but not on others. The objective of the spooler interface is to provide the necessary balance of management control, user control, and security.

User-Oriented Functions

Some of the functions a user can expect to carry out within the spooler system are similar to the administrator's functions. Other functions are more specific to individual users. In some instances, these capabilities are set up by the LAN administrator, and in other cases they are requested by users themselves.

Print Multiple Copies

A user may want to print multiple copies of a document. All copies can be printed on one printer, or they can be distributed over several printers. Using several printers speeds the printing process, and using printers in several different locations makes documents more readily available to the recipients. Spoolers make these printing options possible. Sometimes, a user has two options regarding the printing of multiple copies: The application may be capable of printing multiple copies, and the spooler may also have that capability. Usually when the application is responsible for printing multiple copies, what is essentially one print job is sent to the spooler multiple times. Of course, this method takes up extra space in the spooler files. If the spooler is responsible for printing multiple copies, one copy of the job is sent to the spooler, and the spooler sends it to the printer multiple times. In general, the second alternative is better. Moreover, if the spooler is responsible for printing multiple copies, it may be able to print them more efficiently by using multiple printers. Typically a multiple-copy job created by an application appears to the spooler as a single, long print job.

Print Banners

When printers are being shared, user jobs are interspersed, and there is a good chance that one user will accidentally take the output of another user. This is particularly true when one user has two large jobs and another user has a small job sandwiched between the two large jobs. To help users identify the beginning and ending of their jobs, some spoolers provide an optional **banner page** that contains information in large print identifying the user and the application. Thus banners can be used to identify and separate jobs produced on the same printer. On the negative side, banners increase the amount of paper used. If most jobs are small, printing an extra one or two pages per document represents a large printing overhead.

Print Selected Pages

Sometimes it is helpful to print a subset of the pages of a particular job. For example, suppose you had a long job to print, and the printer ribbon broke after successfully printing 65 pages. It would be more efficient to print the pages that were not successfully printed than to print the entire document. Most spoolers allow users to print selected pages.

NOVELL SPOOLER CONFIGURATION

We could discuss how to configure a spooler from a generic perspective; however, the way in which spoolers operate differs considerably. Therefore, we describe one specific example of a spooler system: the Novell spooler. The latest releases of Novell software de-emphasize the term *spooler* and simply talk about the printing subsystem. However, we continue to use the term *spooler* when discussing the printing capabilities of the Novell system. Novell's printing environment is pictured in Figure 12.4. This figure is the basis for much of the discussion that follows. In our discussion we start at the user end of the print job and work toward the server end.

The CAPTURE Program

Some applications running under a Novell LAN are network-printer aware; that is, they can print directly to the network spooler. To effect this capability, the network admin-

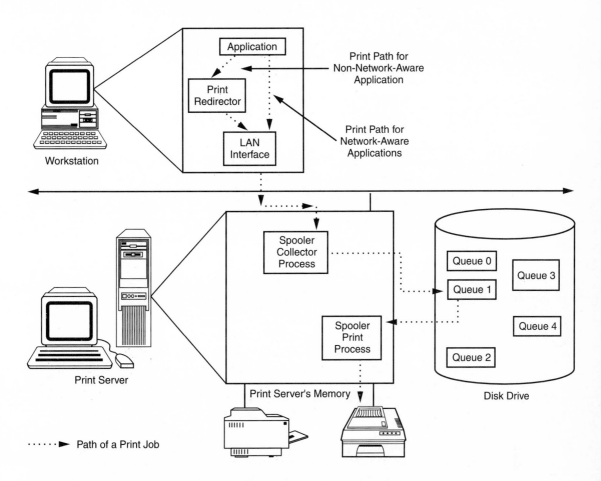

Figure 12.4   The Novell Printing Environment

istrator must properly install the application. With direct printing the user can typically print either to a local printer port or to the network printer. Thus the user can establish several printing paths, such as a local printer port using LPT1 and another port writing directly to the network spooler. The desired path is selected from within the application or a print setup utility.

Other applications are not network aware; that is, they only know how to print to local printer ports, such as DOS's LPT*n* ports. In this instance a printer redirection program is needed to reroute print streams directed to local ports to the network print spooler. Novell's redirection program is called CAPTURE. The **CAPTURE program** runs as a **terminate-and-stay-resident (TSR)** program on each workstation that needs network printing support. Before print redirection can occur, the CAPTURE program must be run and be memory resident. Often this is done through the AUTOEXEC.BAT file when the workstation is started or on an application-by-application basis through an

Table 12.4   Some CAPTURE Parameters

Local = n	The port being monitored. If n = 1 then LPT1 is monitored; if n = 2 then LPT2 is monitored; if n = 3 then LPT3 is monitored. Default is LPT1.
TImeout = n	The timeout interval. The value ranges from 1 to 1000 and represents seconds. Default is no timeout.
Server = <name>	Designates the print server to which CAPTURE is to direct its output. Default is user's default server.
Queue = <name>	Designates print queue to which the output is to be directed.
Job = job	Designates a printer configuration file to use for print job parameters and configuration.
CReate = <name>	Sends the output to a file rather than to a printer.
Form = <name>	Designates a form name or number to be used, such as Form = W2FORM. No default exists.
Copies = n	Directs the number of copies to print. Default is 1 copy.
NAMe = <name>	Provides a user name to be printed on upper half of banner pages. Default is user's logon name.
Banner = <name>	Provides words that are printed on the lower half of banner pages. Default is LST.
NoBanner	Suppresses printing of banner page. Default is banner is printed.
FormFeed	Issues a form-feed character to the printer after the job has completed. Default is form feed enabled.
NoFormFeed	Suppresses a form-feed character after the job is printed. Default is form feed enabled.
Keep	Keeps all print information in the queue even if the application ends abnormally. If an application writing to the spooler fails, a partial print job is, by default, automatically removed from the queue. This parameter keeps partially completed jobs in the event the application or its processor hangs or ends abnormally. Default is to discard the job.
SHow	Shows the printer ports for which CAPTURE is in effect and the parameters specified for each port.

application batch file that starts CAPTURE, starts the applications, and then removes the CAPTURE program when the application terminates.

CAPTURE has a variety of startup parameters, the most important of which defines which printer port is to be monitored. CAPTURE intercepts printed output destined for that port and redirects it to the spooler. Whenever CAPTURE redirects print output for a particular port, that port does not receive any print streams. Therefore, if CAPTURE is intercepting print streams for LPT1, all jobs directed to LPT1 are routed to the spooler, even if there is a printer attached to LPT1.

Some of the parameters that CAPTURE can use are described in Table 12.4. Several of these parameters (including the printer port to be monitored) have default values, which are also shown in Table 12.4. To accept a default setting, the user simply omits the parameter. For example, the default parameter for the local port is L = 1, indicating that port LPT1 is to be monitored. If the user wants CAPTURE to monitor LPT1, then this parameter need not be included in CAPTURE's startup string. For self-documentation purposes, it is usually a good idea to explicitly state the parameters you want to use. If the user wants to use a value other than the default value, the parameter setting must be included in the startup string. Be aware that Table 12.4 does not show all of the CAPTURE parameters.

Table 12.5   Sample CAPTURE Startup Strings

CAPTURE L = 1 TI = 15 Q = PRINTQ2 NB NFF K
CAPTURE L = 2 TI = 15 Q = PRINTQ2 NB NFF K

Once started, CAPTURE stays in memory and directs print jobs to queues until terminated with the **ENDCAP command.** You may want to view the CAPTURE parameters that are in effect. If you run CAPTURE with the SHow parameter, it tells you the ports for which CAPTURE is activated and the parameter settings in effect for each port. Samples of parameters used in CAPTURE starting string are shown in Table 12.5, and the output of the CAPTURE SHow parameter is shown in Table 12.6. If you run CAPTURE without specifying any parameters and CAPTURE is not currently running, it uses the default settings. On a DOS system this means CAPTURE begins capturing print streams destined for LPT1 with no timeout value and no banners printed.

The Print Server Spooler System

The majority of the work of the spooler is done on the file server. It is there that jobs are collected, stored on disk, directed to a printer, and eventually removed from the spooler system. The job is scheduled for printing only after the complete job has been captured in the queue. The LAN administrator can define a variety of queues to meet varied printing needs. Let us now look at how Novell print queues operate. You may wish to refer back to Figure 12.4 during this discussion.

Novell Print Queues

Print queues can be thought of as containers for print jobs. A job directed to a queue is stored in that queue until it is removed. A job is automatically removed when it finishes printing and the hold flag is not on or when the job owner or print queue operator deletes it. A **print queue operator** is a user who has been given the right to manipulate

Table 12.6   Output of CAPTURE Show Parameter

LPT1:	Capturing data to server SERVER	queue PRINTQ2 (printer 0).
	Capture Defaults : Enabled	Automatic Endcap : Enabled
	Banner : (None)	Form Feed : No
	Copies : 1	Tabs : Converted to 8 spaces
	Form : 0	Timeout Count : 15 seconds
LPT2:	Capturing data to server SERVER	queue PRINTQ2 (printer 0).
	Capture Defaults : Enabled	Automatic Endcap : Enabled
	Banner : (None)	Form Feed : No
	Copies : 1	Tabs : Converted to 8 spaces
	Form : 0	Timeout Count : 15 seconds
LPT3:	Capturing Is Not Currently Active.	

jobs in that particular queue. For example, a user or a group manager may be given the right to be a queue operator for queues serving printers in his or her location. The types of things a print queue operator can do are listed in Table 12.7. Some of the print-job parameters that can be changed by the owner of a job or the print queue operator are shown in Table 12.8. Notice in Table 12.8 that a user can make changes to his or her job as long as it does not affect other jobs. The queue operator can do everything a job owner can plus take actions that affect other users, such as changing the order in which jobs are printed and placing a job on operator hold. A job that has been placed on operator hold is scheduled to print only when a queue operator releases the hold. A user cannot release an operator hold for his or her job.

Print queues also offer an element of security. The LAN administrator or queue operator can designate **queue users.** A queue user is a user authorized to direct jobs to that queue. A user cannot direct job streams to a queue unless he or she has been designated as a queue user. Thus, a queue attached to a printer that is used for printing checks can be protected from unauthorized users. If department printers are used, a user in one department can be made a queue user for queues attached to that department's printers but will not be a queue user for queues attached to printers in other departments. Under this arrangement, users in one department cannot tie up printers in other departments.

A printer can be attached to no queue, one queue, or several queues. Figure 12.5 illustrates several configurations. Of course, a queue that is not connected to a printer cannot print jobs. Jobs directed to that queue are held in the queue and not printed. At a later time the queue may be attached to a printer and the jobs stored there can print. Alternatively, the queue may be used for jobs that will never print. For example, a programmer may direct the output of his compiler listing to such a queue. With a print-job perusal program, he can look at the list and locate all of his compiler errors. When the programmer is done looking at the job, he can delete it from the queue.

Print jobs arrive in a queue and are scheduled to be printed. A queue may be connected to several printers to speed the printing of jobs waiting in the queue. The print process prints jobs to whichever printer is available, so two jobs can print from the same queue at once.

A printer can also have several queues servicing it. One reason for this practice is to establish printing priorities. Each queue can be given a queue priority. Thus, the LAN administrator can create an environment wherein users spooling their output to a high-priority queue get better service than users sending their output to a lower-priority queue. If jobs in the high-priority queue are ready to print, they are printed before any ready jobs in the lower-priority queue.

Table 12.7   Functions of a Print Queue Operator

Edit the job parameters for any job in the queue (see Table 12.8)

Delete any job from the queue

Modify queue status by changing operator flags

Change priority of jobs in the queue

Table 12.8   Print-Job Parameters

Parameter	Meaning	Can Be Altered by
Description	Identifies file being printed.	U, QO
User hold	Holds job from printing.	U, QO
Operator hold	Holds job from printing.	QO
Service sequence	Changes priority for printing.	QO
Number of copies	Self-explanatory.	U, QO
File contents	Text or byte stream. With text the spooler interprets formatting such as tabs and format codes. With byte stream application handles formatting.	U, QO
Tab size	Self-explanatory.	U, QO
Suppress form feed	Suppresses a form feed after job prints.	U, QO
Defer printing	Yes or no. Choose *no* if job is to be printed as soon as possible. Choose *yes* and enter target date and time to print later. A large job, for example, can be scheduled to print overnight.	U, QO
Form	Designates that a special print form is required.	U, QO
Print banner	Yes or no.	U, QO
Banner name	Name to print on banner.	U, QO
Banner file	Name of file on banner.	U, QO
Target date	See Defer printing.	U, QO
Target time	See Defer printing.	U, QO
U = user or print job owner		
QO = queue operator		

Queues may be added and deleted as needed. Once created, queues can be attached to and detached from a printer. The ability to create, attach, detach, or delete print queues and the ability to direct print streams to a print queue creates a system that can accommodate almost all printing requirements.

Special Printing Needs

Some installations have special printing needs. Suppose your organization has a unique printer that is not completely supported by one of the standard printer drivers supplied by your network software. Some networks help you overcome this with a utility that allows you to define or enhance a printer-definition file. In a Novell network this utility is called **PRINTDEF.** Novell uses a printer-definition file to describe the functions of a printer, such as underline, bold, near-letter-quality, draft mode, and so on. With PRINT-DEF you can customize a printer-definition file to take full advantage of unique characteristics of your printer. Moveover, if you purchase a new, state-of-the-art printer that is not fully supported by an existing printer-definition file, you can enhance an existing definition to take advantage of your printer's new capabilities.

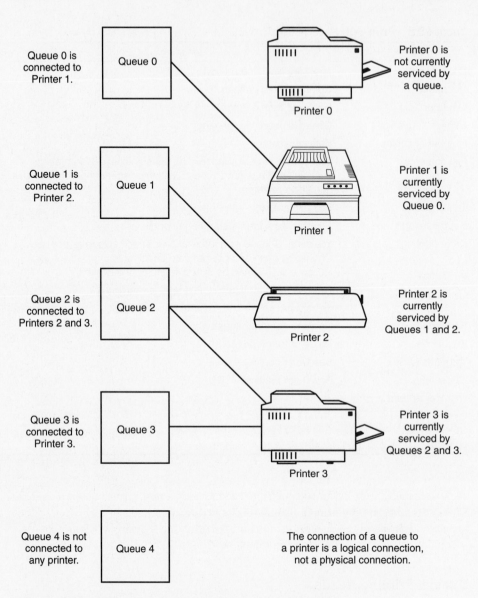

Queue 0 is connected to Printer 1.

Queue 0

Printer 0 is not currently serviced by a queue.

Printer 0

Queue 1 is connected to Printer 2.

Queue 1

Printer 1 is currently serviced by Queue 0.

Printer 1

Queue 2 is connected to Printers 2 and 3.

Queue 2

Printer 2 is currently serviced by Queues 1 and 2.

Printer 2

Queue 3 is connected to Printer 3.

Queue 3

Printer 3 is currently serviced by Queues 2 and 3.

Printer 3

Queue 4 is not connected to any printer.

Queue 4

The connection of a queue to a printer is a logical connection, not a physical connection.

Figure 12.5   Queue and Printer Attachment Configurations

Some print jobs must be printed on special **forms,** such as checks, income tax forms, and invoices. To prevent these jobs from printing on standard paper or on the wrong form, the spooler can allow you to define a form by name and paper size, associate a job with a form name, associate a printer with a form name, prohibit a job from printing on a printer that has not been associated with its form name, and provide assistance in aligning the form on the printer. All of these capabilities are provided within Novell's printer system.

Print Servers

In NetWare, a print server is a **network loadable module (NLM)** running in a file server. One print server process is allowed per file server. A single print server in NetWare 3.*nn* can support up to 16 printers; NetWare 4.*nn* print servers can support up to 256 printers. Network printers can be local, meaning that they are attached to the file server or remote. Remote printers are connected to a dedicated or nondedicated print server. Remote printers run print server applications. In NetWare 3.*nn* the processes are **RPRINTER** and **PSERVER** for nondedicated and dedicated print servers, respectively. In NetWare 4.*nn* a single process, NPRINTER, provides both capabilities.

In another option for connecting printers on a network, dedicated LAN printer adapters allow a printer to be attached directly to the network, as illustrated in Figure 12.5. This solution provides considerable flexibility. The printer can be located anywhere the LAN medium is located and does not require an expensive microcomputer to provide the connection and printer support.

SUMMARY

Setting up a printing environment is one of several keys to creating a LAN that accommodates the needs of all users. On a LAN, printers are shared devices, and software is needed to manage the sharing. The software tool that manages network printing needs is generically called a spooler. In general, a spooler collects print job streams from users and places them temporarily on disk. When a job has been completed, the spooler places the job in an **output queue** for printing, prints the job, and then deletes it from the queue. Most spoolers also provide additional functions, such as security, placing jobs on hold, establishing print job priorities, and so on.

In a Novell network, print jobs are collected in queues. A utility named CAPTURE can route jobs destined for local printers to a network printer. Alternatively, an application that is network aware can write directly to a network queue. Queues may be attached to no printer, one printer, or several printers. A printer can be served by no queue, one queue, or several queues. Moveover, each queue can be given a different priority for printing. This variety of configurations provides the flexibility to meet diverse user needs.

Novell provides some degree of security or exclusivity to the printing configuration. A queue can be restricted to selected users or user groups. A queue user can manipulate his or her job in a queue but cannot perform any action that affects other queue jobs, such as placing his or her job ahead of other jobs in the print order. LAN administrators can designate **queue managers,** who can manipulate all jobs in a queue. Job manipulation includes placing a job on hold, changing its print priority, setting the number of copies to be printed, deferring printing until a specific date and time, changing the target server, and so on.

Key Terms

application program interface (API)

banner page

CAPTURE program

collector program

control sequence

ENDCAP command

first in, first out

forms

hardware interface

high-priority queue

hold

I/O port

low-priority queue

network-loadable module (NLM)

output queue

parallel interface

PRINTDEF

print queue operator

priority system

PSERVER

queue manager

queue user

redirector

RPRINTER

serial interface

small computer system interface (SCSI)

spooler interface

terminate-and-stay-resident (TSR)

timeout interval

Review Questions

1. List three general functions provided by a spooler and explain how each is accomplished.
2. Describe three application-oriented, administrative-oriented, user-oriented, and hardware-oriented spooler functions.
3. What is the function of the print job redirector? Why and when is it necessary?
4. Why would you have several print queues attached to one printer?
5. Why would you have several printers attached to one print queue?
6. Why would you have a queue that is not attached to a printer?
7. Describe two ways to regulate job printing.

Problems and Exercises

1. Write the CAPTURE parameter that
   a. directs the print job stream for LPT1 to a queue named LASER
   b. issues a form feed at the end of the job
   c. suppresses printing of a banner
   d. provides a timeout value of 30 seconds
   Refer to Table 12.4 for a list of some CAPTURE parameters and to Table 12.5 for examples of CAPTURE parameters used in startup strings.
2. The document support group (DSG) in an airplane manufacturing company is responsible for writing and changing airplane manuals and engineering-change notices. Documents range in length from one to several hundred pages. Some documents include graphic images that the application must generate. Generating graphic-image blocks for transmission to the printer can require up to a minute of CPU time. DSG has three printers and wants to share these printers in an optimal manner. Some of their concerns include preventing short jobs from waiting for long manuals to print and problems of interleaving graphic images because of the time it takes to generate graphic images. Suggest a plan for using the three printers that will satisfy DSG's needs. Your plan should include a description of print queues, printers, job types, and timeout intervals.
3. Investigate a LAN system different from Novell's. Compare this system's spooler capabilities with those of Novell.
4. A variety of printing utilities and hardware is available for LANs. Research the literature and describe three of these systems.

Chapter 13

LAN Administration: Backup and Recovery

CHAPTER PREVIEW

A LAN is not a static entity. Data stored on the LAN changes, new applications are added, old applications are retired, users come and go, workstations are added, moved, removed or replaced, servers are added or upgraded, systems fail, and new threats to security and integrity arise. LAN administration is a process of managing such changes, some of which are planned, others unplanned. Adding new users, maintaining security, and modifying the printing environment, topics discussed earlier, are examples of planned changes. Managing unplanned changes—those that arise from unanticipated situations, such as hardware and software failures, power failures, disasters such as fires and floods, and human errors—are the topic of this chapter. The key topics in this chapter are

- data backup
- data recovery
- problem detection
- problem resolution
- diagnostic hardware and software
- disaster planning

By the end of this chapter you should understand some of the unexpected problems that can arise on a LAN, how to deal with those problems, and how to effect recovery.

DATA BACKUP

Data is a valuable corporate resource. It is the raw material from which information is manufactured, and information is the resource that drives corporate decision making. Corporate data resides in many places: in employees' minds, on paper, and in computers. Companies go to great lengths to gather, update, and protect this data.

For years companies have had mechanisms for protecting non–computer-related data. Employees are encouraged to share what they know with other employees or to write down facts known only to them. Organizations make additional copies of hard-copy data as backups in case the original is lost or destroyed. Companies must do the same with their computerized data; that is, they must provide one or more ways to protect its data from accidental and intentional loss and corruption. One way to do this is to create data backups.

Computer systems process data, and most data is subject to change. One of the most critical functions of system administration—on LANs, stand-alone systems, and WANs alike—is preserving the currency and integrity of data. You may have heard the phrase "garbage in, garbage out." This means that if the data used to produce information is not correct, the information produced from that data is also incorrect. Because information is used as the foundation for management decisions, we go to great lengths to keep it from turning into garbage. Moreover, on computer systems we have a variety of objects that help us work with data: programs, user profiles, security settings, logon scripts, command files, and so on. If we take steps to protect the data, we also must take steps to protect the objects used to manipulate that data. Garbage programs and improper security settings operating on good data can turn good data into garbage data.

A **data backup** is a snapshot of a database or files at a particular time. Just as a photograph preserves the image of a scene at a particular instant, a backup provides an installation with a historical copy of the data at one point in time. Have you recently looked at your childhood pictures? They probably bear only partial resemblance to you now. The same is true of data backups; as time progresses they become less like the current image of the data. A backup is produced by making a copy of data, programs, and work files stored on disk. The backup is typically written to other disks or to tapes. Because magnetic tapes are still the most common backup medium, for convenience we may refer to backup images as backup tapes; realize that the backup image may actually be on disk or an optical medium.

The Need for Backups

In computing systems myriad things can happen to corrupt or destroy data or the objects used to manipulate it. A partial list of these things is given in Table 13.1. Some of the items on the list are intentional acts, and others are accidental or circumstantial. Regardless of the cause, a good LAN administration policy must provide a method of **data recovery** to correct data problems. The most common way to restore files to a usable state following a damaging incident is to use backups. In addition to data recovery, backups are also used to archive data, to provide low-cost bulk data storage, and to provide data interchange. Following a brief discussion of the uses of backups, we focus on backup procedures for the recovery of lost or damaged data.

Recovery

If data in a database becomes corrupted or a text file is accidentally deleted, an organization will want to restore the data to a usable state. Backups are the tool most often used to do this. For corrupted program files two alternatives usually exist: restore from backup

Table 13.1   Ways in Which Data Can Be Corrupted

An application program with a logic bug can change data incorrectly.

A user can accidentally erase a file.

A user can accidentally destroy a file by copying a new file over it.

A user can maliciously destroy a file or data in a file.

A system failure can leave the database in a state of partial update.

A disk failure can destroy data or render it inaccessible.

An undetected virus can erase or otherwise destroy data.

A bug in system software, such as the database management system, can cause data loss, unreliable results, or data corruption.

tapes or reinstall the applications from the program disks. Restoring from backup is almost always significantly faster and avoids recreating installation- and user-specific startup and profile data.

Data Archiving

Computer users often want to maintain historical copies of data, a process known as **archiving.** If you use computer software to calculate your taxes, you probably want to archive your tax software and work files to use in case you are audited or to refer back to when preparing next year's return. You probably do not need to permanently keep the data on your disk drives.

Low-Cost Bulk Data Storage

This use of backups is similar to data archiving. The primary difference is that archived data is kept and perhaps never reused, whereas data kept in low-cost bulk data storage can be used periodically. Rather than keeping the data on-line constantly, a disk is used to hold the data temporarily while it is being used and, when no longer needed, the data is removed and stored. This reduces the hardware costs of the system. For example, a research organization may have large volumes of data that have been collected during testing and experimentation. Using backups, researchers can periodically run programs that analyze certain aspects of the data. Once the results of the analysis have been produced, the researchers take several months to evaluate it and determine additional processing needs. Colleges often use low-cost bulk data storage for classes that are taught once per year. Data for these classes are restored to disks during the term in which they are needed and removed when the class is not being taught.

Data Interchange

Before high-speed data communications, one of the primary methods of moving data from one computer to another was to back up the data onto a tape on one system and restore the data to a disk on another system. This is still a viable method for exchanging data today. To do this, of course, the two machines sharing the data must have common hardware and software backup capabilities.

Types of Backups

Backup software may support different classes of backups, including full, partial, differential, and selective backups. A **full backup** backs up all files on a system, volume, or directory. A **partial backup,** sometimes called an **incremental backup,** backs up all files that have changed since the preceding backup. Selection of files to back up on a partial backup is made by looking at an archive bit that is one of the attributes of a file. When a file is backed up, the archive bit is cleared, indicating that it has been backed up. When the file is updated, the archive bit is set, indicating that it has been changed. With a partial backup, only files with the archive bit set are backed up.

A differential backup is similar in some respects to a partial backup. A **differential backup** backs all files that have changed since the last full backup. To compare partial and differential backups, refer to Table 13.2. The table reflects that a full backup was done on Sunday. FileA, FileB, and FileC were updated after the backup on Monday. FileA and FileD were updated on Tuesday. FileE was updated on Wednesday. Finally, the table indicates the files present on daily partial and differential backup tapes. The trade-offs between partial and differential backups are as follows: Partial backups are faster to make and take less tape storage, and differential backups provide faster restoration. With partial backups, the full backup is restored and each partial backup image thereafter is restored. With differential backups, the full backup is restored and then the last differential backup is restored.

Selective backups provide the ability to backup designated files. The files may be indicated by wildcard characters, an exclusion list, an inclusion list, or combinations thereof. For example, a user may want to back up all files that meet the pattern CUST*.DOC in the CUSTOMER directory.

Backups for Static and Dynamic Data

Static data changes infrequently or not at all. An example of static data is a program executable file. The only time a program executable file is changed is when a new release of the product is installed, when patches are made to the code files to fix bugs, or when the code file is infected by a virus.

Whenever new application files are received or existing ones are updated, the first step a LAN administrator usually takes is to make backup copies of the program disks. CD-ROM software distribution has made this step impractical for many of today's users

Table 13.2   Comparison of Partial and Differential Backups

Day	Files Updated	Partial Backup Contents	Differential Backup Contents
Sunday	Full backup completed		
Monday	FileA, FileB, FileC	FileA, FileB, FileC	FileA, FileB, FileC
Tuesday	FileA, FileD	FileA, FileD	FileA, FileB, FileC, FileD
Wednesday	FileE	FileE	FileA, FileB, FileC, FileD, FileE
Thursday	FileA, FIleC, FileF	FileA, FileC, FileF	FileA, FileB, FileC, FileD, FileE, FileF
Friday	FileA	FileA	FileA, FileB, FileC, FileD, FileE, FileF

who do not have writable optical disks or sufficient magnetic disk capacity. For good measure, two backup copies are made: one copy for on-site storage and another for storage at a different location, called **off-site storage.** Storing a backup copy in another location is a safeguard against a catastrophe, such as a fire or flood, that might ruin the data on the computer's disk as well as the backup copies.

Suppose that something happens to static data; for example, a programmer accidentally deletes a program file, or the disk on which it is stored goes bad. To recover from this problem, the LAN administrator must identify and correct the sources of the problem. If a disk had a head crash, it is replaced; if a virus infected the file, the virus is removed from the entire system; if a programmer accidentally deleted the file, security settings are reviewed and possibly changed. After the proper operational environment is restored, say by replacement of a failed disk drive, the backup copy of the data is restored to the system. Because the data has not changed since the backup was taken, the program file is available in the same form as before the problem arose, and recovery is complete.

Dynamic data changes frequently. A database is an example of dynamic data. Data in databases is constantly changed as records are added, modified, or deleted. A backup is a snapshot of data at a particular time, so if a failure occurs that affects dynamic data, the backup for that data probably will not represent the exact state of the data at a point of failure. A backup can accurately represent the state of a database after a failure only if no database updates have occurred since the backup was taken.

Assuming no recovery mechanism exists other than a backup (later you will see several measures some databases use to protect against failures), recovery for dynamic data begins like the recovery for static data: The sources of the problem are detected and corrected, and the backup copy of the data is restored to the disk. However, to fully recover, the database must be brought forward in time to the last consistent state before the failure occurred. This means that the updates that were made after the backup was made must be done again. This can be done by resubmitting transactions posted to the database after the backup was taken or by using some of the special recovery provisions provided by some database management systems that are briefly described later. You may be fortunate and never experience a corrupt file situation. However, experiencing such a failure is a good object lesson: It is much more efficient to perform backup and recovery than to manually redo all the work.

As you can tell, when a failure occurs, having a *current* backup available allows for a fast, comprehensive recovery. In contrast, a dynamic data backup that is a month old may require that a month's worth of work be redone. Backups are a company's insurance policy against data-related disasters and loss. Like insurance, it is better to have them and not need them. When needed, they usually make the difference between a timely return to a productive operation and an arduous, time-consuming system-rebuilding effort with lost work, productivity, and sometimes jobs.

Backup Hardware, Software, and Procedures

Data backups and restorations require both hardware and software. The hardware provides the medium to which the backup is written or from which data to be restored is read. The software provides the logic to write the correct file to the backup medium or to read those files from the backup medium for restoration. Good backup/restore software also provides a variety of options. You may want to refer to Chapter 5 for more information regarding backup hardware and to Chapter 7 for more information regarding backup software.

Making Backups

Key questions facing LAN administrators are, How often should backups be made? What should be backed up? How long should backup copies be saved? Where should backup copies be stored? The ideal answers to these questions are backup everything daily, keep the copies forever, and store copies in at least two separate locations. This ideal is not always practical, however. LAN administration would be much easier if there were one backup/recovery policy that applied universally to all installations; however, life is not always so simple. Each installation needs to formulate a backup policy and backup/restore procedures that allow data recovery from any imaginable data disaster. The recovery must be timely and sufficiently comprehensive to allow the organization to resume productive processing. The definitions of *timely, sufficiently comprehensive*, and *productive processing* vary among organizations, as illustrated by the following examples.

A university LAN that supports student academic work has a cyclic load. During vacations, the system is hardly used. Near the end of a term, the system is often overworked as students rush to meet end-of-term deadlines. (Note that students probably should not rely solely on the LAN backup for recovering their files. In addition, students should backup their files when concluding a work session.) During vacation, having the LAN out of service for several days may not have much of an impact. But losing its services for that long at the end of the semester might have serious repercussions for some students' grades. For this university, the term *timely* has different meanings at different periods.

During the busy period students use a wide variety of applications and files. The term *sufficiently comprehensive* in this case means that most of the lost data must be reconstructed so most of the students can complete their work. During a vacation period, *sufficiently comprehensive* may mean simply having the LAN operational so the LAN administrator can create the files and environment for next semester's classes.

The university defines *productive processing* as all students being able to complete their work at the end of the term. Applications and data files must be recovered to a point that allows this to happen.

Now, consider a lawyer's office that uses a LAN to support its activities. One of the main applications the office uses is word processing of legal documents. The file servers have a large number of inactive files. Wills are maintained on-line for three years after a change, letters are kept on-line for a year, and so on. This means that the number of active documents (the ones currently being worked on) is small in comparison to the bulk of data stored. Moreover, the need to access the older documents is minimal. For the attorney's office, *sufficiently comprehensive* means restoring the active documents and word processing system. Inactive documents can be restored at a more leisurely pace. This is sufficient to allow productive processing for the majority of the staff; that is, the staff can do work of an immediate nature. Timeliness in this case is within a few minutes or hours. Most of the staff can temporarily work on other tasks until the system is restored; however, deadlines do exist and some workers must be able to return to their tasks almost immediately.

As a final example, a LAN being used to control a manufacturing process must be restored quickly to avoid lost production time, costly damage to raw materials, or damage to the processing equipment. In this case getting the system back into operation, even with some data that is not exactly accurate, is probably more cost-effective than completely restoring the entire system before resuming processing. That is, time rather than complete accuracy is of the essence. For the manufacturer *sufficiently comprehensive* means just having the system available to resume direction of the work in progress.

What must be recovered and in what time can differ among applications. The LAN administrator must analyze the backup and restoration alternatives—backup frequency, completeness, and retention—and choose the alternatives best suited to the organization's needs. Let us now look at some of these backup procedure considerations.

Backup Procedures

A backup procedure describes what is to be backed up, when and how backups are taken, the frequency of backups, and the disposition of the backup copies. As described earlier, an application's characteristics are major factors influencing each of these choices. Let us look at each in more detail.

Disposition of Backup Copies

A comprehensive backup procedure ensures that several copies of backups are available and that complete copies are stored in at least two separate locations. Separate locations usually does not mean adjoining rooms; it means off-site storage or the equivalent. Some installations store backups in fireproof vaults. This is not always a viable alternative to off-site storage because floods or explosions, for example, could still damage the backup copies. The objective of off-site storage is to allow recovery from catastrophes that might destroy both computer data and backup copies stored on-site.

Several copies of backups may be needed for another reason. The backup medium itself may go bad and render the backup unusable. For example, a magnetic tape backup may get scratched, stretched, broken, or ruined by exposure to a magnetic field. Each of these circumstances can make the tape unusable. Furthermore, when backing up, you should take steps to ensure that the backup is reliable. A read-after-write backup function may be available in the backup software that checks to see whether the data just written is readable. Another reliability check is to periodically restore backed up data to a test drive to check the reliability of the backup medium and hardware. In this restoration process it is best to do the restoration using a tape drive different from the one making the backup. This checks on the calibration of both drives and guards against backup unit malfunctions. Having a backup to the backup provides a recovery alternative.

Having several generations of backups is also important. An axiom of backup procedures is, "Never immediately recycle your backup media." That is, suppose you decide to use only one tape for backups. Furthermore, suppose that the backup requires the entire tape. What do you suppose happens if a failure occurs while you are making the backup? The answer is that the backup being made is incomplete and the previous backup has been overwritten by the one being made. Hence, no good, complete backup is available.

Keeping a history or several generations of backups is called a **retention policy.** Perhaps one of the most difficult backup policy decisions a LAN administrator must make is how long to retain backups. Three generations of backups are made in the **grandfather–father–son backup method.** When the grandson backup is made, the grandfather backup is recycled and made available for the next backup, the father becomes the grandfather, and so on. This process is illustrated in Figure 13.1. Note that four tape sets are required to maintain three generations of backup. For some installations this may be adequate; however, most companies today have a more comprehensive retention policy. An example of one company's retention policy is outlined in Table 13.3. The tradeoffs you make in formulating a retention policy are based on the volume of data involved, the cost of backup media, the cost of storage, and installation-specific recovery or data-restoration needs.

You can think of backup **comprehensiveness** as the degree of data exactness represented by the backups. A backup with poor comprehensiveness, such as a year-old backup, is probably not a good approximation to the current state of the data. A backup with good comprehensiveness, such as one that is just minutes old, closely represents the current state of the data. Comprehensiveness is a function of the age of a backup and the amount of change in the data since the last backup was made. The older the backup and the higher the volatility of the data, the poorer the comprehensiveness. A good backup plan provides several levels of comprehensiveness. One reason for levels of comprehensiveness is the need to go back in time to retrieve specific data, such as a university's class files used annually. Another reason is that some time may elapse before a data problem is noticed. For example, a newly modified program with a bug that was not detected during testing may have been placed into operation. If the data corrupting bug is not detected for three days, all backups made after the program was used may contain corrupted data. Several backups may have occurred between the time the data was

Table 13.3   A Sample Backup Retention Policy

Backup Policy	
Daily	Back up all files changed since the backup of the preceding day.
	Make two copies; store one copy off-site.
Weekly	Back up all files.
	Make two copies; store one copy off-site.
End of year	Back up all files as of midnight, December 31.
	Back up all files as of midnight at the end of the fiscal year.
	Make two copies; store one copy off-site.

Retention Policy
Retain weekly backups and daily backups for 1 month.
Retain the first backup of each month for 1 year.
Retain the end-of-year backups for 5 years.

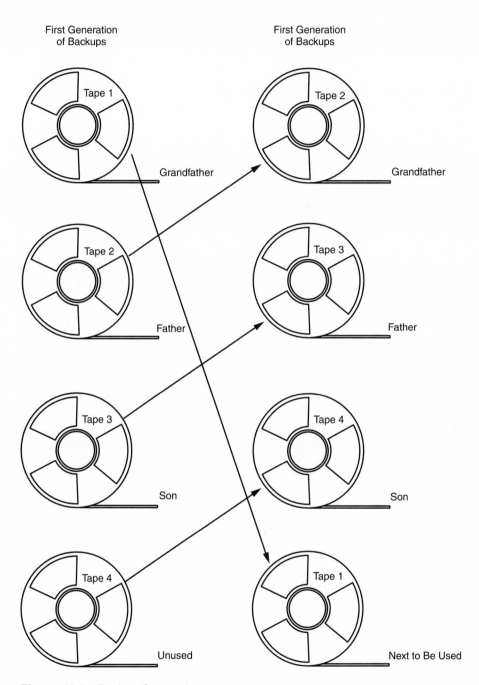

Figure 13.1 Backup Generations

corrupted and the time the corruption was noticed. Recovery may require that several generations of backups be skipped until a backup made before the corruption occurred is found. When used for recovery, older backups require more work to bring the data up to date. Despite the work required, this approach is used if the alternative of fixing corrupted data is more expensive or time-consuming.

Backup Frequency

Static data should be backed up at least twice, and the two versions should be stored in separate locations. A file that has been backed up several times and has not changed need not be backed up again unless one of the backup copies is recycled or is defective. Before such a backup is recycled, a new backup of the static file should be made.

Dynamic files must be backed up more often. Some installations do daily backups; others find that a weekly backup is adequate. You decide the frequency of backups by comparing the time required to do backups with the time required to do recovery. Usually we look at the worst and average recovery scenario when making this decision. For comparison, let us consider two alternatives: daily and weekly backups.

On average, failures occur at about midpoint between one backup being made and the next one taking its place. The best time for a recovery situation to occur is immediately after a backup has been made. In the worst-case scenario, a failure occurs just before the next backup. This worst-case scenario requires you to determine the length and complexity of recovery. If backups have been made weekly, they reflect data that is a week old, and restoration returns the data to that state. Following the restoration, you must somehow repeat the week's work to bring the data to a current state. If daily backups have been made, the worst-case recovery involves redoing what has changed during the day. Assuming a constant workload, a recovery using weekly backups requires seven times as much effort to bring the database to a current status as do daily backups (or five times for a 5-day work week). The backup frequency is seven times as long and the average amount of work to be redone is 3.5 days versus 0.5 days (or 2.5 days versus 0.5 days).

Two other factors influence the frequency of backups: failure rates and timeliness of recovery. If the frequency of failure is low, less frequent backups may be acceptable. If the frequency of failures is high, more frequent backups are called for. If the need to return to operational status immediately is high, then the frequency of backups is greater than if need for an immediate return to operation status is low.

How and When to Make Backups

Once you have determined the frequency of making backups, you must next decide when during the workday you want to make backups. On large systems, some backup utilities allow files to be backed up while updates to that file are being made. This is possible because the system coordinates the backup with before image and after image audit trails, so data integrity is maintained. Because most of today's LAN backup utilities do not provide data integrity protection for on-line backups, it is usually best to create the backups when data is not being modified. This not only promotes data integrity but also reduces LAN overhead while users are most active.

Figure 13.2 illustrates a problem you might experience in making backups while data is being changed. A transaction is moving money from Record A in File 1 to

Record X in File 2. Suppose that a backup was started before this transaction began and that File 1 has already been backed up. On the backup tape the contents of Record A has already been recorded with a balance of $1000. Before the backup gets to Record X in File 2, the transaction begins and ends. When the backup reaches File 2 and records the contents of Record X, the transaction's update has been posted and the balance recorded on the backup is $2000. There is now an inconsistency in the backup.

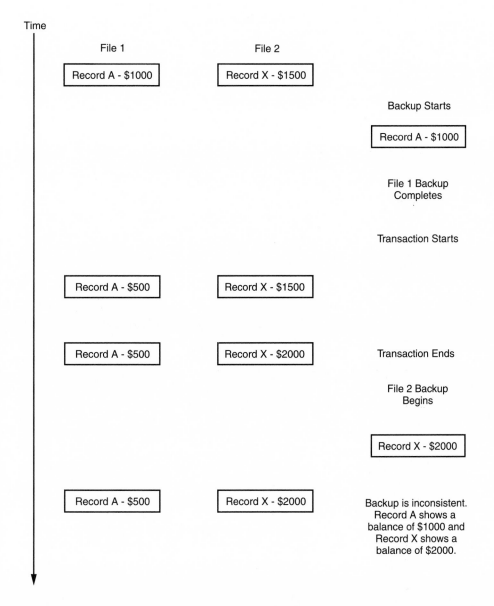

Figure 13.2   Instance of Data Inconsistency During File Backup

Before the transaction there was $1000 in Record A and $1500 in Record X. After the transaction there is $500 in Record A and $2000 in Record X. However, the backup shows $1000 in Record A and $2000 in Record X. To ensure backup consistency, backups should not be made when files are being updated unless the backup utility supports on-line backups. Sometimes, because of the nature of the application, this practice cannot be avoided. For example, a police department LAN may be in continuous operation. For these LANs the backup should be scheduled during the time of lowest activity and, if possible, updates should be deferred between the time the backup is started and the time it is completed.

Many LANs have periods when usage is low and when the LAN is not used at all. These are the best times to make backups because users experience fewer disruptions. For example, for many office LANs the best time to make backups is in the early morning, say between 2 and 6 A.M., either during the work week or on weekends. This time may be the most convenient for LAN users, but it may not be convenient for LAN administrators, particularly for LANs that operate during a typical work period of 8 A.M. to 8 P.M. five days a week. The LAN is essentially unused during the remaining time. A LAN administrator has two options for making early-morning backups: go to work during that time or make unattended backups.

Unattended backups are possible through the backup software itself or through separate software utilities. Some of today's backup systems provide unattended backup capabilities. Typically the LAN administrator specifies to the backup program the date and time the backup must start and the files that must be backed up. The LAN administrator schedules the backup before leaving for the day or has that information recorded for automatic backup. If you have a VCR and have programmed it to backup your favorite program during the week while you are working, you are familiar with this principle. Naturally the LAN must be up and running when the administrator leaves (or the UPS software must be set to start the LAN at the appropriate time), the nodes being backed up and the backup server must be running, the backup medium must be on-line, and the backup program must be running or properly scheduled to run. When the administrator arrives at work the next day, he or she must verify that the backup was satisfactorily completed. Reasons that the backup will not successfully complete include a power outage that shuts down the system, an unformatted tape in the backup unit, and a tape with insufficient data capacity.

If a company's backup software does not provide unattended backup, the LAN administrator can still conduct them. One way to do this is to start a backup remotely. The administrator might use a home computer and modem connection to access the system at the proper time and initiate the backup. Naturally, the preparation steps previously described must be taken first. A more convenient alternative is to buy or write a utility program that automatically invokes the backup. The utility hooks up to the system clock and at a prescribed time starts a batch command file to begin the backup. This is usually more convenient for the LAN administrator than an early-morning telephone call to start the backup.

Companies with large computer systems connected to their LANs have another backup alternative: initiating the backup from a large system. Often large systems have 24-hour operations. The operator of a large computer could initiate the LAN backup from the computer's command console; moreover, if the speed of the link between the large computer and the LAN is high enough, it is possible for the backup to be captured on one of the large system's peripheral devices.

Other Data Reliability Options

Having backups is *always* important. However, there are also optional procedures available that can protect you from some of the situations that ordinarily would require the use of a backup. None of these optional procedures obviates the need for a well-planned and well-implemented backup procedure, but you can lessen the frequency of making backups by using such technologies and procedures as disk mirroring, redundant arrays of independent disks (RAID), fault tolerance, DBMS recovery, recreation and reprocessing, disk editors, and disk utilities.

The first three options improve the reliability and availability of systems and have been discussed in previous chapters. When your system has high reliability, you can reduce the frequency of your backups because the frequency of failures needing data recovery is reduced. Keep in mind, however, that if time is a critical factor in effecting recovery, then time, not reliability, dictates your backup frequency.

DBMS recovery may allow recovery from some problems without resorting to backups. Other database problems may require the use of backups together with the DBMS's recovery mechanisms. The last options—recreation and reprocessing, disk editors, and disk utilities—can also be used when backups are not available or when the problems are limited in scope and time is of the essence. Let us take a closer look at each of these alternatives.

DBMS Recovery

Many DBMSs provide a recovery system that gives you two levels of recovery: **minor fault recovery** and **major fault recovery.** Examples of minor faults include inconsistent data resulting from a CPU failure and transaction failures. Minor faults affect a small portion of the database. Major faults result from head crashes, computer room fires, and accidental deletion of files. Major faults typically corrupt large portions of the database.

When the DBMS provides minor fault recovery, the faults are usually corrected automatically by the DBMS and do not require the use of backups. This type of recovery rolls the database back to a consistent point. For example, if a transaction that updates two records fails after one record has been updated but before the corresponding update to the other record, the completed update is reversed. The update reversal rolls the database back to a consistent state. Minor fault recovery is implemented in several ways. A common method involves writing the images of records before they are changed to a disk file. If a failure occurs, these before images are written back to the database, thus reversing the changes the transaction made. Using before images to provide transaction rollback is illustrated in Figure 13.3.

Major fault recovery usually requires the use of a backup together with database update files to roll the database forward to a consistent, current status. A backup version of the database is coordinated with an audit trail of after images collected by the DBMS. An **after image** is the image of a record after it has been changed by a database transaction and is illustrated in Figure 13.4. Figure 13.5 shows the synchronization of a database backup and the after image audit trail. The after image audit trail is a file to which

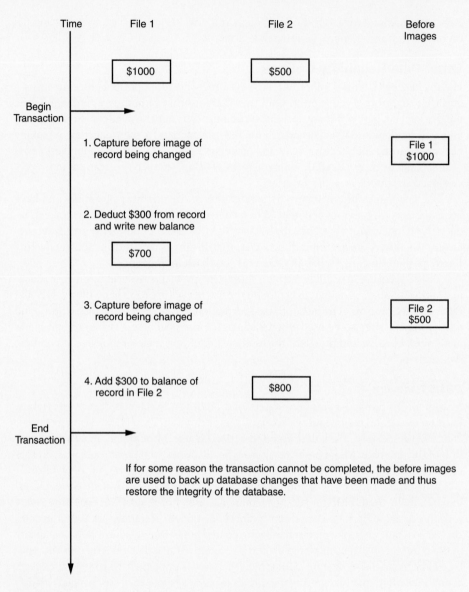

Figure 13.3   Use of a Before Image in a Transaction

after images are written. If a failure occurs, the database backup is first restored, and then the after images are posted to the database to bring the database forward to a current, consistent state. The use of after images avoids the need to reprocess transactions and is much quicker than reprocessing transactions. Restoration using this technique may still be time-consuming because of the volumes of data involved, but the process is mostly automated.

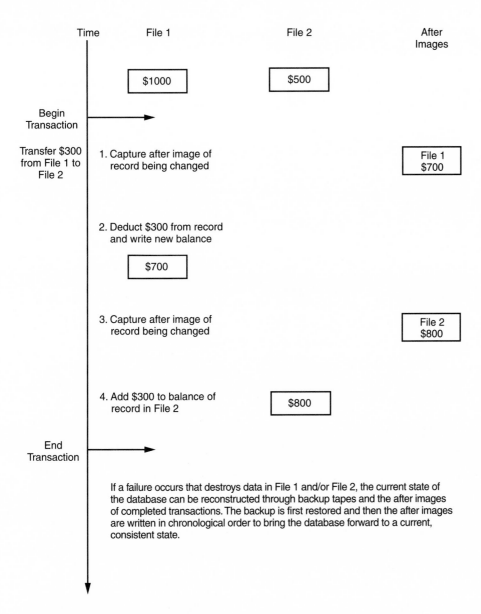

Figure 13.4   Database After Images

Recreation and Reprocessing

If a failure occurs and the company does not have a backup, usually the only alternative is to recreate the data and reprocess transactions. Often this must be done manually and is quite time-consuming. This is the approach organizations have to use when they have not made backups. After using this method one time, an organization usually realizes the

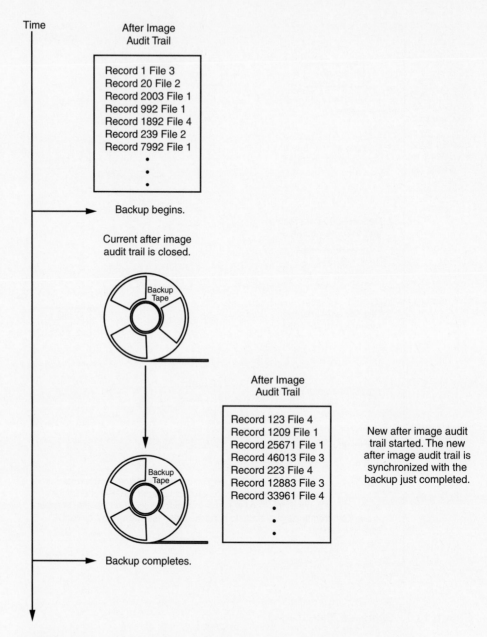

Figure 13.5   Synchronization of Backups and the After Image Audit Trail

importance of making regular backups. Sometimes another option exists. A few companies specialize in extracting data from damaged media. This might be a faster and more economical solution than manual recovery. A good backup policy obviates the need for either of these kinds of recovery. In a recent survey of financial institutions, respondents indicated that their company would be out of business if they had to go 3 to 5 days without their data. The same principle holds for all companies that rely on electronic data, but the time span may differ. Backups may make the difference between profitability and bankruptcy.

Disk Editors

Disk editors allow the LAN administrator to edit a disk at a variety of levels. At the lowest level, a disk editor allows the administrator to edit data at the disk sector level. Examples of this type of editor in a DOS environment are Norton Utilities, Mace Utilities, and PC Tools. Some editors provide editing at higher levels, such as those designed to fix database files and structures. Using a disk editor requires a great deal of expertise by the LAN administrator because it is easy to further corrupt data using these tools.

Disk Utilities

Disk utilities vary widely in scope and capabilities. Generally, compared to a disk editor, a disk utility requires less expertise to use effectively. A disk utility performs certain functions that do not require the administrator to do much more than enter commands. You may be familiar with DOS's CHKDSK and SCANDISK utilities, both of which analyze the disk and fix problems. As another example, Novell provides a utility called BINDFIX that examines the bindery files on NetWare 3.*nn* systems and fixes errors it finds. The **bindery files** are system files that describe the LAN's characteristics, such as user names, passwords, printing configuration, and groups. To use BINDFIX, the administrator simply enters the BINDFIX command, and the utility automatically does its work. DSREPAIR is the NetWare 4.*nn* counterpart to BINDFIX. DSREPAIR fixes problems in the network directory. Every LAN administrator should have one or more of these utilities available to diagnose or fix disk-related problems.

RECOVERY

At some point, *every* LAN fails and recovery must be done. Whenever data or data integrity is lost, it must be restored. Recovery situations vary extensively, so it is unrealistic to try to provide a recovery procedure that encompasses all of them. Generally recovery follows the steps shown in Table 13.4.

Before recovery starts, the cause of the failure should be investigated. Some events are not readily explained, others are obvious. For example, suppose a file disappears from the disk. The LAN administrator may never definitively know the cause. Perhaps it was accidentally deleted by an employee, who is not even aware of erasing it. Recovery in this case might be a simple undelete command that brings the file back immediately. Many of today's OSs have an undelete command. However, the probability of undeleting successfully is inversely proportional to the time between deleting and undeleting the file and the fullness of the disk. If the disk is nearly full, deleted file space is reused more quickly for new files or extensions to existing ones.

In contrast, a disk head crash is an obvious cause of failure. Whenever the source of the problem can be identified, it should be corrected so it does not happen again.

Table 13.4   Recovery Steps

1. Identify and correct the source of the problem.
2. Back up the data that has been corrupted.
3. Restore the most recent, valid backup version of the lost data.
4. Bring the data forward in time until it is both consistent and current.
5. Run diagnostic tests to ensure that the recovery has indeed corrected the problem and that the data is consistent.
6. Document the problem experience, corrective actions, and problems encountered during recovery.
7. Create and implement procedures to prevent similar future occurrences.

When backups are used for recovery, the files on the backup tape typically replace the files on the disk that have been damaged. Sometimes situations arise that prevent successful restoration; for example, the backup tape may have been damaged midway through the reel, and the data on it past that point cannot be read. For this reason, you should attempt to preserve the corrupted data before starting the restoration process. This can be done by backing it up, renaming the files, copying the files to another disk, or using a new disk drive. If a problem occurs during restoration, the corrupted files may provide the next best recovery capability; therefore, they ought to be preserved until you are certain that they are no longer needed. Preserving the files also may help in diagnosing the problem after recovery has been completed.

When you have completed steps 1 and 2 in Table 13.4, you can restore the data from the backup tape. You can restore everything on the backup tape, selectively restore only the files that have been corrupted, or selectively restore only the files needed to put the system back into operation. Less time-critical files can be restored at a more leisurely pace after the system has been restored to operational status. For efficiency, it is best to restore the minimum number of files essential to placing the most critical applications into service. Identification of these files should be a part of the recovery procedure. You must take care when choosing what files to restore and the version of the backup tape used. Often the most recent backups are used because they are the most current. Sometimes older versions must be used because the problem being corrected has gone undetected for some time and may exist on the most recent backup. In this case restoring data from the most recent backup does not correct the problem. Moreover, static data may not be backed up as often as dynamic data. For example, static data will not exist on partial backup images. When restoring static files, you might need to use backup tapes different from those used to restore dynamic data. Again, the recovery procedures should anticipate these situations and contain explicit instructions regarding which backup tapes to use and the order in which to use them. Furthermore, these procedures should be practiced periodically to ensure that administrators are familiar with them and that the procedures continue to meet the recovery needs.

After restoring the data, you must ensure that the problems have indeed been corrected. Again, the data errors may be included on the backup and, if so, are reintroduced during restoration. After you have established that the data is valid, the system can be placed back into operation.

Finally, the failure and the recovery events ought to be reviewed and documented. If necessary, new procedures should be drawn up and implemented to reduce the risk of similar problems occurring.

Low-Level Recovery

Once in a while a disk problem occurs that cannot be corrected by simply restoring files: The disk directory, network directory, or file allocation table may be corrupted. If the problem is localized and can be easily corrected by changing several characters in a file, an index, a disk directory, or the file allocation table, a well-trained technician with the right tools can carry out recovery without resorting to file restoration. The key to this type of **low-level recovery** is having the right tools and knowing how to use them. A well-intentioned but bad attempt to correct a problem in this way can greatly worsen an existing problem. You may know about tools such as Norton Utilities, Mace Utilities, and Central Point Software's PC Tools for DOS file systems. These tools provide ways to recover lost files and correct data errors on DOS disks. Similar tools exist for most LAN operating systems as well. Be aware that the DOS tools will probably not work on server disks when the server is running under an operating system other than DOS.

Again, a word of caution when using these low-level recovery tools. Although they can be helpful in some situations, they can also be harmful to your system if not used correctly. They allow the user to make changes to both system and data areas of the disk and can significantly increase the magnitude of the problem. These tools are never a replacement for backup and recovery procedures.

Diagnostic Tools

Two of the recovery steps outlined in Table 13.4 involve finding errors and their causes. Finding some of these problems is made easier with **diagnostic tools.** Diagnostic tools can be hardware or software oriented, but here we look at the software diagnostic tools only. Hardware diagnostic tools typically require detailed knowledge of the hardware and are used primarily by hardware engineers. We have already mentioned the low-level disk diagnostic and repair tools, such as Norton Utilities, that contain a variety of checks for the integrity of the operating system portions of the disk; in general, they do not check on the integrity of data stored in files.

Diagnostic tools exist for most common database management system disk areas. DBMS diagnostic tools test the integrity of DBMS portions of the database, such as indexes and block structures. Each DBMS has a strategy for storing data and indexes. Associated with this strategy is overhead data used by the DBMS to carry out its operations. This overhead data is transparent to users of the database; the DBMS uses it on the users' behalf, but the users never see it or manipulate it. Overhead data is not immune to corruption. Database diagnostic tools can analyze the overhead data and determine whether it is consistent. If problems are detected, the diagnostic tools reports them and in some cases makes the necessary repairs if the user so directs.

Database administrators often write utility programs to check for the integrity of database data. For example, a retail firm may have customer and order files. Naturally, every order must be placed by a customer, and it would not be valid to have an order record that is not related to some customer record. A database utility or query can be used to check for orders that have no associated customer record. A comprehensive DBMS has data integrity rules that automatically prevent the occurrence of such errors.

Dealing with Errors

Hardware, software, and human errors are to be expected; however, a network administrator should not put up with repetitive errors. Determining error repetitiveness requires organization and documentation.

Every error encountered on a system should be documented. This includes errors classified as user errors. User errors that recur may be an indication of insufficient training or documentation. The best way to track errors is with a problem-reporting system. The problem-reporting system can be manual or computerized. A computerized problem-reporting system is better able to analyze and track problems and spot trends.

Once a problem has been reported and recorded, resolution begins. The problem must be analyzed and its cause determined. Some errors are caused by users, some by software or procedures created locally, and some by software or hardware furnished by a vendor. The first two cases are resolved locally. Errors caused by vendor-supplied hardware or software is usually resolved by the responsible vendor. Problems of this sort are forwarded to the vendor for solution. Responsibility for getting the problem solved, however, remains with the LAN administrator or system support group. Thus, even though the system support person does not solve the problem, he or she is responsible for tracking the progress of the problem, obtaining the solution, and having the corrections installed. A good problem-reporting system assists the support staff in tracking reported problems. We look at problem diagnosis and correction in more detail in Chapter 14.

DISASTER PLANNING

Another component of an organization's recovery procedures and planning is a **disaster plan.** The recovery discussed earlier addressed issues where single components of a system failed. A disaster plan addresses situations that disable major portions of the system (servers, workstations, cabling, and so on). Disaster planning covers situations arising from fires, earthquakes, floods, and intentional acts of system destruction. In disaster planning the LAN administrator should envision all the scenarios that are likely to occur and make contingency plans that lead to quick and efficient resolution of those scenarios.

It is probably true that most organizations have well-defined backup programs in effect. Those that do not will probably implement one after their first recovery incident (if they are still in business). However, few companies have disaster plans. The prudent LAN administrator has at least the rudiments of such a plan in effect. If the right steps are in place, the LAN administrator can have the network up and running at nearly full capacity soon after the disaster has ended. Table 13.5 lists items that should be included in a disaster plan.

Table 13.5   Items Included in Disaster Plan

Insurance	Amount of insurance coverage for software, hardware, and cabling
	Insurance carrier
	Steps required to begin replacing/repairing insured components
Software	Location of off-site storage of software
	Currency of off-site software backups
	Device used to create off-site storage
	Sources of replacement software
	Companies specializing in recovering data from damaged media (backup tapes and disk drives)
Data	Location of off-site storage of data
	Currency of off-site data backups
	Device used to create off-site data storage
	Methods to bring off-site data forward to a current status
	Companies specializing in recovering data from damaged media (backup tapes and disk drives)
Hardware	Workstation configurations
	Server configurations
	LAN topology/wiring diagrams
	Sources of replacement hardware
	Sources for repairing broken hardware
	Location of spare hardware
Environment	Alternative locations for establishing a new network environment
	Minimum requirements for establishing a new network environment
Outside Help	Names of companies specializing in data recovery, setting up a new network, data entry, cabling repair, and so on

A key aspect of a disaster plan is off-site data storage and hardware replacement. Hardware and cabling can be readily replaced from a local computer vendor or other corporate locations, but data, applications, security settings, command files, common carrier data links, and so on are not. If the LAN administrator does no more than provide frequent off-site storage of data, he or she has at least set the foundation for disaster recovery.

After planning for software and data recovery, the LAN administrator should also have plans for rebuilding the system. On the hardware side this may include items such as sources of compatible hardware, identification of hardware at other corporate locations that might be borrowed for emergency use, identification of alternative locations for temporarily or permanently installing the new system, and identification of companies specializing in all aspects of LAN hardware, software, cabling, installation, and data recovery. Having these lists of contacts is important for two reasons.

First, disasters are unpredictable, and a LAN administrator will not know what LAN components need replacement or repair. Second, having a readily available list of sources for replacement, repair, or assistance saves time during the critical recovery period when time is of the essence.

SUMMARY

All LAN systems fail, even systems configured for fault tolerance. Moreover, even if the hardware and software are not prone to failure, the people using them are. Therefore, it is critical that a LAN administrator have a well-planned set of procedures and policies to recover the system following a failure. One of the major components of a recovery policy is data backups.

Backups are used to restore data and programs to a usable state following a failure that has corrupted the data or software. There are many ways in which data can be corrupted. Regardless of the cause of data corruption, the LAN administrator must be able to diagnose the causes, remove the cause of corruption if possible, restore the data to a usable state quickly, and restore the network to operational status. Backups are also used for data archiving, temporary storage, and data exchange.

A good backup policy minimizes the work and time needed to recover lost data. It includes details such as frequency of backups, off-site storage of backups, backup retention, and disposition of the backup medium after it is no longer needed.

Recovery can sometimes be accomplished without the use of backups. Disk editors and disk utilities are available to fix some problems that may occur. These utilities include capabilities such as undeleting files, writing directly to a disk sector, fixing file allocation tables, fixing disk directories, and fixing volume labels. Other utilities are oriented toward patching files in particular formats, such as database index and data files. None of these alternatives are meant as a replacement for taking backups regularly. Improper use of such utilities may compound the problems being experienced.

In addition to backup and recovery plans and procedures, a LAN administrator should also formulate a disaster plan. A disaster plan addresses how to reinstate the network following an event, such as a fire, that disables a major portion of the network. An essential element of a backup policy and disaster plan is off-site backup storage. Off-site storage protects an organization from catastrophes that damage both on-line data and its backups.

Key Terms

after image	diagnostic tools
archiving	differential backup
backup	disaster plan
bindery files	disk editor
comprehensiveness	disk utility
data backup	dynamic data
data recovery	full backup

grandfather–father–son backup method
incremental backup
low-level recovery
major fault recovery
minor fault recovery

off-site storage
partial backup
retention policy
selective backup
static data

Review Questions

1. What is a data backup?
2. Why do we need data backups?
3. Distinguish between backups of static data and dynamic data.
4. Explain four considerations a LAN administrator must weigh when formulating a backup policy.
5. Why might there be differences between backup policies in different companies?
6. How are disk editors and utilities used in recovery?
7. What are the steps a LAN administrator should take in recovering lost data?
8. What is a disaster plan?
9. How does a disaster plan relate to data recovery?
10. Describe three considerations that should be covered by a disaster plan.

Problems and Exercises

1. Suppose an organization had never made data backups during its 1 year in operation. During that time, over 300 MB of data had been accumulated. Suppose further that their server's disk sustained a head crash. How could this organization recover its data? How quickly could the recovery be accomplished? For Problems 2 through 5, consider the following organizational profiles:
   a. A medical office has 10 doctors, 14 nurses, and 6 administrative staff. A LAN is used to record patient visits, billing, and insurance claims. The clinic averages 250 patient visits per day. Each visit results in an average of four records being updated. A paper trail exists describing each patient's visit.
   b. An office of attorneys has 25 attorneys and 40 support staff. Each attorney and support person has a workstation. All correspondence, trial briefs and notes, legal documents, and so on are stored on mirrored server disks. Both current and noncurrent (aged) documents are stored on the disks. Periodically, aged documents must be archived to make room for new work. Much of the current work is time-critical; for example, trial notes are needed for trials in session and contracts are needed for scheduled meetings.
   c. A university LAN is used to support the academic program only. Students use the LAN to prepare assignments for a variety of classes. The students use programs for static data. The students' assignments themselves are, by default, stored on the file server's disks and represent the system's dynamic data. At the beginning of each class, students are warned by their professors that it is the students' responsibility to protect their work files by backing them up to diskette. The university's LAN administrators also have a backup policy.
2. Suppose you are advising each of these organizations regarding a backup policy. Rank them in order of decreasing reliance on frequency of backup (that is, decide which organization would suffer the most from a policy of weekly rather than daily backups). Justify your answer.

3. Outline a backup policy for each organization. Explain any differences among the policies.
4. Suppose each organization experienced a failure that ruined all data on one disk. Explain how each organization would recover from such a problem.
5. Which organization would be most affected by a disaster such as a fire? What suggestions regarding disaster planning would you make for that organization?
6. Examine a utility such as Norton Utilities, Mace Utilities, or a disk utility for a specific LAN system. What low-level recovery capabilities does it provide? What is the skill level expected of a user of that utility?

Chapter 14

LAN Administration: Reactive and Proactive Management

CHAPTER PREVIEW

In the preceding chapters we covered specific, important LAN administration tasks: installation, security, printing, backup, and recovery. Each of these topics is critical to the overall success of a LAN. However, a LAN administrator must perform additional duties to ensure success. These involve solving unanticipated problems (reactive management) and keeping the LAN running at peak efficiency (proactive management). Although LAN administration efforts cannot completely eliminate unanticipated problems, through good planning, network monitoring, network analysis, and network component tuning, a LAN administrator can reduce the need to operate in a reactive mode. The topics you will read in this chapter about include

- problem identification and correction

- system tuning

- capacity planning

- managing system expansion

- network management systems

- network management protocols

REACTIVE NETWORK MANAGEMENT

"The network is down!" is a phrase all too familiar to the experienced network manager. Exactly what does this exclamation from a user mean? A LAN administrator could interpret it to mean that the entire network is not functioning, but this is not always the case. What it does mean is the user is unable to redirect requests on his or her workstation over the network in the usual way. The user may have full stand-alone capability, but the services of the network are not currently available. Myriad reasons, ranging from user error to complete system failure, can cause this to occur. When "the network is down," the network administrator must carry out **reactive network management** to correct the problems experienced by that user.

Consider the LAN illustrated in Figure 14.1. The elements of this system include users, workstations, servers, media, connectors, LAN adapters, and connections to other networks. Each element is subject to failure, which can create network problems. If a problem occurs, the administrator needs the proper tools and the skill to use them to correct problems in a timely way. Correcting a problem efficiently can be difficult in a stand-alone LAN because of the variety of equipment and users involved. A LAN problem could be a user, hardware, software, or cabling error. Furthermore, hardware, software, and wiring errors can be at the server or workstation or between the server and workstation. The difficulty in problem

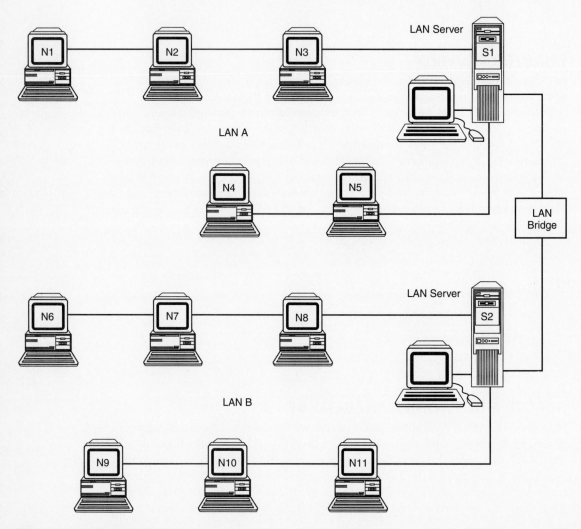

Figure 14.1   Connected LANs

resolution lies in the variety of components and possible causes. Finding and correcting problems becomes even more difficult when administering interconnected LANs. The added difficulty arises from the greater complexity of these networks—the additional interfaces required to make connections between LAN and WAN nodes, the greater variety of data link protocols, media, connectors, and software subsystems that may be responsible for the problem, and the broader knowledge required to diagnose and solve the problem.

Consider one reactive network management problem: Suppose you are a network administrator working at node N1 in Figure 14.1. A user at node N7 reports that he cannot retrieve a file on server S1. Here are a few of the possible causes of this problem:

The user's network software has not been properly started.

The user has forgotten to log onto the network.

The LAN adapter at the user's workstation or the server the user is accessing has failed.

There is a wiring problem.

The server is down.

Security is set incorrectly.

Security is set correctly, but the user has no access rights to the file.

The file does not exist.

The bridge connecting the two LANs is not working correctly.

The LAN administrator must define a set of procedures for finding the problem and correcting it, and he or she must have the appropriate tools to locate the problem. This type of analysis is called problem identification and resolution.

PROBLEM IDENTIFICATION AND RESOLUTION

The following set of procedures is just one of many approaches to solving problems:

1. Information gathering
2. Diagnosis and analysis
3. Problem identification
4. Problem resolution
5. Documentation

The sections that follow give you more details on each step.

Information Gathering

Any failure experienced by a user can be the result of user errors, software errors, hardware errors, inappropriate environment settings, or faulty security. The first step in problem resolution, **information gathering,** involves the identification of various possible causes of the failure. A LAN administrator takes actions similar to those a medical doctor uses to diagnose a patient's problem. The doctor gathers the symptoms and matches them with causes. The LAN administrator must also look carefully at the problem's symptoms and identify possible causes. The administrator can then eliminate some of the possibilities because they do not match all of the symptoms. He or she can investigate a possible cause, test it, and prove whether it is causing the problem. When rejecting alternatives, the administrator must be careful because some problems result from several things being wrong and their mutual interaction. Gathering information forms the basis of the diagnosis and analysis phase.

One way of gathering information is by talking to the user. Because many of the errors a LAN administrator encounters are user-related or operator errors, the beginning questions should be oriented toward validating or refuting this possibility. The term *operator error* covers a variety of problems that cannot be attributed to malfunctions of the network or its resources. An operator error does not always imply that the user is doing something wrong. Here are some examples of incidents usually classified as operator errors:

The user's computer is unplugged.

The user's computer has not been powered up.

The user's keyboard has become unplugged and a screen saver program is in use so touching the keys has no noticeable effect.

The user's AUTOEXEC.BAT file has been modified, and the network interface programs have not been run.

The user is already logged onto another workstation, and the user is limited to only one logon.

Incorrect or incompatible software versions are being used.

Once these sources of errors have been eliminated, the LAN administrator can ask himself or herself, the user, or the user's supervisor any of the following questions:

What are the detailed symptoms of the problem?

What application were you running?

Is running this application within your job scope?

Have you done this task successfully in the past? If so, what is different this time?

What logon ID were you using? Is this the logon ID you should use to do this task?

Have any changes been made to the user's environment recently? If so, what?

What are the implications of not being able to do this?

What is the priority for getting a correction?

The purpose of these questions is to get an understanding of the problem, the user's environment, and the consequences of the user not being able to complete this activity. The consequences are used to set the priority for solving this particular problem.

When preliminary information gathering is complete, the LAN administrator must also learn more about the user's hardware and software environment. Although the administrator probably is familiar with the LAN configuration, it is impossible to remember all the details of each network node; thus, sometimes it is helpful to refresh one's memory regarding details of the hardware and software. The administrator must consult the network documentation to get this information and can use a **configuration management utility,** also called an inventory utility, to get additional current information. A LAN configuration utility maintains hardware and software configurations for all network nodes. Some of the information it collects is given in Table 14.1.

Table 14.1   LAN Configuration Information

General	Number of servers	Number of workstations
	Number of users	Connections to other networks
	Backup devices	Hardware serial numbers
	Purchase dates	Costs
	Support information	Telephone and access numbers
Documentation and Procedures	Type	Location
	Version	
Server and Workstations	Network address	NIC configuration
	Location	Processor type
	Processor speed	Memory
	Disk	Device controllers
	Controller parameters, such as IRQ	BIOS version
	Expansion slots	Ports (used and available)
	Operating system version	Printers
	Directory structures	Startup configuration
Printers	Location	Type
	Spooler data	
Software	Name	Serial number
	Version	License provisions
	Server locations	Support information
Users	Access rights for software and hardware	Logon ID
	User name	Telephone number
	Workstations	Electronic mail address
Network Connections	Type	Configuration
	Location	Nodes connected

Diagnosis and Analysis

The objective of problem diagnosis and analysis is to isolate the source of the problem. This leads to problem identification and solution. If you have taken a programming class, you may have been exposed to a technique called binary search, which is used to search for an item in an ordered list. You probably use a similar technique to look up names in a telephone book or find words in a dictionary. LAN administrators use this technique to isolate the problem to a specific LAN component (user, workstation, cable segment, server, security, software, environment settings, and so on).

A major LAN failure is sometimes easier to resolve than a failure experienced by a single user or group of users. If many users report that the network is down, it is unlikely that the problem is related to a single user or a single workstation. The art of problem determination is somewhat the same in either instance. But the administrator probably begins looking for the problem at different places: For network-wide problems the administrator starts looking at network common resources, such as cabling, LAN adapters, and servers. For user-related problems the investigation usually starts at the user's workstation.

If the preliminary step of data gathering does not lead to a problem solution, the LAN administrator begins the diagnosis and analysis steps. One of the best ways to understand a problem is to observe the user's operating environment. This is easy if the user's office is nearby, but often the user's office is some distance away. Even when the user's office is easy to get to, it may be inconvenient to evaluate the problem there. When analyzing most problems, LAN administrators often must refer to documentation. This documentation is more apt to be located in the LAN administrator's office than at a user location. By using remote control software, a LAN administrator can experience and analyze problems while maintaining access to documentation in his or her own office.

Remote control software allows a user in one location to work with a workstation in another location. Early remote control software had a limited design that allowed two stand-alone workstations to communicate with each other over telephone lines or local lines connected to a serial or parallel port. Most companies offering these products have enhanced their capabilities so a user can connect to another node using network connections as well as telephone links. Thus, a LAN administrator could diagnose and solve problems remotely (for example, from home). A list of the capabilities provided by remote control software is given in Table 14.2.

The principal features of remote control software are the ability to view the monitor of the remote station and the ability to enter commands remotely; basically a remote user can take control of a local workstation. If the administrator can connect to the user's workstation, most problem diagnosis and analysis can be conducted remotely. Moreover, using remote control software can be a good learning experience for users. Users can watch their screen (which is responding to the LAN administrator's remote commands) while the LAN administrator goes through the steps required to solve the problem. This is particularly effective when the problem results from a user error.

If a remote connection is not possible, the LAN administrator usually must go to the user's workstation to further investigate the problem. Inability to make a remote connection can also provide valuable information, such as the cause of a failure of a component along the path to the user or in the user's workstation. If a remote connection

Table 14.2   Features of Remote Control Software

Remote screen display

Remote keyboard entry

Ability for many viewers to be connected to one node

Ability of one viewer to view multiple nodes

Password protection

Audio tone to indicate when someone begins viewing

File transfer

Ability to discover and report the host configuration

Ability to print a memory map of a host

Chat mode, allowing users at both ends to exchange messages over the connection

can be made to the user's workstation, or to workstations adjacent to the user's, the LAN administrator can conclude that the problem is centered at the local workstation or the workstation-to-medium connection; that is, the problem is local to the workstation itself.

When the administrator has gained access to the user's workstation, he or she can begin to analyze the problem. How the administrator proceeds from this point depends on the types of errors being encountered. The first thing that can be checked is the user's ability to log onto the network, and then the security rights to all necessary files, both program and data, and all directories in which the user is working can be checked. Once security settings are established, they seldom change; however, installing new software, adding or deleting users, or other administration activities can result in changes to security settings. Let us look at two examples that might result in changing users' security settings. When new software is placed on a network server, the network administrator must set up security so that users can access the application. In general, program files are secured so they can be run but not copied or modified, most other files are secured as read-only, and perhaps a few files are secured so users can write to them. Setting up security for new applications means giving new access rights to users and groups. Security settings may also need to be changed when a user's job function changes. A payroll administrator who is not allowed to make salary changes may receive a promotion. The administrator's new responsibilities may include making salary changes. This requires a change in the administrator's security settings.

Checking security takes only a few moments and can save several hours of investigation into other potential sources of a problem. If the LAN administrator can run the application while logged onto the user's workstation with the supervisor's ID, it is likely that the problem is in the security setup; a security or user ID problem is the likely cause in this instance because the supervisor ID gives access to all files. If the supervisor ID can successfully avoid the problem experienced by a user ID with lesser security capabilities, it is highly probable that the user has lost access or does not have the proper access to some essential resource.

If security settings prove to not be the problem, the next step in the process of problem diagnosis and analysis begins: determining whether a workstation component (hardware or software) is responsible. One of the easiest ways to demonstrate an error in a local workstation component is to attempt the same process from a workstation near the one the user is unable to use correctly. If the problem is not exhibited at the nearby workstation, it is likely that the original workstation or its connection to the medium is at fault.

Another good technique to use at this point is to duplicate the problem using **known good components.** One of a LAN administrator's tools should be a complete, portable, standard-configured workstation that is known to be good. The administrator brings the known good machine to the user's location and connects it to the network. If the problem does not go away using the portable workstation, then it is likely that the problem is outside the local workstation itself.

A simple, easy way to test the reliability of a LAN adapter is to use a **pocket LAN adapter.** A pocket LAN adapter is portable and provides network connection through the parallel or serial port of a workstation. Often used to attach portable workstations to a network, a pocket LAN adapter is also a useful diagnostic tool for LAN administrators. It is easy to attach and quickly eliminates or identifies the LAN adapter as the problem source. If the user can access the file using the pocket LAN adapter, the problem is probably a broken LAN adapter.

Another source of workstation problems is application and network software. The LAN administrator must check whether the user's workstation is running the proper versions of the proper network operating system software. For example, if the user has just upgraded the workstation's operating system but has not made corresponding changes to the workstation's network operating system software, an incompatibility might exist. Therefore, one diagnostic step is to verify the compatibility of all versions of software being used.

If the workstation is eliminated as the problem, the next step is to check the path between the user and the server, including wiring, hardware, and software. Wiring problems are the most common source of resource request failures, so the LAN administrator should check the wiring first. Wire continuity can be checked with a **cable tester,** which generates a signal on the medium and monitors the signal. Cable testers can determine whether there is a short or break in a cable and pinpoint the problem location within inches. Table 14.3 lists some functions of a cable tester.

Table 14.3   Cable Tester Functions

Cable connectors	RJ45	BNC	AUI
Cable types	Twisted-pair—UTP, STP, CAT 3-5	coaxial cable	
Protocols	Ethernet	Token ring	ARCnet
Printer interface	Serial	Parallel	
Faults detected	Opens	Shorts	Length
	Pair length mismatch	Near end crosstalk (NEXT)	Crossed pairs
	Terminator resistance	Category conformance	Attenuation

It may be that the problem is a hardware malfunction that results in garbled messages. To check for transmission errors, the LAN administrator uses a **protocol analyzer** or a **LAN analyzer.** The protocol analyzer checks message packets for errors and notifies the user of the type and source of errors it receives. Protocol analyzer capabilities are listed in Table 14.4.

Finally, the problem may be related to the server itself. A user may not be able to log on because of a problem with the user ID file or network system files (perhaps the user's ID has even been deleted). In Novell NetWare LAN systems before NetWare Version 4.0, information such as user IDs and passwords is kept in a set of files called **bindery files.** Bindery files are not immune to errors (although they are seldom corrupted). Novell provides a utility, BINDFIX, to examine bindery files and correct any errors it detects.

Identification and Resolution

Once the LAN administrator has correctly identified the problem, it must be corrected. The problem dictates the solution. Because there are so many different types of problems, it is impractical to attempt to discuss here how to solve each one. After the correction is made, the LAN administrator notifies the user that the problem has been corrected and ensures that the user is able to continue with his or her work.

Documentation

Fixing the problem is not the last step in reactive administration. The LAN administrator must also document the problem and its solution. Sometimes one problem occurs several times. Having good documentation of previous problems and their solutions can significantly reduce the time it takes to correct a problem that appears again. Realize that the person who solved the first problem may not be available when a problem reappears. Documentation can assist a new person in solving a problem as well as refresh the memory of the LAN administrator who solved the problem initially.

All the information gathered during the problem-solving process should be documented. You can do this manually, or you can use a **problem reporting and tracking system,** which automates the data-gathering process and provides a fast, efficient mechanism for finding problems of a similar nature, solutions to previous problems, and the status of open problems. A problem reporting and tracking system is a valuable network administration tool. An illustration of a form that might be produced by such a system is shown in Figure 14.2.

Table 14.4   Protocol Analyzer Functions

Utilization statistics	Number of packets sent by a node
Number of packets received by a node	Packet errors
Data logging	Test packet transmission
Packet filtering	Logging of protocol headers
Logging of data portion of packets	Network load statistics
Alarms	Cable testing
Support for multiple protocols	Printed reports

Problem Identifier: _____   Date: ___ / ___ / ___

Received by: _____   Time: ___ : ___ AM/PM

Reported by: _____   Telephone: (____) ____ - _____

Department: _____   Dept. Telephone: (____) ____ - _____

Other Contacts: _____   Telephone(s): (____) ____ - _____

Location: _____

Urgency: ___ Extremely High   ___ High   ___ Moderate   ___ Low

Key Words: _____   _____   _____   _____   _____

Problem Description:

Software Involved: Hardware Involved:

Problem Consequences: Workarounds:

Assigned to: 1. _____   Telephone: (____) ____ - _____   Date: ___ / ___ / ___

             2. _____   Telephone: (____) ____ - _____   Date: ___ / ___ / ___

             3. _____   Telephone: (____) ____ - _____   Date: ___ / ___ / ___

Status: Solution: Date: ___ / ___ / ___

Solved by: _____   Telephone: (____) ____ - _____   Date: ___ / ___ / ___

Installed by: _____   Date: ___ / ___ / ___

Users Notified by: _____   User(s) Contacted: _____

Telephone: (___) ____ - _____   Date: ___ / ___ / ___   Time: ___ : ___ AM/PM

Figure 14.2   Problem Reporting and Tracking Form

PROACTIVE NETWORK MANAGEMENT

Ideally the network administrator anticipates problems and corrects them before they occur. This type of administration is called **proactive network management.** This is not always possible because an administrator cannot usually anticipate hardware and software failures. Some problems, however, result from gradual changes. For instance, the time it takes to transfer a file from a server to a workstation takes increasingly longer as the LAN workload increases. The workload consists of the messages that are transferred over the medium, the processing done by LAN servers, and the work done at the workstations themselves. When the number of messages being transmitted increases and the servers become busier processing those messages, the time it takes to complete a single request such as a file transfer increases. Sometimes the LAN has enough spare capacity to make the time increase scarcely noticeable. But if the LAN is already near capacity performance, additional work can cause significant degradation in performance. A good LAN administrator notices these changes and takes steps to avoid their becoming major problems for the LAN users. This type of administration is called performance monitoring and **system tuning.**

Another LAN administration task is **capacity planning,** which basically is planning for the future. An administrator must gauge the impact of adding new users, adding new applications, and upgrading existing applications and the network operating software itself. As a LAN evolves, additional hardware and software resources often must be added to sustain adequate performance. The administrator must determine what new components are needed, where they must be placed, and who needs access to them.

In carrying out these duties, the LAN administrator must create and maintain documentation of various types. Included among these are procedures and policies covering topics such as backup and restore, recovery, security, adding and deleting users, hardware and software configurations, user profiles, a performance-monitoring database, a system log, and a problem reporting, tracking, and resolution system.

SYSTEM TUNING AND CAPACITY PLANNING

System tuning is the art of monitoring a network, analyzing the statistics gathered from monitoring, and using that information to keep the system running at an acceptable level. Capacity planning is planning for future changes such as additional users or applications and ensuring that the proper resources are available to provide good service when the changes are implemented. Let us first look at system tuning.

Tuning a System

A variety of tools can be used to assist the LAN administrator in tuning a network. In general, these tools gather and analyze network performance data. One of the primary tools used to do this is a **network management system (NMS).** A good NMS has both data collection and analysis components and creates monitors that raise alarms if performance degenerates below certain levels. A network administrator uses the NMS to gather and analyze network performance data. Even when there are no obvious problems to correct, the administrator periodically generates and studies reports on the data gathered. The purpose of this analysis is to identify changes in how the network is operating, identify reasons for these changes, and, if necessary, tune the network to maintain a satisfactory level of service. An NMS plays such an important role in LAN administration that we dedicate an entire section to it later in this chapter.

Another tool used in tuning is a network analyzer. The network analyzer reports on the type and number of packets being sent, the number of transmission errors encountered, and so on. This data can be used to spot system performance problems.

Network use changes over time. It sometimes seems that networks undergo constant change. New nodes are added, new software is introduced, users change their work patterns, LANs may be interconnected, and so on. These changes alter the LAN's workload and can change its responsiveness. For example, suppose that a word processing system is upgraded to a new version. Perhaps the new version requires more memory for the software and has new features, such as graphics support or links to spreadsheets. Some users may move immediately to the new software, and others may remain with the older version. This seemingly insignificant change in user resources can have a noticeable affect on the LAN. With users requesting two different word processing programs rather than one, the file server could be less efficient. The server now has to read two sets of execution files instead of one, disk cache is likely to be used more extensively, and there may be fewer cache hits, resulting in a decrease in server performance. If there were only one version of the word processing software, the file server might satisfy several user needs with one disk access. If the newer version of word processing software has larger execution or operating files, more data must be transferred over the network. If the newer version supports graphics, users may want to transfer large graphic images from their workstation to the server (or vice versa) more often. Even if this one event does not substantially change network performance, a collection of such changes will.

In looking at network performance statistics, the network administrator attempts to find areas where performance is degrading or where other problems seem to be developing. For instance, higher than normal error rates or peak usage bottlenecks are key indicators of potential problems ahead. If any problems are found, the administrator must plan a strategy to resolve them. Sometimes this can be done by **balancing** network components, and sometimes additional hardware components must be added to solve the problem.

Balancing the network is a juggling act of sorts, requiring the administrator to use existing resources but in a slightly different configuration. The administrator may find that one network printer is in constant use while another is idle. Changing the default printer of one or more users to the idle printer may resolve the problem, or moving the low-use printer to another location may make it more convenient and increase its use. Of course, this will not solve the problem if users are overriding the default printer selection and manually directing their output to another printer. If this happens, the administrator should evaluate the printing configuration and attempt to modify it so that default printer selection is the one preferred by each user, keeping in mind the need to balance printing resource requests.

As another example of balancing, suppose two LANs are connected via a bridge, as in Figure 14.1. A **bridge** is a device that connects two similar networks together. If the administrator notices that node N1 on LAN A consistently sends most of its messages to nodes on LAN B, the administrator can transfer node N1 to be part of the configuration of LAN B and reduce the load on the bridge.

A network administrator's first objective is to resolve performance problems by balancing, but if that is not possible or practical, then purchasing or allocating additional hardware may solve the problem. For example, if an administrator notices that the memory swap rate for a file server is too high, he or she can solve the problem in two ways: Reduce the memory pressure on the server by offloading some of its work onto another server or add more memory. Today hardware prices are low enough that it is sometimes cheaper and more expedient to add new hardware than to spend a great deal of time attempting to balance the system. However, funding may not always be available because most companies do not allow for such expenditures in their budgeting process. Some companies tend to budget for direct resources needed because of an increase in the number of users (for example, new workstations and LAN adapters) and ignore the extra burden of network performance needs.

Sometimes, when tuning a system through balancing or adding hardware, several corrective alternatives are available. The primary rule of system tuning is that you should change only one thing at a time. Systems tend to be complicated, and one system component can interact with many other components on the network. When the LAN administrator makes a change in anticipation of improving performance, the change may have a negative effect in another, unanticipated area and actually make the overall system performance worse. If you make several changes at once, it is difficult to determine which change is most responsible for any new problems. The general process of tuning is outlined as follows:

1. Measure system performance; collect and analyze data.

2. Identify possible solutions to a problems.

3. Choose one solution that has the highest merit: the best gain in efficiency and returned performance per cost of implementation, or the quickest and easiest to implement.

4. Install and test the selected solution.

5. Evaluate the results.

6. If performance is still poor go back to step 1.

7. Implement and document the solution.

Tuning requires an in-depth knowledge of the network's hardware and software and the interactions between them. Such knowledge is essential for analyzing data and distinguishing between normal and abnormal results, identifying potential solutions, understanding the implications of the different alternatives, selecting the best solution to try, making the changes, and evaluating the results. A misguided but well-intentioned attempt to improve the system can cause serious problems.

Capacity Planning

Capacity planning is a key responsibility of the network administrator. We have already stated that a network is a dynamic entity. Performance analysis and tuning keep the system running correctly under the existing but perhaps changing workload. Capacity planning is the art of anticipating the workload of the network months or years in advance and taking steps to ensure that the network is able to withstand future loads. Capacity planning is an ongoing activity. Sometimes, however, specific events trigger the need for capacity planning. For example, if a new department is to be added to an existing LAN, the administrator must anticipate the added hardware and software needs and the adjustments that must be made to accommodate the new users while continuing to meet the needs of existing users. If an existing LAN is to be connected to another existing LAN, the administrator must anticipate the change, plan the necessary reconfiguration, order new equipment, plan for the installation of the new equipment, configure and install it, evaluate its performance, and tune the entire network system for optimal performance. In these instances, you definitely do not want to just add the new connections, place the network into operation, and see what happens!

Among the many tools that have been developed for capacity planning on microcomputers, three are particularly effective: performance monitors, simulation models, and workload generators. We cover performance monitors in the section on network management systems later in this chapter. Let us now look at simulation models and workload generators.

Simulation Models

Simulating an object means constructing a model of how the object works and estimating characteristics of the object though working with the model. **Simulation models** can be physical or logical. Automotive and aeronautical engineers often build physical models of cars or airplanes to determine their air flow characteristics. They do this by placing the models in a wind tunnel—a simulated object in a simulated environment. A logical model uses software modules to simulate the performance of objects, thus eliminating the need to build expensive physical models. For example, you can simulate a file server by combining models of the medium, server disks, server CPU, and other server components. You can drive this model by sending it simulated requests and letting the server software simulation modules operate on those requests. By varying the number and type of requests, you can estimate how the server performs in a variety of situations. Naturally these estimates are only as good as the model's ability to accurately represent the server's characteristics. By adding modules representing other LAN components, you can simulate the performance of an entire LAN or even a network of LANs and WANs. Moreover, you can conceivably run the simulation on a single microcomputer.

Simulation models allow the user to describe network hardware configurations and application activities. The model analyzes how the system can be expected to perform under the described conditions. This is useful for estimating response times, processor use, line congestion, and potential bottlenecks. During operational situations, simulation models help determine what size of transaction load will reach or exceed the network's capacity and the effect of adding new applications and nodes to the existing system. A good simulation model in the capacity planning process can avert performance problems at implementation time.

Simulation models vary significantly with respect to the amount of information they provide and the manner in which the user defines the workload. A simple model for cable segment use might interactively prompt the user for the speed of the line, the data link protocol to use, the message size, the average number of messages per transaction, and the number of nodes on the segment. This limited model produces a report indicating the segment performance and the maximum and average response times a user might expect. A comprehensive model, on the other hand, uses a network configuration file and a transaction file as input (both user supplied). The configuration file contains the complete hardware configuration, including disk drives, disk drive performance characteristics, line speeds, data link protocols, node types, and file locations. The transaction file contains a list of transaction types and the activities each transaction performs, such as the number of inputs and outputs to a server's disk and the number of characters transferred between a server and a node.

In addition to the two user-supplied files, the simulation model is driven by software performance characteristics such as LAN operating system overhead, instruction execution times, and disk access times. Such a model outputs information on expected response times, line use, processor use, disk use, and so forth. Essentially the model enables the user to see how the system performs without ever implementing it. For example, if the model predicts that a particular server will have 200 percent use and a response time of 2 minutes, then either a more powerful server or additional servers are needed to support the workload.

The time required to set up a simulation run varies with the amount of detail needed. A detailed, comprehensive model requires a considerable amount of information regarding the application. Usually it is unnecessary to have the correct initial configuration, as the model indicates areas of over- and underuse.

Workload Generators

Whereas the simulation model estimates system use and can be run on a single microcomputer, a **workload generator** actually generates transaction loads for execution on the proposed configuration. If the simulation model and the workload generator were perfect, the results would be identical; in actual practice, however, some variation between the two is likely. A workload generator together with a performance monitor can illustrate how the system will actually function in the proposed configuration. It can also be used for stress testing. Unlike the simulation model, which can be used without an actual system in place, the workload generator requires that you build the network to test it out. It is therefore more often used when acquiring a new LAN.

Like any model, the above models are only as good as the input, the people who use and interpret it, and the closeness of the models to real life. Their value decreases with the amount of time required to use them and increases with their ability to accurately portray an application. This means that they should be used carefully and the results interpreted sensibly.

Planning System Expansion

If, as a result of capacity planning, the network administrator sees a need to add hardware or software, the changes must be planned carefully. System expansion should begin with documentation, hardware and software acquisition, site planning, and site preparation. Configuration of the upgrade (discussed in the next section) includes installation, testing, training, and placing the changes into operation. An upgrade is, after all, a microcosm of a LAN acquisition.

Documentation

As usual, documentation is pervasive. It is performed at each step in the upgrade process. The LAN administrator documents the new hardware and software needs and the justification and costs of the upgrade. Each of the following steps also includes documentation.

Hardware and Software Acquisition

The steps a LAN administrator takes in acquiring the upgrade equipment vary from one organization to another and sometimes depend on the cost of the upgrades. Many organizations, particularly government organizations, have a limited amount that can be spent without obtaining higher approval or competitive bids. If bids must be solicited, the administrator must have a process for evaluating the responses and selecting a choice. Sometimes the acquisition must be done formally via a request for proposals (RFP). The RFP outlines the objectives of the equipment being sought and solicits vendors to provide a solution to the problem. Because the responses may differ significantly, evaluating them and selecting the best one can be a time-consuming process. Remember to ensure that capacity planning and costs associated with this are included in the bidding process.

Site Planning and Preparation

Once the upgrade equipment has been selected, the LAN administrator must plan for its installation. If new hardware is to be added, he or she may have to prepare the hardware location. For example, power outlets may need to be installed, cables may need to be run to the location, and so on.

CONFIGURATION OF HARDWARE AND SOFTWARE UPGRADES

Installing an upgrade is different from installing a new LAN. Installing hardware and software upgrades affects existing LAN users, whereas initial LAN installation is not impeded by the needs of existing users. LAN administrators must plan upgrades carefully to minimize the disruption to LAN users. Often this means doing the installation and testing when the LAN is being used the least, probably on a weekend, on a holiday, or in the early morning. Ideally the administrator can first install and test all hardware and software upgrades on an experimental LAN, that is, a small LAN separate from the production LAN. The experimental LAN is used by LAN administrators and programmers to test new hardware and software before installing them on a production LAN. This approach detects most of the flaws in the installation process and the equipment itself and eliminates many of the causes of delays and user disruptions. Many installations do not have the luxury of an experimental LAN and make all changes directly to the operational system.

Upgrade Configuration Steps

The four steps to configuring an upgrade are installation, testing, training, and making the changes operational. Let us briefly describe these steps and then look more closely at software upgrades.

Installation

When the equipment arrives and the site has been prepared, the new hardware and software can be configured and installed. If the new hardware being installed is for a server, the LAN or a portion of the LAN may have to be taken out of service temporarily. Alternatively, if there are several available servers, the LAN may continue operation but at a reduced capacity. If this is the case, the installation should be scheduled so there is a minimal disruption to the users.

Testing

After the upgrade has been installed, the LAN must be tested. Security settings must be checked to ensure that users have access to all the necessary system components and that the new equipment works correctly and interfaces correctly to other parts of the system. Because the upgrade is intended to solve a particular problem, the LAN administrator should also check to see whether the expectations of the changes were met. If problems are encountered, they may take several hours or even days to correct. Thus, in many cases, testing of this type is done on weekends or during the evening to minimize disruption to system users and business operations.

Training

If new capabilities are added to the LAN, users may need new training to learn how to use them. Training should occur before any of the changes are implemented so users will be ready, not confused, when the changes are made operational. Additional training must be available after the changes have been implemented to help users who missed the initial training session. LAN operators and administrators may also need training in the use and maintenance of the equipment. Ideally users and administrators will complete their training when the new capabilities are made available.

Making Changes Operational

Once the testing and training are completed, the changes are placed into operation. The LAN administrator should closely monitor the system immediately after making changes. The need for additional hardware tuning may surface after the system is used under the normal workload.

Planning Software Upgrades

Planning hardware upgrades and planning software upgrades are equally important. However, software upgrades often have a more disruptive effect on users. Many hardware upgrades, such as adding a new disk to a file server, a new workstation to the network, or a new connection to another network, can be made fairly transparent to users because these changes can be accommodated through drive mappings and startup configuration settings. It is usually not so easy to disguise changes in software; therefore, the LAN administrator must carefully plan the migration of users from one version of software to another. There are many variations in the complexity of upgrading software, and we cannot begin to cover all of them. Therefore, to provide you with a general understanding of the issues, let us examine a specific situation: upgrading from one version of a word processor to a new version. The issues we discuss are similar to those relating to installing a new version of a network operating system, a new workstation operating system, or other application software.

A new software version often has additional functions. Enabling the new functions requires a change in the user's interface and may require changes in the format of files created by the application. Suppose, for example, that your current word processor is a DOS application and you have decided to upgrade to a graphical user interface (GUI) version. You have chosen this change because it has a dramatic effect on the way users can interact with the word processor. Some issues you must deal with are user transition, file compatibility, and reliability.

User Transition

If the software upgrade is for a network or workstation operating system, a user will make the transition from the old software to the new software when the new version is installed. With application software this is not necessarily the case. As the LAN administrator you should make the old and new versions available for some time, perhaps a year or more. Some users resist change or are slow to learn new interfaces, whereas others readily adapt to new situations. You must try to minimize the trauma associated with software changes by giving change-resistant users a reasonable time to make the transition from the old system to the new. With the new word processor, users click an icon in the GUI to start the application rather than typing a command at a DOS prompt, and they use menus, button bars, scroll bars, and other GUI features to work with the document rather than function keys or control key sequences. Eventually, however, you want to have all users converted to the new system, because running several versions of one application requires extra disk space and duplication in support and documentation. To do this, you must work with the company's management team to plan an orderly transition from the old system to the new one.

File Compatibility

Sometimes new software versions require a new file format to accommodate new capabilities. In a word processor, the GUI version may provide new graphics options. A document that uses these new capabilities may be unusable in the old version, or may not be able to display the new graphic images correctly. Of course, this incompatibility can cause problems when documents are worked on by users who are not using the same software version.

Reliability

New software systems are more likely to have bugs than older software because widespread software use uncovers bugs not caught during prerelease testing. These bugs are usually corrected by the software vendor and made available to users. For this reason, it is often wise to pilot a new application for several weeks before making a commitment to widespread corporate use. The LAN administrator and corporate management select a group of users who can begin working with the new application. Only those users have access to the product. After several weeks of error-free use, the application can be made available to other users. The pilot group should be selected so that as many of the capabilities of the new system as possible can be tested. A pilot project not only helps check for reliability but also reveals problems with installation, user configuration, and training.

NETWORK MANAGEMENT SYSTEMS

Earlier in this chapter we described tools a network administrator can use to tune a system. We now take a closer look at one of those tools: a network management system (NMS). An NMS monitors the network operation, gathers network statistics, identifies parameters that are out of tolerance, raises alarms when faults are detected, and, in some systems, suggests ways to correct problems. An NMS therefore allows the LAN administrator to resolve problems that have been reported as well as spot potential problems before they become critical. An NMS is therefore used for both reactive and proactive network management tasks. Table 14.5 lists the functions of a network management system.

Figure 14.3 illustrates the components of a generic network management system. The basic components are devices, device agents or monitors, filters, an alarm or alert,

Table 14.5   Network Management System Functions

Event logging	Alerts and alarms	Expert system problem diagnosis
Graphic user interface	Virus protection	User logon statistics
Message traffic statistics	Server status monitoring	Media monitoring
Workstation status monitoring	Automatic log backup	Network topology graphs
Meter use of software licenses	Trend analysis	Intruder detection

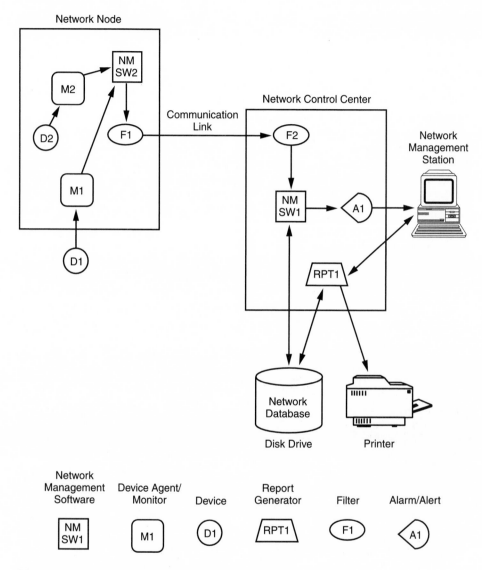

Figure 14.3 Network Management System Components

a report generator, a network control center, a network database, network management software, a network management console, a disk drive, and a printer.

Monitors, or **agents,** located throughout the network, can be dedicated hardware or software devices, or they can be intelligent network devices such as bridges, hubs, or intelligent microcomputer device controllers. For example, an intelligent bridge can collect information about the number of packets that must be switched from one network to another and the stations responsible for the internetwork transfers. A microchannel or EISA disk controller can report disk access statistics. A monitor continually collects information from components for which it is responsible. Naturally the data monitored varies from device to device. Table 14.6 is a list of representative components and their items that can be monitored. Monitors pass their information to network management software components for storage and evaluation.

Network management software collects data from the monitors. The data is usually stored in a database for later analysis. Usually current data is kept in detail form for analysis. After being analyzed, the data should be summarized and stored in a historical database. The historical database is a source of data for spotting network trends that evolve slowly. The network management software also analyzes the data it receives and looks for abnormalities. For example, on a network link a few data transmission errors are likely to occur; however, if the transmission error rate starts to increase, it may indicate the beginning of a problem. When the network management software spots such trends, it forwards out-of-tolerance data to a network control center through a filter. If control is distributed, the system must have several network control centers.

The **filter** receives warning messages, reformats them, forwards the messages to one or more control centers, and suppresses redundant messages. The message may need to be reformatted to make it compatible for the recipient. Realize that today's networks often integrate hardware and software from several vendors. Data collected from this mix of components may be in a format different from that expected by the network control

Table 14.6   Network Component Monitoring

Medium		Server	
	Number of packets	Server	Print queue status
	Packets in error		Status (active/inactive)
	Number of packets by type		CPU busy rate
	Packets per node in and out		Memory utilization
	Percent utilization		Disk busy rate
	Maximum transfer rate		Disk available space
	Packet lengths		Cache hit rate
	Collision rate		Swap rate
	Lost tokens		Queue lengths
			Print activity
Workstations	Status (active/inactive)	**Network Connections (bridges and routers)**	Message traffic
	CPU busy rate		Messages by type
	Disk busy rate		Local versus Internet packets
	Logon user ID		Internet packets per node
	Messages generated		Local packets per node
	Messages received		Error rates
			Path failures
			Path changes
			Routing information

center. Redundant messages are filtered out to prevent the network control center from being flooded by messages regarding the same incident.

The network management software within the network control center analyzes incoming data and displays it for the network administrator. The data usually can be displayed as graphs, tables, or formatted text. When serious out-of-tolerance situations occur, the NMS raises an alarm or an alert. An **alarm** can be an audio signal, a flashing light, a call to a pager, a FAX message, or a message to a remote system. An alarm is an event that attracts immediate attention. An **alert** is less obvious than an alarm. An alert may indicate potential problems by using colors on a color monitor. For example, green can indicate satisfactory situations, yellow can be used for marginal situations, and red can be used for situations needing immediate attention.

The **report generator** allows network administrators to analyze data that has been captured in the network database. This data is useful for spotting trends and for capacity planning.

Network management is a weak spot in many vendor networks, but it is an area in which capabilities are rapidly improving. Sometimes LAN administrators turn to third-party network management tools to effectively monitor their networks. As a network grows, so does the need for effective network management tools. If the network consists of components from multiple vendors, you will need a management system capable of obtaining statistics from them and placing the data into usable formats. Network management systems of this type are called **integrated network management systems.**

NETWORK MANAGEMENT PROTOCOLS

Network management can be complicated, even on homogeneous networks. Network interconnection and a variety of vendor equipment make the management task even more difficult because it is harder to collect and analyze data. Monitoring nodes on one LAN from a node on a different LAN (for example, monitoring a node on a token ring from a network management console attached to a CSMA/CD bus network or from a management console on a WAN) is harder than monitoring nodes on a single homogeneous LAN. To facilitate the exchange of management data among different types of network nodes and devices, a network management standard or protocol is essential. If such standards exist, network designers can build their networks with components that have the ability to capture and exchange management and control data. Two such standards have evolved: the Simple Network Management Protocol (SNMP) and the Common Management Information Protocol (CMIP).

Simple Network Management Protocol

The **Simple Network Management Protocol (SNMP)** is based on the Transmission Control Protocol/Internet Protocol (TCP/IP) discussed in Chapter 16. Since the first product appeared in 1988, it has rapidly gained in acceptance and popularity and is endorsed by companies such as IBM, Hewlett-Packard, and Sun Microsystems. It has also been approved by the Internet Activities Board (IAB).

SNMP has four key components: the protocol itself, the **structure of management information (SMI),** the **management information base (MIB),** and the network management system (NMS). The SNMP protocol is an application layer protocol that outlines the formal structure for communication among network devices. The SMI details how every piece of information regarding managed devices is represented in the MIB. The MIB is a database that defines the hardware and software elements to be monitored. The NMS is the control console to which network monitoring and management information are reported. The SNMP environment is illustrated in Figures 14.4 and 14.5. These figures show a bridge connecting two LANs. We discuss bridges in Chapter 16.

SNMP allows network managers to get the status of devices and set or initialize devices. If problems occur, an event mechanism generates a message that is displayed on the network monitoring console.

As a simple protocol, SNMP has a few shortcomings. Its command set is limited, it has limited provisions for security, and, because there is no strict standard, there are some inconsistencies among different vendors' implementations. The basic premise of SNMP is simplicity. The network agents are therefore intended to be very simple, essentially having the ability to interrogate and set device parameters. They interrogate the parameter values to send them to the network management system and set parameters to control the device. Agents are not intended to filter or analyze the device's data. Despite these deficiencies, most installations use SNMP because of its simplicity and because it was implemented before CMIP.

Common Management Information Protocol

In competition with SNMP is the International Standards Organization's (ISO's) **Common Management Information Protocol (CMIP).** CMIP has a more complex protocol for exchanging messages among network components and has a richer command language and management information base. Therefore, CMIP has the potential for better control and the ability to overcome the limitations of SNMP. In addition, CMIP device agents can be more sophisticated than SNMP agents. A CMIP agent may be given the intelligence to filter and analyze the data it collects. Unfortunately, there are currently no provisions for interoperability of SNMP and CMIP. Because CMIP was developed later than SNMP, operational systems are just beginning to emerge. It will take some time for CMIP to overcome the impetus of SNMP.

SUMMARY

Network management is an important LAN activity. It consists of solving network problems, monitoring performance, tuning LAN components, planning network capacity, and installing new components. Some of these activities are reactive: A problem arises and the LAN administrator reacts to it by analyzing and resolving it. Other activities are proactive: The LAN administrator monitors LAN performance and averts potential problems by anticipating them and taking corrective action before they reach the critical state.

Network management is easier if the manager has the right tools, including problem reporting and tracking systems, network configuration managers, cable testers, protocol analyzers, simulation models, workload generators, network management systems, and remote control software. Each of these tools has a place in different aspects of network management.

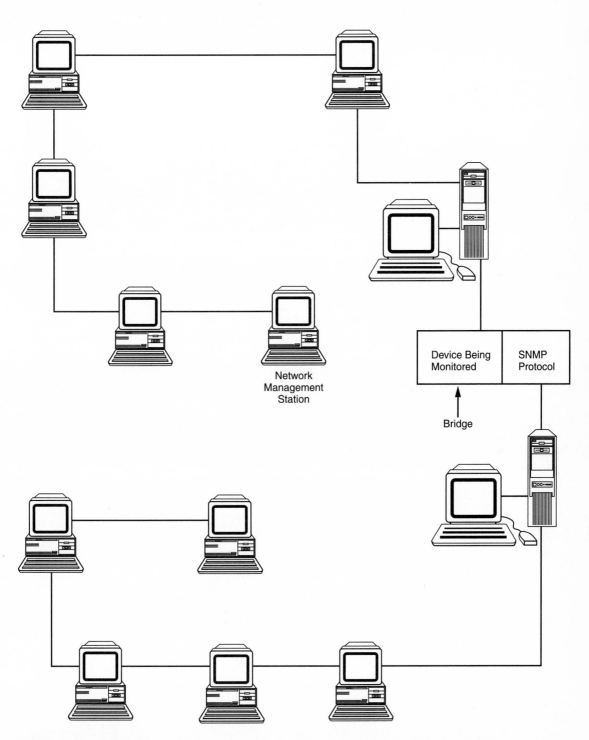

Figure 14.4   SNMP Environment

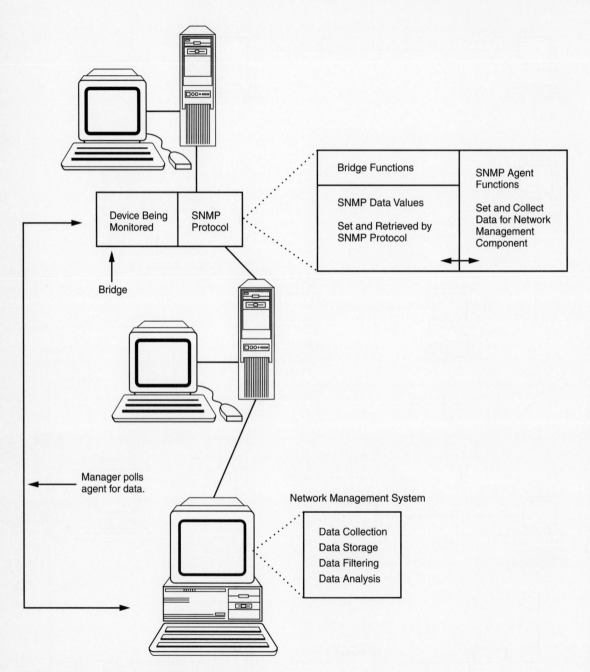

Figure 14.5   Details of SNMP Environment

The essence of network management is managing change. If components break, the manager repairs them. If performance changes, the manager analyzes the system, devises solutions, and implements the solutions. If new applications or users are added, the manager plans for adding network capacity. The solutions range from simple and inexpensive to complex and expensive. Sometimes balancing the load on components is all that is necessary. With the right tools and training, a network manager can keep the network running efficiently and avoid many situations that could develop into critical problems.

Network management can be a complex task, and the task is even more difficult when equipment from different vendors is used. The difficulty arises from creating the interfaces for collecting and formatting performance data. This task is simpler if vendors of network equipment design their components according to a standard. Two network management standards exist: the Simple Network Management Protocol (SNMP) and the Common Management Information Protocol (CMIP). The objective of these standards is to standardize how network management data is reported, stored, and accessed.

Key Terms

agent	monitor
alarms	network management system (NMS)
alerts	pocket LAN adapter
balancing	proactive network management
bindery files	problem reporting and tracking system
bridge	protocol analyzer
cable tester	reactive network management
capacity planning	remote control software
Common Management Information Protocol (CMIP)	report generator
	Simple Network Management Protocol (SNMP)
configuration management utility	simulation model
filter	structure of management information (SMI)
information gathering	
integrated network management system	system tuning
known good components	workload generator
LAN analyzer	
management information base (MIB)	

Review Questions

1. What does a network management system do? What are the components of a network management system? Describe the functions of each network management system component.
2. Why are network management systems necessary?
3. List four tools used to help manage a network.
4. Describe the steps taken in solving a network problem.
5. What functions are provided by remote control systems? By a problem reporting and tracking system?
6. What functions are provided by a configuration management system? By a protocol analyzer? By a cable tester?
7. What is system tuning? Why is it necessary? When is it necessary?

8. Why is it prudent to change only one thing at a time when tuning a system?
9. What is capacity planning and why is it necessary? What are the steps of capacity planning?
10. Describe two tools used to assist with capacity planning.

Problems and Exercises

1. Suppose a user reports an inability to successfully log onto the network. What would you do to help solve this problem? List three likely causes of the problem. What tools would you use to diagnose the problem?
2. Research the literature on a specific network management system. What capabilities does it provide? What networks does it work with?
3. Research the literature on remote control software. What capabilities does it provide? What networks does it work with? Explain how you would use remote control software to diagnose a user's problem.
4. Remote control software allows one to monitor the activities of a workstation anywhere on the network. Thus, remote control software can be used to monitor workers' activities. What problems could arise from the use of this capability? How can LAN administrators and company policies discourage improper use of remote control software? What features does remote control software have to discourage clandestine snooping activities?
5. Suppose you are a LAN administrator. You have just been told that the number of workstations will increase from 25 to 35 because another department will be connected to the LAN. Describe four items that may need to be upgraded to support these new workstations. Explain how the added nodes affect the items you chose.
6. Use a simulation model, such as COMNET III, to model a LAN for the computer science department in your school.
7. Using remote control software, practice diagnosing a problem on a friend's computer.

PART 5

Connecting to Other Systems and Networks

The computing resources of today's organizations are diverse, ranging from a single microcomputer to multiple LANs to WANs that connect all the organization's computing platforms. Chapter 15 examines basic WAN principles, network topologies, and terminology. In Chapter 16 you will build on this knowledge to explore the ways in which interconnection between LANs and WANs is accomplished. We also explore the forefront of LAN technology, one of the most dynamic technologies in the computer industry. In Chapter 17 you will learn about several important but less commonly used technologies that have the potential to become mainstream technologies in the future.

Chapter 15
Wide Area Networks

Chapter 16
Making Network Connections

Chapter 17
Other LAN Technologies

Chapter 15

Wide Area Networks

CHAPTER PREVIEW

In large and small companies alike, LANs have become an integral part of today's data processing environment. A small company's LAN is usually an extension of a stand-alone microcomputer system and represents the company's entire computing system. In contrast, many large companies began their data processing with mainframe or minicomputers and added microcomputers and LANs as extensions of pre-existing computing environments and capabilities. These companies often continue to rely on minicomputers, mainframe computers, and possibly wide area networks (WANs) as well as LANs for their computing needs. In such companies it is not uncommon to establish connections between all the computing platforms to form enterprise networks.

Part 5 of this book focuses on interconnecting LANs with other LANs, WANs, or stand-alone computers. To understand this material, you need to know a little about WANs. In this chapter you will read about some basics of WAN implementations. Topics covered in this chapter include

WAN terminology and topology

functions of the data link layer

WAN data link protocols

functions of the network layer

network routing

IBM's Systems Network Architecture (SNA)

packet distribution networks

differences between LANs and WANs

By the end of this chapter, you will be familiar with the basic principles of WANs, network topologies, and terminology specific to them. This chapter leads to a discussion in Chapter 16 of network interconnections (LAN to LAN, LAN to WAN, and LAN to host computer).

WAN TERMINOLOGY

The world of data communication is rife with terminology, abbreviations, and acronyms. Before we begin our discussion of WAN technology, we define a few common network terms.

Link

The direct connection of two nodes in a network. A link, therefore, connects two computers.

End-to-End Routing

Sometimes when one node wants to send a message to another node, the two are not directly connected. The message must then pass through one or more intermediate nodes before arriving at the final destination. Determining how this is done is called end-to-end routing.

Path

The links that the message traverses. Figure 15.1 shows two paths available for communication between node A and node C (A $\longrightarrow$ B, B $\longrightarrow$ C, and A $\longrightarrow$ D, D $\longrightarrow$ C), with two links on each path.

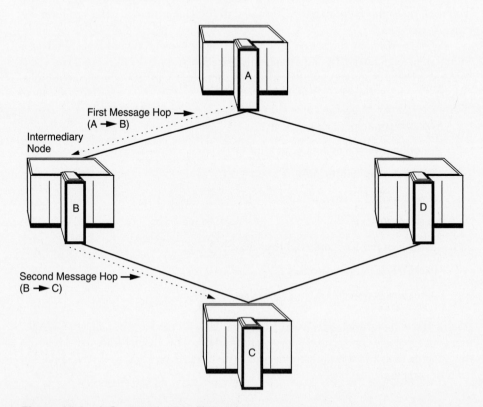

Figure 15.1   A Communication Network

Hop

The number of hops a message takes in going from its source to its destination is the number of links it traverses. Thus a message traveling from node A to node C in Figure 15.1 takes two hops.

Store-and-Forward

A technique used by some networks to send data along a path. Each intermediary node along the path stores the message, sends an acknowledgment of message receipt to the sender, and then forwards the message to the next node on the path. When the sender receives an acknowledgment that the message has been received by the next node, it is no longer responsible for retransmitting the message if an error occurs.

Session

A communication between two users of a network. A user can be a terminal operator, an application, or any other originator of messages. In some systems, sessions are quite formal, with well-defined conventions for establishing, continuing, and terminating the dialogue.

Packet Switching

The technology of transmitting a message in one or more fixed-length data packets.

Packet Distribution Network

A **packet distribution network (PDN)** is sometimes called a **public data network** (also PDN), an **X.25 network** (X.25 is a standard designation), or a **value-added network (VAN).** Henceforth we will use the acronym PDN. A PDN generally connects a user and the nearest node in the PDN. The PDN routes the data packets to their final destination by finding the best route for each packet (packet switching). PDNs are available for public use by a service provider called a common carrier. The common carrier provides the transmission media to connect two users. The advantages of a PDN are an initially low cost for transmission services and a service fee based on the amount of use. The user pays a monthly connection fee plus a charge for the number of messages transmitted. Furthermore, a PDN allows a user to reach most locations in the industrialized world while accessing the service through a local telephone connection. The disadvantages are higher costs than a leased line if message traffic between two points is high and possible congestion and message delays because of message traffic from other companies.

WAN NETWORK TOPOLOGIES

In Chapter 4 we discussed the primary network topologies for LANs: ring, bus, star, and bus with spurs. These topologies can be used by WANs as well. Moreover, WANs can be configured in three additional ways: hierarchical, interconnected, and a combination of these. Most large WANs (those with many nodes) are implemented using these three topologies.

Hierarchical Network

The **hierarchical network** topology, shown in Figure 15.2(a), is also called a tree structure. There is one root node (node A). Several nodes at the second level are directly connected to node A. Each of these nodes can have a number of cascaded nodes attached. This type of network closely resembles corporate organization charts, and corporate computer centers are one place in which this topology can be found. Figure 15.2(a) illustrates such an organization, with the corporate headquarters computer as root node, regional nodes attached directly to the root, district nodes to regional nodes, and branch nodes to district nodes. Corporate reports from a lower level are easily consolidated at the next higher level, and the network generally mirrors the information flow pattern in the corporation. Information flowing from a district in one division to a district in a different division would need to go through the root or corporate node. This topology allows for a great deal of network control.

Interconnected (Plex) Network

An **interconnected (plex) network** architecture is shown in Figure 15.2(b). This topology provides a high degree of flexibility because many paths are available between nodes if a link should fail, so congestion can be avoided. The performance of an interconnected system is generally quite good because direct links can be established between nodes with high amounts of data to exchange. Costs can also be controlled because interconnected topology is capable of the shortest or least expensive configuration. In fact, any of the other topology types can be mimicked by an interconnected topology, although routing and control mechanisms would probably be different.

Combination Networks

A combination of the two topologies just described is sometimes integrated into one network. One such combination is a **backbone network**—for instance, a ring—with spurs attached. The backbone nodes are dedicated to message transfer and data communication, and the other nodes are used for both data processing and data communication. In widely distributed systems with a large number of nodes, this configuration helps reduce the number of hops, the length of the path, and congestion problems. If the backbone is implemented as a ring or with multiple paths available, reliability is also high. A backbone network for a WAN is illustrated in Figure 15.2(c).

Backbone networks are appearing more often in LAN technology as well. The Fiber Data Distributed Interface (FDDI) LAN operates at 100 Mbps, can span distances up to 125 miles, and uses a token-passing ring architecture. FDDI LANs can be used to interconnect a company's departmental LANs in a metropolitan area. For example, a university might use an FDDI backbone to connect the LANs in different departments, or a government agency might use a FDDI backbone to connect departmental LANs in different buildings, as illustrated in Figure 15.2(d). A variation of FDDI uses copper wiring, either shielded or unshielded twisted-pair wires, as the medium. This alternative is known as Copper Distributed Data Interface (CDDI).

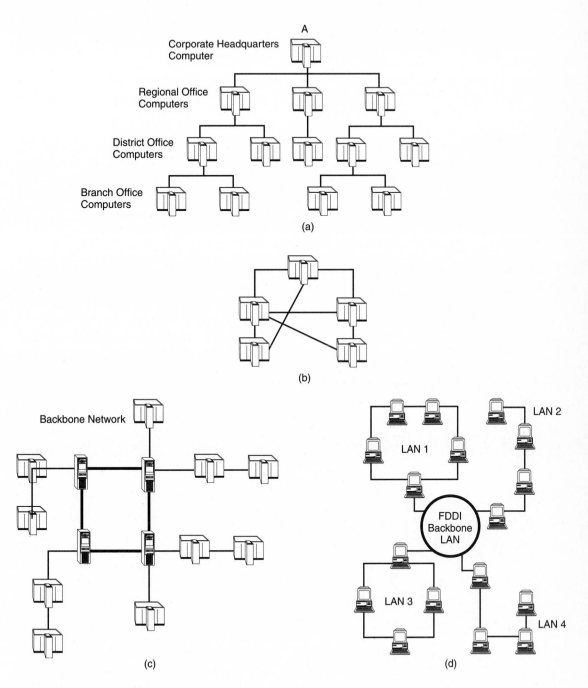

Figure 15.2 Network Topologies

WAN DATA LINK CONTROL PROTOCOLS

In Chapter 1 we introduced the OSI reference model, and in Chapter 4 we looked at functions and examples of the OSI data link layer. In this chapter we look more closely at the data link layer and a data link protocol commonly used in today's WANs. Some of the LAN–WAN connections occur at the data link level, so a cursory knowledge of these protocols is beneficial to understanding how the connections are made.

The two primary methods of passing data from node to node in a LAN are token passing and carrier sense with multiple access and collision detection (CSMA/CD). These methods are seldom used in WANs. Like both of these methods, WAN data link protocols accept a transmission packet from the network layer and add data link control data to the packet. Adding this control information is sometimes called enveloping because the packet is enclosed in the data link control data much like a letter is enclosed in an envelope for transmission. The primary data link control methods used for WANs fall into two general classes: asynchronous and synchronous. In Chapter 4 we briefly discussed asynchronous and binary synchronous protocols. You may want to review those sections at this time. The most common data link protocol used in WANs today is a **bit synchronous protocol.**

Bit Synchronous Protocols

The first bit synchronous data link protocol, **Synchronous Data Link Control (SDLC),** was introduced by IBM in 1972. Since then numerous other bit synchronous data link controls have surfaced, including

> Synchronous Data Link Control (SDLC), from IBM
>
> Advanced Data Communications Control Procedure (ADCCP), an ANSI standard data link protocol (ADCCP is often pronounced "addcap")
>
> High-Level Data Link Control (HDLC), a standard of the International Standards Organization (ISO)
>
> Link Access Procedure–Balanced (LAPB), designated as the data link protocol for X.25 packet distribution networks

All of these bit synchronous protocols operate similarly. SDLC is used in the following discussion as the model for bit synchronous data link protocols because it is used in many IBM installations and thus represents the majority of bit synchronous implementations.

The SDLC Frame

The basic unit of transmission in SDLC is the frame; its general format is presented in Figure 15.3. The **flag field** is used to indicate the beginning and end of the frame. The bit pattern for the flag, 01111110, is the only bit pattern in the protocol that is specifically reserved; all other bit patterns are acceptable. The second field in the frame, the **address field,** is 8 bits wide. The number of unique combinations that can be made from

8 bits is 256, so a maximum of 256 unique addresses are possible. Other data link protocols, such as ADCCP and HDLC, allow the address field to be expanded in multiples of 8 bits, significantly increasing the number of addressable stations per link. The **control field,** also 8 bits long, identifies the frame type as either **unnumbered, informational,** or **supervisory.** Of these three types, only the first two are used to transmit data, with the primary data transport frame being the information frame.

The data field is optional. This field is always omitted for supervisory frames, is optional on unnumbered frames, and is present on information frames. As Figure 15.3 shows, the only restriction on the data field is that the number of bits must be a multiple of eight; each 8-bit group is called an octet. This restriction does not mean that an 8-bit code must be used; in fact, any code is acceptable. But if necessary, the data being transmitted must be padded with additional bits to maintain an integral number of octets. If the data being transmitted consists of five BAUDOT characters, at 5 bits each, only 25 bits would be required for the data and an additional 7 bits would have to be appended to complete the last octet.

Following the optional data field is a **frame check sequence** for error detection, which is 16 bits long. The final field of the frame is the flag that signals the end of the message. The bit pattern for the ending flag is the same as that for the beginning flag, thus allowing the ending flag for one frame to serve as the beginning flag for the next.

SDLC is a positional protocol; that is, each field except the data field has a specific length and location relative to adjacent fields. Thus, there are no special control characters (except for the flag characters) to delimit the data or headings in the message. For control frames, which are either unnumbered or supervisory, the control function is encoded in the control field. Unnumbered frames have 5 bits available to identify the control function, so 32 different function types are available. The supervisory frame has only 2 bits available, so a maximum of 4 functions can be defined.

Number Sent (Ns) and Number Received (Nr) Subfields

As shown in Figure 15.4, in information frames the control field contains two 3-bit fields known as the **number sent (Ns)** and **number received (Nr)** subfields. The Ns and Nr counts are used to sequence messages. Three bits allow for eight numbers, 0 through 7. When transmitting an information frame, the sender increments the Ns field value. The Ns or Nr number following 7 is 0; thus, the number sequence cycles through those eight values. The Nr field is used for acknowledging receipt of messages. Every time a message is received, the receiver increments the Nr count, which represents the number of the frame expected next. Thus an Nr count of 5 means message number 5 should arrive next. The Ns and Nr counts are compared every time a frame is received to make sure that

Flag 01111110	Address (1 or more octets)	Control Field (8 or 16 bits)	Data (Optional Octets)	Frame Check Sequence (16 or 32 bits)	Flag 01111110

Figure 15.3 SDLC Frame Format

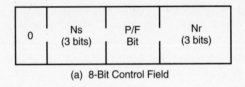

(a) 8-Bit Control Field

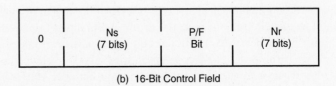

(b) 16-Bit Control Field

Figure 15.4 Expansion of Control Field in SDLC Frame

no messages have been lost. This scheme allows seven messages to be sent before an acknowledgment is required.

Although the ability to receive up to seven frames without acknowledgment improves performance, it also places a burden on the sender, which must be ready to retransmit any unacknowledged frames. Because this requires that messages be saved in the sender's buffers until acknowledged, this can create problems for systems with small buffers or memory.

Both ADCCP and HDLC allow the control field to be expanded to provide for larger Ns and Nr counts, as illustrated in Figure 15.4. When the control field is expanded to 16 bits, the Ns and Nr fields can both be 7 bits long; this allows 128 sequence numbers, and up to 127 messages can be transmitted before being acknowledged. This is especially beneficial with satellite links, where because of the propagation delay for response, a small number of unacknowledged frames could create undesirable delays. Consider the effect of the Ns and Nr sizes for satellite transmission. Satellite signals incur a one-way propagation delay of approximately a quarter of a second. If 10,000-bit blocks are being transmitted on a 1 Mbps satellite link, then theoretically 25 blocks could be transmitted every quarter of a second. With 3-bit Ns and Nr fields, only 7 blocks could be sent before waiting for an acknowledgment. In this case transmission time for 18 blocks would be lost, limiting the available capacity.

WAN NETWORK LAYER FUNCTIONS

As discussed in Chapter 1, the OSI network layer performs three major functions: routing, network control, and congestion control. These functions are the same on LANs and WANs. Whereas the data link layer is concerned with getting data between two adjacent nodes, the network layer is concerned with end-to-end routing, or getting the data from the originating node to its ultimate destination. In many networks data may take a variety of paths to go from the originating node to the destination node. The network layer must be aware of alternative paths in the network and choose the best one. Which path is best depends on a variety of factors, some of which are congestion, number of intervening nodes, and speed of links.

Network control involves sending and receiving node status information to and from other nodes to determine the best routing for messages. Where priorities are associated with messages, it is the responsibility of the network layer to enforce the priority scheme.

Congestion control means reducing transmission delays that might result from overuse of some circuits or from a particular node in the network being too busy to process messages in a timely fashion. The network layer should adapt to these transient conditions and attempt to route messages around such points of congestion. Not all systems can adapt to the changing characteristics of the communication links, however. In some instances, specifically broadcast-type systems, there is very little that can be done to overcome this problem.

Message Routing in a WAN

Message routing, one of the functions of the network layer on both LAN and WAN systems, is accomplished differently on WANs than on LANs. The two primary methods of routing a message from node to node in a LAN are token passing and CSMA/CD. Token passing sends a message from node to node until it circulates around the ring or bus. In CSMA/CD the message is broadcast to each node simultaneously. The nodes to which the message is addressed accept the message, and the others ignore it. Using such methods in a WAN is often not practical. The speeds of WAN links are usually much slower than those of a LAN, and the time it would take for a message to circulate among all nodes would be prohibitive; moreover some nodes may not be on the path to the destination node, and sending a message to those nodes is not productive. Therefore, WANs typically use different message routing methods.

Routing is achievable through a number of algorithms used to direct messages from the point of origination to final destination. Because messages in a WAN are not usually broadcast to all nodes as in a LAN, the path a message takes in reaching its destination must be determined by one or more network nodes. Determination of message routing can be either centralized or distributed. Routing itself can be either static, weighted, adaptive, or broadcast and is governed by a network routing table resident at each node. The **network routing table** is a matrix of other nodes together with the link or path to that node. Thus if a message destined for one node arrives at some other node, the network routing table is consulted for the next node on the path between the two nodes. Network routing tables can also contain more information than just the next link (such as congestion statistics).

Let us look at the varieties of WAN routing techniques, starting with how routes are determined.

Centralized Routing Determination

In **centralized routing,** one node is designated as the network routing manager to whom all nodes periodically forward such status information as queue lengths on outgoing and incoming lines and the number of messages processed within the most recent time interval. The routing manager is thereby provided with an overview of network functioning, where bottlenecks are occurring, and where facilities are underused. The routing manager periodically recalculates the optimal paths between nodes and constructs and distributes new routing tables to all nodes.

This form of network routing determination has many disadvantages. The fact that the routing manager must receive many messages from the other nodes increases the probability of congestion, a problem that can be exacerbated if the routing manager is itself a node used to accept and forward messages. And networks are sometimes subject to transient conditions, as when the internode transfer of a file saturates a link for a short period of time. By the time this information is relayed to the routing manager and a new routing is calculated, the activity may have already ceased, making the newly calculated paths less than optimal. Moreover, some nodes will receive the newly calculated routing tables before others, leading to inconsistencies in how messages are to be routed. For example, suppose that under the old routing mechanism the route was A $\longrightarrow$ B $\longrightarrow$ D $\longrightarrow$ X, whereas the new path is A $\longrightarrow$ C $\longrightarrow$ D $\longrightarrow$ X, as shown in Figure 15.5. The new path from node B to node X is B $\longrightarrow$ A $\longrightarrow$ C $\longrightarrow$ D $\longrightarrow$ X. Now if node B receives its new routing chart while node A is still using the old chart, then for a message destined from A to X, A will route it to B and B will route it back to A, continuing until A receives the new routing table. In addition, transmission of the routing tables themselves may bias the statistics being gathered to compute the next routing algorithm.

An additional problem with centralized routing calculations is the large amount of processing power needed; a considerable amount of CPU time can be consumed. Reliability of the routing manager is also an important factor. If this node fails, then either the routing remains unchanged until the system is recovered, or an alternative routing manager must be selected. The best situation is to have alternative routing managers available in case the primary routing node fails. The routing manager sends the alternative nodes "I'm alive" messages at predefined intervals. If the backup manager fails to

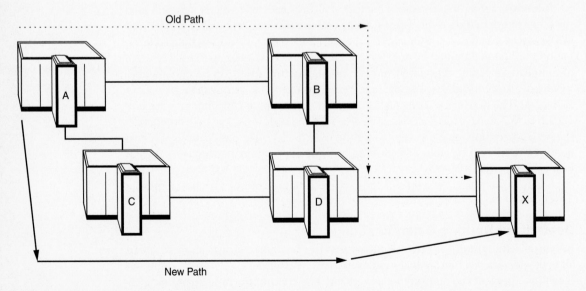

Figure 15.5   Centralized Routing

receive this message within the prescribed interval, it assumes that the manager has failed and takes over. The backup routing manager's first responsibility is to broadcast the fact that network status messages should now be routed to it.

Distributed Routing Determination

Distributed routing determination relies on each node to calculate its own best routing table, which requires each node to periodically transmit its status to its neighbors. As this information ripples through the network, each node updates its tables accordingly. This technique prevents the potential bottleneck at a centralized route manager, although the time required for changes to flow through all of the nodes may be quite long.

In addition to the two approaches to route determination, several message-routing techniques are available. The primary ways we can route messages are static routing, weighted routing, adaptive routing, quickest link, best route, and broadcast routing.

Static Routing

The purest form of **static routing** involves always using one particular path between two nodes; if a link in that path is down, then communication between those nodes is impossible. That is, between any two nodes there is only one path: the link between them. If the link is down, the available network software cannot use any of the potential alternative paths. Fully interconnected networks sometimes use this approach, but fortunately this type of system has largely disappeared. In general, static routing now refers to the situation in which a selected path is used until some drastic condition makes it unavailable, at which time an alternative path is selected and used until the path is manually switched, a failure occurs on the alternate path, or the original path is restored.

Weighted Routing

When multiple paths exist, some implementations use **weighted routing,** in which each path is weighted according to perceived use. The path is then randomly selected from the weighted alternatives. For example, Figure 15.6 shows three paths from node A to node X via nodes B, C, and D. Suppose the network designers had determined that the path through node B would be best 50 percent of the time, through node C would be best 30 percent of the time, and through node D would be best 20 percent of the time. When a message is to be sent from node A to node X, a random number between 0 and 1 is generated: If the random number is 0.50 or less, the path through node B is used; if the random number is greater than 0.50 and less than or equal to 0.80, the path through node C is selected; otherwise the path through node D is used. The path may alternate, but each path is used with the same frequency as in the routing tables. This type of routing can be changed only by altering the route weighting in the routing tables.

Adaptive Routing

Adaptive routing, occasionally called **dynamic routing,** attempts to select the quickest or best current route for the message or session.

The simplest adaptive routing technique is to have a node pass along the message as quickly as possible, with the only restriction being not to pass it back to the sending

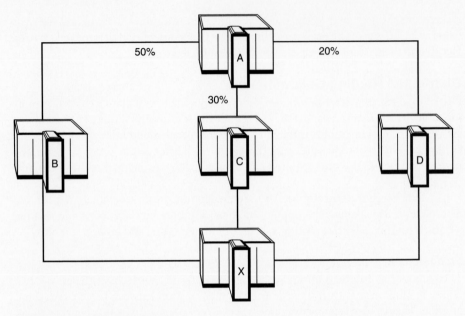

Figure 15.6　Weighted Routing

node. Thus the receiving node looks at all potential outbound links, selects the one with the least amount of activity, and sends the message out on that line. There is no attempt to determine whether that link will bring the message closer to its destination. This technique is not very efficient and can cause messages to be shuffled to more nodes than necessary, thereby adding to network congestion. The message could conceivably be shifted around the network for hours before arriving at its destination. The advantage of this technique is its simplicity, because routing tables do not need to be maintained. Even though it is the simplest to implement, it is not a viable routing method for most WANs.

The more intelligent adaptive routing techniques attempt to select the best route, as determined by one or more of the following parameters; the number of required hops, the speed of the links, the type of link, and congestion. Routing of this type requires current information on the status of the network. If a node is added to the network or if one is taken off the network, that information must be relayed to the nodes doing route calculation. Knowing the speed of the links as well as the number of hops is important. Traversing two links at 4800 bps is more costly than traversing one link at 2400 bps. The line time for both is the same, but some time is lost in receiving and forwarding the message. Link congestion occurs when message traffic on a link is heavy (similar to freeway congestion during the rush hour). Avoiding congested areas prevents messages from being stuck on inbound and outbound queues. In the configuration of Figure 15.7, if node B is transmitting a file to adjacent node C, the route from node A to node C through B is the shortest but probably not the quickest at that time. The route through nodes E and D would be more efficient because the link from B to C is congested.

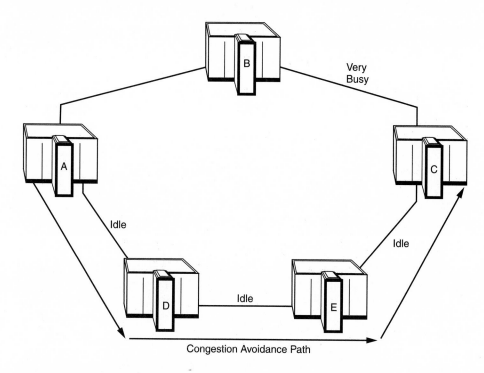

Figure 15.7 Adaptive Routing

Broadcast Routing

A third type of routing is **broadcast routing,** exemplified by CSMA/CD and token passing. Routing is quite easy: The message is broadcast to all stations, and only the station to which the message is addressed accepts it.

IBM'S SYSTEMS NETWORK ARCHITECTURE

Vendor offerings play a major role in network implementation and configuration, and almost every major computer vendor offers a networking capability. Many of today's LANs conform to established industry standards. Often, however, networks are proprietary to the vendor and do not conform to established standards. Of course, this makes attaching equipment from other vendors more difficult because the other vendors must build their equipment to conform to corporate standards that are more subject to change than industry standards. Vendor networks compete with each other, with packet switching or X.25 networks, and with common carrier networks.

The following section is devoted to one particular network that has become a de facto industry standard, IBM's **Systems Network Architecture (SNA).** Currently most networks being designed on IBM mainframe systems use SNA. Other vendors' equipment interfacing with an IBM network is likely to do so via an SNA interface. Many computer manufacturers have implemented or are implementing the ability to attach to an SNA network as some type of SNA node.

A network based on SNA consists of a variety hardware and software components in a well-defined configuration. The objective of any network is to enable users to communicate with one another. SNA users are entities with some degree of intelligence—either people working at a terminal or operator's console or applications providing services for other programs or terminal users. A terminal is not a user, although the terms *terminal operator* and *terminal* are often used synonymously. SNA has been developed to provide communication paths and dialogue rules between users. This is accomplished via a layered network architecture similar to the OSI reference model.

Hardware Components

SNA defines four distinct hardware groupings called **physical units (PU).** The four physical units are numbered 1, 2, 4, and 5, with no PU currently assigned to number 3. These device types are listed in Table 15.1.

The hardware configuration consists of IBM or IBM-compatible CPUs, communication controllers, terminal cluster controllers, and terminals, printers, or workstations, connected by any type of medium. Other vendors' equipment may also be included in the network if it conforms to the SNA protocols. The preferred data link protocol is the bit synchronous SDLC, but accommodations have been made for asynchronous protocols and character-oriented synchronous protocols.

Logical Units and Sessions

Users of SNA are represented in the system by entities known as **logical units (LU).** An LU is usually implemented as a software function in a device with some intelligence, such as a CPU or controller. The dialogue between two system users is known as a session. As agents of the users, the LUs are involved in establishing communication paths between users who want to establish a session.

Session Types

Many different types of sessions can be requested, such as program to terminal, program to program, or terminal to terminal. Each of these categories can be further stratified as to terminal type (interactive, batch, or printer) and application type (batch, interactive, word processing, or the like). To further complicate matters, one logical unit can represent several different users, and a user can have multiple sessions in progress concurrently.

Table 15.1   SNA Physical Units

Physical Unit	Hardware Component
Type 1	Terminal
Type 2	Cluster controller
Type 4	Communications controller
Type 5	Host processor

Suppose a terminal wants to retrieve a record from a database. The terminal must use the services of an application program to obtain the record. Each user—the terminal and the database application—is represented by a logical unit. The terminal LU issues a request to enter into a session with the database application LU. The application LU can either accept or reject the session request. Rejection typically occurs for security reasons, because the requesting LU lacks authority to establish a session with the application LU, or because of congestion, meaning that the application LU has already entered into the maximum number of sessions it can support. If the session request is granted, then a communication path is established between the terminal and the application. The two users continue to communicate until one of them terminates the session. Figure 15.8 shows several sessions between users communicating through their respective logical units.

LU Types

Seven LU types have thus far been defined within SNA. These are numbered from 0 to 7, with the definition for LU type 5 omitted. It is important to note that the LU types refer to session types, not to a specific LU. Thus one specific LU can participate in a type

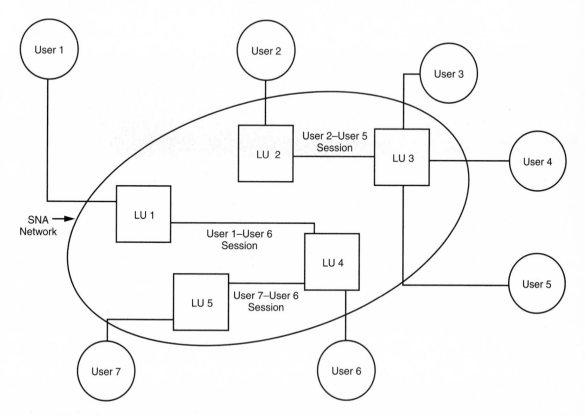

Figure 15.8   SNA Sessions and Logical Units

1 LU session with one LU and a type 4 LU session with another. For two LUs to communicate, they must both support and use the same LU session type.

Of the seven LU types, all but LU types 0 and 6 address sessions with hardware devices such as printers and terminals. LU type 6 is defined for program-to-program communication. It has evolved through two definitions, LU 6.0 and LU 6.1, to its current definition, LU 6.2. LU 6.2 has recently been given considerable attention as a key SNA capability. There are several significant aspects of LU 6.2.

LU 6.2 defines a program-to-program communication interface that is more general and can have wider uses than the interfaces provided by the hardware-oriented LU types. Program-to-program sessions provide a communication path for applications distributed over multiple nodes. The two applications do not have to be in the same node to communicate with each other. This capability supports transaction processing systems with multiple processing nodes. For example, Figure 15.9 shows an application in workstation A in LAN 1 communicating through an SNA LU 6.2 session with an application in workstation X on LAN 2.

Because a program-to-program interface is more generic than a session type involving specific hardware devices, other vendors' equipment can enter into SNA sessions with an application process running in an IBM processor as long as the communicating program in the vendor's processor adheres to the session rules. For example, an application on a microcomputer could enter into a session with an application running on an IBM node or another microcomputer.

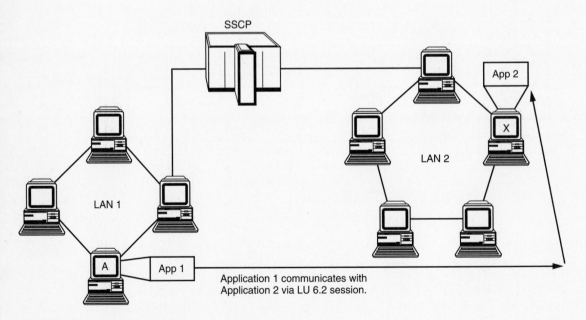

Figure 15.9   LU 6.2 Interface

PACKET DISTRIBUTION NETWORKS

The concept of a packet distribution network (PDN) was first introduced in 1964 by Paul Baran of the Rand Corporation. Baran defined a process of segmenting a message into specific-sized packets, routing the packets to their destination, and reassembling them to recreate the message. In 1966 Donald Davies of the National Physics Laboratory in Great Britain published details of a store-and-forward PDN. IN 1967 plans were formulated for what is believed to be the first PDN, ARPANET, which became operational in 1969 with four nodes. The ARPANET has since expanded to more than 125 nodes and was renamed NSFNET.

PDNs specify several different packet sizes, most commonly 128, 256, 512, and 1024 bytes. All packets transmitted conform to one of the available packet lengths. Individual users subscribe to a service providing one of the available packet sizes. Eliminating large variations in packet size makes management of message buffers easier and evens out message traffic patterns.

PDN Terminology

A PDN is a packet-switching WAN variously called an X.25 network, a value-added network (VAN), or a public data network. The terms *packet distribution* and *packet switching* both refer to how data are transmitted (that is, as one or more packets with a fixed length). The X.25 designation stems from CCITT's X.25 recommendation, which defines the interface between computer equipment and data circuit-terminating equipment (DCE) for devices operating in the packet mode on public data networks. The term *public data network*, which derives from the X.25 recommendation, is somewhat of a misnomer because packet-switching networks have also been implemented in the private sector. When the network is public, users subscribe to the network services much as they subscribe to telephone services. The term *value-added network* is used because the network proprietor adds not only a communication link but also message routing, packet control, store-and-forward capability, network management, compatibility between devices, and error recovery.

The general configuration of a PDN is given in Figure 15.10. Some CCITT recommendations covering different aspects of PDN access and use are listed in the figure at the points where they apply.

PDN Advantages and Disadvantages

PDNs have several advantages: The user is charged for the amount of data transmitted rather than for connect time. Applications that send low volumes of data over a long period will find the charges for a PDN lower than for either leased lines or switched lines. The PDN also gives access to many different locations without the cost of switched connections, which usually involve a charge for the initial connection plus a per-minute use fee. Access to the PDN is usually via a local telephone call, which also reduces costs (that is, until telephone companies begin using measured billing). Network maintenance and error recovery are the responsibilities of the PDN.

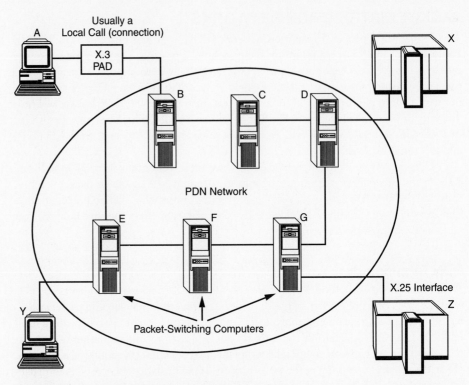

Figure 15.10   PDN General Configuration

PDNs also have disadvantages: Because the PDN is usually shared, users must compete with each other for circuits. Thus it is possible for message traffic from other users to impede the delivery of a message. In the extreme case a virtual circuit to the intended destination may even be unobtainable. This is also true for a switched connection from a common carrier. If the number of data packets to be transferred is great, then the cost of using a PDN can exceed that of leased facilities. Because the PDN is controlled by its proprietor, the individual user is unable to make changes that might benefit an individual application, such as longer messages or larger packets, longer message acknowledgment intervals, and higher transmission speeds, all set by the PDN administrators.

Frame Relay

X.25 was a product of the 1970s, when the reliability of data communication links were much worse than they are today. Characteristics of the telecommunication network at that time were analog switches and copper media with poor error characteristics. To provide effective communication with error-prone links, considerable error checking was built into the X.25 protocol. When data is transmitted from one node to another though several intervening nodes, acknowledgments are required at each link, which introduced extra overhead in the protocol. Thus in Figure 15.10, if node A transmits to node X, the following acknowledgments may be required:

B to A	C to B	D to C	X to D	for sending
D to X	C to D	B to C	A to B	for acknowledgment

The overhead of the X.25 protocol results in the transmission speed being limited to 64 Kbps or less (although that speed may increase). Consequently, X.25 is not well suited to some forms of transmission such as voice and video, where frames must arrive close together. In contrast to 1970s communication networks, most networks today use digital switches and fiber optic cable. Consequently, the likelihood of errors is much less. Frame relay takes advantage of the additional reliability by reducing the amount of error checking during transmission. Error checking is essentially end-to-end rather than node-to-node. Consequently, frame relay can support speeds up to 2 Mbps and higher speeds are likely.

Frame relay operates at the data link layer, whereas X.25 operates at the network layer. Frame relay provides capabilities for congestion control that allow the service to be maintained during periods of congestion and minimize the possibility of one user monopolizing the network at the expense of other users. Frame relay is the heir apparent to X.25 services.

COMPARING WANS WITH LANS

The primary difference between a WAN and a LAN is distance. A LAN serves a limited geographical area, typically within one building or building complex. The maximum allowable distance a LAN can cover varies with the system, but it is generally a few miles, sometimes depending on the type of medium used or by one or more standards. A WAN can cover a large geographical area, or it can be limited to a small area. In the latter case it is distinguished from a conventional LAN in that the network technology can be used without change to set up a geographically distributed network. Distance is not the only feature distinguishing a LAN from a WAN. Other distinguishing factors may include topology, data link protocol, routing algorithm, media, ownership, and transmission speed. Let us briefly look at each of these factors.

Topology, Protocols, and Routing

LAN topologies are usually bus, ring, or star. Sometimes the topology is a combination of these, such as a bus with spurs. WAN topologies are typically hierarchical or interconnected, although rings and stars are also used. Hybrid topologies consisting of combinations of several topologies are also common. For example, a WAN with hundreds of nodes may use a backbone ring network to provide efficient transmission over long distances. The subnetworks attached to the backbone ring may use hierarchical, star, and interconnected topologies. LAN data link protocols are usually CSMA/CD or token passing, whereas WANs use asynchronous or synchronous protocols. The protocol of choice for most WANs today is a bit synchronous protocol such as HDLC. In a LAN, routing is either broadcast with CSMA/CD or always-transmit-to-your-neighbor node in token passing. A variety of routing algorithms are used in WANs, and WAN routing is often more complex than LAN routing. WANs often use an adaptive routing technique, meaning that the routing may change based on conditions such as congestion, failed links, and failed processors, or a probability function for weighted routing.

Media

LAN media are usually twisted-pair wires, coaxial cable, fiber optic cable, or one of the new wireless media. Although mixed-media networks are possible, a single LAN usually uses a single medium type. WAN media are often obtained through a common carrier and may consist of a variety of media, such as telephone wires, fiber optic cable, coaxial cable, microwave radio, and satellite. A company implementing a LAN usually evaluates the media and selects the one that best meets its needs. For WANs a company typically selects a service level based on speed and error characteristics and allows the common carrier to use its variety of media to meet these performance characteristics.

Ownership

A LAN is almost always privately controlled with respect to hardware, software, and media. A WAN, on the other hand, usually consists of computer hardware and software owned or controlled by the user, together with media and associated data communication equipment provided by a common carrier. It is not always the case that a WAN uses media provided by a common carrier; sometimes WANs are implemented as totally private networks. One such network is Commodity News Service (CNS) in Kansas City. CNS provides information on commodities such as wheat, gold, silver, and coffee. Some of CNS's subscribers live in rural agricultural areas. In some of these areas CNS has installed its own communication lines to provide its services. In Canada an electric utility uses lines it owns to communicate between geographically distributed centers, and some railroad companies also have private, geographically distributed communication lines. Most often WANs using private media are those having nodes located in a small geographical areas. It is common to have WANs that use both private media and media obtained from a common carrier.

Transmission Speed

LAN nodes are connected via a high-speed communication path. The speed typically is at least 1 Mbps and often higher. Transmission speeds for WANs vary widely and, like those of LANs, are constantly increasing. However, the usual transmission speeds for long-distance connections are generally less than LAN speeds. Common WAN speeds are 9600 bps, 56 Kbps, and 1.54 Mbps. Speeds of 1.54 Mbps result from a transmission service known as T-1. Higher speeds of 6.3 Mbps (T-2), 45 Mbps (T-3), and 281 Mbps (T-4) are also available but are too expensive for most companies. For example, a 1992 tariff request for a common carrier for T-1 lines was $2500 per month plus $3.50 per mile; for T-3 links the cost was $16,000 per month and $45 per mile. Under this tariff the monthly cost for a 100-mile link would be $2850 for T-1 and $20,500 for T-3.

A variety of different speeds are often found in one WAN. Referring back to Figure 15.5, the speed of the connection between nodes A and B might be 9600 bps, and the speed of the connection between nodes A and C might be 56 Kbps. If the transmission path between nodes A and D is through node B, then the overall speed of transmission is limited by the speed of the lowest communication link, link A–B in this case.

LAN–WAN INTERCONNECTIONS

The differences between LANs and WANs just cited present considerable obstacles to LAN–WAN interconnection. When we connect a LAN to a WAN, many of these differences must be reconciled. The interconnection must be able to accommodate significant differences in transmission speeds, data link protocols, transmission media, and perhaps internal data codes. LAN speeds can be 10,000 times faster than WAN speeds. The format of a LAN message can be different from that of the WAN to which it is connected, and the interconnection must translate messages from one protocol format to the other. The type of media and the connectors used to attach stations to the media can differ, and the interconnection must provide for connection to both LAN and WAN media. Although internal data codes are not a part of WAN technology, sometimes mainframe computers attached to a WAN use the EBCDIC code, whereas LAN computers most commonly use the ASCII code. Thus code translation may be an essential function for LAN–WAN connections.

SUMMARY

LANs do not always exist in isolation. Many companies having LANs also have large stand-alone computing systems and WANs. These various platforms can be interconnected to form an enterprise network of LANs and WANs or LANs and large host systems. Because of the need to interconnect LANs and WANs, LAN administrators should be aware of the basics of WAN technology.

WANs and LANs often differ in topology. LANs usually use a bus, ring, or star topology. WANs typically use a hierarchical or interconnected topology. Hybrid networks consisting of several subnetworks with differing topologies are also possible in WANs. For example, some WANs with a large number of nodes use a ring backbone network to provide faster service between nodes that are geographically dispersed. Attached to the backbone ring may be subnetworks that use a hierarchical, star, or interconnected topology.

The data link protocols most often used by large systems, so WANs are asynchronous and synchronous. Asynchronous transmissions send one character at a time and the sending and receiving stations are not synchronized with each other. Synchronous transmissions send a block of data at a time and the sending and receiving stations are synchronized so the data bits can be recognized correctly. In general, synchronous protocols are more efficient than asynchronous protocols. Both are widely implemented and provide means for interfacing to microcomputers and LAN nodes. The data link protocol of choice for most of today's WANs is a bit synchronous protocol. Several variations of bit synchronous protocols exist. Some of these variations are HDLC, SDLC,

ADCCP, and LAPB. Bit synchronous protocols are preferred because they are efficient, provide good error detection, and allow any bit sequences to be transmitted as data (transparency).

The network layer is responsible for message routing, and there are a variety of methods for doing so. Routing can be determined by a centralized routing manager, or this function can be distributed among all or several nodes. Common routing algorithms include static, weighted, adaptive, and broadcast.

A variety of WAN implementations exist. In this chapter we looked at two specific implementations: a PDN and IBM's Systems Network Architecture (SNA). Both are significant because of the large number of computers, large and small, that have interfaces to these networks. A PDN is a public network. A service provider provides a customer with an interface to the PDN. The PDN is responsible for services provided by the OSI physical, data link, and network layers (that is, for functions such as node-to-node connections, error detection, and message routing). Because many systems interface to PDNs, a PDN can serve as a common connection interface for computers.

SNA is one of the most common WAN architectures, so many different companies have built hardware and software interfaces for SNA networks. These interfaces exist for large and small systems alike. Thus microcomputers equipped with the right hardware and software are able to communicate with nodes on an SNA network. One interface, the LU 6.2 program-to-program interface, is particularly attractive because it is designed to allow a program on one computer to communicate directly with a program on another computer. Thus SNA is important not only as a WAN architecture but also for network interfaces.

Key Terms

adaptive routing
address field
backbone network
bit synchronous protocol
broadcast routing
centralized routing
control field
distributed routing
dynamic routing
end-to-end routing
flag field
frame check sequence
hierarchical network
hop
informational frame
interconnected (plex) network
link
logical unit (LU)
LU 6.2

network routing table
number received (Nr)
number sent (Ns)
packet distribution network (PDN)
packet switching
path
physical unit (PU)
public data network (PDN)
session
static routing
store-and-forward
supervisory frame
Synchronous Data Link Control (SDLC)
Systems Network Architecture (SNA)
unnumbered frame
value-added network (VAN)
weighted routing
X.25 network

Review Questions

1. Distinguish between a link and a path.
2. What does end-to-end routing mean?
3. Describe two WAN topologies.
4. What are the advantages of an interconnected network?
5. What is a backbone network? What advantages does a backbone network provide?
6. What is the format of an SDLC frame?
7. How are the Ns and Nr counts used in the SDLC protocol?
8. What functions are performed by the OSI network layer?
9. What are the advantages and disadvantages of centralized routing calculations? Of local route determination?
10. Distinguish between static and adaptive routing.
11. What are the advantages and disadvantages of the quickest link routing algorithm? What are the problems inherent in the quickest link routing method?
12. Describe the weighted routing algorithm.
13. Why are only three layers defined for PDNs? Do the other OSI layers exist? Explain.
14. What are the four types of physical units in SNA? What is the role of each in the network?
15. What is a half-session layer in SNA? What is its purpose? Explain how a session is established in SNA.
16. Compare a LAN and a PDN.

Problems and Exercises

1. WAN end-to-end transmissions tend to be much slower than LAN transmissions. Suppose that a 1000-byte message needs to go from node A to node D in Figure 15.5 and that the path is A $\longrightarrow$ C and C $\longrightarrow$ D. How long will it take for the message to arrive at node D? How long would it take in a CSMA/CD LAN operating at 10 Mbps? Assume that the 1000-byte message includes all necessary enveloping data and that the speed of the links is 56 Kbps.
2. A hierarchical topology is used by some companies because it mirrors the corporate organizational structure. Would such a topology be effective for a network of university computers? Explain your conclusion.
3. Bit synchronous protocols allow multiple messages to be exchanged before an acknowledgment is received. Suppose node A must send five 1000-byte messages to node B over a 9600-bps link. Suppose further that a message acknowledgment requires 8 bytes of data. What is the time difference between sending five messages and getting one acknowledgment and sending five messages and getting five acknowledgments?
4. Suppose that the connection between node A and node B in Problem 3 was a satellite link in which the time to send a message from node A to node B is 1/4 second. What is the time difference between getting one acknowledgment and getting five acknowledgments in this instance?
5. Suppose a company established a ring WAN with 10 nodes and with all links having a speed of 9600 bps. Suppose the company also decided to use a token-passing media access control protocol like that used in LANs. Calculate the average and maximum time a given node must wait to get the token, assuming no other station has a message to send. Assume the token length is 8 bytes. Make the same calculations for a 16-Mbps token ring.
6. Suppose that the quickest link routing method was used for the network in Figure 15.5. Explain how a message from node A to node X could loop through the network forever. Would the same problem occur for messages from node X to node A?

7. A PDN is more cost-effective than leasing lines when the number of packets being sent is less than a certain number, called the breakeven point. Suppose that a leased line between node A and node B is $1000 per month and that the charge for a PDN between the same two points is a $400 flat monthly fee plus $2 for every 1000 packets transmitted. What is the breakeven point in packets?

8. Suppose that in Problem 7 your company's transmission requirements are right at the breakeven point. Would you pick a leased line or a PDN connection? Justify your answer.

Chapter 16

Making Network Connections

CHAPTER PREVIEW

Most organizations have diverse computing resources, ranging from single microcomputers to multiple local and wide area networks that connect hundreds of computers of varying types: microcomputers, minicomputers, mainframes, and supercomputers. Today a large organization may have several microcomputer LANs, a WAN of large computers, and perhaps connections to public computer networks. When one organization has a variety of computers and networks, those computers must be interconnected. Interconnection provides better use of hardware and software and allows users to communicate easier. Thus a LAN may need to be connected to another LAN, one large host computer, a WAN, remote workstations or terminals, or public networks. In this chapter we cover the principal ways interconnections are accomplished. Topics you will read about include

LAN-to-LAN connections

repeaters, bridges, routers, and gateways

the TCP/IP protocol suite

LAN-to-host connections

IBM system connections

internetwork connection utilities

The focus of this chapter is internetworking: LAN-to-LAN, LAN-to-WAN, and LAN to host. The reason for having a LAN and a WAN or a LAN and a host should be apparent. Let us now see why we might have multiple LANs.

LAN-TO-LAN CONNECTIONS

There are a variety of reasons why a company has several LANs and several ways in which they are connected. By definition a LAN serves a limited geographical area. Most LAN specifications place a limit on the length of the medium used and the number of nodes per LAN. Companies that have LANs in separate geographical locations or LANs that cover distances greater than the maximum medium distance allowed, or companies with more nodes that can be accommodated by one LAN, must segment their network into two or more LANs. When this is done, the users will probably need to be able to make inter-LAN exchanges. Users on one LAN may want to exchange e-mail messages with users on the other LAN, or a user on one LAN may want to use resources located on the other LAN. Thus one reason for having several LANs is distance. But distance or geographical separation is not the only reason for having several interconnected LANs.

LANs sometimes provide department-level computing. A company that is interested in department-level computing might implement a LAN for each department or for groups of departments. For example, consider a computer software manufacturer with departments for software development, documentation, software support, accounting, personnel, payroll, and marketing. Most companies like this go to great lengths to protect the integrity of their new products and sensitive data. Often details of new developments must be protected even from some of the company's employees. Having separate LANs allows the company to split functions and gives an additional level of security. For example, the software company might have one LAN shared by software development and documentation because they work closely together, one for software support (separating support staff from developers), one for accounting (to protect billing and customer data), one for personnel and payroll (to protect the confidentiality of employee data), and one for marketing. This separation reduces the likelihood that software the company develops can be inadvertently or intentionally made available to customers through the support or marketing LAN. Likewise, personnel information can be protected more easily if it is on a separate LAN. Thus another reason for having multiple LANs is departmental computing or separation of functions.

In many companies microcomputers were introduced as stand-alone systems. Workgroups in some of these companies independently created LANs with several nodes. Later these companies realized there would be advantages to connecting those LANs. Because these LANs began independently, with no corporate direction or standard for LANs, the job of connecting them is more complex than if they were homogeneous. Thus a third reasons for LAN connections is to consolidate independent LANs that were formed in an ad hoc manner. Superficially this reason is similar to the preceding one: connecting departmental LANs. The difference is that department-oriented LANs are a planned separation, and workgroup-oriented LANs simply evolved.

A fourth reason for connecting multiple LANs is the number of LAN users. A LAN with hundreds of users might provide poorer performance than the same LAN with tens of users. Even when more users are added, the responsiveness of a LAN must be maintained. Responsiveness can be maintained by adding more resources to an existing LAN—more memory, more disks, another server—or by splitting the LAN into two or more smaller LANs. When a LAN is split, a proper balance must be sought; however, an even balance is not always attainable because of distances and physical location or because of different sizes of workgroups. Because inter-LAN communication involves more overhead than intra-LAN communication, users and resources should be grouped on the separate LANs in a way that reduces the amount of inter-LAN messages. Often members of a department communicate with each other more than with members of other departments. Thus, splitting a LAN because there are many users being served often results in a configuration similar to splitting along departmental or workgroup lines.

Let us now look at the specific ways in which LANs or LAN segments can be connected.

THE OSI REFERENCE MODEL REVISITED

In Chapters 1, 4, and 15 we specifically discussed various layers of the OSI reference model. You may wish to refer back to those chapters at this time to review the details of the model. When a LAN is connected to another network or computing system, the connection interface may occur at several OSI layers. However, even though the connection interface may be implemented at, say, the network layer, all node-to-node connections must always have a connection at the physical level, and a data link protocol must be involved in sending the data over the medium at the physical level.

What do we mean when we say that the connection interface is made at the network layer, the data link layer, or the physical layer, and so on? An interface that operates at the physical layer is called a **repeater.** Repeaters must be sensitive to the signals on the medium. They must know and obey all the physical layer connections. However, repeaters have no sense of what they are forwarding; all they are forwarding is electrical signals, light pulses, or radiated frequencies. For all a repeater knows, the signal being forwarded might be noise (and it sometimes is).

An interconnection that operates at the data link layer is called a **bridge.** Bridges must know about the data link protocol. When a message arrives at a bridge, the bridge examines the data link header placed on the message by the sending node. It uses information in the header to determine where to forward the message. An interconnection that operates at the network layer is called a router. The router must know the protocol used at the network layer. It uses this information in much the same way as a bridge. Let us now look at some of the details of how each of these interconnection methods works.

Repeaters

Every LAN has a distance restriction. One of the IEEE 802.3 standards specifies a maximum segment length of 500 meters. If you want to span longer distances, you can use a repeater to connect two segments. The standard allows for a maximum of four repeaters, for a total distance of 2500 meters per LAN. The relationship between a repeater and the OSI model is illustrated in Figure 16.1, and Figure 16.2 illustrates two repeaters connecting three segments in an IEEE 802.3 network.

As signals travel along the medium, they lose strength through attenuation. Weak signals can result in transmission errors. A repeater accepts a signal, regenerates it, and passes it along at full strength. A repeater is a simple hardware device. It does not buffer messages or know about MAC protocols or data packets; it simply gets a signal, renews it, and passes it on. Moreover, a repeater does not separate one segment of the network from another. That is, if a station in segment 1 and a station in segment 3 of the network shown in Figure 16.2 try to transmit at the same time, a collision occurs.

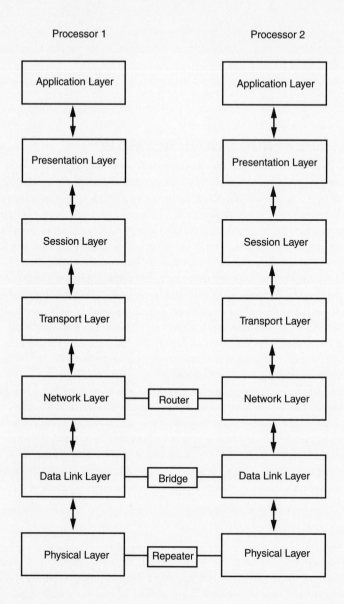

Figure 16.1   A Repeater, Bridge, and Router and the OSI Reference Model

A list of repeater capabilities and characteristics is given in Table 16.1. Note that one of the capabilities of some repeaters is media transfer. You can change media, say from twisted-pair wires to fiber optic cable, at a repeater junction; however, the MAC protocol is the same even though the medium changes. The LAN administrator must also keep in mind that a change in the medium can result in a change in the overall length of the LAN.

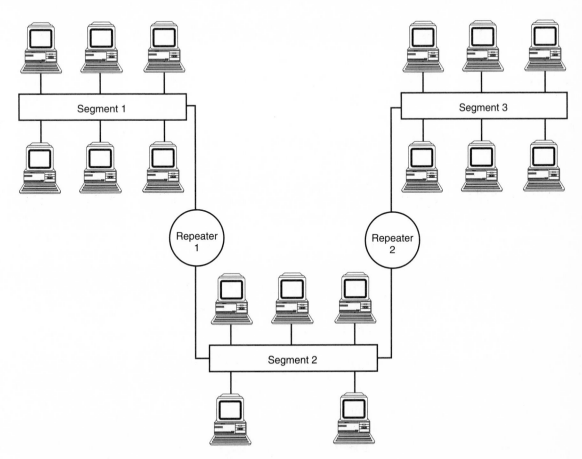

Figure 16.2 Repeaters Connecting Three LAN Segments

Bridges

The relationship between a bridge and the OSI model is illustrated in Figure 16.1. Although this figure shows a bridge at the data link layer, the data is still transmitted from the data link layer down to the physical layer, over the medium to a physical layer and up to the data link layer. Such a connection can use a variety of physical layer implementations. If the MAC protocol is the IEEE 802.3 CSMA/CD protocol, the bridge can use twisted-pair wires, coaxial cable, fiber optic cable, or wireless media. Often the networks being connected use the same medium; however, in some instances the media of two LANs being connected by a bridge may differ. For example, two Ethernet LANs, one using coaxial cable and one using twisted-pair wires, may need to be connected. Some bridges provide connectors that allow for the connection of different media.

Early bridges were used to connect two networks, each of which used the same MAC protocol. For example, a bridge might connect two token ring LANs or two IEEE 802.3 LANs. Today bridges also connect LANs having different MAC protocols. These newer

Table 16.1   Repeater Characteristics and Capabilities

Media transfer, such as coaxial cable to twisted-pair wires

Multiple ports allowing one repeater to connect three or more segments

Diagnostic and status indicators

Automatic partitioning and reconnection in the event of a segment failure

Manual partitioning

Backup power supply

bridges must be able to reformat packets from one data link protocol to another. You should be aware that the use of the term *bridge* can vary. Sometimes a bridge is defined in the original sense: a device connecting two identical networks using identical MAC protocols. Others use the broader definition: a device used to connect two networks at the data link layer. For example, you may read about bridges that connect a token ring to an Ethernet LAN. Sometimes a device providing this capability is called a **brouter** or **multiprotocol bridge.** Figure 16.3 illustrates two LANs, LAN A and LAN B, using a token-ring protocol. These two rings may be configured around departments, one ring per department, or around distance, if the distance spanned by the workstations is greater than what can be supported by a single LAN. Regardless of the reason for having two rings, it is likely that a node on LAN A will want to communicate with a server on LAN B or that a user on LAN A will want to send mail to a user on LAN B. A bridge can provide these abilities.

Early bridges blindly forwarded all message traffic from one LAN onto another LAN. Unlike these early bridges and repeaters, today's bridges are selective in what they do. Only internetwork packets are forwarded by a bridge, as illustrated in Figure 16.4. The bridge in Figure 16.3 can be used to move data packets between the two LANs. It accepts packets from both LANs, transfers LAN A packets addressed to nodes on LAN B to LAN B, and transfers LAN B packets addressed to nodes on LAN A to LAN A. These basic bridge functions plus additional functions are listed in Table 16.2.

To do its job, a bridge must know about the addresses on each network. Because the bridge knows the MAC protocol being used, it can find the source and destination addresses and use them for routing. (We use the term *routing* here to describe the process of the bridge deciding to which LAN the message must be transferred. In using this term we do not imply that the bridge is performing the functions of a router.) Upon receiving a packet and extracting the destination address, the only additional information the bridge must know is the LAN to which the destination node is connected. This is determined in several ways. Older bridges blindly transferred each message onto both LANs or required network managers to provide a network routing table. The **routing table** contains node addresses and the LAN identifier for the LAN to which the node is connected. Network interconnection can be more complex than a single connection of two networks. Figure 16.5 shows four LANs connected with four bridges. A network routing table for bridge B1 in Figure 16.5 is shown in Table 16.3. These older bridges are static regarding their ability to forward messages. If a new node is added to one of the networks, the routing tables in all bridges must be updated or the new node will not be able to receive inter-LAN messages.

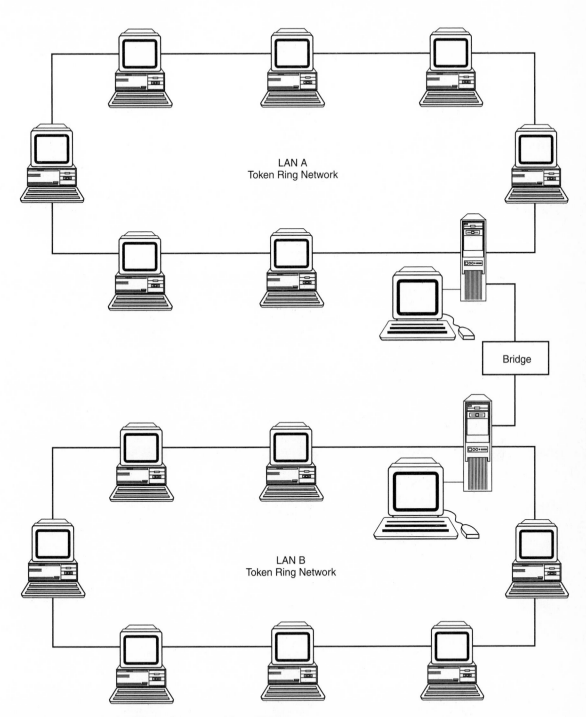

Figure 16.3   Token Rings Connected by a Bridge

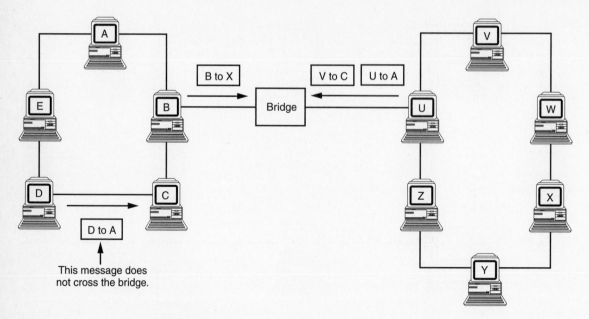

Figure 16.4 Bridge Packet Forwarding

Most bridges being sold today are called **learning bridges,** or **transparent bridges.** A learning bridge builds its routing table from messages it receives and does not need to be loaded with a predefined routing table. Essentially the network administrator just connects the bridge and the bridge is immediately operational. To understand how bridges

Table 16.2   Basic Bridge Functions

Packet Routing Function	1. Accept packet from LAN A.
	2. Examine address of packet.
	3. If packet address is a LAN A address, allow the packet to continue on LAN A.
	4. If packet address is a LAN B address, transmit the packet onto the LAN B medium.
	5. Do the equivalent for LAN B packets.
Additional Functions	Media conversion
	Learning
	Remote connection
	Signal conversion
	Speed conversion
	Packet statistics
	Token ring to Ethernet conversion

of this type work, let us take another look at the bridge configuration Figure 16.5: four LANs (A, B, C, and D), four bridges (B1, B2, B3, and B4), and five nodes (N1, N2, N3, N4, and N5). Each bridge has two ports labeled P1 and P2. Some bridges may have more than two ports; bridge B2 has a third port, P3. This configuration has at least two paths between each LAN. For example, LAN A can get to LAN D via bridges B1 and B3 or directly via bridge B2; LAN D can get to LAN C directly through either bridge B4 or B2 or indirectly through bridges B3, B1, and B2.

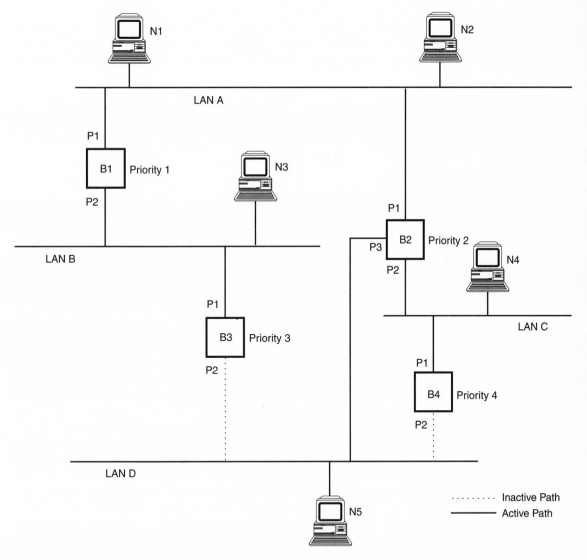

Figure 16.5   LAN Bridge Routing with Active and Inactive Paths

Table 16.3   Bridge B1's Network Routing Table

Node	Port	Comments
N1	P1	
N2	P1	
N3	P2	
N4	P1	Bridge B2 Routes
N5	P1	Bridge B2 Routes

We start by explaining how a bridge works in a simple, generic sense. Let us assume that each bridge has a fully developed routing table, like that shown for bridge B1 in Table 16.3. Note also that each node has only one route. If a route changes for some reason, the bridge updates its routing table to show the new route. Some networks use routing algorithms that allow multiple active paths between two nodes, but this is not typical of bridges.

Looking again at Figure 16.5, suppose that bridge B1 receives a packet from N1 destined for N2. Recall that each MAC packet contains the address of the sender and recipient. Because the bridge is aware of the data link protocol, it finds the source and destination addresses in the packet. The bridge examines its routing table for the destination address. In this case the destination address is local because both the source and destination addresses are on LAN A. Thus the bridge essentially does nothing. In a token-passing LAN the bridge may need to forward the packet to the next node on the LAN on which the message was received. In a CSMA/CD LAN the bridge does nothing because packets are broadcast to all nodes simultaneously.

Now suppose that bridge B1 receives a packet on port P2 from LAN B with a source address of N3 and a destination address of N2 (on LAN A). The bridge again consults its routing table for the destination address and finds it to be a nonlocal node. The routing table shows the outbound port on which to send the packet (P1 in this instance). The bridge simply takes the packet as received and transmits through port P1 onto LAN A (if the LANs have different MAC protocols, the bridge reformats the packet to make it compatible with the receiving MAC protocol). Similarly, if bridge B3 receives a packet from node N5 with a destination of N2, it consults its routing table, finds that the path to N2 is port P1, and transmits the packet to LAN B. Bridge B1 on LAN B receives this packet, consults its routing table, and forwards the packet to LAN A through port P1. At this point you may be wondering why bridge B4 did not also transmit the packet onto LAN C or why bridge B2 did not also transmit it and cause a duplicate packet. The answer lies in how bridges operate and learn. Two algorithms, spanning tree and source routing, are used.

The Spanning Tree Algorithm

Spanning tree algorithms, in which bridges exchange routing information with each other, can be used on any type of LAN. The spanning tree algorithm has been evaluated by the IEEE 802.1 Media Access Control Bridge Standards Committee. The committee selected the spanning tree algorithm as the standard for all IEEE 802 LAN standards.

In developing the algorithm for spanning trees let us first look at a simple case. You may wish to refer back to Figure 16.5 during this discussion. Recall that each LAN packet contains the source address and the destination address. If bridge B1 receives a packet on port P1, the bridge assumes that the source address is a node local to LAN A. Because a bridge receives all network traffic on a LAN to which the bridge is connected (bridge B1 gets all message traffic on LANs A and B), a bridge soon learns all of the local node addresses from the source addresses in these messages. If a source address is not found in the bridge's routing table, the address is added to the table.

Suppose node N3 in Figure 16.5 sends a message to node N2. If the destination address N2 is already in B1's routing table, the bridge forwards the packet accordingly. If the destination address is not already in the bridge's routing table, the bridge needs to locate the address. It does this by sending the packet out on all ports other than the one on which it was received, which is called **flooding** (the packet is also sent to all nodes on the LAN on which it was received). In this instance, the packet is transmitted on port P1.

Flooding ensures that a packet arrives at its destination by sending it along all possible paths. The bridge eventually receives either an acknowledgment that the packet was received or a message from the receiving station. The acknowledgment contains the address of the original recipient, N2 in this case. From this acknowledgment, the bridge can determine the direction in which the node lies, and it adds this information to its routing table.

Sometimes a path may become unavailable, or new bridges or paths may become operational, which may cause routing information to change. To keep routing as efficient as possible, each bridge sends status messages periodically to let other bridges know of its current state. Also, status messages are sent immediately if the topology changes.

Now we consider a more complex situation, in which multiple bridges are connected to the same network and there may be multiple paths between LANs and perhaps multiple ports per bridge, as illustrated in Figure 16.5. If node N5 sends a message to node N2, is the packet sent via bridge B2 or via bridges B3 and B1, or even via bridge B4 and then bridge B2? To reconcile such decisions, each bridge is given a priority. If two or more bridges are available, the bridge with the highest priority is chosen. If the path along that route is disrupted, the path can change and the highest priority alternative path is activated. We consider in more detail how this occurs.

A bridge has at least two ports. An active port accepts packets from the LAN end of the port, and an inactive port blocks or does not accept packets from the LAN end of the port. An inactive port still can be used to transmit packets. However, these packets must originate from the bridge end of the port. Each bridge is assigned a priority by the administrator.

The bridge with the highest priority is designated as the root bridge. Each bridge has an active port in the direction of the root bridge. Other ports are active or inactive depending on the priority of the bridge and the configuration. Figure 16.5 also shows the priority of each bridge (with 1 representing the highest priority) and the active and inactive paths. A port is active if its path is active; otherwise it is inactive. All bridges have their port in the direction of the root bridge active. Therefore, packets from the root direction can be forwarded and received. For all other cases, the active port from a LAN is toward the bridge with the highest priority. Ports on the root bridge are always active. Thus, in Figure 16.5, LANs A and B choose bridge B1's ports as the active ports. LAN C is connected to two bridges, B2 and B4. B2 is chosen because it has the higher priority, and B2's port P2 is active. B4's port P1 is also active because P1 is in the direction of the root bridge. LAN D is connected to three bridges, B2, B3, and B4. Because B2 has the highest priority, it is chosen as the active bridge. Ports P2 on bridges B3 and B4 are inactive and do not accept packets from LAN D.

The advantages of the spanning tree algorithm are that it is MAC-layer–independent, bridges can learn the topology of the network without manual intervention, and paths can change if an existing path becomes inoperable or if a better path is introduced. The algorithm overhead is the size of the routing table for networks with many communicating nodes, and the extra network traffic resulting from status messages and flooding.

Source Routing

In practice, spanning tree algorithms have been more commonly used for CSMA/CD LANs, and source routing is more common for token-passing LANs. Source routing is an IEEE standard used as a routing algorithm for token-passing networks.

Source routing relies on the sending station to designate the path for a packet. In Figure 16.5, suppose node N5 wants to send a packet to node N2. If N2 is in N5's routing table, the packet is sent along that route; otherwise, N5 must "discover" the best route to N2. N5 does this by sending a **discovery packet** on all routes available. In this case, the discovery packet is sent on port P2 of bridge B4, port P3 of bridge B2, and port P2 of bridge B3. Each bridge, in turn, transmits the packet on each port except the one on which the packet was received. Moreover, each bridge appends its information to the packet. Thus, node N2 receives several packets, each containing the identity of each bridge through which the packet traveled. All of these packets are returned to node N5. N5 selects the path from all the alternatives returned. In our example, node N5 will probably receive four discovery packets with paths B4–B2, B2, B3–B1, and B4–B2–B3–B1. Upon receiving the four responses from its discovery packets, node N5 chooses one. B2 would probably be the best route because there is only one bridge through which the message must pass. Realize, however, that path B3–B1 might be faster if B2's connections on ports P1 or P3 are slower than the connections for bridges B3 and B1.

After N5 discovers the path to node N2, whenever node N5 needs to transmit to node N2, it appends the selected routing information to its packet. Each bridge along the way investigates this information to determine by which route to send the packet.

You might have already noticed that the algorithm as just explained has one possible fault. The discovery packet sent from bridge B4 reaches bridge B2, and B2 sends the packet out on ports P3 and P1. The packet on port P3 is directed back to LAN D and again reaches bridges B4 and B3. A mechanism must be in place to prevent discovery packets from looping through the network. This is accomplished in one of two ways. First, a maximum number of hops is specified. If the maximum is set to 10, then a packet that has not reached its destination after traversing 10 bridges is discarded. The second way to prevent a loop is to discard a packet that recirculates through the same bridge. For example, one of N5's discovery packets goes from B4 to B2 and then back to B4. When B4 finds that it has already handled that packet, it discards the packet.

The advantage of the source routing algorithm is that bridges are not responsible for maintaining large routing tables for extensive networks. Each node is responsible for maintaining routing information only for the nodes with which it communicates. The disadvantages are the overhead of sending numerous packets during discovery and the extra routing data that must be appended to each message.

Other Bridge Capabilities

In the preceding discussion the relative locations and the media of the interconnected LANs were not described. The LANs might have been geographically separated or confined to a small area. You can also purchase bridges that accommodate media differences. For example, suppose that in Figure 16.6 LAN A uses coaxial cable and LAN B uses twisted-pair wires as the medium. You could select a bridge that has BNC connectors for coaxial cable on one port and RJ-45 connectors for twisted-pair wires on the other port.

You also have bridge options for connecting geographically distributed LANs. A variety of interconnection possibilities exist. The most common of these are listed in Table 16.4. Usually the speed of the connection between remote LANs is much slower

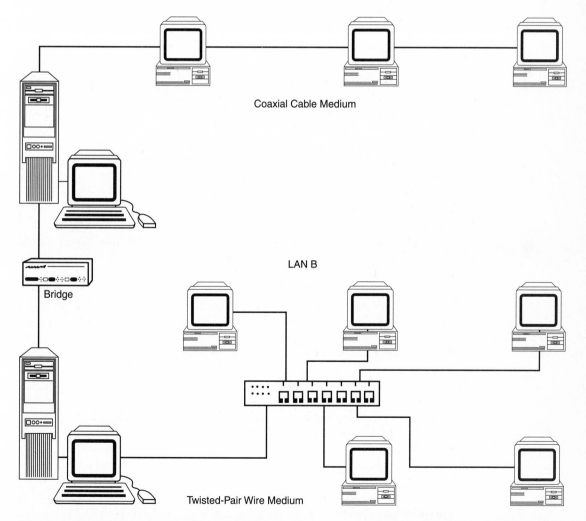

Figure 16.6   Medium Conversion with a Bridge

Table 16.4   Remote Bridge Connection Alternatives

RS-232 serial lines	RS-422 serial lines at 19.2 Kbps to 2 Mbps
Synchronous transmission at 56 Kbps or 64 Kbps	T-1 Line at 1.5 Mbps
Fractional T-1 at multiples of 64 Kbps	X.25 packet-switching network
Integrated services digital network (ISDN)	

than the speed of either LAN. This speed difference can result in the bridge becoming saturated with messages if there are many internetwork packets. Bridges have memory that allows some messages to be buffered. The memory buffer helps reconcile the differences in transmission speed. If too many messages arrive in a short period, the buffer becomes full. Packets that arrive when the buffer is full are lost. Note also that this condition can occur when two local LANs are connected. A bridge must do some minor processing to determine where a packet must be routed. Except for very slow LANs, the processing time can exceed the arrival rate. Thus bridges connecting LANs experiencing high packet arrival rates can also become saturated.

Routers

Routers operate at the network layer of the OSI reference model. The network layer is responsible for packet routing and for collecting accounting information. Some networks use a static routing algorithm, meaning that packet routing between two nodes never changes. In a CSMA/CD bus LAN, a packet is broadcast to every node; in a token ring a packet is transmitted from one node to the next node in the ring. In some networks several routing paths may be available, as illustrated in Figure 16.7. The network layer is responsible for routing an incoming packet for another node onto an appropriate outbound path. Thus a packet that arrives at a node in a network similar to the one shown in Figure 16.7 arrives at the physical layer and moves up to the network layer through the data link layer. If the packet is not for an application on the receiving node, the network layer determines the outbound path for the packet and sends it down to the data link layer, which formats the packet with the proper data link control data (perhaps a different data link protocol than that of the arriving packet). The data link layer then passes the packet down to the physical layer for transmission to the next node on the path to the final destination.

An interconnection interface that operates at the network layer is called a **router.** A router is not sensitive to the details of the data link and physical layers. Thus it can be used to connect different types of networks, such as a token ring LAN to an IEEE 802.3 LAN or a LAN to a WAN. Although the network interconnection is established at the network layer, you must realize that data link and physical layer services are also involved. A router looks at the destination address of a message, determines a route the message should follow to reach that address (possibly passing through two or more networks), and provides the addressing that the network and data link layers along the route require for delivery. For example, a Novell network uses a protocol called **Sequenced Packet Exchange/Internetwork Packet Exchange (SPX/IPX)** to transfer

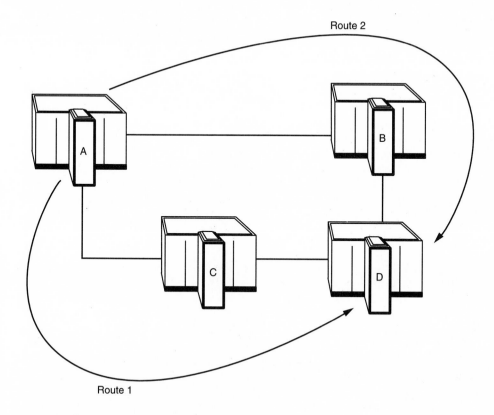

Figure 16.7 Alternative Routes in a Network

packets between nodes. SPX operates at the transport layer and IPX at the network layer. Another protocol used by many networks is the **Transmission Control Protocol/Internet Protocol (TCP/IP).** TCP/IP is the protocol used on the Internet. An SPX/IPX router cannot forward TCP/IP packets, and a router that knows only the TCP/IP protocol cannot forward SPX/IPX packets. For two nodes to exchange data using a router, they must both share a common network protocol. Figure 16.1 shows the relationship between a router and the OSI layers.

A variety of network protocols are used for network interconnection. For example, Novell's native network protocol is SPX/IPX, which can be used to establish the common basis of communication between a Novell token-ring LAN and a Novell CSMA/CD LAN. However, SPX/IPX can not be used as a routing protocol in WANs and in LANs provided by other network vendors if those networks do not support the SPX/IPX protocol. The network administrators must find one network layer protocol supported by at least one node on each network. Several internetwork protocols have been developed, but the most common of these is Transmission Control Protocol/Internet Protocol (TCP/IP). As a result, we use TCP/IP as our router example.

TCP/IP

Transmission Control Protocol/Internet Protocol (TCP/IP) was developed by the Advanced Research Projects Agency of the United States Department of Defense. Originally designed as an internetwork protocol, it has evolved over time into a suite of protocols addressing a variety of network communication needs, one of which is that of a router. Note that TCP/IP is not just a microcomputer protocol. On the contrary, it was developed on large systems and was later transported to microcomputers. Because TCP/IP runs on such a wide variety of platforms, it is an ideal choice for a routing protocol. Other functions provided by the TCP/IP protocol suite include file transfer, electronic mail, logons to remote nodes, and network management protocols. It has become the current networking standard architecture.

Using TCP/IP's routing capabilities, users can be on the same network or different networks, they can be on networks that are directly connected to each other by a bridge or router, or they can be on networks with one or more intermediate networks. Figure 16.8 illustrates how networks might be connected using TCP/IP. In the figure, workstations that function as routing nodes are denoted by Rn and nonrouting nodes by WSn. Internetwork connections are made through specific network nodes, so node R1 on network A has a physical connection to node R2 on network B, and node R3 on network A has a physical connection to node R4 on network C. These networks can be either LANs or WANs, and routing nodes that communicate directly with each other must share a common data link protocol and a physical link. That is, we speak of routers operating at the network level, but for messages to pass from one node to another, they must pass through the data link and physical layers of each computer. The key is that the information needed to determine how to forward the message is understood by the network layer's logic. For example, in Figure 16.8 let us momentarily assume that network A is a CSMA/CD LAN, network B is a token-ring LAN, and network C is a WAN. Nodes R1 and R2 must share a common data link protocol and medium, and nodes R3 and R4 must share a common data link protocol and medium. A key concept surrounding routers is that they are independent of the data link protocols used between any two nodes.

As the abbreviation implies, TCP/IP consists of two distinct protocols, the transmission control protocol and the internet protocol. The TCP operates at the transport layer, and the IP operates at the network layer. Let us look at the functions of each protocol.

The IP provides a connectionless datagram service. In a connection-oriented transmission, a virtual circuit is established for the session and packets are all sent over that circuit. When you telephone someone, a circuit is established and your calling session uses that circuit until you are done and then the circuit is torn down and the facilities used to form the circuit are available to other subscribers. In a connectionless transmission service, no virtual circuit is established; instead, the delivery mechanism (the IP in this example) makes a "best effort" attempt to deliver the message. It is possible that a packet will be lost during transmission. Detecting this loss and initiating recovery is not the responsibility of the IP.

The TCP is the protocol responsible for guaranteeing end-to-end message delivery. Thus, if a packet is lost during transmission, the TCP, not the IP, is responsible for

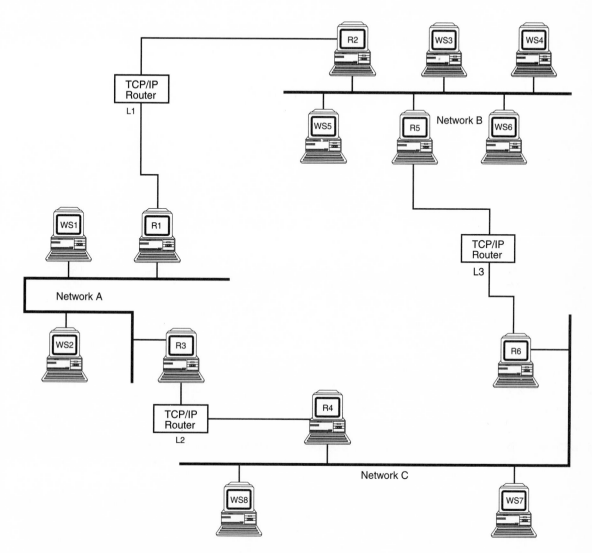

Figure 16.8   LANs Connected with TCP/IP Routers

resending the message. The TCP also guarantees that individual packets arrive in the correct order. Thus, the primary functions of the TCP are to provide message integrity, provide acknowledgments that a complete message has been received by a destination node, and regulate the flow of messages between the source and destination nodes. In addition, the TCP may divide the message into smaller transmission segments. Usually these segments correspond to an IP transmission packet.

Let us now look at how the TCP and IP cooperate in sending a message from one node to another. The following example serves as a model for the functions of a generic router. Suppose that in Figure 16.8 node WS1 on network A needs to send a message to node WS5 on network B. The procedure followed by the TCP/IP protocol in carrying out this transmission is as follows:

1. The TCP in node WS1 receives a message from an application. The TCP attaches a header to the message and passes it down to the IP in node WS1. The message header contains the destination address and error-detection fields, such as a cyclic redundancy check (CRC) and a message sequence number. These are used to ensure that the message is received without errors and that messages are received in the proper sequence or can be reordered into the proper sequence.

2. Node WS1's IP determines whether the destination is an internetwork address. If the address is on the local network, such as node WS2, then the IP passes the message to the local network routing facility, which transports the message to the proper node. If the destination is a node on another network, the IP finds the best path to the destination and forwards the message to the next IP node along that path. In this case the IP in node WS1 sends the message to node R1.

3. The IP at node R1 receives the message, examines the address, and determines the address of the next node, R2 in this example. The IP breaks the message up into packets of the appropriate size, adds a header to each packet, and passes it down to the data link layer. The data link layer appends its transmission information and transmits the packets over the link between R1 and R2.

4. The data link layer at R2 receives a packet, strips off the data link layer control data, and passes the message to R2's IP. If the destination is local to that IP's network, as it is in this instance, the IP delivers it to the local network routing facility for delivery. If the destination is on another network, the IP determines the next node along the path and sends the message to it. For example, if the node address were WS7, the packet would be routed to node R5 and then to node R6. Ultimately the message arrives at the destination node.

5. When the message arrives at the final destination node (through the services of the IP and local network routing facilities) it is passed up to the TCP. The TCP decodes the header attached by the sender's TCP. The receiving TCP checks for errors, such as message sequence or CRC errors. If no errors are detected, the TCP determines the destination program and sends the message to it.

On the path from source to destination, the message passes through several IP nodes and traverses links with several different data link protocols. The routing protocol, TCP/IP in this example, is responsible for generating the destination address and intermediate addresses along the way and for ensuring the correct delivery of the message.

From the preceding discussion you should realize that a LAN node that must communicate with a node on another network must run both the TCP and IP software. Most of today's LAN operating system vendors have this available in DOS, Windows, OS/2, and UNIX versions. This software and associated utilities are also available from independent software vendors. Moreover, a variety of TCP/IP utilities can be found in the public domain and are thus available at little or no cost.

Gateways

The interface between two dissimilar networks is called a **gateway.** A gateway is basically a protocol converter. It reconciles the differences between the networks it connects. With repeaters, bridges, and routers, the communicating nodes share a common protocol at the physical, data link, or network layer, respectively. Suppose that it is necessary to connect two nodes that do not share a common protocol. In this instance a gateway or protocol converter can make the interconnection. Naturally the gateway must be able to understand the protocol of the two nodes being connected and also be able to translate from one protocol to the other. The components of a gateway are the network interfaces and the logic that carries out the conversion necessary when moving messages between networks. The conversion must change the header and trailer of the packet to make it consistent with the protocol of the network or data link to which the message is being transferred. This may include accommodating differences in speed, packet sizes, packet formats, and so on. For example, suppose that both a LAN and a WAN can interface to an X.25 network. The X.25 network can then serve as an intermediary and allow the stations on the LAN and WAN to communicate. This type of network has two gateways, one from the LAN to the X.25 network and one from the X.25 network to the WAN, as illustrated in Figure 16.9.

Choosing the Right Interface

We have defined three network interconnections: repeaters, bridges, and routers. How do you choose the right one? In general, you should choose the connection at the lowest OSI level possible. Thus, a repeater is usually preferable to a bridge, and a bridge is usually preferable to a router. As you move up the OSI layers, your connection must be more intelligent, do more work, and have a lower packet exchange rate. These are not the only deciding factors, however.

A bridge can replace a repeater, and a router can replace a repeater or a bridge; however, the opposite is not always true. A repeater cannot always substitute for a bridge and a bridge cannot always substitute for a router. If you have the option of using a repeater, you might instead choose to use a bridge. This decision makes sense if the bridge can handle the message traffic and if you already have the bridge components. A bridge also allows some LAN isolation capability that a repeater does not provide. Thus, you might choose a bridge over a repeater to provide an extra level of network security.

SWITCHES AND VIRTUAL LANS

One general trend of LANs has been ever-increasing speeds. The higher speeds are a consequence of placing more users on a single LAN, adding bandwidth-hungry applications such as audio and video, and integrating LANs with other LANs, WANs, and the Internet. LANs falling into these categories have the potential of becoming

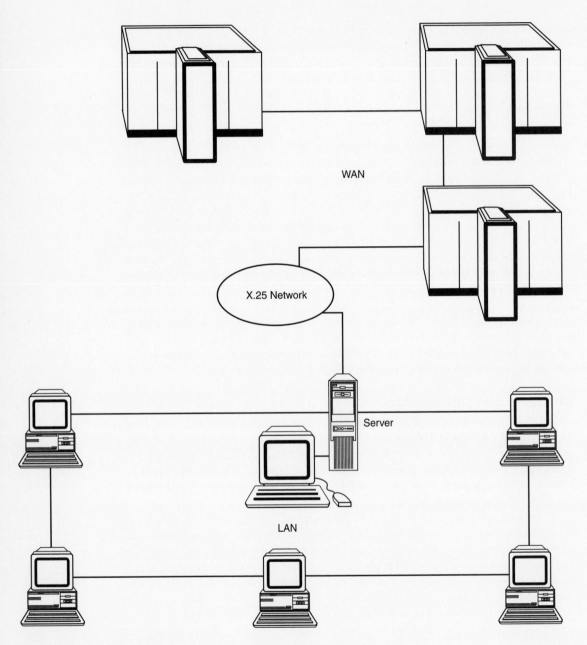

Figure 16.9   LAN–WAN Interconnection Using an X.25 Network

congested. Two solutions to this problem are increased speeds and LAN segmentation. However, the baseband characteristics of most LANs mean that only two stations can communicate with each other at any given point. An additional solution to the speed and congestion problem exists: LAN switches.

LAN switches work similarly to the way in which a telephone switch works. In the idle state you are not connected to anything except the telephone switch and cannot communicate with anyone until a circuit is set up. When you dial someone's number, the complete transmission capacity of the telephone network is not dedicated to your call; instead, a connection is made between your telephone and the telephone of the person you are calling and a single circuit is used, leaving other circuits available to other subscribers. This type of technology is also being used to increase the capacity of Ethernet and token-ring LANs. A switch is illustrated in Figure 16.10. Let us now look at how switches operate and how they can help solve some medium congestion problems.

LAN switches, also called **switching hubs,** look much like standard wiring hubs. For simplicity, we use a CSMA/CD switching hub in our example. A standard wiring hub sends each frame it receives to all other ports on the hub. Only one network node can transmit at one time. With a switching hub nodes are connected to the hub in the same manner as with a standard hub. No additional hardware is required for the node-to-switch interface and the node itself does not know the type of the hub (switching or standard) to which it is connected. Suppose a node attached to a switching hub transmits a packet. The switching hub examines the data link header of the packet and obtains the destination address. The switch then establishes a dedicated connection

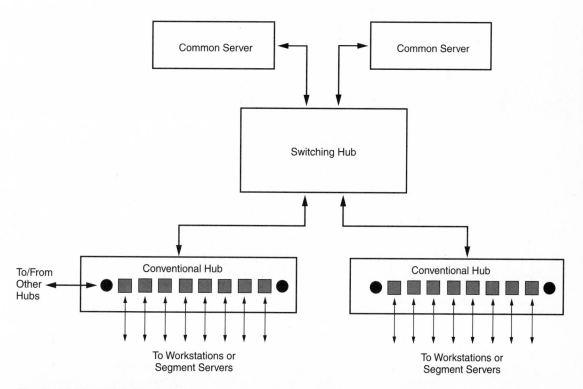

Figure 16.10   A LAN Switch

between the sender's port and the recipient's port and the two communicate. In the meantime, similar sessions can occur between other nodes attached to other ports.

The difference between an 8-port standard hub and an 8-port switching hub, both operating at 10 Mbps, is that only one 10-Mbps transmission can occur on the standard hub, but up to four 10-Mbps connections can occur simultaneously on the switching hub. A few words of caution are in order here. In a dedicated server LAN with only one server, all communication is between clients and the server. A switching hub may not provide any benefit in this instance. Furthermore, although theoretically four connections are possible on the 8-port switching hub, the likelihood of using all four connections is low. Realize also that switches are used on much larger LANs than we used in this simple example. In general, switches operate in the following way:

The frame enters switch.

The switch looks up the destination address in a table.

The switch sends the frame to the addressee's port.

Multiple simultaneous cross-connections are possible.

An n-port hub can support $n/2$ simultaneous connections.

The aggregate data rate of an n-port switch is $n/2 \times X$, where X is the port speed.

Collisions are avoided.

Although all switches operate in the same general way, there are two distinct architectures in use: **cut-through switches,** also known as cross-point switches, and **store-and-forward switches.** Cut-through switches can be faster than store-and-forward switches because they do not need to await the arrival of a complete packet before beginning packet forwarding. Cut-through switches wait only long enough to read destination address from the data link header and then begin forwarding the packet. This results in lowering the time the switch is occupied with the packet. The disadvantage to this is the switch does not do error checking; it sends packets as quickly as possible and the switch may forward bad packets. Furthermore, cut-through switches are best for small packets; the larger the packet size, the less the throughput increase over store-and-forward switches.

Store-and-forward switches are essentially high-speed bridges. The switch maintains an address table for each port. A store-and-forward switch collects and stores an entire packet before beginning the forwarding operation. Store-and-forward switches have a higher delay before beginning to forward packets than cut-through switches; however, before forwarding a packet a store-and-forward switch checks the CRC error code and forwards only error-free packets.

Switches may perform port-based switching or segment-based switching. With port-based switching only one address per port is allowed. These switches are cheaper and provide faster address lookups than segment-based switches. Segment-based switches allow multiple addresses per port and hence can be used to segment the

LAN. Address lookups are slower than for port-based switching and segment-based switches are more expensive, but they also can provide more flexibility. The overall cost per node of segment switches may be less because multiple nodes can be associated with one port. Each segment-based switch has a maximum number of addresses it can accommodate and there is also a maximum number of addresses per port. For example, one 24-port switch allows 8192 addresses in total and a maximum of 1024 addresses per port.

Some switches provide a combination of high- and low-speed ports, say some 10-Mbps ports and some 100-Mbps ports. Another possible switch feature is a limited degree of fault tolerance provided by backup power supplies and hot-swappable modules. With hot-swappable modules, failed switch modules can be replaced while the switch is operating. Switches have another benefit: the ability to create virtual LANs.

The benefits of switching hubs can be significant. Some benefits of switching hubs are given in Table 16.5.

Virtual LANs

In the LANs we have been discussing thus far, the LAN is defined by the attachment of nodes to the medium. Switches offer another capability: the ability to define LANs based on switch addresses. Such LANs are called **virtual LANs.** A virtual LAN is illustrated in Figure 16.11. Note that nodes are collected together based on addresses to form a virtual LAN rather than by how they are connected.

The benefit of virtual LANs is the ability to collect existing computers into a virtual LAN and to move workstations about while maintaining their virtual LAN connection. Because LANs are identified by addresses or switch ports and not by physical connections, LAN nodes can be moved from one location to another and remain on the same virtual LAN without having to change connections at the wiring hubs. If one user changes to another workgroup, the change from one virtual LAN to another is done by changing virtual LAN switch addresses, not by cable changes. At present there are no standards covering virtual LAN implementations but if the technology spreads standards will be developed. Thus, today's implementations are vendor specific and lack of interoperability of different vendor switches in support of virtual LANs is a potential problem. Some vendors use ports to determine what constitutes LAN segments. In this

Table 16.5   Some Benefits of Switching Hubs

Efficient network segmentation to balance traffic.

Good price/performance.

Availability of shared and dedicated bandwidth.

Support of new technologies such as asynchronous transfer mode and other network protocols.

Preservation of investment in cabling and LAN adapters.

Devices can communicate at NIC speeds as long as necessary.

Provide bridging and routing as well as integration with faster technologies, such as FDDI, 100 Mbps Ethernet.

Multiple connections can be established concurrently.

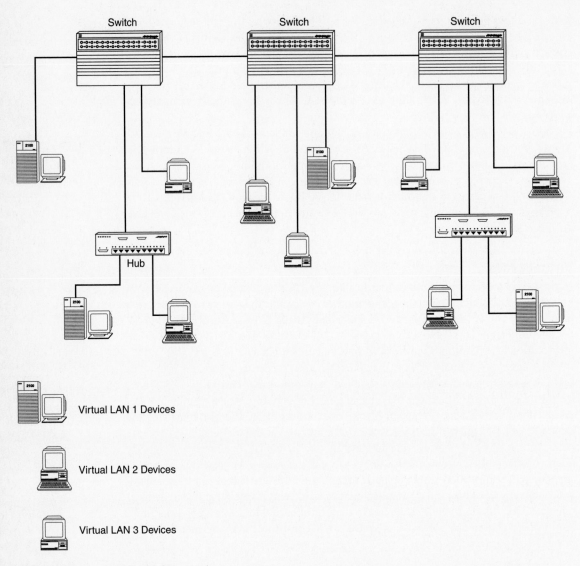

Figure 16.11 A Virtual LAN

implementation, multiple ports may be collected to form a virtual LAN; all nodes attached to the same port must be on the same virtual LAN. Other vendors use packet tagging to identify member nodes of a virtual LAN. Each packet has a vendor-specified tag attached. Tags are unique to nodes and are used to determine the virtual network to which a node is attached. A third approach uses the MAC addresses of nodes to segment the nodes into virtual LANs. As you probably noted, these three techniques will not work together and the packet tagging of one vendor will probably not be compatible with the packet tagging of another.

Asynchronous Transfer Mode

Asynchronous Transfer Mode (ATM) is a high-speed switching technology used to provide services for LAN and WANs alike. It is commonly used to supply backbone network capabilities and to provide high-bandwidth communication between nodes for transmission of full-motion video with voice and computer-aided design applications. ATM was developed as part of the broadband ISDN specifications. Originally, ATM speeds were set at 155 and 622 Mbps but other speeds such as 25 and 45 Mbps are available and very-high-speed switches allow transmissions faster than 1 Gbps.

ATM uses high-speed digital switches, fiber optic cables, and full duplex transmission to attain its high throughput. ATM networks transmit small, fixed-size frames called cells (as opposed to the term *packets* used in X.25, frame relay, and other protocols). A cell is 53 bytes long and usually carries 47 or 48 bytes of data; the remaining 5 or 6 bytes is called the header. The header is used to provide flow control, cell type identification, addressing, and error checking. In setting up ATM on a LAN, additional equipment, such as switches, cabling, and channel service unit/data service unit (CSU/DSU), must be deployed. As of this writing, LAN adapters do not connect to ATM switches, but that is likely to change. Thus a company's investment in ATM technology is more extensive than the investment in switching hubs.

ATM specifies four protocols (originally there were five), each of which is oriented to a specific class of service. These protocols are called adaptation layers and are designated AAL-1, AAL-2, AAL-3/4, and AAL-5. The adaptation layers are designed to identify and support various classes of services such as a constant bit rate for video and voice (AAL-1), time-sensitive variable bit rates for packetized voice (AAL-2), transmissions where delays can be tolerated but error checking is important (AAL-3/4), and services similar to AAL-3/4 but with a reduced need for error checking. For networks requiring extremely fast transmission, the best options today are ATM and gigabit Ethernet. Figure 16.12 illustrates one LAN implementation of ATM.

LAN-TO-HOST CONNECTIONS

The preceding discussion explored ways of connecting networks together—specifically, ways in which a LAN can be connected to another LAN or to a WAN and ways of connecting nodes to each other via switches. For some companies there is another LAN connection need, that of connecting a LAN to a stand-alone computer.

Many companies entered the microcomputer age with a large computer already installed. As these companies grew in their use of microcomputers and then installed one or more LANs, the large computer continued to play an important role in their computing needs. For example, a large computer, which we will call a host, might be used for payroll or existing database applications. Even companies that replaced or are replacing the host with LAN technology go through a period when both computing environments exist. Companies that use hosts and LANs usually need to exchange data between the two environments. This can be done via media exchange. For example, data on the host can be copied onto a diskette or tape and transferred to the LAN and vice versa. Often a LAN–host direct connection is a more efficient way to do this. Figure 16.13 illustrates a host computer connected to a LAN.

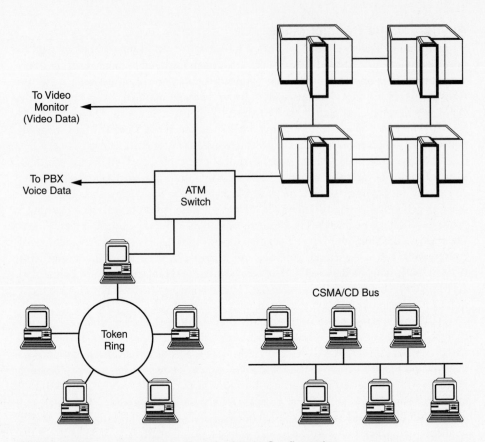

Figure 16.12   Asynchronous Transfer Mode Configuration

Before discussing the ways in which the LAN–host connection can be made, let us look at several ways in which a LAN user can interact with a host. In Figure 16.13 a user at node N1 might need to view, update, or evaluate data that is stored in the host's database. This user has three basic options: Do the work on the host, do the work on LAN workstation, or a combination of both. A user at node N2 might need to send an e-mail message to a user at terminal T1. A user at node N3 might need to run an application that exists only on the host. The application may be available only on the host for a variety of reasons: It has not yet been implemented on the LAN, it needs special hardware available only on the host (such as a typesetting machine), it requires computing power beyond that which is available on the LAN, and so on.

The three preceding examples cover most of the general connection needs of LAN users. These needs can be summarized as follows:

using host data

using host applications

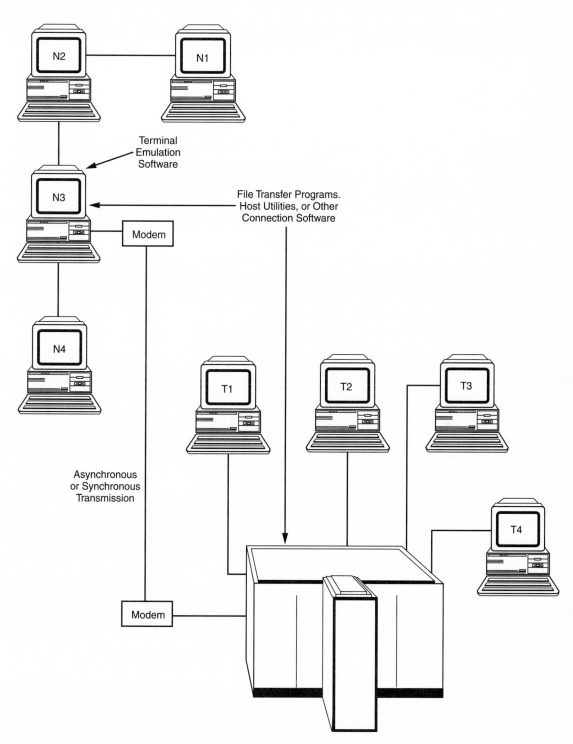

Figure 16.13 LAN-to-Host Connection

transferring data from the host to the LAN

transferring data from the LAN to the host

using host hardware or software resources

communicating with host users

It is just as likely that a host user will have the same basic needs for LAN resources. You have already read about two ways in which a LAN–host connection can be made, using routers and gateways. Let us now look at some other ways to make these connections.

The Host as a LAN Node

Some hosts have the ability to connect to the LAN as a node. This is the most effective way of establishing the connection. The host can thus operate as a server, providing all the needs listed in the previous section. Unfortunately this is not always an option, so we must look at other capabilities.

Asynchronous Connections

Virtually every computer has the ability to send and receive using an asynchronous data link protocol. You are probably familiar with the serial port on a microcomputer; it is an asynchronous communication port. Because most computers support the asynchronous data link protocol, it is sometimes used to link a microcomputer to a host. Usually a microcomputer attached to a host asynchronously operates in one of two modes: file transfer or terminal emulation. A list of **terminal emulation** software capabilities is given in Table 16.6.

Dedicated Connection per Microcomputer

Host computers can usually accommodate many asynchronous connections. Small minicomputers usually support 32 or more, and large mainframes can accommodate hundreds.

Table 16.6   Common Features of Asynchronous Communications Software

Scripts
Mouse support
File transfers (Compuserve, XModem, YModem, Kermit)
Terminal emulation (ANSI, DEC VT 220, IBM 3101, TTY)
Electronic mail
Phone directory
Capture of data to a disk
Text editor
Password security

One way to connect a LAN node to a host is to provide a **dedicated connection** between a port on the host and each microcomputer needing a host connection.

A dedicated connection provides direct host access, and the microcomputer does not use LAN resources for communicating with the host. The typical connection has the microcomputer appear to the host as though the microcomputer were a host terminal. In addition to the serial port, the microcomputer needs terminal emulation software to establish the connection and carry on a host session. Terminal emulation software is available from many sources and has the ability to emulate a wide variety of terminals. With dedicated connections the LAN administrator and data processing department can easily control which LAN nodes have access to the host. Nodes without a direct connection cannot make a host connection.

A dedicated connection has several disadvantages. First, as with all asynchronous connections, the speed of the link is slow. Asynchronous speeds can be over 100,000 bps but typically for microcomputer connections they are 33.6 Kbps or less. If many LAN nodes must communicate with the host, many host ports are required. This not only reduces the number of ports available to the host's terminal users but also is somewhat costly. The cost of host ports can be significant and having a large number of ports is burdensome for microcomputers that need only occasional access.

Multiplexing

A **multiplexer** is a hardware device that allows several devices to share one communication channel. Multiplexing is typically used to consolidate the message traffic between a computer and several remotely located terminals, as illustrated in Figure 16.14. This technique can also be used to allow several microcomputers to share a communication link to a host processor.

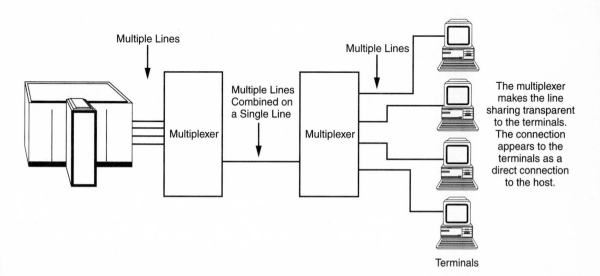

Figure 16.14   A Multiplexer

Shared Asynchronous Connections

In some applications each LAN node needs occasional access to the host, but the number of concurrent connections is far fewer than the number of LAN nodes. In such situations a dedicated line per node is excessive. A better solution is to share asynchronous connections. The most common way to share connections is via a **communications server,** as illustrated in Figure 16.15.

In the figure the communications server has four connections to the host. A microcomputer needing host services requests a connection through the communications server. If all four ports are in use, the request is denied. If a host port is free, the request is honored and the microcomputer is connected to a vacant host port. You might note that the communications server functions much like a telephone switch.

Communications servers also provide connections for remote hosts. The usual way a connection is made to a remote host is via a modem connection. The line to the remote host may be dedicated or switched. A dedicated line is continuously available; a switched line connection is established on an as-needed basis. The typical example of a switched line is a dial-up telephone line. The link between two devices is made via a telephone call, remains active during the length of the session, and is broken when the session is completed. Rather than providing each LAN node with a dedicated modem,

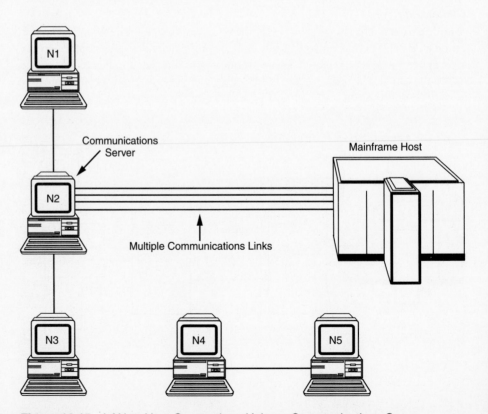

Figure 16.15   LAN-to-Host Connections Using a Communications Server

the communications server can provide **modem sharing.** The technique for doing this is much like the sharing technique described in the previous paragraph.

Other Types of Host Connections

Asynchronous connections are common because they are easily implemented and are supported by most host systems. The only host-specific characteristic is the type of terminal being emulated or file transfer software. Other vendor-specific connections exist.

IBM System Connections

Because of the dominant role played by IBM systems, many network connections are based on IBM software and hardware technologies. These connections might also work on non-IBM equipment because many manufacturers of large computers support one or more IBM communication protocols. Two of the most common IBM interfaces are described here.

IBM-3270 Emulation

One of the mainstays of IBM's communication networks is the family of 3270 terminals. The family consists of a variety of terminals, printers, and cluster controllers. The communication protocol used for 3270 devices is a synchronous protocol, either the Binary Synchronous (BISYNC) Protocol or the Synchronous Data Link Control (SDLC) protocol (discussed in Chapter 15).

IBM-3270 emulation can be effected through a communications server or through individual LAN nodes. When implemented at individual LAN nodes, a synchronous communication controller must be installed in the microcomputer. The controller provides the necessary line interface. If a communications server is used, the server must have a synchronous communication port. Aside from the protocol interface, the connection works much like the asynchronous connection described earlier.

LU 6.2 Connection

For many years IBM networks have been designed around IBM's Systems Network Architecture (SNA), which is discussed in Chapter 15. In SNA users communicate through sessions, and a variety of session types are defined. Logical units (LUs) represent users in establishing, using, and ending a session. One type of session allows programs to communicate with other programs. This type of session is called an LU 6.2 session. Support for LU 6.2 sessions is available for microcomputers and is being increasingly used to establish host connections. The advantage of an LU 6.2 interface is that a microcomputer application can communicate directly with a host application or with an application on another network node (as opposed to the microcomputer simply acting as though it were a terminal).

INTERCONNECTION UTILITIES

Having the ability to establish network connections is one part of communicating among networks. Another part is having utilities that help you exploit those connections. Many such utilities are available. Some are commercial products, and others are available in the public domain for little or no cost. Some utilities you may find useful are briefly described here.

File Transfer Utilities

File transfer utilities allow you to move files between network nodes. File transfer capabilities are an intrinsic part of many routers; part of the TCP/IP protocol suite is a file transfer capability. Kermit is another file transfer utility that runs on a wide variety of computer platforms. It uses asynchronous communication links to transfer ASCII format files. Three common microcomputer file transfer utilities are XMODEM, YMODEM, and ZMODEM. Kermit, XMODEM, YMODEM, and ZMODEM are often included in terminal emulation programs.

Remote Logon

Remote logon utilities allow users to log onto a remote system. A remote logon essentially establishes a remote user as a local user on the **remote node.** Once a user has successfully logged onto the remote node, commands issued by that user are processed and acted on by the remote node rather than by the local node. When the user logs off the remote node, the session is reestablished on the local node.

Remote Control

In Chapter 14 we describe **remote control** utilities as a diagnostic tool. We mention them here because some remote control packages also provide connection services, allowing users to transfer data between nodes.

REMOTE ACCESS

Remote access is a capability common to many of today's LANs. Through remote connections, LAN administrators can resolve problems from their home or other work locations, users can perform some of their work at home and telecommute, and travelers can conduct work while away from the office. Often the connection to the LAN is via switched telephone connections but connections might also be via ISDN connections, frame relay, the Internet, or leased T-1 lines. Two types of remote access are possible: remote node and remote control.

Table 16.7   Remote Control Program Features

DOS and Windows support	Scripts for repetitive tasks	Security
Support for different monitors	Clipboard capabilities	Compression
File transfer	File management (delete, copy)	Password encryption
Host PC reboot	Access restrictions by drive, directory, file	Printing at either end
Host ability to view remote screen	Sending graphics changes only	

Table 16.8   Remote Node Features

Sanity check feature to avoid huge downloads	Statistics	Management
Call-back option	Fault tolerance	Automatic reconnection after lost connection
User name / password different from network	Permanent download of executable files	Disconnection if inactive for defined period
Automatic session resumption after reconnection	Limits on user connect time	Dial-out

Remote control uses the same software that is used for remote diagnostics. Remote control allows for telecommuting, remote support and diagnostics, file transfer where the size of the file being transferred is small (because of low link speeds), and remote network administration. Remote control requires a computer at both ends of the connection and remote control software to manage the connection. The remote node dials into a modem to which the LAN node is attached; we call the LAN node the local node. Once the connection is made, the local node does all the processing and the remote node receives the monitor display and sends keyboard commands. Files can be transferred, but the communication speed of telephone connections is usually 33.6 Kbps or lower and large file transfers are time-consuming. A variety of remote control software packages are available. Some of the features you might expect in these packages are given in Table 16.7.

With remote node technology for remote access, the remote dials directly into a network communications server rather than to a designated node. The remote session is implemented via software services on the server. The communications server acts as a router and the processing is performed at remote node rather than at a LAN node. This type of connection is generally slower than remote control because more data must be transferred over the communication link. This type of connection is good for e-mail and small file transfers and it is much more efficient if the application software is stored on the remote node. Note that placing applications on the remote node may affect software license costs. Some remote node features are given in Table 16.8.

SUMMARY

LANs are not necessarily isolated islands of computing. Often there is a need to connect several LAN segments: homogenous but separate LANs, heterogeneous LANs, LANs to WANs, or LANs to a host. These connections can be made in many ways.

Repeaters are used to connect segments of a homogenous LAN. The main reason for doing this is to extend the length of the LAN medium. Repeaters operate at the physical level. They simply accept a signal from one segment, amplify or regenerate the signal, and forward it onto the next segment.

Bridges connect homogenous but distinct LANs. A bridge operates at the data link (MAC) level. A bridge receives a packet, looks at its destination address, and, if the address is a node on a LAN other than the one on which the packet was received, transmits the packet onto another LAN. Most of today's bridges are learning bridges. Learning bridges can adapt to changes in network paths.

Routers operate at the network layer and can connect homogenous or heterogeneous networks. A router receives a message, determines the address of the destination, and chooses a route for the message to take. The message may travel through several intermediate networks to reach the destination. Different data link protocols may be used in moving the message from the source to its recipient. Because they operate at the network layer, routers are independent of data link protocols.

Gateway is a name applied to network connections between heterogeneous networks. A gateway must perform translation functions such as packet formatting, speed conversion, and error checking.

LAN switches can be used to help segment LANs and to increase the aggregate speed of a LAN using traditional wiring hubs. A switch forms a connection between two communicating nodes and allows other nodes to also enter into a communication session. Thus, multiple transmissions can be in progress simultaneously. In most conventional LANs only two stations can communicate at any time. Some switches also allow the creation of virtual LANs where the LAN is defined by node or port addresses rather than by physical connections. Asynchronous transfer mode (ATM) switches provide a wide range of speeds and are used in companies where extremely high speeds are necessary and for network interconnections.

Sometimes LAN nodes must be connected to a host machine. Some hosts can connect directly to the LAN and operate as LAN nodes. Asynchronous connections are common and easy to implement but are quite slow. Synchronous connections offer greater speed but usually require additional microcomputer hardware.

Remote access is becoming a common LAN need. Remote access allows users to connect to the LAN from a distance. Two general kinds of remote access are available: remote control and remote node. With remote control, the remote user provides keyboard inputs and receives screen output while the work is done by a computer directly connected to the LAN. File transfers are also allowed. With remote node, the processing is done primarily at the remote node. This usually requires more communication between the remote node and LAN resources. Because the communication speed between the remote node and the LAN is usually low, remote node connections are usually more time-consuming than remote control sessions.

Because of the wide variety of connection services available, you should be able to find ready-made solutions to most of your LAN connection needs.

Key Terms

asynchronous transfer mode (ATM)	flooding
bridge	gateway
brouter	IBM-3270 emulation
communications server	learning bridge
cut-through switch	modem sharing
dedicated connection	multiplexer
discovery packet	multiprotocol bridge
file transfer utility	remote access

remote control
remote logon utility
remote node
repeater
router
routing table
Sequenced Packet
  Exchange/Internetwork Packet
  Exchange (SPX/IPX)

source routing
spanning tree algorithm
store-and-forward switch
switching hub
terminal emulation
Transmission Control Protocol/Internet
  Protocol (TCP/IP)
transparent bridge
virtual LAN

Review Questions

1. Give two reasons why a company might have two LANs in the same general location. Identify the OSI level at which each of the following operates.
   a. bridge
   b. repeater
   c. router
2. What does a repeater do? Under what conditions can a repeater be used?
3. What does a bridge do? Under what conditions can a bridge be used?
4. What does a router do? Under what conditions can a router be used?
5. Compare the capabilities of repeaters, bridges, and routers.
6. Describe how TCP/IP sends a message from a node on one network to a node on another network.
7. Besides providing network interconnections, list three other functions you might find in TCP/IP.
8. What is a gateway?
9. Compare store-and-forward switches and cut-through switches.
10. Compare ATM switches and switching hubs.
11. What is a virtual LAN?
12. How are virtual LANs formed?
13. Describe three distinct LAN-to-host interfaces.
14. What are the advantages and disadvantages of asynchronous LAN-to-host interfaces?
15. Describe two common types of microcomputer interfaces to IBM systems.
16. Describe the two basic ways of setting up remote access. What are the advantages and disadvantages of each?

Problems and Exercises

1. Evaluate the following LAN situations. State whether the LANs can be consolidated with a repeater, a bridge, or a router. Give all possible types of connections. State which connection alternative you would choose, and state why you would choose it.
   a. A token ring and token bus.
   b. Two IEEE 802.3 LANs. One LAN has a total cable span of 1000 m and the other has a total cable span of 2500 m.
   c. Two IEEE 802.3 LANs. Each has a total cable span of 1000 m. Assume that the cable being used meets the IEEE 802.3 standard for maximum segment lengths of 500 m and a maximum distance of 2500 m per LAN.
   d. Three Novell LANs. One LAN is an ARCnet, one is a token ring, and one is a CSMA/CD bus.

2. Suppose your company has two IEEE 802.3 LANs, one in your eastern office and one in your western office (the distance between them is several hundred miles). The company wants to connect these LANs so users can more easily exchange data. The data being exchanged is primarily small messages, such as e-mail messages and small data files. Occasionally a file several megabytes in size must be exchanged, but in these situations, the exchange is not time-critical (for example, it could occur overnight). Devise a way to connect these LANs. Describe the type and speed of the communication channel you would use to make the connection. Explain your decision.

3. Suppose the two LANs described in Problem 2 were different (a token ring and a CSMA/CD bus). Would your decision be different? Explain any differences and the reason for your decision.

4. Suppose the situation in Problem 2 were different in that the large files (2 MB or less) had to be exchanged within 2 minutes or less. Would your solution to the connection be different? Explain any differences and the reason for your decision.

5. Suppose a company has two large computers connected by a synchronous communication line with a speed of 56 Kbps. These computers are geographically separated, one in the eastern office and one in the western office. Each of these locations also has a LAN. The company wants to allow all computer users to communicate (those connected to the LANs as well as those connected to the large computers). Can the connection be made using the existing communication link? Explain your answer.

6. Assuming that the existing communication link described in Problem 5 were used for the long distance connection, answer each of the following.
   a. How can the LANs be connected to the large systems?
   b. Describe the changes a LAN packet undergoes as it moves from a LAN to a large system to the other large system and then to the other LAN. Assume that the LANs are homogeneous.

7. Suppose you need to set up a virtual LAN. Explain the steps you would go through to do so. Describe the hardware you would need and the options your hardware supports. Explain why you chose the hardware.

8. Suppose you need to set up remote access capabilities on your LAN. Describe the hardware and software that must be available at the LAN and remote end and what type of communication services would you use for each of the following:
   a. employees who are traveling
   b. an employee who will work at home a great deal of the time
   c. a remote office housing five workers

Chapter 17

Other LAN Technologies

CHAPTER PREVIEW

In the preceding chapters we concentrated in the technologies that are commonly implemented in today's LANs. But LAN technology, both hardware and software, is one of the most dynamic technologies in the computer industry. Microcomputer LAN technology is about 16 years old, and in that time we have already seen many new technologies emerge and others become obsolete. This trend will continue. In this chapter we look at several technologies that are important but less commonly used and a few that are on the frontiers of today's technology. These technologies fill a critical need in a small percentage of today's LANs and have the potential to be mainstream technologies in the future. Some of the topics covered in this chapter include

nondedicated servers

peer-to-peer LANs

diskless workstations

ISDN

high-speed LANs

multimedia on LANs

Internet connections

mobile computing

NONDEDICATED SERVERS
AND PEER-TO-PEER LANS

Many of today's LANs use client/server technology with dedicated server nodes. This is certainly true of most large LANs. The average number of nodes per microcomputer LAN is 6.3. This implies that there are many LANs with six or fewer nodes. For these small LANs, dedicating an expensive server machine (which will probably be underused) reduces the cost-effectiveness of the network. Two other technologies—nondedicated servers and peer-to-peer LANs—provide users an alternative to dedicated servers.

413

Often on a small LAN the most expensive and powerful computer is used as a dedicated server. The server might be idle much of the time. For example, it is hard to imagine four users in a typical office keeping a dedicated server busy most of the time. A few LAN operating systems allow you to have a **nondedicated server,** which works as both a server and a workstation. Usually, a nondedicated server is the workstation with the most resources. Because a nondedicated server also functions as a workstation, it can be used more effectively.

The advantage of nondedicated servers is more effective use of resources, but there are also some disadvantages. Naturally a nondedicated server must divide its workload between its application work and its server work. Sometimes it might be very busy in both roles. In these instances both classes of users, those using the server as a server and those using the server as a workstation, experience some service degradation. If these conflicts occur too often, the LAN administrator should think of making the server dedicated. Another disadvantage of nondedicated servers is the increased likelihood of server failures. Simply running both applications and server software increases the possibility of failures because the server is doing more and the environment is more complicated. However, the most probable source of nondedicated server failure is the user's application or the user him- or herself. If the application gets locked up, the server may be unable to attend to its server duties. If the user powers the server down or unintentionally formats the server's disk, the server's function also are disrupted.

Taking nondedicated servers one step further leads us to **peer-to-peer** LANs. In a peer-to-peer LAN, any or all nodes can operate as servers. This type of LAN is quite common when the system has few workstations. Artisoft's LANtastic, Microsoft's Windows 95 and NT client OSs, IBM's Warp Connect, and Novell's Personal NetWare are a few examples of peer-to-peer networks.

Personal NetWare runs under the DOS operating system, so it essentially runs as a DOS application and uses the DOS file management system. This is a benefit because you can quickly install the network software on an existing DOS system without reformatting the disk. The disadvantage is that you are limited to the file attributes and the limited multiprocessing of a DOS system. Because DOS has few file attributes, you cannot store important file and directory information such as the owner ID of a file, file-protection attributes such as execute-only, or directory attributes such as create and open (see Chapter 11).

Personal NetWare allows you to designate each node as client only, server only, or both. Thus you can tailor the network to the types of computers and users. A server node does more work and uses more system resources (such as memory) than a client node. Capabilities that Personal NetWare provides include logon security, user account restrictions, message distribution to users, print spooling, disk and directory mapping, and auditing of network activities such as user logons, user logoffs, system file backups, and interfaces to other Novell NetWare systems.

In general, the main benefit of peer-to-peer networks is the low cost per node, usually under $200 for both hardware and software. Some lower-cost, lower-performance networks use the microcomputer's serial or parallel ports for communication. This type of connection can reduce the cost per node to $100 or less. Personal NetWare supports only 25 nodes, but several peer-to-peer LANs support many more nodes. For instance, Artisoft manufactures one of the leading peer-to-peer LANs that allows 300 users per network.

DISKLESS WORKSTATIONS

Diskless workstations have been available for quite some time; however, their use is likely to expand. As the name implies, a diskless workstation has no local disk drives. These nodes boot their operating systems from a server, and all disk reads and writes are to server disks. There are many advantages and a few disadvantages to this approach.

The initial advantage of diskless workstations is cost. The computers do not need disks, so they may cost as much as $300 less. The only component that needs to be added to the configuration is a LAN boot ROM, which allows the system to be booted from a server disk rather than from a local disk. Cost savings also accrue from lower maintenance costs. Because disks are mechanical devices, they are more likely to fail than most electronic components, so a computer without disks should need fewer repairs. Management control is another significant advantage of diskless systems. Because users have no local disks, they cannot introduce viruses, install personal software and files, illegally copy software, and copy sensitive corporate data to a diskette for personal reasons. Moreover data cannot be lost because a user failed to back up work-critical files that resided only on his or her local disk, and the LAN administrator can control the types and versions of software being used on the network.

Diskless workstations also have a few disadvantages. In the absence of a server, the workstation is nearly useless: It cannot boot an operating system without a server, so network attachment is essential to making the computer operational. Moreover, without disks, programs cannot be started without a server. Because users have no local disks for personal or temporary files, the use of the server's disk is increased and may lead to higher server costs. Furthermore, the number of vendors selling diskless systems is somewhat limited, so purchasers do not have as wide a selection from which to choose. Finally, the node cannot be removed to another corporate location and be used as a stand-alone system without disk drives, and if the server fails, the node cannot be used locally until the server is brought back into service.

ISDN

Integrated services digital network (ISDN) is a digital communications service offered by several common carriers. It can be found in most major computer-using countries. ISDN provides high-speed data circuits that can carry a variety of communications data, including voice. ISDN service is just beginning to make its presence known. Extensive availability is planned for the future. ISDN will probably have an impact on LAN implementations. It can serve as the medium for small and large LANs alike. Most of today's ISDN services provide lower-speed links, most commonly 56 Kbps and 1.5 Mbps. This is considerably below the speeds of most current LANs; however, higher-

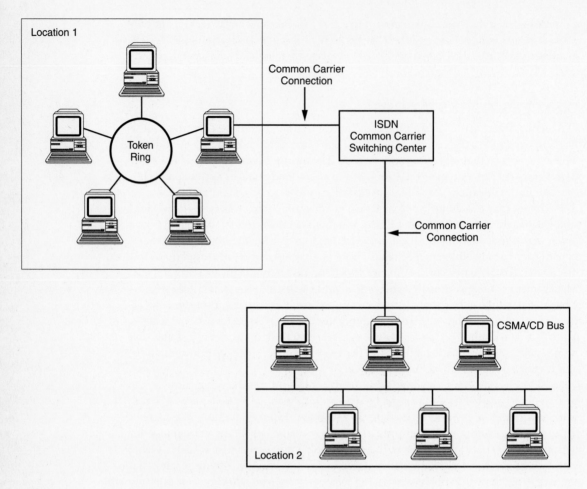

Figure 17.1 LAN Interconnection Using ISDN

speed links are planned for the future. ISDN may become the medium for some LANs and for others a means for LAN interconnection, as illustrated in Figure 17.1.

DIGITAL SUBSCRIBER LINE

Digital subscriber line (DSL) service is a switched digital service that started in the mid-1990s. The service provides very high-speed transmission rates over switched telephone wires. Several DSL alternatives are available, and the service class is some-times generically called xDSL. The x in xDSL stands for the class of service. One such service, asymmetric DSL (ADSL), provides different transmission speeds for up-loading and downloading data. This optimizes performance in connections where the data traffic is heavier in one direction than another. For example, when I access the

Internet, I typically receive many more characters than I send. ADSL is an ideal so-lution for this type of communication. ADSL speeds range from 32 Kbps to 8 Mbps downstream and from 32 Kbps to 1 Mbps upstream. Other classes of DSL services in-clude the following:

Rate adaptive asymmetric (RADSL)

High-bit-rate (HDSL)

Symmetric (SDSL)

Very high-bit-rate (VDSL)

With VDSL, a telephone customer within 1000 feet of the telephone exchange of-fice will eventually be able to attain speeds of 51 Mbps. Because xDSL services provide very high data rates, it is likely that xDSL services will become the high-speed switched communication of choice.

HIGH-SPEED LANS

The first **high-speed local area networks (HSLANs)** were LANs that served a wider ge-ographical area than typical office LANs, up to 200 km (125 mi). LANs that serve a wider area, say 100 mi or more, are called **metropolitan area networks (MANs).** In ad-dition to serving wider geographic areas, MANs also operate at speeds much greater than most of today's office LANs. The MAN speed most common today is 100 Mbps, but even greater speeds can be expected in the not-too-distant future. The most common MAN is the Fiber Distributed Data Interface (FDDI) LAN. FDDI, specified by the American National Standards Institute (ANSI) standard, is a token-ring LAN operating at 100 Mbps on fiber optic cable. Moreover, shielded twisted-pair wires are now being used to provide FDDI-equivalent technology. This variation of FDDI is called the Copper Data Distributed Interface (CDDI) or the Shielded Twisted-Pair Wire Distributed Data Interface (SDDI). This technology is also being implemented on unshielded twisted-pair wires. However, CDDI does not support the long distances of FDDI. The maximum dis-tance between nodes on fiber is 2 km (60 km with high-grade fiber) whereas the maxi-mum distance between nodes for copper is 100 m. The maximum network span for fiber is 200 km, but it is considerably less for CDDI. The actual distance spanned depends on the configuration—either direct connection or wiring hubs—and the number of nodes allowed. The maximum number of nodes for FDDI is 500. FDDI is more expensive than 100-Mbps Ethernet. Consequently, it has lost some of its market niche in office LANs. One of its primary roles is as a backbone network.

The FDDI family of technologies is not the only HSLAN proposal. The IEEE 802 LAN standards committee has also developed specifications, IEEE 802.6, for a MAN. The IEEE 802.6 standard has also been adopted by ANSI. The standard is also called the Distributed Queue Dual Bus (DQDB) standard.

As the name DQDB indicates, the architecture uses two buses. Each bus is unidi-rectional, meaning that data is transmitted in one direction on one bus and in the other

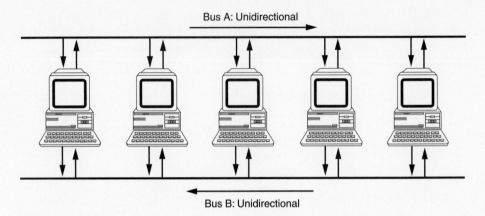

Figure 17.2 Dual Bus MAN

direction on the second bus, as illustrated in Figure 17.2. Each node must therefore be attached to both buses. The specification also allows for a variation called a looped bus. The looped bus still uses two one-direction buses; however, each bus forms a closed loop, as illustrated in Figure 17.3. The speeds defined in the standard depend on the medium used (45 Mbps with coaxial cable and 156 Mbps with fiber optic cable). Distances up to 200 mi are supported.

Another high-speed LAN possibility that is currently being standardized is a 1-Gbps Ethernet. As the demand for bandwidth continues to increase this fast LAN technology will be needed.

It is difficult to accurately predict which of the new technologies will dominate the industry, but one thing is sure: HSLANs will become more common. They will be used to provide faster delivery for large LANs, as backbone networks to connect separate LANs in a building complex or a metropolitan area, and, as you will read in the next section, for LANs providing multimedia services.

MULTIMEDIA ON LANS

Multimedia technology extends a computer's capabilities by adding audio and video. Multimedia is much more than just the ability to produce sound, pictures, and animation on a computer. The promise of this technology is the full integration of audio and video into existing software. Additional hardware is needed to bring these capabilities to a computer. The minimum requirements for a multimedia personal computer (MPC) include a CD-ROM drive, an audio board, a computer with a fast processor, a high-resolution color monitor, and ample memory and disk capacity. Multimedia technology is rapidly expanding on both stand-alone microcomputers and LANs. In this section we do not discuss the details of multimedia technology; instead, we examine its impact on LANs.

Multimedia on LANs is already being used. A multimedia server on a LAN delivers digitized audio and video signals to client workstations capable of supporting the

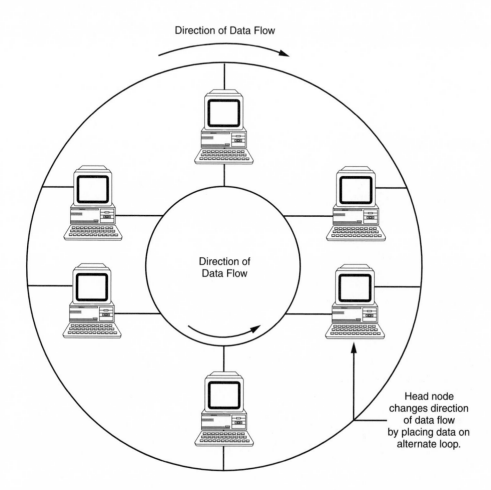

Direction of Data Flow

Direction of
Data Flow

Head node
changes direction
of data flow
by placing data on
alternate loop.

Figure 17.3 Dual Bus Loop MAN

technology. The issue is not whether multimedia can be done on LANs but how to do it successfully. The main problem with this technology today is the speed of the common LAN. Today's Ethernet LANs operate at 10 Mbps, and token rings operate at 4 or 16 Mbps, both of which are inadequate for extensive use of multimedia. Full-motion video to a monitor with a resolution of 640 × 480 picture elements (pixels) and 24-bit true color at a frame rate of 30 frames per second requires a data rate of 240 Mbps. This is much faster than common LAN speeds. Still-frame video and audio signals do not require such high bit rates, but sustained transfers of 16 to 384 Kbps are needed for the duration of many multimedia video and audio sessions. At the higher rate, 30 users would require more than the entire capacity of a 10-Mbps LAN. Moreover, LANs operating at 10 Mbps are not designed to sustain that 10-Mbps data rate because of overheads in the data link protocol, transmission errors, and delays in media access. Obviously changes must made in LAN technology to support these sustained, high data rates.

A combination of several techniques is necessary to realize the full potential of multimedia for large numbers of users. Among these are data compression, higher-speed networks, LAN segmentation, and the asynchronous transfer mode switches described earlier.

Data Compression

Data compression reduces the number of bits that need to be transferred. You may be familiar with this technology through disk compression programs that approximately double the storage capacity of disk drives. An 80-MB disk might be able to store 160 MB of data with compression. If data are compressed before transmission and then decompressed at the receiving end, the demand on the transmission media can be significantly lowered. Compression/decompression chips are available that perform these two operations faster than software. Equipping multimedia clients and servers with compression/decompression capability will help by reducing the number of bits being transferred.

Higher-Speed Networks

Even with compression, the capacity of LANs running under 20 Mbps still can be strained by several concurrent multimedia users. Several high-speed LAN options are available to accommodate these users, as described in an earlier section.

LAN Segmentation

Even 100-Mbps LANs cannot meet the needs of large numbers of concurrent multimedia users. To allow for greater number of concurrent multimedia users, LANs may need to be broken down into small segments, as illustrated in Figure 17.4. Each multimedia segment can be served by a dedicated multimedia server or by a multimedia server on a high-speed backbone network. Both of these options are shown in Figure 17.4. Because each segment has few users, the data-carrying capacity of each segment is not exceeded. It is even conceivable that one intensive multimedia user will need his or her own LAN segment.

MOBILE COMPUTING

A new capability that LAN administrators must deal with is mobile computing. Mobile computing is similar to remote access computing, and they share some of the same LAN connection features. However, traditional remote computing uses wire-based media, whereas mobile connections use wireless media or telephone lines. For many years, computer professionals have had mobile computing capabilities. It started with portable terminals and then portable computers, followed by a need to remotely connect portable computers to LANs. In this way, personnel who are out of the office can still connect to the LAN and send or receive their e-mail messages and perhaps perform

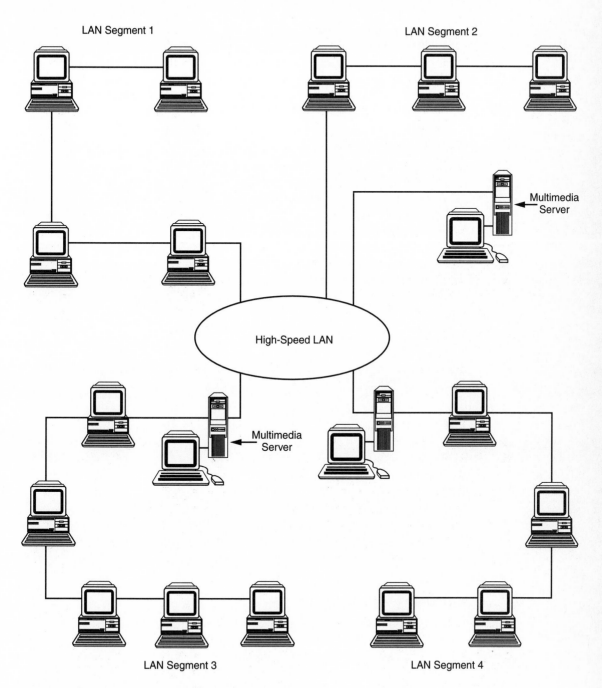

Figure 17.4 Multimedia LAN Configurations

other tasks. The current disadvantage of mobile LAN connections is the speed of the link. LAN connections must be made over telephone lines, via cellular technologies, or perhaps via one of the newer technologies oriented to mobile computing. However, regardless of the connection medium, speeds still are orders of magnitude slower than LAN speeds.

Some of the applications of mobile or remote LAN connections include the entry of orders directly from the customer location, checking on the status of vending machines, transmissions from sensors in areas that might be hazardous for humans, and a myriad of other applications. The following communication facilities currently are available to mobile users.

Wireless Modems

Wireless modems are now available for speeds up to 33.6 Kbps.

Circuit Switched Cellular

Circuit switched cellular (CSC) is the standard analog cellular telephone facility. It is available in almost all major metropolitan areas and supports speeds up to 14,400 Kbps, with higher speeds likely to follow. To use this capability, your cellular telephone must have an RJ-11 jack and a wireless modem. CSC was designed for voice use and is unreliable for digital transmission of the high error rates.

Cellular Digital Packet Data

Cellular digital packet data (CDPD) is a digitized cellular service providing speeds higher than those available on CSC. CDPD is based on the Internet protocols and uses idle voice channels on CSC nets. Some cellular providers are adding this capability to their networks.

RAM Mobile Data and Ardis

RAM is a service of Bell South Mobile and RAM Broadcasting; Ardis is a mobile service provided by Motorola and IBM. Both are digital packet networks based on proprietary network protocols. Both provide speeds up to 19.2 Kbps.

As time progresses, demand for mobile LAN connections will grow and the technology will probably respond to the demand with new, higher-speed services.

INTERNET ACCESS

Many companies are now connected to the Internet. Internet connections serve not only as a source of information but also as a way of marketing and advertising products. Naturally, LAN nodes need to connect to the Internet as well. Most leading LAN vendors offer Internet gateways. Internet connections, however, cause additional concerns, including security, worker productivity, and corporate liability.

An Internet connection can be traversed in two directions. By default, if company employees can access the Internet, then outsiders can access the corporate network as well. When setting up Internet connections, management must address the security issues of outsiders gaining access to corporate data. To prevent undesirable outside access, security fences called firewalls must be installed. There are a variety of ways firewalls can be implemented, and the details of these implementations are beyond the scope of this book. In essence, they all do the same thing: block messages from unauthorized users or computers from entering the company's enterprise network. A generic illustration of how this can be accomplished is given in Figure 17.5.

Employee productivity may suffer as a consequence of and Internet connection. There are many interesting places to visit on the Internet, and some employees may decide

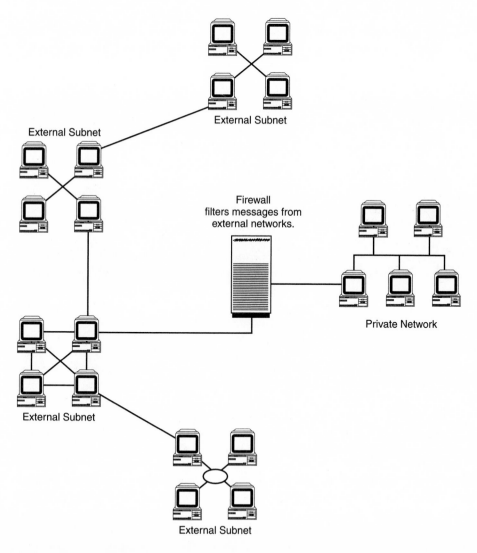

Figure 17.5   A Firewall

to spend their time "surfing the Net" in addition to using the Internet as a business tool. This is not a new phenomenon; stand-alone and networked computers have games that also can occupy an employee's time. Still, Internet access adds another possible diversion for employees.

Legal issues are a third concern companies may face as a consequence of Internet connection. The Internet as a business entity is new enough that legal implications are not yet established. We do know, however, that there is legislation regarding pornography and the Internet. What has yet to be decided is the liability a company has if their Internet site becomes a repository of illegal text and graphics (perhaps stored by an employee without the company's knowledge). What is the company's liability if software is illegally copied from its computers? What are the issues surrounding international law? Who is responsible if a minor accesses pornographic materials through a school or public access facility such as a library? Issues such as these will probably be resolved as test cases are brought to court.

SERVERS

In earlier chapters we talked about servers primarily in the context of file, printer, and database services. Other types of services are also available.

In Chapter 16 we mentioned communications servers. Communications servers provide several varieties of services, most commonly modem pooling. Modem pooling allows one or more modems to be shared by users, just as a printer is shared among users. Rather than dedicating a modem to each user who is likely to need such services, **modem pooling** allows several modems to be attached to one server. When a user needs to use a modem, the server connects the user to one of the pooled modems if one is available. The user can then use the modem as though it were locally attached. The advantage of this is the ability for many users to have modems available without purchasing a modem for each user. Moreover, the server can regulate use of the modems by placing restrictions on who can use them.

Remote access servers, also mentioned in Chapter 16, provide a way for remote users to connect to the LAN and use its services. Remote LAN use via an asynchronous (modem) connection is limited to transfers of small amounts of data. It is impractical to download large program files because the speed of the connection is too slow. Waiting 20 minutes for a word processing program to be loaded over a slow communication link is not realistic. Access servers allow the full services of the LAN to be used remotely without such time delays. This is effected by having all the processing done at the LAN end of the connection and by passing only keyboard and display data over the communication link. Of course, files can also be transferred to the remote system, but large file transfers tend to be time-consuming. See Chapter 16 for additional details of remote hosts.

Another method for remote access is remote control software. Using this technique, remote users can connect to idle workstations and operate in much the same way as they would using a remote access server. Remote control software is described in Chapter 14.

Table 17.1 FAX Server Capabilities

Ability to interface with electronic mail systems

Automatic routing of incoming FAX messages to recipients

Detection/correction of line errors

Security via password protection

Automatic redial for busy numbers

Recognition of pages not received and transmission of only missing pages on reconnect

Collection of accounting statistics (user information, number called, duration, and so on)

The use of facsimile (FAX) transmissions grew rapidly in the latter half of the 1980s. FAX transmissions are not always from one FAX machine to another. FAX images can be stored on a computer's disk and either printed, displayed on a computer screen, or transmitted to another computer or FAX machine. Computer management of FAX images has grown as fast as the use of FAX itself. LAN users can share the use of FAX facilities with a **FAX server.** Capabilities of FAX servers are listed in Table 17.1.

TECHNOLOGY AND NETWORK MANAGEMENT

As time progresses, network management will become both easier and harder. It will become harder because LANs will be larger, the software (both application and system), will be more complex, and interoperability between a LAN and other devices or networks will increase. Network management will become easier because network management systems will be more sophisticated and will provide the network administrator with more assistance in monitoring, diagnosing, and tuning the network.

The most promising technology in network management systems is expert system technology. An **expert system,** one example of artificial intelligence technology, encapsulates the talents of an expert within a software system. A network management system with an expert system component can diagnose system parameters, suggest corrective measures, and automatically or through manual selection carry out one of the suggested corrective measures.

SUMMARY

The field of data communications is rapidly changing, and nowhere is this change more apparent than in microcomputer LAN technology. Some of our existing technologies will become obsolete and be replaced with newer ones. In the preceding chapters the focus was on common LAN features. Many specialty capabilities exist, and to cover them all in detail here is impractical. Some of the less common technologies are high-speed LANs, asynchronous transfer mode, diskless workstations, peer-to-peer LANs, a variety of server technologies, wireless technologies, expert systems in LAN management, multimedia on LANs, and other medium alternatives such as ISDN. Each of these capabilities is available today. Some of them may become leading technologies tomorrow.

Key Terms

expert system

FAX server

high-speed local area network (HSLAN)

metropolitan area network (MAN)

modem pooling

multimedia

nondedicated server

peer-to-peer LAN

Glossary

Acronyms

For a more thorough definition of a term, please refer to the Key Terms glossary.

ACU	Auto-Call Unit
ADCCP	Advanced Data Communications Control Procedure
ADMD	Administrative Management Domain
ADSL	Asymmetric Digital Subscriber Line
AM	Amplitude Modulation
AMP	Asymmetrical Multiprocessing
ANSI	American National Standards Institute
API	Application Program Interface
APPN	Advanced Peer-to-Peer Networking
ARP	Address Resolution Protocol
ASCII	American Standard Code for Information Interchange
ATM	Asynchronous Transfer Mode
BCC	Block Check Character
BCD	Binary Coded Decimal
BISYNC	Binary Synchronous Communications (also BSC)
BIU	Bus Interface Unit
BNC	Bayonet–Neill–Concelnan (a coaxial cable connector)
BPS	Bits per Second
BSC	Binary Synchronous Communications (also BISYNC)
CAD	Computer-Aided Design
CAI	Computer-Aided Instruction
CAM	Computer-Aided Manufacturing
CCITT	Consultative Committee on International Telegraph and Telephony
CDDI	Copper Distributed Data Interface
CICS	Customer Information Control System
CIU	Communications Interface Unit
CLNP	Connectionless Network Protocol
CMIP	Common Management Information Protocol
CMIS	Common Management Information Service
CPU	Central Processing Unit
CRC	Cyclic Redundancy Check
CRT	Cathode Ray Tube
C/S	Client/Server
CSMA/CA	Carrier Sense with Multiple Access and Collision Avoidance
CSMA/CD	Carrier Sense with Multiple Access and Collision Detection
DBMS	Database Management System
DCE	Data Circuit-Terminating Equipment
DCE	Data Communications Equipment
DCE	Distributed Computing Environment
DES	Data Encryption Standard
DFS	Distributed File System
DPSK	Differential Phase Shift Keying
DSL	Digital Subscriber Line
DTE	Data Terminal Equipment
EBCDIC	Extended Binary-Coded Decimal Interchange Code
EDI	Electronic Data Interchange
EIA	Electronic Industries Association
E-mail	Electronic Mail
ESDI	Enhanced Small Drive Interface
FCS	Frame Check Sequence
FDDI	Fiber Distributed Data Interface
FDM	Frequency Division Multiplexing
FEP	Front End Processor
FM	Frequency Modulation
FMS	File Management System
FQDN	Fully Qualified Domain Name
FSK	Frequency Shift Keying
FTP	File Transfer Protocol
GDSS	Group Decision Support System
GUI	Graphical User Interface
HDLC	High-Level Data Link Control
Hz	Hertz
IDE	Integrated Drive Electronics
IEEE	Institute of Electrical and Electronic Engineers

IP	Internet Protocol
IPC	Interprocess Communication
IPX	Internet Packet Exchange
ISDN	Integrated Services Digital Network
ISO	International Standards Organization
LAN	Local Area Network
LAPB	Link Access Protocol, Balanced
LATA	Local Access and Transport Area
LLC	Logical Link Control
LRC	Longitudinal Redundancy Check
LU	Logical Unit
MAC	Media Access Control Protocol
MAU	Multistation Access Unit
Mbps	Million Bits per Second
MIB	Management Information Base
MIPS	Million Instructions Per Second
MNP	Microcomputer Network Protocols
MTA	Message Transfer Agent
MTBF	Mean Time Between Failures
MTTR	Mean Time to Repair
MUX	Multiplexing
NAU	Network Addressable Unit
NCP	Network Control Program
NFS	Network File System
NIA	Network Interface Adapter (also NIC)
NIC	Network Interface Card (also NIA)
NMS	Network Management System
NOS	Network Operating System
ODI	Open Data-link Interface
OLE	Object Linking and Embedding
ORB	Object Request Broker
OS	Operating System
OSF	Open Software Foundation
OSI	Open Systems Interconnection reference model
PAD	Packet Assembly/Disassembly
PBX	Private Branch Exchange
PC	Personal Computer
PCI	Protocol Control Information
PCM	Pulse Code Modulation
PDN	Packet Distribution Network
PDU	Protocol Data Unit
PERT	Program Evaluation and Review Technique
POP	Point of Presence
PPP	Point-to-Point Protocol

PRMD	Private Management Domain
PSE	Packet Switching Equipment
PSK	Phase Shift Keying
PU	Physical Unit
PUCP	Physical Unit Control Point
PVC	Permanent Virtual Circuit
QAM	Quadrature Amplitude Modulation
RAID	Redundant Arrays of Independent Disks
RBOC	Regional Bell Operation Company
RFI	Request for Information
RFP	Request for Proposal
RFQ	Request for Quotation
RFS	Remote File Sharing
RIP	Routing Information Protocol
RJE	Remote Job Entry
RMON MIB	Remote Monitoring Management Information Base
RPC	Remote Procedure Call
SAA	System Application Architecture
SAP	Service Access Point
SBT	Six-Bit Transcode
SCSI	Small Computer System Interface
SDLC	Synchronous Data Link Control
SDU	Service Data Unit
SMDS	Switched Multimegabit Data Service
SMI	Structure of Management Information
SMP	Symmetrical Multiprocessing
SMTP	Simple Mail Transfer Protocol
SNA	Systems Network Architecture
SNADS	SNA Distribution Services
SNMP	Simple Network Management Protocol
SONET	Synchronous Optical Network
SPX/IPX	Sequenced Packet Exchange/Internet Packet Exchange
SQL	Structured Query Language
SSCP	Systems Services Control Point
SSR	Spread-Spectrum Radio
STDM	Statistical Time Division Multiplexing
STE	Signaling Terminal Equipment
STP	Shielded Twisted-Pair
SVC	Switched Virtual Circuit
TCP	Transaction Control Process
TCP/IP	Transaction Control Protocol/Internet Protocol
TDM	Time Division Multiplexing
TSAP	Transport Service Access Point

UA	User Agent	**VTAM**	Virtual Telecommunications Access Method
UPS	Uninterruptible Power Supply		
UTP	Unshielded Twisted-Pair	**WAN**	Wide Area Network
VDT	Video Display Terminal	**WATS**	Wide Area Telecommunications or Telephone Service
VDU	Video Display Unit		
VHF	Very-High-Frequency radio waves	**XNS**	Xerox Network System
VRC	Vertical Redundancy Check	**XTP**	Xpress Transfer Protocol

Key Terms

100Base-X   An IEEE 802.3 specification for 100-Mbps transmission over unshielded twisted-pair wires.

100VG-AnyLAN   An IEEE 802.12 specification for 100-Mbps transmission over unshielded twisted pair-wires. In contrast to 100Base-X, 100VG-AnyLAN provides a node priority capability called demand priority.

10Base2   An IEEE 802.3 specification for baseband transmission at 10 Mbps over thin coaxial cable segments of 200 m.

10Base5   An IEEE 802.3 specification for baseband transmission at 10 Mbps over thick coaxial cable segments of 500 m.

10Base-T   An IEEE 802.3 specification for baseband transmission at 10 Mbps over twisted-pair wires.

access method   A software subsystem that provides input and output services as interface between an application and its associated devices. It eliminates device dependencies for an application programmer.

access security   Security that controls a user's access to data. The controls may regulate a user's ability to read and update data, to delete files, and to run programs.

access server   An interconnection utility that allows microcomputers to access LAN resources from remote locations.

access time   The total time required in accessing a disk, including seek time, latency, and transfer time.

active hub   A node connection hub used in an ARCnet LAN that provides signal regeneration and allows nodes to be located up to 2000 ft from the hub.

active node   A node capable of sending or receiving network messages.

active port   The status of a bridge port that will accept packets from the LAN end of the port.

acoustic coupler   An acoustic coupler converts digital signals to analog and analog to digital. It is used mostly in switched communications and uses the telephone handset to pass data between a terminal or computer and the acoustic coupler.

adapter   A device that connects one system to another and allows the two systems to interoperate.

adaptive routing   A routing algorithm that evaluates the existing paths and chooses the one that will provide the best path for a message. Routes may change because of congestion and path failures.

address   A set of bits that uniquely identifies an object. Addresses may be numbers or character strings. For example, on the Internet an address may be represented by a 32-bit number usually represented in writing as a dotted quad in the form 123.001.144.010, where each component is a number between 0 and 255. The same address may be represented as a string of characters such as MYSERVER.COMPANY.COM. String names are usually converted to their numeric equivalent by an address resolution procedure because numeric addresses are typically used by the network and data link layer protocols.

address resolution protocol (ARP)   A protocol used to convert an IP address to the hardware address of a node. For example, if a node on an Ethernet network has an IP address, an internet message will refer to the IP address. The ARP protocol is used to convert the IP address to a hardware address so the message can be delivered over the Ethernet network.

Administrative Management Domain (ADMD)   A domain that represents a private electronic mail system corresponding to a public delivery network in the X.400 standard hierarchy.

Advanced Data Communications Control Procedure (ADCCP)   An ANSI standard bit-oriented data link control. Pronounced "add-cap."

Advanced Peer-to-Peer Networking (APPN)   An IBM network technology that allows two nodes to communicate directly with one another. Under IBM's Systems Network Architecture, communication between two entities generally requires the involvement of the Systems Services Control Point (SSCP), which runs in an IBM host computer. With APPN, the involvement of the SSCP and host node are not required.

Advanced Program-to-Program Communication   In IBM's Systems Network Architecture (SNA), this is the ability of two programs to communicate with each other via an LU 6.2 session.

after image   The status of a record after it has been processed.

agent   A device component that collects data for the device, which is then stored in the management information base (MIB). In client/server computing, an agent performs information preparation and exchange on behalf of a client or server process. In electronic mail systems, agents can act on behalf of users to operate on mail. For example, a vacation agent could automatically file mail messages and forward them to another user.

aggregate data rate   The amount of information that can be transmitted per unit of time.

alert   A signal given by the network management system that a statistic, such as current line status, line quality, or number of retries on the line, has changed since the last status report. Also known as an alarm.

American National Standards Institute (ANSI)   A U.S. standard-making agency.

American Standard Code for Information Interchange (ASCII)   A code that uses 7 or 8 bits to represent characters. One of the two common computer codes. See also **Extended Binary-Coded Decimal Interchange Code.**

amplitude   The height, magnitude, or energy of a waveform.

amplitude modulation (AM)   One method of changing the properties of a wave to represent data.

analog line monitor   A diagnostic tool that monitors and displays the analog signals on the communication circuit or on the data communication side of the modem, enabling the user to check for noise and proper modulation.

analog transmission   Refers to measurable physical quantities, which in data communication take the form of voltage and variations in the properties of waves. Data is represented in analog form by varying the amplitude, frequency, or phase of a wave or by changing current on a line.

AppleTalk   Apple Computer's proprietary LAN implementation for linking up to 32 Macintosh systems in a CSMA/CD LAN at 115 Kbps.

application layer   One of the layers of the International Standards Organization's reference model. The functions of this layer are application dependent.

Application Program Interface (API)   In LANs, the interface between application programs and the network software.

ARCnet   LAN implementation based on Datapoint's attached resource computer network.

Asymmetrical Digital Subscriber Line (ADSL)   A common carrier service that allows high-speed data transfer over standard telephone lines. Speeds of 1.5 Mbps in one direction are possible over one twisted-pair line and up to 7 Mbps over two twisted pairs. ADSL is touted as one of the high-speed access capabilities to remote LANs and the Internet.

asymmetrical multiprocessing   A type of multiprocessing in which processors are dedicated to different functions, such as an I/O processor and the main CPU. Compare with symmetrical multiprocessing.

asynchronous transfer mode (ATM)   A high-speed transmission protocol in which data blocks are broken into small cells that are transmitted individually and possibly via different routes in a manner similar to packet switching technology.

asynchronous transmission (Async)   The oldest and one of the most common data link protocols. Each character is transmitted individually with its own error detection scheme, usually a parity bit. The sender and receiver are not synchronized with each other. Also known as start–stop protocol.

AT&T divestiture   In 1984 AT&T was broken up into independent RBOCs and a separate AT&T company. The divestiture ended the regulated monopoly of AT&T and freed AT&T and the RBOCs to enter into business areas previously denied to them.

attenuation   A weakening of a signal as a result of distance and characteristics of the medium.

authentication   A process in which a system user is required to provide or verify his or her user identification to gain system access.

authorization   A security procedure that ensures that the entity making a request is allowed to carry out all the activities implied by the request.

Auto-Call Unit (ACU)   A device used to place a telephone call automatically without manual intervention.

backbone network   A network used to interconnect other networks or to connect a cluster of network nodes.

backup software   Software that is responsible for reading the files being backed up and writing them to the backup device.

baluns   Adapters that change coaxial cable connectors into twisted-pair wire connectors, allowing transfer from one medium to another or from a connector for one medium to a different medium.

bandwidth   The difference between the minimum and the maximum frequencies allowed. Bandwidth is a measure of the amount of data that can be transmitted per unit of time. The greater the bandwidth, the higher the possible data transmission rate.

baseband transmission   Sends the data along the channel by means of voltage fluctuations. The entire bandwidth of the cable is used to carry data.

batch   A style of computing in which inputs are collected over time and then processed as a group. Processing is carried out without interaction with a user.

Baudot   A code obtained from the telegraph industry that is used in data communication with telegraph lines or equipment originally designed for telegraphy. It is limited in its number of representable characters.

baud rate   A measure of the number of discrete signals that can be observed per unit of time.

before image   The status of a record before it has been processed.

benchmark   A test in which one or more programs are run on a proposed hardware configuration to verify the ability of the hardware to meet a system's application requirements.

binary coded decimal (BCD)   A coding scheme for the storage of data in digital computers. The code may be either 4-bit or 6-bit.

Binary Synchronous Communications (BISYNC or BSC) protocol   A transmission protocol introduced by IBM as the data link protocol for remote job entry. It later became a de facto standard for many types of data transmission, particularly between two computers. Data is transmitted a block at a time, and the sender and receiver need to be in time with each other. Specific control characters are used to indicate beginning of text, end of text, start of header, and so on.

bit   A binary digit, either 0 or 1.

bit-oriented synchronous data link protocol   A data link protocol in which one or more bits are used to control the communication link. Bit synchronous protocols are commonly used on both LANs and WANs.

bit parallel transmission   The simultaneous transmission of bits over a wire medium.

bit rate   One method of measuring data transmission speed (in bits per second).

bits per second (bps)   The number of bits that can be transferred over a medium in 1 second (a measure of data transmission speed).

bit stuffing   The implementation of transparency in SDLC through bit insertion.

bit synchronous protocol   A data link protocol in which one or more bits are used to control the communications link. Bit synchronous protocols are commonly used on both LANs and WANs.

block   A contiguous group of bits or bytes. Often messages are broken into blocks of a specific size for transmission over a data communications line.

block check character (BCC)   In the error detection methods of longitudinal redundancy check (LRC) or cyclic redundancy check (CRC), an error detection character or characters, called the BCC, is appended to a block of transmitted characters, typically at the end of the block.

block mode   A mode in which data is entered and transmitted in one or more sets or blocks.

breakout box   A passive, multipurpose diagnostic device that is patched or temporarily inserted into a circuit at an interface.

bridge   The interface used to connect networks using similar data link protocols.

broadband transmission   A form of data transmission where data is carried on high-frequency carrier waves; the carrying capacity of the medium is divided into a number of subchannels (video, low-speed data, high-speed data, voice, and so on), allowing the medium to satisfy several communication needs.

broadcast message   A message sent to all users on a network.

broadcast radio   Uses AM, FM, and short-wave radio frequencies, with a total frequency range from 500,000 to 108 million cycles per second. Its primary applications include paging terminals, cellular radio telephones, and wireless LANs.

broadcast routing   Routing in which the message is broadcast to all stations. Only the stations to which the message is addressed accept it.

brouter   A term used to describe bridges that can connect two LANs using different data link protocols.

buffer overflow/overrun   A situation that arises when the buffer is either too small or too full to receive the transmitted data. In either case there is no place to store the arriving characters, and the data is lost.

bus   A communication medium for transmitting data or power. A LAN topology.

bus interface unit (BIU)   In a LAN, the bus interface unit provides the physical connection to the computer's I/O bus.

byte count protocol   A type of synchronous protocol that delineates data by including the number of characters being transmitted within the message.

cable tester   A diagnostic tool used to detect faults in cables by generating and monitoring a signal along the cable.

cache memory   High-speed memory that improves a computer's performance.

callback unit   A security device for switched connections. It operates by receiving a call, verifying the user, severing the call, and calling the user back.

call clearing   The process that dissolves a switched virtual circuit.

carrier sense with multiple access and collision avoidance (CSMA/CA)   A media access control technique that attempts to avoid collisions.

carrier sense with multiple access and collision detection (CSMA/CD)   A media access control technique that attempts to detect collisions and is the most common access strategy for bus architectures.

carrier signal   A wave that continues without change. The carrier signal can be modulated by a modem so a receiver can interpret the information.

Carterphone case   A U.S. case regarding attaching devices to a telephone company's network.

CCITT V.10 and V.11   Electrical interfaces for data transmission.

CCITT V.24   A functional interface similar to RS-232-C.

CCITT V.25   A specification for establishing and terminating sessions with an auto-call unit.

CCITT V.28   A specification for electrical interface similar to that of RS-232-C.

CCITT V.32   A modem standard specifying trellis encoding techniques to represent signals.

CCITT V.34   A modem standard for speeds up to 28.8 Kbps using trellis encoding.

CCITT V.35   A standard for data transmission at speeds up to 48,000 bits per second using a 34-pin connection.

CCITT V.42   A modem standard that defines error-checking capabilities using cyclic redundancy checking.

CCITT X.20 and X.21   Standards that cover the interface between DCE and DTE for packet distribution networks.

CCITT X.24   A functional interface for packet distribution networks.

centralized routing   A routing algorithm in which one node in the network is charged with the responsibility of determining the path between nodes in the network. It determines the routing tables and distributes them to each other node.

central processing unit (CPU)   The processing components of a computer. The components of the CPU are control, arithmetic logic unit, and memory.

Centrex service   A telephone company service that provides PBX capabilities to a company. With the Centrex service, the PBX equipment is located on the telephone company's premises.

character count termination   A transmission termination technique where a transmission is complete when a specified number of characters have been received. Allows the computer to save the data in blocks and avoid buffer overflow.

character synchronous protocol A type of synchronous protocol oriented toward specific data codes and specific characters within those codes.

checksum A technique used to check for errors in data. The sending application generates the checksum from the data being transmitted. The receiving application computes the checksum and compares it to the value computed and sent by the sending station.

cipher text The encrypted version of a message or data.

circuit Either the medium connecting two communicating devices or a path between a sender and a receiver where there may be one or more intermediary nodes. The exact meaning depends on the context.

client A software application that requests services from the server in a client/server computing environment. Some systems may call the client a requester.

client/server protocol An application framework in which the processing load is divided among several processes called clients and servers. Clients issue requests to servers, which provide specialized services such as database processing and mail distribution. Within this framework, clients are able to concentrate on business logic and servers can use specialized hardware and software that allow them to provide services more efficiently. When clients and servers are located in different computers, application processing is distributed over multiple computers and, in effect, the network becomes the computer.

closed system A proprietary system wherein the interface specifications are not made readily available to other manufacturers. Thus, a closed system does not provide support for OSI or ANSI standard protocols and interfaces.

cluster controller A device that manages multiple terminals by buffering data transmitted to and from the terminals and performing error detection and correction.

coaxial cable A transmission medium consisting of one or two central data transmission wires surrounded by an insulating layer, a shielding layer, and an outer jacket. Coaxial cable has a high data-carrying capacity and low error rates.

code independence The ability to successfully transmit data regardless of the data code, such as ASCII or EBCDIC.

collision In a CSMA/CD media access control protocol, a collision occurs when two stations attempt to send a message at the same time. The messages interfere with each other, so correct communication is not possible.

common carrier A public utility that provides public transmission media, such as the telephone companies and satellite companies.

Common Management Information Protocol (CMIP) Guidelines issued by the ISO for creating network management software products. Also known as the Communications Management Information Protocol.

Common Management Information Service (CMIS) An ISO standard for services to be provided by a network management system. CMIS and CMIP form the ISO network management protocol.

communication controller A computer that serves as a front-end processor for a host machine. The communication controller provides the data link protocols and the physical devices attached to communication lines.

communications interface unit (CIU) In a LAN, the communications interface unit provides the physical connection to the transmission medium.

communications server A server that monitors connections to the host by determining whether there is a free port to make the connection and granting or denying the request accordingly.

compact disc read-only memory (CD-ROM) An optical disk technology in which data can be read from the compact disc. Often used to distributed software and documentation.

computer-aided design (CAD) An application of computers in the design process. One component is computer drafting.

computer-aided instruction (CAI) The use of computers to facilitate the education process.

computer-aided manufacturing (CAM) The use of computers to solve manufacturing problems. CAM includes robotics control, machine control, and process control components.

computerized branch exchange (CBX) A private branch exchange using a computer as controller.

concentrator A computer that provides line-sharing capabilities, data editing, polling, error handling, code conversion, compression, and encryption.

conditioning A service provided by telephone companies for leased lines. It reduces the amount of noise on a line, providing lower error rates and increased speed.

conducted media Media that use a conductor such as a wire or fiber optic cable to move a signal from sender to receiver.

congestion control The reduction of transmission delays.

Connectionless Network Protocol (CLNP) The counterpart to the Internet Protocol (IP), this protocol provides message services such as message priorities, route selection parameters, and security parameters.

connector Establishes the physical connection between the computer and the medium.

consistency A consistent system is one that works predictably with respect both to the people who use the system and to response times.

Consultative Committee on International Telegraph and Telephony (CCITT) An international standard organization.

contention A convention whereby devices obtain control of a communication link. In contention mode, devices compete for control of the line either by transmitting directly on an idle line or by issuing a request for line control.

contention mode A mode in which the host and the terminal contend for control of the medium by issuing a bid for the channel.

context data A requirement of multithreaded processes that entails unifying the work by keeping track of the completed parts and of parts yet to be worked on, and ensuring that an interrupted transaction is restarted at the correct point.

control center A network component responsible for monitoring the network and taking corrective action when necessary.

control signals Signals that are exchanged between a sender and receiver to establish, maintain, and terminate connections, communications, and the flow of data.

conversational mode A mode in which the terminal and the host exchange messages.

cooperative computing A data-processing model in which two or more processes collaborate on the processing necessary for a single transaction or application. The cooperating processes may reside in different computers.

Copper Distributed Data Interface (CDDI) An ANSI LAN standard for twisted-pair-wire LANs spanning a distance of approximately 200 km and providing speeds of 100 Mbps. An extension of the fiber distributed interface LAN.

corporate license A license that gives a corporation unlimited use of software at all locations.

CPU time The amount of time required for the CPU to execute the processing instructions, including those executed by the database management system, operating system, data communication software, and application programs.

critical path The sequence of events in a project that takes the longest to complete.

crosstalk Distortion or interference on one channel by the signals of a different channel.

current loop A transmission technique that uses changes in current flow to represent data. Does not require a modem and operates at speeds up to 19.2 Kbps.

Customer Information Control System (CICS) A TCP provided by IBM. Its primary function is as an interface between terminal users on one side and application programs or the database on the other.

cyclic redundancy check (CRC) An error detection algorithm that uses a polynomial function to generate the block check characters. CRC is a very efficient error-detection method.

daisy chain A connection arrangement in which each device is connected directly to the next device. For example, a daisy chain of devices A, B, C, and D might have A connected to B, B connected to C, and C connected to D. Also known as cascading.

database management system (DBMS) A system that organizes data into records, organizes records into files, provides access to the data based on one or more access keys, and provides the mechanism for relating one file to another.

database server A computer that allows microcomputers on a network to request database processing of records, returning a single-figure answer rather than the set of records essential to determining the answer.

data communication   The transmission of data to and from computers and components of computer systems.

data communication equipment (DCE)   One class of equipment in data communication, including modems, media, and media support facilities.

data compression   Data compression is used to reduce the number of characters or bits in a message. A common form is repeating character compression, in which long strings of repeating characters are replaced by the repeating group and the repeat count. Compressing data allows fewer characters to be transmitted and improves line efficiency, increasing the effective aggregate data rate.

Data Encryption Standard (DES)   An algorithm that uses an encryption key to transform data, called plain text, into an encoded form, called encrypted or cipher text.

data flow control layer   Layer 5 in IBM's SNA networks. The data flow control layer provides a set of protocols between two users. These protocols provide for the orderly flow of information between the two users.

datagram   One type of connection option for a PDN. The message fits into the data field on one packet. There is less accountability for packet delivery than for other connection types.

data link control layer   Layer 2 in IBM's SNA networks. The data link control layer is responsible for protocols in node-to-node transfers, such as synchronous and asynchronous transmissions. The data link control layer is also responsible for error detection and recovery across a link. Similar in function to the OSI Reference Model data link layer.

data link layer   One of the layers of the ISO's OSI reference model. The data link layer is responsible for node-to-node-message transfers.

data link protocol   Convention that governs the flow of data between a sending and a receiving station.

data switch   A device implemented on sub-LANs to provide connections between microcomputers.

dataset/modem   Short for modulator-demodulator. A device that changes digital signals to analog signals for transmitting data over telephone circuits. Also used for some fiber optic transmission (digital fiber optics do not require a modem) and any transmission mode requiring a change from one form of signal to another.

data terminal equipment (DTE)   The second class of equipment in data communication, including terminals, computers, concentrators, and multiplexers.

deadlock   A state that exists when two or more processes are unable to proceed. It occurs when two or more transactions have locked a resource and request resources that other involved processes already have locked.

dedicated printer   A printer that can be used only by a person at the workstation to which the printer is attached.

dedicated server   One or more computers that operate only as designated file, database, or other types of servers.

dibits   A transmission mode in which each signal conveys two bits of data.

differential phase shift keying (DPSK)   A modulation technique that uses phase modulation. DPSK changes phase each time a 1 bit is transmitted and does not change phase for 0 bits.

digital branch exchange (DBX)   A digital PBX.

digital private branch exchange (DPBX or DBX)   A private branch exchange that transmits data in digital format.

digital subscriber line (DSL)   A service that provides high-speed data transfers over telephone lines. A variety of DSL services are planned, including asymmetrical (ADSL), high-speed (HDSL), and rate-adaptive (RADSL). Predicted speeds range up to 8 Mbps.

digital transmission   A transmission mode in which data is represented by binary digits rather than an analog signal.

direct sequencing   Sends data out over several different frequencies simultaneously to increase the probability of success.

discovery packet   A packet sent by the sending station on all available routes to evaluate and determine the best route from the information collected by the packet.

disk caching   Similar in function to cache memory except that main memory serves as a high-speed buffer for slower disk drives.

disk drive interface/controller   Sets the standards for connecting the disk drive to the microprocessor and the software commands used to access the drive.

diskless workstation A workstation that has no local disk drives, reducing the ways in which a virus can be introduced.

disk mirroring A fault-tolerant disk storage strategy in which data is written to two independent disk drives. If one drive fails, the remaining drive allows processing to continue.

disk seek enhancement An I/O optimization technique that reduces the head movement during seeks and improves performance.

distortion The change of transmitted signals resulting from noise. Distortion can result in transmission errors.

Distributed Computing Environment (DCE) A standardization for middleware established by the Open Software Foundation that specifies the use of remote procedure calls, security, name services, and messages for client/server computing.

distributed database A database wherein data is located on two or more computing systems connected via a data communication network. The fact that data is distributed should be transparent to database users.

Distributed File System (DFS) Network software responsible for making network resources available to multiple users regardless of their location in the network.

distributed processing The geographic distribution of hardware, software, processing, data, and control.

distributed query processing A condition in which a user at one node can start a query involving data on other nodes.

distributed routing determination A routing algorithm in which each node calculates its own routing table based on status information periodically received from other nodes.

distributed transaction management In a distributed database, a transaction may be operated on by several processes in different computer nodes. Transactions of this type must be managed by the distributed database system to ensure database integrity either by completing the transaction or by reversing any updates done by a transaction that cannot be completed.

distribution list A predefined list of individual users in a workgroup, represented by a single E-mail address, that replaces the need to enter each user's address when sending a message to the entire workgroup.

document coauthoring system A system that allows two or more workers to work on one document concurrently.

document management system A system that helps an organization manage and control its documents.

domain In IBM's SNA, the network components managed by a Systems Services Control Point.

dotted quad The four-octet address representation on the Internet.

double buffering Used when buffer overflow/overrun occurs to avoid losing characters.

downloading The process of transferring data or an application from the server to the workstation.

DS1/T1 through T4/DS4 High-speed data transmission circuits from a common carrier.

dumb terminal A terminal that passively serves for input or output but performs no local processing.

duplexed servers The fault-tolerance technique in which one server can fail and another is available to continue working.

echo The reflection or reversal of the signal being transmitted. Also used to define a transmission convention in which the receiver of data sends the data back to the sender to assist in error detection.

echo suppressor A device that allows a transmitted signal to pass in one direction only, thus minimizing the echo effect.

effectiveness A measure of how well a system serves users' needs.

electronic appointment calendar A workgroup productivity tool that is stored on the network so that users can consult each other's appointment calendars.

electronic bulletin board A software system that allows users to post electronic messages. Electronic bulletin boards are often accessed by a switched telephone connection and serve as a clearinghouse for software and hardware exchange and as a medium for information exchange.

electronic conferencing An application that assists users in arranging and conducting meetings electronically.

electronic mail (E-mail)   An on-line service equivalent to the postal system that allows users to send and receive messages from other users electronically.

electronic meeting systems   Network software that allows participants to exchange machine-readable information in the form of graphics, text, audio, and full-motion video.

emulator   A diagnostic tool that enables the user to check for adherence to a specific protocol.

encryption   A process in which transmitted data is scrambled at the sending location and reconstructed into readable data at the receiving end.

end office   A telephone company office to which a subscriber is connected. Also called a class 5 office.

Enhanced Small Device Interface (ESDI)   A disk drive interface for microcomputers. Generally provides good performance and is often used as the interface for LAN server drives. See also **small computer system interface.**

enterprise network   A network of two or more LANs connected to each other, or one or more LANs connected to a WAN.

environment variable   A parameter stored by an operating system or program. The data and time are two environment variables commonly stored by an operating system. In a LAN, environment variables can be used to tailor the user's interface to the LAN.

ergonomics   The science of designing equipment to maximize worker productivity by reducing operator fatigue and discomfort while improving safety.

Ethernet   A LAN implementation using the CSMA/CD protocol on a bus. The IEEE 802.3 standard is based on Ethernet. One of the most popular LAN implementations.

exclusive open mode   A file open mode in which an open request is granted only if no other user has the file opened already.

Extended Binary-Coded Decimal Interchange Code (EBCDIC)   A code that uses 8 bits to represent a character of information. One of the most common computer codes. See also **American Standard Code for Information Interchange.**

external specification   Specifications detailing end-user interfaces to a system and information available to the user.

facsimile   (FAX) transmission Electronic transmission of a document image.

fault tolerance   A combination of hardware and software techniques that improve the reliability of a system.

Fiber Distributed Data Interface (FDDI)   An ANSI LAN standard for fiber optic LANs spanning a distance of approximately 200 km and providing speeds of 100 Mbps.

fiber optic cable   A transmission medium that provides high data rates and low errors. One or more glass or plastic fibers are woven together to form the core of the cable. This core is surrounded by a glass or plastic layer called the cladding. The cladding in turn is covered with plastic or other material for protection. The cable requires a light source, most commonly laser and light-emitting diodes.

file exchange utilities   A workgroup productivity tool that allows files to be easily copied from one network node to another.

file management system (FMS)   A system that provides a subset of a database management system's capabilities. An FMS provides functions such as storage allocation and file access methods for a single file.

file server   A computer that allows microcomputers on a network to share resources such as data, programs, and printers. The file server's software controls access to shared files, as opposed to the operating system of the microcomputer.

file transfer protocol (FTP)   A capability of the TCP/IP protocol suite that allows files to be transferred from one node to another over the network.

file transfer utility   An intrinsic part of many routers, this utility allows files to be moved between network nodes.

filter   A software component used to screen and format data sent to the management center.

flooding   A technique used by a bridge to locate a destination address not present in the bridge's routing table by sending a packet out on all possible paths. An acknowledgment from the receiving station contains the destination address of the packet, which can then be added to the bridge's routing table.

flow control   A mechanism used by network protocols to provide message pacing so the sender does not send data faster than the receiver is able to accept it.

fractional T-1, T-3   A T-1 service that fills the void of high-speed transmission options between 64 Kbps and 1.5 Mbps by providing a portion of T-1 line to customers. Fractional T-3 service provides the same capability by allowing a user to subscribe to some of the 28 T-1 lines that constitute a T-3 line.

frame   A term used to describe a transmission packet in bit-oriented protocols.

frame relay   A fast packet switching protocol that is similar to X.25 packet switching. Frame relay does not perform as exhaustive error checking as X.25 and is thus able to switch packets at a higher rate than X.25.

framing protocol   A type of synchronous protocol that uses reserved characters or bit patterns to delineate data and control fields within the message.

frequency division multiplexing (FDM)   A technique that divides the available bandwidth of the circuit into subchannels of different frequency ranges, each of which is assigned to one device.

frequency hopping   Data is transmitted at one frequency, the frequency changes, and the data is transmitted at the new frequency. Each piece of data is transmitted over several frequencies to increase the probability that the data will be successfully received.

frequency modulation (FM)/frequency shift keying (FSK)   One method of changing the characteristics of a signal to represent data. The frequency of the carrier signal is changed. Often used by lower-speed modems.

front-end processor (FEP)   A communication component placed at the host end of a circuit to take over a portion of the line management work from the host. Also called a communication controller or a message switch.

full duplex   A data transmission mode in which data is transmitted over a link in both directions simultaneously.

Fully Qualified Domain Name (FQDN)   The computer.domain notation used to specify addresses in the Internet.

functional specification   An agreement between management and designers outlining design objectives, such as the product to be produced, and design constraints, such as time and cost.

functional testing   Testing individual modules to ensure that they produce the desired results.

function keys   Additional keys found on some terminals that transmit specific character sequences to the host.

gateway   The interface used to connect two dissimilar networks or systems by providing conversion from one network to another.

Gbps   A billion bits per second.

geosynchronous orbit   A satellite orbit in which the satellite is stationary with respect to the earth. The satellite is always positioned over the same location.

group decision support system (GDSS)   System that assists individuals and groups in the decision-making process and helps them set objectives.

groupware   A collective of workgroup productivity tools that allows a group of users to communicate and to coordinate activities.

guardbands   Subchannel separators that are implemented in frequency division multiplexing to avoid crosstalk.

half duplex   A data transmission mode in which data can travel in both directions over a link but in only one direction at a time.

half-session layer   Represents a single layer (transmission control, flow control, and presentation service) in the four-layer definition of SNA functional layers.

handshaking   an asynchronous protocol that allows two nodes to identify each other and establish the session flow control.

Hertz (Hz)   The term used to denote frequency; 1 hertz is 1 cycle per second.

heterogeneous   In networks, a network made up of a variety of equipment, particularly equipment and software from a variety of vendors.

hierarchical topology   A network topology in which the nodes are arranged hierarchically. Also known as a tree structure.

High-Level Data Link Control (HDLC)   A positional synchronous protocol that operates in full duplex mode in both point-to-point and multipoint configurations. Data is transmitted in fixed-format frames consisting of start flag, address, control information, block check character (CRC), and end-of-frame flag. HDLC is an ISO standard similar to IBM's SDLC.

host   A processor that provides support and services to terminals or other processors.

hub   A wiring concentrator for connecting workstations on a token ring or 10Base-T local area network.

Hush-a-Phone Case   A U.S. case that set a precedent regarding attaching equipment to telephone networks.

identification   Information assigned to a specific user of a system for security and control purposes. User identification ranges from simple user names to high-security measures such as voice print and fingerprint identification.

IEEE 802.1 High-Level Interface Subcommittee   The high-level subcommittee that addresses matters relating to network architecture, management, and interconnections.

IEEE 802.2 Logical Link Control (LLC) Subcommittee   This subcommittee defines the functions of the logical link control sublayer of the OSI Reference Model data link layer. The objective of the LLC Subcommittee is to provide a consistent, transparent interface to the MAC layer so that the network layers above the data link layer are able to function correctly regardless of the MAC protocol.

IEEE 802.3 standard   A standard that covers a variety of CSMA/CD architectures that are generally based on the Ethernet.

IEEE 802.4 standard   A subcommittee that sets standards for token bus networks.

IEEE 802.5 standard   A subcommittee that sets standards for token-ring networks.

IEEE 802.6 standard   A metropolitan area network standard similar to the FDDI family of technologies. The IEEE 802.6 standard has also been adopted by ANSI. The standard is also called the distributed queue dual bus (DQDB) standard. As the name DQDB indicates, the architecture uses two buses. Each bus is unidirectional, meaning that data is transmitted in one direction on one bus and in the other direction on the second bus.

IEEE 802.7 Broadband Technical Advisory Group   This group provides guidance and technical expertise to other groups that are establishing broadband LAN standards, such as the 802.3 subcommittee for 10Broad36.

IEEE 802.8 Fiber Optic Technical Advisory Group   This group provides guidance and technical expertise to other groups that are establishing standards for LANs using fiber optic cable.

IEEE 802.9 Integrated Data and Voice Networks Subcommittee   This committee sets standards for networks that carry both voice and data. Specifically, it is setting standards for interfaces to the Integrated Services Digital Networks (ISDNs).

IEEE 802.10 LAN Security Subcommittee   This committee addresses the implementation of security capabilities such as encryption, network management, and the transfer of data.

IEEE 802.11 Wireless LAN Subcommittee   This committee sets standards for multiple wireless transmission methods for LANs.

IEEE 802.12 Demand Priority Access Method Subcommittee   This subgroup developed the specifications for the 100VG-AnyLAN protocol. The protocol specifies 100-Mbps speeds over twisted-pair wires.

impulse noise   A noise characterized by signal spikes. In telephone circuits it can be caused by switching equipment or by lightning strikes and in other situations by transient electrical impulses such as those occurring on a shop floor. Impulse noise is a common cause of transmission errors.

inactive node   A node that may be powered down and is incapable of sending or receiving messages.

inactive port   A bridge port that will not accept packets from the LAN end of the port.

Information Superhighway   A national information system geared toward moving the raw materials (data) and finished goods (information and ideas) of information to their needed locations.

infrared transmission   Uses electromagnetic radiation of wavelengths between visible light and radio waves. It is a line-of-sight technology used to provide local area connections between buildings and is also the medium used in some wireless LANs.

Institute of Electrical and Electronic Engineers (IEEE)   A professional society that establishes and publishes documents and standards for data communication. IEEE has established several standards for LANs, including the IEEE 802.3 and IEEE 802.5 standards for LAN technology.

Integrated Services Digital Network (ISDN)   The integration of voice and data transmission (and other formats such as video and graphic images) over a digital transmission network. This network configuration is proposed by numerous common carriers.

integrated testing   A procedure that ensures that all parts of a system are functionally compatible.

intelligent terminal   A terminal that has both memory and data processing capabilities.

interactive   A computing paradigm in which users interact with the programs.

interconnected (plex or mesh) network   A network topology in which any node can be directly connected to any other node.

intermodulation noise   A special form of crosstalk, which is the result of two or more signals combining to produce a distorted signal.

internal specification   Specifications or "blueprints" for developing a software system.

International Standards Organization (ISO)   An organization that is active in setting communication standards.

Internet   A specific collection of interconnected networks spanning more than 40 countries throughout the world. An internet (with a small letter *I*) is any interconnection of two or more computer networks.

Internet Packet Exchange (IPX)   The network layer protocol used by Novell NetWare LANs.

interoperability   The ability of all network components to connect to the network and to communicate with shared network resources.

interrupt   A signal issued by hardware or an application requesting a service from the operating system.

interrupt characters   A set of characters that terminate a message or cause an interruption in transmission to perform a special action, such as a backspace.

inventory software   A management tool used to collect LAN component data, such as network addresses and CPU types, that will assist a network administrator in managing and fixing a network.

inverse multiplexer   A mux that provides a high-speed data path between two devices by separating data onto multiple lower-speed communication circuits.

I/O driver   The part of the operating system that manages the input/output subsystem by providing low-level access to devices.

I/O optimization   A variety of ways to optimize the task of file access, which increases the performance of the server.

Kbps   A thousand bits per second.

Kerberos   An authentication service developed for open, distributed systems. Kerberos was developed by the Massachusetts Institute of Technology.

Kermit   A file transfer protocol commonly used for file transfers between a PC and another node.

key disk   A security system in which a flexible disk must be in the disk drive when the application is run.

LAN analyzer   A diagnostic tool that monitors network traffic, captures and displays data sent over the network, generates network traffic to simulate load or error conditions, tests cables for faults, and provides data helpful for system configuration and management.

LAN Server (IBM)   An example of LAN software that runs under an existing OS (OS/2).

laser   A light source for fiber optic transmission.

latency   The average time required for the requested data to revolve under the read/write heads.

learning bridge   Bridge that builds its own routing table from the messages it receives, rather than having a predefined routing table. Also known as a transparent bridge.

leased lines   Lines leased from common carriers. Lines are leased when the connection time between locations is long enough to cover the cost of leasing or if speeds higher than those available with switched lines must be attained.

license agreement   An agreement that covers the rules under which you are allowed to use a product.

light emitting diode (LED)   A source of light for fiber optic transmission.

line monitor   A device used to diagnose problems on a communication link. Also known as a protocol analyzer.

link   The circuit established between two adjacent nodes, with no intervening nodes.

Link Access Procedure–Balanced (LAPB)   A bit synchronous protocol similar to high-level data link control. LAPB is the protocol specified for X.25 networks.

Local Access and Transport Areas (LATA)   The region served by a regional Bell operating company (RBOC). Following the divestiture of AT&T the U.S. was divided into local access and transport areas. LATAs are not rigidly defined, but calls within a LATA are handled exclusively by the RBOC (the call is not handled by a long-distance carrier but still may be a toll call).

local area network (LAN)   A communication network in which all of the components are located within several kilometers of each other and that uses high transmission speeds (generally 1 Mbps or higher).

Local Distributed Data Interface (LDDI)   An ANSI proposal for high-speed LAN standard.

local procedure call   In programming, one procedure in a program can call another procedure in the same program. The called procedure carries out a processing task for the calling procedure. Generally, the two procedures exchange information through a list of parameters that are passed between the calling and the called procedure.

locks   Record or file-level control that overcomes the problem with file open contention.

log file   A monitoring tool used for both diagnostic functions and predictive or management functions.

logical link control (LLC)   A sublayer of the OSI reference model data link layer. The logical link control forms the interface between the network layer and the media access control protocols.

logical unit (LU)   In IBM's SNA, a unit that represents a system user. Sessions exist between LUs or between an LU and the SSCP. Several types of LUs have been defined.

longitudinal redundancy check (LRC)   An error-checking technique in which a block check character is appended to a block of transmitted characters, typically at the end of the block. The block check character checks parity on a row of bits.

LPT*n*   A parallel printer port on an IBM-compatible personal computer. There are three available parallel printer ports: LPT1, LPT2, and LPT3.

LU 6.2   An SNA logical unit type representing a program-to-program session.

mail agent   A software module that can automatically act on behalf of a user to forward mail or alert other users that the recipient is unavailable.

management information base (MIB)   A database that defines the hardware and software elements to be monitored in the SNMP.

mark   In data transmission, the equivalent of a 1 bit.

matrix switch   A device that allows terminal connections to be switched among the available processors.

Mbps   A million bits per second.

mean time between failures (MTBF)   A measure of the average amount of time a given component may be expected to operate before failing.

mean time to repair (MTTR)   The average amount of time required to repair a broken piece of equipment and restore it to service.

Media Access Control (MAC) protocol   A sublayer of the OSI reference model's data link layer. The MAC protocol defines how a station gains access to the media for data transmission. Common MAC protocols are carrier sense with multiple access and collision detection (CSMA/CD) and token passing.

medium   In data communication, the carrier of data signals. Twisted-pair wires, coaxial cables, and fiber optic cables are the most common LAN media.

menuing software   A management tool used to provide users with options via a menu of choices.

message logging   Also called safe storing, this recovery system writes the message to a file before acknowledgment so the message may be reviewed or recovered later if necessary.

message sequence numbers   A system in which each transmitted message is given a sequential number, allowing multiple messages to be transmitted without acknowledgment.

message transfer agent (MTA)   An interface between E-mail user agents.

metering software   A monitoring tool used on LANs to enforce adherence to software license agreements by keeping track of the number of times an application is executed.

metropolitan area network (MAN)   The subject of the IEEE 802.6 standard. Similar in nature to the FDDI LAN specification.

Microcomputer Network Protocols (MNP)   A set of modem protocols providing for data compression and error checking, such as MNP Level 4 and MNP Level 5.

microwave radio   A method of transmitting data using high-frequency radio waves. It requires a line of sight between sending and receiving stations. Capable of high data rates, microwave is used for WANs and wireless LANs.

middleware   A software interface that functions as an intermediary between clients and servers.

mirrored disks   A fault tolerance technique in which two disks containing the same data are provided so that if one fails, the other is available, allowing processing to continue.

mobile computing   Has expanded the role of broadcast radio in data communication. It requires a wireless medium such as cellular radio, radio nets, and low-orbit satellites.

modem   Short for modulator–demodulator. A device that changes digital signals to analog signals for transmitting data over telephone circuits. Also used for some fiber optic transmission (digital fiber optics do not require a modem), and any transmission mode requiring a change from one form of signal to another.

modem eliminator   A device that allows data transmission over short distances without a modem. Provides for signal timing as well as data transmission.

modem turnaround time   The time required for a modem to make the transition from sender to receiver on half-duplex links. It includes the time for the old sender to drop the carrier signal, for the new sender to recognize that the carrier signal has been dropped, and for the new sender to raise the carrier signal that must be detected by the new receiver.

modular expansion   A system that allows the user to upgrade from a small system to a more powerful system by adding more of the same type of processor to the existing system.

multidrop   See **multipoint connection.**

multimedia technology   Technology that extends a computer's capabilities by adding audio and video to data.

multimode graded-index fiber   Acts to refract the light toward the center of the fiber by variations in the density of the core.

multimode step-index fiber   The oldest of the fiber optic technologies, in which the reflective walls of the fiber move the light pulses to the receiver.

multiple access   The ability for nodes to access a medium that is not carrying a message.

multiplexer   A hardware device that allows several devices to share one communication channel.

multiplexing   A line-sharing technology that allows multiple signals to be transmitted over a single link.

multipoint connection   A connection in which several terminals share one communication link.

multistation access unit (MAU)   In an IBM token-ring LAN, a MAU is used to interconnect workstations.

multithreading   The capacity of a process to work on multiple requests at once.

NetView   IBM's network management system. NetView has three major subsystems: NetView, NetView/PC, and NetView/6000.

NetWare   A leading example of the integrated LAN operating system software approach by Novell.

network   Two or more computers connected by a communication medium, together with all communication, hardware, and software components. Alternatively, a host processor together with its attached terminal, workstations, and communication equipment, such as transmission media and modems.

network adapter   A network interface card.

network addressable unit (NAU)   In IBM's SNA, any device that has a network address, such as a logical or physical unit.

network architecture   The way in which media, hardware, and software are integrated to form a network.

network configuration tool   A monitoring tool used to plan the optimum network configuration with respect to sources and types of circuits.

network control   Involves the sending and receiving of node status information to other nodes to determine the best routing for messages.

network control center   The organization responsible for monitoring and controlling the network.

Network Control Program (NCP)   A data communication program that helps manage a communications network. Specifically, a program that runs in IBM's 37xx line of communication controllers.

network directory services   A database that contains the names, types, and network addresses of network resources. Examples of resource types include users, printers, and servers. The directory database may be replicated on several network nodes, thus allowing users and processes to locate resources they need to complete their work.

Network File System (NFS)   A distributed file system developed by Sun Microsystems that is also compatible with DOS and UNIX-based systems.

network interface card (NIC)   An adapter that establishes the link between the LAN medium and the host computer's bus.

network layer   One of the layers of ISO's OSI reference model. The network layer is responsible for end-to-end message routing.

network loadable module (NLM)   In a Novell NetWare 386 system, NLMs can be linked to the network operating system to provide capabilities such as utilities, disk drivers, and file services. Independent software vendors can provide usual network value-added services through NLMs. See also **value-added process.**

network management   Software, hardware, procedures, and human activities for monitoring, controlling, and fixing networks.

network management system (NMS)   A combination of hardware and software used by network supervisors to monitor and administer a network.

network manager   An individual or management team responsible for configuring, planning, tuning, and establishing standards and procedures for a network.

network routing manager   A designated node that oversees network functioning, locations of bottlenecks, and use of facilities.

network routing table   In the process of message transmission, a table in which the network layer looks up the destination address to find the next address along the path.

network statistics   Information, such as error rates, data rates, and the number of retransmission attempts resulting from errors, that is collected to analyze network performance trends.

network topology   A model for the way in which network nodes are connected. Network topologies include bus, ring, and star.

neutral working   A method of transmitting data in a current loop, where current represents a 1 bit and the absence of current indicates a 0 bit.

next received   See **number received.**

next sent   See **number sent.**

node   A processor in a network, either a LAN or a WAN.

noise   Disruptions to data transmission that can result in errors in the data being transmitted. There are several types of noise, such as impulse, white, and echo.

nondedicated server   A computer that can operate as both a server and a workstation.

null modem   A cable in which the transmit and send leads are crossed. A null modem allows two devices to communicate over short distances (typically 50 ft or less) without using a modem.

number received (Nr) subfield   In bit synchronous transmission such as HDLC, a field on the transmission frame and on the receiver's system used to represent the frame sequence number the receiving station expects to receive next.

number sent (Ns) subfield   In bit synchronous transmission such as HDLC, a field on the transmission frame and on the sender's system used to represent the frame sequence number being transmitted.

Object Request Broker (ORB)   A standardization for middleware established by the Object Management Group that ensures hardware and software independence by locating a server that is capable of satisfying a client's request.

octet   A group of 8 bits used in bit synchronous protocols. Data, regardless of its code, is treated as octets.

office automation systems   A special case of a distributed system, with both data and processing distributed among several different components.

open architecture   Architecture whose network specifications are available to any company. This allows a variety of companies to design hardware and software components that can be easily integrated into new and existing networks.

Open Software Foundation (OSF)   A foundation dedicated to formulating specifications for open system architectures.

Open Data-link Interface (ODI) A protocol independent specification used in LANs. The ODI specification allows multiple data link protocols to exist on a network.

open system See **open architecture.**

Open System Interconnection (OSI) Management Framework The part of the OSI Reference Model standard that provides the model for network management standards.

Open Systems Interconnection (OSI) Reference Model A seven-layered set of functions for transmitting data from one user to another, specified by ISO.

Operating System (OS) The overall manager of the computing system that performs all of its functions transparent to the application program and the programmer.

OS/2 Operating system for IBM and IBM compatible microcomputers. OS/2 extended version contains LAN management capabilities and data communication interfaces.

pacing See **flow control.**

packet A unit of data transmission. The packet consists of the data to be transmitted together with the headers and trailers affixed by the various layers in the OSI Reference Model.

packet assembly/disassembly (PAD) A function in a packet switching network that breaks messages into packets for transmission and reassembles packets into messages at the message's destination.

packet switching The transmission of a message by dividing the message into fixed-length packets and then routing the packets to the recipient. Packets may be sent over different paths and arrive out of order. At the receiving end, the packets are reordered. Routing is determined during transmission of the packet. Also known as packet distribution network (PDN), public data network, X.25 network, or value-added network.

packet switching equipment (PSE) Equipment that accepts and forwards messages in a packet distribution network.

parity check/vertical redundancy check (VRC) The same as parity error checking. For each character transmitted, an additional bit, the parity bit, is attached to help detect errors. The bit is chosen so that the number of 1 bits is even (even parity) or odd (odd parity).

parity data In RAID technology, additional data that provides the ability to reconstruct data that has been corrupted.

passive hub A node connection hub used in an ARCnet LAN that does not provide signal regeneration, so nodes can be located no more than 100 ft from the hub.

password A secret expression used by authorized persons to prove their right to access a system.

path A group of links that allows a message to move from its point of origin to its destination.

path control layer The third layer in IBM's SNA. Path control provides end-to-end routing.

peer layers Corresponding layers in the OSI Reference Model. For example, the network layers in two nodes are peer layers.

peer-to-peer A type of communication in which any two devices can communicate on essentially equivalent basis. A peer-to-peer architecture is a LAN option that allows nodes to communicate on an equal basis and share resources (as opposed to a server-based LAN).

performance monitor A monitoring tool that provides snapshots of how a system is actually functioning, which helps the network management team identify trends in the use or misuse of the network.

permanent virtual circuit (PVC) One of three types of connection for a packet distribution network. A PVC provides a permanent link (such as a leased line) between two nodes. It is usually selected when two nodes require continual transmission.

phase jitter A variation in the phase of a continued signal from cycle to cycle.

phase modulation A change in the phase of a carrier signal. Commonly used alone or in conjunction with amplitude modulation to provide high-speed transmission (4800 bps and higher).

phase shift keying (PSK) A form of phase modulation.

physical control layer Layer 1 in IBM's SNA networks. The physical control layer covers physical interfaces similar to the physical layer of the OSI Reference Model.

physical layer One of the layers of ISO's OSI reference model. The physical layer specifies the electrical connections between the transmission medium and the computing system.

physical security   Measures, such as door locks, safes, and security guards, taken to deny physical access to restricted areas.

physical unit (PU)   In SNA, a hardware unit. Four physical units have been defined: Type 5, host processor; Type 4, communication controller; Type 2, cluster or programmable controller; and Type 1, a terminal or controller that is not programmable.

Physical Unit Control Point (PUCP)   In IBM's SNA, a PUCP resides in nodes that do not contain a Systems Services Control Point. The PUCP is responsible for connecting the node to and disconnecting it from the network.

plain text   The unencrypted or properly decrypted version of a message or data. Plain text is intelligible. Also known as clear text.

point of presence (POP)   A point at which a transfer is made from a local telephone company to the long-distance carrier in the U.S. telephone network.

point-to-point connection   A connection using a communication line to connect one terminal or computer to a host computer.

point-to-point protocol   A protocol that allows routers to establish data link connections and to exchange configuration information.

polar working   One method used to implement current loop transmission.

polling   The process of asking terminals whether they have data to transmit.

port concentrator   A device that allows multiple input streams from a multiplexer to be passed to the host through a single communication port.

port selector   A device that helps determine which users are granted access to applications when the number of potential terminal users far exceeds the number of available lines. Also known as a data switch.

positional protocol   A type of synchronous protocol that delineates fields by the use of fixed-length fields on the message, by indicating the size of the message with a character count embedded in the message, or both.

presentation layer   One of the layers of ISO's OSI reference model. The presentation layer addresses message formats.

presentation service layer   Layer 6 in IBM's SNA networks. The presentation service layer is involved in formatting data received from and sent to a user.

primary center   A telephone company class 3 station. A primary center is one station higher than a toll center.

printer driver   A software module that determines how to format data for proper printing on a specific type of printer.

print server   A computer that allows several users to direct their printed output to the same printer.

private branch exchange (PBX)   Telephone switching equipment located on corporate premises and owned by the corporation. A PBX allows telephone calls within an office to be connected locally without using the telephone company's end office or transmission circuits.

private lines   Communication lines owned by a user, or communication lines leased from a common carrier.

private management domain (PRMD)   A domain that represents a delivery and interconnection network corresponding to a company in the X.400 standard hierarchy.

program evaluation and review technique (PERT)   A technique that tracks a project's progress to determine its critical path and to monitor personnel, schedules, and project resources.

project management system   A management tool that assists in planning projects and allocating resources.

propagation delay   The amount of time it takes for a signal to travel from its source to its destination.

protected open mode   A file open mode that is granted only if no other user has already been granted exclusive or protected mode.

protocol   Convention used for establishing transmission rules. Protocols are used to establish rules for delineation of data, error detection, control sequences, message lengths, media access, and so on.

protocol control information (PCI)   A header attached to a service data unit. The protocol control information and the service data unit (SDU) form a protocol data unit (PDU).

protocol converter   A special-purpose device that allows a terminal to look like a different type of terminal in order to facilitate interconnection between different computer systems.

protocol data unit (PDU) A unit of information exchanged between peer protocols in the OSI Reference Model.

protocol stacks A protocol stack allows a collection of protocols to interoperate. The stack defines the order of operation of the protocols. The top of the stack is oriented toward the application layer while the protocols at the bottom of the stack deal with communication protocols, such as those at the data link and network layers.

proxy agent Software that provides an interface between different network management protocols.

public key encryption An encryption algorithm. Two keys are created, the public and private keys. Encryption is accomplished with the public key. Decryption is done with the private key.

pulse code modulation (PCM) A method for transmitting data in digital format.

quadbits A technique in which each signal carries four bits of data. Requires 16 different signals.

quadrature amplitude modulation (QAM) A modulation technique using both phase and amplitude modulation.

queuing time The amount of time the transaction must wait in queues for service.

radiated media Media that use radio waves of different frequencies or infrared light to broadcast through the air or space.

random access memory (RAM) The primary memory storage of a computer. The CPU obtains instructions and data from RAM and updates RAM when data changes.

read-only memory (ROM) Computer memory that may be read but not modified. Used to store programs or data not subject to change.

receiver A device or user that is the destination of a message.

recovery The act of restoring a system to operational status following a failure.

redirector A software module that intercepts and reroutes network application I/O requests before they get to the workstation's OS.

redundant arrays of independent disks (RAID) A fault-tolerance disk storage technique that spreads one file plus the file's checksum information over several disk drives. If any single disk drive fails, the data stored thereon can be reconstructed from data stored on the remaining drives.

regional Bell operating company (RBOC) The AT&T divestiture resulted in the formation of RBOCs and a separate AT&T company. An RBOC is responsible for local telephone services within a region of the US.

regional center A class 1 telephone station.

reliability The probability that the system will continue to function over a given time period.

remote control software A diagnostic tool that allows a LAN administrator to remotely view a user's monitor and take control of the user's keyboard.

remote data access (RDA) An OSI standard that defines a service that allows application programs to access data located on another node. RDA is intended to allow such access independent of the database management systems or operating systems being used.

remote file sharing (RFS) A distributed file system that is supported only by UNIX-based systems.

remote job entry (RJE) An application of data communication. Batches of data are collected at a remote site and transmitted to a host for processing. In early implementations the input was card format and the output was printer format (between the remote terminals and the host processor).

remote logon facility A network utility that allows users to log onto a remote system, thereby establishing the user as a local user on the remote node.

remote monitoring management information base (RMON MIB) An SNMP standard that describes nine different device groups. A vendor must choose an appropriate group for a device adhering to this standard and is required to support all the data objects defined for that group.

remote procedure call (RPC) A remote procedure call is similar to a local procedure call except that the calling and called procedures are not a part of the same program. The called and calling procedures may be located in the same computer or in different networked computers.

repeater A device used to amplify signals on a network. Repeaters allow the medium distance to be extended.

request for information (RFI) An informal method of investigating hardware and software solutions by presenting a brief statement of a problem to be solved and a list of questions soliciting solutions to the problem.

request for proposal (RFP) Sometimes called a request for quotation (RFQ), a formal document describing the problem to be solved and asking qualified vendors to submit plans and costs for solving the problem.

response time The amount of time required for a user to receive a reply to a request. Usually the time elapsed between the user pressing the Enter key to send the request (or the equivalent) and the return of the first character of the response.

reverse channel Allows transmission in both directions on a line that is essentially half duplex. The reverse channel generally has a lower transmission rate than the forward channel and is used to acknowledge receipt of data. Reverse channels help reduce the need for modem turnaround.

ring topology A network configuration commonly used to implement LANs. The medium forms a loop to which workstations are attached. Data is transmitted from one station to the next around the ring. Generally the access protocol is token passing.

root bridge The bridge assigned the highest priority.

router A network interconnection device and associated software that links two networks. The networks being linked can be different, but they must use a common routing protocol.

routing An algorithm used to determine how to move a message from its source to its destination. Several algorithms are used.

routing information protocol (RIP) One of the protocols used by routers to exchange routing information and thus update their network routing tables.

routing table An information source containing node addresses and the identification of the path to be used in transmitting data to those nodes.

RS-232-C standard An Electronic Industries Association (EIA) standard for asynchronous transmission.

RS-366 standard An Electronic Industries Association (EIA) standard for automatic-call unit interface.

RS-449 standard An Electronic Industries Association (EIA) standard that improves on the capabilities of RS-232-C.

satellite radio transmission Transmits data via very-high-frequency (VHF) radio waves and requires line-of-sight transmission between stations.

sectional center In the telephone network, a class 2 station.

security Controls implemented by network management to delay unauthorized access to a system.

seek time In disk accessing, the time it takes to move the read/write heads to the proper cylinder.

serial binary transmission The successive transmission of bits over a wire medium.

server In client/server computing, the software application that provides clients with the services they request. A computer that provides LAN services.

server license A license that allows an application to be installed on one server.

service data unit (SDU) The basic data unit consisting of data assembled at the application layer. Protocol control information is attached to the SDU forming a protocol data unit.

session The dialogue between two system users.

session layer One of the layers of ISO's OSI reference model. The session layer is responsible for establishing a dialogue between applications.

shared open mode A file open mode that allows several users to have a file open concurrently.

shared printer A printer controlled by a server and available to designated users.

shielded twisted-pair (STP) wires Twisted-pair wires that have a metallic or foil outer covering shield around them to reduce the probability of noise affecting the signal transmitted over the wires.

signaling terminal equipment (STE) Node used to provide an interface between two different packet switching networks.

simple mail transfer protocol (SMTP) A protocol within the TCP/IP protocol suite. SMTP is an application layer protocol used to implement mail services and message transfer.

Simple Network Management Protocol (SNMP) SNMP provides a guideline for creating network management software products. SNMP has four key components: the SNMP protocol, structure of management information (SMI), management information base (MIB), and the network management system (NMS).

simplex transmission A mode of data transmission in which data may flow in only one direction. One station is always a sender and another is always a receiver over a simplex link.

simulation model A monitoring tool that allows the user to describe network and system activities and to receive an analysis of how the system can be expected to perform under the described conditions.

single-mode transmission The fastest fiber optic technique, in which the light is guided down the center of an extremely narrow core.

single threading A technique in which only one operation is processed at a time.

site license A license that gives the user unlimited rights to use the software at a given site.

Six-Bit Transcode (SBT) A six-bit computer code developed by IBM primarily for RJE.

sizing The analysis conducted to determine the amount of hardware required to support a system. Sizing must consider the system throughout and the required transaction response times during peak processing periods.

small computer system interface (SCSI, pronounced "scuzzy") A microcomputer interface used for disk drives and other peripherals. A SCSI disk drive typically provides good performance, and SCSI drives are often used as interfaces to LAN server drives.

smart terminal A terminal that can save data entered by the operator into memory.

SNA distribution services (SNADS) An SNA facility that provides asynchronous distribution of documents throughout a network.

socket A combination of a transmission control protocol (TCP) port number and an internet address. Sockets are used in TCP/IP and other systems to provide connections between two entities.

software license agreement A document provided by the software vendor that specifies the rights and restrictions of using the software.

source routing A learning bridge algorithm in which the sending node is responsible for determining the route to the destination node. The routing information is appended to the message and the bridges along the route use the routing information to move the message from the source to destination.

space Asynchronous transmission term for a 0 bit.

spanning tree A method by which learning bridges build their own routing table.

spanning tree algorithm A learning bridge algorithm in which bridges exchange routing information with one another. Based on the routing information thus received, each bridge maintains a routing table that shows how to route messages to other LANs.

spooler A software system that collects printer output (typically on disk) and schedules the data for printing. (SPOOL is an acronym for Simultaneous Peripheral Operation On Line.)

spread-spectrum radio (SSR) The primary application for data communication is for use with wireless LANs. It has a characteristic reliability in environments where signal interference is likely.

STARLAN A configuration similar to the basic star topology in that each workstation is connected to a wiring hub. The primary medium used for implementations is twisted-pair wires.

start bit In asynchronous transmission, the line state is changed from one state to another to indicate that a bit is about to arrive. The change in line state represents 1 bit, called the start bit. The start bit is a 0 bit, also known as a space.

star topology A network topology using a central system to which all other nodes are connected. All data are transmitted to or through the central system. Also known as star network.

star-wired LAN A variation of star topology in which a wiring hub is used to form the connection between network nodes.

static routing A form of routing in which one particular path between two nodes is always used.

statistical time division multiplexing (STDM) A technique that provides improved time-sharing efficiency by transmitting data only for lines with data to send, rather than allowing idle lines to occupy carrying capacity of the communication circuit. Also known as a stat mux.

stealth virus   A computer virus that has the ability to change its signature or identity, thus making the virus more difficult to detect and eradicate. Also known as a polymorphic virus.

stop bit   In asynchronous transmission, after the start bit, character bits, and optional parity bit are transmitted, a stop bit (a 1 bit) is sent to end the character.

store-and-forward system   When transmitting data between two nodes, the messages are logged at intermediate nodes, which then forward them to the next node.

StreetTalk (Banyan)   A database that provides network directory services.

stress testing   A procedure that ensures that the system can sustain the designated workload.

Structured Query Language (SQL)   A relational database language developed by IBM and later standardized by ANSI.

Structure of Management Information (SMI)   A component of the SNMP that details how information is represented in the management information base (MIB).

subarea   A portion of an SNA network consisting of a subarea node (a host node or communications controller, PU Types 5 and 4, respectively) together with all of the network resources supported by the subarea node.

sub-LAN   A network that provides a subset of LAN capabilities, primarily peripheral sharing and file transfer, but has lower data transfer rates and transparency than a LAN.

subnet   The first set of numbers in an Internet address representing the network identification of a node's network.

switched connection   A communication link established when one station dials a telephone number to connect to another station. A switched connection uses voice circuits. The circuit exists for the duration of the session.

switched multimegabit data services (SMDS)   A high-speed connectionless digital transmission service.

switched virtual circuit (SVC)   One of three types of circuits in a packet distribution network. When a session is required between two users, an end-to-end circuit is determined and allocated for the duration of the session. Similar to a switched connection.

symmetrical multiprocessing   A type of multiprocessing in which the multiple processors share memory and peripheral devices and in which the workload is evenly distributed over the available processors. Compare with asymmetrical multiprocessing.

synchronous   A transmission protocol where the sender and receiver are synchronized. Data is generally transmitted in blocks, rather than a character at a time, as in asynchronous transmission.

Synchronous Data Link Control (SDLC)   An IBM positional synchronous protocol that operates in full-duplex or half-duplex mode in both point-to-point and multipoint configurations. Data is transmitted in fixed-format frames consisting of start flag, address, control information, block check character (BCC), and end-of-frame flag.

synchronous protocol   See **synchronous.**

Systems Network Architecture (SNA)   IBM's architecture for building a computer network. Encompasses hardware and software components, establishing sessions between users, and capabilities such as office and message/file distribution services.

Systems Services Control Point (SSCP)   In IBM's SNA, the process that controls a domain. It is responsible for initiating network components, establishing sessions, and maintaining unit status.

T-1 communications   A high-speed (1.54-Mbps) common carrier service. T-1 service is also known as DS-1 signaling.

T-2 communications   A high-speed (6.3-Mbps) common carrier service. T-2 service is also known as DS-2 signaling.

T-3 communications   A high-speed (45-Mbps) common carrier service. T-3 service is also known as DS-3 signaling.

T-4 communications   A high-speed (274 Mbps) common carrier service. T-4 service is also known as DS-4 signaling.

telecommunication   The transmission of data by electromagnetic systems, including telephone, telegraphy, video, and computer data transmission.

TELNET   A TCP/IP protocol that allows entry from a keyboard to be passed from a local system to a remote system. Through this protocol, an application on the remote node believes that it is communicating with a locally attached device.

terminal   An input/output device that can be connected to a local or remote computer called a host computer.

terminal emulation   A software program and a hardware interface that allow one microcomputer to function as a variety of terminals in support of changing requirements.

terminator   A resistor at a cable end that absorbs the signal and prevents echo or other signal noise.

think/wait time   The amount of time an operator waits or thinks while entering data for each transaction.

throughput   The amount of work performed by a system per unit of time.

time division multiplexing (TDM)   A technique that divides transmission time by allotting to each device a time slot during which it can send or receive data.

timeout interval   A period of time allowed for an event to occur. If the event does not happen, the timeout expires and the process initiating the event is notified.

time-staged delivery system   Software that allows users to identify a transmission package, designate one or more recipients of the package, and specify a delivery priority.

token   A special frame that is passed between nodes on a LAN. The node that receives the token has the right to transmit data. In some LANs only one token is allowed to circulate. In MANs such as FDDI, several tokens may circulate at one time.

token passing   A media access control protocol in which a string of bits called a token is distributed among the network nodes. A computer that receives the token is allowed to transmit data onto the network. Only the stations receiving a token can transmit. Token passing is implemented on ring and bus LANs.

token-passing bus   A LAN architecture using a bus topology and token-passing media access control protocol.

token-passing ring   A LAN architecture using a ring topology and token-passing media access control protocol.

toll center   In the telephone network, a toll center is a class 4 switching office. Also called a class 4 station.

topology   The physical layout of a network. Common LAN topologies are bus, ring, and star. Common WAN topologies include star, hierarchical, and plex or interconnected.

transaction   A user-specified group of processing activities that either are entirely completed or leave the database and processing system in the same state as before the transaction was initiated.

transaction control process (TCP)   A process that receives inputs from terminals and routes them to the proper application processes. TCPs also may edit input data, format data to and from a terminal, log messages, and provide terminal job sequencing. Examples include IBM's CICS and Tandem's Pathway. Also called a teleprocessing monitor or message control system.

transaction log   Records all of the data received, used in recovering from failures and in system auditing.

transaction routing   The routing of a transaction received from a terminal to one or more application programs.

transaction service layer   Layer 7 of IBM's SNA networks. Transaction service addresses application level processing.

transceiver   A device that receives and sends signals. A transceiver helps form the interface between a network node and the medium.

transfer time   The amount of time required for the data to be sent over the channel to the CPU's memory.

transmission control layer   Layer 4 of IBM's SNA networks. Transmission control addresses initiating and terminating sessions, flow control, and message sequencing for end-to-end reliability. Transmission control contains functions found in the session and transport layers of the OSI Reference Model.

Transmission Control Protocol/Internet Protocol (TCP/IP)   A suite of internetwork protocols developed by the U.S. Department of Defense for internetwork file transfers, electronic mail transfer, remote logons, and terminal services.

transparency   The ability to send any bit string as data in a message. The data bits are not interpreted as control characters.

transparent access   The ability of a user to access distributed files as though they were located on the user's local node.

transparent bridge   A learning bridge. Transparent bridges are able to use information contained in the data link packets to determine the path along which to send packets.

transponder   In satellite communications, a transponder receives the transmission from earth (uplink), amplifies the signal, changes frequency, and retransmits the data to a receiving earth station (downlink).

transport layer   One layer of ISO's OSI reference model. The transport layer is responsible for generating the end user's address and for the integrity of the receipt of message blocks.

transport service access point (TSAP)   An address used by the transport layer to uniquely identify session entities.

trapdoor encryption   An encryption algorithm that uses large prime numbers and two keys, one key made public and the other kept secret by the message recipient. The public key encrypts the data, and the private key decrypts the cipher text. Also known as the public key method.

tribits   A method of modulation that allows three bits to be represented by each signal.

TTY   Teletypewriter. Used to describe a terminal that mirrors the capability of a teletypewriter device. A dumb terminal.

twisted-pair wires   A type of wire that consists of pairs of wires (typically two or four pairs) in a LAN. Each pair of wires is twisted together to reduce noise from adjacent pairs and to enhance their ability to transmit data. Twisted-pair wires can be shielded or unshielded.

uninterruptible power supply (UPS)   A backup power unit that continues to provide power to a computer system during the failure of the normal power supply. A UPS is often used to protect LAN servers from power failures.

unipolar signaling   A digital transmission signaling technique that uses a single voltage to represent a 1 bit and zero voltage to represent a 0 bit.

UNIX   A popular multiuser operating system. UNIX is available on a wide variety of hardware platforms and has numerous capabilities that make it effective as a network operating system.

unshielded twisted-pair (UTP) wires   A type of twisted-pair wire that has no metallic outer covering to shield the wires from external interference.

uploading   The transfer of files or programs from the terminal to the host.

user agent (UA)   A mail agent that allows a user to compose a message, provides recipient addresses, and receives messages.

user logon script   A set of actions to be taken when the user logs on, such as setting search paths and initial menus.

user profile   Information needed to define the applications and transactions a user is authorized to execute.

V.nn   One of a variety of CCITT protocols.

value-added process (VAP)   In a Novell NetWare 286 system, VAPs become extensions of the network operating system on servers. A VAP is used to provide services such as network printing and gateway communications.

video display unit (VDU)   A terminal that uses a technique such as a cathode ray tube or a liquid crystal display to represent data. Also called a video display terminal (VDT) or cathode ray tube (CRT).

Vines (Banyan)   An example of LAN software that runs under an existing OS (UNIX).

virtual circuit   A connection, established when setting up a communication session, between a sender and a receiver in which all messages are sent over the same path.

virtual routing   No permanently established path exists; instead each node consults its routing table to determine which node should next receive the message.

Virtual Telecommunications Access Method (VTAM) One of IBM's telecommunication access methods.

virus detection software   Software that analyzes a system and attempts to discover and remove any viruses that have infected the system.

weighted routing   When multiple paths exist, each is given a weight according to perceived use. A random number is generated to determine which of the available paths to use based on their weights.

white noise   One source of data communication errors. It results from the normal movements of electrons and is present in all transmission media at temperatures above absolute zero. Also known as thermal noise and Gaussian noise.

wide area network (WAN)   A network that typically covers a wide geographical area and operates at speeds lower than LAN speeds.

Wide Area Telecommunications or Telephone Service (WATS) An inbound or outbound telephone service that allows long-distance telephone service. In the U.S. the inbound service is associated with the 800 area code toll-free numbers.

Windows NT A leading example of the integrated LAN operating software approach by Microsoft.

wireless LAN A LAN implemented without using conducted media. A wireless LAN may use spread-spectrum radio, broadcast radio, microwave radio, or infrared light transmission to connect the workstations together. Some LANs may use both conducted and wireless media.

wiring hub Used by some LAN implementations to provide node-to-node connection.

workgroup software Often called groupware, this software facilitates the activities of a group of two or more workers by reducing the time and effort needed to perform group tasks such as meetings, office correspondence, and group decision making.

workload generator A monitoring tool that generates transaction loads and pseudo-application processes for execution on a proposed configuration to illustrate how a system will actually function.

workstation A term applied to microcomputers or personal productivity devices.

write once, read many (WORM) A type of optical drive that allows the user to write to the medium one time. Data written cannot be erased or changed; it can only be read.

X.25 network A network defined by CCITT X.25 standard. An X.25 network uses packet switching, and is also known as a packet switching network or value-added network. See packet switching network.

X.400 standard A standard developed by CCITT that provides a platform for the implementation of a worldwide electronic message-handling service.

X.500 standard A standard that specifies the procedure for creating a directory system to maintain electronic mail user names and their network addresses as well as the names and addresses of other network resources such as printers and servers.

Xerox Network System (XNS) A peer-to-peer Ethernet LAN standard developed by the Xerox Corporation. Some attributes of XNS are used in Novell NetWare LAN operating systems, such as the IPX protocol.

Xpress Transfer Protocol (XTP) An extension of TCP/IP that enhances performance by reducing the amount of processing and allowing some functions to be worked on simultaneously.

zero-slot LAN A low-speed LAN using standard microcomputer components that do not require an additional slot on the motherboard for a LAN adapter.

Index

A

Access control rights, 269
Access matrix, 266, 266t
Access rights, 259, 259t
Access security
    LAN software and, 154
Access time, 118
Active hub, 89, 90f
Adaptive routing, 363–364, 365f
Address field, 358
Address Resolution Protocol
    (ARP), 167–168
After images, 215, 313, 315f
    audit trail, 316f
Agents, 343
Aggregate data rate, 68
Alarm, 345
Alert, 345
American National Standards
    Institute (ANSI), 99
American Standard Code for
    Information Interchange
    (ASCII), 6
American wire gauge (AWG), 56
ANSI fiber distributed data inter-
    face (FDDI) standard, 106
ANSI looped bus LAN, 102, 103f
Antivirus programs, 176f, 276
Application layer, 15, 17–18
Application program interface
    (API), 46, 141–142, 213, 213f,
    287
Application software, 139–140,
    201–232
Archiving, 303
ARCNET, 61, 90f
    connections in, 129, 132f
Artisoft
    LANtastic, 198–199
Asynchronous connections, 404t,
    404–406

Asynchronous Transfer Mode
    (ATM), 401, 402f
Attributes, 271–273, 272t–273t
Audit, 194
    sample events, 194t
Authentication, 258
AUTOEXEC.BAT file, 246
AUTOEXEC.NCF file, 248t

B

Backbone network, 82, 84f, 356,
    357f
Backup, 122, 301–317
    data inconsistency in, 310–312,
        311f
    disposition of, 307–310
    frequency of, 310
    need for, 302–303
    procedures for, 307–313
    synchronization of, 316f
    types of, 304, 304t
Backup devices, 122t, 122–124
Backup software, 183
Balancing, 336
Baluns, 128–129
Bandwidth, 104
Banner page, 292
Banyan
    Vines, 169, 197–198
Baseband transmission, 104, 106
Batch file, 247t
Batch processing, 215
Before images, 215
Bindery, 188
Bindery files, 317, 333
Biological identification and
    authentication, 258
Bit synchronous protocol, 358–360
Bridge, 326f, 336, 380f, 381–390
    functions of, 384t
    medium conversion with, 389f

    packet forwarding, 384f
    remote connection alternatives,
        390t
    routing, with active and inac-
        tive paths, 385f
Broadband transmission, 104–105
    frequency allocations, 105f
    standards and use, 105–106
Broadcast radio, 64–65
Broadcast routing, 365
Brouter, 382, 383f
Browser, 23–24
Bus interface unit (BIU), 128
Bus topology, 85–88, 87f

C

Cable tester, 332, 332t
Cache memory, 119
Capacity planning, 334–335,
    337–339
CAPTURE program, 292–295
    parameters of, 294t
    sample startup strings, 295t
    show parameter, output of, 295t
Carrier sense with multiple access
    and collision avoidance
    (CSMA/CA), 96
Carrier sense with multiple access
    and collision detection
    (CSMA/CD), 95–96, 96t
    versus token passing, 107t
Category 1 wire, 57
Category 2 wire, 57
Category 3 wire, 57–58
Category 4 wire, 58
Category 5 wire, 58
Cellular digital packet data
    (CDPD), 422
Centralization, 203, 205f
    disadvantages of, 203–205
Centralized routing, 361–363, 362f

Certified mail, 223
Channels, 242
Character framing, 91, 92f
Cipher text, 265
Circuit switched cellular (CSC), 422
Client, 22
Client/server application models, 214f
Client/server computing, 207–214
    advantages of, 209–212
    LAN, 210f
    in mainframe computer, 207, 208f
    peer-to-peer, 211f
Client/server dialogue, 174–176
Client/server model, 17
Client/server protocol, 149
Client/server technology, 212–214
Coaxial cable, 5, 39, 56f, 60–62, 61f
    connecting wiring hubs, 61, 62f
Code independence, 94
Collector program, 287
Collision, 95
Combination networks, 356, 357f
Common carrier, 21
Common Management Information Protocol (CMIP), 346
Communication
    elements of, 3–7, 4f
    LANs and, 30, 32f
Communication network, 354f
Communications interface unit (CIU), 128
Communications server, 406f, 406–407
Comprehensiveness, 308
Computer viruses, 32, 273–278, 275t
Concurrent logons, 264
Conducted media, 55–63
CONFIG.SYS file, 246, 248t
Configuration management utility, 329, 329t
Connectors, 58–60, 59f, 128
Consistent state, 215
Contention, 29, 95–96, 150–154
    problems in, 150, 151f

Control field, 359–360, 360f
Controller, 118
Control sequence, 286
Copper Distributed Data Interface (CDDI), 82, 417
Copyright laws, 156
Corporate license, 159
Critical path, 224
Crosstalk, 57, 70–71
Cutover, 251
Cut-through switches, 398
Cyclic redundancy check (CRC), 74–75, 93

D
Data access control, 266–267
Data and device access security, 261
Data backup, 302. *See also* Backup
Database management
    in distributed systems, 217–221
Database management system (DBMS), 35, 144
Database servers, 114–116
Database software, 214–217
Data communications, 3–26
Data compression, 420
Data corruption, 303t
Data encryption standard (DES), 265
Data link layer, 16, 19
Data link protocols, 91–94
Data preparation, 249
Data recovery, 302–303
Data switch, 28–29, 29f, 282, 282f
DBMS recovery, 313–314
Deadlock, 152–153, 153f
Deadly embrace, 152–153, 153f
Decentralized systems, 203, 204f
Deciphering, 265
Decryption, 265
Dedicated connection, 405
Diagnostic tools, 319–320
Differential backup, 304, 304t
Digital subscriber line (DSL), 416–417
Directories
    attributes of, 271–273, 273t
Directory rights, 271

Disaster plan, 320–322
    items in, 321t
Discovery packet, 388
Disk caching, 119, 120f
Disk drive interface, 118
Disk editors, 317
Diskless workstations, 32, 124, 415
Disk seek enhancement, 177–178, 178t
Disk server, 114, 115f
Disk swapping, 120
Disk utilities, 317
Distributed Computing Environment (DCE; Open Software Foundation), 213
Distributed database, 217–221
    rules for, 218t, 218–221
Distributed file systems, 205–207
    objectives of, 206t, 206–207
Distributed queue dual bus (DQDB), 102, 102f, 417–418, 418f–419f
Distributed routing, 363–365
Distributed systems, 201–203
    database management in, 217–221
    evolution of, 203–205
Distribution list, 222
Document coauthoring, 226–227
Document management, 226–227
Domain services, 196
Downloaded, 44
Downsizing, 33, 33f–34f, 228
Duplexed servers, 179
    fault-tolerant, 179, 180f
Dynamic data, 305
Dynamic routing, 363–364, 365f

E
Echo, 71
Effective rights, 267
EIA/TIA-568 standard, 57
Electronic calendar, 36, 224
Electronic conferencing, 36, 224
Electronic mail (e-mail), 36
    server, 209
    systems, 221–224

Electronic meeting systems (EMS), 37
Electronics Industries Association (EIA), 57
Elevator seeking, 191
E-mail. *See* Electronic mail
Encapsulation, 17
Encryption, 265
ENDCAP command, 295
End-to-end routing, 354
Enterprise network, 22–23, 169, 170*f*, 171
Enveloping, 17
Error
    dealing with, 320
    impact of, 72*f*
    sources of, 69–71
Error correction, 76–77
Error-correction codes, 76
Error detection, 7, 72–76
Error prevention, 71
Ethernet, 61, 86
    message formats, 92, 93*f*
Exclusive open mode, 150–151
Expert system, 425
Explicit rights, 269
Extended Binary Coded Decimal Interchange Code (EBCDIC), 6–7

F

Facsimile machines, 133
Fake logon, 263
Fault tolerance, 178–181
FAX server, 425, 425*f*
Fiber Distributed Data Interface (FDDI), 82, 417
Fiber optic cable, 5, 39, 62–63, 63*f*
File/directory tree structure, 269, 270*f*
File rights, 267, 267*t*
    determination of, 268–271, 269*t*
Files
    attributes of, 271–273, 272*t*
File servers, 114, 116*f*
File transfer utilities, 408
Filter, 344

Firewall, 423, 423*f*
First in, first out, 291
Flag field, 358
Flooding, 387
Floppy diskette drives, 123
Flow control, 18
Folders, 195
Forms, 298
Frame check sequence, 359
Frame relay, 370–371
Full backup, 304
Full-duplex mode, 18
Functional testing, 250

G

Gateway, 395, 396*f*
Generic server table, 166, 167*t*
Grace logons, 263
Grandfather-father-son backup method, 308, 309*f*
Group decision support systems (GDSS), 36, 227
Group manager training, 253
Groups, 259
Groupware, xv, 33–34, 221–227

H

Half-duplex mode, 18
Hamming codes, 76
Hard disk drives, 123
Hardware interfaces, 286
Hardware upgrades, 340–342
Hierarchical network, 356, 357*f*
High-priority queue, 291
High-speed buffer, 285–286
High-speed local area network (HSLAN), 417–418
Hold, 288
Hop, 355
Host
    LAN connection to, 401–407, 403*f*
    as LAN node, 404
Host computer, 7
Host language interface, 144
Hot-swappable, 127
Hubs, 127–128
Hypertext, 23

Hypertext Markup Language (HTML), 23

I

IBM
    IBM-3270 emulation, 407
    network operating systems, 197
    system connections, 407
    Systems Network Architecture (SNA), 365–368
Identification, 258
IEEE standards, 99–104
    802.3, 87, 100–101, 240, 241*t*
    802.4, 87, 101
    802.5, 82, 101
    802.12, 87, 103–104
Impulse noise, 70
Incremental backup, 304, 304*t*
Informational frame, 359
Information gathering, 327–329
Infrared light, 5, 39
Infrared transmission, 65–66
Inherited rights filter (IRF), 268
Institute of Electrical and Electronic Engineers (IEEE), 99
    standards. *See* IEEE standards
Integrated drive electronics, 118
Integrated network management systems, 345
Integrated services digital network (ISDN), 415–416, 416*f*
Interconnected (plex) network, 356, 357*f*
Interconnection utilities, 407–409
International Standards Organization (ISO), 9
International Telecommunications Union (ITU), 99
Internet, 23
    access to, 422–424
Interoperability, 174, 198–199
Interrupt, 174
Interrupt request (IRQ), 244
Intranets, 23–24
I/O interfaces, 142
I/O optimization, 177–178
I/O port, 282

IP protocol, 165, 166f
IPX protocol, 165, 166f

K

Key disk, 156
Known good components, 332

L

LAN adapters, 41, 125–126
LAN administration
 backup, 301–317
 printing environment, 281–300
 proactive network management, 334–335
 reactive network management,
  325–327
 recovery, 317–320
 security, 260–273
 users and groups, 257–260
LAN administrator
 responsibilities, 254t
 training, 253–254
LAN analyzer, 333
LAN environment, 42–43, 43t,
 145–146
LAN installation, 235–256
 administrative details of,
  235–240
 tasks in, 240–251, 241f
LAN system, 53–54
LAN system software, 163–185
LANtastic (Artisoft), 198–199
Latency, 118, 142
Learning bridge, 384
License agreement, 154, 157–159
 owner's rights, 159–160
License control, 159
Light-emitting diode (LED), 62–63
Links, 5, 354
Local area network (LAN), 8,
 21–22, 27–50
 characteristics of, 37t, 37–40
 connected, 326f, 326–327
 connected by router, 163, 164f
 connected with LAN, 377–379
 connection to host, 401–407,
  403f
 costs of, 41–43, 42t

decisions regarding, 106–109
hardware, 113–135
high-speed (HSLAN),
 417–418
interconnected with WAN, 11f,
 373, 396f
media, 39, 39f–40f, 54–55, 55t,
 69t
media selection criteria, 66–69,
 67t
node-to-medium connection in,
 128–130, 129f
operating system, 177–181
peer-to-peer, 413–415
printer configurations, 189,
 190f
printing configurations,
 282–283, 283f
rationale for, 27–34
segmentation of, 420
selection criteria, 41t, 41–48
standards, 98–104
support and maintenance agreements for, 239–240
virtual, 399–400, 400f
versus WAN, 10t
versus WANs, 371–373
Locks, 152
 waiting for release of,
  152, 152f
Logical link control (LLC), 89
Logical units (LU), 366, 367f
 types of, 367–368
Logon restrictions, 264–265
Logon script, 252, 260
Longitudinal redundancy check
 (LRC), 73–74, 74t–75t
Low-level recovery, 319
Low-priority queue, 291
LU 6.2, 368, 368f, 407

M

Magnetic tape drives, 123–124,
 124t
Mail administrator, 222
Mail agent, 209
Mailbox, 222
Major fault recovery, 313

Manageability, 47, 48t
Management information base
 (MIB), 345
Maximum rights mask, 271
Media access control (MAC) proto-
 cols, 39, 54, 89, 95–98
 token passing, 96–98, 98t
Medium, 5–6
Medium conversion
 with bridge, 389f
Medium installation, 243–244
Message, 4
 receiving, 19–21
Metropolitan area network (MAN),
 9, 22, 417
Microsoft network operating sys-
 tems, 195–197
Microwave radio, 65
Middleware, 213
Minor fault recovery, 313
Mirrored disks, 178, 179f
Mobile computing, 420–422
Modem pooling, 424
Modem servers, 133
Modem sharing, 407
Monitors, 343
Multimedia, 418–420, 421f
Multiplexer, 405, 405f
Multiprotocol bridge, 382, 383f
Multistation access unit (MAU,
 MSAU), 85, 85f–86f
 connections in, 129, 131f
Multithreading, 148
Mutation engine, 278

N

NetWare (Novell), 166, 176
 data access security in, 267t,
  267–268
NetWare Loadable Modules
 (NLMs), 194
NetWare 3.x (Novell), 187–191
 installation, 247
NetWare 4.x (Novell), 187,
 191–195
 installation, 247
Network, 7–9
Network analyzer, 335

Network component monitoring, 344*t*

Network directory, 168–174
possible contents of, 171*t*

Network directory structure, 172*f*
distributing and replicating, 173*f*

Networked systems, 205

Network interface card (NIC), 125–126

Network interface software, 164, 165*f*

Network layer, 16, 19

Network loadable module (NLM), 299

Network management
proactive, 334–335
reactive, 325–327

Network management protocols, 345–346
simple (SNMP), 345–346

Network management system (NMS), 335, 342–345
components of, 343*t*
functions of, 342*t*
integrated, 345

Network of computers, 8, 9*f*

Network operating system (NOS), 145, 163, 177–181
common capabilities of, 198*t*
implementation, 187–200
multiple, complications with, 199*t*

Network routing table, 19, 20*f*, 361

Node, 5

Noise
and data communications signal, 70*f*

Nondedicated servers, 413–415

Novell. *See also* NetWare
network operating systems, 187–195
print queues, 295–297
spooler configuration, 292–299, 293*f*
SUPERVISOR ID in, 259

Novell Directory Services (NDS), 191

sample objects and properties, 193*f*
sample tree, 191, 192*f*

Number received (Nr), 359–360, 360*f*

Number sent (Ns), 359–360, 360*f*

O

Object Request Broker (RB), 213

Octet, 92

Off-site storage, 305

100VG-AnyLAN, 87

On-line transaction processing, 215

Open modes, 150–151, 152*t*

Open networks, 154

Open standards, 10, 154

Open Systems Interconnection (OSI) Reference Model, 9–21, 379–395
formatting, 17*f*
function of, 16–19
functions of layers of, 15–16
layers of, 12*f*

Operating system (OS), 139, 163

Operating system software, 140–144

Operator training, 253

Optical disk drives, 123

OS/2 Warp Connect, 197

OS/2 Warp Server, 174

Output queue, 299

P

Packet distribution network (PDN), 355, 369–371, 370*f*
advantages and disadvantages of, 369–370
frame relay in, 370–371

Packet switching, 355

Parallel interfaces, 286

Parity check, 72–73, 73*t*

Parity data, 178

Partial backup, 304, 304*t*

Passive hub, 89, 90*f*

Password, 258

Password administration, 262–264
suggested policy for, 262*t*

Path, 5, 354

Payment schedule, 238

Peer-to-peer LAN, 413–415

Peer-to-peer network, 187

Penalty clauses, 239

Performance testing, 250

Personal NetWare (PNW; Novell), 187–188

Personal productivity software, 34–35

Physical layer, 16, 19

Physical security, 261

Physical units (PU), 366, 366*t*

Plain text, 265

Plenum cables, 59–60

Pocket LAN adapter, 332

Polymorphic viruses, 278

Portability, 31

Presentation layer, 15, 18

Presentation services, 35

Preventive maintenance, 239

Primary business software, 228

PRINTDEF, 297

Printer driver, 126

Printer interface, 286

Printers
and LANs, 126–127
new, support for, 286–287
queue configurations, 296, 298*f*

Printer sharing, 28*f*

Printing environment, 281–300
creating, 283–284
stand-alone, 284*f*

Print-job parameters, 297*t*

Print queue operator, 295–296
functions of, 296*t*

Print servers
in NetWare, 299

Priority system, 291

Private data, 249

Proactive network management, 334–335

Problem(s)
diagnosis and analysis of, 330–333
identification and resolution of, 327–334

Problem reporting and tracking system, 333
    forms in, 334f
Processor bus, 121, 121t
Processors, 121
Processor speed, 121
Productivity software, 34–37
Program Evaluation and Review
    Technique (PERT), 224–226,
    225f
    chart of installation activities,
    241f
Progress payments, 238
Protected open mode, 151
Protection clauses, 239
Protocol analyzer, 333, 333t
Protocols, 16, 107–109, 108t
PSERVER, 299
Public data, 249
Public data network (PDN), 355
Punchdown block, 57
Purchase contract, 236–239

Q

Queue managers, 299
Queue users, 296

R

Reactive network management,
    325–327
Read-after-write, 178
Receivers, 5, 6f
Recovery, 317–320
    low-level, 319
    steps in, 318t
Recovery facilities, 217
Recreation, 315–317
Redirector, 147, 287
    functions, 147f
Redirector implementations, 174,
    175f
Redundant arrays of independent
    disks (RAID), 178, 179f
Remote access, 408t, 408–409, 409t
Remote control, 408
Remote control software, 330–331,
    331t
Remote logon utilities, 408

Remote node, 408
Repeaters, 61, 379–380, 380f–381f
    characteristics and capabilities
    of, 382t
Report generator, 345
Reprocessing, 315–317
Requester/server protocol, 149
Resource sharing, 27–30, 28f–31f
Response time, 67–68
Restorative maintenance, 239
Restricted number of concurrent
    users license, 158–159
Retention policy, 308, 308t
Retry limit, 77
Ring topology, 82–85, 84f
RJ-45 jack, 58, 59f
Routers, 390–391
Routing, 5
Routing algorithm, 5
Routing table, 382, 836t
RPRINTER, 299

S

Security, 48, 260–273
    data and device access, 261
    operating system and,
        143–144
    physical, 261
    system access, 261
Security utilities, 273, 273t–274t
Seek, 142
Seek time, 118
Selective backup, 304
Sender, 4, 6f
Sequence checks, 75–76
Sequenced Packet
    Exchange/Internetwork Packet
    Exchange (SPX/IPX), 390–391
Serial interface, 286
Server(s), 22, 32, 424–425
Server disk drives, 116–118
Server license, 159
Server memory, 119–121
Server operating systems, 176–177,
    177t
Server platforms, 113–122
Server request queue, 148, 148f
Server software, 176–183

Server/workstation communica-
    tions, 163–168
Services Advertising Protocol
    (SAP), 166–167
Session, 15, 355
Session layer, 15, 18
Shared open mode, 151
Shared read-only mode, 151
Shared update mode, 151
Shielded twisted-pair (STP), 56f,
    56–57
Shielded Twisted-Pair Wire
    Distribution Data Interface
    (SDDI), 417
Signatures, 278
Simple Network Management
    Protocol (SNMP), 345–346
    environment, 347f–348f
Simplex transmission, 18
Simulation models, 337–338
Single-threading, 149
Single-use, multiple-workstation
    license, 158
Single-user, single-workstation
    license, 158
Site license, 159
Site planning, 242–243
Small computer system interface
    (SCSI), 118, 286
Software, 139–162
    application, 201–232
    classes of, 139–145
    functions of, 145–149
    license agreement. *See* License
        agreement
    location, 145, 146f
    requirements for shared usage,
        149–154
    server, 176–183
    standards, 154, 228–230
Software protection, 154–160
Software upgrades, 340–342
    planning, 341–342
Source routing, 388
Spanning tree algorithms,
    386–388
Spooler, 29, 181–183, 182f,
    284–292

administration-oriented functions of, 288–291
application-oriented functions of, 287–288
functions of, 285t
hardware-oriented functions of, 285–287
Novell configuration, 292–299, 293f
options for, 183t
printing alternatives, 288, 289t
user-oriented functions of, 291–292
Spooler interface, 291
Spread-spectrum radio (SSR), 65
SQL server, 114–116, 117f
StarLAN, 89
STARTNET.BAT file, 247t
Star topology,90f, 88f, 88–89
Startup files, 247
STARTUP.NCF file, 249t
Star-wired LAN, 88f, 88–89, 101
Static data, 304
Static routing, 363
Statistical reports
from spooler, 289–290, 290t
Store-and-forward, 355
Store-and-forward switches, 398
StreetTalk, 169, 197
Structured query language (SQL), 115–116
Structure of management information (SMI), 345
Supervisory frame, 359
Swapping, 141
Switches, 128, 395–401, 397f
Switching hubs, 397–398
benefits of, 399t
Symmetrical multiprocessing (SMP), 121
Synchronous Data Link Control (SDLC), 358
frame, 358–359, 359f
System access security, 261
System expansion
planning, 339–340
System Fault Tolerance (SFT) Level III (Novell), 180, 180f

System programming, 260
Systems Network Architecture (SNA; IBM), 365–368
sessions in, 366–367, 367f
System tuning, 334–337

T
TCP/IP protocol, 167
Telecommunications Industries Association (TIA), 57
Terminal emulation, 404, 404t
Terminal network, 7–8, 8f
Terminal servers, 133
Terminate-and-stay-resident (TSR), 293
Terminators, 85
in bus network, 130, 133f
Testing, 250–251
Thicknets, 61
Thinnets, 61
Timeout interval, 287–288
Timeout value, 262
Time-staged delivery systems, 227
Token passing, 82, 96–98, 98t
versus CSMA/CD, 107t
Token-passing bus, 97f, 97–98
Token-passing ring, 82, 84f, 86f, 97
with bridge, 382, 383f
Topology, 54, 81–89, 83f, 107–109, 108t
WAN, 355–356, 357f
Training, 251–254
Transaction, 215, 216f
using before images, 216, 217f, 314f
Transaction processing, 215
Transaction rollback, 216
Transceiver, 128, 130f
Transfer time, 118
Transition Tracking System (TTS), 189
Transmission Control Protocol/Internet Protocol (TCP/IP), 391–395, 393f
Transparency, 94
Transparent bridge, 384
Transport layer, 15–16, 18–19

Transport services access point (TSAP), 18
Trustee rights, 267
establishment of, 271
Twisted-pair wires, 39, 56f, 56–60, 58f
layout, 59f

U
Uninterruptible power supply (UPS), 130–133, 181
Unnumbered frame, 359
Unshielded twisted-pair (UTP), 56–57
Upgrade configuration, 340–342
steps in, 340–341
User configuration options, 149–150, 150t
User ID, 258
Users, 258–259
User training, 251–252

V
Value-added network (VAN), 21–22, 355
Vertical reduncancy check (VRC), 72–73, 73t
Vines (Banyan), 169, 197–198
Virtual LANs, 399–400, 400f
Virtual memory, 120, 141
Virus detection software, 32
Viruses, 32, 273–278, 275t
detection of, 275–277
eradication of, 277–278
introduction of, 275
protecting against, 275–278

W
Warp Server Advanced (WS), 197
Weighted routing, 363, 364f
What-if analysis, 35
White noise, 70
Wide area network (WAN), 8, 22, 353–376
centralized routing in, 361–363, 362f
data link control protocols, 358–360

distributed routing in,
363–365
interconnected with LAN, 11f,
373, 396f
versus LAN, 10t, 37, 371–373
message routing in, 361
network layer functions,
360–365
topologies, 355–356, 357f
Windows 95, 195

Windows NT Server (NTS),
195–197
Wireless LANs, 103
Wireless media, 55, 63–66
connecting LANs in two buildings, 243f
frequencies, 66f
Wiring hub, 127
Work-flow automation software,
224–226

Workgroup productivity software,
34–37
Workgroup software, 221–227
Workload generator, 339
Workstation, 22, 28
Workstations, 124–125
WORM technology, 123

X

X.25 networks, 22, 355